a chronology
from biblical to modern times
with photographs, maps and charts

Adrian Wolff

Israel, A Chronology

The right of Adrian Wolff to be identified as author of this work has been asserted by him in accordance with the Copyright, Designs and Patents Act of 1988.

ISBN 978-0-9798149-0-7
Printed in Israel

Adrian Wolff
Israel, 2008
www.israeltours.co.il
adrianwolff72@gmail.com

First printing January 2008, reprint October 2008
Second Edition 2010, reprint, 2011,
Third Edition 2013 A5 size, reprint 2014
Fourth Edition 2017

CONTENTS

Contents

Contents

Contents

5

8. List of maps

Contents

2. FOREWORD

> "Remember the days of yore, Understand the years of generation after generation. Ask your father and he will relate it to you, your elders and they will tell you." (Deuteronomy 32:7).
>
> "Hashem (God) will give strength to His nation, Hashem will bless His nation with peace." (Psalms 29:11).

Adrian Wolff has been a **Licensed Tour Guide** and lecturer in Israel for some years, leading groups or individuals around his country, showing them the rich and intricately woven tapestry of its long history combining so many different threads from different peoples and religions. This richness can be dazzling and at times, overwhelming. He had never planned to write a book. It was the dearth of tourists during the Second Intifada (Arab Uprising) from 2000 until 2005 that brought about more free time and less income. He began to lecture, attending courses in Military History and started to research this book. Originally, twelve pages of chronological data consisting of two pages each on six separate subjects were prepared to assist when touring. These pages have expanded into the present book. Each chapter can be read separately, according to the reader's interest.

The book concentrates on the important subjects in the history of Israel, from prehistoric times with the formation of the Jordan Rift Valley until the present day. This book is of use both to newcomers to the history of the region and to those readers who are already knowledgeable about the subject, but who want the convenience of an aid-memoiré. As a reference book it is easily readable yet serves as a comprehensive guide to the history of Israel that categorizes and places all the events in a clear and clearly accessible historical perspective in a clear and logical form. The reader is invited to enjoy the Biblical Quotations that bring alive its historical content and location.

The text highlights important facts in **bold** and summaries in shaded boxes integrated into the text together with maps and photographs to illustrate the area, events, and actors during the relevant periods.

You will find a summary of Judaism, Christianity and Muslim theology with a wide use of **Biblical, New Testament** and **Koranic** quotations where relevant. Appendixes summarize certain events to include charts of data. An Index displays an easy reference and cross-reference according to years, people and events. The reader is invited to open the **fold-out maps** found inside the back cover. They assist the reader to find a specific location while reading. The Overlords chapter is an overview of

Middle Eastern history.

Adrian is honored to have as an intellectual mentor, Anton Felton Esq. who has encouraged him all through by saying, 'Take one of the subjects and expand, then take another'. During the many hours of research he always had the personal goal of presenting the manuscript to him. Soon he was to find there are no short cuts. Anton helped him make this happen.

There are others who read sections and gave their invaluable comments and input – Col. (Res.) Paul Keidar, Lt-Col (Res.) Yossi Abboudi, Dr. Patricia Morris, Stephen Schulman, Jim Anderson, Ian Hamilton, Moss Eker, Joseph Sweeney and my father Dr. Jack Wolff (ל"ז). Also am grateful to my mother Mavis Wolff (ל"ז), our daughter Dr. Maya Wolff, Judy Romano, George Balot, Uri Shevah Judaica, The Ha'mapalim Museum at Atlit, the Estate of Lt. E Noel Symonds and Timothy Guy for use of their photographs. Thanks to Vivienne Silver-Brody (www.viviennesilver-brody.com) of Silver Print Gallery Collection, Ein Hod for the use of various photographs from her book "Documentors of the Dream, Pioneer Jewish Photographers in the Land of Israel 1890-1933".

The author also thanks his wife Emma, and daughters Maya and Meirav for their patience and support. *"An accomplished woman who can find? Far beyond pearls is her value...She opens her mouth with wisdom and the teaching of kindness is on her tongue...her children have risen and praised her...Many women amassed achievement, but you surpassed them all"* . (Proverbs 31:10, 26, 28, 29).

Adrian Wolff
Israel, 2008

The Third Edition, A5 size, is revised and updated, increased number of charts and number of photographs. Additions to the text include a brief history of anti-Semitism, Jewish traditions and symbols, Israel's economic progress and agricultural development, and summary of Overlords of the Middle East.

The Fourth Edition is revised and updated. Chapter 2 Exodus 1300-1050BCE and Chapter 20 WW I and Mandate 1914–1928 are re-written, with many more additions and photographs throughout the text.

Adrian Wolff
Israel, 2017

3. INTRODUCTION

1. A Short History of Israel from geological time to the present

> *"Hear O Israel, Hashem is our God, Hashem is the One and Only."* (Deuteronomy 6:4). שמע ישראל
>
> *"...and they left to go to the land of Canaan."* (Genesis 12:5).
>
> *"All the Children of Israel went out and the assembly gathered together as a single man, from **Dan to Be'er Sheva**."* (Judges 20:1).
>
> *"...for I have made you the father of a multitude of nations...I will ratify My covenant between Me and you and between your offspring after you, throughout the generations, as an everlasting covenant, to be a God to you and to your offspring after you."* (Genesis 17:5-7).

Jews have since about 1750BC lived continuously in Israel defined in the Bible as **The Land of Israel** or *"Eretz Israel* ארץ ישראל*"* (I Samuel 13:19). Greeks call the region *Ioudaia* (Judea); the Romans, *Iudaea* (Judaea); Christians, *Terra Sancta* (The Holy Land); and Arabs, *Palestine*.

Israel spans between two super-powers of the ancient world - in the east, the Assyrians occupying the Fertile Crescent; and later the Babylonians in Mesopotamia; and to the west, Egyptians along the Nile River with their famous temples, pyramids and ancient agriculture. Its location between the sea (Mediterranean) and the desert (Judean and Jordan) defines its strategic importance to control the Trade Route from east to west (and from west to east) passing through Israel between the Judean Hills and the coast. When Moses brought the Children of Israel to the Jordan River, they were already a nation, with their universal jurisprudence - a code of social norms to assist in everyday life - a guide of how one should behave. At this early period in Israel's nationhood, they are familiar with the words of Moses, later written in the Books of Deuteronomy and Leviticus. The social and legal norms described in these two books are the basis for modern western laws.

Jews do not always control the Coastal Plain (due to Philistine presence) therefore cannot obtain precious hard metals (iron, copper) to manufacture weapons for defense as the Land of Israel is poor in natural resources and raw materials. *"There was no **smith** (חרש) in the entire Land of Israel...Thus it was on the day of war that there was not to be found sword or spear in the possession of any people who were with Saul and Jonathan."* (I Samuel 13:19,22). King Solomon, around 970BCE constructs fortress cities with horse stables at crossroads of Megido, the border-city at Hazor in the Upper Galilee and at Gezer overlooking the Ayalon Valley on the road from the port of Jaffa to Jerusalem. The Assyrians conquer and absorb the Kingdom of Israel in 722BCE as consequently these large ancient cities are abandoned and cease to have any importance. The Children of Israel (**Israelites**) are transferred to the east, dispersed and disappear for eternity. The Babylonians conquer the Kingdom of Judah destroying the First Temple in 586BCE, exiling many of the Children of Judah (**Jews**) to Babylon. A minority return 50 years later when Cyrus, King of Persia defeats the Babylonians (Cyrus Cylinder in British Museum). The Jews arise against foreign occupiers - the Greeks in 165BCE and the Romans in 66CE(AD) to control their land and destiny.

The Roman Army defeats the Jews in 70CE(AD) after a four-year war, destroying King Herod's Jewish Holy Temple carrying off the Golden Menorah to Rome. The catastrophic results of the Jewish Revolt (66-70) and Bar Kochba Revolt (132-135) are expulsion to the Diaspora as Jews now no longer constitute the majority of the population in Judea. Romans rename the region 'Palestine' in 135 after the Philistines who disappeared 800 years earlier. Twice the Temple has been destroyed (586 BCE and 70CE). Large powerful empires occupy and control the Land of Israel and incorporate it into their empires - Assyrian, Hellenic, Roman, Byzantine, Muslim, Crusader, Mamluk, Ottoman and British. Yet, beyond all odds the Jews still survive.

After a hiatus of nearly 2000 years lasting from 70 to 1948, the Jews once again control The Land of Israel. How do they endure in the Diaspora as a people, a nation, a philosophy, a religion, with their own spoken and written language while all the other ancient (western) peoples and empires have disappeared? The answer is the direct connection between '*the people of the Book*' (the Jews) with '*the Book*' (the Bible), unconnected to a physical or cult object, united by their spiritual omnipresent belief. **Jews, survive in foreign lands as an ethnic culture due to Jewish belief – monotheism** "...*and bring you into the bond of the covenant*" (Ezekiel 20:37). And **Jewish 'Tradition' based on the 'the family'.** "...*these matters that I command you...you shall teach them thoroughly to your children*" (Deuteronomy 6:6,7).

J-J Rousseau states about Jews "*They have mingled with all peoples.. have no rulers, yet they are always a people...of all the systems of legislation now known to us, only this one has undergone all tests, has always been steadfast.*"

Israel does not derive its legitimacy from sympathy over the Holocaust, but from international law. On 29 November 1947, the UN voted to create two separate countries, one Jewish and the other Arab. The British leave as the Jews gain independence on 15 May 1948, opening the Gates of Zion. Immediately five Arab countries invade the infant state. Many new immigrants are Holocaust survivors fleeing persecution from their neighbors. Simultaneously entire Jewish communities in the Arab world virtually disappear, over 800,000 flee persecution, leaving penniless for a new life in Israel and other western countries.

2. Jerusalem

> "*Please take your son, your only one, whom you love - Isaac - and go to the land of Moriah.*" (Genesis 22:2).
>
> "*Solomon then began building the Temple of Hashem in Jerusalem on Mount Moriah.*" (II Chronicles 3:1).
>
> "*If I forget you, O Jerusalem, let my right hand forget its skill. Let my tongue adhere to my palate, if I fail to elevate Jerusalem above my foremost joy.*" (Psalms 137:5-6).
>
> "*For from Zion will the Torah come forth, and the word of Hashem from Jerusalem.*" (Isaiah 2:3).
>
> "*...according to the Law of Moses...they brought Him to Jerusalem to present Him to the Lord...to offer a sacrifice...according to...the law of the Lord, 'A pair of turtledoves or two young pigeons.*" (Luke 2:22,24).
>
> "*That repentance and remission of sins should be preached in His name to all nations, beginning in Jerusalem.*" (Luke 24:47).
>
> "*...found Him in the temple.*" (Luke 2:46).
>
> "*Jesus went into the temple of God and drove out all of those who bought and sold in the temple.*" (Matthew 20:12,14).
>
> The Koran does not mention explicitly the word 'Jerusalem'.

For over 3000 years, Jerusalem has had continual settlement while the major capitals of ancient empires Babylon, Nineveh, Luxor, Sparta, and Persepolis are ruins. Jerusalem, holy to all three monotheistic religions, is located on the watershed (divide) where rainwater will flow either westwards towards the green Coastal Plain onto the Mediterranean Sea or eastwards into the brown Judean Desert and the Dead Sea. Rainwater flows sporadically in the wadis only during the rainy winter months. The Gihon Spring in the Kidron Valley is the only perennial source of water. Situated in the Judean Hills, Jerusalem nearly 800 meters above sea level, giving rise to difficult non-motorized transport is never a commercial center, not located on any Trade Route. Its status has always endured as a religious pilgrimage center.

Jerusalem, is originally a small Canaanite city-state, politically aligned with Egypt. It is where the Jewish Patriarch Abraham prepares to sacrifice his son Isaac on Mt. Moriah. Following the return of the Children of Israel from their sojourn in Egypt, Joshua conquers Eretz Israel without capturing Jerusalem. King David proclaims Jerusalem in about 1000BCE to become the eternal capital and spiritual center of the Jewish people. "*David then captured Zion Fortress which is (called) the City of David.*" (II Samuel 5:7). Also I Chronicles 11:5. King Solomon (son of King David) builds The First Temple in 970BCE directly over the 'rock/Foundation Stone' on Mount Moriah, and after his death, the Kingdom is split into Israel and Judah. King Nebuchadnezzar exiles the Jews to Babylon, destroys the First Temple in 586 BCE. "*By the rivers of Babylon, there we sat, and also wept when we remembered Zion."* (Psalms 137:1). After fifty years in exile the Children of Judah, now known as Jews (*Yehudim* יהודים in Hebrew) return to Zion and rebuild the Temple. Jerusalem falls in 332 BCE, this time to the army of Alexander the Great as his forces march eastwards bringing Greek culture, mathematics and philosophy to the Near and Middle East. The Maccabis, under the leadership of Judah the Maccabi recapture Jerusalem in 165BCE, gaining control of the Jewish Holy Temple. Yet another super-power looms in the west and in 63BCE, the Roman General Pompey captures Jerusalem. King Herod in 23BCE builds The Second Temple on Mount Moriah. Daily animal sacrifices take place on the Temple Mount, Jerusalem, the capital of the Jewish people in the Land of Israel. *"My House will be called a house of prayer for all the peoples."* (Isaiah 56:7).

According to Christian belief, in about 30CE Jesus Christ is condemned, crucified and buried on *"a place called Golgotha, that is to say, Place of the skull."* (Matthew 27:33). Jerusalem is the site of the battle in 70CE between the Jews and the Roman Army, culminating in the sacking and destruction of the Second Temple and the conflagration that raged through the city. After the devastating results of the failed Bar Kochba Revolt (132-135CE), the Romans ban Jews from Jerusalem, changing its name to *Aelia Capitolina*, and the name of the territory of *Iudaea* (Judea) to **Palestina** after the Philistines who disappeared 800 years earlier. **Jerusalem remains after the Destruction of the Temple, the Jewish spiritual capital and Jewish prayers are always directed towards the Temple Mount**. The Midrash Tanhuma Kedoshim 10 states, *"The Land of Israel is the center of the world. Jerusalem is at the center of the Land of Israel. The Temple is the center of Jerusalem"*.

Some three-hundred years after the Crucifixion, Christians construct large impressive Byzantine-style churches in The Holy Land at traditional sites related to the life of Jesus. In Jerusalem, they construct The Church of the Holy Sepulchre over Golgotha (The Hill of the Skull), the Crucifixion site and the Tomb of Jesus Christ, signifying the holiest spot for all Christians, the Nea (new) Church, and on Mt Zion, St. Mary's Church over the site of The Last Supper. Byzantines severely limit and often curtail Jewish presence in Jerusalem. Muslims conquer Jerusalem in 638 allowing Jews to return during the Early Arab Period. The Muslim caliph of Damascus Abed al-Malik constructs in 691 a shrine to Mohammed in Jerusalem over the 'rock' on the Temple Mount to represent the spot where Muslims believe his horse placed its footprint before his ascent to heaven. The Koran does not use the word Jerusalem nor is it during any of the Arab Periods the capital or main-city of Arab Palestine.

Crusaders control Jerusalem from 1099 before they are defeated in 1187. Again, in 1229 the Crusader pilgrims control the Holy Christian sites in

Jerusalem for over a decade. They regard Jews as infidels whose presence in Jerusalem is almost non-existent during the Crusader Kingdom.

Jews return to Jerusalem in the Later Arab Period during Ottoman Rule. Once again, they together with other non-Muslims (Christians) must pay the compulsory head-tax (*jizya*) or convert to Islam. All the inhabitants live within overcrowded conditions in the Old City Walls until 1860 when Jews begin to construct residential buildings opposite the Jaffa Gate. From 1880 onwards, increased Jewish presence in Jerusalem results from the First Immigration Movement (Aliyah Alef), when many Jewish suburbs or quarters are constructed west of the Old City, and once again they become the majority inhabitants of Jerusalem.

Following the four hundred years of direct Ottoman control from Istanbul the British capture Jerusalem before Christmas 1917 ending persecution of non-Muslims and corruption by the Civil Authorities. A municipal ordinance enforces the construction of all buildings with Jerusalem stone facade, creating a uniformity of style. Arabs riot against Jewish presence.

In Israel's War of Independence in 1948, The Jordanian Arab Legion conquers the Jewish Quarter and the Western Wall in the Old City as the new Israeli Army is not sufficiently strong. Jordan controls the eastern sector including the Old City, the Temple Mount, the Western Wall, Church of the Holy Sepulchre, Dome of the Rock and al-Aqsa mosque. The Jordanians also capture the Jewish suburbs north of Jerusalem in Atarot and Neve Ya'akov.

Jerusalem, the capital of the State of Israel, a divided city from 1948 until 1967, with its government and administration controlling in the western sector only. Jerusalem is united following the Israeli military victory in the 1967 Six-Day War. The municipal borders expanded, new suburbs and public buildings constructed. Arabs find work places in western Jerusalem but social integration is restrained. Peace does not prevail as terrorist activities all too often punctuate the lives of the citizens of Jerusalem.

3. The Crusaders

"I bring you good tidings of great joy which will be to all people. For there is born to you this day in the city of David a savior who is Christ the Lord." (Luke 2:10,11).

"In the beginning was the Word, and the Word was with God, and the Word was God." (John 1:1).

"Him they compelled to bear His cross...they had come to a place called Golgotha, that is to say, Place of a Skull...Then they crucified Him." (Matthew 27:32-35).

"And he laid Him in a tomb which had been hewn out of the rock, and

rolled a stone against the door of the tomb." (Mark 15:46).

In 312 at the Edict of Milan, Emperor Constantine I (The Great) converts to Christianity, now the official religion of the Roman Empire, the beginning of the **Byzantine Period**. The Parthians (Persians) and then the Muslims defeat the Christian Byzantines in The Holy Land, destroying the churches. Europe is in the Dark Ages, a period of feudal society. Peasants work the land and owe their services to the feudal lord, may not leave their village, marry or own property without the lord's permission.

In 1095, the Byzantine Orthodox Emperor residing in Constantinople asks for help from the Catholic Pope in Rome to regain territory lost to Muslim forces, including Jerusalem. The Emperor claims Christian pilgrims are assaulted during their pilgrimages to the Church of the Holy Sepulchre in Jerusalem. When the Pope announces a Crusade to *"free Jerusalem from the infidel"* he is asked, *"But where is Jerusalem?"* *"Hummm, hummm"*, replies the Pope. Christian Europe is not certain what to call the area where Jerusalem is located, so they call it *'The Holy Land'* or *'Terra Sancta'* in Latin, controlled by the Muslim Fatimids in Cairo. The Pope offers to pardon and rescind all sins, debts and tax payments to fighters, warriors, cavalrymen, medieval gladiators who participate in the Crusades as soldiers of Christ. Crusader kings from Western Europe organize and lead various military campaigns, seeking a desire for exotic women, jewels, lands with serfs and slaves, fortresses and above all power, wealth and authority. The Crusades are often portrayed as a chivalrous period with brightly colored clothes, worn by proud members of various heroic, gallant orders as tens of thousands of Christian nobles and peasants take the cross to distant shores in search of glory, honor and passion. They regard Constantinople as a free, wealthy treasure chest, awaiting plunder. They scarcely think for a moment of hardships before them on hazardous overland journeys, where most of them die in foreign lands far from home before ever reaching The Holy Land. Eventually the minority of the Crusaders arrive to experience many difficulties, repeatedly under assault from the various Arab caliphs and sultans.

The Crusaders rebuild their ruined churches in the new Romanesque and later, Gothic style on the same sites of the destroyed Byzantine Churches. Restored Crusader churches, castles and fortresses can be visited today. The Crusaders are less wealthy than the Byzantines and due to external Muslim pressure, they feel the necessity to construct churches speedily, usually smaller than the original Byzantine ones using large stone floor-slabs dissimilar to the original mosaic-covered floors. Many lords and barons travel with their ladies and retinues of servants, cooks, musicians, pages, etc. The early church gains its power through its exclusive path through the priest to salvation through faith in Christ their Messiah Jesus and through Him to God. As the majority of Christians are illiterate until mid-19th century (universal education laws), the life of Christ is painted on the interior walls of the church for people to see, learn and remember.

The Byzantine and Crusader Periods are not pleasant times for Jews living within the Christian world. Why should a Crusader travel thousands of kilometers to kill the 'infidel' in Jerusalem when he can kill a Jew living along the Pilgrimage Route and save his soul? Anti-Jewish pogroms initiated by various Crusaders in Europe, force many Jews to flee northwards and eastwards. In The Holy Land, many Jews flee to Egypt.

The Crusades begin with the disastrous 'People's Crusade' in 1096. These barbarians enjoy a festival of slaughter along their route to Constantinople. The Emperor in Constantinople bars these vagrants from entering his capital and sends them on to Anatolia, soon to be annihilated. The First Crusade in 1099, the only Crusade to be victorious in battle, captures Jerusalem and The Holy Land. Soldiers of the Second Crusade attack a Christian ally in Damascus in 1148 and never arrive in The Holy Land. King Richard I in the Third Crusade never conquers or controls Jerusalem and negotiates a treaty in 1192 permitting Christians pilgrims the right to pray in Jerusalem as pilgrims, not conquerors.

The Fourth Crusade is another disaster with Christian (Catholic) fighting Christian (Orthodox) in Constantinople in 1204, creating a permanent rift between Western Latin Catholics and Eastern Orthodox. The Children's Crusade of 1212 ends with the children perishing on their way overland towards Constantinople, others using a more southern route are sold in North Africa by unscrupulous mariners. The Fifth Crusade lands in Egypt with the hope of exchanging Crusader gains for the Kingdom of Jerusalem now in Muslim hands. This Crusade is another hopeless and costly disaster ending in its defeat in Egypt in 1221. The Sixth Crusade obtains without bloodshed Christian rights to Jerusalem and Bethlehem in 1229. However after a decade the Muslims discontinued these privileges. The Seventh Crusade of 1248 follows the same pattern of the Fifth Crusade, only with worse consequences, resulting in a larger Crusade military defeat and a larger ransom paid for the freedom of the king. The Eighth Crusade ends feebly in the sands of the Tunisian desert in 1270. After two hundred years in 1291, the Muslims defeat the Crusaders expelling them from The Holy Land, demolishing numerous churches and ports to prevent Crusader soldiers and logistic materiel arriving by sea.

Europe now has a different economic and social climate compared to the First Crusade 200 years earlier. The Crusaders return to Europe bringing with them the original Hellenic cultural and academic ideas originating from Greece brought to the Orient by Alexander the Great. International trade between Europe and the East increases the importance of Constantinople as a gateway to the Orient.

From a Christian standpoint the 200-year Crusader Period is filled with hazards and unsuccessful adventures. In reality, it was a period of suffering, death, and disease in remote lands far from home, where other curious languages and customs dominate. They find many of the resident population in The Holy Land to be Orthodox Christians not Latin Catholics whose customs are dissimilar and whose interpretation of the Trinity (the Father, the Son and the Holy Spirit) differs from theirs in the west. All Crusades, except the First and Sixth Crusade are hopeless disasters in which the Crusaders never achieve their goals of conquering and controlling Jerusalem. From the Muslim point of view, the Crusades are a minor 200-year invasion, temporally upsetting the 'status quo' between the various Muslim rulers of the time. The Crusaders had no influence whatsoever, making no impression on life in Muslim-controlled territory - they came, they were defeated, they left.

By the middle of the 14th century the Black Death in the Middle East spreads to Europe killing 30% of the population, creating a shortage of serfs who rebel against the feudal system. A rise in the mercantile middle class in Christian Europe leads towards an Age of Industrialization, Age of Discovery and Age of Enlightenment, increasing new material wealth, while new ideas flourish. Europeans open new overland Trade Routes along the Silk Road to China, north of Muslim controlled territory. In 1498, Vasco da Gama, a Portuguese maritime explorer is the first European to sail from Lisbon via the Cape of Good Hope to India and return, discovering the new maritime route to the East. A larger proportion of tonnage transported by ships reaches its destination when compared to the Overland Trade Routes even after taking into account losses caused by shipwrecks and pirates. The new maritime routes result in declining Muslim income received from charging tolls and taxes along the Overland Trade Routes (the Silk Road is now in Muslim hands), and now with fewer goods moving, there is less to pillage and steal. The Muslim world remains static in its religious environment, while only Istanbul remains a rich and glorious city due to its trade with Europe. Non-Muslims (Orthodox Christians) are the majority of the population of Istanbul until after World War One. The influence of wealth in Europe results from new trade opportunities with the Orient and Western Hemisphere bringing new economic impetus as European cities grow and with new social orders.

While Europe grows economically, it ignores the Muslim world until Napoleon in 1798 attempts to control the route from the Mediterranean Sea through the Red Sea to the Orient. Arabia remains feudal, not attracting any European interest until the invention of the petrol-driven internal combustion engine in the later part of the 19th century and the sudden need to control the sources of petroleum.

4. Islam

> *"I swear there is no God but Allah and Mohammed is his messenger (prophet)."* (Shahadah, Islamic basic creed).
>
> *"He it is who has sent His messenger with the guidance and the religion of truth, that He may cause it to prevail over all religion. And Allah sufficient as a witness."* (Koran 48:28 The Victory).
>
> *"And fight them until persecution is no more, and religion is all for Allah."* (Koran 8:39 Spoils of War).
>
> *"Let those fight in the way of Allah who sell the life of the world for the other. Who so fights in the way of Allah be he slain or be he victorious, on him We shall bestow a vast reward."* (Koran 4:74 Women).
>
> *"O Children of Israel! Remember My favour wherewith I favoured you and how I preferred you to (all) creatures."* (Koran 2:122 The Cow).
>
> *"When Moses said to his people: Oh my people (Children of Israel), Remember Allah's favor to you, how He placed among you Prophets and He made you kings and gave you that He gave not to any (other) of (His) creatures (the Bible). O my people! Go into The Holy Land (Eretz Israel) which Allah has assigned for you."* (Koran 5:20,21 The Table Spread).
>
> *"And we said to the Children of Israel, dwell in the land, but when the promise of the hereafter comes, we shall bring you together out of the various nations."* (Koran 17:104 The Children of Israel).

During the 6th and 7th centuries most inhabitants of the Middle East, Europe and North Africa are heathens (pagans) except Christians living within the Byzantine Empire, and Jews who live mainly in towns and ports along the various Trade Routes. In the year 610, a new monotheistic religion Islam, whose followers Muslims or Moslems, emerges in the sands of Arabia. The Muslims forces defeat the Byzantine Army in The Holy Land in 638. The Byzantine Christian Empire will remain in Constantinople until their defeat by the Ottomans in 1453.

Muslims believe Allah (God) made Mohammed the last messenger (prophet) giving them absolute rights over the infidel (non-believers), as other monotheistic non-Muslims are granted security, but disposed of their weapons, armor, horses and ordered to pay a heavy annual tribute - the *jizya.* جِـزْيَة . *"He it is who has sent His messenger with the guidance and the religion of truth, that He may cause it to prevail over all religion. And Allah sufficient as a witness."* (Koran 48:28). *"And slay them wherever you find them."* (Koran 2:191). *"Fight those of the disbelievers who are near to you, and let them feel harshness in you."* (Koran 9:123). Muslim extremists believe a person's death in battle makes him a martyr so ensuring his place in heaven. *"Religion with Allah (is) The Surrender (al-Islam) (to His will and guidance)...Who so disbelieves the revelations of Allah (will find that) lo! Allah is swift at reckoning."* (Koran 3:19). *"Fight against such of those who have been given the Scripture (Jews) as believe not in Allah nor the Last Day (Christians)."* (Koran 9:29). Apostasy from Islam is punishable by death. Examples taken from the Holy Koran of Islam's role to force supremacy over the non-Muslim world are: 3:151; 8:12; 8:56-60; 33:26-27.

Setting out from Medina and later Mecca, the Muslims convert the local heathen population in their sweep to convert the world to Islam. *"Take not the Jews and Christians for friends."* (Koran 5:51). *"And fight them until persecution is no more, and religion is all for Allah."* (Koran 8:39). In their eyes the rest of the world is populated by infidels (*kaffrs*) waiting to be conquered by Islam. Muslim fundamentalists believe in the principle of holy war, the jihad, in which the territory under Muslim rule, the *dar al-Islam* دار الإسلام (the house of Islam) is in a permanent state of war with all other territory, the *dar al-Harb* دار الحرب (the house of war). This state of jihad can only end when the *dar al-Harb* submits to Islam. In less than 100 years, the Muslim Empire, *'ummah'* أمة in Arabic, will be victorious extending from Arabia to Persia in the east; to North Africa and Spain in the west. The Muslim invasion of Gaul halts in 732 at The Battle of Tours. A common language, Arabic facilitates unity and a common culture.

Muslims are tolerant of religious practices of those non-Muslims or *'dhimmī'* ذـمـي who reside within the *'ummah'* but looking back through history, often non-Muslims are sometimes restricted as shown by:

- Non-Muslims pay a special head and property tax - *jizya*.
- Restrictions on professions and administrative positions.
- Restrictions on dress code.
- Non-Muslims may not build a religious structure taller than a mosque.
- Non-Muslims are not permitted to own a weapon.
- Non-Muslims may not own a horse, forced to travel by donkey or mule
- A *'dhimmi'* (non-Muslim) is not allowed to be a witness at a trial. Muslims can falsely accuse a Jew or Christian of defying Islam, to which he may not defend himself. (See Peters).
- Non-Muslims cannot testify before a Muslim court and receive less compensation than a Muslim.
- Muslim men may marry a non-Muslim spouse, but a Muslim woman may not marry a non-Muslim man.
- Frequently in Jerusalem, new non-Muslim religious buildings (church, synagogue) may not be constructed. Existing building may be repaired
- Forbidden to perform non-Muslim religious practices in public.
- May enter bathhouses only wearing a special sign around their neck.
- Cannot inherit property from a Muslim, or bequeath their property to their children.

In extremist Muslim society, women are protected from outsiders. It views Christianity as decadent for its belief in the Virgin Mary. Until the 20th century a women could never head a Muslim regime – a 'sultana' did not exist, while in the Christian world very powerful women lead their countries – Isabella in Spain, Elizabeth I in England, and Catherine in Russia. The history of the various caliphates and sultanates demonstrates rulers always absolute, frequently ruthless, many gaining control though violent means, building magnificent mosques and empires supporting many of the leaders in opulence. Muslim capitals are grand when the Silk Road is active and the major Trade Routes pass through these cities.

Churches are converted into mosques (Hagia Sophia in Istanbul, Church of St. John in Damascus). In Jerusalem, the 5th Umayyad caliph Abed al-Malik ibn Marwayn residing in Damascus constructs the Dome of the Rock over the Holiest Site for the Jews on Mt. Moriah, the Temple Mount. Christians and Jews are often restricted in constructing new or renovating old religious buildings.

Life for both Christians and Jews, living under various Caliphates (Umayyad, Abbasid, Fatimid) and Sultanates (Ayyubid, Seljuk, Mamluk and Ottoman) is remembered for its suffering, persecution, lack of personal safety, corruption of officials and forced conversion. The Golden Age for Jews living in a Muslim world occurs in Spain after the Muslim invasion in 711 and improves after the Umayyad take over in 755. Their conditions deteriorate with the Almoravids in the late eleventh century and deteriorates under the Almohads in the mid-twelfth century.

The Muslim world stagnates once Europeans discover the New World (Columbus, 1492) and sea route to India (da Gama, 1498). Europe develops economically and socially during industrial and technical revolutions. Muslim lands remain culturally stagnant, many subsistence illiterate farmers and nomads, lacking sufficient investment in infrastructure or industrial development until the mid-20th century. The Muslim world falls further behind the west in science, education, commerce, social and democratic freedom with no freely elected parliament and government, frequently ruled by corrupt ruthless dictators.

Many Arab leaders are military leaders or dictators. Freedom of speech is limited, and often fundamentalist terrorism is encouraged in non-Muslim regions bordering on Muslim countries (Kashmir in India, Indonesia, Malaysia, Thailand, Philippines, Southern ex-Russian Republics, Sudan, and Nigeria). The Koran (3:28, 9:3, 16:106, 60:4) permits misleading non-believers (*taqiyya* تقية dissimulation and *kitman* كتمان secrecy, concealment) to advance the cause of Islam - by gaining the trust of non-believers.

The Arabs are offered and reject an independent Palestinian State four times.

1. The British propose in 1937 to divide Palestine west of the Jordan River into two separate states. Arabs reject Samaria, Judea and the

Negev. The Jews accept the Coastal Plain and parts of the Galilee. The British are to control Jerusalem and Bethlehem.

1. A UN Resolution of 1947 offers a two-state solution whereby the Jews control the Coastal Plain, Upper Galilee, Beit She'an and Jezreel Valleys and Negev. The Jews accept the resolution. Jerusalem is to be held as international territory. The Arabs reject the offer of Lower Galilee, Judea and Samaria, Jaffa and Gaza.

2. After the Arab defeat in the 1967 Six-Day War, the Israel government unanimously proposes to withdraw to pre-war lines on conclusion of a peace agreement. The Arabs reply with three refusals - no recognition, no negotiations, and no peace with Israel.

3. In 2000 at the Camp David peace negotiations, Israel offers of over 90% of the West Bank, 100% of Gaza, and the East Jerusalem suburbs, rejected by Yasser Arafat, the Palestinian Authority leader.

The Jordanians after 1948 destroy all the synagogues in the Old City, Jerusalem. In 2000 a frenzied Muslim mob destroys the Jewish Holy Site, Joseph's Tomb in Shehem/Nablus. In the same year Muslims attack another Jewish Holy Site, Rachel's Tomb in Bethlehem forcing the Israelis to turn the structure into an armed fortress to protect Jewish pilgrims. Muslims hurl rocks from the Temple Mount at Jewish worshippers praying at the Western Wall plaza. Various Imams (Muslim preachers) in Gaza and other locations preach in their Friday morning sermons *'Slaughter to the Jews'* (*itbach al-Yehud*) and praise the Muslim suicide bombers. The terrorists mainly attack soft-targets such as restaurants, busses, shopping malls, banquet halls, with drive-by shootings and bombings.

Today the State of Israel, as an independent Jewish state is rejected by Muslim extremists, located within territory once controlled by Muslims (the *ummah*), even though Jews have continuously settled in The Land of Israel for over 3000 years. The Muslim nationalist movement does not recognize any border and is still intent in eradicating the State of Israel. Muslim leaders do not recognize Israel as 'The Jewish State'.

5. The Jewish Pioneers

"I established My covenant with them to give them the land of Canaan." (Exodus 6:4).

"I am with you...wherever you go, and I will return you to this soil; for I will not forsake you." (Genesis 28:15).

"I brought you into a fruitful land, to eat its fruit." (Jeremiah 2:7).

"I gather in the House of Israel from the peoples among whom they were scattered...and they will dwell on their land." (Ezekiel 28:25).

"I will plant them upon their land and they will never again be uprooted from their land that I have given them." (Amos 9:15).

Emancipation. History of the Pioneers during the late 19th century begins when Jews in both Eastern and Western Europe establish organizations to encourage Jews to immigrate (Aliyah in Hebrew, *'to go up'*) to Eretz (The Land of) Israel. This movement is successful in establishing the independent Jewish State, The State of Israel on May 15, 1948.

The post-Napoleonic era brings substantial civil reforms. Western Europeans living in the 19th century have emancipation, freedom, universal liberties. Jews are allowed to move out of the ghettos and many move to large towns. Emancipated Jews start to appear in the first ranks of the arts and sciences. The 19th century brings growth of literacy, increased newspaper readership and population growth. In addition an epoch of considerable industrial production, a spread of technology, economic growth, increased incomes and colonial expansion. In Europe, the increasing urbanized populations establish emerging socialist and liberal movements to include many Jews such as Moshe (Moritz) Hess in Germany. Millions immigrate to America to take up new opportunities, unhindered by traditional prejudices. Most of the European population is illiterate until mid-19th century as universal education becomes available in the west. Jews have always been literate, *"You shall teach them thoroughly to your children"* (Deuteronomy 6:7). "וְשִׁנַּנְתָּם לְבָנֶיךָ וְדִבַּרְתָּ בָּם"

In Western European, Jews are eager to gain more civic rights, in the hope to be accepted as equals. Many reside outside of the ghettos of European cities, study at universities, follow professions, and even stand for public office. Now Jews are permitted to argue their client's case in Judicial Courts and Jews are appointed judges. However, acceptance into Christian society as equals is still doubtful, encouraging many talented Jews to convert to Christianity as a means to further their professional, academic or business standing. In spite of assimilation in Western Europe and in America, some Jewish leaders are of the opinion that Jews can only be free from persecution in their own country, Eretz Israel.

The situation for Jews in Western Russia and Poland (The Pale of Settlement) where most of European Jewry reside differs from those living in emancipated Western Europe. Limitations are imposed on their movement, education, profession and dress while restrictions on land ownership prevail. Jews are forced into compulsory military service in 1827 lasting 18-25 years (reformed in 1874 to 'only' six years service) or given an alternative of converting to Christianity or purchasing their freedom or emigrate. In the late 19th and early 20th centuries, the local illiterate hoodlums enjoy Jew-bashing during many anti-Semitic pogroms in Russia and Ukraine. This encourages hundreds of thousands of Jews, both secular and religious, to immigrate to America, Great Britain, Australia, Argentina, and South Africa while a minority chooses Eretz Israel as their destination.

Before 1880 Jews living in Eretz Israel are mainly religious, waiting for messianic redemption, almost totally urban dwellers, living in four main centers - Jerusalem, Tiberias, Safed and Hebron. The Jews from Eastern Europe immigrate to Eretz Israel, to *"possess the Land that Hashem swore to your forefathers to Abraham, Isaac, and to Jacob, to give them and their children after them."* (Deuteronomy 1:8). They wish to *"to be free people in our own land."* (Hatikva, Israeli National Anthem). They are the 'Pioneers', *'halutzim '*(חלוצים).

Jews immigrating during the First Aliyah (immigration) in 1882 to Eretz Israel find it underdeveloped with subsistence production, using agricultural techniques unchanged for centuries. The Land of Israel is devoid of infrastructure, impoverished and definitely not *"a land of wheat, barley, grape, fig and pomegranate; a land of oil-olives and date-honey. A land where you will eat bread without poverty."* (Deuteronomy 8:8,9) nor *"A land flowing with milk and honey"* (Joshua 5:6).

In the 19th century, Eretz Israel is a province (vilayet) within the Turkish Ottoman Empire, controlled by administrators directly appointed from Istanbul. Jews and Christians living within the Ottoman Empire have religious freedom but are subject to discrimination in the courts and forced to pay the head-tax (jizya), payable by all non-Muslims. Lack of economic and industrial development in Eretz Israel results in primitive conditions, centuries away from the situation in Europe. Forests have been cut to supply wood for the various wars and for railway sleepers on the Hejaz Railway.

The pioneering Jews purchase land, dig wells, plant crops and reap the success of their efforts, often many die from malaria or Arab terrorism. The Pioneers agricultural and urban activities are in direct conflict with Arab nomads who for centuries have moved their flocks along natural pastures. Conflicts will erupt as Jews view their legal purchase of land as ownership, contrary to the Arab nomad's traditional values.

The British government in the Balfour Declaration, 2 November 1917 is initially in favor of the Zionist cause viewing "*with favour the establishment in Palestine of a national home for the Jewish people*" (Balfour Declaration) as British and Commonwealth Forces conquer Eretz Israel in 1917/1918. They bring their traditional British methods of administration and government, noted for law and order, together with an almost total elimination of bribery and corruption. Jewish immigration to Eretz Israel increases, together with the promotion of British interests. A Jew living in Eretz Israel can purchase land, work in agriculture or live within an urban society, follow a profession of his or her choice and climb the social ladder without assimilation or religious stigma. The Jewish settlers build new towns to accommodate the immigrants. New agricultural settlements - collective farming communities (kibbutz in

1910); and small farm-holdings (moshav in 1920) are established, mainly in outlying areas that will define the borders of the future country.

During the British Mandate period the Jewish authorities (Zionist Executive) obtain unlimited immigration of Jews to Eretz Israel (known as the Yishuv during this period) to escape anti-Semitism in the post-Russian Revolution era. The duties of the British Army and Police in Eretz Israel are primarily an Imperial Police Force. The British troops are not familiar with the background to the political situation and are uninvolved in the emerging Zionist nationalism in Eretz Israel. Concurrently, Arab nationalism begins to surface and is violently opposed to any Jewish presence in Eretz Israel between the Jordan River and the Mediterranean Sea as they view the Jews as a threat to their control of Palestine. Influenced by these Arab riots in 1929, the British government alters its policy, imposing restrictions on Jewish immigration in 1930. Consequently, the Jews of Eretz Israel become disillusioned with the official British Foreign policy, which they feel, appeases the Arabs.

With the rise of Hitler and the subsequent Holocaust of European Jewry, many Jews try to flee Nazi-controlled territory, only to find the Gates of Zion officially closed to them by British Foreign policy. The British Foreign Office pressurizes the governments of Yugoslavia, Bulgaria, Greece and Turkey to not permit Jews fleeing from persecution to enter these countries on their way to Palestine. The Jewish authorities organize various methods of illegal immigration to circumvent British naval patrols. In addition, in the post-WW II period until May 1948, many thousands of Jewish Refugees, now living in Transit Displacement Camps in Europe, are barred from legally entering Eretz Israel.

The Zionist leaders press for independence, which does not fall in line with British policy in the eastern Mediterranean. The period of 1948 is the beginning of the Cold War as British Foreign Policy supports buffer states against the Communist threat in South East Asia including Malaya, Singapore, Burma and Hong Kong. In the Middle East and the Eastern Mediterranean, the British wish to have influence in Palestine, Jordan, Aden, Cyprus and Malta, while they disengage from Egypt and Iraq. India and Pakistan receive independence from the British Empire in 1946.

The British depart from Palestine on 14 May 1948 as Jews prepare to celebrate the first independent Jewish State after nearly 2000 years of exile since the Destruction of the Second Temple by the Romans in 70 CE. Five Arab neighboring countries prepare for war to drive the Jews into the sea. The British calculate the Israelis will contain the local Arab terrorism but not withstand the invading armies of the Arab countries, which they expect will destroy the infant Jewish State. The pro-British Jordanian monarch, King Abdullah I will then rule all Palestine and move his capital from Amman to Jerusalem. The Jordanian Arab Legion is led and trained by 40 British officers (Sir John Glubb Pasha) and armed together with The Transjordan Frontier Force which operates openly within the British Army. During this period, all Hagana (Jewish Defense) activities are termed illegal by the British and possession of weapons carries the death penalty.

Before departing, the British withdraw from many strategic locations (Safed, Gesher, Latrun, Nevi Yusha, Rosh Pina, Iraq-Suidan (Metzudat Yoav)), etc. without informing the Zionist Executive. The British do not prevent Arab armies from five Arab countries (Egypt, Jordan, Syria, Iraq and Lebanon plus others) from invading before the end of the Mandate. Outnumbered in manpower and weapons, the Jewish Defense Organization (Hagana), and later renamed the Israel Defense Force successfully repulses the invading Arab armies and contains local terrorism. The Jews cannot afford the luxury of a defeat, which would result in another Holocaust. One-percent of the total Jewish population (a very high proportion) is killed during Israel's War of Independence. Ten percent of the total Jewish population of Israel is displaced during this war. During the 1948 War of Independence, the Israelis capture the Galilee in the north and Negev in the south, but lose control of the Holiest Site for all Jews, the Temple Mount including the Western Wall as well as the Jewish Quarter of Jerusalem.

The infant Jewish State is not to live in peace with her neighbors as Arab terrorism continues unabated, encouraged by Arab leaders, resulting in five major wars within 30 years. The Syrians are not content with remaining on the eastern side of the cease-fire lines on the Golan Heights, and two years after Syria signs the Armistice Agreement, their forces invade in 1951, capturing No-Man's Land up to the Jordan River and Hamat Gader. Until 1967, the Syrians would frequently shell Israeli civilian settlements along the border in the Upper Galilee.

6. The Arab-Israel Conflict

"When you draw near to a city to wage war against it, you shall call out to it for peace. But if it does not make peace with you, but makes war... with you, you shall besiege it..and you shall smite all its males by the blade of the sword. Only the women, the small children, animals that will be in the city...(is) the booty of your enemies." (Deut. 20:10,12,13,14).

"They will beat their swords into plowshares and their spears into pruning knives; nation will not lift sword against nation, nor will they learn war anymore." (Micah 4:3).

"Take not the Jews and Christians for friends." (Koran 5:51)."*and fight them until persecution is no more, and religion is all for Allah."* (Koran 8:39)."*Fight against such of those who have been given the Scripture as believe not in Allah."* (Koran 9:29).

The Arab war of extermination against Jewish settlement in the Land of Israel has gone on for decades. The Palestinian media continuously incite their people to hatred of the Jews and murder of Israelis. More Israelis are killed in terror attacks during the period 1948–1967 (Independence to the Six-Day War), than after the so-called 'Occupation' period from 1967-1993 (the signing of the Israel - Palestinian Authority Agreement in 1993). See Appendix 6.11 'Numbers killed by Arab terror attacks in Israel'. The intentional killing of civilians is a crime against humanity and not a legitimate form of protest. This official and unofficial terrorism is encouraged and financed by various Muslim countries.

Muslim Fundamentalists, the present Palestinian Hamas and Hezbollah leaderships do not recognize the 1967 borders, still seek to destroy the State of Israel. Despite over 4,000 Hezbollah missiles fired from Lebanon into Israel, the world leaders in 2006 criticize Israel's military reaction. Similarly they remain silent during the 6 years that Qassam rockets from Gaza were fired into Israel resulting in Operations in Gaza Cast Lead in 2009, Pillar of Defense in 2012 and Protective Edge in 2014.

The rise of radical Islamism sees Israel's destruction as the fulfillment of its religious destiny. The unending anti-Semitism in the world has now transformed itself into anti-Israelism. Whatever Israel does, it will be criticized endlessly, by both western and democratic countries, repressive and autocratic. The Palestinians never recognize the borders as defined in 1949 or 1967, now in 2017 demand Israeli withdrawal to the pre-1947 lines, but do not recognize Israel as 'The Jewish State'.

King Abdullah I of Jordan, President Anwar Sadat of Egypt and Lebanese Phalange Christian leader Pierre Gemayel were assassinated when they attempted to recognize and make peace with Israel.

Prof. Norman Bentwich writes of the then British Secretary of State for the Colonies Mr. Winston Churchill's visit to Palestine following Arab riots in Palestine in early 1921 and his meeting with an Arab deputation. Churchill told the delegation that Britain was committed to the Balfour Declaration of 1917. He continued "*The Jews who are scattered over the world, should have a national center where some of them may be re-united; and that center must be in the Land of Palestine, with which over more than 3000 years they have been intimately associated.*"

(See Appendix 6.6 'Overlords of the Middle East'.)

4. DATES AND GLOSSARY

4.1 Dates

BCE = Before the Common Era, refers to **BC**.

CE = the Common Era, refers to **AD**

Different dates have been found relating to the same events in the various texts used in my research. This is especially evident in occurrences Before the Common Era (BCE or BC). Also many of the 'early dates' are approximate as I have attempted to place the people and places in chronological order.

4.2 Israel

- 'Israel' is referred by the name used by the particular people at the time.
- Biblical Hebrew for 'Land of Israel' is **Eretz Israel** (I Samuel 13:19).
- After the Fall of the Kingdom of Israel, the Kingdom of **Judah** remains.
- Greek Period - **Ioudaia = Judea**
- Roman Period - **Judaea = Judea**
- Post-Hadrian Roman Period (135 CE) - **Palestina**
- Arab Period - **Palestine**. Palestine is never an independent territory
- Crusader Period, **Terra Sancta – The Holy Land**
- Ottoman Period 1516–1917, a Vilayet (province) of Beirut, Mutasarreflik (sub-district) of Jerusalem, controlled directly from Istanbul. Turks are not Arabs. An independent state 'Palestine' never exits
- Jews refer to pre-1918 Palestine as '**Eretz Israel**'
- British Mandate – **Palestine**
- Jews living in British Mandate Palestine refer to Eretz Israel as the '**Yishuv**'.

4.3 God

The word "Hashem", 'the Name', refers to God. Exodus 3:14. See Moses 1240 BCE.

4.4 The Bible

The **Bible** refers to the 24 books of the **Tanach**, the Torah, Prophets and Writings of the Hebrew or Jewish Bible. Christians name this book the **Old Testament**. All quotations are taken from 'Tanach, ArtScroll Series', Mesorah Publications, Ltd. NY. Quotations are in **blue.**

Temple I = First Temple. Temple II = Second Temple

The **New Testament** refers to the 27 books of the **Christian Bible** including the 4 Gospels. All quotations are taken from The MacArthur Study Bible, New King James version'. Word Publishing. USA. Quotations in **purple**.

Koran quotations taken from 'The Meaning of the Glorious Koran'. A Mentor Book. Quotations in **brown.**

4.5 Christian Sects

Christian sects have slightly different approach to Christian subjects.

27

4. 6   Terrorist attacks in Israel. Mention only 'major' terrorist incidents.

4. 7   Spelling

I have attempted to be consistent in use of terminology and spelling and applied standard accepted American and Turkish spelling. The reader is cautioned that many different spellings of non-English words are found in various texts e.g. Umayyad or Omayad; Mamluk or Mameluke.

Aaron = Aharon
Acre = Acco, St. Jean d' Acre (Crusader)
Afek = Aphid
Akaba = Aqaba
al-Qaeda = al Qaida
Amman = Rabat Amman
Armistice Line = Agreed Disengagement Lines 1949
Arsuf = Apollonia, Arsur (Crusader)
Atlit = Castiau Pelerin (Crusader)
Babel = Babylon
Be'er Sheva = Beer Sheva
Beit She'an = Beth Shean
Beybars = Baibars = Baybars
Bible = Old Testament
BCE (Before the Common Era) = BC
Caesarea = Cesaire (Crusader)
Capernaum = Kfar Nahum
CE (Common Era) = AD
Christian Bible = New Testament
Diaspora = Jews living outside Israel
Djemal Pasha = Jamal Pasha
Ein Gedi = En Gedi
Elijah = Eliyahu = Elias
Eretz Israel = The Land of Israel
Ethics of the Fathers = Pirkei Avot
Etzel = Irgun. Support active retaliation against Arab attacks, also Lehi
Fatah = PLO (Palestine Liberation Organization)
Fatih = Conqueror (Turkish)
Feisal = Faisal, Fayzid, Feysal
Ferman = Firman (Turkish edict)
Francis = Francois
Frederick = Friedrich
Gamaliel = Gamliel
Green Line = 1949 Armistice Border
Hagana = pre-State Jewish Defense Organization
Haifa = Haifas (Crusader)
Hamas = Gaza Branch, Muslim Brotherhood
Hashem = God
Hebron = Hevron, St. Abraham ville Ebron (Crusader)
Hezbollah = (Party of God, party of Allah). Radical Shi'a Islamists
Holy Land = Terra Sancta
Hussein = Husayn

IAF = Israel Air Force
IDF = Israel Defense Force
Intifada = Palestinian Arab uprising
Itzhak = Izhak = Yitzhak = Isaac
Jaffa = Joppa, Yafo, Yafa, Japhe
Jamal Pasha = Djemal Pasha
Jean = John
Jewish Agency = administer development of the Jewish National home
Jezreel = Yezreel, Esdrelon
JNF = Jewish National Fund (KKL)
Judea = Judah
Judas (Latin) = Judah (Hebrew)
Kalikia = Qalqilya
Kaza = Ottoman sub-district
Kinneret = Sea of Galilee
Koran = Quran
Lod = Lydda, St. Jorge de Lidde (Crusader)
Mattatiyahu = Mattathias
Megido = Megiddo
Mishna = Mishneh
Moab = Moav
Mohammed (not the Prophet) = Mahmud, Mehmed, Mehmet
Omayad = Umayyad
Pirkei Avot = Ethics of the Fathers
PLO = Palestinian Liberation Organization = Fatah
Pontius Pilate = Pontias Pilatus
Purple Line = Israel/Syrian Golan border
Rafiah = Rafia, Rafa, Raphia
Ramle = Ramla, Rames (Crusader)
Safed = Zefat, Saphet (Crusader)
Sancak = Sanjak = Ottoman district
Sebastia = Sabaste (Crusader)
Shehem = Nablus, Naples (Crusader)
Shi'ite = Shi'a Muslims
The Holy Land = Terra Sancta = Israel
Tiberias = Tabarie (Crusader)
Tyre = Tyr (Crusader)
'Umar = Omar
Umayyad = Omayad
Vilayet = Vilajet = Ottoman province
Wadi = Dry river bed, seasonal flow
Wilhelm = William
Yavne = Jabneh, Yibna, Jabneel, Jamnia, Iberian
Yehuda = Judah
Yishuv = pre-State Jewish settlement and institutions in Israel
Yohanan = Johanan
Yonatan = Jonathan
Zevulun = Zebulun
Zippori = Sephoris, Le Saforie
1967 Border = Status on 4 June 1967 (dissimilar to 1949 Armistice)

5. A History of Israel

Chapter 1. In the beginning. Up to 1310 BCE

בראשית ברא אלהים את השמים ואת הארץ. והארץ היתה תהו ובהו..." בראשית 1:1,2
"In the beginning of God's creating the heavens and the earth, when the earth was astoundingly empty..." (Genesis 1:1,2)

From 'chaos', order is 'created'. The first sentence comprises 7 words and 28 letters. The number 28 in Hebrew is כח, means *'strength'*.

Note: **BCE** (Before the Common Era) = **BC** (Before Christ)
CE (The Common Era) = **AD** (Anno Domini = After Christ)

Chronology Summary
Archaeological Eras

Lower Paleolithic	500,000 - 120,000 years ago
Middle Paleolithic	80,000 - 35,000 years ago
Upper Paleolithic	35,000 - 15,000 years ago
Mesolithic	15,000 - 8000 BCE
Pre-pottery Neolithic	8000 - 5500 BCE
Pottery Neolithic	5500 - 4500 BCE
Chalcolithic	4500 - 3500 BCE
Early Bronze Age	3500 - 2200 BCE
Middle Bronze Age	2200 - 1550 BCE
Late Bronze Age	1550 - 1200 BCE
Iron Age from	1200 BCE

Historical Periods

Canaanite	3500 - 1730 BCE
Patriarch	1730 - 1550 BCE
Israelite	1550 - 1220 BCE
Judges	1020 - 922 BCE
Kingdom of Israel	922 - 722 BCE
Kingdom of Judah	922 - 586 BCE
Babylonian	586 - 332 BCE
Hellenic	332 - 165 BCE
Hasmonean (Maccabi)	165 - 63 BCE
Roman	63 - 37 BCE
Herodian	37 BCE - 70 CE
Roman	70 - 325
Byzantine	325 - 638
Early Muslim	638 - 1099
Crusader	1099 - 1291
Mamluk	1291 - 1516
Ottoman	1516 - 1918
British Mandate	1918 - 1948
Israel	1948 +

Millions of years ago the Negev was covered by the ocean. Later continents are formed leaving hard limestone and dolomite rock deposits over softer sandstone sediments. Asymmetrical folds produce hump-shapes ridges. Over time erosion removes the hard layers outcrops exposing the underlying sandstone.

4m years ago. The **Dead Sea** Valley is created as the earth's crust opens, causing the Judean Mountains to fold downwards into the valley (below sea level). Seawater from the Mediterranean (Tethys) Sea flows through the Yizre'el (Jezreel) and Jordan Valleys to the tongue-shaped Sodom Sea in the Dead Sea area below sea level. In the Negev the sandstone is drained towards the Dead Sea though a single outlet forming a deep transverse valley, known today as Ancient Erosion Craters or in Hebrew as *Makhtesh*. The Craters are renown for their multi-colored rocks and sand - black, grey, purple, red, and yellow.

The Ramon Crater is 40 by 9 kms and 500 meters deep
The Large Crater is 10 by 5 kms
The Small Crater is 7 by 5 kms with steep cliffs

Ramon Crater   Adrian Wolff

0.9-0.7m years ago. **Homo erectus** remains are discovered in Lower Pleistocene strata at Ubeidiya (Afikim), northern **Jordan Valley,** south of Sea of Galilee (Kinneret in Hebrew). Stone and sharpened cutting tools are made from flint, basalt and dolomite pebbles.

0.5 m years ago. Uplift in the Eastern Mediterranean forces up the Carmel Mountains eastwards, elevates Yizre'el (Jezreel) Valley above sea level, closing the Sodom Sea from the Mediterranean. The **Dead Sea** (Salt Sea in Hebrew) is created and Mt. Sodom is formed.

Salt deposits on the Dead Sea shore   Adrian Wolff

Floating in the Dead Sea   Timothy Guy

400,000+ years ago. Teeth found in a cave near Rosh Ha'ayin appear to be from a vegetarian early human, pre-Neanderthal and pre-Homo sapiens.

100-10,000 years ago. Evidence of **Neanderthal Man** living in the Taboun Caves, Carmel Mountains. 25-50 inhabitants populate the caves and engage in hunting local animals - fallow deer, gazelles, and wild cows. Their diets consist of wild (emmer) wheat, barley and oats harvested with razor-sharp flint-rock blades. Skulls found indicate both Early Man (Homo Sapiens) and Neanderthal families overlap at this site, with evidence of homo sapiens remains predate those of Neanderthal.

20,000 years ago. The earth's surface steadily warms. The **Sodom Sea**, a closed sea, water level declines as water evaporates, results in the salt content of the **Dead Sea** to increase to 30-32% (oceans have 2-3% salt content). The Jordan River flows from Mt. Hermon in the Golan (2,224 meters), through the Hula Valley in the Upper Galilee, the Sea of Galilee (-210 meters) to the Dead Sea (-392 in 1930, falling to -430 meters in 2016). Evaporation is greater than the fresh water flow, as the Dead Sea level recedes over the past decades. See Table 6.13.

12,000c Evidence of a prehistoric village is uncovered at the Ein Gev River in the Kinneret area. Findings of human remains, flint tools, artworks, animal remains, bone and grinding stone tools. This village includes cultural characteristics typical of both the Paleolithic (Old Stone Age) and Neolithic (New Stone Age) Periods as humans begin to shift from mobile hunter-gatherers to more stable agricultural societies.

8000c Beginning of the **domestication of plants (by women) and animals (sheep, goats, dogs)** in **Mesopotamia** along the Tigris and Euphrates Rivers. The use of primitive sickles, reaping knives, simple hoes and digging sticks. Plants previously self-pollinated, are now cultivated grains. The domestication of animals, creates surpluses, thereby freeing people from the continual daily activity of finding food to eat. **A division of labor leads to specialization, increased efficiency and production**. People live in small communes begin to pursue other activities such as pottery, wood carvings and leather working. Man begins to till the soil allowing more moisture from the first rains to penetrate and reach the seeds, thereby enhancing decomposition and aeration producing increased nutrients and minerals, improving soil fertility. Different chromosomes are found between wild and cultivated plants.

8000c Early cultivated plants in the Middle East are: Wheat ('emmer') for baking (see Aaronsohn 1910), barley, legumes, lentils, chick peas, bitter vegetables, flax (for oil and fibers for textiles). Rice originates from the Far East, reaches the Middle East during the Roman Period. Citrus originates in India and East Asia. Cultivation of domesticated **barley** grown in semi-arid northern Negev and eastern Samaria, possessing a stiffer, non-brittle stalk that does not break as easily as 'wild barley'. Barley ears remain in the soil until the next season preventing dispersion since the seed is disentangled from the stem only by thrashing using mechanical or physical methods. Wheat's nutritional value is greater than barley, is easier to mill, but requires higher quality soil and increased rainfall, growing in the more fertile central and northern valleys and hills in Samaria and Galilee. A three-week period of collection and harvest of cultivated wheat is enough to support a family. A cultivated pea pod unlike the wild pea does not split when it dries.

8000c One of the first towns, **Jericho** is founded near the Jordan River, at the northern end of the Dead Sea. Not all the inhabitants are food gatherers as some have other vocations, or trades, including carpentry, masonry, leather working, jewelry making and trading activities. The manufacture of sun-dried mud bricks.

7-5000c **The Neolithic pre-Pottery era**

4500c **Chalcolithic Period** is characterized by the Stone and then the Copper Ages. Villages and towns begin to appear in **Mesopotamia** along the Tigris and Euphrates Rivers. Egypt adopts the solar calendar. The establishment of calendar dates is important for the timing of planting and harvesting of crops according to the flooding of the Nile. They produce grinding tools, mortars, pestles, basalt bowls, carnelian jewelry. Settlements are uncovered in the Negev, Ein Gedi, Coastal Plain, Galilee, Golan, Judean Hills (Motza, Abu Ghosh) and Jerusalem (Shuafat, Beit Vegan).

3500c **Canaanite Period I.** The rise of city-kings and villages in Canaan. The **potter's wheel** (storage of liquids and grains) is found at archaeological sites in Kish and Sura in Mesopotamia originating from the 2nd half of the 4th millennium BCE. Copper and bronze replaces stone and clay tools and ornaments.

3100c The **Invention of Writing** in Mesopotamia. The beginning of hieroglyphics and cuneiform as pictures represent words. Ancient writing uses a hammer or chisel on stone or clay. As most people are right-handed, it is easier to carve or hit symbols from right to left. With the invention of paper, there less smudging when writing from left to right with quill and ink, as used in modern languages.

2500 **Canaanite Period II.** Evidence of trade between Canaan and Egypt, including copper mined in Sinai and Timna near Akaba.

2050 **Glass** in Mesopotamia. Glass vessels appear from 1500BCE.

2000 **The Middle Bronze Age**. The **Amorites**, nomadic tribes from Arabia invade Canaan. A period of political stability in Egypt. The **Execration Texts** found in **Egypt**, from XII Dynasty identify

"*Rushalimum*" (Jerusalem in English, Yerushalai'im in Hebrew) as a Canaanite City. Note: The Hebrew word '*Yerushala'im*' ירושלים= *ir shalom* = city of peace. Some inscriptions made on bowls and on clay figurines mention cities and ethnic groups within Egypt's control and influence, listing Pharaoh's potential enemies in Cush (Sudan), Libya, Canaan, Phoenicia, southern Syria and Egypt; in Canaan at Megido, Hazor, Kedesh, Acre, Ashkelon.

18thc   From 18th to 16th centuries the **Hyksos** originally from Asia, invade Mesopotamia, destroy Babylon and make their way to Canaan and conquer Egypt. Their usage of **horses and chariots** having **wheels with spokes** assists their army's mobility and maneuverability. 'Sea Peoples' in the southeastern Mediterranean conquer them. Semi-nomads move westwards along the Fertile Crescent towards Canaan.

Tel Megido, Jezreel Valley   Adrian Wolff

18thc   **The Biblical Period.** Following The Great Flood, "*God said to Noah...I establish My covenant with you and your offspring after you...my rainbow in the cloud, and it shall be a sign of the covenant between Me and the earth.*" (Genesis 9:8,13). God gives Noah and his descendants seven **ethical values and principles** to obey. **The Seven Noahide Laws** are universal for all people who are responsible to ensue that, "*This obligation, to teach all the peoples about the Laws of Noah is incumbent upon every individual in every era.*" (Mishna Torah 8:10).
   1. Prohibition of idolatry.
   2. Prohibition of murder.

3. Prohibition of incest and adultery.
4. Prohibition of eating flesh from a living animal (cruelty).
5. Prohibition of theft.
6. Bless the Divine Name – forbidden to curse God.
7. Mankind is must establish a legal code and fair court system.

US Congress in 1991 officially recognizes The Seven Noahide Laws

1730 **The Patriarch Period. Abraham** *"departed...from Ur Kasdim to...the land of Canaan...I will make you a great nation...Abram...passed to...Shehem...Moreh....Hashem (God) appeared to Abram and said 'To your offspring I will give this land'."* (Genesis 11:27-29,31;12:2,6,7). **The word 'Hashem' refers to God.** See Moses 1240BCE.

Map 1. The Fertile Crescent – Ancient Kingdoms and Trade Routes, 3 – 1 millennium BCE

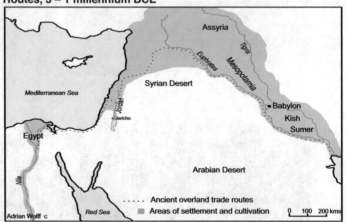

18th c *"He relocated to...Beit-el...built an altar to Hashem...There was famine...Abram descended to Egypt".* Later he returns to Canaan*"...with his wife (Sarai)...and Lot...to Beit-el...There was quarreling between the herdsmen of Abram's livestock and the herdsmen of Lot...So Abram said to Lot (his nephew)...Please separate from me. If you go left then I will go right, and if you go right then I will go left...So Lot chose for himself the whole plain of the Jordan, and Lot journeyed from the east; thus they departed...Abram moved his tent...(to the west) Mamre...Hebron...he built...altar to Hashem..."Abram the Ivri."* (Genesis 10:19; 12:8,10; 13:1-3,7-11,18; 14:13). Ivri derives from Hebrew עבר - 'the other side' (of the Euphrates).

18th c After meeting with the King of Sodom, Abraham meets King of Salem, Malchi-zedek in Jerusalem. (City of peace = עיר שלום)

36

Genesis 14:18 tells how Malchi-zedek, welcomes Abraham with *"bread and wine"*.

18thc   *"To your (Abraham) descendants have I given this land, from the river of Egypt, to the great river, the Euphrates...Abraham said 'My Lord, Hashem (Elohim).* Addressing God as my Lord, showing his acknowledgement and allegiance to respect and revere Hashem. *"You shall be a father of a multitude of nations, your name shall no longer be called Abram, but your name shall be Abraham...I will ratify My covenant between Me and you and between your offspring after you, throughout their generations, as an everlasting covenant, to be a God to you and to your offspring after you."* (Genesis 15:2,18,19; 17:1-7).

18thc   Abraham prepares to sacrifice his son **Isaac** on **Mt. Moriah** in Jerusalem, to *"Please take you son...Isaac and go to the land of Moriah, bring him up there as an offering."* (Genesis 22:2). The original Hebrew Biblical text uses the word *'oleh'* (offering) as Hashem does not intend Abraham to 'sacrifice' his son Isaac. The term 'to go up' (oleh) refers to the journey up to Jerusalem. *"Abraham called the name of that site 'Hashem Yireh, as it is said on that day, on the mountain Hashem will be seen"* (Genesis 22:14). Yireh = 'Hashem will see'. The original name Shalem and Yireh are joined into Yerushalaim ירושלים (Jerusalem). The sacrifice of Isaac begins the everlasting covenant between Abraham and Hashem (God), declaring *"I know that you are a God-fearing man."* (Genesis 22:12).

18thc   Hittites also reside in Canaan. *"Sarah died in Kiryat Arba which is Hebron...Ephron the Hittite responded to Abraham...weighed out...four hundred silver **shekels**...Abraham buried Sarah his wife in the cave of the field of the Machpelah facing Mamre...Hebron...confirmed as Abraham's estate for a burial site."* (Genesis 23:2,10,16,17,19,20).

18thc   Stockbreeders are found in Judah and Samaria, but not in the Coastal Plain of Canaan.

17thc   *"**Rebecca**...saw Isaac...he married Rebecca...the children agitated within her...'Two nations are in your womb; two regimes...shall be separated...pass from one regime to the other, and the elder shall serve the younger."* (Genesis 24:53,54,62,64,67; 25:20-23).

17thc   *"The first...**Esau**...brother...Jacob...Esau became...(a) hunting...Jacob abiding in tents. Isaac loved Esau...but Rebecca loved Jacob...Esau came in from the field...exhausted...Jacob said 'sell, as this day, your birthright to me...Esau spurned the birthright."* (Genesis 25:25-33).

17thc "*Jacob...dreamt...ladder...its top reached heavenward...'I am Hashem, God of Abraham and...Isaac, **the ground upon...you I will give it and to your descendants**.*" (Genesis 27:28; 28:10-13).

17thc "*Laban...had two daughters...**Leah** and...**Rachel**...Jacob worked seven years for Rachel...Laban...took Leah his daughter and brought her to him...Laban said 'Such is not done in our place, to give the younger before the elder...for the work you will perform for me yet another seven years.*" (Genesis 29:16,18,20,22,26,27).

Map 2. Abraham's travels in the Land of Canaan

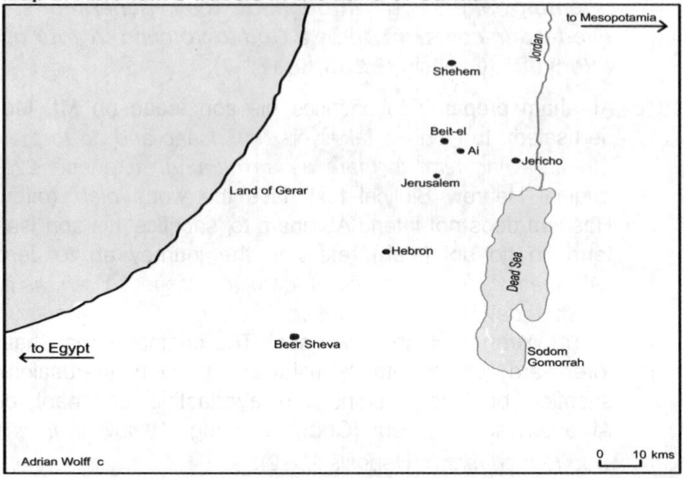

17thc "*Jacob arrived...at...Shehem...He bought...land...for one hundred kesitahs. He...proclaimed, 'God, the God of Israel...go up to Beit-el; (בית אל=House of God) I will make there an altar to God...Hashem said to him, 'Your name is Jacob. Your name shall not always be called Jacob, but **Israel** is your name.*" (Genesis 33:18-20; 35:3,10, also Genesis 32:29). **'Israel' ישראל in Hebrew is *Ya'shar-el* = straight to God. Another meaning is 'to prevail' ישרה over the Divine angel אל. The Bible uses the words '*Bnei Israel*'–the Sons of Israel (Jacob) = The Children of Israel or Israelites.**
The name 'Israel' in Hebrew combines the names of all three Patriarchs and four Matriarchs.

י = יצחק, יעקב Isaac, Jacob
ש = שרה Sarah
ר = רבקה, רחל Rebecca, Rachel
א = אברהם Abraham
ל = לאה Leah

17thc "*The sons of Jacob were twelve. The sons of Leah: Reuben, Simon, Levi, Judah, Issachar and Zebulun. The sons of Rachel:*

38

Joseph and Benjamin. The sons of Bilah, maidservant of Rachel, Dan and Naphtali. And the sons of Zilpah, maidservant of Leah: Gad and Asher." (Genesis 35:22-26). Jacob' daughter Dinah is born to Leah. (Genesis 34:1). Dinah is 'defiled by Shehem' (Exodus Chapter 34).

17thc   *"They journeyed from Beit-el...to Ephrat, when Rachel went into labor and had difficulty in her childbirth...her soul was departing,...she called his name Ben Oni (son of my mourning), but his father called him Benjamin. Thus Rachel died and was buried on the road to Ephrat, which is Bethlehem.* **Jacob set a monument over her grave;** *it is the monument of Rachel's grave until this day."* (Genesis 35:16-20). **This custom of placing a stone on a grave continues until today.**

Tel Be'er Sheva, Mud-Brick Walls   Adrian Wolff

17thc   *"Esau had taken his wives from...Canaanite women...settled on Mount Seir; Esau, he is Edom."* (Genesis 36:1,8). Note: Edom, or adom = red in Hebrew, see Genesis 25:25. Edom in the area southeast of the Dead Sea and Arava Valley has reddish colored mountains. *"Jacob settled...in the land of Canaan."* (Genesis 37:1).

1550   **Late Bronze Age. The Israelite Period**.
       Joseph son Jacob is sold by his brothers to *"Ishmaelites...for twenty pieces of silver...then...brought...to Egypt...became a successful man."* (Genesis 37:28; 39:2,4).

16thc   The Pharaoh of Egypt has a dream he is unable to interpret. *"So Pharaoh...summoned Joseph...Seven years are coming-a great abundance throughout...Egypt. Then seven years of famine will arise...will ravage the land...See! I have placed you in charge of all the land of Egypt. And Pharaoh removed his ring from his hand and put it on Joseph's hand. He had him dressed in garments of fine line and he placed a gold chain upon his neck. He also had him ride in his second royal chariot and they proclaim before him 'Avrech".* "*The earth produced during the seven years of abundance by the handfuls. He gathered all food of the seven years...and he placed food in the cities...Joseph amassed grain like sand of the sea...until he ceased counting, for there was no number."*" (Genesis 41:14,25,29,30,41,42,47-49, 54).

16thc There is famine in Canaan. "*but in all the land of Egypt there was bread.*" (Genesis 41:54) "*So Joseph's brothers-ten of them-went down to buy grain from Egypt. But Benjamin, Joseph's brother, Jacob did not send along with his brothers.*" (Genesis 42:3,4).

16thc Joseph confronts his brothers "*...let one of your brothers (Simon) be imprisoned...while you...bring provisions for...your households. Then bring your youngest brother (Benjamin).*" (Genesis 42:19,20,29). The brothers return to Canaan. "

16thc "*The brothers set out...to Egypt...Joseph said to his brothers, 'I am Joseph. Is my father still alive?...it is me, whom you sold into Egypt...They...came to land of Canaan to Jacob their father...I shall go and see him before I die.*" (Genesis 43:15; 45:1,3,4,25,28).

16thc "*Have no fear of descending to Egypt, for I shall establish you a great nation there.*" (Genesis 46:3) "*They took their livestock and their wealth which they had amassed in the land of Canaan and they came to Egypt–Jacob...all his offspring...Pharaoh...let them settle in the region of Goshen'...they were fruitful and multiplied.*" (Genesis 46:6,7; 47:5,6,27).

16thc "*Jacob called for his sons...these are **the tribes of Israel, twelve.**" (Genesis 49:1,28). Later, on their return to Canaan after their Exodus from Egypt, the descendants of the twelve sons of Jacob live in specific areas of the Land of Israel, known as the **Twelve Tribes** (the Israelites).

16thc "*(Jacob) instructed them to...bury me with my fathers…(in) the field of Machpelah...(together with)...Abraham and Sarah...Isaac and Rebecca...and...Leah*". (Genesis 49:29,30,31). "***Joseph died...*** *buried in Shehem.*" (Genesis 50:22,26. Joshua 24:32).

1482 The Egyptians under Pharaoh **Thutmose III** invade Canaan. Inscriptions found at Karnak in Egypt describe the cities he captures - Jaffa, Afek, Megido, Hazor.

1450 **Phoenicians,** sea-traders of olive oil, wine, cedar wood and copper, colonize in the Eastern Mediterranean use a single-letter script **alphabet,** later adopted by the Greeks. Phoenicians are termed by the Greeks *phoinikes,* 'red-people' from the reddish-purple dye they extract from murex mollusks. They construct the ports of Sidon, Tyre and Dor.

1367 Pharaoh **Akhenaten** (Amenhotep IV 1350–1334) worships a single deity, Aten, constructs a new city, Akhet-Aton (today's Tel el-Amarna) on the Middle Nile, with temples at Karnak, official buildings and splendid palaces. His wife is Queen Nefertiti. Their son **Tutankhamen,** pharaoh of Egypt (1352-1348) restores ancient pagan god worship.

14thc Letters written in cuneiform on clay tablets from local kings to the Pharaoh in Egypt are found in Akhenaten's Holy City at Tel **el-Amarna** in the **Middle Nile Valley.** They express the social and political relations between Egypt and various city-states, announcing the growing dangers of tribes invading from Canaan. Canaanite city-states loyal to the pharaoh are: Acre, Shimon, Achshap, Megido, Shehem, Afek, Gezer, Gat, 'Urusalim' (Jerusalem) and Lachish. Egyptians under **Pharaoh Seti I** (rules 1318–1304) conquer the Hittites in Canaan at Megido, Beit She'an, Acre (later known as Ptolemais), Hazor, Kedesh, Tyre and Sidon. Further evidence found engraved on a clay tablet written in Akkadian cuneiform script is found at **Tel Afek,** sent by the governor of Ugarit in Syria to the Egyptian governor ruling Canaan on behalf of the Pharaoh of Egypt.

Chapter 2. Exodus to Land of Israel 1300 – 1022 BCE

1300 It is generally believed the **Children of Israel** are under bondage in Egypt during the reign of Pharaoh Ramses II (1304–1227). They contribute to the construction of the temples at Abu Simbel along the Nile River. *"A new king arose over Egypt, who did not know Joseph...Egypt enslaved the Children of Israel with crushing hardness."* (Exodus 1:8,13).

1240 Amram marries Yochevet, have three children, Aaron, **Moses** and Miriam (I Chronicles 5:29; Exodus 6:20). Moses marries Zipporah, have a son Gershon. *"Moses...arrived...Horeb (Horev). An angel of Hashem appeared...**was burning in the fire but the bush was not consumed**."* God tells Moses, *"I shall...rescue it from...Egypt and to bring it up...**to a land flowing with milk and honey**...I shall dispatch you (Moses) to Pharaoh...take My people, the Children of Israel out of Egypt."* (Exodus 2:21,22; 3:1,2,7,8,10).

1240 Jews believe God cannot be defined in physical terms whatsoever, therefore God is known as **'The Name'**, **Hashem in Hebrew**. *"You shall not make a carved image nor any likeness of that which is in the heavens above or on the earth below or in the water beneath the earth."* (Exodus 20:4). Moses asks *"God...'what is His Name?"...'Hashem answers Moses 'I shall be as I shall be' (aehiye asher aehiye* אהיה אשר אהיה *YHVH Yahva, (also JHVH)...This is my Name forever."* (Exodus 3:13,14). God exists outside to time, and as such, we cannot apply any concepts of change to Him. The letters of 'the Name' יהוה (**YHVH**) is never pronounced as it is spelled. During prayer 'the Name' is pronounced *Adonai* אדוני (my Lord), other Hebrew names are *Eheyeh, Yah, El, Elohim* אלוהים, *Elohai, Shadai.* (See Kabbalah 1570).

13thc *"The king of Egypt will not allow you to go...I shall strike Egypt."* (Exodus 3:19,20). *"Moses and Aaron...said to Pharaoh...Send out My people."* (שלח את עמי in Hebrew, Let my people go!) (Exodus 5:1).

Ten plagues are brought upon the Egyptians.
1. **Blood** *"I shall strike the waters that are in the River, and they shall change to blood."* (Ex. 7:17)
2. **Frogs** *"I shall strike your entire boundary with frogs."* (Ex. 7:27)
3. **Lice** *"...become lice throughout the land of Egypt."* (Ex. 8:12)
4. **Vermin**. *"The houses of Egypt shall be filled with the swarm (vermin), and even the ground upon which they are."* (Ex. 8:17)
5. **Livestock epidemic** *"On your livestock...horses...the*

donkeys...camels and...flock–a very severe epidemic. Hashem shall distinguish between the livestock of Israel and the livestock of Egypt and not a thing that belongs to...Israel will die." (Ex. 9:3,4)

6. **Boils** *"Boils and blisters, erupting on man and beast."* (Ex. 9:10)
7. **Hail** *"I shall rain a very heavy hail, such as there has never been in Egypt."* (Ex. 9:18)
8. **Locusts** *"I shall bring a locust-swarm into your border. It will cover the surface of the earth."* (Ex. 10:4,5)
9. **Darkness** *"There was a thick darkness throughout the land of Egypt for a three-day period."* (Ex. 10:22)
10. **The death of the firstborn** will '**pass-over**' the Children of Israel. The festival of Passover, in Hebrew Pesach פסח. *"Every first-born in...Egypt shall die...But against...Israel ...neither man nor beast... know that Hashem will have differentiated between Egypt and Israel."* (Ex. 11:5,7)

13ᵗʰc Pharaoh finally surrenders allowing the Children of Israel to leave. Pharaoh *"called to Moses and Aaron...'go out...the Egyptians...granted their request-so they emptied Egypt. The Children of Israel journeyed from Ramses to Succoth, about 600,000 men on foot, aside from children". "They baked the dough that they took out of Egypt into* **unleavened cakes**,...*they were driven from Egypt...could not delay, nor had they made provisions." "Remember this day...you departed from Egypt, from...bondage...* **chametz** *(leavened bread) may not be eaten". "Hashem shall bring you to...a* **land flowing with milk and honey**". *"For a seven day(s)...shall you eat* **matzot**, *and on the seventh day there shall be a festival to Hashem".* (Exodus 12:31,32,36-39; 13:3,5,6). Jews continue to celebrate **Passover (Pesach)** Seder, 1st Festival of Freedom. *"remember that you were a slave in the land of Egypt...your God has taken you out."* (Deuteronomy 5:15).

On Passover Eve the family partakes in reading and singing the Passover story (Haggadah), eating a festive meal with wine.

The Seder table has five items:

1. Three Matzot (unleavened bread) representing the Kohen (priests), Levites and Israel. The bread is 'unleavened' as they left in a hurry before their bread could 'rise' in the ovens.
2. Roasted meat bone commemorating the Passover offering.
3. Bitter herbs - (maror) symbolizing the slavery in Egypt. (Ex.12:8)
4. Haroshet - chopped apples, nuts, wine and cinnamon or nutmeg resembling the mortar used for bricks.
5. Karpas - parsley and egg dipped in salt water eggs to symbolize Spring and rebirth.

13thc *"God did not lead them by way of the...Philistines...turned...toward the way of the wilderness to the Sea of Reeds'."* (Exodus 13:17,18). The earliest translation of the Tanach into Greek, known as the Septuagint, expedited in Alexandria in the 3rd century BCE, translates the original Hebrew words *Yam Suff,* the **Sea of Reeds** as *Erythra Thalassa,* the **Red Sea**. The mountains in the Red Sea area are of a reddish color.

*"Hashem went...in a **pillar of cloud**...a **pillar of fire**."* (Exodus 13:21). *"Make...two silver **trumpets**...summoning the assembly and to cause the camps to journey."* (Numbers 10:2). *"He (Pharaoh) harnessed his chariots and...He took six hundred elite chariots...and he pursued the Children of Israel...Moses...lift up your staff and stretch out your arm over the sea and split it; the Children of Israel shall come...on dry land...and the water was a wall for them on their right and on their left. Egypt pursued and came after them...He removed the wheels of their chariots and caused them to drive with difficulty...Moses 'Stretch out your hand over the sea and the water will go back upon Egypt, upon its chariots and upon its horsemen...there remain not one of them...Deep waters covered them."* (Exodus 14:6–8,15–28; 15:5).

They did not have enough to eat in the Sinai desert. *"We remember the **fish** we ate in Egypt, **cucumbers, melons, leeks, onions and garlic**."* (Numbers 11:5). *"shall rain for you food (**manna**) from heaven...and pick each day's portion on its day."* (Exodus 16:4). *"**Manna** was like **coriander seed**...grind it...tastes of **dough kneaded with oil**."* (Numbers 11:8).

13thc *"Amalek came and battled Israel in Refidim...when Moses raised his hand, Israel was stronger, and when he lowered his hand Amalek was stronger...Joshua weakened Amalek and its people with the sword's blade..."Hashem said...I shall erase the memory of Amalek from under the heavens...**Hashem maintains a war against Amalek from generation to generation**."* (Ex. 17:8-15).

13thc **Moses climbs Mt. Sinai to receive the Ten Commandments and Ark of the Covenant**. *"to the top of the mountain."* (Ex.19:20). *"**For a commandment is a lamp and the Torah is light**."* (Proverbs 6:23). *"Moses...skin of his face had become radiant (קרן)".* (Ex.34:29). Jeromes' Vulgate translates the Hebrew singular word (keren קרן- radiant) into plural 'Horns' (קרנים).

The Ten Commandments Exodus 20:1-14
1. Belief in God *"I am Hashem, your God, Who has taken you out of the land of Egypt, from your house of slavery."*
2. Prohibition of idolatry *"You shall not recognize the gods of*

others in my presence. You shall not make yourself a carved image nor any likeness of that which is in the heavens above or on the earth below or in the water beneath the earth. You shall not prostate yourself to them nor worship them, for I am Hashem, your God-a jealous God **who visits the sin of fathers upon their children to the third and fourth generations**, for My enemies, but who shows kindness for thousands (of generations) to those who love me and observe my commandments."

3. Prohibition of vain oaths "You shall not take the Name of Hashem, your God in vain, for Hashem will not absolve anyone who takes His name in vain."

4. The Sabbath "Remember the Sabbath day to sanctify it. Six days shall you work and accomplish all your work, but the seventh day is Sabbath to Hashem, your God; you shall not do any work - you, your son, your daughter, your slave, your maidservant, your animal, and your covert within your gates - for six days Hashem made the heavens and the earth, the sea and all that is in them, and he rested on the seventh day. Therefore Hashem blessed the Sabbath day and sanctify it."

5. Honoring parents "Honor your father and mother so that your days will be lengthened."

6. Prohibition against murder "You shall not kill."

7. Prohibition against adultery "You shall not commit adultery."

8. Prohibition against kidnapping/stealing "You shall not steal."

9. Prohibition against bearing false witness "You shall not bear false witness against your fellow".

10. Prohibition against theft "You shall not covet your fellow's house. You shall not covet your fellow's wife, his manservant, his ox, his donkey, nor anything that belongs to your fellow."

The exact location of Mount Sinai (*har-Horeb*) is unknown, cannot become a Jewish pilgrimage site. The Christian Monastery at Mt Sinai is a Christian site from the Byzantine Period. Moses, known as the greatest of all prophets, is given the Divine Law. *"Never again has there arisen in Israel a prophet like Moses."* (Deuteronomy 34:10). "He gave Moses the **two Tablets of Testimony**." (Exodus 31:18)...*the Declarations...**inscribed...on two stone Tablets**...Moses finished **writing the words of this Torah**...commanded the Levites, the bearers of the Ark of the Covenant of Hashem. **Take this book of the Torah...place it at the side of the Ark of the Covenant** of Hashem." (Deuteronomy 4:13; 31:24-26), in the Tabernacle constructed by Bezalel, son of Uri, son of Hur. This portable Temple, used in the desert during the conquest of the land of Israel, contains other vessels used in the physical worship of God. (Exodus 38:22).

The Ark of the Covenant. (Two Tablets of the Ten Commandments). Moses is instructed by Hashem to "...*make a Sanctuary (dedicated) for Me...make an Ark of acacia wood...you shall place in **the Ark the Testament-tablets**...make a screen for the entrance of the Tent, of turquoise, purple and scarlet wool, and twisted linen. You shall make make for them the Screen five pillars of acacia wood and cover them with gold...and cast for them five sockets of copper.*" (Exodus 25:1; 26:34,36,37). Gold represents Divine Light, silver denotes innocence (Zechariah 6:11).

"When they will encamp, every man at his camp and every man at his banner (flag). (Numbers 1:2;44;46;52).

The Menorah–a Jewish Symbol "...*make a menorah (oil-lamp candelabra) of gold...three branches (on each side)...its lamps seven*" (Exodus 25:31,32,37). "*take olive oil...to kindle a **continual (everlasting) lamp**...an eternal decree for your generations.*" (Leviticus 24:1-4). (See -952,-516,70,204. Tabernacle, Altar and burning incense in Exodus chapters 26, 27, 30).

13th c   Hashem commands Moses "*you shall teach them and they shall perform in **the land that I give them, to possess it**.*" (Deuteronomy 5:28). "*The Torah...is the heritage...of the nation...**tribes** of Israel.*" (Deuteronomy 33:4,5). **Man has intellectual power, is able to think, make decisions, act with free will, creator of his own destiny.** We have been given "***the tree of Knowledge of Good and Bad...Man has become like the Unique One among us, knowing good from bad.***" (Genesis 2:9; 3:22). **The 'land' refers to the Land of Israel,** *Eretz Israel* **in Hebrew. No word or letter may be added or subtracted from the Torah, The Five Books of Moses.**

The written Torah has 613 commandments and prohibitions, 248 positive and 365 negative. A human body has 248 limbs, and 365 nerves and veins. The Torah has social codes which lay down the rules of a Jewish 'way of life' to cover all aspects of one's daily life from birth to death to include Sabbath, circumcision, diet, feasts etc. All people are equal, chosen in God's image (Genesis 1:26-27). Man alone can guide his actions through reason. Jews believe when a person transgresses he must make amends for his wrongdoing, repent, and atone. Jews contend that all righteous people whatever their belief, have a place in heaven, in contrast to Christianity and Islam that believe only their true believers go to heaven in the after-life.

The basis of Jewish belief is found in '*Shema Yisrael*' שמע ישראל

"Hear, O Israel: Hashem is our God, Hashem is the One and Only. You shall love Hashem, your God with all your heart, with all your soul, and with all your resources. And these matters that I command you today shall be upon your heart. You shall teach them thoroughly to your children and you shall speak of them while you sit in your home, while you walk on the way, when you retire and when you arise. Bind them as a sign upon your arm (Teflilin-phylacteries) and let them be ornaments between your eyes. And write the on the door-posts (mezuzah) of your house and upon your gates." (Deuteronomy 6:4-9).

Tefillin (phylacteries) are a pair of black leather boxes containing Hebrew parchment scrolls to connect your head, heart and hand.

Mezuzah is affixed to the right doorpost in a Jewish home, as a declaration and reminder of faith. A handwritten scroll is placed inside inscribed with the verses of the Shema prayer. The name of God, *Sha-dai* שד"י appears on the reverse side of the parchment, is an acronym for Hebrew *"Guardian of the doorways of Israel."*

Tallit (prayer shawl) is used during morning prayers with fringes (tzitzit) to serve as a constant reminder of our obligations to Hashem and to others.*"...make themselves tzitzit on the corners of their garments, throughout the generations...upon each corner a thread of **turquoise** wool." (Numbers 15:38).*

Red/Crimson thread *"...the midwife took a crimson thread and tied it to his hand..." (Genesis 38:28,30).*

Jewish Theology

1. The Bible, The Tanach contains - Torah, Prophets and Writings.
2. Believe in God and God alone.
   "Hashem is our God, Hashem is the One and Only." (Deut. 6:4). *"You shall not recognize the gods of others in My presence."* (Deut. 5:7). The Hebrew letters designating the concept of God (Hashem) are יהוה (JHVH), which relates to the past היה, the present הוה, and the future יהוה. Hashem was, is and will be at the same instant, beyond the dimension of time. The final letter of this concept is a 'hey' ה, the fifth letter of the Hebrew alphabet, symbolizing the five fingers of the hand, to receive what Hashem is giving.
3. Goodness, Creation
   Before 'creation' the earth was empty, without form תהו ובהו. God is concealed עלם from the universe עולם, existing before and after creation. Hashem created the universe for the purpose of bestowing 'good'. *"Hashem saw that He had made*

and behold it was very good". (Gen 1:31) וירא אלוהים כי טוב. "*Hashem is good to all; His mercies are on all His works.*" (Psalms 145:9). Human actions are a free choice, as we have full responsibility for them. By doing 'good', man has the opportunity to draw 'close to Hashem'. *"I made the earth and I created Mankind upon it"* (Isaiah 45:12).

4. God cannot have any human form, structure or plurality whatsoever. Iconolatry is forbidden.

    "You will not be able to see My face" (Ex. 33:20). "*You shall not make yourself a carved image of any likeness of that which is in the heavens above or on the earth below or in the water beneath the earth.*" (Deut. 5:8). "*I Shall Be As I Shall Be.*" (Ex. 3:14). God cannot be born, die, suffer, and 'become flesh'.

5. God is for all peoples. "*Hashem is good to all.*" (Psalms 145:9).

6. Atonement. The Torah tells us of various sins perpetrated by man. We alone have to atone for our sins, to act and rise above our sins by using the Ten Commandments as our guide. "*Fathers shall not be put to death because of their sons, and sons shall not be put to death because of their fathers.*" (Deut. 24:16). Death cannot bring forgiveness to a person's sin. "*Do not desire the death of the wicked one, but rather the wicked one's return from his way, that he may live. Repent from your evil wicked ways.*" (Eze. 33:11). A Jew is expected to repent and ask forgiveness from a person he has wronged. On the Day of Atonement he asks atonement from God who is omnipresent.

7. The Messiah will "*bring forth justice to all nations.*" (Isaiah 42:1).

8. The Messianic Age will bring the ingathering of the exiles. "*He will raise a banner for the nations and assemble the castaways of Israel; and he will gather in the dispersed ones of Judah from the four corners of the earth.*" (Isaiah 11:12).

9. The Messiah will arrive "*It will happen in the end of days.*" (Isa 2:2) bringing peace on earth. (Isa.11:6-9), from the House of David. "*Bethlehem - Efrata - ..from you some one will emerge for Me to be a ruler over Israel.*" (Micah 5:1).

    "*Rejoice greatly, O daughter of Zion! Shout for joy, O daughter of Jerusalem! For behold, your king will come to you, righteous and victorious is he, a humble man riding upon a donkey.*" (Zech. 9:9). The Messiah can arrive at any time without warning. A donkey is less ostentatious than a horse.

10. The Bible does not state the Messiah will be a god or God-like. The concept of the Messianic Age gives mankind optimism for the future.

11. We should conduct our daily lives to be honest, considerate in our dealings with man and respectful in our perspective with

God. "*Hashem is the earth and its fullness, the inhabited land and those who dwell in it...Who may ascend the mountain of Hashem and who may stand in the place of his sanctity? One with clean hands and pure heart; who has not sworn in vain by My soul, and has not sworn deceitfully. He will receive a blessing from Hashem and just kindness from the God of his salvation*" (Psalms 24:1,3,4,5).

"*You shall love your fellow as yourself.*" (Leviticus 19:18).

"*For God will judge every deed—even everything hidden—whether good or evil.*" (Ecclesiastes 12:14).

12 Judaism sees each person as being potentially righteous. "*All of Israel has a portion in the world to come.*" (Mishna Sanhedrin 10:1)

Albert Einstein states "*Try and penetrate with our limited means the secrets of nature and you will find that, behind all the discernible laws and connections, there remains something subtle, intangible and inexplicable.*" "*Every one who is seriously involved in the pursuit of science becomes convinced that a spirit is manifest in the laws of the Universe - a spirit vastly superior to that of man.*" "*The most important human endeavor is the striving for morality in our actions...(to) give beauty and dignity to life.*" "*The bond that has united the Jews...is, above all, the democratic ideal of social justice coupled with the ideal of mutual aid and tolerance among all men.*" (Walter Isaacson.*Einstein*)

Jewish prayer."*Blessed are You, Hashem our God, King of the universe, Who has kept us alive, sustained us and brought us to this season.*"'*she'hianu,ve'kimanu, ve'higanu le'zeman ha'zeh'*.
ברוך אתה יי אלהינו מלך העולם שהחינו וקימנו והגיענו לזמן הזה.

Jewish Tradition in daily life are expected to keep the commandments of the Tanach. Responsibilities begin with the care of individuals in the home-to provide and educate children, honor parents and participate in social and community responsibilities. "*All Jews bear responsibility for one* כל ישראל ערבים זה לזה *another*". (Shavuot 39a). Giving charity is part of Jewish communal life. "*When you harvest of your land, you shall not complete your reaping to the corner of your field...for the poor...shall you leave them*". (Leviticus 19:9,10). A Rabbi was asked "*what was at the basis of Jewish education*". He answers: "*Questions. We teach our children to make questions*".

The Sabbath is 'holy' since it is devoted to spiritual rather than worldy affairs. "*The Sabbath (is) an eternal covenant for their generations...Six days shall you work and accomplish all your work, but the seventh day is Sabbath to Hashem, your God; you shall not do any work...for six days Hashem made the heavens* *and the earth...he rested on the seventh day."* (Exodus 20:8; 31:16). **Enjoy Sabbath and give to charity** *"Eat rich foods and drink sweet beverages, and send portions to those who have nothing prepare..and to engage in great rejoicing."* (Nehemiah 8:10-12). לכה דודי פני שבת נקבלה. *"Come my friend to meet the bride, let us welcome the presence of the Sabbath as a bridegroom rejoices over his bride."* (Jewish liturgy, Rabbi Shlomo Alkabetz, 1584).

Sabbatical *"For six years you may sow your field...prune your vineyard...and gather in its crop. But the seventh year shall be a complete rest for the land."* (Leviticus 25:3-4).

Sabbath Kiddush (wine blessing) Cup, Uri Shevah   www.uriart.co.il

Moses proclaims the laws and values must be remembered. They are coded in the Book of Deuteronomy and Leviticus as relevant jurisprudence for The Children of Israel's new life in their land. The **Children of Israel** (Bnei Israel בני ישראל) are now **The People of Israel** (Am Israel עם ישראל) as Jews are now a nation possessing a legal structure regarding how a person **should** (not **must**) behave and be judged. Moses translates the most intense idealism of social behavior into practical concepts into the details of everyday life. His everlasting ethical imperatives are with us today as these laws are the basis of western culture and social behavior. Moses warns the nation. Those who do *"not cleanse completely, recalling the iniquity of parents upon children to the third and fourth generation"*. (Numbers 14:18).

Examples of Social Laws taken from the Tanach.
1. **Age and Respect.** *"In the presence of an old person you shall*

rise." (Lev. 19:32).

2. **Alcohol over-indulgence.** *"Do not drink intoxicating wine...that you not die."* (Lev. 10:9).

3. **Borrowing, restitution.** *"If a man shall borrow...he shall surely make restitution."* (Exodus 22:13).

4. **Bribes.** *"Do not accept a bribe."* (Exodus 23:8).

5. **Business Honesty.** *"You shall have correct scales, correct weights, correct dry measures, and correct liquid measures."* (Lev. 19:36).

6. **Charity.** *"You shall not harden your heart or close your hand against your destitute brother...open your hand to your brother, to your poor, and to your destitute in your land."* (Deut. 15:7,11).

7. **Cleanliness/hygiene.** *"Cover your excrement."* (Deut. 23:14).

8. **Criminal Behavior.** *"The iniquities of the wicked one will trap him, and he will be suspended in the cords of his sins."* (Prov. 5:22).

9. **False Accusations.** *"Distance yourself from false word."* (Ex 23:7).

10. **Foolishness.** *"Do not answer a fool according to his foolishness, lest you be considered like him."* (Prov. 26:4).

11. **Honesty.** *"Confess their sin that they committed."* (Num. 5:7).

12. **Judgement.** *"Do not execute the innocent or the righteous."* Ex. 23:7. *"...not show favoritism in judgement, small and great alike shall you hear; you shall not tremble before any man."* (Deut. 1:17).

13. **Hospitality.** *"Men were standing...so he ran toward them...and bowed toward the ground...'Let some water be brought and wash your feet, and recline beneath the tree. I will fetch a morsel of bread that you may sustain yourselves, then go on."* (Gen. 18:1–5).

14. **Lies.** *"You shall not bear false witness against others."* (Ex. 20:13)

15. **Murder.** *"You shall not kill."* (Ex. 20:13; 21:12).

16. **Negotiations.** *"When you draw near to a city to wage war against it, you shall call out to it for peace."* (Deut. 20:10).

17. **Payments.** *"You shall not be late in paying."* (Deut. 23:22).

18. **Respect, Consideration for others and Equality of Mankind.** *"You shall love your fellow as yourself."* (Lev. 19:18).

19. **Respect for Elders.** *"Honor your father and mother."* (Ex 20:12)

20. **Sabbath.** *"...the seventh day...you shall not do any work - you, your son, your daughter, your servant, your animal."* (Ex. 20:10,11).

21. **Social and Moral Behavior.** *"You shall not be a*

gossipmonger...you shall not stand aside while your fellow's blood is shed." (Lev. 19:16).

22. **Strangers**. "You shall not taunt or oppress a stranger." (Ex. 22:20).

23. **Testimony**. "A single witness shall not stand up against any man for any iniquity or for any error, regarding any sin that he may commit; according two witnesses or according to three witnesses shall a matter be confirmed." (Deut. 19:15).

24. **Theft**. "You shall not steal...not covet...anything that belongs to your fellow (man)." (Ex. 20:13).

25. **Worker's payment**. "A worker's wage shall not remain with you overnight until morning." (Lev. 19:13).

Pirkei Avot פרקי אבות - Ethics of the Fathers

The Mishna (Oral Bible) is written in the 1-2 century CE. One of the tractates, Pirkei Avot containing six chapters, is completely devoted to Jewish morals, values and ethics. Parents and educators should teach them to the next generation and be role models.

"Engage not in much gossip" 1:5

"Associate not with the wicked" 1:7

"He who does not increase his knowledge, decreases it." 1:13

"Say little and do much." 1:15

"Receive all men with a cheerful countenance." 1:15

"The world is preserved by truth, by judgement and by peace."1:18

"Be honorable to oneself...bring oneself honor from mankind." 2:1

"An excellent thing is the study of the Torah combined with some worldly occupation". 2:2

"The wise man does not speak before him who is greater than he in wisdom, and does not break in upon the speech of his fellow, he is not hasty to answer." 5:10

13thc Moses says "Provide for yourselves distinguished men who are wise, understanding and well known...shall appoint them as your heads." (Deuteronomy 1:13). **Hashem defines the borders of the Land of Israel, 'Eretz Israel' ארץ ישראל** in the Bible. "This is the land that shall fall to you as an inheritance, the land of Canaan according to its borders." (Numbers 34:1-6).

Festivals "...say to them: Hashem's appointed festivals." (Leviticus 23:1,2) "And Moses declared the appointed festivals of Hashem to the Children of Israel." (Lev. 23:44).

Passover-Pesach "For a seven-day period you shall eat matzot...For in the month of spring you went forth from Egypt." (Ex. 34:18). "This day shall become a remembrance for you and you shall celebrate it as a festival for Hashem, for your *generations.*" (Ex.12:14). At the festive meal Jews eat symbolic foods - bitter herbs, 4 cups of wine, shank bone of lamb, hard-boiled eggs and haroshet (fruit and nut paste to resemble mortar).

Shavu'ot On Mt. Sinai Moses "*...wrote...the words of the covenant the Ten Commandments...the two Tablets of the Testimony....You shall make the Festival of Weeks with the first offering of the wheat harvest.*" (Exodus 34:22, 28, 29). (Leviticus 23:15, 22).

Rosh Hashana "*In the seventh month, on the first...month there shall be a rest day, a remembrance with shofar blasts.*" (Lev 23:24)

The **Shofar** symbolizes: Hope for the future, Ascension of the Divine Presence, Time to celebrate a holiday. "*Make music for God...make music for our king...For God is King of all the earth.*" (Psalms 47:6).

Yom Kippur "*On the tenth day of this month is the Day of Atonement...you shall not do any work on this day...to provide you atonement before Hashem, your God.*" (Lev. 23:27,28). The Holiest Day of the Jewish Calendar, fasting from sundown to sundown, about 25 hours. The service begins with the words '*Kol Nidre*' - *All vows.* A Jew seek 'atonement' (to repent and not repeat the sin) to amend for any wrongs committed during the year for his sins against God and other human beings.

Succot "*On the fifteenth day of this month is the festival of Succot, a seven-day period for Hashem...You shall take for yourselves the fruit of the citron tree, the branches of date palms, twigs of a plaited tree, and brook willows and you shall rejoice before Hashem...You shall dwell in booths.*" (Lev. 23:34,40,42). "*Provide you* **rains** *in their time, and the land will...produce...the tree of the field will give its fruit.*" (Lev. 26:4).

The Jewish Calendar has 354 days in the year, 28 days each month, 12 months in the year. There are 7 leap every 19 years, with an additional month (Adar Bet) in years 3,6,8,11,14,17,19.

13thc Moses sends twelve spies on a reconnaissance mission into Canaan to discover the capabilities of the resident tribes and in addition, their reactions towards foreign conquerors. (Numbers 13:2,17-19). Moses prepares to enter Canaan. "*Possess the Land that Hashem swore to your forefathers to Abraham, Isaac, and to Jacob, to give them and their children after them.*" (Deut. 1:5,8).

13thc **The Census.** "*Take a census...who were coming out of...Egypt...the countings of the sons of Israel: Six Hundred and one thousand, seven hundred and thirty.*" (Numbers 26:1,2,4,51).

1210 Moses appoints a successor "*Take yourself* **Joshua,** *son of*

Nun" (Numbers 27:18).

1210   Moses "*Ascend(s) mount Nevo,...in...Moav, which is before Jericho, and see the Land of Canaan that I have given to the Children of Israel as an inheritance...from a distance shall you see the land, but you shall not enter there.*" Moses is buried in an unknown grave which cannot become a pilgrimage site. "*no one knows his burial place to this day.*" "*Never again has there arisen...a prophet like Moses.*" (Deut. 32:49-52; 34:6; 34:10).

1210   **Return and conquest of the Land of Israel (Eretz Israel). Joshua** leads the Children of Israel to invade Canaan. "*The entire people...will return to the land of your inheritance...from the desert and Lebanon until the great river, the Euphrates River, all the land of the Hittites until the Great Sea toward the setting of the sun...to observe, to do according to the entire Torah...make your way successful, and...act wisely*". (Joshua 1:2,4,7,8). They cross the Jordan River near Jericho. "*The waters descending from upstream stood still...the Kohanim, the bearers of the Ark...all Israel crossing on dry ground until the entire nation finished crossing.*" (Joshua 3:15,16,17; 4:10,19). They encamp near Gilgal (Joshua 4:19). Shortly thereafter encircle seven times and conquer Jericho. "*Blew the shofars...wall fell in its place...burned the city and everything that was in it.*" (Joshua 6:11-24). Fertile agricultural fields, abundant with fruit and fresh water surround the oasis of Jericho.

Jurisprudence.
A suspect is innocent until proven guilty. Joshua states, "*prepare for yourself a city of refuge...where a killer may flee.*" (Joshua 20:2,3). "*So that the killer will not die until he stands before the assembly for judgment.*" (Numbers 35:12).

12thc   **Joshua does not settle the Jebusite city-state of Jerusalem**, not being attractive economically or strategically. Later King David will conquer Jerusalem. Joshua defeats the rulers of city-states in the **south**, to include Ai, Libnah, Lachish, Gezer, Eglon, Hebron and Debir. In the **north** Joshua captures Dor, Hazor and "*to the plain of Gad in the valley of the Lebanon at the foot of Mount Hermon...the mountain...lowland...plain...waterfalls...wilderness...in the south...up to the border of Edom...the Dead Sea....Ma'aleh Akrabim... Zin...to Kadesh-Barnea...Kedesh in the Galilee...Shehem...Kiryat Arba...Bezer...Ramot...and Golan.*" (Joshua 10; 11: 2,10,17; 12:8; 15:1-3; 20:7,8). Evidence of scorching is found at Tel Hazor. The entire Land of Israel is divided among the descendants of the **Twelve Tribes** who made the exodus from Egypt. (Joshua chapters 13 to 19). His troops and followers "*shall drive out the Canaanite even though they have iron* *chariots and are strong."* (Joshua 17:18).

12thc   Joshua instructs the Children of Israel to worship Hashem and follow His Commandments. (Joshua 24:14,17,18,19, 20). He leads them to prosperity, to establish borders and provinces.

Map 3. Territory of the Twelve Tribes 12th century BCE

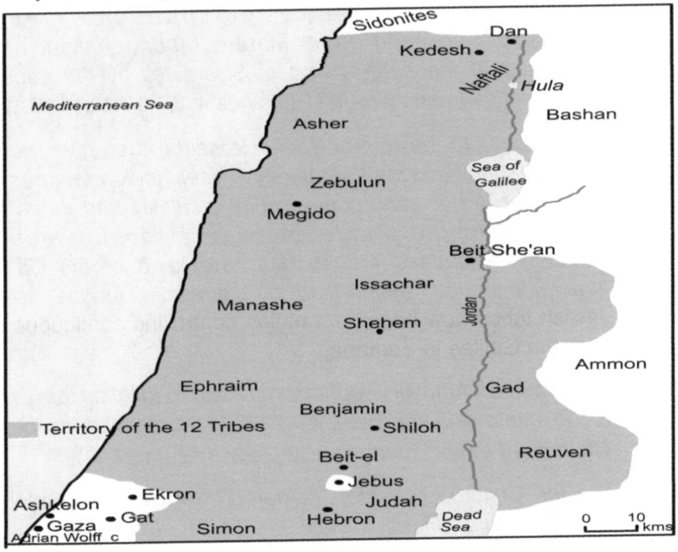

1200c **Iron Age** 1200 – 1020 **Age of the Judges of Israel**.

1175   **'Sea People'**, related to the Minoans and Mycenaeans from the Aegean invade Canaan, settling in five cites - Ashdod, Ashkelon, Ekron, Gat, and Gaza (I Samuel 5). Known as **Philistines** (*Pelishtim* in Hebrew), traders who possess iron, a commodity unavailable to the Children of Israel who inhabit the mountainous areas of Judah and Samaria. The Philistines leave no language, literature, nor inscriptions. They will disappear from history following the Babylonian invasion and conquest of Judea, Samaria and Egypt during the 6th century BCE.

12thc   The Children of Israel continue their conquest of Canaan. (Judges 3:31). Canaanites who settled in the Lower Galilee are wedged between the Jewish tribes in the Upper Galilee and those in Samaria. The Children of Israel follow **Deborah** *"a prophetess, the wife of Lapidot...lived...in Mt. Ephraim, and the Children of Israel would go up to her for judgment."* (Judges 4:4,5). Sisera, a leader of King Jabin's Canaanite army possesses iron chariots, is enticed into a narrow gorge near Mt. Tabor in the Lower Galilee. The prophetess Deborah leads them to victory. "*The general...Sisera... (had) nine hundred chariots.*" (Judges 4:3). "*Deborah...summoned Barak, son of Avinoam of Kedesh Naftali and said...go...toward Mount Tabor...take...ten thousand men from...Naftali and from...Zevulun. I will draw toward you, to the Kishon Brook, Sisera, the general of Jabin's army, with his chariots and his multitude...Barak...and ten thousand men...and Deborah...descended from Mount Tabor...chased after the chariots...and the entire camp of Sisera fell by the edge of the sword, not even one was left.*" (Judges 4: 3,4,6,7,10,14,15,16).

12thc   "*Sisera fled...to the tent of **Yael**...He said to her 'give me a bit of water to drink because I am thirsty'...Yael...took a tent peg, placed a hammer in her hand came to him stealthily and drove the peg into his temple...while he was sleeping deeply and exhausted.*" (Judges 4:17,19,21). "*The hand of the Children of Israel...destroyed Jabin, king of Canaan.*" (Judges 4:24). The Jewish tribes now become a nation controlling contiguous territory from the Galilee to Samaria,.

12thc   "*All of Midan, Amalek...Jephthah crossed to the Children of Ammon to do battle against them...and (they) were subdued before the Children of Israel.*" (Judges 6:33; 7:23; 8:12; 11:32,33).

1120   "*All the Children of Israel...gathered...**from Dan to Be'er Sheva** and the land of Gilead, to Hashem at Mitzpah.*" (Judges 20:1).

Tel Dan, Canaanite entrance. Note clay brick arch over entrance. Adrian Wolff

1120   "*The Children of Dan...came upon Laish...struck them down by the sword and burnt the city...They named the city Dan.*" (Judges 18:26,27,29). A city is constructed at (Tel) Dan to include a large entrance gate using a keystone at the apex of the arch. Over one-thousand years later Roman architecture will use the arch with a key-stone as the standard construction method to support a roof.

12thc The Children of Israel continue to be in conflict with the Philistines. **Samson** is born to a supposedly infertile woman Manoah and to Zorah of the Dan tribe. *"you are barren and not given birth, but you shall conceive and give birth to a son...For the boy shall be a* **nazirite** (נזיר = *pure, cannot be tempted) of God from the womb, and he will begin to save Israel. From the hand of the Philistines"* (Judges 13:3,5). Samson's miraculous birth to a barren, infertile woman is a sign of his holiness and source of his strength. Samson is deceived by Delilah's treachery exposing the secret to his strength. *"If I would be shaven, my strength would leave me....The Philistines seized him and gouged out his eyes. They brought him down to Gaza and bound him in copper fetters...The hair on his head began to sprout after he had been shaved...Samson...leaned with force, and the building collapsed on the governors and on all the people inside it."* (Judges 16:17,21,22,30).

1060 In an effort to gain control the hinterland of the Coastal Plain towards the port of Jaffa, the Children of Israel battle the Philistines at Afek near the headwaters of the Yarkon River in the Sharon Plain. They are defeated in the Battle of Eben-ezer as the Philistines capture the Ark of the Covenant. *"When the Ark of the Covenant of Hashem arrived at the camp, all Israel sounded a great shofar blast and the ground shook...So the Philistines fought. Israel was smitten...Thirty thousand foot soldiers fell from Israel, the Ark of Hashem was taken...and the two sons of Eli, Hofni and Pinhas, died."* (I Samuel 4:5,10,11).

Various ailments afflict the Philistines in their towns of Ashdod, Gat and Ekron. The Philistines assume the cause to be a result of their capture of the Ark of the Covenant at Afek, which now is in their possession. (I Samuel 5). The Philistines place the Ark of the Covenant on a *"new wagon...and put the golden objects...the cows set out on the direct road to Beit Shemesh...the men of Kiryat Ya'arim (west of Jerusalem) came and brought (it)...to the house of Abinadab...designated Elazar his son to guard the Ark."* (I Samuel 6:7,11,12 7:1).

1050c The Jewish Prophet **Samuel**, son of Hannah and Elkanah is born. *"She named him Samuel (Shaul me'el = requested of God) for 'I requested him from Hashem."* (I Samuel 1:20). Samuel spoke *"If you are returning unto Hashem...then remove the foreign gods...serving Him alone; then He will rescue from the hand of the Philistines....When the Philistines approached for the battle with Israel...so that they were defeated by Israel."* (I Samuel 7:3,10).

Chapter 3. King Saul to King Solomon 1022 – 933 BCE

1022 - 922 Kings of Israel, the Monarchy Period

11thc *"**Samuel**...appointed his sons judges...were swayed by profit... perverted justice...the elders...gathered...said, 'Give us a king to judge."* (I Samuel 8:1,3,4,6).

11thc *"**Saul** was exceptionally goodly...Samuel took a flask of oil and poured some onto Saul's head...all the people shouted 'Long live the king...made Saul king...in Gilgal."* (I Samuel 9:2; 10:1,24; 2:15).

11thc Philistines control the Coastal Plain and **Trade Routes** with Egypt (south), Lebanon, and Assyria (north). The Israelites, located in the hills of Samaria and Judah have limited trading for essential commodities. Shortage of iron and copper, used to manufacture weapons of war is a serious drawback in their strategic position to defend themselves against neighboring enemies.

11thc *"The Philistines gathered to wage war against Israel, with thirty thousand chariots, six thousand cavalry and foot soldiers as numerous as the sand of the sea."..."Now there was **no smith** (חָרָשׁ)to be found anywhere in the entire **Land of Israel (Eretz Israel)** ארץ ישראל...on the day of war...there was not to be found sword or spear...(with) any people who were with Saul and Jonathan."* (I Samuel 13: 5,19,22).

11thc *"The Philistines assembled their camps for war...standing on the mountain on one side and Israel...on the other...the valley was between them. **Goliath** of Gat, his height six cubits...a **copper** helmet...wearing **armor** of mail; the weight...was five thousand shekels...a copper shield on his legs and a copper neck-guard between his shoulders. The shaft of his spear was like a weaver beam and the **blade** of his spear weigh six hundred iron shekels."* (I Samuel 15:2,3,18; 17:1-7). Saul's army is assembled from the villagers, shepherds and farmers residing in the area. Jesse (ישי) from Bethlehem requests his younger son **David**, a shepherd to *"hurry...to your brothers* (in the army of Saul)*...inquire after the welfare of your brothers."* (I Samuel 17:17,18).

1010c Goliath humiliates Saul with a challenge. *"Choose yourselves a man...if he can fight me and kill me, we will be slaves to you; and if I defeat him and kill him, you will be slaves to us and serve us. Give me a man and we will fight together".* (I Samuel 17:8,9,10). Saul has no reply. *"Saul and all Israel heard these words of the Philistine...were terrified and greatly afraid."* (I Samuel 17:11).

1010c David volunteers to fight Goliath. *"David...took his staff...picked out five smooth stones from the brook and put them in his shepherd's bag and in the knapsack, and his slingshot...in his hand...The Philistine peered and saw David, and he derided him, for he was youth.* David informs Goliath and Philistines the Israelites cannot be subdued by force. *"You come to me with a sword, a spear and a javelin – but I come to you with the Name of Hashem...that you have ridiculed...The whole earth will know that there is a God in Israel...*Perhaps David is predicting survival of the Jewish nation! *"...David...took a stone...and slung it and struck the Philistine (Goliath) in the forehead...he fell upon his face, upon the ground...the Philistines saw that their hero was dead, and they ran away."* (I Samuel 17:32,40,42,45,46,48,49,51).

11thc David marries *"Michal daughter of Saul loved David"* (I Samuel 18:20,27). King Saul is uncomfortable with David's popularity and charisma, pursuing him as he flees. David spares Saul by *'stealthily cut off a corner of Saul's robe...*(proving his loyalty)*...David...did not permit them to rise up against Saul."* (I Samuel 24:5,8).

11thc King Saul is continuously in battle against the Philistines who control the Trade Route along the coast. King Saul's sons Jonathan, Avinadav, and Malchi-shua are killed in battle against the Philistines at **Mount Gilboa** in the Jezreel Valley. (I Samuel 31:1-5). When his situation in battle against the Philistines appears to be hopeless *"Saul took his sword and fell upon it...his three sons...all of his men, died together on that day...the Philistines...severed his head...they hung up his remains upon the wall of Beit She'an."* (I Samuel 31:4,6,8,9,10). (II Samuel 1:6,10).

1006 King David unites **the northern The Ten Tribes** in **Israel** and **the southern Two Tribes** in **Judah** into one united kingdom. *"All the tribes of Israel came to David...sealed a covenant with them in Hebron...and they anointed David...ruled over all of Israel...administered justice and kindness to his entire people."* (II Samuel 5:1,3; 8:15). He defeats external enemies and leaves his successor a united, secure, prosperous kingdom.

1006 **Weapons of War.** David's troops include *"men...armed with **bows**, both right-handed and left-handed, in **slinging stones or shooting arrows** with a bow...**shields** and buckles...bearers of shields and **spears**."* (I Chronicles 12:2,9,34,38). King David is able to expand his empire as Egypt is currently in a state of civil war as infighting temporarily weakens its super-power status.

10thc The Israelites are mainly agriculturalists, a minority live in the towns Shehem, Bethlehem and Hebron. Only after Jerusalem is conquered and becomes the capital, does the relative importance of towns become influential, together with urban occupations such as carpentry, leatherwork, metalwork, textiles, jewelry and the visible results of the importance of trade - building of storerooms and striking of coins. Clay seals found in the NW Negev describe kings, rather than lone chieftains ruling over this area.

998 King David will not allow a 'foreign-controlled enclave' to exist within his realm, and therefore the Jebusite Hittite city-state of Jerusalem has to be conquered. His forces enter through the gutter *"tzinor"* at the Gihon Spring. Then King David moves his **capital** from Hebron to **Jerusalem**, settling on Mount Zion (the City of David) in an area called the 'Ophel'. (II Samuel 5:3,5-9; 7:24), uniting the House of Israel.

10thc King David makes a treaty with the Phoenicians. *"Hiram, king of Tyre, sent a delegation to David with cedar wood, and carpenters, and masons of wall-stones, and they built a palace for David."* (II Samuel 5:11), also I Chronicles 14:1.

10thc **Musical instruments**. The Ark of the Covenant is brought from Kiryat Ya'arim to the City of David. *"with **harps, lyres, drums, timbrels and cymbals**."* (II Samuel 6:3,5,12,14,15;15:29). *"**shofar...lyre...harp...drum...dance...organ...lute...cymbals...trumpets**...a ten-stringed instrument...lyre, with singing accompanied by a harp."* (Psalms 150:1-5; 92.4).

10thc King David defeats *"Philistines...Moab...Aram...Edom...Ammon."* (II Samuel 5:17-25; 8:1,2,6,14;12:26). King David controls the Coastal Plain. His influence stretches from Damascus, the Euphrates in the east and to Egypt in the west, with Jerusalem, center of his empire.

10thc King David makes a population **census** in his realm. *"Travel around among all the tribes of Israel, **from Dan to Be'er Sheva**, and count the people."* (II Samuel 24:1,2). An inscription uncovered at Tel Dan in 1993, bears the words *"House of David King of Israel"*

10thc King David purchases a *"threshing floor (Mt Moriah) from (Araunah) in order to build an **altar** to Hashem...for fifty silver **shekels**."* (II Samuel 24:21,24). (See Deuteronomy 25:4; Micah 4:12, 13; Jeremiah 15:7). King David does not construct a Temple in Jerusalem. *"When your days are complete...He shall build a Temple."* (II Samuel 7:12, 13). King David had conquered various tribes and kept their booty e.g. (II Samuel 4:20). This acquired wealth/booty cannot be used to construct a Temple, which must be financed by internal 'Jewish' funds or donations.

970   King David conquers Jerusalem. Solomon, son of David and Batsheva becomes king, expands and builds the city. King Solomon is forever known for his wisdom and judgement, is the reputed author of Proverbs, Ecclesiastes and the Song of Songs. *"requested understanding, to comprehend justice* (to distinguish between good and evil)*...Solomon ruled...from the (Euphrates) to the land of the Philistines, until the border with Egypt, they brought tributes and served Solomon all...his life."* (I Kings 3:9,1-13; 4:1,7; 5:1)

961   **King Solomon constructs a Temple on Mt. Moriah where the Jewish Patriarch Abraham had previously prepared to sacrifice his son Isaac.** *"Hiram, king of Tyre...cut down cedars...from Lebanon...to place the Ark of the Covenant of Hashem...two Cherubim out of olive wood...overlaid...with gold...throne where he would judge...valuable stones...the two pillars of copper."* (I Kings 5:15,16,17,20-23; 6:1,2,19,23,28; 7:7;9; 10;15) (II Chronicles 3:1).

Map 4. Jerusalem, King Solomon's Temple 952 BCE

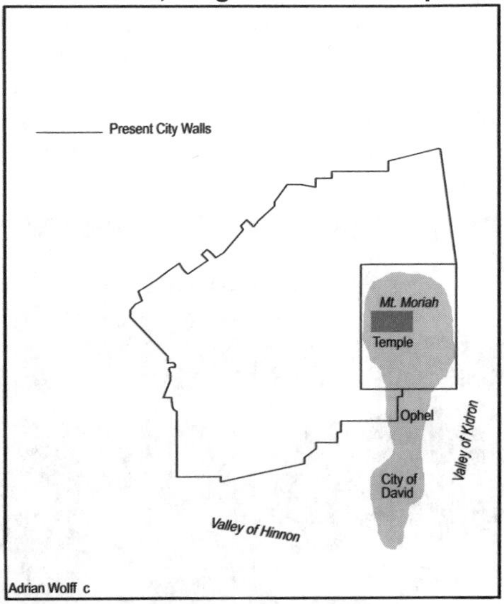

952   **The First Temple** is completed. *"Solomon...bring(s) up the Ark of the Covenant...from the **City of David, which is Zion**...to the Inner Sanctum of the Temple, to the Holy of Holies, to beneath the wings of the Cherubim...spread their wings over...the Ark.* (I Kings 8:1,6,7). *"an **Altar**...of acacia wood...cover...with gold...the **Tabernacle** of ten curtains – twisted linen with turquoise, purple and scarlet wool-with a design of cherubim."* (Exodus 26:1; 30:1; 30:3,5,6). The priests are commanded to perform a **daily animal**

sacrifice in the Temple. (Exodus 20:21). **Incense** represents the Jews responsibility and desire to serve God in manner pleasing to Him. "S*pices–stacte, onycha and galbanum–spices and pure frankincense*. (Exodus 30:34-36). High Priests wear pants, a tunic, sash, turban, robe, garment worn over the robe (ephod), breastplate (hosen) with 12 different gemstones, and a miter (ceremonial headdress). *"For My House will be called a house of prayer for all the peoples."* (Isaiah 56:7). **Non-Jews are welcome to pray at the Western Wall today. Animal sacrifices at the Temple are not restricted to Jews (Leviticus 1:2).**

10th c King Solomon constructs an impressive large palace adjoining the Temple Mount and City Walls are built around Jerusalem. The estimated **population** of Eretz Israel is half-a-million inhabitants, two-thirds in the northern (Israel) and one-third in the southern (Judah) territory. He *"builds his...palace, the Milo and the wall of Jerusalem; Hazor...Megido;Gezer...Beit Horon, Ba'alat...Tadmor...and...Lebanon."* (I Kings 7:1; 9:15,17,18,19).

10th c All three Solomonic fortified cities command the entrances to valleys (Hazor the Hula, Megido the Jezreel Valley, and Gezer the Ayalon Valley) The entrances to have a straight entrance to allow entry of horse and carriage. The city gate has a double-door, three pairs of piers and a fighting overhead platform. See Deuteronomy 12:17; II Kings 23:8; Proverbs 14:19, 31:31; Psalms 118:19.

Tel Hazor, entrance to the Water System   Adrian Wolff

10th c The **Gezer Calendar,** attributed to the Solomonic period is engraved on a small limestone tablet in early **paleo-Hebrew** and testifies to the use of Hebrew writing in the 10th century BCE. Ancient (paleo) **Hebrew** script originates from Phoenician script used in Judea during the First Temple Period until the Destruction of the First Temple. The calendar lists agricultural tasks performed during the different seasons, identified by months.

10thc *"King Solomon made a fleet in Etzion-geber, which is near Elot. On the coast of Sea of Reeds, in the land of Edom...they came to Ophir and took gold from there."* (I Kings 9:26,28). **Note: The original Hebrew clearly states '*Yam Suff*' ים סוף - The Sea of Reeds, not the Red Sea.** Edom/Adom = Red. (See Esau 15thc BCE, Moses 1240 BCE).

10thc *"The queen of Sheba...arrived in Jerusalem with a large entourage, with camels bearing very large amounts of spices and gold and precious stones."* (I Kings 10:1,2).

10thc During the reign of King Solomon, both Jerusalem and the empire flourishes. He *"made a great throne of ivory, and overlaid it with sparkling gold...made silver in Jerusalem (as common) as stones."*, and collects gold and taxes. *"King Solomon had four thousand stables of horses for his chariots and twelve thousand horsemen...assembled chariots and horsemen, he had one thousand four hundred chariots...and...twelve thousand riders, he kept them in chariot cities."* (I Kings 10:18; 10:27; 10: 26).

Megido, Horse Trough   Adrian Wolff

933 King Solomon dies *"...and was buried in the City of David his father. His son Rehoboam reigned in his place."* (I Kings 11:43).

Chapter 4. Israel and Judah 933 – 722 BCE

933   The Kingdom previously united by King David is now divided into two separate kingdoms. **Judah** in the south from 933 until 586BCE includes Jerusalem. **Israel** in Samaria and Galilee north of Jerusalem from 933 until 722BCE.

933   Rehoboam (Rehavam), son of Solomon, **King of Judah** (933-917). (I Kings 12:21).

Map 5. Division into Two Kingdoms 933 BCE

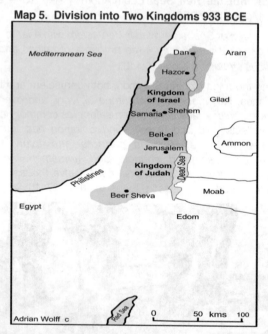

933   Rivalry for the central position of Jerusalem between King Solomon's son Reheboam and Solomon's general, Jeraboam strains the relationship between Judah and Israel. **Judah**, whose capital Jerusalem is traditionally the more important religious domain of the two; while **Israel**, spanning the northern, milder and wetter climatic zone, is wealthier from the sale of its agricultural produce (fruits and wheat). *"For the whole area (of Galilee) is excellent for crops and pasture and rich in trees of every kind...every inch of it has been cultivated...not a parcel goes to waste"*. (Josephus Flavius).

"Rehoboam went to Shehem...to make him king...Jeroboam..spoke 'Your father made our yoke (of taxation) difficult; now you

alleviate...that he placed upon us, and we will serve you...King Rehoboam took counsel with his elders,.... Saying 'How do you advise; what word to respond'...They respond (favorably)...speak kind words...they will be your servants...The king responded harshly...ignored the advise of the elders...saying 'My father made your yoke heavy, and I shall add to your yoke! My father chastised you with sticks; I will chastise you with scorpions." (I Kings 12-14). *"There was warfare between Rehoboam and Jeraboam, all the days."* (I Kings 14:30). The Twelve Tribes were never reunited.

933 Jeraboam (Yeravam) **King of Israel** (933-912) *"built Shehem."* (I Kings 12:25)."*Rehoboam remained in Jerusalem...built up cities for defense in Judah...placed rulers and storehouses of food, oil and wine...(stored) shields and spears...Judah and Benjamin remained his."* (II Chronicles 11:5,11,12).

Rivalry between the two kingdoms weakens their stand against potential enemies as they reject a unified alliance. The tribes conquered by King David east of the Jordan River (Moab, Edom, Ammon) break their allegiance to Jerusalem, simplifying the invasion by Egypt.

10thc Rehoboam of Judah pays Shishak of Egypt a large ransom not to attack Jerusalem. *"He took away the treasures of the Temple...the king's palace...He also took the golden shields."* (I Kings 14:25,26).

10thc Jeraboam practices idolatry by building two altars to rival the Temple in Jerusalem. *"He made two golden calves..these are your gods...he placed one in Beit-el and one in Dan,"* (I Kings 12:28,29). *"Jeroboam...sinned and caused the multitude to sin"* (Ethics 5:21).

Tel Dan, Israelite Altar   Adrian Wolff

917 *"There was warfare between Rehoboam and Jeraboam, all the days of (Aviyam's) life."* (I Kings 15:6).

9thc **Aramaic** is spoken in the Middle East. Jews speak paleo-Hebrew.

875 Jehoshafat (Yehoshafat), of Judah, (875–851). *"made peace with the king of Israel (Ahab)."* (II Kings 22:43; 22:45). He establishes a Legal Court. *"judges in the land...no corruption nor favoritism nor acceptance of bribes."* (II Chronicles 19:5,6,7). *"Jehoshafat built Tarshish ships to travel to Ophir for gold, but he did not go, because the ships broke down at Etzion-geber"* (Gulf of Akaba). (I Kings 22:49).

882 King Omri King of Israel (882-874), builds a Royal Palace in his new capital in Samaria. (I Kings 16:24).

874 Ahab (Ahav) son of Omri, King of Israel (874–853) increases his alliance to Sidon. *"took a wife, Jezebel daughter of Ethbaal, king of the Sidonians...worshipped the baal (idols, gods)...prostrated himself...erected an altar for the baal in the temple he built in Samaria."* (I Kings 16:30,31,32).

860+ **Age of the Prophets** Elijah, Elisha, Yonah, Amos, Hosea, Isaiah.

9thc **Elijah (Eliyahu) the Prophet** in the Kingdom of Israel, during the reign of King Ahab (Ahav). He confronts Ahab's idolatry and predicts drought years. *"Elijah, the Tishbite...of Gilead, said to Ahav...there will not be dew, nor rain during these years."* (I Kings). Elijah challenges the false gods of King Ahab. *"If Hashem is the God, go after Him, and if the baal, go after him...given two bulls... cut it and put it on wood, but not apply fire...You shall call out in the name of your gods and I shall call out in the name of Hashem, and which ever God responds with fire, He is the true God'...fill four jugs with water and pour them over the elevation offering and over the wood'...A fire of Hashem descended and consumed the...offering...Wood...stones...earth...water...The entire people saw and fell on their faces and exclaimed 'Hashem, He is the God...Elijah said...'Seize the prophets of baal. Let none of them escape...Eliyahu took them down to the Kishon River and slaughtered them."* (I Kings 17:1;18:21;18:23-40). The Prophet Elijah castigates King Ahab suggesting his behavior should not be different from any citizen's. *"The word of Hashem came to Elijahu the Tishbite...Ahab has humbled himself before Me?".* (I Kings 21:28,29). King Ahab improves the defenses of Megido.

853 King Ahab is killed in battle against **Assyria**. *"A man (of Aram) drew his bow...hit the king...between the joints of his armor".* (I Kings 22:34,37). The strength of the Kingdom of Israel is temporary *"...when Ahab died, the king of Moav had rebelled against the king of Israel."* (II Kings 3:4,5). Mesha reestablishes the independence of Moav (Moab).

9th C   Prophet **Elisha**, a man of God (Ish Elohim) performs miracles, returning a Shunamite woman's son to life (II Kings 4:8-35). *"Naaman...of the army of...Aram...was a great warrior – a leper... Elisha (said)...'bathe seven times in the Jordan; your flesh will become normal again and you will be cleansed"* (II Kings 5:1;10).

851   Jehoram (Yehoram), son of Jehoshafat King of Judah (851–844). *"Jehoram...(marries) Ahab's daughter (Athaliah)...he did what was evil in the eyes of Hashem."* (II Kings 8:16,18).

844   Sibling rivalry. Yehu, King of Israel (843-816) kills his brother Jehoram (II Kings 9:24). Ahaziah, son of Jehoram King of Judah (844–843).

843   Yehu kills his nephew Ahaziah (II Kings 9:27). Athaliah, Queen of Judah (843-837), is wife of murdered King Jehoram and mother of Ahaziah, hides her grandson Yehoash, (Ahaziah's son) for six years during her rule. (II Kings 11:1-3).

837   Athaliah is executed by the priests for worshiping idols. Jehoash (Yehoash), son of Ahaziah King of Judah (837-798). *"...was seven years when he became king."* (II Kings). During this period the Temple is repaired. King Jehoash's reign is marked by bribery, and in addition he *"took all the sacred objects...and sent them to Hazael king of Aram."* (II Kings 11:18; 12:1; 12: 19).

Map 6. The Assyrian Empire 9 – 7th centuries BCE

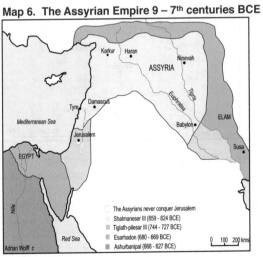

795   The battles between the two kingdoms Israel and Judah continue. Jehoash of Israel defeats Amaziah of Judah when his forces destroy the Jerusalem city walls and loot riches from the Temple and Palace. (II Kings 14:13,14). His servants kill King Jehoash. (II Kings 12:21,22). Amaziah, King of Judah 798-782.

782   **Azariah (Uzziah),** son of Amaziah, King of Judah, born 808, rules 782-740. Known as Azariah in II Kings and Uzziah in II Chronicles. The city of Jerusalem prospers during his reign. King Azariah/ Uzziah reduces the Philistines to become his vassals. He controls the Trade Routes through his kingdom. "*He built up Eilat.*" (II Kings 14:22; 15:3). "*He...did battle against the Philistines, breaching the wall of Gat...of Yavne, and...of Ashdod...The Ammonites presented a tribute to Huzzah...the(n) approach(ed) Egypt...became exceedingly powerful...*"*Uzziah built towers in Jerusalem...in the wilderness...dug many wells...livestock in the lowlands and...plains...field(s)...vine(s)...in the hills and Carmel.*" (II Chronicles 26:6,8,9,10).

Map 7. Trade Routes 1st Millennium BCE – 1st Millennium CE

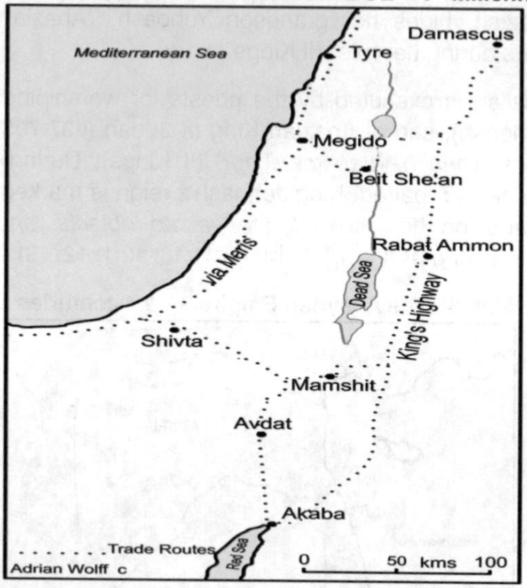

8thc   **Weapons of War.** "*Uzziah has an army of warriors...with **shields, spears, helmets, armor, bows and catapults to sling stones.** He installed devices in Jerusalem, designed by creative people, to be stationed on the towers and on the corners, to shoot arrows and large rocks...he...fortified himself...until he was strong.*" (II Chronicles 26:11,14,15). "*His heart became haughty...He betrayed Hashem, he entered the Sanctuary of Hashem to burn incense upon the Incense Altar.*" (II Chronicles 26:16). He is punished as "*He was a leper until the day of his death, and dwelt in a place of asylum.*" (II Kings 15:5).

745   Tiglat-pilesar III (rules 744-727) king of the Assyrians usurps the throne from his brother, unifying Assyria with Babylonia,

conquering and subjugating all the kingdoms surrounding his territory, forcing them to pay an annual tribute. He exiles the newly conquered rich and educated subjects to other parts of his empire. He will capture Egypt to control the east-west Trade Route.

745 Amaziah, a priest of the Temple at Beit-el "*said to* ***Amos'*** *Go flee to the land of Judah. Eat bread, there you may prophesy. But do not continue to prophesy in Beit-el.*" (Amos 7:12,13).

735 Prophet Hosea castigates decay within Israel. "*Israel has forsaken the Benevolent One...the enemy will pursue him...Rejoice not Israel...for you have strayed from your God.*" (Hosea 8:2,3; 9:1).

735 Prophet **Isaiah** chides against idol worship. "*My people does not comprehend...They have forsaken Hashem.*" (Isaiah 1:2; 1:4). The Judges are righteous, while many of the kings sinned and ultimately bring the nation down.

733 Assyrian troops of Tiglat-pileser III capture the towns of Kedesh, Yiron, Merom, Hazor and Megido in the Kingdom of Israel. "*In the days of Pekah, king of Israel, Tiglath-pileser king of Assyria came and took Ijon, Abel-beth-maacah, Janoah, Kedesh, Hazor, Gilead and the Galilee and all the lands of Naftali.*" (II Kings 15:29).

733 "*Rezin...of Aram (Damascus) and Pekah* (752-732)...*of Israel went to do battle against Jerusalem, they besieged Ahaz,(King of Judah) but could not defeat him.*" (II Kings 16:5, Isaiah 7:1)

733 Ahaz of Judah entices Assyrian Tiglat-pileser III with wealth from the Temple to assist him against Aram and Israel. (II Kings 16:7,8).

732 Pekah king of Israel is assassinated. King Hoshea (732-722) pays a large tribute to Tiglath-pileser III not to attack Israel.

727 Tiglat-pileser III dies, Shalmaneser V is King of Assyria, (rules 727-722). King Hoshea of Israel turns his alliance towards Egypt and ceases to pay the tribute to the Assyrians. "*Then the king of Assyria (Shalmaneser V) discovered that Hoshea had betrayed him...Assyria then invaded the entire country; he went up to Samaria and besieged it for three years.*" (II Kings 17:4,5).

727 Despite the grave situation facing the Kingdom of Judah, Isaiah is optimistic stating "*those that crossed the (Euphrates) river with the king of Assyria...will be destroyed...Do not be afraid of Assyria, My people who dwell in Zion (Judah), though he will strike you,*" (Isaiah 7:20; 8:4; 10:24). The Prophet Isaiah preaches against Israel forming an alliance with Egypt foreseeing a civil war. "*Egyptians to fight Egyptians.*" (Isaiah 19:2,3). Isaiah warns of the imminent fall of the Kingdom of Israel. "*My people is being exiled*

because of ignorance..."Woe to those who speak of evil as good and of good as evil." (Isaiah 5:13, 20).

722   **Fall of the Kingdom of Israel**. King Shalmaneser V dies in Samaria. King Sargon II of Assyria (722-705) conquers the Kingdom of Israel, including Gezer and has full control of the Trade Route from the Fertile Crescent to Sinai.

Map 8. Fall of the Kingdom of Israel 722 BCE

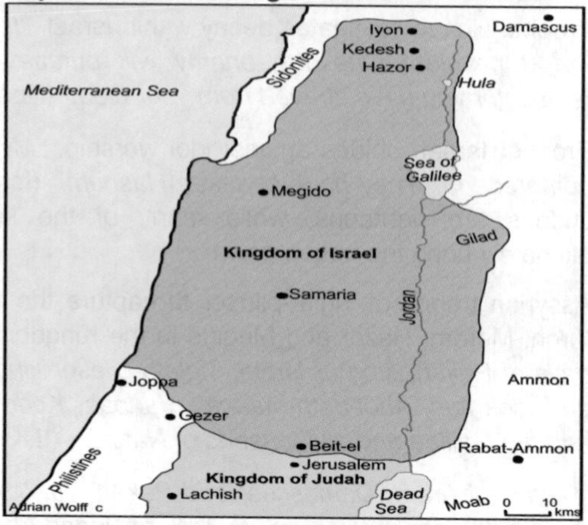

722   *"In (the reign of) Hoshea, the king of Assyria (Sargon II) captured Samaria and exiled Israel to Assyria. He settled them in Halah, in Habor...in the cities of Media...the Children of Israel sinned...worshiped...idols...forsook all the commandments of Hashem, their God...and worshiped the Baal...Hashem...removed them...**none remained except the tribe of Judah**...Israel had torn itself away from the House of David."* (II Kings 17:6,7,11-12,14-15,16,18,20-21). *"Aram from the east and the Philistines from the west, they have consumed Israel with every mouth."* (Isaiah 9:11). *"...those who are lost in the land of Assyria...will prostrate themselves to Hashem on the holy mountain in Jerusalem."* (Isaiah 27:13).

722   **The Assyrians transfer The Ten Tribes of Israel to Assyria, and from there they disperse, to disappear for eternity**. They deport leaders, wealthy and educated of the conquered population to other parts of the empire, substituting local inhabitants with peoples from other parts. This transfer or relocation is made to prevent a local rebellion and uprising against Assyrian rule, bringing stability and central control to the area. The immigrants are usually subdued and do not rise against their conquerors. Jewish inhabitants of Israel are replaced by other subjects

transferred from the Assyrian Empire to Shehem, to become known as **Samaritans**. *"Assyria brought people from Babylonia..Cuthah...Avva...Hamat...Sephardim...settled in...Samaria in place of the Children of Israel...too possess Samaria and dwelled in its cities...do not know the law of the God of the land."* (II Kings 17:24,26).

As a group, Samaritans begin to follow the *'mitzvot'* (blessings) and embrace many Jewish traditions. They recognize the Five Books of Moses (Torah), celebrate Shavu'ot, Succot and during Passover they offer a sacrifice on Mt. Gerizim, above Shehem. Samaritans do not recognize The Temple in Jerusalem, call themselves 'Israelites' and maintain their traditions, language and script similar to Ancient Hebrew. Their leader has the title of 'High Priest'.

Samaritan religious Principles
- One God, the God of Israel, One Prophet, Moses ben Amram.
- One Holy Script – the Torah (First Five Books of the Bible).
- Believe in the 'Taheb', a prophet similar to Moses, a descendent of Joseph who will appear at 'the end of the days'.

Samaritan Traditions
- To live in the Land of Israel.
- Males are circumcised.
- Compulsory participation in the sacrifice on Mt. Gerizim.
- Celebrate the Sabbath as written in the Torah.
- Adhere to the laws of impurity as prescribed in the Torah.

Synagogue Khirbet, Samara (Samaria) (copy)   Adrian Wolff

Chapter 5. Fall of Judah, Hellenic Rule 722-169 BCE

722   Before the Fall of the Kingdom of Israel in 722BCE various conflicts and battles between Israel and Judah result in neither side making significant territorial gains. Jerusalem, located in Judah, consistently remains the all-important spiritual center of the Jewish people, even though the northern Israel is wealthier than the southern semi-desert of Judah. Many residents of the newly conquered Israel now move to Judah, swelling the population of Jerusalem. The entire region is under the ever-increasing threat from the north-east in **Assyria,** expanding along the Trade Route towards the other super-power of this era, Egypt. Judah is forced to pay an annual tribute to forestall the Assyrians from attacking Jerusalem who formally control most of the surrounding region.

722   Judah seeks a strong leader to save them from the menace of the newly created all-powerful Assyrian juggernaut. *"Therefore, my Lord Himself will give you a sign. Behold, the maiden (עלמה) will become pregnant and bear a son, and she will name him Immanuel...the child will know to abhor evil and choose good."* (Isaiah 7:14,16).

Important Note:

1. Jewish understanding

For Jews the '*sign*' is the birth of a leader who will save Judah from the Assyrian threat. This strong leader is born to a pure, young '*maiden*'. Jews are referring to the new king to be, Hezekiah. The original Hebrew word '*almah*' (עלמה) means a '*maiden*'. Hebrew for virgin '*betula*' (בתולה) Isaiah uses only in Chapter 47:1. Immanuel means '*God is with us*', referring to the prophecy that **Judah will be saved** from these threats.

2. Christian understanding

The King James and New International Version translate the original Hebrew word '*almah*' as a *virgin*. The New English Bible uses "a *young woman*". Christian theology believes the '*sign*' denotes the prophecy '*God is with us*' referring to the birth of Jesus Christ, the Christian Messiah who **will save mankind** born to a pure maiden, a virgin. This passage is a cornerstone of Christian theology. Words '*Jesus, a man from the Galilee, or Nazareth*' do not appear anywhere in the Bible (Tanach).

722   The Prophet Isaiah predicts *"For a child has been born to us, a son has been given to us and the dominion will rest on his shoulder; the Wondrous Adviser, Mighty God, Eternal Father, called his name Sar-Shalom (Prince of Peace); upon the one with the greatness in*

dominion and the boundless peace that will prevail on the throne of David and on his kingdom, to establish it and sustain it through justice and righteousness, from now to eternity." (Isaiah 9:5,6).

Important Note:

1. Jewish understanding

For the Jews the *'child has been born'* refers to the future King Hezekiah. *'Dominion'* refers to Judah will survive the Assyrian challenge on its independence. *'The Mighty God, Everlasting father'* refers to God who has sent the *'Prince of Peace'*, Hezekiah to save Judah. He is from the lineage of King David.

2. Christian understanding

Similar to the Jewish view of the Messiah coming from the lineage of King David, Christians believe these verses strengthen their prophecy of the birth of Jesus, the coming Christian Messiah, a Son born in Bethlehem, home of David to Mary the Virgin Mother. Christians translate the Hebrew word *'hamishra'* as government, not dominion, implying Jesus will rule the entire world. Christians liken *'Everlasting Father'* to Jesus who will be an eternal father to His people. *'The Prince of Peace'* is Jesus who will obtain peace with God and among all nations.

716   Hezekiah, son of Ahaz, King of Judah (716-687). *"He observed His commandments"* (II Kings 18:6), is successful in his endeavors, becoming a wealthy sovereign. *"treasure houses for silver and gold, precious stones, spices, shields...silos for...grain, wine..oil...stables for...animals...herds. He made....cities...had abundance of flocks of sheep and cattle."* (II Chronicles 32:27-29).

705   Assyrian Sargon II is killed in battle in northern Persia. **King Hezekiah** of Judah joins the coalition against the Sargon II's son, Sennacherib (704-681). Hezekiah condemns the hypocrisy of idolatry. *"The kings of Assyria have destroyed all the countries...Hashem, our God, save us from his hand, then all the kingdoms of the world shall know that You are Hashem."* (Isaiah 37:18-20). Hezekiah becomes independent from the Assyrians and Philistines. (II Kings 18:7,8).

702   King Hezekiah builds an additional wall in Jerusalem to protect the inhabited areas outside the existing wall. (II Kings 19:34). *"He also prepared much weaponry and shields."* (II Chronicles 32:5). The Assyrian approach Jerusalem. *"Hezekiah saw...Sennacherib...was headed for battle against Jerusalem...decided to stop up the waters of the springs that were outside the city."* (II Chronicles 32:2,3). The only perennial source of water for Jerusalem is located in the Kidron Valley, beneath the city walls in the east. To protect this valuable source of life-giving water, Hezekiah decides against

constructing walls around the spring since the city will lose its strategic advantage of height. He decides to "*bring the water source into the city.*" (II Kings 20:20) to construct a **Water Tunnel** from the **Gihon Springs** outside the walls to the **Siloam Pools**, diverting the headwaters inside the city. (II Chronicles 32:30, Isaiah 22:11). An upper pool already exists at the spring. A new tunnel is constructed into the strata of the hill, hewn from both ends, an absolutely amazing feat, carved in a squiggly line, 533 meters in length, 45 meters beneath the surface. An inscription is chiseled in the tunnel where the two sides meet. "*...when the tunnel was driven through...each man toward his fellow...heard the voice of a man...was an overlap in the rock on the right and on the left. And when the tunnel was driven through...the water lowered from the spring toward the reservoir for 1200 cubits and the height of the rock above the head of the quarryman was 100 cubits.*" The original inscription is exhibited in Istanbul. A copy is displayed in the Israel Museum, Jerusalem. Stones are placed over the spring source to hide its location from the enemy. **This water tunnel still operates today, 2700 years later**, a physical example of the Bible and First Temple Period.

Hezekiah's Water Tunnel, Jerusalem (1st Temple Period)   Adrian Wolff

702   Prophet Isaiah predicts the Assyrians will not conquer Jerusalem. "*Not enter this city...not shoot an arrow...not approach it with a shield and... not a ramp against it. On the route by which he came he will retreat, but he will not enter this city...I shall protect this city.*" (Isaiah 37:33,34).

701   King Sennacherib invades the Coastal Plain, conquering the **Philistines who disappear from history,** turns eastwards towards

Judah including Lachish. *"Sennacherib...attacked all the fortified cities of Judah and captured them."* (Isaiah 36:1). A stone relief depicting this victory is displayed in the British Museum showing the conquest of 46 walled towns. At Tel Lachish an ostracon (pottery shard) is found containing an inked ancient Hebrew script.

701   King Hezekiah is forced to pay a heavy tithe to dissuade King Sennacherib from attacking Jerusalem. (II Kings 18:13-16). King Sennacherib sends a representative to *"not listen to Hezekiah...make peace with me."* (Isaiah 36:16). *"The people remained silent...a command from the king saying do not answer him."* (Isaiah 36:21). Isaiah promises victory to King Hezekiah (Isaiah 37:6). King Sennacherib lays siege to Jerusalem, but is unable to breach the city walls, nor is he successful in locating a source of fresh water due to the construction of the underground water tunnel diverting the water into the city. His troops and horses do not have sufficient quantities of clean drinking water. *"An angel of Hashem went out and struck down one hundred eighty-five thousand (people) of the Assyrian camp. The rest arose (early) in the morning and behold - they were all dead corpses."* (Isaiah 37:36). (II Chronicles 32:21).

701   After his soldiers' perish in the camp outside Jerusalem (on Mt. of Olives), Sennacherib withdraws, returning to Nineveh in Assyria. (Nineveh the Assyrian capital is near Mosul by the Tigris River in Kurdistan, northern Iraq). On his return to Assyria, Sennacherib is assassinated. (II Chronicles 32:21), (II Kings 19:35,36).

701   **Judah is of marginal importance in the Near East balance of power, devoid of natural resources, not located on any major trade route.** The redemption of Jerusalem is saved from the enemy. It leads the Holy City to *"Clear the way of Hashem, make a straight path in the desert, a road for our God. Every valley will be raised, and every mountain and hill will be lowered, the crooked will become straight and heights will become valley."* (Isaiah 40:3,4)

Important Note:
1. Jewish understanding
'Clear the way of Hashem' leads to the Holy City, Jerusalem. Belief in Hashem, to live accord God's Commandments.

2. Christian understanding
'Clear the way' for the revelation of the Christian Messiah. The way to eternal life is through belief in Jesus, the 'Son of God'.

701   Hashem consoles Isaiah *"I am Hashem. I have called you with righteousness, I will strengthen your hand, I will protect you, I will set you for a covenant to the people, for **a light to the nations**...I*

Am what I Am (YHVH), that is My Name, I shall not give My glory to another, nor My praise to graven idols." (Isaiah 42:6,8).

701   Isaiah predicts the independence of Judah continues while the Assyrians are victorious in Egypt. (Isaiah 20:4). The **'Ingathering of the Exiles'**. *Bring My sons...and My daughters from the ends of the earth...all the nations gathered together and all the regimes assembled."* (Isaiah 43:5,6,9).

687   King Manashe is in conflict with Isaiah and has him murdered, later he repents (II Chronicles 33:15,16).

637   Josiah (Yosiah) (637–608). His reign is marked with religious revival, he is known to be righteous, restoring the Temple to its glory. (II Kings 23:2,4). Josiah conquers limited areas of Israel while the population of Jerusalem increases.

624   **Jeremiah** (Yermiyahu) 25:1-3 tells of his 23 years of prophecy. He prophesies a disaster forthcoming to the Kingdom of Judah because of the capricious, inconsistent and disobedient beliefs of the leaders of Judah. An example of Jeremiah's preaching of righteous behavior is to *"Administer justice and righteousness, and save the robbed from the hand of the oppressor, do not taunt and do not cheat the stranger...and do not spill innocent blood."* (Jeremiah 22:3).

Ancient Hebrew Seal, end 1st Temple Period.   Israel Antiquities Dept.

7thc   First written Torah (The First Five Books) is completed in Babylon.

605   **Nebuchadnezzar** king of the **Chaldeans (Babylonia)**. The Babylonians defeat both the **Assyrian and Egyptian armies** at Carchemish in Northern Assyria while Jerusalem is spared (Jeremiah 46:2).

602   *"Nebuchadnezzar...invaded (Judah)...bound him (Yehioakim) in chains...take him...to Babylonia...brought vessels of the Temple...to Babylonia."* (II Kings 24:1) (II Chronicles 36:6,7). He rebuilds the ruined city of Babylon in Mesopotamia.

598   Jehoiachin (Yehoiachin), son of Jehoiakim, (598–597). **'The First Exile to Babylon'.** *"Nebuchadnezzar, king of Babylonia came up to wage war against Jerusalem...took him (Yehoiachin) (captive)...removed...all the treasures of the Temple...the king's palace...exiled all of Jerusalem...no one left except for the poorest of the common people."* (II Kings 24:10-15). **The Prophet Ezekiel** expands a vision for the **'Return to Zion'** שיבת ציון. *"I will assemble you from all the nations and gather you in from the lands where you have been scattered and give you the Land of Israel."* (Ezekiel 8:10; 11:17; 28:25), bringing hope and triumph. Ezekiel expands the reason for **atonement** *"I do not desire the death of the wicked one, but rather the wicked one's return from his way."* (Ezekiel 33:11). **Ezekiel, in chapters 40 to 46 describes in detail his vision of a new Temple.** A 'traditional' tomb of Ezekiel is located in Kifl, Iraq. The first chapter of the book of Ezekiel is titled 'Discipline of the Chariots' מסע המרכבות, which according to Kabbalists, contains the secrets to prophesy.

Map 9. Jerusalem Before Fall of The First Temple 586 BCE

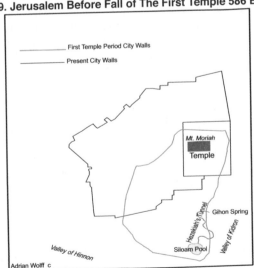

597   **Zedekiah,** (597–586). *"(Nebuchadnezzar) then crowned Mattaniah, (Yehoiachin's uncle, brother of Yehoahaz and Yehoiakim) in his place, and changed his name to Zedekiah."* (II Kings 24:17). The Prophet **Jeremiah** opposes any rebellion against Babylon

predicting dire consequences. (Jeremiah 20:5). Jeremiah refuses to be silenced, continuing to give powerful public orations against corrupt regimes. Citizens believe existence of the Temple in Jerusalem is enough to save them, although they still worship idols. *"Do not follow the gods of others, worshipping them...Now correct your ways and your deeds and heed the voice of Hashem your God."* (Jeremiah 25:6; 26:13).

595   King Zedekiah pronounces his loyalty to Nebuchadnezzar of Babylonia and the Jews return to Jerusalem. (Jeremiah 27:12).

586   Jeremiah continues to preach against the rule of King Zedekiah and the futility of confronting the Babylonians, suggesting submission without battle. *"Babylon will definitely come here, and he will destroy this land and eliminate man"* (Jeremiah 36:29). **Jeremiah predicts the Return to Zion** *"...they will come together from the Land of the north (Babylonia) to the Land that I have given (Eretz Israel) as a possession to your fathers."* (Jeremiah 3:18). Zedekiah foolishly makes an anti-Babylonian alliance with the Egyptians. (Jeremiah 37:5,7,8). Judah has an estimated 700,000 inhabitants. Zedekiah imprisons but does not kill Jeremiah (Jeremiah 37:15,16; 38:16,24).

586   After 2 and half years of siege, Nebuchadnezzar breaches the walls on 17 day of Tamuz captures Jerusalem a second time, **destroying The First Temple on the Ninth day of the month of Av** (*Tisha B'Av*). *"Nebuchadnezzar...of Babylonia...came to wage war against Jerusalem...the famine in the city..."***burned the Temple of Hashem**...palace...every great house...walls of Jerusalem...smashed." (Jeremiah 52:4-6; 13,14; 39:6-8,10) "*He burned the Temple of Hashem, the king's palace and all the buildings of Jerusalem, and every great house he burned in fire. And the walls of Jerusalem all around"..."The remainder of the people who were left in the city...were sent into exile"..."some of the poor people of the land...left to be workers in vineyards and in the fields."* (II Kings 25: 9-12). The Temple is plundered (Jeremiah 52:17-23), *"And Judah was exiled from its land."* (Jeremiah 52:27). (II Kings 25:21). *"because they forsook the covenant...of God and prostrated themselves to the gods of others and worshipped them."* (Jeremiah 22:8,9).

586   The sons of King Zedekiah are killed before his eyes. Babylonians then blind him before he is exiled together with the Jewish population to Babylon. (II Kings 25:1-7). King Zedekiah *"...will not die by the sword. You will die peacefully (in Babylon)."* (Jeremiah 34:4,5). Gedaliah, the last Jewish governor is murdered.

586   **The Babylonian Period. Second Exile to Babylon**. Jerusalem is destroyed, ceasing Jewish Administration. Traders and educated people are forced to leave for Babylonia. The population of Jerusalem decreases, is poorer, with a lower level of economic activity (commerce and trade). (Nehemiah 1:3). **The Ark of the Covenant originally brought to Jerusalem during the reign of King David and placed in King Solomon's Temple** and the High Priest's garments including the breastplate (hoshen) now **disappear for eternity.** King David had predicted an exile in Babylon "*By the rivers of Babylon, there we sat, and also wept when we remembered Zion...If I forget you, O Jerusalem, let my right hand forget its skill. Let my tongue adhere to my palate, if I fail to recall you, if I fail to elevate Jerusalem above my foremost joy.*" (Psalms 137:1,5,6). **The Temple is destroyed ceasing the pronouncement of the name of God YHVH by the High Priest inside the Holy of Holies of the Temple on the Day of Atonement. Jews begin to refer to God as '*Adonai*', my Lord, or '*Elohay Yisrael*', God of Israel.** Jews do not have a physical sign to refer to God, alluding by means of different words or letters.

Jewish exiles in Babylonia become known as 'B'nei Yehuda', the 'Sons of Judah' or 'Yehudim' יהודים **in Hebrew, or 'Jews' in English.** "*Nehemiah...inquired of them about the Jews* היהודים*...the remaining ones, who remained in captivity*". (Nehemiah1:1,2). Babylonian Jewry assume the role of leader of the Diaspora communities as great Torah learning schools (yeshivot) are opened at Sura, Pumbedita (Faluja) and Nehardea.

586   Jeremiah remains with Gedaliah at Mizpah, encourages the remaining Jews in Judah not to be afraid of Nebuchadnezzar, dissuading them unsuccessfully, against travel to Egypt. (Jeremiah 40:4,6; 42:10-12). Subsequently the Babylonians conquer Egypt in 584 and Moav, Amnon, Edom, Damascus, Kedar, Hazor and Elam. (Jeremiah 46:24; ch 49).

586   Jeremiah continues to give hope "*the offspring of the House of Israel...from all the lands wherein He had dispersed them...will dwell in their own land (Eretz Israel).*" (Jeremiah 23:7,8). The Prophet Jeremiah introduces a note of optimism by predicting the Babylonian exile to last for a fixed period, "*This entire land shall be in ruin and desolation...will serve...Babylon for seventy years... your children will return to their border.*"(Jeremiah 25:11; 29:10; 31:16)

Jewish Prayer methodology begins during the Babylonian Period. The aim of prayer is 'to increase the awareness of God' and is an integral part of daily life. Prayer need not to be performed inside a synagogue and can be recited in any language. A formal prayer service requires a quorum of at least 10 adult Jewish men (post bar mitzvah age 13), known as a *minyan*. Traditional Jews sway during prayer. Scholars explain since God is spiritual, the human body's movement represents engulfing the material human form with the Holy Spirit (ru'ach ha'kodesh). The Hebrew word ru'ach רוח spirit, also means wind.

Jews settle in Kurdish areas of northern Mesopotamia (Iraq) speak Aramaic. Shrines of Jewish prophets are found - Yonah in Nonevah, Nahum in A'gosh, Daniel in Kirkuk, Queen Esther and Mordechai in Hamadan. The two-year **Operations Ezra and Nehamia** (1948-1950), airlifts 120,000 Jews from Iraq to Israel, ending the rich, successful and continuous Jewish life in Babylonia/Iraq for over 2500 years.

6thC   *"Nebuchadnezzar...dreamt...my spirit is agitated to know my dream."* Daniel says, *"Bring me before the king, and I will tell the interpretation."* (Daniel 2:1,2,24; 8:16; 9:22).

561   *"Evilmerodach, (Nebuchadnezzar's son-Balthazer)...of Babylonia...released Jehoiachim from prison."* (II Kings 25: 27-30), also (Jeremiah 52:31).

539   King **Cyrus** II the Great (biblical name Koresh) (born between 590 and 580, dies 529) of Persia and Media defeats all opposition and enters Babylon unhindered. He rules from India to Egypt. Persians follow the Zoroastrian religion, are multicultural and allow previously conquered peoples to return to their homelands. He makes a public declaration granting Jews the right to return to Judah and rebuild their Temple in Jerusalem. **The Cyrus Cylinder**, discovered in Babylon in 1979, inscribed in Akkadian declares "*I Cyrus King of Babylonia...and I built for them (Jews) a permanent Temple. I gathered all their inhabitants and restored their place of residence.*" (Displayed in the British Museum, London).

538   **The Persian Period**
Jewish exiles to return, known as *'shivat zion'* in Hebrew, **the 'Redemption to Zion,** to their original homeland in Judah. Unique in history is a people/race voluntary moving to their roots. The majority decide to remain in the fertile and wealthy environment of Babylonia, while the minority, including the poorer, and priests (Kohenim and Levis) 'Return to Zion'. (II Chronicles 36:23).

6thC   **Aramaic becomes the official language of the Persian Empire and gradually replaces paleo-Hebrew in both Jewish holy scripture and secular writings.**

536   Jews begin **rebuilding the Temple**, perform sacrifices and return Holy Vessels from Babylon. "*Cyrus king...commanded...to build...a*

Temple in Jerusalem...the Children of Israel...(settled) in the cities...and they built the Altar of the God of Israel." (Ezra 1:2-4; 3:1,2; 6:3-5; ch 3).

6thc — Daniel refuses to deviate from his faith in Hashem. King Darius (reigns 522-486) of Persia (the Mede) places him in a Lion's Den where he is unharmed. (Daniel 6:23,24,29).

516 — Reconstruction of *"This Temple was completed...(in) the sixth year of the reign of King Darius."* (Ezra 6:15) is dedicated to Hashem and daily animal sacrifices performed once again. A new **Golden Menorah** is made, perhaps similar to the original Solomonic.

5thc — Persian king *"Ahasuerus (Xerxes reigns 486-465) reigned from Hodu (India) to Cush (Ethiopia) a hundred and twenty-seven provinces"* (Esther 1:1), also over Greece. The Persians used the Phoenician fleet who in return, receives control of the eastern Mediterranean cost. All foreign provinces under Persian rule are independent, constituting part of the Persian federation, with its extremely wealthy capital Shushan (Sura). (Esther 1:6,7).

5thc — Ahasuerus halts The Temple construction until payment of taxes. (Ezra 4:21,24). *"Haman sought to destroy all the Jews...throughout the entire kingdom of Ahasuerus - the people of Mordechai."* Queen Esther tells Ahasuerus *"This wicked Haman"* plans genocide against the Jews, *"so they hanged Haman on the gallows that he had prepared for Mordechai."* (Esther 7:6,10; 8:5,7). This is not 'by chance', as Jews believe 'it is all for the good' - הכל לטובה.

Charity. *"The Jews gained relief from their enemies...from one of sorrow to gladness and from mourning to festival, to observe them as days of feasting and gladness, and sending delicacies to one another **and gifts to the poor**...These days of Purim should never cease among the Jews."* (Esther 9:22,28). Their traditional graves of Esther and Mordechai are at Hamadan (Hegmataneh) in Persia.

445 — Persians appoint Prophet **Nehemiah** as governor of Jerusalem, rebuilding of the walls and fortifications of Jerusalem. (Nehemiah 2:17,18, Chapter 3). The existence of walls represents a city, and/or a regional center. Nehemiah rigorously enforces **Sabbath enjoyment**, observance and charity. *"Go, eat rich foods and drink sweet beverages, and send portions to those who have nothing prepare..and to engage in great rejoicing."* (Nehemiah 8:10-12). Public reading of the Torah every Monday, Thursday and Saturday.

435 — Prophet **Ezra** the Scribe leaves Babylon for Jerusalem rebuilding the community for Torah study, leading **The Great Assembly** (Supreme Court of the Jewish People). **He asserts the Torah to**

be property of the entire Jewish Nation and is publicly recited before assemblies of people in every town and village in the Diaspora with standardized prayers and services. Houses of prayer, a **synagogue** is found within Jewish communities to include Torah teaching and studying. (Nehemiah 8;2,3). **The Hebrew word for synagogue בית בנסת, Beit Knesset means a 'house of assembly, NOT 'a house of worship'**. During this period the Jewish population of Judea becomes more vibrant and secure. **The two Books of Chronicles are compiled, describing History of the Jews until Prophet Ezra**.

332   **Alexander the Great** (356–323 rules 336-323), King of Macedonia, known as one of the greatest generals ever, conquers all territory from Macedonia, the Middle East, Egypt, Fertile Crescent, Persia to the Indus River in India.

The Hellenic Period as Greeks spread knowledge and understanding. Greek becomes the official language replacing Aramaic. Greek concept of the **'polis'**, an independent city is introduced throughout the empire, with a governor overseeing all Greek Civil Administration, town planning (grid) and city functions. Greek temples are built in high, commanding positions, seen from all quarters of the city. Greek cities have palaces, markets, industrial and residential quarters, academies, gymnasiums, while theater and cultural events are promoted. Alexander encourages his troops to marry local women introducing Hellenic culture to complement and continue the local customs in areas of his conquest. Hellenic troops conquer but do not damage Jerusalem.

Increase in trade: From Egypt - wheat, papyrus, linen, glass. From Africa - elephants, ivory and ostrich feathers. From Arabia and Persia – carpets. From India – cotton. From China - silk.

4thC   **Hebrew remains a spoken and written language of the Jews, enjoying religious freedom, allowing Jews to live according to their customs, exempt from taxes during a fallow year. Alexander refuses to recognize the Samaritans as Jews.**

323   Alexander the Great dies suddenly in Mesopotamia without leaving a successor, causing a split, dividing the empire between his generals **Antioginus** I Cyclops in Macedonia, **Ptolemy** in Egypt and Judah, and **Seleucus** I Nicator in present-day Syria and areas north of Judah.

315   Eretz Israel is once again a disputed area, the border between the Ptolemaics and Seleucids. **Ioudaia** in Greek, or Judah in Hebrew is overrun by the new Seleucid king, **Antigonus I** (382–301) gaining tariffs and taxes from the east-west trade along the Trade

Routes and particularly along the 'Via Maris' on the Coastal Plain of Judea. Ptolemy I retreats southwards to Sinai and Egypt. Antigonus' son, Demetrius is appointed governor of Judah.

312   **Ptolemy I** of Egypt gains control of Jerusalem and Eretz Israel from the Seleucids. The local Jews refuse to fight on Sabbath and are taken as prisoners to Alexandria.

275   Ptolemaics summon seventy or seventy-two Jews from Eretz Israel to Alexandria for the sole purpose of translating the Tanach (Bible) into Greek, known as the **'Septuagint' (seventy)**.

261   Antiochus II, (287-246), the Seleucid king (rules 261-246), imposes heavy taxes on Jewish Priests in Jerusalem and farmers of Judah.

Map 10. Hellenic Control – Disputed Territory 4th - 3rd century BCE

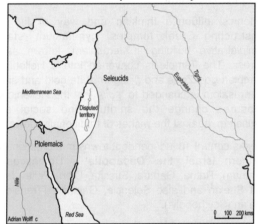

220   Simon II, son of Onias I, High Priest of the Sanhedrin Jerusalem, known as 'Simon the Just of the Great Assembly.' (*Ha'knesset ha'gadol* in Hebrew). He preaches, 'Upon three things the world is based: Torah, Divine service, and the performance of good deeds'.

217   Antiochus previously one of Ptolemy IV's commanders, defects to the Seleucid, known as King Antiochus III, (242–187) plans to conquer Egypt. In large battle of antiquity at Rafah (Rafiah/Raphia) in Gaza, Antiochus III with 68,000 troops battle 75,000 Egyptians of Ptolemy IV. Over 300 elephants are brought to the combat area, little cavalry is used. The Seleucid phalanx is surrounded forcing their retreat northwards. Battle ends in a stalemate without either side making any territorial gains. Ptolemy's situation is short-lived.

198   Antiochus III (Seleucid) (in Syria of today) defeats Ptolemy V (Ptolemaics) at the Battle of Panias (Banias) conquers all Judea.

Jews of Jerusalem welcome Antiochus III. *Jews...demonstrated friendship...**live according to the laws of their own...exemption from taxes for three years**...those citizens who...have become slaves... grant...freedom."* (Joseph Flavius, The Jewish War = JF).

175   Antiochus IV Epiphanes (the Mad) (215–164 BCE) introduces Greek customs in Ioudaia (Judah) currently populated almost entirely by Jews. The minorities are remnants of various Canaanite tribes. The Greeks persecute any High Priest resisting Hellenic influence. Conditions for Jews deteriorates, forbidding Jewish observance of Sabbath, celebration of religious festivals, performing circumcision, or keeping dietary laws. Failure results in death. **There is a split between Jews who maintain their steadfast traditions and customs, and Hellenized Jews who accept Greek culture.**

175   Hellenics influence thinking and way of life in Jerusalem, constructing Greek temples, gymnasium, statues and the administrative building in Jerusalem, known as the **Acra** or fortress. The Temple is converted into a Hellenic shrine to the Olympian god Zeus and pillaged of its gold and silver. The status of Jerusalem is changed to '*polis*' - of the Hellenic Empire. These measures change the spiritual and social atmosphere in Jerusalem, against the wishes of traditionalist Jews.

175   Greeks control 10 independent towns in a crescent-shaped area in northern Israel, the **'Decapolis'** - Damascus, Philadelphia (Amman), Rafna, Gadara, Sussita, Dion, Pella, Jerash, Canatha, Beit She'an and also Seleucia, Galaditis (Transjordan) and Beit She'an (Scythopolis).

174   Jason is appointed High Priest in place of his brother Onias III. He promises Antiochus IV a considerable increase in tax income.

171   Menelaus, an ardent Hellenist, is appointed High Priest in Jerusalem, changing from representing Jewish interests to becoming an official of the Hellenic (Seleucid) administration. When Menelaus is unable to fulfill his financial obligations to Antiochus IV Epiphanes, he is banished to Antioch where he is tried and put to death. The Seleucids appoint Eliakim (Alcimus) High Priest.

169   *"Antiochus IV Epiphanies stormed the City...to loot...plundering the Sanctuary and stopped the continuous succession of daily sacrifices."* (JF). They plunder the Temple in Jerusalem, removing the golden altar, the lamp, gold and silver.

Chapter 6. Maccabi and Hasmonean 167 – 40 BCE

Hellenics consider *'only beautiful is good'*, while Judaism views *'only the good is beautiful'*. *"Wisdom. Where can it be found?...Precious gold cannot be exchanged for it and its price cannot be weighed in silver. It cannot be compared to...gold or...shoham or sapphire...exchange be (in) golden articles."* (Job 28:12,15–17).

167   **Antiochus IV Epiphanes (the Mad, the Wicked)** (215–164) stations Seleucid troops in the Hellenic Administration building the **Acra** fortress, opposite the Temple securing their position in Jerusalem and plunder more Temple treasures. *"And they built the City of David with a great strong wall, and with strong towers and made it a fortress (Acra) for them."* (I Maccabees 1:35-38).

They place a statue of the Greek god Dionysus inside the Jewish Temple, erecting a temple to the Greek god, Zeus Olympius. Any opposition results in death. Jews are antagonized, especially the demand they bow down to Greek idol gods. Antiochus IV prohibits Torah study, Sabbath observance and circumcision and forces *"sacrificing swine on the altar."* *"Bacchides...(a) command(er of)...plunged recklessly into every form of iniquity."* (Josephus Flavius. The Jewish War = JF).

167   Persecution of Jews continues. A revolt begins in Modi'in (Modi'im), triggered when **Mattatiyahu (Matthew) the Maccabi,** kills a representative of the Seleucid king about to execute an order to sacrifice a pig to a Greek god and eat its flesh. *Mattatiyahu...raised a tiny force consisting of his five sons and himself, and killed (a messenger of) Bacchides (Antiochus' representative)...Fearing...he fled to the hills...many people joined him...gave battle, defeated Antiochus' generals and chased them out of Judaea."* (JF).

The Hebrew word Maccabi מכבי is an acronym for "מי כמכה באלם יהוה-*Who is like You among the heavenly powers Hashem!'* (Exodus 15:11). **The Maccabi rebellion is initially religious against Hellenic Administration pressurizing Jews to follow Greek religious customs. Soon this revolt becomes nationalistic to strive for Jewish autonomy.** Mattatiyahu with his five sons travel from towns to villages overturning altars of foreign gods, encouraging Jews to revolt against the oppressive Hellenic conquerors. One son, **Judah (Judas Maccabeas) the Maccabi** *"allying himself with Rome"* (JF) attacks Hellenics, not in open battlefield, but while they march, ill-prepared for a surprise attack, using guerrilla tactics, armed with farming implements such as mace and sling. Isolated Seleucid patrols are ambushed and destroyed as assailants take their weapons. Seleucid garrison in Jerusalem is isolated from the coast

167 Apollonius leads reinforcements from Samaria towards Jerusalem. Judah with 600 men surprise the numerically superior, better trained and armed Hellenic force, blocking their march. Hellenic troops become surrounded unable to use their heavy weapons in the wadi (gorge) and become trapped. Apollonius and many of his troops are killed, losing all their weapons.

166 Seleucid forces under Seron travel from Lod (Lydda) to relieve Greek forces embattled in Jerusalem. Judah the Maccabi, at the Battle of Beit Horon ambushes them as they trudge up the hill. Surviving Hellenic troops retreat to the Coastal Plain.

165 **Beginning of the Maccabean/Hasmonean Period/dynasty**. After his father Mattatiyahu dies, Judah the Maccabi assumes command in 165 until 160.

Summary of the eight battles of Judah the Maccabi
167 Gaphna, Shomron (Samaria). Judah defeats Apollonius.
166 Beit Horon, Shomron (Samaria). Judah defeats Seron.
165 Emmaus. Judah defeats Gorgias, the largest Hellenic defeat.
165 Beit Zur, Gush Etzion. Lysias forces Judah to withdraw. Judah conquers Jerusalem.
162 Beit Zecharia. Judean Hills. Lysias defeats Judah, Elazar is killed.
162 Beit Horon. Judah defeats Nicanor.
162 Givon, Jerusalem Hills. Judah defeats Nicanor.
161 Beit Horon. Battle of Eleasa. Bacchides defeats Judah, is killed

165 Gorgias plans a surprise attack against Judah encamped at Mitzpah, NW of Jerusalem. Judah learns of Hellenic troop movements, defeating and pursuing them to Gazara. Hellenic troops return to their camp at Emmaus, finding it in flames, retreating to the coast, unsuccessful in recapturing Jerusalem. Emmaus is Greek for the Hebrew word *'hama'* (hamaus).

165 At the Battle of Beit Zur near Marisa in Edema, Lysias with 30,000 troops, thirty elephants, cavalry and chariots force Judah to withdraw to the Gophna Hills north of Jerusalem. Judah conquers Jerusalem, encouraging his followers to protect their lives and fight their adversaries even on the Holy Sabbath. The oil in the Temple lamp should have lasted one day but miraculously lasts for eight days. This **festival of lights**, known as the **Festival of Hanukkah,** is the **Second festival of freedom for the Jews** (the First being

Passover, the Exodus from Egypt and the Third, Independence in 1948). The altar is rebuilt and daily sacrifices are resumed to rededicate the Temple. The Festival of Hanukkah occurs on the 24th of the Hebrew month of Kislev - in December of this year. For Jews, the lighting of Hanukkah candles symbolizes the triumph over injustice and evil.

164   Antiochus IV Epiphanes dies shortly after completing a successful campaign against the Parthians (Persians) in the east.

163   Judah attacks Yavne (Jamnia). At Jaffa (Joppa) they torch ships to avenge the death of Jewish inhabitants drowned by the local gentiles. Then capture Hebron and Marisa bringing the Coastal Plain, Idumea and Gilad into the Hasmonean Empire.

Map 11. The Maccabi Empire 2nd century BCE

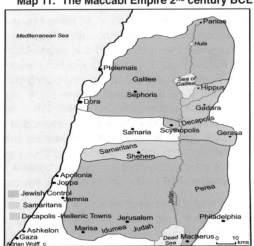

162   Lysias, defeats the Maccabis in the Battle of Beit Zechariah, north of Beit Zur in the Judean Hills south of Jerusalem. Elazar, the youngest Maccabi brother is killed, crushed by a war elephant as he "*struck the beast's under-belly.*" (JF).

162   Seleucids breach the Temple walls of Jerusalem, controlling the Acra, a strong fortress facing the Temple Mount reminding the Jews that their land is still occupied. Bacchides places Alcimus on the throne and several Jewish leaders are slaughtered. Judah defeats the Hellenics at the Beit Horon road. He defeats Nicanor in the Battle of Capharsalma, near Givon (west of Jerusalem).

161   Judah dies in the Battle of Eleasa near Beit Horon. Judah's brother Jonathan takes over leadership 160-142. The High Priest Eliakim (Alcimus) a traitor, dies in Jerusalem.

161   Yohanan (John), the eldest of the five Maccabi brothers is killed by hostile tribesmen while transporting goods to the Nabateans in Perea, east of the Jordan River.

152   Jonathan exploits the decline in Seleucid rule to establish himself in Jerusalem. The Greek garrison is expelled and the Acra is cleansed of heathen cults. He repairs the fortifications to the Temple Mount, is appointed High Priest and governor of the Jews. Hasmoneans control Judea, Gezer and Jaffa. *"Jonathan...strengthen(s) his authority...(by) securing his position by this friendship with Rome."* (JF).

150-100 A separate Jewish sect, **Essenes** are disturbed by Hellenic influences, establish their community of about 200 at **Qumran** on the NW shore of the Dead Sea, living according to the Torah. They are led by their charismatic, enigmatic leaders 'The Teacher of the Righteous'*'moreh ha'zadik'*. The ascetic Essenes are *"Contemptuous of wealth...none...better off than the rest...surrender their property to the order...Always wear white... Before the sun rises do not utter a word on secular affairs, but offer to Him traditional prayers...work assiduously till an hour before noon...when they again meet in one place and donning linen loincloths wash all over with cold water...When women bathe they wear a dress...go back to work till evening...Persons...are not immediately admitted...has to demonstrate his strength...will never hide anything from members of the sect or reveal any of their secrets to others...abstain from seventh-day work more rigidly than any other Jews."* (JF). The scrolls describe the community's laws.

Essenes lead a communal life with a central dining hall, assembly hall, ritual bath (separately for both men and women), laundry room, stable, pottery workshop and watch tower. The scriptorium (writing room) contains desks and inkstands. They follow a 364 day solar calendar, unlike the 354-day Jewish lunar-based calendar. Their conservatism can be seen by the use of paleo-Hebrew script in the Leviticus Scroll found in the Qumran Caves (See Qumran 1947). This community will endure the harsh dry, hot climate until 68CE when the Romans conquer Qumran. See Essenes 68; and Dead Sea Scrolls 1947; 1995.

146   The **Romans** are eroding Hellenic influences in the Mediterranean while the Parthians (Persians) are defeating the Seleucids in areas of present-day Syria and Jordan. The Romans finally defeat and destroy Carthage killing 150,000 and taking 25,000 prisoners in the last of the Punic Wars. They welcome the Jewish Revolt against Hellenic Rule and are reputed to assist them during the

Hasmonean Period. Jews welcome Roman pressure on the Hellenics forcing their withdrawal from Eretz Israel.

142   Tryphon lures Jonathan to Beit Shikma, where he is killed, buried at Modi'in. Simon, last brother is appointed High Priest (142–135).

142   The **Sanhedrin,** Greek for *'an assembly that sits in judgment'* is established in Jerusalem. This **Supreme Court has authority over all Jews and Jewish customs including over those living in the Diaspora.** The 120 Sanhedrin members are known as *'anshei knesset ha'gedola'* (men of the great assembly). Ten members from each of the Twelve Tribes. The Israeli Knesset (parliament) today has 120 members.

142   Simon defeats the Hellenics at the Battle of Kidron, removes them from the Jerusalem Acra.

141   The Maccabi (Hasmonean) Revolt against the Hellenics ends when Seleucids are powerless to continue fighting. Hasmoneans control the Galilee, Samaria, Judea, Edom, Ammon and Moav. Hasmoneans use a five-pointed **Shield (Star) of Solomon** symbol

135   Ptolemy (son of Abulus) governor of Jericho assassinates Simon the Maccabi, (his father-in-law) together with his sons Judah and Mattatiyahu while they attend a banquet at Docus near Jericho. None of the five Maccabi brothers die from natural causes.

135   **Yohanan** (Johanan-John) **Hycranus,** son of Simon (135–104), conquers areas beyond the Jordan River to Madaba. He obliterates the town of Samaria, a Hellenic center and occupies Beit She'an (Scythopolis). Jews are free to reside in all Galilee. Jerusalem, capital of the empire flourishes economically from income collected, including an annual tax of half-a-**shekel** from each inhabitant. Jews control most of Eretz Israel, the Coastal Plain (except Ashkelon), eastern districts beyond the Jordan River (Perea), comprising almost all the area from Lake Merom in the Lebanese mountains to the border with Egypt. For the next six decades, no enemy approaches Jerusalem.

135   **Sages in Jerusalem** become renowned and influence Jewish thought throughout the Jewish world. The Temple becomes the magnetic ritual and religious center for a large population under the influence of Judaism. Coins are minted, trade flourishes and various crafts are developed in the city. The Hasmonean palace is built, Temple towers strengthened and a bridge connecting the Upper City with the Temple Mount. Monuments, the Tomb of the Sons of Hezir, of Zechariah, and of Jason are constructed in memory of these priests.

112 Yohanan Hyrcanus defeats both the **Samaritans and Idumeans** (Beit Guvrin area) **who are forcibly converted to Judaism to ensure their loyalty. Antipater,** father of the future King Herod, is from Idumea.

104 Judas Aristobulus I, reigns for one year (104-103). **He is the first Hasmonean to wear a crown and call himself 'king', a title that by tradition belonged only to David's descendants**. Judas Aristobulus I continues to promote Hellenic life-style and customs, causing opposition within the royal house. The king imprisons his mother and murders his brother. He conquers the gentile population of the Galilee and Mount Hermon area which he forcibly converts to Judaism.

103 Alexander Yanai (Janaeus), (a brother of Judas Aristobulus I) (103–76) marries Alexandra (Shlomzion), widow of his brother. Alexander Yanai completes the conquest of Eretz Israel including the via Maris Trade Route and ports including Ashkelon.

103 Two distinct rival divisions emerge within Judah. The **Perushim or Pharisees** the majority, middle/lower classes who regard the Temple as the high authority of instruction, the observance of Jewish rituals, Torah study and validity of the Oral Law (Mishnah). The aristocracy and landowners support the monarchy and High Priest. The other group the **Zadukim or Sadducees,** originating from the priestly house of Zadok is less conservative, more democratic, wealthier priests, merchants and aristocrats, accepting only Torah-based precepts, its supremacy over the Oral Law. A Civil War erupts in Judah.

76 Alexandra (Salome/Shlomzion) queen (76-67). During her reign Sadducees and Pharisees make a reconciliatory peace with political, religious harmony and renewed Torah study. *"The* **Pharisees**...*more pious...and stricter in the interpretation of the Law." "Alexandra, being devoted to religion (allowed the Pharisees to) become(ing) the effective rulers of the state."* (JF).

76 Queen Alexandra appoints her son Hyrcanus II, High Priest despite not being a forceful person.

67 Queen Alexandra dies. A civil war erupts between her sons Aristobulus and Hyrcanus, both intent on holding the title of king.

67 Aristobulus II (67-62) receives military training and gains support from the Sadducees, being more aggressive and ambitious than his brother Hyracanus who is no match when *"the bulk of his army deserted him and went over to Aristobulus."* (JF), as riots and civil war ensures. Antiptater the Idumean, (father of Herod, see 112

BCE) advises Aretas III, king of the Nabateans (87-62), at Petra, their capital in Perea (Transjordan) *"to receive Hyracanus and restore him to his throne."* (JF). The Nabatean kingdom has increased in strength and expands its frontiers.

66   Aristobulus II appoints himself king and High Priest.

64   Aristobulus II defeats both Hyrcanus II and the Nabateans at Papyron near the Jordan River when Roman troops in the area intervene, allowing Aristobulus II to remain king.

63   **The Roman Period.** Roman General **Pompey** (106–48) suddenly changes his allegiance and favors Hyrcanus II, the weaker puppet of the two brothers as he ousts Aristobulus II. Pompey assembles a 3-month siege on **Jerusalem,** finally attacking from the north towards the Temple Mount on the Sabbath Day. The Jewish priests do not make military preparations on the holy day continuing their religious service as if no danger looms. *"Not even when the Temple was being captured and they were being butchered round the altar did they abandon the ceremonies ordained for the day...putting the service of God before their own preservation"* (JF). Josephus Flavius states over 12,000 Jews are killed this day. Pompey is filled with admiration at the fortitude of the Jews, does not desecrate the Holy of Holies. No *"sacred treasures did he lay a finger, and only one day after the capture he instructed...to purify the Temple and perform the sacrifices."* (JF).

63   Aristobulus II surrenders, is exiled to Rome. Roman general *"Gabinus next reinstated Hyrcanus II in Jerusalem"* (JF), who governs the country as a Roman tributary with the title of High Priest controlling Judea, Galilee, Idumea and Perea to the east of the Jordan River. The Coastal Plain, port cities, Samaria and Beit She'an (Scythopolis) are all annexed to Rome (to control the Trade Routes), subject to the Roman Proconsul in Syria. Antipater becomes adviser to Hyracnus II controlling the administration and is actually the real power holder. Within two centuries Rome controls from Gibraltar to Crimea, from Hadrian's Wall to the Euphrates. **Judea is an agricultural and textile producer.**

63   Jewish war captives are brought to Rome, rapidly emancipated due to their skills, literacy and partly due to their religious customs (Sabbath and kashrut observance), which their masters find inconvenient. Jews refuse to attend Roman theaters and games.

Roman Administration

1. Roman conquerors apply a practical administration not based on philosophical theories.

2. **'Pax Romana'** allows personal freedom of all inhabitants ruled by an administration based on 'law and order'.

3. 'All roads lead to Rome' signifies the contribution of goods (wheat, olive oil, etc) and valuables (gold, silver, etc) from all territories within the empire for the upkeep of the imperial capital, Rome.

4. Inhabitants living within the Empire have little reason to rebel, as Rome controls their economic and political needs through local kings and governors, responsible directly to Rome.

5. The Roman Armies conquer, protects, develops areas, and guards all borders against invasion. They also provide food (cultivate), carry mail and marry locals.

6. Religious freedom is available to all. Jews of Judea (and in other parts of the empire) may follow Sabbath observance, not practiced by any other peoples at this time, are also permitted religious freedom including to 'go up to' Jerusalem during the three pilgrimage festivals - Passover, Succoth and Shavu'ot.

7. Roman aqueducts increase agriculture production, bring water to towns which increase in size, improve public hygiene.

8. Romans construct places of entertainment for their citizens such as theaters, amphitheaters, and hippodromes. Gladiator fights and horse races take place.

9. Roman prosperity depends upon provincial exploitation.

10. Roman schools teach Latin and Greek grammar, Greek language, music, history, astronomy, mythology and philosophy.

11. A Roman governor is appointed, frequently corrupt.

12. Judea is heavily taxed.

61   King Aristobulus, together with other conquered kings and prisoners are paraded in a victory celebration in Rome, where he is put to death.

60   Malichus, Nabatean King (60-30). See 40, 30BCE.

57   Herod (73-4BCE) together with his brother Phasael, sons of Antipater (adviser to Hyracanus II) are sent to study in Rome where they meet Mark Anthony, a Roman leader. Herod's mother is princess Cyprus, daughter of the Nabatean King Malichus I. Gabinius a personal friend of Pompey, is governor in Judea (57-55)

55   Hyrcanus II influences Jewish communities living in the Nile Delta to support Julius Caesar (100–44) in his conflict with Pompey. "*Egyptian Jews…(in the district of) Onias…Antipater induced them not only to oppose the army but even to furnish supplies.*" (JF). Julius Caesar is victorious over Pompey, restoring Hyrcanus II some political powers previously removed by Pompey.

53   Crassus, governor of Syria, plunders the Temple in Jerusalem.

51   Ptolemy XII dies, leaving the throne to 18-year-old Cleopatra and her brother, the 10-year-old Ptolemy XIII. She rules 51-30.

48   **Julius Caesar** defeats Pompey's superior forces at the Battle of Pharsalus in central Greece. Caesar offers leniency to the defeated troops, sparing them all. Pompey flees to Egypt where he is assassinated.

48   Antipater courts Julius Caesar who allows Jews to control Jaffa and the Yisre'el/Jezreel Valley (Esdraelon Plain). In appreciation of Jewish support in his power struggle against Pompey, he releases Jews from military service. Jewish Roman citizens are estimated to be nearly 10% of the Roman population in the Middle East.

47   Cleopatra tries to maneuver a claim to Ein Gedi and Dead Sea region in an effort to control the fragrance (from persimmons), cosmetic and medicinal production of this area. *"...along the bank of the stream were many trees...the water...sweetened...(the fish) may live...from Ein Gedi to Ein Eglaim...fruit...for food...leaves for healing."* (Ezekiel 47:8-12). In the Dead Sea area there are *"black lumps of asphalt...float...useful not only for caulking ships but also for curing bodily sickness."* (JF).

47   Hyrcanus is named 'ethnarch' (subordinate-governor) and Antipater is appointed Procurator of **Iudaea (Judea).** Antipater maneuvers his son Phasael into position as governor of Jerusalem and his other son Herod governor of the Galilee as *"Hyracanus is paralysed with fear, every minute expecting Herod to March against him with an army at his back."* (JF). Herod is made a Roman citizen, quickly putting down a revolt against the Roman administration, executing the leader **'Hezekiah of the Galilee'** and rebels. (See Judah 4BCE).

45   Julius Caesar brings Cleopatra to Rome as his mistress.

44   Pompey's supporters Cassius and Brutus, against his command, assassinate Julius Caesar on the **Ides (15) of March** 44. This is an aristocratic conspiracy to restore republican freedom, resulting in a civil war. Jews mourn him as their own, grateful for his sympathetic legislation, protecting Jews in exercising their faith. Remembered for: enacting laws against excessive interest rates, establishing laws of bankruptcy, stabilizing the currency by basing it on gold. Restores old temples, builds new ones, public libraries, theaters, roads, canals. Reduces excessive taxation, has a census taken, makes land allotments to fathers of three children, allows liberty of conscience and worship, establishes public libraries, builds roads

across Italy, allows all freemen of Italy to become equal citizens with those of Rome, appoints provincial governors according to ability, forgives surrendering foes, commits the **'Julian Calendar'** of 365 days, an extra day in February every fourth year.

43   Cassius levies high taxes in Judea and sells the inhabitants of four towns into slavery. "*Herod...brought his quota of one-hundred talents from Galilee and earned Cassius' hearty approval.*" (JF).

43   Malichus, king of the Nabateans poisons Antipater, fearing Cassius would make Herod king of Judea. See 30BCE.

42   Octavian (63BCE-14CE) and **Mark Anthony** (83-30BCE) defeat Julius Caesar's assassins Brutus and Cassius at Philippi (NE Greece of today) who commit suicide.

42   Cleopatra VII (69-30BCE) realizes the weakness of Egypt (compared to Rome) and seduces Mark Anthony as a means to pursue her position of power. She marries him in 32BCE.

42   **Herod** marries Miriam (Mariamme I), (the daughter of Alexander (brother of King Antigonus), a granddaughter of Hyrcanus II), banishing his previous wife Doris, a Samaritan, together with her son Antipater II.

40   Mark Anthony rejects demands for removal of Herod and appoints both Herod and Phasael as joint 'tetrarchs' (subordinate governors) in Judaea. Citizens of Jerusalem revolt against Herod and Phasael

40   Parthians invade, and with Hasmoneans defeat and temporarily expel the Romans from Jerusalem. Parthians place (Mattathias) Antigonus, son of Aristobulus II as king (ruling for 4 years 40-37 when he is defeated and killed). King Antigonus places Herod's brother Phasael in prison where he commits suicide (some say murdered). The aged High Priest Hyrcanus is mutilated, exiled from Judea and taken to Parthia.

40   Herod flees to Herodian, south-east of Jerusalem, then to Masada where his family and 800 followers find refuge. King Antigonus besieges Masada, (Josephus Flavius Jewish War 1:12:2). Antigonus' troops withdraw due to scarcity of fresh water at the Dead Sea. Herod leaves his family at Masada traveling to Alexandria, Rhodes and Rome where he is well received.

Chapter 7. King Herod 37 – 4 BCE

37 **Herodian Period**

Mark Anthony convenes the Senate *"introduced Herod...his own loyalty to Rome...making Herod king."* (Josephus Flavius, The Jewish War = JF). **The Roman senate approves Herod as king of Judea** (born 73, reigns 37-4BCE). The Jewish majority in Judea prefer a Hasmonean ruler. Herod pays Rome a generous annual stipend, raising high taxes resulting in poverty, ill-feeling and resentment. He defeats Antigonus' forces in Jericho. Together with Roman assistance rescues his family and friends from the siege at Masada, and proceeds to **capture Jerusalem**. Herod *"bestowing honors on those who had taken his side...the supporters of Antigonus he liquidated."* (JF). The conquered ruler Antigonus, the last Hasmonean king, is executed.

37 Roman rulers, including those who begin their rule as beneficial, often end as debauched and despotic, requiring the protection from a personal army, the Praetorian guard. Rome's leaders customarily eradicate rivals by killing them and their family. Many Roman generals and leaders (Pompey, Julius Caesar, Augustus) use their positions to accumulate vast personal wealth. Bribery is the norm as a means to be elected to the Roman Senate. Divorce is very common amongst Roman aristocracy as husbands look to a wife as a stepping-stone to higher power or wealth (what's new!). Roman Army conscripts its citizens in March each year serving for 25 years. Some auxiliary logistics forces are locals who do not enter into battle. Roman soldiers are encouraged to marry local brides. After their release from military service, they receive land to farm and cultivate. Roman theaters do not use topographical features as engineering aids having self-standing stalls and rows, unlike Greek theaters built on a natural gradient of the mountain slope. Roman law provides a coherent legal system to support economic activity throughout the empire.

37 Jews of Judea are opposed to the high taxes needed to support Herod's grandiose lifestyle, constructing six palaces, numerous exotic architectural structures resembling Rome. Examples of Herod's mania and tyranny and his lack of morality, which is not dissimilar to the leaders in Rome is seen by his actions as he murders family members, the remaining Hasmonean dynasty, 46 leaders of the Sanhedrin and eradicating all opposition. He surrounds himself with Greek-speaking learned people, poets and historians and is a patron of the arts. He controls the Jewish

administration of Judah, without the responsibility of security and intrusions on the borders, which is under Roman Army control.

• Jonathan, his wife's brother (also named Aristobulus) is drowned at Jericho in 35BCE, due to his popularity as High Priest.

• Herod murders his wife's grandfather, former King Hyrcanus II in 31BCE.

• Herod executes his uncle.

• Herod marries Mariamme I in 37BCE, executes her in 29BCE, her (Mariamme's) mother Alexandra in 28BCE, and his sons Alexander and Aristobulus are strangled at Sebaste in 7BCE.

• Herod executes his son Antipater II from his first wife Doris (marries in 47BCE) five days before his death in 4BCE.

"*Vast numbers...executed...tortured...individuals...cities...Jewish blood to gratify foreigners...reduced his people to poverty and utter lawlessness.*" (JF).

Summary of King Herod's Period.

The Jews never recognize Herod as 'A Jewish King'. He exterminates the Hasmonean Dynasty. The kingdom expands to previous Hasmonean borders except the Greek Decapolis cities in the Galilee and parts of Perea east to the Jordan River. The economy grows due to increased trade, while he funnels heavily taxed income into public works and constructs 6 palaces in Judea, and about 20 sites outside his realm in Perea, Tyre, Tripoli, Asia Minor, and Greece, making strategic alliances with neighboring rulers should he flee his own kingdom. King Herod controls state-owned copper mines in Cyprus; lends money to neighboring rulers.

At Caesarea, in honor of Emperor Augustus Caesar, he constructs (22-10BCE) a port **Caesarea Maritima,** one of the three largest ports in the Eastern Mediterranean with a 600-meter pier out to sea as no natural bay is suitable. The other two large ports are Leptis Magna in Libya and Alexandria (population 500,000) in Egypt. Tariffs are collected on all exported and imported goods while communication routes are improved. An aqueduct is constructed from the Carmel Mountains 12-kilometers away. After Herod's death Caesarea becomes the Roman capital and governor's official residence of Judea in 6AD.

In his capital **Jerusalem**, Herod has absolute power seeking to avoid conflict with Jewish traditional customs. He purges the Sanhedrin (Jewish High Council) to become solely an academic and religious council, depriving it of all executive power. From 23 BCE, reconstructs and expands **The Second Temple,** one of the largest structures in the world. Mt. Moriah is flattened in the north, extending the southern platform using of arches to increase its area. Water is conveyed from the Bethlehem area by an aqueduct to the Temple, stored in subterranean cisterns under the southern Temple area. The Greek Acra, the central administrative building, now called the **Antonia Fortress** (named after Mark Anthony) is expanded with walls 60 meters high and four towers. It is the official administrative building and residence of the Roman Governor in Jerusalem. He constructs three defensive **towers** - Phasael (Herod's brother), Miriam (Herod's wife) and Hippicus (Herod's friend) in an area of the Tower of David to protect his palace. Josephus describes these towers as being taller than the light-house at Alexandria. The Psiphonus Tower (at Zahal Square today) at 35 meters high has a view of the Dead Sea (described as the 'west sea', meaning west of the Nabateans). Judea, devoid of marble, is imported from Marmara in Turkey, used extensively in all of his palaces and especially in the Temple. *"He who has not seen the Temple of Herod, has never see a beautiful building"* Babylonian Talmud, Baba Batra, 4a: Shemot Rabba 36:1).

Map 12. King Herod's Construction Projects 37 – 4 BCE

At the **Dead Sea** King Herod controls the perfume trade, a sought after fragrance from persimmons grown in this area. Salt is mined, used for the preservation of foods, as a sealant, and glue. The Dead Sea water level reaches the cliffs in the north-west making no land bridge possible along the western shore, using small boats. The salts and muds have therapeutic qualities, are exported. (Ezekiel Chapter 47). Fragrances (frankincense and myrrh), originating in Yemen, pass through Judea on to the Mediterranean.

At **Herodian**, Herod constructs a 25 meter mausoleum on top of this man-made hill, seen from afar. This is the only site bearing his name. He scoops soil from the incline and piles it atop the peak resembling a volcanic cone. The palace is built in the inside with a surrounding wall. "*Encircled the top with round towers...a palace so magnificent.*" (JF). He rebuilds **Samaria** with "*6000 colonists*" (JF) and renames it **Sebaste** (Greek for Augustus) in honor of the emperor. Herod assists construction at Cos, Rhodes, Astons, Sparta, Nicopolis and Antioch.

36   "*The (Hasmonean) high priest Jonathan first built a fortress and named it Masada.*" (JF). Herod builds **Masada** (a UNESCO World Heritage site) from 36 to 30BCE into an impregnable fortress, 450 meters above the present level of the Dead Sea. Masada is located along the Trade Route from Edom, Moab, and the Arava, to Ein Gedi and Jerusalem. Herod plans Masada as a safe-house for himself and his family should Jewish subjects revolt against his despotic rule "*...and more terrible danger from the Egyptian queen Cleopatra. For she did not conceal her intensions but constantly appealed to Anthony, begging him to destroy Herod and requesting the transfer to herself of the Kingdom of Judaea...he did not yield to her demands, hopelessly enslaved as he was by his passion for her*". (JF). Herod destroys the Hasmonean structures on the mountaintop previously constructed by King Alexander Yanai (103–76BCE) whose coins are found on the site. He constructs intricate aqueduct systems diverting the sporadic rain waters through channels allowing the water to flow into 12 cisterns dug into the hillside and additional cisterns are chiseled into the bedrock on the plateau holding over 40,000 cubic meters of fresh water. "*He had cut in the rock numbers of great tanks to hold water.*" (JF). In severe desert conditions (average 50 millimeters of rainfall a year) Herod has the technology to bring sufficient quantities of water up onto the plateau. Roman-style bathhouses consist of a dressing-room (apoditerium), cold-room (fridgedarium), temperate-room (tepidarium) and a double-floored hot steam room (caldarium) where steam is blown under the floor and escapes through clay-chimneys in the walls. A concave roof prevents droplets of hot water falling on your head. A 550 cubic meter swimming pool at the Western Palace has a canvas roof (tarpaulin). (See Roman Bath Houses 135). Herod builds a **3-tiered palace** on the northern corner with "*a sunken road led from the place to the hill-top,*

invisible from the outside", and another **(Western) palace** in the west serving as an entertainment center for visiting guests. *"The plateau was of rich soil...the king reserved it for cultivation."* Archaeologists have located twenty-nine **storage rooms, a synagogue and columbarium** (dovecotes) for protein, carrying messages and providing nutrients for vegetation.

33   Mark Anthony divorces Octavian's sister Octavia, to peruse the charms of Cleopatra.

31   **Earthquake** in Judea *"destroyed 30,000 people and cattle."* (JF).

31   Upon his return from Parthia, the aged Hyrcanus II (his wife's grandfather) is executed under orders of Herod.

31   *"Cleopatra had (killed all)...her own family...extended her acquisitiveness to Jews...worked in secret to get their king Herod, put to death. Anthony was sober enough to realize...the killing...was utterly immoral...He sliced off large parts of their territory, including the palm-grove at Jericho in which balsam is produced, and gave them to Cleopatra."* (JF). Cleopatra *"begging (Anthony) to destroy Herod and requesting the transfer to herself of the kingdom of Judea."* (JF).

31   **Octavian (Augustus= sacred)** (63BCE-14CE) is threatened by Anthony's partnership with Cleopatra to make Alexandria the new capital of the Roman Empire, reducing Rome's status. Octavian defeats the fleets of Mark Anthony and Cleopatra at the naval **Battle of Actium** off Greece (2 September). Following their defeat both commit suicide the following year 30BCE in Alexandria, Egypt, Anthony by the sword and Cleopatra by holding an asp to her breast. Anthony is 53 and Cleopatra 39. Egypt is annexed to the Roman Empire. Octavian rules as consul from 31 until 27BCE when he takes on the title **Augustus Caesar.** In 23BCE he receives imperial power of the tribune. He encourages the visual arts; restores existing buildings; constructs new buildings – Pantheon, Teatro di Marcello, Ara Pacis (Altar of Peace).

30   Herod fears his friendship with Mark Anthony would damage his standing with Octavian. *"Herod...sails to Rhodes...sought audience (with Augustus)."* (JF). Herod tells Octavian *"found me fighting loyally by his side...As it was I sent him all the reinforcements I could and many thousand sacks of corn; and not even after his defeat at Actium did I desert my benefactor...I told him there was only one way of retrieving his disasters-Cleopatra's death."* (JF). Octavian *"replies 'You are perfectly safe and your throne is now more securely yours. You deserve to rule over many subjects after showing such loyalty to your friend'."* (JF). He confirms Herod will

remain King of Judea. *"Herod welcomed him (Octavian) for the first time with his kingly wealth, rode by his side when he inspected his army near Ptolemais (Acre)..."Caesar...restored to his kingdom the area sliced off by Cleopatra and added Gadder, Hippus, and Samaria...Gaza, Anthedon, Poppa, and Strato's Tower."* (JF). **Romans call the territory Iudaea (Judea).**

30   Herod had not forgotten *"Cassius instructions...surrounded Malichus* (Nabatean king who poisoned his father Antipater, (see 43 BCE) *and hacked him to death."* (JF).

29   Herod accuses his wife Miriam (Mariamme I), daughter of the Hasmoneans Alexander and Alexandra of plotting to poison him. She is executed. Herod weds Malthace of Samaria.

28   Obodas III king of Nabatea constructs towns along the **Spice Route in the Negev** – Mamshit, Avdat, Shivta, and Nitzana (See Nabateans 363). The towns have tent-like dwelling units in the desert conditions - door facing east, with high opening westwards to allow a cross-breeze to cool the interior.

27   Octavian takes the title **Augustus** (your eminence) **Caesar**. Herod constructs **Sebaste** (Augustus in Greek) to honor the emperor.

24   King Herod marries Miriam II, daughter of Boethas of Egypt.

23   In **Jerusalem** King Herod constructs various public stadiums for Roman-style entertainment - hippodrome, theater and amphitheater. He reconstructs and expands the Temple Mount, **The Second Temple is** to reconcile his subjects, perpetuate his name and make his capital Jerusalem, one of the largest cities in the Eastern Mediterranean. The physical area is increased and height of the new 'Holy of Holies' building (*Kodesh Ha'kadashim* קדש הקדשים) is doubled. *"In the fifteenth year of his reign, he restored the existing sanctuary and round it enclosed an area double the former size, keeping no account of its costs and achieving magnificence beyond compare...The High Priest's breastplate...secured by two round gold brooches...twelve more stones in four groups of three...He did not normally wear these vestments: he put on less ornate garments except when he entered the inmost shrine, which he did once a year-alone-on the day observed by all as a fast or God...**Whoever has not seen Jerusalem in its splendor has never seen a fine city.** The Temple offered everything that could delight the eye and the heart. Sheeted in heavy gold plate on every side...From the very top rose sharp gold spikes to prevent birds from perching on the roof and soiling it...a palace...named Antonia in honor of Anthony. His own place, built in the Upper City."* (JF).

Drainage Canal, beneath a stairway down Ophel Slope   Adrian Wolff

The Western Wall, Jerusalem   Adrian Wolff

Josephus tells how after construction of the Temple had begun, King Herod sends an emissary to Rome to request building permission. The emissary takes his time traveling and obtaining a meeting with the relevant authorities in Rome. They told him 'if you have not begun, don't; if you are in the construction stage, stop; and if you have finished, there is nothing to be done'. After eight years the infrastructure is complete and the buildings another three years. An annual tax of two **shekels** is imposed on all Jews for the maintenance and upkeep of the Temple. Money-changers assist pilgrims to convert their currencies to pay for the tax and for a sacrificial animal. A sheep market exists for daily sacrifices.

The Temple Mount has a natural gradient sloping southwards. The northern area is flattened extending the platform 40 meters into the southern Tyropoeon (Cheesemakers) Valley using four levels of vaults with extensive underpinnings with arches to maintain the level of the platform, creating subterranean cisterns (later known during the Crusader Period as Solomon's Stables). The total area is 144,000 m². Northern Wall is 300, Southern Wall 280, Western Wall 488, Eastern Wall 480 meters.

A portico containing columns 15 meters high surrounds the Temple Mount. The southern section has two halls each three floors high, the royal basilica. The outer forecourt for trade and secular activities is open to both Jews and non-Jews. A higher enclosed level contains the sacred area of the inner forecourt 250 x 260 meters, accessible only to Jews, is divided into three parts: 1. The Priest's Court (Kohanim, Levites) contains an altar for sacrifices and the Holy of Holies. 2. The Court of Israel (the men's section). 3. The Women's Court. A wall of huge stones taken from the limestone quarries in the northern part of the city (outside Herod's Gate of today) surrounds the Temple Mount. Stones of the outer wall average 1-1.2 meters high and 1-3 meters wide. The stones have a smooth frame approximately 2 centimeters wide, with a rough interior. The largest stone discovered is 13.6 meters long, 3.5 meters high and approximately 3.5-4.5 meters deep weighing an estimated 500 tons, not situated at base level, is actually moved to its current position. Dry construction methods are used with closely joined courses, each course spaced 2 centimeters inward.

The **'Holy of Holies'** structure (*hakadosh hakadashim*) constructed over the 'rock or foundation stone' on Mt. Moriah, is 70 meters tall (one of the tallest buildings in the ancient world), where Abraham prepared to sacrifice his son Isaac 1700 years earlier (Genesis 22:2). The Priest's Court covered by white marble facade and gold lintels, has a menorah standing at its entrance. The High Priest (*ha'cohen ha'gadol*) enters the Holy of Holies only once a year, on Day of Atonement, Yom Kippur, when he utters the name of YHVH (Ex. 3:13). Original Ark of the Covenant had disappeared during the Babylonian exile. "*No fly was seen in the slaughter house...no rain never quenched the fore of the wood-pile on the altar; neither did the wind overcome the column of smoke that arose...never did serpent or scorpion injure anyone in Jerusalem.*" Pirkei Avot V:8.

'**The Western Wall**', 488 meters long today is the closest part of the exterior Wall to the Holy of Holies. 'The Wailing Wall' is 60 meters where the faithful pray and some leave personal notes (here it is 'local mail!!'). Jewish pilgrims lament the Destruction of the Holy Temple. The Herodian Wall has 19 courses both below and above the current plaza level. The courses seen today are Herodian with Umayyad Arab, Mamluk and Ottoman levels built above the original rectangular stones.

Pilgrims' notes placed in the Western Wall   Adrian Wolff

Wilson's Arch found under the Muslim Quarter is named after British cartographer and geographer Sir Charles Wilson (see 1864). A shaft dug by British archaeologist Sir Charles Warren (see 1867) under Wilson's Arch exposes 14 layers of rectangular Herodian stones. Warren names the vaulted passageway 'the secret passage'. According to Jewish tradition, the **Southern Wall** is where, the 'just' will enter through the Hulda Gate on the Day of Judgement. Umayyads block the gate in the 8th century to prevent such an occurrence. The main entrance is from the southeast gate and exit from the southwest. Jews always pray facing the Holy of Holies. Pilgrims exit backwards, as it is forbidden to turn one's back on the Holy of Holies.

Robinson's Arch named after the American biblical geographer Edward Robinson (1794-1863) delineates the arch over the Tyropoeon Valley (Valley of the Cheese makers). The staircase leads up to the Temple Mount and the bridge connects the Temple

Mount with the Upper City. Jewish Zealots destroy the arch in 70 CE during Jewish War to prevent the Roman troops entering the Temple Mount. The inscription visible today on the Western Wall is from Isaiah 66:14 "*You will see and your heart will exult*".

Southern Wall steps, Hulda Gates, Temple Mount   Adrian Wolff

Robinson's Arch   Adrian Wolff

Water. Rains fall only during the three winter months and no perennial streams flow through the Jerusalem area. Rainwater is collected from rooftops and drains constructed to channel the water into cisterns cut into the bedrock, plastered with lime to prevent seepage. Engineers devise ways to convey large quantities of water to the Temple to fulfill the laws relating to cleanliness and purification for the population, estimated at 100,000 in addition to the large numbers of pilgrims ascending upon Jerusalem during the three pilgrimage festivals. A further high demand for water is needed for the daily animal sacrifices. Canals lead water from outside the walls to reservoirs inside the city. A dam is constructed in the Valley of Hinom and the pool at Siloam (the only source of perennial water) is expanded. Two ancient aqueducts to Jerusalem exist - the lower from the A'roub springs north of Hebron, and an upper east of Etzion, south of Bethlehem. The walls are plastered with lime and covered with stone slabs to prevent evaporation. King Solomon's Pools on the upper aqueduct are located roughly midway between the A'roub springs and Jerusalem, a distance of 10 kilometers as the crow flies, circumnavigating 15 valleys, totaling 44 kilometers. The average gradient is one per mille (1000). The lower aqueduct passes Bethlehem, Sur Bahir, Government House, and Sultan's Pool along the slope of Mt Zion to a reservoir at the southern side of the Temple Mount, 68 kilometers with an average gradient of only 0.45 meters per mille including through a tunnel.

Map 13. Herodian Jerusalem – 2nd Temple Period up to 70 CE (AD)

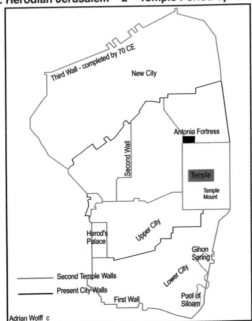

23   Herod sends his sons Alexander and Aristobulus, (of his second wife Mariamme I), to complete their education in Rome.

22   An additional example of Herod's nepotism is seen when Herod appoints Boethos, the father of his wife Miriam II as High Priest. Later this year King Herod marries Pallas.

22   At a Phoenician port Strato's Tower, King Herod *"constructed a harbor bigger than Piraeus."* (JF), (22–10BCE) *"The...sea-board from Dora to Joppa, midway between which the city lies was without a harbor."* (JF). The port **Caesarea** Maritima, named after his patron Emperor Augustus Caesar, the largest on the eastern Mediterranean coast, will be the first port to export the winter crops when the spring sailing season begins. Herod collects substantial income from taxation levied on goods imported and exported through Caesarea to and from the East along the Trade Routes.

The Port
- The entrance has two 80-90 meter towers, with a lighthouse, topped by statues, mark the opening into the port.
- A southern 600-meter and a northern 300-meter breakwater are constructed with sluice gates for drainage to prevent silting.
- Storage vaults are found in the harbor.
- A chain controls entry and exit while taxes are collected.
- Local exports – wine, olive oil, flax, grain, figs, dates.
- Double-walled wood forms are towed into position over a foundation of boulders. Concrete in baskets set under water.
- Imported items for export in the Mediterranean – silks, spices.

At Caesarea, Herod constructs impressive Roman-style architectural structures - palace, bath-house with all the facilities befitting a Roman capital town, circus (in Latin, hippodrome in Greek), theater, amphitheater and temple (to Augustus). Herod's palace has a fresh-water swimming pool overlooking the sea. The theater seats 4000 spectators, a 3-tiered high backdrop wall on the stage (*scaenae frons*). The hippodrome 250 x 50 meters, seats 10,000 spectators is used for horse and chariot races. Starting gates are seen today. *"He entirely rebuilt (Strato's Tower) with white stone, and adorned with the most magnificent palaces...He had blocks of stone let down into 20 fathoms of water...Upon the marine foundation...constructed above the surface...a breakwater...circular terrace...as a broad promenade for disembarking passengers...At the harbor-mouth stood colossal statues, three on either side...Facing the harbor-mouth stood Caesar's temple remarkable for its beauty and grand proportions, it contained a colossal statue of the emperor...The rest of the buildings – amphitheater, theater, public places-were constructed in a style worthy of the name which the city bore."* (JF).

Caesarea, Theater   Adrian Wolff

Caesarea, Herod's fresh water Swimming Pool   Adrian Wolff

King Herod becomes president of the Olympic Games held in Caesarea for chariot races and gladiator competitions. Like all Roman games, there is a small or no charge for entrance. *"The king also instituted four-yearly games. His bounty...was a gift...to the whole world, where the fame of the Olympic Games penetrates...he not only accepted the post of president of the quadrennial celebration...but he endowed them for all time with revenues...He instituted...offering prizes of the highest value...not the victors only, but also those who obtained second and third place."* (JF).

Caesarea, Hippodrome   Adrian Wolff

Caesarea, Aqueduct   Adrian Wolff

20   Caesarea has no water sources. A 12-kilometer long **aqueduct** is constructed to convey water from springs at Shuni, at the southern end of the Carmel range. The aqueduct has a very shallow gradient as it traverses the flat 'plain', cuts through a hill before reaching the beach on its way to Caesarea. Shuni will become a Roman resort with a theater, bathing pools with multi-colored mosaics and marble statues.

20   Herod builds a small temple, Caesarea Philippi at the Banias springs, one of the sources of the Jordan River in honor of his patron Augustus Caesar. This temple is close to the Greek sacrificial cave and Temple dedicated to Greek god Pan. Note: Pan = Panias = Banias.

17   King Herod travels to Rome to meet the Roman authorities and returns to Jerusalem together with his sons Alexander and Aristobulus.

15   Marcus Vispanius Agrippa, Herod's a close friend, visits Judea, received stately to please his father-in-law Augustus. Herod names his son after Agrippa. Herod entertains his guests lavishly in his various palaces offering them wine from Italy, apples from Cumae and Italy, preserved onions, fish source from Spain, all served in fine tableware to include silver cups.

15   The Temple in Jerusalem is completed. Workers to construct a northern Third Wall called Bezetha, enclosing the New City.

14   King Herod quarrels with his sons Alexander and Aristobulus. Herod restores favor to his eldest son, Antipater II and to his first wife Doris.

Church of the Annunciation, Nazareth   Adrian Wolff

6   *"Now in the sixth month the angel Gabriel was sent by God to a city of Galilee named **Nazareth,** to a virgin betrothed to a man whose name was Joseph, of the house of David. The virgin's name was Mary...the angel said to her, 'Rejoice, highly favored one, the Lord is with you, blessed are you among women.'...You will conceive in your womb and bring forth a Son, and shall call His*

name Jesus. He will be great, and will be called the Son of the Highest, and the Lord God will give Him the throne of His father David." (Luke 1:26-32). Also Matthew 1:21, 23.

6   *Mary...entered the house* (in Ein Kerem) *of Zacharias and greeted* **Elizabeth** *(your relative has also conceived)...'His name is John (= gracious)...Immediately his tongue loosed.* (Luke 1:39,40,36,63,64).

6   Probable birth date of Jesus in **Bethlehem**. Beit Lehem=House of Bread in Hebrew; Bayt Lahm=House of Meat in Arabic. The date 4 BCE is also used to denote His birth. *"A decree went out from Caesar Augustus that all the world should be registered. This census first took place...so all went to be registered everyone to his own city. Joseph also went up from Galilee, out of the city of Nazareth, into Judaea, to the city of David, which is called* **Bethlehem**...*to be registered with Mary, his betrothed wife, who was with child...She brought forth her first born Son, and wrapped Him in swaddling cloths and laid Him in a manger, because there was no room for them in the inn."* (Luke 2:1-7).

6   *"The angel said...I bring you good tidings of great joy, which will be to all people. For there is born to you this day in the city of David a savior, who is Christ the Lord."* (Luke 2:10,11). *"...**Jesus** was born in Bethlehem of Judaea in the days of Herod the king."* (Matthew 2:1). The Hebrew name Joshua is 'Ye'hoshua' יהושע. The Greek translation uses the Galilean pronunciation Joshu'a ישוע (redeemer/deliverer). The Hebrew word Mashiah' משיח is Messiah, literally meaning 'anointed one'.

6   *"Wise men came to Jerusalem...seen His star in the East and have come to worship Him...they had opened their treasures, they presented gifts to Him: gold, frankincense and myrrh."* (Matthew 2:1,2,11).

6   *"And when eight days were completed for the circumcision of the Child, His name was called Jesus...according to the law of Moses were completed, they brought Him to Jerusalem to present Him to the Lord...and to offer a sacrifice according to what is said in the law of the Lord, 'A pair of turtledoves or two young pigeons."* (Luke 2:21,22,24).

6   According to the New Testament *"Herod the king...was troubled'* by the birth of Jesus, and *"had secretly called the wise men...and search carefully for the young child,"* (Matthew 2:3,7,8) causing the Christian Holy Family to *"flee to Egypt and stay there."* (Matthew 2:13). *"Then Herod...was exceedingly angry and he sent forth and put to death all the male children who were in Bethlehem and in all its districts, from two years old and under."* (Matthew 2:16).

6   *"After the killing of Mariamme I (29BCE) and her sons he would spare no one." "Hating his children more than any father had ever done, Herod hated his brother far more." "His anger descend first on Doris...stripped her of all her adornments.* Herod's son Alexander *"told them not to rest their hopes on Herod, a shameless old man who dyed his hair...but to turn to Alexander, who would succeeds to the throne whether Herod liked it or not."* (JF). King Herod *"sent his sons* (Alexander and Aristobulus by his wife Miriam (Mariamme I) to Sebate (Samaria)...*orders that they should be strangled'. "No one guessed that Herod would be so barbarous as to murder his children."* (JF). Herod's son Antipater II now is the undisputed heir.

6   Herod breaks with the Pharisees sect executing many members.

5   King Herod divorces Mariamme II.

4   **'Judah of the Galilee'**, son of 'Hezekiah of the Galilee' (See 47 BCE) and Mathias son of Margalus are rabbis in Jerusalem. *"Although it was unlawful to have in the Sanctuary images...or likeness of any living thing, the king (Herod) had put up over the Great Gate a golden eagle (Roman symbol). This the rabbis now urged them to cut down, saying that even if danger was involved it was glorious thing to die for the laws of their fathers. The king had the rebels burnt alive."* (JF). Their followers become known as **Kana'im or Zealots** (Rebels).

4   *"Sickness spread through his entire body, accompanied by a variety of painful symptoms."* (JF). Herod arrives in Jericho..."*sent for his sister Salome...said 'I know the Jews will greet my death with wild rejoicings, but I can be mourned on other people's account and make sure of a magnificent funeral...These men under guard - as soon as I die, kill them all - let loose the soldiers...then all Judaea and every family will weep for me."* (JF). Herod then executes Antipater II, son of his first wife Doris. King Herod dies in Jericho in late March five days after his son's execution. Herod had instructed the slaughter of the High Priests upon his death to prevent them usurping the dynasty. *"Before the military knew that Herod was dead, Salome went out with her husband (Alexas)...freed the prisoners...king had ordered to be murdered. She told them the king had changed his mind and was permitting them to go home again."* The Romans are quick to intervene. There are celebrations of joy and relief upon his death. Herod is buried in Herodian in the Judean Desert, east of Bethlehem. *"Everything possible was done by Archelaus to add to the magnificence...There was a solid gold bier, adorned with precious stones and draped with the richest purple...body wrapped*

in crimson...a golden crown and a scepter by the right hand." (JF). His tomb is discovered in 2007.

4   Following Herod's death Archelaus (another of Herod's sons) claims *"he would endeavor in every way to show himself kinder to them than did his father."* (JF). A crowd *"clamored for a lightening of direct taxation...the release of prisoners...they were for men who...had died for the laws of their country and for the Temple...Archelaus realized that the crowd could no longer be restrained without bloodshed; so he sent his whole army against them, the infantry in a body through the City; the cavalry through the fields... killing about 3000"* (JF).

4   *"When Herod was dead, behold, an angel of the Lord appeared in a dream to Joseph in Egypt saying 'Arise take the young Child and His mother, and go to the land of Israel'...And he came and dwelt in a city called **Nazareth**."* (Matthew 2:19,20,23).

4   Judea descends into anarchy following Herod's death. The various Roman governors oppress the Jews. The High Priests establish their personal militias to control The Temple, resulting the resignation of the Sanhedrin in 28CE.

4   Four different Jewish groups struggle for supremacy of the leadership.

1. The **Pharisees**, from the Hebrew word 'perushim = separatists led by the rabbis and Sanhedrin. They maintain ritual purity and resist from 'pleasures of the secular'.
2. The **Sadducees** reject the 'Oral Law' and the leadership of the rabbis. Many of their followers are wealthy priests, occasionally purchasing their position and befriend Romans.
3. The **Zealots** are passionate nationalists, break away from the Pharisees, wanting to confront the Romans.
4. The **Sicarii** (= dagger) anarchists against the establishment. They resort to theft and terrorism as a means to achieve their objectives. They carry small daggers under their cloaks, assassinating Romans, wealthy Jews, and priests, then blend into the crowd.

The First Temple is destroyed due to idol worship, illicit relationships and murder. The Jewish Sages attribute the Destruction of the Second Temple to baseless hatred that prevailed amongst the Jews of Judea.

4   The Romans retain the Herodian dynasty and divide Herod's kingdom between three of his sons and his sister.
'Ethnarch' and 'tetrarch' refer to a subordinate governor status.

1. Archelaus 'ethnarch' of Judaea, Samaria, Idumea, Caesarea and Sebaste. Archelaus is not given title of king. In 6CE Emperor Augustus deposes Archelaus and annexes his territory.

2. Philip 'tetrarch' in Golan includes Caesarea Philippi (Panias) until 34CE. Philip is the only of Herod's sons to rule until his natural death.

3. Herod Antipas 'tetrarch' in Galilee and Perea (Gilad and Edom) until 37CE. Antipas builds the town of Tiberias on the western shore of the Sea of Galilee and Zippori a regional center on the via Maris in the Lower Galilee. Antipas' stepdaughter is the notorious Salome-Herodias, who, according to the New Testament is responsible for the death of St. John the Baptist. "*Give me John the Baptist's head here on a platter.*" (Matthew 14:8).(Matthew 14:1-12. Mark 6:14–26)

4. Salome rules the cities of Yavne and Azotus in the Coastal Plain and Phasaelis in the Jordan Valley.

5. Aristobulus another son of Herod does not rule any territory. Agrippa his son, is appointed King I in 37CE=(AD).

4   A Roman Procurator rules Judea subordinate to the Legate in Syria, while **the Judaean administrative capital moves to Caesarea in 6AD**. Roman garrisons with legionaries are dispersed throughout the territory. The office of the Jewish High Priest, rigorously subordinated to the Romans, is prevented from obtaining any independent authority and is given license to control only Jewish traditional matters. The Jews wish to live within an independent Jewish territory, are eager to expel the Roman invading conquerors of Judea (Eretz Israel). During the three Jewish pilgrimage festivals (Passover, Shavu'ot, Succot), the Roman Procurator will transfer himself from the Roman capital of Judea in Caesarea to Jerusalem, to take command of the Roman garrison should the Jews riot against the Roman authority.

Chapter 8. Jesus and His Followers 6 - 65 CE (AD)

CE Common Era = AD

6   Widespread disturbances throughout Judea as various groups of Jewish rebels rise against the Roman authorities for autonomy.

6   The ethnarch (subordinate governor) Archelaus is deposed. Judea, Idumea and Samaria are annexed into a Roman province. The capital is moved from Jerusalem to Caesarea. Coponius procurator

6   Jesus *"was 12 years old..(His parents)..went up to Jerusalem..they found Him in the temple."* (Luke 2:42,46).

10   Hillel (75 BCE–10CE), the famous Talmudic teacher in Jerusalem is known to tell his students *"You shall love your fellow as yourself."* (Leviticus 19:18). Later in (Pirkei Avot I:14; II:8) *'If I am not for myself, who will be?"*. *"More schooling, the more wisdom."*

14   Emperor Augustus Caesar dies in Rome, is remembered for establishing a constitutional government, centralizing power in Rome, with stability and prosperity. Permits religious freedom for the Jews. Succeeded by his step-son, **Tiberius** (rules 14–37CE) by his wife Livia, who is a successful administrator. Jesus Christ is crucified during his reign.

17   Herod Antipas honoring Roman Emperor Tiberius, founds Tiberias on the Sea of Galilee, built on ruins of Rakkat, an ancient town of the Naftali tribe, causing Jewish religious leaders to forbid Jewish residence, fearing a unsuspected construction over a Jewish grave. Tiberius expels the Jews of Rome, rescinds in 29.

26   **Pontius Pilate** Roman procurator of Judea (26–36). *"Conveyed to Jerusalem the images of Caesar known as sigma...caused great excitement among the Jews...do not permit any graven image...in the City...rushed off to Pilate in Caesarea...When Pilate refused, they fell prone...remained motionless...soldiers surround(ed) the Jews...Pilate declaring that he would cut them to pieces unless they accept the images of Caesar...the Jews...bent their necks, shouting they were ready to be killed rather than transgress the Law. Amazed at the intensity of their religious fervor, Pilate ordered the sigma to be removed."* (**Josephus Flavius, The Jewish War = JF**). Jews oppose foreign oppression and look for salvation, hoping perhaps the Messiah will deliver them from the Roman yoke.

28   **Baptism of Jesus** in the Jordan River by his cousin **St. John the Baptist**. *"baptized by him in the Jordan, confessing their sins...he will baptize you with the Holy Spirit."* (Matthew 3:5,6,11).

28 Jesus returns to **Nazareth**, *"He came to Nazareth where He had been brought up. As His custom was, he went into the synagogue on the Sabbath day, and stood up to read."* (Luke 4:16). Congregants reject Jesus when His claims to be the Messiah. *"All those in the synagogue when they heard these things, were filled with wrath...and thrust Him out of the city."* (Luke 4:21,28,29).

28 Mother of Jesus, Mary is invited to a wedding in **Cana**, near Nazareth. She attends together with Jesus and his friend Simon, a fisherman from Capernaum (Kfar Nahum). Jesus performs **His First Miracle**. *"There was a wedding in Cana of Galilee, and the mother of Jesus was there. Now both Jesus and His disciples were invited to the wedding...they ran out of wine...Jesus said to them 'Fill the water-pots with water'...was made wine."* (John 2:1,2,3,7,9).

Capernaum, Orthodox Church   Timothy Guy

28 Simon impressed by the Miracle at Kfar Cana, invites Jesus to visit his home in **Capernaum**, on shore of the Sea of Galilee where He continues to perform miracles. *"He entered Capernaum...and it was heard that He was in the house. Immediately many gathered together...He preached the word to them. Then they came to Him, bringing a paralytic who was carried by four men...Then Jesus saw their faith, He said to the paralytic, 'Son, your sins are forgiven you.'...'But you may know that the Son of Man has power on earth to forgive sins'. He said to the paralytic, 'I say to you arise, take up your bed and go to your house. Immediately he arose, took up the bed...so that all were amazed."* (Mark 2:1-12). Capernaum is located on the border of the province where customs and taxes are collected at the crossing to and from the Golan. *"As Jesus...saw a man named Matthew sitting at the tax office."* (Matthew 9:9).

28   At Capernaum Jesus prophetically predicts His sacrifice for the Sins of Mankind. He claims one's soul will go to heaven by becoming a 'believer' of Jesus the Messiah. "*I am the bread of life...which comes down from heaven, that one may eat of it and not die...If anyone eats of this bread, he will live forever; and the bread that I shall give is My flesh, which I shall give for the life of the world...Whoever eats My flesh and drinks My blood has eternal life and I will raise him up at the last day...He who eats My flesh and drinks My blood abides in Me, and I in him. As the loving Father sent Me, and I live because of the Father...These things He said in the synagogue as He taught in **Capernaum**.*" (John 6:48,50,51,54,55,59).

28   The Kinneret basin is "*wonderful...in its beauty...the rich soil...there is not a plant that does not flourish...walnuts...palms...figs and olives...is watered by a spring with great fertilizing power, known locally as Capernaum (Kfar Nahum)...breeds fish.*"(JF).

28   **Jesus walks on the water.** Every afternoon during the summer months a strong westerly wind blows at the Sea of Galilee. "*The boat was now in the middle of the sea, tossed by the waves,...for the wind was contrary...Jesus went to them, walking on the sea...Jesus spoke to them saying 'Be of good cheer, It is I, do not be afraid'...Then those who were in the boat came and worshipped Him saying, 'Truly You are the Son of God'.*" (Matthew 14:24-33). Also Mark 1:16-18; 6:34-45.

Church of the Primacy, Ancient Port, Sea of Galilee   Adrian Wolff

28   At Tabgha on the NW shore of the Sea of Galilee, Jesus performs the miracles of the **Multiplication of the Loaves and Fish**. "*He departed from there by boat to a deserted place by Himself...when*

the multitudes heard it, they followed Him on foot...Jesus went out...He saw a great multitude, and...was moved with compassion for them and healed their sick....do not need to go away...give them something to eat...they said. 'We have here only five loaves and two fish'...He took the five loaves and the two fish, and looking up to heaven, He blessed and broke and gave the loaves to the disciples and the disciples gave to the multitudes...Now those who had eaten were about five thousand men, besides women and children." (Matthew 14:13-21). Greek for **fish** is **i ch th u s** = I**e**sous **Ch**ristos **th**eou **u**sios **s**oter = Jesus Christ, Son of God, Savior.

Mosaic Fish and Bread, Church of the Multiplication   Adrian Wolff

28   At **Mt. of Beatitudes (=blessed)** *"Jesus departed from there...and went up the mountain and sat down there. Then the great multitudes came to Him, having with then the lame, blind, mute, maimed, and many others and they laid them down at Jesus' feet and He healed them."* (Matthew 15:29,30).

Jesus names the Twelve Apostles. Apostle in Greek = messenger. *"He went out to the mountain to pray and continued into the night in prayer to God...He called His disciples...from them He chose twelve...He named apostles: Simon, whom He also named Peter, and Andrew his brother; James and John; Philip and Bartholomew; Matthew and Thomas; James, the son of Alphaeus, and Simon called the zealot; Judas, the son of James, and Judas Iscariot, who also became a traitor."* (Luke 6:12–16). (Matthew 10:2–4). Matthew and John are the Gospels. Tradition tells that 11 of the 12 Apostles are martyred.

Feeding the masses, "*Jesus called His disciples...'I have compassion on the multitude...with Me three days...have nothing to eat'...Jesus said to them 'How many loaves do you have?' and they said 'Seven and a few little fish'...He took the seven loaves and the fish and gave thanks, broke them and gave them to His disciples and the disciples gave to the multitudes. So they ate and were filled...Now those who ate were four thousand men, besides woman and children.*" (Matthew 15:29-38).

Church of the Beatitudes   Adrian Wolff

28   Death of St. John the Baptist. "*When Herod's (Antipas) birthday was celebrated, the daughter (Salome-Shulamit) of Herodias danced...he promised...to give her whatever she might ask. She...said, 'Give me John the Baptist's head here on a platter.'*" (Matthew 14:6-8). Mark 6:22-25. This episode in The New Testament has inspired many artists and musicians.

28   Jesus visits **Caesarea Philippi**, (Banias) at the foothills of Mt. Hermon, a natural spring, one of the three sources of the Jordan River. "*Philip (tetrarch' in Golan) also had built Paneas, a city at the fountains of the Jordan, he named it Caesarea.*" (JF).

28   At Banias Peter (Simon) proclaims Jesus as the Messiah and foresees His resurrection. **The First Vision of Messiah.** "*When Jesus came into the region of Caesarea Philippi, He asked His disciples saying 'Who do men say that I, Son of Man', Simon Peter answered and said 'You are the Christ, the Son of the living God.*" (Matthew 16:13,16). **The First Revelation of the Church,**

Simon becomes St. Peter. Jesus tells Simon "*You are Peter, and on this rock I will build My church...and I will give you the keys to the kingdom of heaven, and whatever you bind on earth, will be bound in heaven, and whatever you loose on earth will be lost in heaven.*" (Matthew 16:18,19). The original Christian Bible (New Testament) is written in Greek. The Greek word '*Petrus*' means '**rock**'. Christians understand this to be Jesus commanding Peter to continue the preaching and succession of Jesus. Catholics understand this to refer to a 'head' of the church - the future popes.

Map 14. Jesus' Ministry in the Galilee 28 – 30

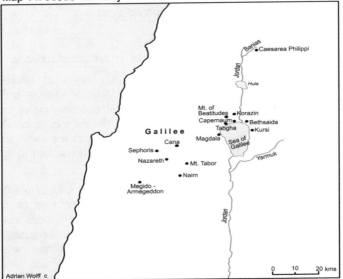

Adrian Wolff c

28   **The First Vision of His Crucifixion and Resurrection.** "*Jesus and His disciples went out to the towns of Caesarea Philippi...Peter...said to Him 'You are the **Christ**' (=Messiah)...And the Son of Man must suffer many things...and be killed and after three days rise again.*" (Mark 8:27-31).

Note: **The Greek word 'Christos' or Christ in English as He receives the 'chrisma' meaning 'anointed one (the Messiah), nomination, confirmation, unction'.** The New Testament uses the phrase '*Son of Man*'. **Jesus referring to His humanity – that God has a representative in the form of a man, Jesus.** This phrase is frequently found in the Book of the Jewish Prophet, Ezekiel 2:1,3,6,8; 3:1,3; and 4:1. The original Hebrew words '*bnei Adam*' (בני אדם) translated into literal English is '*son(s) of man*', meaning *'people'* collectively such a community, inhabitants, multitude, populous, population and not directly to one person only, or the 'son(s) of a man'.

30   In Alexandria, the Jewish philosopher Philo Judaeus (20 BCE-50 CE) compiles an interpretation of the Septuagint translation of the Torah. He writes of eight essential principles of spiritual religion.

        1. Existence of God
        2. His unity
        3. Divine providence
        4. Creation of the world
        5. Unity of the world
        6. The existence of incorporeal ideas
        7. Revelation of the Law
        8. Eternity

Philo's nephew Tiberius Alexander, procurator of Judea 46 to 48.

30   Queen Helena, daughter of King Izates of Abiabene in Mesopotamia, influenced by a Jewish teacher Ananias, converts to Judaism. Helena is the mother of "*Monobazus, king of Adiabene, beyond the Euphrates.*" (JF). Queen Helena moves to Jerusalem where she builds a palace on the Ophel, in the lower southeast city. (The palace is seen in the model of Jerusalem at the Israel Museum, Jerusalem).

30   Jesus climbs **Mt. Tabor** with Peter, John and James to pray. Suddenly a cloud engulfs Jesus and in the rays of light. He reappears speaking to both Moses and Elijah. "*Jesus took Peter, James and John and led them up on a high mountain...and He was transfigured before them. His clothes became shining, exceedingly white, like snow...And Elijah appeared to them with Moses and they were talking to Jesus.*" (Mark 9:2-4). Also Matthew 17:1-11; Luke 9:28-20. In this **Transfiguration** of Jesus, Christian belief foretells of the Crucifixion and Resurrection of Jesus that "*The Son of Man has risen again from the dead.*" (Matthew 17:9). This event occurs forty days before the Crucifixion is the period of **Lent** (according to Catholic tradition).

30   Jesus travels towards Jerusalem. **The Parable of the Good Samaritan**. "*A man went down from Jerusalem to Jericho, and fell among thieves, who stripped him of his clothing, wounded him, and departed, leaving him half dead...a priest came down that road...he passed by on the other side. Likewise a Levite...came and looked...a Samaritan...saw him, he had compassion. So he went to him and bandaged his wounds, pouring oil and wine, and set him on his own animal, brought him to an inn, and took care of him.*" (Luke 10:30-34).

30   **Jesus teaches His disciples to pray.** "*...as He was praying in a certain place...His disciples said to Him, 'Lord, teach us to pray.*" (Luke 11:1).

"*Our Father in heaven, Hallowed be Your name.*
Your kingdom come. Your will be done. On earth as it is in heaven.
Give us day by day our daily bread,
And forgive us our debts as we forgive our debtors.
And do not led us into temptation, But deliver us from the evil one.
For yours is the kingdom and the power and the glory forever,
Amen". (Matthew 6:9-13 and Luke 11:2-4).

30   "*Jesus went into the temple of God and drove out all of those who bought and sold in the temple, and overturned the tables of the moneychangers and of those who sold doves...the blind and the lame came to Him in the temple.*" (Matthew 21:12,13,14). **Money-changers** assist pilgrims to purchase sacrificial animals and trading items.

Dominus Flevit, Mt. of Olives   Adrian Wolff

30   Jesus arrives for the Passover pilgrimage festival predicting the destruction of Jerusalem, "*He sat on the Mount of Olives opposite the Temple*" (Mark 13:3). "*saw the city and wept*" (Luke 19:41). "*When you see Jerusalem surrounded by armies, you know that its desolation is near.*" (Luke 21:20). Dominus Flevit=the Lord wept.

30   Romans are apprehensive of a Jewish uprising and any opposition is violently oppressed. During the Passover Jewish pilgrimage festival, the Roman governor **Pontius Pilate** travels from his capital of Judea in Caesarea to Jerusalem to command the Roman

troops. A stone is found at Caesarea with the inscription "*Tiberiem Pontius Pilatus praefectus Judeae*" Pontius 'Pilate, governor of Judea during the reign of Tiberius', exhibited in the Israel Museum.

30 **The Last Supper.** At a dinner in an 'Upper Room on Mount Zion' in Jerusalem Jesus, a charismatic preacher from Nazareth in the Galilee tells his followers He foresees His Crucifixion and preaches His immortality. *"show you a large upper room...they prepared the Passover."* (Mark 14:15,16). *"As they were eating, Jesus took bread, blessed it and broke it and gave it to the disciples and said 'Take, eat, this is My body. Then He took the cup, and gave thanks, and gave it to them, saying 'Drink from it, all of you for this is My blood. For this is My blood of the new covenant, which is shed for the many remission of sins."* (Matthew 26:26,27,28).

Garden of Gethsemane, ancient olive trees   Timothy Guy

30 **Christ predicts Peter's denial.** *"Peter, the rooster shall not crow this day before you will deny three times that you know me."* (Luke 22:34). After the meal, Jesus and his disciples walk in the Kidron Valley to Gethsemane on the lower slope of Mt. of Olives. *"Jesus came with them to a place called Gethsemane".* (Matthew 26:36). Gat Shemenim in Hebrew=oil press. **The Trinity.** *"Go therefore and make disciples of all the nations, baptizing them in the name of the **Father, and of the Son and of the Holy Spirit**, teaching them to observe all things that I have commanded you."* (Matthew 28:19,20). This site is designated by Christians where Jesus is betrayed. *"Jesus...went out with His disciples over the brook of Kidron, where there was a garden...And Judas betrayed Him...for Jesus often met there with His disciples."* (John 18:1,2). *"His betrayer had given them a signal saying, 'Whomever I kiss, He is*

the One; seize Him and lead Him, away safely'...Then they laid their hands on Him and took Him." (Mark 14:44,46) *"Then Simon Peter, having a sword drew it and struck the high priest's servant and cut off his right ear...Jesus said to Peter 'Put your sword into the sheath."* (John 18:10). *"For all who take the sword will perish by the sword."* (Matthew 26:52).

30   Jesus is taken to a Jewish Priest Joseph Caiaphas (appointed by the Romans). *"Then Annas sent Him bound to Caiaphas, the high priest."* (John 18:24). Jesus' followers proclaim Him to be **King of the Jews'**. Jewish priests are only responsible for Jewish civil affairs, not with a subject of national leadership and cannot give a death sentence. The Roman Governor, Jewish ruler, and High Priest all unanimously oppose this young preacher, a popular Galilean leader. As Jesus originates from the north, the authorities may have thought he has connections with the Cana'im (rebels) like Yohanan from Gush Halav.

Church of All Nations, Gethsemane, Mt. of Olives   Adrian Wolff

30   **The Trial of Jesus,** held in the Antonia Fortress, the Roman Administration building, the Roman Governor Pontius Pilate accuses Jesus. *"Are You the King of the Jews?....Jesus answered, 'You say rightly that I am a king. For this cause I was born, and for this cause I have come into the world."* (John 18:33,37). *"The chief priests of the Jews said to Pilate,' Do not write, 'The King of the Jews', but He said 'I am king of the Jews."* (John 19:21). *"One of us should die for the people, and not the whole nation should perish."* (John 11:50). Romans do not understand the concept or

meaning of a 'Messiah', hence Pilate uses the word 'king'. Jesus says *"for they do not know what they do.* (Luke 23:34).

30   **The Crucifixion.** The sentence is death. Roman citizens are beheaded (St. Paul) while non-Roman citizens are crucified (St. Peter), a Roman, not a Jewish practice. All crucifixions and burials take place outside of the city walls. In Jerusalem, on a hill shaped like a skull called **Golgotha** (skull in Hebrew) Jesus is crucified together with two robbers outside the Second Wall. *"And He, bearing His cross went out to a Place (hill similar to) of a Skull, which is called in Hebrew Golgotha, where they crucified Him, and two others with him, one on each side and Jesus in the center."* (John 19:17). *"Jesus cried out...My God, My God, why have You forsaken me?"* (Mark 15: 34). (Matthew 27:38). *"There were also women looking on from after, among them were Mary Magdalene, Mary the mother of James the Less and of Joses, and Salome."* (Mark 15:40). Letters **INRI** appear on Christian crosses depicting Jesus on the Cross, signifying *'Iesu Nazareth Rex Iudaeum'* Latin for 'Jesus of Nazareth, King of the Jews'.

30   **The Burial of Jesus.** *"The day before the Sabbath, Joseph Arimathea...went to Pilate and asked for the body of Jesus...he bought fine linen, took Him down, and wrapped Him...And laid Him in a tomb which had been hewn out of the rock, and rolled a stone against the door of the tomb."* (Mark 15:43-47). **The Resurrection of Jesus.** *"The first day of the week Mary Magdalene went to the tomb early...Mary stood outside...weeping...she stooped down and looked at the tomb....She turned around and saw Jesus standing there and did not know that it was Jesus. Jesus said to her 'I am ascending to My Father and your Father and to My God and to your God."* (John 20:1-17).

30   **Jesus appears to the Disciples**. *"The same day at evening, being the first day of the week....**Jesus came and stood...and said to them, 'Peace be with you'**...He showed them His hands and His side. Then the disciples were glad when they saw the Lord."* (John 20:19).

30   **Jesus appears at Emmaus.** *"...two of them were traveling...to Emmaus...Jesus Himself drew near and went with them. But their eyes were restrained, so that they did not know Him...So they...returned to Jerusalem...saying 'The Lord is risen."* (Luke 24:13,16,33,34).

30   **The Ascension of Jesus.** Jesus ascends to heaven from the Mount of Olives where *"He blessed them, that He was parted from them and carried up to heaven."* (Luke 24:51). *"He was received up*

into heaven." (Mark 16:19), occurring 50 days after the Crucifixion *"the Day of Pentecost had come...all in one place. And suddenly there came a sound from heaven...a...wind...and they were filled with the Holy Spirit."* (Acts 2:1-4).

Christian Theology

1. Christians believe in both the Jewish and Christian Bibles, known by them as The Old and New Testaments. Jews do not recognize the New Testament. *"Do not...came to destroy the Law or the Prophets...but to fulfill."* (Matthew 5:17).

2. Christians believe in One God, manifested Himself to the Christian world in **The Trinity** - The Father, the Son and the Holy Spirit, to assist them to better understand His nature. (See Ephesians 4: 4-6).

   ▪ The Father refers to God, known as Jehovah (YHVH),.

   ▪ The Son refers to Jesus - God in human form, equal to God. *"And the Word became flesh and dwelt among us."* (John 1:14) *"No one has seen God at any time. The only begotten Son, who is in the bosom of the Father, he has declared Him."* (John 1:18). Also see Nicaea 325; and 1054 'filioque'.

   ▪ The Spirit refers to God being with us, present in all Christian lives. *"Make disciples of all nations, baptizing them in the name of the Father...the Son and...the Holy Spirit, teaching them to observe all things that I have commanded you."* (Matthew 28:19,20).

3. Jesus equates Himself to God. Christians believe Jesus is a human incarnation of God, often referred to as the 'Son'. *"He who has seen Me has seen the Father...I am in the Father, and the Father in Me."* (John 14:9,10). *"You are the Son of God. You are the King of Israel."* (John 1:49). *"In the beginning was the Word, and the Word was with God, and the Word was God. He was the beginning with God."* (John 1:1).

4. Jesus Christ is the Messiah and Son of God, to return to establish His kingdom on earth. *"Are you Christ, the Son of the Blessed? Jesus said, 'I am and you will see the Son of Man sitting at the right hand of the Power, and coming with the clouds of heaven'."* (Mark 14:61,62). *"You are the Christ, the Son of the living God."* (Matthew 16:16). *"God was His Father, making Himself equal with God."* (John 5:18). *"I and My father are one."* (John 10:30).

5. Jesus is the savior. *"I did not come to judge the world, but to save the world."* (John 12:47). His believers will be rewarded at the Last Judgement to a life in paradise. *"...anyone not written in the Book of Life was cast into the lake of fire."* (Rev. 20:15).

6. Christians believe the Messiah has already arisen in the human form of Jesus Christ. *"And He will bring forth a Son, and you shall call His name Jesus."* (Matthew 1:21). *"Peter answered and said to Him 'You are the Christ."* (= Messiah) (Mark 8:29).

7. Jesus sacrifices his life for the sins of mankind. *"The bread that I shall give is My flesh, which I shall give for the life of the world."* (John 6:51). Also Matthew 26:26-35; Luke 22:14-20.

8. Christians accept a total belief in Jesus as a way of life. *"He who believes in the Son has everlasting life; and he who does not believe the Son shall not see life."* (John 3:36).

9. Only through Jesus can a Christian know God. *"I am the way, the truth and the life. No one comes to the Father except through Me."* (John 14:6).

10. A Christian is saved from damnation through belief in Jesus as in death a Christian participates in the Resurrection of Christ. *"For when you were slaves of sin...For the end of those things is death. But now having been set free from sin and have become slaves of God."* (Romans 6:20,21).

11. Jesus alone is without sin. *"He made Him who knew no sin to be sin for us, that we might become the righteous of God in Him."* (2 Corinthians 5:21).

12. Christians believe Jesus will return again in a 'Second Coming' to complete the salvation of all believers. *"Christ was offered once to bear the sins of many. To those who...wait for Him He will appear a second time, apart from sin, for salvation."* (Hebrews 9:28).

13. A Christian should behave by, *"Let love be without hypocrisy. Abhor what is evil. Cling to what is good. Be kindly affectionate to one another with brotherly love."* (Romans 12: 9,10).

14. Original sin condemns a person to 'Hell' for eternity. The only escape is to accept Christ, the Savior. *"though one man sin entered the world, and death through sin, and thus death spread to all men, because all sinned."* (Romans 5:12). *"For when you were slaves of sin...For the end of things is death. But now having been set free from sin."* (Romans 6:20,21,22). Catholics see very person as a habitual sinner, redeemed only by the Son of God, Jesus Christ.

Christians believe a person becomes a 'Christian' by choice through confession of faith in Jesus Christ. Many churches baptize new believers who are encouraged to share the Gospel (Good News) with the unbelieving world with the goal of bringing them to Christ. Christians view The Old Testament (Tanach) as incomplete. The New Testament codifies salvation, redemption and justification of Jesus, The Son of God. Since Jews reject Jesus as the Christ or Messiah, therefore according to Christians, Jews cease to be the conduit to God.

The expression 'knock on wood' is to figuratively touch the Cross of Jesus. A gentle 'Tap on Wood,' originates in areas where the sound of church bells was banned under Muslim rulers.

30   After the Crucifixion of Jesus, **St. Peter** becomes leader of the new sect. According to Catholic belief, the Pope represents the 'Eternal Being' on Earth, their highest authority. St. Peter is the first Apostle performs a miracle. *"At Joppa (Jaffa)...a certain disciple named Tabitha...became sick and died...Peter...knelt down and prayed. And turning the body he said 'Tabitha arise'. And she opened her eyes and when she saw Peter she sat up."* (Acts 9:36,37,40)

30   St. Peter performs the first baptism of a gentile, a Roman centurion Cornelius stationed at Caesarea, the Roman capital of Judea. *"...they entered Caesarea. Now Cornelius was waiting...As Peter was coming in, Cornelius met him and fell down at his feet...Peter answered 'Can anyone forbid water, that these should not be baptized who have received the Holy Spirit, just as we have. And he commanded them to be baptized in the name of the Lord."* (Acts 10:24,25,47,48).

34   Philip, son of Herod dies a natural death while ruling as tetrarch (subordinate governor) in the Golan.

36   Saul, a tentmaker, rug and carpet weaver, born in Tarsus, southern Anatolia, is a vigorous opponent of Christianity, participates in the stoning of St. Stephen, the first Christian martyr. Stephen announces the destruction of the Temple and return of Jesus. *"And they cast him out of the city and stoned him...laid down their clothes at the feet of a young man named Saul. And they stoned Stephen."* (Acts 7:58,59).

37   Gaius **Caligula**, Roman emperor (born 12, rules 37–41) views himself as a god. Reckless spending, instability and terror in Rome characterize his reign. He protects Jews living in Rome. while he instigates callous murders of Jews in Judea and Alexandria, disregarding Jewish sentiments, provokes near rebellion.

37   Caligula removes Herod Antipas' control in the Galilee and Perea. Romans appoint **Agrippa I**, son of Aristobulus, (the murdered son of King Herod and Mariamme), ruler of Judea 37-44. Agrippa I is known for his scrupulous observance of the Mosaic code. His personal charm and his popularity brings hope to the oppressed Jews of Judea. He authorizes the continued construction the Third Wall north of Jerusalem, to include agricultural areas.

38   Philo, a Jewish philosopher from Alexandria travels to Rome to plead to emperor Caligula to cease forcing the Jews to erect statues in honor of the the emperor, to treat him as god, to construct altars and temples (including in Jerusalem). He also appeals on behalf of Alexandria's Jewish population for protection continuous attacks by Alexandria's Greeks.

39   Jews comprise 20% of the 100,000 inhabitants of Alexandria. The Roman prefect **Avillus Flaccus** allows the local Hellenics to place a statue of a god in the synagogues in Alexandria, victimizing Jews for refusing to worship Emperor Caligula. He annuls Alexandrian citizenship for the Jews, as Greeks kill Jews and torch their homes. Caligula orders the governor in Syria, Petronius to place a golden statue of himself (Caligula) in the Jewish Temple in Jerusalem. *"He ordered...(to) erect his statues in the Temple; if the Jews refused...to execute the objectors and enslave...the population...They pleaded their Law and ancestral customs and explained that it is not possible for a graven image of God, much less of a man, to be placed in the Temple...If he wished set up the images in their midst, he must first sacrifice the whole Jewish race: they were ready to offer themselves as victims with their wives and children."* (JF). King Agrippa I travels to Rome to dissuade Caligula, citing possible riots by Jews in Judaea. The murder of Caligula in Rome in 41 saves the completion of the statue.

39   Saul converts to Christianity and changes his name to **Paul.** *"As he journeyed he came near Damascus and suddenly a light shone around him from heaven...and when his eyes were opened he saw no one...A man named Ananias coming in put his hand on him, so that he might receive his sight...and he received his sight at once, and he arose and was baptized."* (Acts 9:3,8,12,18). **St. Paul** is responsible for promoting Jesus' ministry. He travels from Caesarea to Antioch, Cyprus, Thessalonica, Athens, Corinth, Ephesus and finally to Rome in an effort to convince the Jews to follow Jesus' beliefs. The Jews violently oppose him as described in the Book of Acts chapters 13-20. *"They stoned Paul and dragged him out of the city."* (Acts 14:19).

39   In an attempt to succeed in converting non-Jews, St. Paul makes a complete break from Judaism and Jews. He annuls the Mitzvot (Blessings) of the Torah, canceling the practice of circumcision, promotes proselytism amongst non-Jews and declares Sunday not Saturday to be the Holy Day of Rest. *"They have been informed... you teach all the Jews who are among the Gentiles to forsake Moses, saying that they ought not to circumcise their children nor walk according to their customs."* (Acts 21:21). *"On the first day of*

the week, when the disciples came together to break bread." (Acts 20:7). St. Paul preaches to Christians that observance of Judaism is not necessary for salvation. *"Let it be known to you that the salvation of God has been sent to the Gentiles."* (Acts 28:28). He continues *"For the love of money is a root of kinds of evil"* (1 Timothy 6:10). **St. Paul and his followers are considered non-Jewish and become followers of Christ or Christians.**

Steps at Caesarea Port.St. Peter, St. Paul may boarded to Rome.Timothy Guy

41   **The term Christian is first used at Antioch in Anatolia.**

41   Caligula is murdered in Rome by officers of the Praetorian Guard, members of the Roman Senate and of the imperial court. Emperor Claudius (born 10, rules 41-54), is Caligula's uncle, restores Jewish rights allowing them to live according to their own laws. *"On Agrippa he at once bestows the entire kingdom of his forebears...wealth poured into Agrippa's treasury."* (JF).

44   King Agrippa I the popular Jewish monarch dies. The Romans transfer authority to his son **King Agrippa II**. Romans continue to rule by procurator **Cuspius Fadus** (44-46) in a period of maladministration and exploitation of the Jewish subjects in Judea.

46   Romans appoint a Jew, Tiberius Alexander as procurator 46-48.

48   **Ventidus Cumanus** procurator in Judea 48-52, *"whose governorship was marked by disturbances and further disaster to the Jews."* (JF).

50   **Gospel** (godspel) means 'good tidings' in early English. **The Gospels originally written in Greek are known as the**

'Evangelion'. The First Gospel is written (50-70) by **St. Matthew** describes the history of Jesus from His birth; Authority; Miracles; Commissioning of the Twelve Apostles; Crucifixion; Resurrection and Ascension to Heaven. Catholics believe the symbol of St. Matthew to be 'God's Angel'.

50 The Second Gospel of Jesus (50-70) by **St. Mark** (founds Copts in Cyrenaica) describing the life of Jesus; His Activities; Miracles; Ministry until the empty tomb is discovered and Resurrection. Catholics believe St. Mark's symbol is 'A Lion with Wings'.

52 **Felix** procurator in Judea (52-60). Roman tax collectors and wealthy landowners exploit the Jewish population in Judea. There are confrontations between the Jews and Hellenics in Caesarea.

52 Zealots/Rebels (See 66 Sicarii) become increasingly active, descending from hilltops, looting houses of Roman sympathizers, putting the occupants to death. The Romans are unsafe, even in Jerusalem where Zealots "*mingle with festive crowds, concealing under their garments small daggers with which they stabbed their opponents*" (JF) and disappear in a crowded street.

52 Armed clash between Jews of the Galilee and Samaritans at Gema in Samaria. "*Claudius found the Samaritans guilty and ordered their three most powerful men to be executed.*" (JF).

54 Nero, Caesar (54-68) in Rome. "*Nero lost his balance and abused his good fortune outrageously. He put to death in succession his brother, wife, and mother.*" (JF).

58 St. Paul insults the Jewish priesthood in Jerusalem, and is dragged from the Temple. A Roman officer saves him when St. Paul claims to be a Roman citizen "*But I was born a citizen*" (Acts 22:28). He is sent "*...to Caesarea...and bring him safely to Felix the governor.*" (Acts 23: 23,24) where he is kept under house arrest for two years, before he sails for Rome.

60 **Porches Festus**, procurator in Judea 60-62.

60 In Rome St. Paul continues to attempt the conversion of the local heathens/pagans to his new religion, Christianity. "*For I am not ashamed of the gospel of Christ, for it is the power of God to salvation for everyone who believes...The just shall live by faith.*' (Romans 1:16,17). "*The righteousness of God, through faith in Jesus Christ, to all and on all who believe. For there is no difference, for all have sinned and fall short of the glory of God...through the redemption that is in Christ Jesus...by His blood, through faith, to demonstrate His righteousness.*" (Romans 3:22,24,25). through the goodness and mercy of Jesus Christ who

offers salvation, "...*we also eagerly wait for the Savior the Lord, Jesus Christ.*" (Philippians 3:20).

60   The Third Gospel by **St. Luke** describes the life of Jesus from the Annunciation by the Angel Gabriel in Nazareth; His Ministry in the Galilee; journey to Jerusalem; The Passion Week; Crucifixion; Resurrection and Ascension of Jesus on Mt. of Olives. St. Luke also writes the Book of the Acts of the Apostles. Catholics believe the symbol of St. Luke to be 'A Bull with Wings'.

62   **Albinus** procurator (62-64) is "*guilty of every possible misdemeanor...with official actions that meant widespread robbery and looting of private property or with taxes that crippled the whole nation.*" (JF).

64   **It is important to note religion is not predominant in the Roman way of life that is tolerant of various religions and cults within the Roman Empire. Frequently Jews are exempt from emperor-worship. Judaism is recognized allowing them special privileges such as protecting their right to Sabbath rest, prayer, the celebration of Jewish festivals and pilgrimages and their eating customs (kashrut). At this time, the Jews are the only peoples in the world to observe a weekly 'day of rest', the Sabbath. Some educated Romans observe the Jewish Sabbath as a day of worship and rest.**

The Roman authorities reject Christianity because they attempt to convert Roman heathens to their new religion, unlike the Jews who do not seek converts. Christian allegiance is to Christ, not to the emperor. The catacombs in Rome are secret places where Christians pray and bury.

64   Roman authorities widely persecute Christians and oppose St. Peter's missionary activities sentencing him to death. St. Peter, originally from Capernaum, a non-Roman citizen, requests to be crucified upside down, not to equate himself with Jesus. The Pieta in St. Peter's Church, Rome is built over the assumed site.

64   The Roman Procurator **Gessius Florus** (64-66) in Judea "*indulged in every kind of robbery and violence...he showed himself the most heartless of men...he stripped whole cities, ruined communities...as he himself received a rake-off.*" (JF). Florus is short collecting taxes for Rome and seizes gold from the Jewish Temple. Riots begin and within a short period Jewish insurgents seize the Temple Mount. A spirit of revolt is spreading against the Romans in Judea.

Chapter 9. Jewish War and Fall of Masada 66 - 73

66   Romans allow Jews religious freedom (but do not try to convert them!!). The **Jewish Revolt** is nationalistic against Roman oppression begins in Caesarea *"with a predominant Greek population"* when Romans and gentile (Hellenic) neighbors attack *"in the middle of their seventh-day (Sabbath) ceremonies"* (JF) slaughtering 20,000 Jewish residents, while some survivors flee towards Narbata, a few kilometers northwards. The news of the slaughter reaches Jerusalem, as Jews begin rioting which quickly spreads to other parts of the Judea. *"The Jews expected all their Mesopotamian brethren to join their insurrection. (The) Roman supremacy was being challenged by the Gauls on their borders, and the Celts were restive-in fact after Nero's death disorder reigned everywhere."* (Josephus Flavius, The Jewish War = JF).

The Roman governor **Gessius Florus** wishes to loot Jewish possessions and seize the Temple in Jerusalem. The Jews march towards the Antonia Fortress, the Roman Administrate building in Jerusalem protesting Roman oppression and taxes. Florus encourages his soldiers to provoke the Jews into rioting, lusting for blood, charge the protesters killing 3600 Jews. The Jews begin a revolt throughout Judea, joining the Zealots. The more reasonable elements, the Sages try to dissuade the Jews from resorting to violence. Jews roam the rural areas and forests.

66   Jews comprise approximately 10% of the total population of the Roman Empire. The Rebels assume two external factors will assist them in their fight again the Roman empire:
1. The local Jews residing the Middle East will rise up against Roman rule. They do unsuccessfully in Syria and Alexandria.
2. The Parthian Empire (247 BC–224 AD) will attack the Romans from the east.

66   Approximately 100,000 Jews reside in Jerusalem (Prof. Mordechai Gichon). Their numbers will increase substantially during the **Jewish War** as Jews flee the conquering Roman Army. Rome has over 1,000,000 inhabitants while all other major cities in Europe are very small in comparison (around 10,000 inhabitants). The **population** of Judea has 1.2 million inhabitants. Nero is emperor 54-68. **Elazar**, son of the High Priest Hananiah (Ananias), captain of the Temple persuades all priests to refuse any offerings in the Jewish Temple for or on behalf of non-Jews, thereby discontinuing the daily sacrifice in the name of the Roman Emperor. Rebels capture and torch the Jerusalem Roman administrative building,

the Antonia Fortress. The surviving Roman troops in Jerusalem flee the **Rebels/Zealots** to Herod's Palace, take refuge, and are eventually butchered.

66   Another group, the Galilee **Sicarii** (rebels) led by **Menachem**, son of 'Judah of the Galilee', capture the Masada fortress by the Dead Sea and together with their newly acquired war booty, arrive at Jerusalem to support the Jewish revolt. Every settlement where Jews are the majority, they rise in revolt against the Romans. Wealthier Jews do not support a revolt predicting a futile attempt against the powerful Romans will result in tragedy. Young and poorer Jews accuse them of cowardice. **King Agrippa II** summons the people to the Assembly urging a delegation to travel to Rome. *"The* (procurators) *of Rome are unbearably harsh...on them you are going to make war...the same procurator will not be here forever and his successors are almost sure to be more reasonable. But once set on foot, war can to easily be either broken off or fought to a conclusion without disaster...Look at the far-flung empire of Rome and contrast your own impotence...while their arms have triumphed over the whole world...the danger threatens not only ourselves but also those who live in other cities; for there is not a region in the world without its Jewish colony...Spare the Temple...At the end of his speech he burst into tears as did his sister* (Bernice)." (JF).

66   The Jews of Beit She'an (Scythopolis), the wealthy trade, weaving and dying center are opposed to the revolt, nevertheless *"the Scythopolitians...slaughtered...more than 13,000...and looted the property...caused all the other cities to take arms against their Jewish colonies. In Ashkelon 2500 were put to death, in Ptolemais (Acre) 2000...of all the towns in Syria there isn't one that hasn't exterminated its Jewish inhabitants...and tortured to death in Egypt."* (JF).

66   *"The first Caesar and all of his successors allowed the privileges to the Jews from Alexander's time onwards to be diminished... (Roman) soldiers rushed into the Delta where Jews were concentrated,"* (JF) killing, looting and burning, leaving 50,000 corpses.

66   **Cestius** Gallus the Roman Governor (Imperial Legate) of Syria sends troops to Jerusalem. Roman troops insufficient in number, are forced to withdraw, only to be surrounded by forces of Simon, Bar-Giora in a gorge (wadi) at Beit Horon on the road from the coast to Jerusalem. *"The steep slope made it impossible for mounted men to charge...on both sides there were cliffs and ravines...No one could find a way to flee."* (JF). Romans lose over

six thousand soldiers with their weapons and equipment, including the 'Eagle standard', symbol of the Roman Empire. Jews immediately make preparations to defend Jerusalem from the inevitable Roman onslaught. Jewish commissioners are directed to the provincial centers to prepare defenses, while all men of military age are given armed training and new coins are struck. Inscriptions on coins found in Jerusalem attest to the reason for The Jewish Revolt - nationalism – *'the freedom* (חירות) *of Jerusalem'* and *'the redemption* (גאולה) *of Zion'* - 'to be free people in their own land.' (Israel's national anthem).

66   *"The people of Damascus, learning of the destruction of the Roman force...fell upon the Jews...10,500 they slaughtered."* (JF).

67   **Yohanan**, son of Levi, from Gush-Halav (Johanan of Gischala) fervently opposes the appointment of Joseph ben Mattathias (37-100), governor of the Galilee, to lead the revolt against the Romans as he has no formal military training. Nevertheless leaders in Jerusalem over-rule his opinion. The leadership assumes since he was educated in Rome he has knowledge of Roman methods. *"Josephus knew that the invincible might of Rome was chiefly due to unhesitating obedience and to practice in arms...a long period of training...no indiscipline dislodges them from their regular formation, no panic incapacitates them, no toil wears them out...They never give the enemy a chance to catch them off their guard...a large number of engineers with all the tools for needed building. Times for sleep, guard-duty and reveille are announced by trumpet-calls, and nothing is done without orders...on the battle field, changing direction promptly as required and whether attacking or retreating move as one man."* (JF).

67   Roman emperor Nero sends **Vespasian**, an able Roman general, conqueror of Britain, together with his son Titus to direct the war against the Jews, bringing additional Roman Legions from Egypt, landing with 60,000 soldiers and advanced war material at Ptolemais (Acre). He begins to conquer the Galilee, Golan and Perea to prevent the large Jewish communities in Mesopotamia assisting the rebels with manpower and materiel.

67   Many Jews flee to the safety of Jerusalem. There is no unity as their energies are wasted in internal conflicts, split between the extremists and moderate elements. The rebels impose *"Terror...no one thought of anything but his own safety."* (JF). Zealots and Sicarii fight each other, as thousands of Jews are killed. Zealots ignite the Jerusalem food stores, condemning its population to starvation, simultaneously preventing Jews from leaving.

67   The High Priest Ananus rebukes the rebels *"When houses were ransacked, nobody cared...they seized their owners too, and dragged through the middle of the City...they have seized...the Temple...as a citadel or fort...Ananus roused the populace against the Zealots...They started pelting each other with stones in the streets and in front of the Temple and by hurling spears at long range...This citizen army was later destroyed by John of Gischala (Yohanan of Gush Halav)."* (JF). The rebels invite Idumaeans who together with Ananus *"turning to the City they plundered every house and killed anyone they met"* (JF).

67   **The Fall of Yodfat.** Roman troops under Titus march through the Galilee to Yodfat (Jotapata). Jewish defenses led by **Joseph ben Mattathias** withstand the first Roman attack *"ordered boiling oil to be poured on the soldiers under the shields"* (JF) but after an 48-day siege, the situation becomes desperate. The Zealots demand all the defenders to commit suicide rather than become enslaved to the Romans. Joseph ben Mattathias offers to draw lots to kill each other. By chance or chicanery Joseph ben Mattathias is left with one other man and convinces him to surrender the city to the Romans *"he persuaded this man also, under a pledge, to remain alive...Vespasian ordered the city to be demolished."* (JF). Joseph ben Mattathias, taken prisoner to the Roman capital Caesarea, tells the Roman General Vespasian *"...I come to you as a messenger of greater destinies...You will be Caesar, Vespasian, you will be emperor and your son here...for you, Caesar are master not of me only, but of land and sea and the whole human race."* (JF). Vespasian enjoys the flattery, believing this prophecy. He immediately conscripts Joseph ben Mattathias as his assistant and historian, later to become known as **Josephus Flavius**, author of **'The Jewish Wars'** which remains the basic historical document of this period. Josephus admits he is not popular with the Jews *"some reviled him as a coward, some as a traitor."* (JF).

67   The Galilee *"is excellent for crops or cattle and rich in forests of every kind...the whole country is cultivated and fruitful from end to end."*(JF). Before the autumn rains both Yodfat and Zippori (Sephoris), an important regional center in Lower Galilee falls finalizing Roman control in the entire Galilee. Zealots escape death from the Romans making their way into Jerusalem where they reinforce the extremists. Suspected Roman sympathizers are killed, while the administration of Jerusalem now falls into the hands of Yohanan of Gush Halav.

67   Vespasian declares *"The Jews, though extremely bold and contemptuous of death, have neither discipline nor experience in war, and are nothing but a rabble, not fit to be called an*

army." (JF). Josephus portrays Vespasian as compassionate when at Tiberius, he receives a representation of 'elders' who appeal to "*spare the citizens, who have been friendly to the Romans at all times and punish only those responsible for the revolt*". At Tarichaeae (north of Tiberius) "*Titus, having disposed of the culprits, took pity on the residents and put an end to the slaughter.*" (JF).

Gamla, Golan   Adrian Wolff

67   **The Fall of Gamla.** Hasmonean King Alexander Yanai originally builds Gamla in 81BCE, as the regional capital of the Golan. A synagogue and mikva (ritual bath) are constructed. "*For it was situated upon a rough ridge of a high mountain, with a kind of neck in the middle, where it begins to ascend, it lengthens itself and declines...like a camel* (gamal in Hebrew)". (JF). Vespasian now turns his attention to the Jewish town of Gamla in the Golan after the defenders hold out against a force previously sent by King Agrippa II. The Romans with approximately 40,000 troops face 10,000 men, women and children at Gamla. On their first attack Roman soldiers manage to penetrate the defenses of Gamla, are ambushed, suffer heavy casualties when the roofs collapse they retreat. After a seven months siege "*they were short of supplies...were starving.*" (JF). On 22 November 67 the Romans successfully undermine a tower on the northeast, which collapses, allowing troops easy entry into Gamla.

"*The Jews inflicted heavy casualties on their attackers, rolling down rocks and hurling missiles..(then) a tempest, which carried the Roman shafts up to them but checked and turned aside their own....whether they resisted or tried to surrender their fate was the same...Despairing of their lives and hemmed in on every side, multitudes plunged headlong with their wives and children into the ravine...Four thousand which had been slain by the Romans, while those who flung themselves over the cliff were found to exceed five thousand."* (JF).

Coins found at Gamla are inscribed '**to the redemption of Jerusalem the holy**." These coins link the heroic stand against the Romans at Gamla with the campaign to save Jerusalem. The Romans conquer Gamla on 23 November 67 which is never resettled again. By the end of 67 all the Galilee and Golan is now in Roman hands. Gamla is rediscovered after Israeli conquest of the Golan in 1967.

67   St. Paul, a Roman citizen, is beheaded for preaching Christianity and attempting to convert local heathens to his new religion. This site, on the banks of Tiber outside the walls of Rome is known as 'The Three Fountains' as his head bounced three-times and fountains appeared. Here the Basilica of St. Paul is constructed.

68   Nero, emperor of Rome dies, leaving a bankrupt economy and administration. Galba, an aged 'old republican' is emperor (68-69).

Qumran Caves   Adrian Wolff

68   The **Essenes**, (see 150BCE) living at Qumran by the NW shores of the Dead Sea, are a religious sect, believe in the coming of the Messiah. During the Jewish War, they are followers of the Zealots. Realizing the Romans will arrive at their settlement, they hide their texts in caves near their settlement. *"Their spirit was tested to the*

utmost by the war with the Romans, who racked and twisted, burnt and broke them, subjecting them to every torture yet invented in order to make them blaspheme the Lawgiver or eat some forbidden food, but could not make them do either or ever once fawn on their tormentors or shed a tear. Smiling in their agony and gently mocking those who put them on the rack." (JF).

Their scrolls are discovered in 1947, known today as the **'Dead Sea Scrolls'**. They are the oldest copies of the Bible which has not been changed in any way over the past 2000 years. (See Dead Sea Scrolls 1947; 1965. Essenes -150). Some Christians believe St. John the Baptist to have lived with the Essenes. The Dead/Salt Sea is not mentioned in the New Testament. Nor have any of the Dead Sea texts mention the words St. John, Jesus, or Nazareth.

68   Perea, Judea, Idumae, Gerasa are subdued to the Romans.

69   Hebron, Beit-el and all the Judean highlands are under Roman control, leaving only Jerusalem, Herodion, Masada and Macherus (on the eastern shores of Dead Sea) under Jewish control. The **population** of Jerusalem swells to 120,000-150,000 as Jews flee for their safety from other regions of Judah to fight the Romans.

69   Yohanan of Gush Halav strengthens the fortification of Jerusalem to withstand a siege and defend the Temple. His forces number about 8,400 fighters. Followers of Simon bar Giora defend the Upper City, now joined by extremists led by Menachem, son of Judah of the Galilee who previously seized Masada from the Romans in 66. Simon's forces number around 15,000 fighters. Forces of Elazar ben Hanan also reinforce Simon's troops. A Civil War breaks out between the supporters of Simon bar Giora who try to dislodge the Zealots of Yohanan of Gush Halav from the Temple Mount, resulting in food granaries going up in flames, hastening the famine in the besieged Jerusalem. *"She was destroyed by internal dissensions."* (JF).

69   During this year (69), there is a rapid succession of Roman emperors. The unpopular Roman emperor Galba is murdered in Rome, replaced by Otho who commits suicide after his defeat in battle by Vitellius' Rhineland army. Shortly after his appointment as emperor, Vitellius is defeated in battle. Vitellius, known for his excessive eating and cruelty is assassinated. Vespasian is in Alexandria preparing for the final battle against the Jews when news reaches him of Vitellius' assassination. Vespasian realizes he is virtually unopposed to become the new emperor, hurries to Rome after sending his son Titus, governor of Egypt, to complete the conquest of Jerusalem. On his arrival in Rome, the popular General Vespasian is appointed emperor and proclaims the

beginning of the Flavian Dynasty (69-96). Josephus Flavius' prediction comes true as his chains are removed. Vespasian restores finances, while consolidating Roman conquest in Judea, Britain and Germany. He initiates large construction projects in Rome such as the Colosseum.

70   **The Fall of Jerusalem.** Titus, son of Vespasian attacks Jerusalem with four Legions comprising over 65,000 Roman armored foot soldiers, not including additional cavalry, artillery (catapults, ballistas, mortars) and logistical support soldiers. Jewish forces of 40,000 soldiers and irregulars do not have armor, cavalry, artillery or siege towers, but are successful in face to face fighting against the Roman centurions. The divided Jewish Zealot rebel leaders are Eleazar, son of Simon; in The Temple complex, with Yohanan of Gush Halav in the Temple Mount. The Sicarii, Simon son of Giora in the Upper City and parts of the Lower city. Yohanan *"never failed to set fire to the houses that were stocked with grain and supplies...almost all the grain-enough to support them through many years of siege-went up in flames...John (Yohanan) purloined the scared timber for the construction of engines of war."* (JF).

Titus constructs Roman Army camps in the area between Mt. Scopus and the Mt. of Olives for the Fifth and Eleventh Legions. The latter Legion will be relocated to another camp west of the Three Towers (Jaffa Gate of today). Addition camps are built north of the city for the Fifteenth (near Schneller camp today) and the Tenth (X) Legion along the lower slopes of Mt of Olives (near Gethsemane). After rupturing the Second Wall the Romans build a rampart-wall encircling Jerusalem, patrolled to contain the Jews inside the city preventing anyone leaving, fresh food supplies reaching the defenders and Jewish reinforcements entering. The starving Jewish population ate cooked leather, horses, their saddles and dung. The defenders believe God is on their side and will deliver them in some miraculous fashion as He had done in periods of their forefathers.

The Lower City is captured after a breach in the walls, while the Upper City and Temple Mount continue to hold out. On orders from Titus, the Antonia Fortress the administrative building and residence of the Roman Governor in Jerusalem is destroyed to prevent Jewish fighters taking positions. Jewish defenders throw corpses over the walls to avert disease and epidemic breaking out within the city. By the summer the situation becomes desperate with critical shortages of food, resulting in suspension of daily sacrifices at the altar for the first time since the triumph of Judah the Maccabi over two hundred years earlier. *"Some crossed over...*

knowing the fate that awaited them but regarding death at enemy hands as a deliverance, compared to starvation." (JF).

Titus sends Josephus Flavius unsuccessfully to convince the Jews to surrender. *"Titus showed his anxiety to save the City and the Sanctuary by inviting the insurgents to come to terms...Titus Caesar...over and over again he delayed the capture of the city and prolonged the siege in the hope that the ringleaders would submit."* Titus *"had offered the Jews peace and self-government with amnesty for all offenders, but they had rejected concord in favor of strife; peace in favor of war, plenty and abundance in favor of hunger."* (JF). Titus does not want the Temple to be destroyed, to keep it as a symbol of Rome's glory.

The more moderate Zealots open the Temple Gates on Passover allowing Passover sacrifices. Extremists enter, killing the moderates, now controlling the entire Temple Mount. Elazar's ben Simon's followers are eradicated.

The **Fall of Jerusalem and the Destruction of The Second Temple** takes place on the ninth day of the month of Av (*Tisha B'Av*), the exact anniversary of the destruction of Jerusalem and Fall of the First Temple by Nebuchadnezzar in 586 BCE.

- The Upper City (in the Jewish Quarter of the Old City today) is populated by the priests and wealthy.
- The Lower City (City of David) populated by the 'regular population.
- The New City in the north is the first are to fall to the Romans.

Zealots of Yohanan of Gush Halav destroy the rampart between the Upper City and the Temple Mount. The Temple is stormed by the conquering Roman troops who ignite its contents causing a huge conflagration continuing over one month, destroying the Temple Mount and Herod's Palace. *"The end was precipitated..one ...entered the building...when Caesar (Titus) rushed out to restrain the troops thrust a firebrand, in the darkness, into the hinges of the gate. At once a flame shot up from the interior, Caesar and his generals withdrew, and there was none left to prevent those outside from kindling the blaze. Caesar shouted and waved to the combatants to put out the fire, but his shouts were unheard as their ears were deafened with greater din...Thus against Caesar's wishes, was the Temple set on fire...While the Temple blazed, the victors plundered everything that fell in their way and slaughtered wholesale all who were caught. No pity was shown for age, no reverence for rank."* (JF). Sacred Temple items are *"handed from the sanctuary, lamp-stands (Menorah), tables, basins, and cups, all of solid gold and very heavy...curtains, vestment of the chief priests with precious stones...spices which were blended and daily burnt as incense."* (JF).

Western Wall stones felled by Roman troops   Adrian Wolff

The Upper City holds out for another month before it too, is conquered. Titus now would not allow the starving Jews in the Upper City to surrender - they were all slaughtered, igniting their houses together with the corpses.

Titus *"Caesar ordered the whole city and all the Temple to be razed to the ground leaving only the loftiest towers, Phasael, Hippicus, Marianne* (in the area of the Tower of David today) *and the portion of the wall enclosing the city on the west. The latter as an encampment of the garrison that was to remain."* (JF), used as the headquarters of the Roman Tenth Legion to control Jerusalem. The symbol of the Tenth Legion (X) is the Golden Eagle, a species prevalent in the Judean and Negev deserts. Part of a column with an inscription Legion X still remains as a lamp-standard in an alley at Jaffa Gate.

Titus does not rebuild Jerusalem. The VI Roman Legion remains in the Megido area in the Lower Galilee.

70   Most Jews of Jerusalem are either killed, executed or perish from hunger. Many of the survivors are sold into slavery or sent into exile. *"The total number of prisoners taken throughout the entire war amounted to 97,000 and of those who perished during the siege, from the first to the last, 1,100,000".* *"John, starving with his brothers in the sewers...Simon was kept for the triumphal*

141

procession and ultimate execution...Those who had taken part in the sedition and terrorism...were executed...of the youngsters he picked out the tallest and handsomest to be kept for the triumphal procession; of the rest, those over seventeen were put in irons ands sent to hard labor in Egypt, while the great numbers were presented by Titus to the provinces to perish in the theaters by the sword or by wild beasts; those under seventeen were sold". (JF).

Roman Column. Legion X, Jaffa Gate area. Adrian Wolff

70   All prisoners (100,000) over the age of 17 are sent to work till they perish in the Egyptian copper mines, those under 17 are sold as slaves. Other are sent to Roman circuses where they are forced to contest against hungry lions for the pleasure of the Roman spectators. Seven hundred of the most attractive Jewish youths are chosen to be marched in Titus' victory parade in Rome. Over 1,000,000 Jews die from disease, hunger or battle.

70   Titus celebrates his victory with gladiator games in an orgy of violence at Caesarea, the Roman capital of Judea. *"Many of the prisoners perished here, some thrown to wild beasts, others forced to meet each other in full-scale battles...exceeded 2500...nothing amazed the spectators as much as the behavior of young children; for not one could be constrained to call Caesar lord".* (JF).

70   All Jews had previously paid a voluntary head-tax payment to the Temple, now a compulsory **'Fiscus Judaicus'** (Jewish Tax) *"of 2 drachmas a head"*.(JF) to the *Imperium Romanum* (Roman Empire) of Judea (see 96).

70   The **'Golden Menorah'** from the Second Temple is taken to Rome by Titus as war booty, displayed in a museum showing items captured by his conquering forces. The Golden Menorah remains in Rome until the beginning of the Fall of the Roman Empire when in the 4th century Emperor Constantine transfers all the valuables from Rome to his new capital in Byzantium (Constantinople). Procopius of Caesarea (500-554) writes about the Roman emperor Justinian (see Jon E Lewis) *"the treasures of the Jews, which Titus...had brought to Rome after the capture of Jerusalem...Jews...said "These treasures (are) expedient to carry into the palace in Byzantium. Indeed it is not possible for them to be elsewhere than in the palace of Solomon....When this had been brought to the Emperor, he became afraid and quickly sent everything to the same sanctuaries of the Christians in Jerusalem."* A legend tells of Venetian Crusaders abducting the Golden Menorah as payment for their maritime services during the disastrous failed Fourth Crusade in 1202-1204. The Golden Menorah, of considerable weight in gold, is melted down and consequently disappears, lost for eternity.

Golden Menorah, Arch of Titus. Israel Philatelic Bureau.
Model at Western Wall

70   Until the Destruction of the Temple the majority of inhabitants in Jerusalem are Jews, now after the conquest by Titus, they will become the minority until 1870. After the Fall of Jerusalem during the next 50 years, few Jews will reside in Jerusalem which is populated by Hellenics and Roman soldiers. The last pockets of

Jewish resistance in Herodian in the Judean Desert and Machareus in Perea (east bank of the Dead Sea) fall to the Romans. Titus refuses a petition from Antioch to expel their Jews.

70 **Unlike the situation in Jerusalem, the population of Judea remains predominately Jewish**. After the destruction of the Temple, all daily animal sacrifices cease, and the concept of the High Priest is eliminated as the Sadducees dissolve. The conquest of Judea together with the Fall of Jerusalem, the Destruction of The Second Temple and the subsequent eradication of all Jewish resistance ending at Masada (see 73CE) does not close our history books on the Jews, Jewish life, Jewish philosophy or Jewish theology. This catastrophe is an unfortunate episode which will not annihilate the Jews.

70 Jews can no longer can go to the Temple to sound out learned priestly advice or receive a Jewish legal opinion from an erudite priestly interpretation of the Tanach (Bible), as the central judicial system no longer exists. Yet Jews survive as a unified 'race' due to the constitution and universal legal code of social behavior - Tanach and Talmud.

A legend tells of how **Rabbi Yohanan ben Zakai** of the Hillel Academy in Jerusalem, despite the Roman siege, escapes from besieged Jerusalem, in a coffin borne by his disciples. The Roman General and future emperor Titus permits Rabbi Yohanan ben Zakai to settle and teach in Yavne (Jamnia) the new home of the Sanhedrin, where he continues the tradition of Torah study and its interpretation, begin writing the Jewish **Oral Code**, thereby ensuring the survival of Judaism replacing any geographic, cultural and language differences amongst Jews spread out in the Diaspora. Through the establishment of this academy, a method is found to continue the many ceremonies and regulations previously performed only in the Temple and adopt them in Jewish life outside Jerusalem. The distinctive theological figure in Jewish history until the Fall of the First Temple is **'the Prophet'**. After the Jews returned from Babylonian exile in 538BCE, the political leadership of the Jewish people is represented by the position of the **High Priest**, (and priests 'Kohanim') at The Temple whose position is frequently usurped by a king during the Hasmonean Period. Now after the Destruction of the Second Temple, the aristocracy and priesthood vanishes and its place is taken is taken by the **Rabbis** to teach and interpret Jewish Law. The Jews will always have a spiritual center in the Torah and pray towards Jerusalem.

70 Sages continue to compile laws, commentaries and traditions. The monumental compilation of **Jewish law (*Halacha*)** and **customs**

(*agada*) are the intellectual and philosophical cornerstones that make up the Oral Law (**Mishna**) and Commentary (**Gemara**) which together comprise the **Talmud**. Learned rabbis will spread out and enter the multitude of Jewish communities in Eretz Israel and in the Diaspora. Local Jewish courts residing in Jewish communities can decide legal judgment according to Jewish Law. After the Fall of Jerusalem all Temple rituals cease and are substituted by prayer leadership of the rabbis. Teaching of the Torah is transferred to the home or seminary. **In the post-Temple era the recognized representative of the Jews is not a king, warrior, or landowner, but is a student or scholar.** The Sanhedrin is now reconstituted by members chosen by their ability rather than by their political influence in Jerusalem.

Already in the 4th century BCE the Jewish Prophet Ezra encourages public reading of the Torah and praying in 'lesser sanctuaries'. The Temple is now in ruin and Jews are prevented from rebuilding the magnificent structure, yet Jewish life continues to flourish in all Jewish communities, centered around the **synagogue,** which becomes the epicenter of Jewish communal life both in Eretz Israel and in the Diaspora. "*They shall make a Sanctuary for Me – so that I may dwell among them.*" (Exodus 25:8). The synagogue is a house of prayer, of education, of study, a meeting point, a place to receive alms and charity and a hostel to accommodate an 'out of town Jewish traveler'. **The 'Ark' of a synagogue faces the Temple in Jerusalem, with a raised platform (bimah) for reading the Torah.** Larger synagogues have a ritual bath (mikveh), and a *genizah* for storing sacred manuscripts and ritual objects. Knowledge of a common language, Hebrew, allows members of Jewish communities to communicate with one another. Jewish travelers from the orient can converse with Jews in the west. This is evident with the discovery in Spain of textiles, glass and beads originating in China. "(See Elkan Adler).

71   Titus sails to Rome, constructing the Arch of Titus, engraved with images of Jewish captives carrying vessels of the Temple. Yohanan of Gush Halav is imprisoned for life, Simon ben Giora is executed. Sages claim that Titus dies a slow and painful death caused by a brain tumor.

73   **The Fall of Masada.** King Herod constructed at Masada 100 years earlier a palace on the northern side. Herod, despised by the Jews, realized that should he ever need to flee, Masada is inaccessible to an army and his private palace, secure. "*Herod equipped this fortress as a refuge for himself...danger from the Jewish masses, who might push him off his throne.*" (JF).

Masada, view from Dead Sea   Adrian Wolff

After the Fall of The Temple in Jerusalem in 70, rebels (Sicarii) flee to Masada, a lone hill-top in the Dead Sea Valley where they declare independence from Roman control. **The Roman Empire will not tolerate an independent colony within territory under their control, however remote and small the rebellious site**.

Masada, The Roman Camp on the western side   Adrian Wolff

The Romans are determined to have full territorial and administrative control. Therefore Jewish resistance at Masada is doomed to capitulate, notwithstanding how long it takes to conquer the lone hill-top rising 400 meters above the surrounding desert on the western side of the Dead Sea. Josephus Flavius estimates 10-15,000 Roman soldiers from Legion X under the command of General Flavius Silva the new governor, build eight camps around Masada, *"for not only food brought from a distance...even drinking water...as the neighborhood possessed no spring"* (JF), now enclosed by a one-meter high wall to prevent entry and exit of the defenders led by Elazar ben Yair. Nevertheless defenders do manage to sneak out undetected by descending the 'snake-path' on the eastern slope.

Masada, Southern Cistern   Timothy Guy

Masada, Storage Rooms   Adrian Wolff

The Romans have no knowledge of the large food stocks and water supplies available to the defenders. *"The provisions stored inside...enough to last for many years...weapons of every kind."* Herod had left *"a quantity of weapons of every kind...enough for 10,000 men as well as un-wrought iron and bronze and a store of lead."* (JF). Dove-rearing is used on a large scale for protein and fertilizer. It takes Jewish slaves eight months using stones, tamarisk timber and gravel filler to construct a 'ramp' on the western slope. The rebels hurl burning torches and sling stones at the slave-workers below, protected by portable shelters. Romans now employ battering rams and siege engines against the fortress wall. Josephus Flavius describes how the wind turned the Sicarii (Zealots/Rebels) fire-arrows against themselves.

Masada, The Roman Ramp on the western side   Adrian Wolff

73   Realizing their situation to be hopeless, on the first day of Passover, the 15th day of the Hebrew month of Nisan in the year 73, the leader of the Jewish revolt, **Elazar ben Yair** makes a speech before all the Jewish residents who have held out on the mountain top of Masada for nearly three years.

They choose suicide to slavery. *"Brave and loyal followers! Long ago we resolved to serve neither the Romans nor anyone other than God Himself, who alone is the true and just Lord of mankind. The time has now come that bids us prove our determination by our deeds. At such a time we must not disgrace ourselves. Hitherto we have never submitted to slavery, even when it brought no danger with it. We must not choose slavery now, and with it penalties that will mean the end of everything if we fall alive into the hands of the Romans...In our case it is evident that day-break will end our resistance, but we are free to choose an honorable death with our loved ones...Let our wives die un-abused, **our*** *children without knowledge of slavery. After that, let us do each other an ungrudging kindness, preserving our freedom as a glorious winding-sheet. Let our possessions and the whole fortress go up in flames...One thing only let us spare - **our store of food; it will bear witness** when we are dead to the fact that we perished, not though want but because, as we resolved at the beginning, we chose death rather than slavery...Let us die un-enslaved by our enemies, and leave this world as free men in company with our wives and children...The husbands tenderly embraced their wives and took their children into their arms, and gave the longest parting kisses to them, with tears in their eyes. Yet at the same time did they complete what they had resolved on"*. Then lots are taken for the final suicides. *"Then they chose ten men by lot out of them, to slay the rest; every one of whom laid himself down by his wife and children on the ground, and threw his arms about them, and they offered their necks to the stroke to those who by lot executed; and when the ten had, without fear, slain them all, they made the same rule for casting lots for themselves...So these people died with this intention that they would not have so much as one soul among them all alive to be subject to the Romans...they died defending their freedom, not betraying it."* (JF).

At dawn Roman soldiers break into the fortress wall and hear no human sounds from the defenders, finding 960 bodies, the result of the mass suicide. *"Saw nobody as an enemy, but a terrible solitude on every side, with a fire within the palace, as well as perfect silence".*(JF). This story is told by *"an ancient woman and another...with five children who had concealed themselves in caverns underground, and had carried water to drink, and were hidden there when the rest were intent upon the slaughter of one another."* (JF). The 29 food stores and water marks in 12 cisterns identify the fact that the besieged population can hold out for many more months. *"For there has been a mass of corn, amply sufficient for years, abundance of wine and oil, besides every variety of pulse and piles of dates."* (JF). The Roman soldiers *"admired the nobility of their resolve, and the way in which so many had shown in carrying it out without a tremor an utter contempt of death... the whole country had been subdued"* (JF).

73   Titus *"instructed to pull down the Jewish sanctuary in the district of Onias (in Egypt)."* (JF).

Chapter 10. Roman and Byzantine Rule 81 - 570

81   **Domitian** (81-96) succeeds Titus as emperor, extracts sever taxes (Fiscus Judaicus) on Jews.

90   **St. John** writes the Fourth Gospel describing the life of Jesus; preparation of the disciples; His Crucifixion; Resurrection and Ascension. *"In the beginning was the Word, and the Word was with God, and the Word was God. He was in the beginning with God"*. (John 1:1,2). St. John claims *"I am the Alpha and the Omega, the First and the Last."* (Rev.1:10,11;6;22:13). Christians believe nothing is outside Christ's knowledge as He is the beginning and the end. *"I am the first, and I am He, who will be with the last (generations)"*. (Isaiah 41:4). Alpha and Omega are the first and last letters of the Greek alphabet. This symbol is found in many churches. Catholics believe the symbol of St. John to be 'An Eagle'

Alpha and Omega, North Church, Shivta   Adrian Wolff

96   Emperor Nerva (96-98) frees the Fiscus Judaicus (Jewish Tax).

98   Rabbi Gamliel II, a descendant of Hillel, is elected Patriarch or *Nasi*, Yavne Sanhedrin head, represents Jews before the Romans.

106   The Nabatean Empire, its capital Petra, in Perea (Jordan) falls to the Romans, known as *Provincia Arabia*. Nabatean traders and cities will survive for another 6 centuries. See Nabateans 363, 640.

115–117 The **Second Jewish Revolt**. Jews in Alexandria and Cyrenaica revolt against the Romans who swiftly suppress the insurgents.

131   Roman Emperor **Hadrian**, (76-138, emperor 117-138) is known as an intellectual, a singer, dancer, musician, painter, sculptor, writer

of grammar and poems. He is a practical administrator, visiting most territory under his control. Hadrian visits Jerusalem and instructs the local Roman Governor to forcibly integrate the Jewish population into the Roman Empire. Various anti-Jewish edicts are announced banning the ritual of circumcision, preventing Bible study, together with the cessation of Sabbath observance.

132   Simon Bar Kozeba, called by his followers **Bar Kochba** (son of a star), leads the **Third Jewish Revolt** to obtain Jewish Independence in Judea, successfully defeats the Romans. Jewish coins are struck to commemorate the liberation of Jerusalem. Romans send the Egyptian Twelfth Legion Deiotariana to put down the revolt only to be forced to retreat. The various Jewish communities notify each other of their success against the Romans by lighting fires from hilltops, quickly communicating their message. This festival is commemorated each year on to the Hebrew date, **Lag B'Omer,** the 33rd day of the 'Omer'. The Jewish revolt spreads to Libya, Cyprus and Mesopotamia, suppressed by the overwhelming power of the Roman Empire. During the Bar Kochba Revolt the Christian population does not rise against the Romans. Open display of Christianity is suppressed.

134   Emperor Hadrian orders the Governor of Britain, Gaius Julius Severus with 35,000 soldiers of the Tenth Legion to methodically destroy any resistance in Judea. **Simon Bar Kochba** writes from the Wadi Muraba'at caves in the Judean Desert to Joshua Ben Galgula in ink on papyrus using Aramaic-Hebrew script *'if any man of the Galileans...is ill-treated, I will put irons on your feet.'*

135   Torah scholar and teacher **Rabbi Akiva** ben Joseph (50-135) lives as an illiterate shepherd until age 40. His teachings lay the foundation of the *Mishna* (Oral Law), and Kabbalah text "Book of Formation' *Sefer Yetzrirah'*. He preaches *"What ever God does is for the best"*, (Talmud Brachot 60b) and *"You shall love your neighbor as yourself."* (Leviticus 19:18). He supports the new Jewish uprising. He and nine of his followers are captured, brought to the Roman capital, Caesarea, where they are tortured to death.

135   The Jews are defeated, many killed, enslaved or exiled leaving a destitute population and desolate territory. Torah teachers are condemned to death. Simon Bar Kochba is killed at Beitar, Jerusalem is sacked. During the Roman and following Byzantine Periods Jews are forbidden to reside in or visit Jerusalem, other than a pilgrimage on the Ninth day of the month of Av (*Tisha B'Av*), to commemorate the Fall of both Temples, and visit on the Day of Atonement. All Torah teachers could be put to death. Yehuda ben Baba's Tanach study is banned and many flee to **Usha** in the

Galilee where they secretly continue to teach their students and reorganize national Jewish life. A story is told how Rabbi Yehuda ben Baba remains stationary in front of the Roman soldiers who come to arrest him at Usha, thereby allowing time for his disciples to flee. Over 980 Jewish communities are destroyed in Judea and a million Jews die in the revolt. **For the first time in Jewish History, Jews are in a minority in Eretz Israel, never to renounce their claim to the Land of Israel.**

135 Emperor Hadrian passes laws to obliterate the memory of the Jews. The names previously used for the territory, Judea and Samaria are abolished now called Syria/**Palestina** (Palestine) for the first time, after the Philistines who disappeared during the end of the Assyrian Period over 800 years earlier. The name Palestine is later taken by Christian literature. Josephus Flavius refers to Philistines as '*Palaistinoi'*. Hadrian rebuilds Jerusalem into a pagan Roman citadel. The name of Jerusalem is changed to **Aelia Capitolina** (Hadrian's clan name). Building construction, dormant since 70CE, is renewed. Roman towns follow the grid plan with the main road the **cardo** and the **decumanus**. A forum parades is built where the two main roads meet includes a market.

1. The north-south artery, the *cardo* is constructed from the main gate in the north (Damascus Gate of today) to Mt Zion.
2. The west-east artery *decumanus* from the Three Towers (Jaffa Gate today) to the Temple Mount, reaches St. Stephen's Gate.
3. A Roman temple to Aphrodite is constructed on the small hill (Golgotha) off the *cardo*, where, during the Byzantine Period, the Church of the Holy Sepulchre is constructed.
4. The Roman Forum is constructed in the area along the *cardo*, meeting the *decumanus*, in the Christian Quarter of today.
5. A Roman temple to Jupiter is constructed on the Temple Mount on Mt. Moriah over the site of the destroyed Jewish Temple.
6. An arch commemorating Roman victory over the Jews is built on the *decumanus* (via Dolorosa today). Christians believe from this arch (constructed 100 years after the Crucifixion) the Roman governor Pilate stated 'Behold the man-*ecce homo'.*

Roman Bath-houses. Roman towns are characterized with a public 'bath-house', similar to today's Country Club, having an important position in Roman society as the chief meeting point, even at Masada (see 36BCE) in severe desert conditions. Romans bath every day with mixed bathing allowed and entrance without payment. The complex includes a dressing room; a *palestra* for games (wrestling, jumping, play ball), a massage room, a steam-room, warm bath with soap, cold bath, rubbing the body with oil.

Club rooms for dice games, library and reading rooms, and musicians, orators or poets perform.

Roman Agriculture uses damming wadis and terracing hillsides to irrigate crops, also in desert conditions.

Jerusalem, Roman Cardo   Judy Romano

Beit She'an, Roman Street, Cardo   Adrian Wolff
Diagonally placed paving stones assist wheeled vehicles passing over imperfections.

Beit She'an, Roman Theater   Adrian Wolff

Beit She'an, Roman Amphitheater   Adrian Wolff
Lowered arena and entrance tunnels for contestants - human and animal

135   Simon ben Gamliel, *Nasi* (president) of the Synod 135-165.

138   Emperor Hadrian dies, his successor Antonius Pius (138-161)
       discontinues his policies. Antonius Pius' rule brings peace and
       prosperity to Rome, extending Roman citizenship and commerce
       throughout the empire. Both Emperor Antonius Pius and his
       successor Emperor Marcus Aurelius (emperor 161-180) are
       favorable towards Jews and Jewish religious practices within the
       Empire, allowing functions of the Sanhedrin to continue.

Beit She'an, Public Latrines   Adrian Wolff

155   Polycarp, the Bishop of Smyrna is martyred for refusing to burn incense for the emperor.

Beit She'arim   Adrian Wolff

165   Roman soldiers murder Simon ben Gamliel, succeeded by his son Yehuda Ha'Nasi (the president), (165-217), reputed to be a personal friend of the Roman Governor who allows him to live in **Beit She'arim** (UNESCO Heritage Site 2015) and later in **Zippori.**

2nd-4thc Evidence of the banning of Jewish residence in Jerusalem during the post-Hadrian Roman Period is found in the catacombs at **Beit**

She'arim near the Haifa Bay. Jews wishing to be close to the arrival of the Messiah are not permitted to bury their dead on the Mount of Olives in Jerusalem. An alternative site at Beit She'arim becomes the central Jewish necropolis housing sarcophagi of wealthy Jews from many parts of the Middle East, awaiting their transfer to burial in Jerusalem. The Jewish town of Beit She'arim is destroyed in 352 during a Jewish uprising against the Romans.

2ndc   During the Bar Kochba Revolt **Rabbi Shimon bar Yochai**, a student of Rabbi Akiva, is sentenced to death for anti-Roman sentiments. He flees together with his son Eliezer to Peki'in in northern Galilee, hiding in a cave, allegedly for 12 years. During their solitary sojourn, they concentrate on Torah interpretations. He writes the outline of the **Mishna,** included in the original version of Rabbi Yehuda Ha'Nasi. He is reputed to receive 'Divine Inspiration' רוח הקודש. His teachings compose the **Zohar** "The Book of Splendor", the basis of Jewish spiritual philosophy, **Kabbalah,** were hidden, uncovered in the 13th century, edited by Rabbi Moshe de Leon 1238-1305. Rabbi Shimon bar Yochai becomes a Sanhedrin emissary to Rome to plead the abolition of the anti-Jewish decrees against Jewish religious observance. He dies on the 33rd day of the Omer (Lag be'Omer) buried at Mt. Meron together with his son, a pilgrimage site for Kabbalist Jews.

Kabbalah expounds the process of creation, the nature of divinity and the origin of the fate of the soul.
Three Characteristics of the Soul are:
1. **Nefesh (soul)** – the living body function.
2. **Ruach (spirit)** – passions and dynamic emotions.
3. **Neshema (breath)** – defining our personal identity.

The **Zohar** 'The Book of Splendor' identifies two higher levels Chaya (living) wisdom, and Yehida (uniqueness). The central literature of Kabbalah, arranged according to the weekly Torah portions is composed of five volumes, originally in Aramaic, contain the utterances and commentaries of Rabbi Shimon bar Yochai. The section "*Idra Rabba*" The Greater Assembly, expounds profound mysteries concerning the revelation of the Divine and two descriptions of the Seven Places in the celestial Garden of Eden

193   Roman Severus Emperors Septimus (193-211) and Alexander (211-235) are sympathetic towards Jews who favor their ascent to power, granting citizenship to non-Roman Jewish citizens.

204   Rabbi **Yehuda Ha'Nasi (the prince) 135-219** the Sanhedrin (Higher Religious Authority) head '*Rabbeinu HaKadosh*', our Holy Rabbi. He studies the Torah under his father, Rabbi Yehudah ben

Ilai of Usha, Rabbi Yaakov ben Kurshai, and Rabbi Shimon bar Yochai in Tekoa. He establishes his first Torah academy at Sh'faram, in Beit Shearim, and later moves to Zippori (Diocaesarea), Lower Galilee where he writes the codification of traditional Jewish jurisprudence, completing the first **Mishna, the Jewish Oral Law detailing how a Jew should live his daily life.** He is buried in the necropolis in Beit She'arim.

The Mishna is divided into six sections.

1. **Seeds** or *Zera'im.* Laws relating to agriculture, seeds, sabbatical year, portion given to workers and poor.

2. **Festivals and Seasons** or *Mo'ed.* Laws relating to ceremonies, rituals, observance, Sabbath, religious festivals, fast days, etc.

3. **Women** or *Nashim.* Laws relating to betrothals, marriage contracts (*ketuba*), divorce, married life. This is one of the first written documents relating to women's rights.

4. **Damage** or *Nezakim.* Civil and Criminal Laws. Damages, theft, labor relations, usury, real estate, partnerships, tenant relations, inheritance, court composition, jurisdiction, testimony, punishment.

5. **Holiness** or *Kedoshim.* Laws relating to the Temple - sacrifices, offerings and donations.

6. **Purification** or *Tahorot.* The purity of vessels, dwellings, food and personal hygiene.

Before the Fall of the Temple, Jews would go up to the Temple in Jerusalem to get advice or a judgment from a Priest. After the Destruction of the Temple problems arise defining settlements. The issue is not what a man MUST do and what he must not do, but rather what a man SHOULD do and should not do. Regardless of his position in society a Jew is expected to study the Jewish Code. He may work in the fields or at a trade during the day while studying early in the morning and in the evenings. Physical work is suspended after the spring harvest and autumn crops to enable the students to study for a month each time. This tradition will continue unbroken from the 2nd century.

All the regulations are for a person's physical, mental and psychological health. For example *"You shall not round off the edge of your scalp."* (Leviticus 19:2). Religious Jews follow this biblical regulation by not shaving their 'side-burns'. This is a 'physical rule' as the carotid artery is close to the skin in the temple area, if heedlessly shaved can cause accidental suicide. Legal disputes on business or matrimonial matters are not specifically mentioned in the Tanach (Bible). The Mishna encompasses civil and penal laws, religious laws, daily life, rituals on Sabbath and festivals, dietary regulations and gender relations. Special institutions such as bath-house (*mikvah*) and ritual slaughter are kept according to strict regulations. A Mikvah must contain at least 40 Sa'ah (750 liters) of natural rain, spring, lake, or sea water, or melted snow.

Zippori, Water System   Adrian Wolff

Herodian Mikvah at Western Wall area, Jerusalem   Adrian Wolff

All opinions in the Mishna are a guide for an individual's physical, mental or psychology well-being. It is essential to bathe in a **ritual** bath or *mikvah* at least once a week, and always before the Sabbath. The mikvah has to be plastered and in direct contact with the ground, not less than forty *seah* (1.0 meters) wide and at least 3 *amot* (1.2 meters) deep.

Jews perform the traditional **Jewish Wedding ceremony**. Before a marriage ceremony takes place, the **ketuba**, the Jewish Marriage Contract written in Aramaic is signed in the presence of the bridegroom and two witnesses not related to the couple and to each another (Deuteronomy 19:15). The *ketuba* originates during this period and is one of the first written documents protecting woman's rights by making divorce costly to the husband and also guarantees the woman's rights to property after the death of her husband. The groom purchases the ring which he places on the bride's finger during the ceremony, reciting The *ketuba* is universal and still used today in every Jewish marriage without regard to location or denomination (orthodox, reform etc.).

Wedding in the desert at sunset, under a 'chupah   Adrian Wolff

The wedding ceremony always takes place under a '*chupah*' *"for this will be a canopy over all."* (Isaiah 4:5) *"let the bridegroom go forth from his chamber and the bride from her canopy".* (Joel 2:16). *"She then took the veil and covered herself'"* (Genesis 24:65). Four staves hold an elevated cloth canopy symbolizing the home. The ceremony may be held outside, weather permitting. During the wedding ceremony the rabbi reads aloud the contents of the *ketuba* and then the couple drink wine. Jewish Law requires only one ring given by the bridegroom to the bride to represent the wholeness achieved through marriage and the hope for an unbroken marriage. The bridegroom recites "*You are consecrated to me with this ring according to the Law of Moses and Israel."* On conclusion of the ceremony the bridegroom breaks (stamps/ crushes) a glass to symbolize the destruction of the Temple, and man's short life on earth.

Jewish Burial is conducted before sundown of the day of death. The eyes and mouth is closed, arms and hands extended alongside the body, thoroughly washed in salty, warm water, hair and beard combed, toes and fingernails cleaned and trimmed. The body, dressed in a simple shroud without seams, buttons, pockets or knots, is laid to rest in the earth *"for you are dust and to dust shall you return."* (Genesis 3:19). *"Naked did I emerge from my mother's womb, and naked I shall return there."* (Job 1:21). The body is buried with the head towards Jerusalem, awaiting the advent of the Messiah. The family sit for a seven-day (shiva) period of mourning, when relatives and friends visit and bring food. Judaism teaches that life is a divine gift to be cherished in itself, not a testing ground for the world to come. There are no last rites, nor anointing of the dead. Judaism is more concerned with fulfilling the commandments of Hashem in this world than with any rewards in the World to come. Kabbalists believe the soul is immortal. *"Rachel died and was buried on the road to Ephrat, which is Bethlehem. **Jacob set a monument over her grave;** it is Rachel's grave until this day."* (Genesis 35:16-20). **This custom for a Jew to place a stone on a grave continues until today.** It is impossible to dig a grave in the rocky surfaces in Judea. Most graves are above ground, covered with local rock (which aren't scarce like flowers, found only in spring) Another factor is - the more stones, the less chance of a beast digging for the cadaver.

Hamsa (see **Menorah** 1240BCE, 952BCE, 516BCE, 70CE). The hand is used as a symbol in Judaism, Christianity and Islam (Fatima's hand). The five-branched menorah or Hamsa (five) has been a Jewish expression of the Divine. His right hand He made the heavens His love and mercy. His left hand He made the earth and wrath. *"If I forget you, O Jerusalem, may my right hand lose its cunning"* (Psalms 137:5). Kabbalist use the Hand of God as a metaphor to explain the cause of evil on the world. The hand is a symbol of strength *"with a strong hand and an outstretched arm"* (Deuteronomy 5:15), Hashem took Israel out of Egypt. Five-branched menorahs (hamsa) are found in the 2nd century synagogue in Avalim (Israel); with Hebrew inscriptions in the murals of the 3rd century Dura Europas Synagogue in Syria; on a 4th century seal in Avignon; on a 5th century Spanish tombstone and at the 5th century synagogue at Capernaum; on the mosaic of the 6th century Beit Alpha Synagogue. Six-branched menorah are seen today outside Jewish homes in Djerba, Tunisia. A eleven-branched menorah is carved in stone in the synagogue in Katzrin.

220 *"Rabbi Gamaliel, son of Rabbi Yehuda Ha'Nasi said, 'An excellent thing is the study of the Torah combined with some worldly occupation.'"* Pirkei Avot II:2.

249 During Emperor Decius' reign (249-251) a 'certificate of sacrifice' to traditional gods is required of Christians. Failure results in death.

303 Emperor Diocletian (284-305) persecutes Christians, destroys Churches and their holy books.

312 **Legalization of Christianity becoming the official religion within the Roman Empire,** announced at the **Edict of Milan** in an agreement between the two co-emperors, Licinius and the new convert to Christianity, **Constantine** (Emperor Constantine I the Great) (See 330). Constantine is reputed to have had a vision of a blazing cross inscribed 'By this, Conquer' before his decisive battle with Maxentius outside Rome. He has a long spear made in gold and precious stones, on the top a crown and two letters (P and X in Greek, R and CH in Latin) indicating the name of Christ. He seeks Divine assistance, greater than weapons or a army. He allows freedom to worship Christianity and construction of churches. All confiscated Christian property is returned. The persecution and martyrdom of Christians ending their public execution, condemnation to death in public areas, confiscation of property and banishment.

Constantine defeats Licinius in battle in 324, ascribing his success to his conversion to Christianity. **Pagans living within the Roman Empire begin to convert to Christianity following the official conversion of Emperor Constantine, uniting the different peoples of the empire.** The Jews, a minority, are persecuted

324 Emperor Constantine I moves his capital from Rome to his new capital in Byzantium, a Greek city on the Bosphorus, joining the Black and Aegean Seas. The Roman Empire is split with two emperors. Rome is bankrupt, having a militarized state with an ineffective army, parasitic inverted aristocracy and hostile peasantry. Constantine transfers his wealth and the Golden Menorah to Byzantium. Barbarians had previously crossed the Danube in 230, and successfully cross the Rhine in 406.

325 Representatives of Christianity at the Council of Nicaea (Iznik today) meet to solve Christian theological disputes, incorporating the word *'of the substance'* into a creed, signifying the equality of the Son (Jesus Christ) with the Father (God). (See 800; 1054).

327   Queen **Helena** (St. Helena), mother of Emperor Constantine, a devout Christian, travels to Palestine, identifying original Christian Holy Sites connected with Jesus, constructing Byzantine-style churches on these sites. The large **Church of the Holy Sepulchre** is built over a small hill resembling a skull, known as Golgotha (skull = gulgolet in Hebrew) (John 19:17) off the Roman cardo, where Christians believe Jesus is Crucified. Queen Helena locates, under the Roman Temple of Aphrodite, what she believes to be the '**True Cross**' on which Jesus is crucified. The True Cross is sawn into three pieces - one remains in Jerusalem; one sent to the Pope in Rome, and the third segment to the emperor residing in Constantinople. In time, devout Christian pilgrims to Jerusalem cut off a piece as a souvenir, until it completely disappears.

4thC   During the Byzantine Period Christian pilgrimage to the Holy Land is encouraged, gaining momentum as they wish to be close to sites associated with Jesus' life. Jerusalem, no longer a pagan city, is transformed into a Christian monument, while Jews remain prohibited from entering except on the Ninth day of the Hebrew month of Av (Fall of both First and Second Temple). Throughout the Byzantine Period there is no construction on the Temple Mount, left in ruins, as predicted by Jesus "*Your house is left to you desolate*" (Matthew 23:38).

330   The **Byzantine Period** begins when Byzantium, now renamed **Constantinople**, standing at cross-roads between Europe and the east is declared capital of the Roman Empire.

330   Eusebius (260–340), the first bishop of Caesarea writes Martyrs of Palestine Onomasticon (Christian sites and geography) and Ecclesiastical History.

335   The completion and dedication in Bethlehem of the Church of the Nativity over the Grotto of the Nativity, the accepted birth site of Jesus. In addition completion of the Church of the Holy Sepulchre over the hill of Golgotha in Jerusalem, site of the Crucifixion.

351   Taxes are increased to support the opulent lifestyle of the inept, inefficient and increasingly mismanaged Byzantine regime. Anti-Byzantine sentiments increase in Palestine. Emperor Constantine II instructs general Ursicinus to put down the rebellion in Beit She'an, slaughtering the Jewish population. The Jewish learning schools in Zippori, Tiberias, Lod and Beit She'arim never recover.

4thC   **Traditional Byzantine, Orthodox and Catholic anti-Semitism.** Christians believe Christ's death was a necessary part of God's purpose for salvation. Various popes (not all) promote the concept of the devil and all his hosts of hell removing God for being held accountable for the world's failures. A Christian is part of Christ's mystical body and the Jews a part of Satan's mystical body. Judaism questions the nature and existence of the Christian hell, so threatening the very powerful tool of the pope and priests-of eternal damnation. If you sinned in this world, your immortal soul will go to hell. The Cross signifies Christ's suffering and death with salvation and eternal life, previously unavailable to humanity. Accusations against Jews of ritual murder of young children is a re-enactment of Christ's passion. The fact that Jews do not accept Christ as the Messiah is a challenge to Christians' belief in the Revelation, therefore a Jew must convert to Christianity or be killed. Violence is legitimized and encouraged against Jews who are demonized and alienated. *"anyone not written in the Book of Life was cast into the lake of fire."* (Revelations 20:15).

Early Christian writers (the Church Fathers) fear Christians are becoming attracted to Judaism. **John Chrysostom** (c347-407), Archbishop of Constantinople compares the synagogue to a pagan temple, representing the source of all vices and heresies. He preaches that Jews are collectively responsible for the death of Christ and are in league with Satan. His anti-Semitic sermons use quotations from the gospels of St. Matthew and St. John.

St Augustine (354–430) sees the Jews blindness and refusal to recognize the truth of Christianity, making them willful instruments of the Evil One. His most pernicious statement states because of the Jews' failure to convert, they should be left alive to live in degrading, humiliating conditions, thus symbolizing the church's triumph over synagogue (Strasbourg Cathedral statues). Jews should never forget, to suffer as a perpetual reminder of their murder of Christ, to be converted at the 'End of the Days', an essential precursor to the Second Coming. *"Blessed are you when men hate you, and when they exclude you"* (Luke 6:22).

The first part, **The Inferno** (Italian for Hell) of Dante Alighieri's 14th century poem '*Divine Comedy*' describes his journey through Hell, telling of the unending agonies of the damned. His work does **not** mention any Jews among the heretics and usurers.

Popular Anti-Jewish Beliefs - all fallacious
1. The Blood Libel and Ritual Murder
2. Desecration of the Host
3. Jews as Devils
4. The Jewish Smell
5. The Wandering Jew
6. Polluted Jewish Blood
7. Well Poisoning

8. Jewish World Conspiracy
9. Jewish Stubbiness
10. Jewish Laziness
11. Expulsions

Examples of official anti-Semitism during the Byzantine Period
• Theodosius II (408-450) excluded Jews from public office.
• Fifth century Jews are massacred by Christians, stirred by clerics to destroy synagogues and convert Jews.
• Jews must be punished and degraded.
• No new synagogues may be constructed.
• A Christian may not go to a Jewish physician
• Heraclitus (610-641) prohibits any public exhibition of Judaism.
• 580 King Recared of Spain. Jews are excluded from official positions
• 616 King Sisebut of Spain. Prohibits open practice of Judaism.
• 626 King Dagobert of France expels all Jews.

From the 5th century, the church decided self-inflicted pain (scourging one's own body), would help save one's soul, imitating Jesus' suffering on the cross. In 1267 the Vienna Council decrees that Jews must wear the *pileum cornutum* (horned hat), and in France they are required to wear identity badges.

Byzantine Church at Kursi, Sea of Galilee   Adrian Wolff

362   In his counter-reaction towards Christianity, Emperor **Julianus II** The Apostate (350-363), writes to Patriarch Hillel II (330-365) to allow the Jews to return to Jerusalem and rebuild the Temple. Julianus is killed in battle against Parthians (Persians) at Samara on the Tigris River before any pro-Jewish proposals materialize.

363   Severe **earthquakes** in Palestine. Buildings are damaged in Jerusalem and the Roman governor's residence in Zippori.

Emperor Jovian (331-364, rules 363-364) bans Jews from living in Jerusalem.

363　**The Spice Route.** The **Nabateans** are a people of ancient Arabia and Jordan (See 160 BCE, 64 BCE and 106 CE). They hold a monopoly of the rich overland **Caravan** trade along the **Spice Route** beginning in Yemen, passing through Arabia, the Negev and onto the Mediterranean coast at Gaza, a distance of about 2500 kilometers, taking roughly three months in each direction. The caravan route is preferable to sailing northwards up the Gulf of Akaba due to unfavorable winds. They are reputed to speak their own language, similar to Aramaic, later develops into Arabic. They follow the dominant religion of the area at the particular period. The Nabateans kept secret of a route from Petra through the Negev to Gaza, a 60-day journey, especially the location of water sources in the desert. Their knowledge of these wells and the routes through the mountain passes provide them with lucrative income and shortens the journey by at least three days. Only those camel drivers familiar with Nahal Nekarot passageway can find their way through the Ramon Crater.

Byzantine South Church, Shivta　　　　　　　Adrian Wolff

Nabateans originally live in tents and the only permanent structures they build are religious shrines (Avner Goren). From the Roman Period onwards they construct permanent settlements, their capital at Petra, Jordan with additional settlements along the desert trade routes in the Negev at Nitzana (Nessna), Mamshit (Mampsis), Avdat (Oboda), Shivta (Sobata) and Rehovot (Rehovot ba-Negev). Nabateans are the major traders, merchants and caravan guides in the Negev until the entry of Muslims. During the

Byzantine Period, elaborate churches are constructed using imported marble from Mamara, Turkey, displaying wealth. Their urban architecture does not follow typical Roman town planning as the streets of Nabatean desert towns follow the topography to allow rainwater to be channeled into plaster-lined cisterns. Nabateans disappear after 640 following the invasion of Islam.

Byzantine Baptism Pool, Mamshit   Adrian Wolff

Water. Nabateans use irrigation methods in an arid climate, cultivate agriculture by growing barley (feed for Arabian horses they breed and sell to travelers for quick communication, not for defense purposes). They store water in impermeable plastered cisterns and in water-filled jars to enable travelers to cross inhospitable deserts. Pips found at various Nabatean sites show a variety of fruit trees, olive trees and vines in addition to field crops (barley). Numerous wine and olive presses are constructed, found at these sites today. Nabateans build dams and walls along the hill slopes to channel rainwater run-off into the fields. Using this method 50-100 millimeters of annual rainfall from a relatively large catchment area is directed into small, cultivated plots. The water flows towards each tree and is contained in a surrounding basin, eventually seeping into the loess soils of the Negev. Today, Israelis successfully irrigate vines, citrus, almonds and olives using the brackish underground water in the Negev.

Spices. Nabateans trade in desirable Christian ceremonial commodities **Frankincense** and **Myrrh** indigenous to Arabia, used in perfumery and incense, found in Yemen and in the Oman desert plateau bordering the green mountains of the Dhofar region.

Christians value frankincense as the Magi bring gifts to the Christ child and symbolizing His divinity. *"wise men from the East came to Jerusalem, saying 'where is He who has been born King of the Jews? For we have seen His star in the East and have come to worship Him"* (Matthew 2:1,2). Myrrh, darker in color, richer aroma used to perfume the royal mummies in Egypt, is a main ingredient in the sacred anointed oil of the Jews used in the Temple. Myrrh is also used for medicinal purposes to treat ailments. In addition, wine and olive oil are exported. Nabateans trade in cinnamon originating in the Far East.

Water channel in desert town, Shivta, Negev   Adrian Wolff

Stone roof construction, Mamshit   Adrian Wolff

Wine press in desert town, Shivta, Negev   Adrian Wolff

Camels. Camels after 1000BCE, become domesticated for transportation valued as pack or riding animals, for their wool, milk, hides and meat. They have soft, wide-spreading large diameter two-toed feet to assist them to walk on soft sand. They have adapted to the harsh dusty desert climate by possessing double rows of eyelashes, haired ear openings and the ability to close their nostrils. Camels can subsist on coarse, sparse food such as thorny plants and dried grasses. They store fat in their humps and can exist without food and water for many days. Camels lose their body weight slowly and regain their lost weight within a quarter hour of drinking. Their body temperature is 39°C assists their survival in the heat. Camel caravans are composed of up to 1000 camels on a single trek. One-third of the camels carry loads, one-third are substitute carriers while the remaining third are expected to die during the journey. Only female camels are used for caravan transportation, as the males are too unruly and undisciplined, especially should a female camel reach menstruation.

Caravansary. Nabateans establish a well-organized system of caravan stops, *caravansary* to provide food and shelter for travelers, at Metzad Nekarot and Ein Saharonim in the Ramon Crater. The caravansary is usually a square enclosure comprising a massive wall, with small windows near the top. A heavy gate, the sole access is wide and high enough to allow entry of a laden camel. The ground floor is used for storing bales of merchandise and upstairs rooms for lodging. Nabateans supply food and medical care to merchants and camels and provided replacement camels. A sick or injured camel can mean the loss of 150 kilograms of merchandise. Nabateans create an intricate military system with military camps at central points, forts and watchtowers along the roads to protect the caravans from highway robbers.

The Talmud is the 'interpretations', a guide to 'a way of life' for everyday behavior. Jewish laws relate to rituals, family, ethics, and philosophy. The Hebrew word *Talmud* means 'study' or 'learning' and is composed of legal codes made up of the **Mishna** or Oral Law, supplementing the written Laws of the Torah; and the **Gemara** comprising the explanation and commentary of the Mishna. The Jerusalem Talmud, written in Western Aramaic dialect, notifies the central spiritual and symbolic importance of Jerusalem. Construction of synagogues in the Galilee and Golan.

395   Theodosius I (347-395). **The Roman Empire splits into two separate sects.** West the **Latins** in Rome. East the **Byzantines** in Constantinople. Greek remains the official language in the east.

425   Following Patriarch Gamliel IV death, Emperor Theodosius II (401-450, rules 408-450), suspends the Jewish Patriarchate, consequently the Sanhedrin ceases to exist.

425   **The Mishna is codified, Jewish calendar fixed, Jewish teaching and learning schools (*yeshivot*) exist throughout the Jewish world in sufficient strength to assume the continuation of Jewish life in Eretz Israel and the Diaspora.**

Kfar Nahum Synagogue   Adrian Wolff

438   Empress Eudocia, wife of Emperor Theodosius II, is exiled to Palestine where she rules (441–460), constructing of the Church of St. Stephen, the Church of St Sophia, Church of the Redemption,

and the Church of St John the Baptist. Jerusalem City walls are extended and Jews are once again allowed to reside.

458   Rome is plundered by its own inhabitants, taking materials from public buildings, destroying temples, monuments, palaces for constructing private buildings.

476   German vandal invaders under Odoacer/Odovacer conquer Rome, removing Romulus Augustus. Constantinople, with a large middle-class population, continues to thrive economically charging a 10% tax on all passing trade.

482   Justinian (482-565) is the last Byzantine Emperor to speak Latin, thereafter the emperors all spoke Greek.

493   Rome declines due to class struggles, moral decay and corruption, stifling taxes to pay for luxurious excesses of the leaders, extensive wars and a disintegration of leadership and administration. The Ostrogoths, under King Theodoric kill the Roman King Odovacar, capture Rome **ending the Roman Empire in the west**. After the destruction of Rome, the sole defender of the Christianity is the Eastern Orthodox Church remaining the official religion of the Byzantine Empire, based in Constantinople.

495c   **Babylonian Talmud,** based on the Jerusalem Talmud is completed by Rabbis Yose and Ravina who are in contact with their colleagues in Eretz Israel. The Babylonian Talmud, influenced by Persian Law is written in Eastern Aramaic dialect in the famous learning academies of **Pumbedita** and **Sura** in Mesopotamia. These famous Jewish schools of Torah study continue to teach uninterruptedly until 1950 when Iraqi Jews flee anti-Semitic persecution, plunder and murder.

502   An **earthquake** razes buildings in the Latrun and Acre areas.

520   Construction of a synagogue at **Beit Alpha** at the foothills of Mt. Gilboa. The finely laid mosaic floor depicts the two panels of the Holy Ark, the sacrifice of Isaac, a shofar and the sign of the Zodiac. Many large synagogues are constructed in the Galilee and Golan.

521   A Samaritan lawyer Silvanus negotiates a truce between rebelling Samaritans in Beit She'an and the Byzantine authorities.

529   The Samaritan population revolts against Byzantine rule. The Jewish population of Beit She'an is massacred by their non-Jewish neighbors.

534   Emperor Justinian I (483-565) rules in Constantinople (527-565), known for his internal policy as the codifier of laws, an administrator, reformer and legislator. He publishes the *Codex*

Justinian in 534 incorporating legislation used until the end of the Byzantine Empire. *"Justice is the constant and perpetual wish to render to every one his due."* Institutes, I.i.1. His civil policies are biased towards the majority of his subjects who are Orthodox Christians. Emperor Justinian persecutes all non-orthodox Christians, pagans, heretics and also the Jews living within the Byzantine Empire. He initiates the construction of many public buildings in Constantinople including the large, magnificent Hagia Sophia Church in Constantinople. Elaborate drainage systems are constructed together with underground cisterns.

534 Procopius writes 'History of the Wars". Upon reaching Byzantium with Gelimer (king of the Vandals, who is captured by Belisarius) *"....And there was also silver weighing many thousands of talents and all the royal treasure...among these were **the treasures of the Jews,** which Titus, the son of Vespasian, together with certain others, had brought to Rome, after the capture of Jerusalem. And one of the Jews seeing these things, approached one of those known to the emperor and said: "These treasures I think it inexpedient to carry into the palace in Byzantium. Indeed, it is not possible for them to be elsewhere than in the place where Solomon, the king of the Jews, formally placed them. For it is because of these that Gizerie captured the palace of the Romans (in Libya), and that now the Roman army has captured that of the Vandals. When this had been brought to the ears of the Emperor, he became afraid and quickly sent everything to the sanctuaries of the Christians in Jerusalem".* (see Menorah 70).

Map 15. Christian Influence 6th century

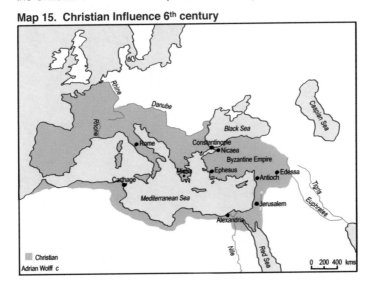

541-544 Recording of an epidemic plague stretching from Mesopotamia to the Middle East and North Africa.

543 The Nea Church in Jerusalem is dedicated during Emperor Justinian's reign, the largest basilica (115 x 70 meters) in The Holy Land also called 'The New Church of St. Mary, Mother of God'. The church is depicted on the 6th century mosaic map of Jerusalem found on the floor of the St. George's Church in Madaba, Jordan. The mosaic shows the walls of Jerusalem including Mt. Zion within the city boundary.

551 An **earthquake** in the Dead Sea area. Petra is destroyed.

553 Emperor Justinian forbids Jews to read their sacred texts in Hebrew, limiting to Greek or Latin translations only. Other Byzantine anti-Jewish measures and restrictions are enacted by Heraclius 632, Leo II in 721, Basil I in 873, and Romanus I in 932.

555 Samaritans revolt in Caesarea, burn churches. Byzantines put down the revolt, massacring thousands.

566 Lombardic pagan tribes from Asia Minor invade and conquer northern Italy (566-568), convert to Christianity and forgo their Germanic language for Latin.

Chapter 11. The Birth of Islam 570 - 661

570   **Mohammed**, son of Abdullah and Aminah is born in Mecca, Arabia. Mohammed's father dies before he is born and his grandfather Abdul Mutalib becomes his guardian until he dies, when his uncle Abi-Talib is named his custodian. Local inhabitants are all members of the Quraysh tribe, pagan worshippers of a large black meteor stone found in Mecca, and in addition, they are reputed to worship a tree and water.

595   At age 25 Mohammed marries his employer, Khadiga about 40 years old, a widow of a merchant. She gives birth to a daughter Fatima, who will marry Ali Ibn Abi-Talib, son of Mohammed's uncle.

610   Mohammed retires to Mt. Hira near Mecca to meditate for a month each year, known as the holy month of Ramadan. Mohammed receives his first revelations from angel Gabriel at Mt. Hira, now begins to preach his new monotheistic religion to local pagans in Mecca. *"...Gabriel. For he it is who has revealed to your heart by Allah."* (Koran 2:97). Mohammed believes he is the messenger (prophet) of God, called 'Allah' by all Muslims. *"I swear there is no God but Allah and Mohammed is his messenger (prophet)."* (The Muslim creed). *"Praise be to Allah, Lord of the words."* (Koran 1:1).

613   Chosroes II Parviz, Persian (Parthian) Emperor (606-628). During the Perso-Byzantine War he conquers the Fertile Crescent, invades western Christian Byzantine territory including Palestine. Jews living within the Byzantine Empire have been persecuted for centuries, now assist Chosroes II to defeat the Byzantines to occupy Jerusalem damaging the Church of the Holy Sepulchre, destroying the Nea Church, taking the 'True Cross' into exile.

622   **The Rise of Islam.** Mohammed continues to preach his vision of monotheism and attempts to convert the local pagans (Quraysh) in Mecca to his new religion, **Islam**, whose followers are **Muslims or Moslems**. Followers believe a person can reach 'The Garden of Eden' (*Jinat eiden*) in after-life through morality, piety and honesty. The religion is without temples and ceremony as **the faithful surrender to Islam**. Sinners will be punished and damned in hell in after-life ('*jehenom*'). The Quraysh threaten to kill Mohammed for attempting to convert them, make a pact (*al-Aqabah*) expelling him into exile, never to return to Mecca. On 20 June 622 Mohammed and his followers depart from Mecca for Yathrib, an oasis 400 kilometers to the north where he establishes the '**ummah**' - the Muslim community (empire). Yathrib becomes known as Medinat

al-Nabi, 'the town of the Prophet', later shortened to Medina. Muslims refer to Mohammed's 'flight from Mecca to Medina' as the **Hijra** (emigration), and recognize this year (622) as **the first year of the hijra**, the Islamic calendar.

The Muslim Year

The Muslim calendar begins in the year 622 when Mohammed and his followers are exiled from Mecca to Medina.

8th month - Haj to Mecca with animal sacrifice.

9th month - Ramadan, fasting month, commemorates Mohammed's meditation.

10th month - Shawwa, begins with joyous feast id-el-Fitr.

12th month - Dhul Hijjah, Haj ceremonies.

The Muslim calendar is based on the lunar calendar of 336 days, 12 months and 29/30 days in the month. There is no leap year.

622   Jews are wealthy, respected by the local Arabian tribes for their religion, culture, and literacy, living in the oases of Teyma, Khaybar, and Yathrib (Medina). Jews of Medina are Banu Qaynuqa (blacksmiths, goldsmiths, iron-mongers, jewelry), Banu Nadir (date plantations), Banu Qurayza (wine merchants).

Mohammed is attracted to (Yathrib) **Medina**, due to its large Jewish population, who do not worship idols unlike other pagan centers in Arabia. He anticipates they will be tolerant of his new monotheistic religion.

624   Mohammed attempts to convert Medina's Jews meeting little success. He decapitates the Jewish poet, Ka'b Ibn al-Ashraf, head of the Banu Nadir, 'Kill every Jew you can'. At the Battle of Badr, an oasis, outnumbered followers of Mohammed defeat the Quraysh. "*Slay the idolaters wherever you find them.*" (Koran 9:5). Mohammed views this conquest as Allah's allowing theological permission to eradicate any opposition. "*Ye (Muslims) slew them not, but Allah slew them.*" (Koran 8:17).

626   Muslims besiege and defeat the Jewish tribe of Bani Nadir in Medina whose survivors emigrate northwards to Edri in Jordan. "*The mightier will soon drive out the weaker; when might belongs to Allah, and to His messenger and the believers.*" (Koran 63:8). Remaining Jewish tribes are forced to pay an annual tribute (**jizya**), the non-Muslim head-tax. Non-fighting conquered residents are forced to assist to pay a tax to finance wars.

627   Muslims agree to allow the Jewish tribe of Bani Qurayza (Valley of the Villages) to leave Medina, but on their departure slaughter the men and take women and children to slavery. "*Those are they whom Allah has cursed...(Mohammed) will find for him no*

helper." (Koran 4:52). Remnants of the Jewish population of Medina area flee northward for Nazir, Kainula and Kaliza in Arabia. Jewish tribes in Qurayza and Nadir are called by the Arabs al-Kahinan (Kohen - priests).

629   Muslims attack Jews living in the Khaybar region, are forced to deliver half their palm groves to Muslim leaders. Over 600 men and women are killed, while their children are taken as slaves, taking all their possessions. Muslims expel all remaining Jews of Arabia. Any Jew who chooses to remain is forced to convert to Islam or be killed. *"And fight them until persecution is no more, and religion is all for Allah."* (Koran 8:39).

629   Byzantine Emperor Heraclius (575-641) defeats the over-extended Parthians (Persians). He re-conquers Palestine, once again becoming Christian territory, returning to Jerusalem with the relic of the 'True Cross'. The Byzantines begin to repair the destroyed churches but are unable to be rebuilt and restored before the Muslim invasion of Palestine. Both Byzantine and Persian armies are exhausted in their long conflict, allowing a newcomer (Islam) to enter the power vacuum. Byzantines massacre many Jews for supporting the Parthians and for their refusal to convert to Christianity, while others are expelled. In 632 Heraclius decrees the forcible conversion of Jews to Christianity. Additional anti-Jewish measures taken by Byzantine Emperors are: Leo III in 721, Basil I in 873 and Romanus Lepapenus I in 932.

630   Mohammed together with Abu Bakr and 10,000 Muslim followers pledge a *jihad* (holy war) against the Quraysh of Mecca. They return, capture Mecca, rescinding the previously agreed pact of 622 the *al-Aqabah,* made by Mohammed with the Quraysh (never to return to Mecca). The Koran permits two forms of misleading non-believers known as *taqiyya* تـقية dissimulation and *kitman* كـتمان secrecy, concealment, to advance the cause of Islam, gaining the trust of non-believers. *"Allah is free from obligation to the idolaters."* (Koran 9:3). *"Go forth, light-armed and heavy-armed, and strive with your wealth and your lives in the way of Allah."* (Koran 9:41). *"Those who disbelieve (in Allah)...will not be raised again."* (Koran 64:7). Local Quraysh pagans are forcibly converted to Islam as the Muslim call to prayer is heard in Mecca. *"Save those who repent before you overpower them."* (Koran 5:34). The ***Ka'aba*** is now in Mohammed's hands, claiming the 'black stone' originates from the Garden of Eden, given by Allah to Adam, is brought to Mecca by the angel Gabriel.*"Adam, Dwell...in the Garden and eat freely."* (Koran 2:35).

Originally the meteoric black stone is thought to be larger than its present size 30 centimeters high. Today the *Ka'aba* is covered by glass, enclosed in a large tent made from silk 13x10x15 meters, called *kiswah*. A sacred mosque (*al-Masjud al-Haram*) is constructed over the *ka'aba*. Entry by non-Muslims into the *ka'aba* area is strictly forbidden. Muslims claim Abraham (Ibrahim in the Koran) blessed this stone, making pilgrimage the **haj,** with animal sacrifice obligatory for all Muslims. "*Perform the pilgrimage and visit (Mecca) for Allah...keep your duty to Me.*" (Koran 2:196,197). "*We made the House (at Mecca) a resort for mankind and a sanctuary (saying): Take as your place of worship the place where Abraham stood (to pray)". "domestic animals...to be brought as an offering to the Ka'aba.*" (Koran 5:95).

630   The defeat of the Quraysh and other pagan tribes in Arabia gives Mohammed and his followers increased prestige and honor among the various illiterate tribes who quickly convert to Islam. They join forces to capture all the small, non-unified, independent tribes living in Arabia bringing all this area under Muslim control by 632.

632   Mohammed makes a final pilgrimage to Jabel (Mt.) Arafat outside Mecca. Muhammad receives revelations, the Ayah ('Word of Allah'), which comprise the Koran, the basis of the religion. The Muslim prophet Mohammed dies suddenly in Medina on 8 June 632 without leaving a successor, or a spiritual leader.

Mohammed's tomb in Medina is named *Jama'a al-Nab (*Tomb of the Prophet). **Mecca, where Mohammed is born, is the holiest place for Islam. Medina, where Mohammed dies, is the second holiest site.** Two mosques are located near Ji'irrana, a village located between Mecca and Ta'af in Arabia. One is the al-Masjid al-Adna, (the closer mosque) and the other al-Masjid al-Aqsa, (the farther mosque, mentioned only once in the Koran). Prophet Muhammad's night-time journey from the 'holy mosque' of Mecca to al-Aqsa, is referring to the mosque in Ji'irrana.

632   **Abu Bakr,** (caliph 632–634) who assisted Mohammed to conquer Mecca, is the 1st Caliph of the four Rashidun Caliphs or successor. He is the spiritual and political leader of all followers of Islam representing the Muslim prophet, Mohammed. Mohammed's son-in-law, Ali Ibn Abi-Talib initially objects to Abu Bakr's appointment, conceding in the name of Muslim unity.

The Rashidun Caliphate 632 - 661
- Based in Mecca
- Rashidun means the righteous, guided ones
- Capture: Arabia, Palestine, Alexandria, Damascus

- Defeat Byzantines in Palestine in 636, capture Jerusalem in 638
- Nabatean traders convert to Islam
- Koran written and finalized in 651 (after Mohammed's death)
- Only one of the four 'Rashidun' caliphs dies naturally

633　Patriarch Bishop Sophronius bans Jews from Jerusalem.

634　Rivalry for the position of Caliph or successor continues as Abu Bakr eradicates his opposition. He dies in 634. 'Umar ibn Hata'ab (another reputed father-in-law of Mohammed), the 2nd Rashidun Caliph (634–644), moves his forces northwards to conquer Palestine, Jerusalem, Damascus, westwards to Alexandria and Libya and eastwards into Mesopotamia. The first battle in The Holy Land (Palestine) takes place at Dathin (near Ramle) with victory against the Byzantines. 'Umar receives help from Khaled Abu al-Walid of Mesopotamia, whose forces arrive after only 18 days of travel. Following this battle Muslims continue their conquest by capturing Gaza, Rafiah, Samaria, Nablus, Lod, Yavne, Jaffa, and Beit Guvrin, with the exception of Jerusalem and Caesarea, the present Byzantine capital in Palestine.

635　Muslim forces capture Damascus.

636　After 12,000 Christians change sides, Muslims defeat the **Byzantines** at the Battle of Ijnadein at Tell al-Jamua near the Yarmuk River in southern Golan. Christian forces withdraw from Palestine and Syria but continue to hold Caesarea and Jerusalem.

637　'Umar is victorious against the Persians at Kadesia (Kadisiya), in the lower Euphrates River.

638　After a two-year siege, 'Umar ibn Hata'ab captures Byzantine **Jerusalem**, Muslims call *'medinat beit hamidrash'* (place of the temple). All non-Muslims are forced to wear recognizable clothing, and their ownership of a horse is forbidden. The defeated non-Muslim inhabitants are forced to pay a 'head-tax' *jizya* for their freedom from slavery. Initially Muslims ban Jews and Christians from living in Jerusalem, later allowed to resettle. Christians are permitted freedom of worship and right of passage to leave for Byzantine territory. All Christian Holy Sites remain controlled by the Christian Authorities. Caliph 'Umar ibn Hata'ab constructs a wooden mosque on Harem esh-Sharif (Temple Mount) on the Mount Moriah, in Jerusalem.

640　Forces of Islam overrun the wealthy Christian **Nabatean** towns in Palestine (Nitzana, Shivta, Mamshit, Avdat, Rehovot, Halutza) and Transjordan (Petra) forcing their inhabitants convert to Islam, severing cultural ties with the Christian world. The Negev is disconnected from its previous trade centers, reducing the demand for commodities transported (frankincense, myrrh, wine) along the Spice Route used in Christian ceremonial practices. Nabateans abandon their towns in a dusty, dry climate. The sharp decline in trade and population causes the irrigation systems and dams to be in a state of disrepair. The Nabateans completely disappear between 640 and 800 becoming desert nomads grazing their flocks of goats and sheep. Their towns are not destroyed, to be found partly intact by archaeologists in the 19th century. In the 12th century, King Baldwin I constructs a fortress outside the ancient site of Petra, lost until in 1812, when Johann Burchardt, a Swiss explorer, by chance stumbles on the town.

Summary of Muslim influence

1. Starting from Arabia, Muslims conquer territory along the North African coast to Spain in the west; to Chinese border in the east; to Hungary, Ukraine in the north; to Zanzibar in the south.
2. Language - Arabic, also used in prayers, replaces Greek.
3. Science - Muslims apply the sciences brought from Greece to the east in the fields of philosophy, sciences, mathematics, medicine, and astronomy. Europe remains in the Dark Ages.
4. Culture - The Muslims incorporate the Greek/Hellenic culture.
5. Muslims forcibly attempt to convert heathens, pagans, Christians and Jews.
6. Palestine stagnates during this period, is not developed economically or culturally.
7. In Palestine, Byzantine Regional capitals are changed:

	Byzantine	Muslims
Center	Caesarea	Lod, Ramle
North	Beit She'an (Scythopolis)	Tiberias (Tamarin)
East	Petra	Philadelphia (Amman)

Note: Jerusalem has no administrative position.

641   Muslim forces, after a four-year siege capture Caesarea, the Byzantine capital of the Palestine, by creeping through a secret passage in the south-east. Ashkelon, a Byzantine Mediterranean Sea port falls. **All Byzantine presence in Palestine ends.**

642   Muslim forces capture Alexandria in 639 and all Egypt in 642. Previously during the Byzantine Period, Christian Copts are the majority of the population. The Arab general who captures Alexandria reports it contains 40,000 tax-paying Jews.

644   Mu'awiya ibn Safian of the Umayyad tribe, governor of the Damascus (640-660), admiral of the Muslim fleet in the Mediterranean Sea, sends a slave to assassinate the Rashidun Caliph 'Umar ibn Hata'ab while he is praying. 'Uthman ibn Affan 3rd

Rashidun Caliph (644–656) of the Umayyad tribe, a son-in-law of Mohammed, rivals Ali ibn Abi-Talib.

Goats in the Negev   Adrian Wolff

651   **Writing of the Koran.** Followers of Mohammed compose his sayings and record them in writing as the Muslim Holy Book, the **Koran** with 114 chapters (sura) and verses (aya'a). The Koran is not written in chronological order, but by size of chapter (*sura*) in descending order according to the number of verses, except for the first chapter, the *Shahadah*. The final version of the Koran is completed in 651 and no new additions are accepted. The Mecca Koran, comprising 92 chapters or *sura,* covers Mohammed's period in Mecca from 610 until 622. The Medina Koran, comprising 22 chapters or *sura,* covers Mohammed's period in Medina from 622 until 632. Adam, the first man, is revered as a prophet.

Muslim Customs and Belief - The Five Pillars of Islam

1. **'*Shahadah*'. Faith.** The cornerstone of Islamic **faith** is the *shahadah* expressing love and fear, together with the Unity and Oneness of Allah (God). Mohammed is the last prophet and messenger of Allah. "*I swear there is no God but Allah and Mohammed is his messenger (prophet).*" The Islamic creed.

2. **'*Salat*'. Prayer.** A Muslim must **pray** every day. Sunnis pray 5 times, Shi'ites 3 times daily. "*Establish worship...and bow your heads with those who bow.*" (Koran 2:43). "*When the call is heard for prayer of the day...haste unto remembering Allah and leave your trading.*" (Koran 62:9). Muslims are assisted in their prayers by counting the verses of the Koran using beads, or *masbaha,* to bless Allah. The *masbaha* is divided into 3 groups of 33 beads, representing the 99 blessings of Allah.

3. **'*Ramadan*'. Fasting.** Muslims mark the Revelation of the Prophesy of Mohammed by partaking in compulsory daytime

fast during the entire month of Ramadan. *"Fasting is prescribed for you...(during) the month of Ramadan."* (Koran 2:183,184,185). Submit to this discipline and deprivation.

4. *'Haj'.* All Muslims are expected to make a **pilgrimage** (*haj*) to Mecca at least once during their lifetime. *"Perform the pilgrimage and visit Mecca for Allah...keep your duty to Me."* (Koran 2:196,197).

5. *'Zakat'.* **Charity.** All Muslims are expected to make **charitable** donations (2.5%) to other Muslims. These donations are usually not directed towards non-Muslims or to non-Muslim organizations or causes. *"...pay the poor-due."* (Koran 2:43).

Customs of Islam

1. Muslims pray facing Mecca. Friday is their Holy Day of the week. The preacher (*Imam*) gives a sermon (*kutba*).
2. The Koran makes no reference to male or female circumcision.
3. Eating of pork is prohibited. Ritual *(halal)* slaughter of meat.
4. Drinking of alcohol is forbidden.
5. Covering of head and or face of women in public.
6. Simple grave, body on its right side, head towards Mecca.

Haj to Mecca

1. A Muslim upon his pilgrimage the *haj* to Mecca,s has to dress in two layers of seamless white cloth, bare their right shoulder and cover their head, similar to the dress code during the 8th century
2. Only men may enter the *Ka'aba*, (160 by 100 meters). Women are forbidden. If they venture into Mecca they must cover all their body as no naked flesh may be exposed.
3. Non-Muslims are not permitted to enter the *Ka'aba*.
4. Muslims circle the *Ka'aba* seven times anti-clockwise, attempt to touch and kiss the 'black stone' (today has a glass protection). Then through a corridor beside the *Ka'aba*, where according to Muslim tradition, Ibrahim's wife searched for water finding the *Zamzum* well. It is customary to drink from this well.
5. The night between the 7/8th of the month of Ramadan, pilgrims walk to Jabel (=Mt.) Arafat to hear a sermon and pray to Allah.
6. On the night of the 10/11th of Ramadan is the festival *id al-Adha*, symbolizing the sacrifice of Ishmael. Ibrahim (Abraham) is told to sacrifice Ishmael and not Isaac. *"Make mention...of Ishmael. Lo! He was the keeper of his promise, and the messenger (of Allah), a prophet."* (Koran 19:54).
7. At Maladefa pilgrims collect stones in divisions of seven, hurling them at three pillars at Mina, which represent the devil, Satan.
8. The pilgrim returns to Mecca and repeats the circular walk around the *Ka'aba,* and along the corridor to the *Zamzum* well.

9. The pilgrim then travels to Medina, the second most holy site for Muslims, to visit Mohammed's grave.

10. On the last night of the month of Ramadan, on the 29th or 30th (depending on the full moon), all Muslims partake in the feast *id al-Fattir*, lasting three days to commemorate the ending of the month of fasting during Ramadan.

Jews in the Koran

Muslims who are familiar with the Bible and New Testament write portions of the Koran. Tales describe Adam, Noah, Abraham (Ibrahim), the Sacrifice of Isaac (claim Ishmael is sacrificed), Jacob (Ya'akub) and the Exodus of the Children of Israel led by Moses (Musa) regarded by Muslims to be a prophet. **Jerusalem is not mentioned in the Koran, neither by the Arabic word al-Kuds nor by the Hebrew word *Yerushala'im* or by names given by various peoples at the time.**

1. **The Covenant made by God to the Children of Israel**
   Koran chapter (sura) 5, verse (aya'a) 20, 'The Table'. *"Allah (God) made a covenant with the Children of Israel and when Moses said to his people 'Oh my people, remember Allah's (God's) favor to you how he placed among you prophets and he made you kings and he gave you what he has not given to any other creature" (The Ten Commandments)."*

2. **The Land of Israel is given by God to the Children of Israel**
   Koran 5:21, 'The Table'. God (Allah) tells Moses *"Go into the Land (Eretz Israel) which Allah (God) has assigned for you."*

3. **Gathering of the exiles (Jews) in the Land of Israel**
   Koran 17:104, The Night Journey (Children of Israel). *"We said to the Children of Israel, dwell in the land, but when the promise of the hereafter comes, we shall bring you together gathered out of various nations".*

4. **The Bible is given to the Children of Israel**
   Koran 29: 27, The Spider. *"We gave him Isaac, and Jacob, and we established on his descendants the priesthood and the scriptures (Bible) among his seed (Children of Israel)."*

5. **Belief in Biblical Commandments**
   Koran 46:12 The Wind Carved Sand-hills, al-Ahkaf. *"there was the Scripture of Moses an example and mercy, and this is a confirming Scripture in the Arabic language, that it may warn those who do wrong and bring good tidings for the righteous."*

6. **Persecution of Jews.** (Koran 4:160). *"Because of the wrongdoing of the Jews, we forbade them good things...because of their much hindering from Allah's way".*

Christianity in the Koran. Jesus is viewed as a 'prophet', not Messiah. *"They slew him not nor crucified"* (Koran 4:157).

"Christians say: The Messiah is the son of Allah...Allah fighteth against them. How perverse they are". (Koran 9:30). Names found in the Koran - Gabriel, Amram (Abraham), Maryam, Zecharia (father of John), Yohanan (Hanna, Yehia).

651   **Prophets in Islam.** Muslims regard both Moses and Jesus as prophets, with Mohammed the very last. Various sects have grown from Islam - Druze, Alawites, Bahai'is and Ahmeds, all believe their particular leaders to be the last prophet. These sects are excommunicated from mainstream Islam.

651   Non-Muslims *'dhimmi'* are allowed to reside under Muslim rule, forced to pay a compulsory head and property tax, the *'jizya'.* *"Fight against those who have been given the Scripture as believe not in Allah (Jews) nor the Last Day (Christians)...follow not the religion of truth until **they pay the tribute** (jizya)."* (Koran 9:29).

655   Muslims led by Admiral Mu'awiya ibn-Safain defeat the Byzantine fleet off the Alexandria coast at the Battle of the Masts (*Dahat al-Suwari*), halting their attempt to regain a foothold in Egypt.

Painted entrance of home awaiting Haj participant, Jerusalem. Adrian Wolff

656   Caliph 'Uthman ibn Affan is assassinated by followers of Mohammed's son-in-law Ali ibn Abi-Talib, who becomes the 4th Rashidun Caliph (656–661). Unity within the *ummah* (Muslim empire) collapses, never to be re-established as civil war begins. Muslims are split into 3 divisions - **Sunni, Shi'ite (Shi'a), Khariji**, each sect divided on their opinion to appoint a ruler of all Muslims.

Muslim Sects
1. Sunni Muslims
   1. Originate from Mohammed's tribe the Quraysh in Mecca, forced converts to Islam.

2. The majority of Muslims are Sunni Muslims.
3. Stress model behavior and guidance. *Sunna* are words and deeds of Mohammed.
4. Collection of *hadiths* written by the Prophet Mohammed.
5. Establish schools - Hanafis, Malikis, Shafis, Hanbalis.
6. A council in Cairo presently controls Sunni Muslims.
7. Fundamentalists - Muslim Brotherhood, Hamas, Taliban, al-Qaeda, Boko Haram, Jamiat al-Islami, Islamic Jihad Union.

2. Shi'ite Muslims = Shi'a Ali

1. About 10% of all Muslims are Shi'ite Muslims.
2. The name Shi'ite is derived from *Shiat Ali*, after Ali ibn Abi Talib, son-in-law of Mohammed, designated his blood-line successor.
3. Shi'ite Muslims regard their form of Islam as the pure representation of Mohammed's original thoughts.
4. Shi'ites practice public weeping and self-flagellation on the anniversary of the assassination of Ali ibn Abi-Talib.
5. Divided into sub-sects - Druze, Imanis, Ismailis, Bahai'i, Nizaris, Assassins *(Hashishia)*, Zaidis, Allawites.
6. Council in Iran.
7. Fundamentalists - Muhudejadin, Taliban, Hezbollah, Islamic Jihad, Islamic State, Salafists, Ansar, Quds Force.
8. Legally allowed to marry a girl aged 9 or 11 years old, depending on country.
9. The religious rulers command the political arena.

3. Holy Places for Shi'ite Muslims

Shi'ite Muslims pilgrimage sites at al-Najaf and Karbala in Iraq where Ali Ibn Abi-Talib, and Hussein his grandson, are assassinated by Sunni Muslims. Qum and Mashed in Persia.

4. Differences between Sunni and Shi'ite Muslims

1. **Islamic Law.** Shi'ites believe the sayings of the Imams are a source of divine inspiration and the '*hadiths*' can only be deemed valid if transmitted by Imams.
2. **Jurisprudence and unprecedented legal cases.** Shi'ite Imams use deductive reasoning (*aql*) rather than analogy (*qiyas*). Imams in both sects, enjoy freedom in legal opinion.
3. **Authority.** Sunnis reject the concept giving Shi'ite Imams absolute power and possess complete knowledge.
4. **Ritual.** Sunni Muslims pray 5 times a day, Shi'ite 3 times a day, partake in minor pilgrimages to tombs of the 12 Imams. Shi'ites mourn the slaying of Ali ibn Abi-Talib and his son Hussein.

656 Khariji in Mesopotamia believe in piety and are sincere to the Islamic cause. Rule of Islam is firstly religious and the head of the Muslims does not have to be either a member of Mohammed's

family (Shi'ite) or a member of the converted Quraysh (Sunni). The Khariji Muslim sect believe only Allah can decide man's destiny and Muslims must strictly follow the Islamic code, therefore rejecting all other Muslim sects. The Khariji maintain only through a *jihad* or holy war can they control the territory they conquer, convert non-Muslims to Islam, and are entitled to kill any infidel or non-believer (*kaffr*) who refuses Islam. The Khariji Muslim sect establishes Religious Courts.

Map 16. The Islamic Empire 7ᵗʰ century

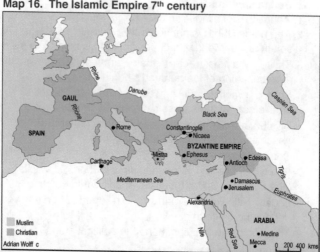

> **Khaiji** (also khawarij)
> 1. Reject the validity of Ali ibn Abi-Talib, son-in-law of Mohammed as the hereditary leader of Muslims and oppose his successor the Umayyad Caliph Mu'awiya ibn-Sufian. Any Muslim, not necessarily a descent from Quraysh or Ali may become the leader (caliph) of the Muslim community.
> 2. Believe only Allah decides, not man, and therefore reject other Muslim sects.
> 3. Believe in the Sixth Pillar of Islam - the *jihad* or holy war, to control territory they conquer, convert all non-Muslims to Islam, and kill any infidel (kaffr) refusing Islam.
> 4. Only accept literal interpretation of Koran.
> 5. Fundamentalists beliefs.
> 6. Khaiji puritanism and idealism finds followers in Iran and Arabia.

661   Severe **earthquake** in Palestine causes extensive damage to many buildings including churches and synagogues in Jerusalem, Jericho, the Jordan Valley and other centers.

Chapter 12. The Early Arab Period 661 - 1094

661   At the **Battle of Kufah** on the Euphrates River, Mu'awiya ibn Safain executes his cousin Caliph **Ali ibn Abi-Talib**, son-in-law of Mohammed, the last Rashidun caliph. A split in Islam between bloodline (**Shi'ite**) and non-bloodline (**Sunni**) sects for control of Muslim leadership. The tomb of Caliph Ali ibn Abi-Tallin, the Shi'ite founder, at al-Najaf in Iraq is a Shi'ite Muslim pilgrimage site, the second holiest city to Shi'ites, after Mecca .

Mu'awiya I, the 1st Umayyad Caliph (661–680), transfers the center of Islam to Damascus to rival the caliph in Mecca, begins construction of The Dome of the Rock.

Umayyad Caliphate 661–750, continues in Spain 756–1031.
- Umayyads are descendants of Umayya ibn Abed Shams, from the Quraysh tribe.
- Umayyads are **Sunni** Muslims, have a white banner.
- The Umayyad capital in Damascus rivals the Mecca caliph.
- Umayyads collect taxes from non-Muslims, the *jizya*.
- The Umayyad Empire expands from Persia to Spain.
- 90% of all Jews live in Muslim lands - Persia and Mesopotamia.
- Umayyads have no administrative experience. Use Christian and Jewish advisors.
- Arabic language is used for prayer and administrative purposes.
- Muslim coinage, the gold dinar is introduced.
- Umayyads build the first Arab town in Palestine, Ramle on the via Maris. Restore coastal towns and rebuild roads.
- On the Temple Mount in Jerusalem, Umayyads construct the Dome of the Rock and the first al-Aqsa mosque.
- *Dhimmis* may not ride a horse, employ a Muslim, carry a weapon, build new places of worship, inherit from a Muslim. Must wear special clothing.
- Abbasids annihilate the Umayyad Caliphate in 750, who remain in Spain until the end of their dynasty in Cordoba in 1031.

673   Muslim forces fail to capture the Byzantine capital, Constantinople.

7thc   90% of all Jews live in Muslim lands in Mesopotamia and Persia.

680   Yazid ibn Mu'awiya assassinates his father, 2nd Umayyad Caliph.

680   During the **Battle of Karbala** (near ancient Babylon), Sunni Umayyad supporters ambush and kill Hussein (Husayn) (629-680), grandson of Mohammed, younger son of Ali ibn Abi-Talib,

(Mohammed's son-in-law), for refusing to pledge allegiance to Caliph Yazid I. Hussein's tomb in Karbala is a pilgrimage site for Muslim Shi'ites. The lineage from Mohammed comes to an end. This causes an irreconcilable split between Shi'ite and Sunnis over the rights to the inheritance of Muslim leadership. Changes in Muslim leadership sometimes occurs violently.

Umayyad Bridge, Yavne   Adrian Wolff

680   Ali's elder son Hassan (Hasan) (625-680), previously renounces his claim to the caliphate, lives in Medina.

682   Abdullah Ibn al-Zubayr of Hejaz and Mesopotamia rebels against Caliph Yazid ibn Mu'awiya of Damascus, disallowing Umayyads Sunnis to fulfill the Haj in Mecca and Medina, one of the five basic Islamic commandments. In order to justify choosing Jerusalem as their alternative pilgrimage site, the Umayyads move the concept of the al-Aqsa mosque from near Ji'irrana in Arabia to Jerusalem, adding the legend of the night time journey of Mohammed. (See 632, 691). Sunnis now consider Jerusalem their third holiest city.

683   Mu'awiya II ibn Yazid, 3rd Umayyad Caliph (683-684). Anarchy and violence between Shi'ite and Sunni Muslims continues.

684   Marwayn ibn al-Haham, 4th Umayyad Caliph (684–685), continuing anarchy. Umayyad Muslim pilgrims make a perilous journey to the ka'aba in Mecca, in an area ruled by another Muslim leader.

685   Abed al-Malik ibn Marwayn. 5th Umayyad Caliph (685–705), unifies the Umayyad Empire, ending internal revolts. Muslim coins, the gold dinar are issued. Arabic is the official language, used for administrative purposes.

691   The Dome of the Rock (Qubbet el-Sakhra) in Jerusalem is the third holiest site to Islam after Mecca and Medina. **Jerusalem is not mentioned anywhere in the Koran and in addition the Koran does not specifically say Mohammed ever visited Palestine.**

Consequences of the rivalry between counter-Caliph Abdullah ibn al-Zubayr in Mecca and the Umayyad Caliph in Damascus **Abed al-Malik** result in Muslim Holy Sites in Arabia not being within Umayyad (Sunni) territory. Abed al-Malik needs an alternative pilgrimage site enticing pilgrims to visit Jerusalem within his territory, rather than make the dangerous journey to Mecca and Medina controlled by a rival caliph. Some 60 years after Mohammed dies in Medina, a Muslim legend claims Mohammed 'ascends to heaven' from Jerusalem on his horse al-Burak as his horse's hoof touches this rock on Mt Moriah before going to heaven during his mysterious night journey. al-Buraka an Aramaic word, from Babylonian Talmud circa 500CE describing the Jewish Messiah will arrive on a donkey (Zechariah 9:9). Muslims identify this quotation *"Glorified be He Who carried His servant by night from the Inviolable Place of Worship to the Far Distant Place of Worship"* (Koran 17:1).

The Dome of the Rock, Jerusalem   Adrian Wolff

The 5th Umayyad caliph Abed al-Malik ibn Marwayn residing in Damascus, orders the construction 688-691 of a shrine in Jerusalem, the **Dome of the Rock (Qubbet el-Sakhra)** directly over the same 'rock' on Mt. Moriah where Jewish Patriarch Abraham prepares to sacrifice his son Isaac. Also directly over the Foundation Stone of the Jewish Holy Temple constructed by King Solomon in 952 BCE, 1700 years earlier. Abed al-Malik wishes to counterbalance the Christian Holy Site in Jerusalem, the Church of the Holy Sepulchre and creates a Muslim holy site in the city.

During the Byzantine period, the Temple Mount is used as a garbage dump, symbolizing Christianity's victory over Judaism.

Muslims call the Temple Mount 'Haram al-Sharif', the Place of Respect. The architecture of the Dome of the Rock is octagonal, similar to the original Church of the Holy Sepulchre, displaying typical Byzantine architecture with Persian and Syrian influences. The Dome of the Rock is the oldest Muslim structure (shrine) still standing in its original form. The Crusader Templar Knights Order convert the Dome of the Rock into a church 'Templum Domini' (God's Temple), cover the 'rock' with marble and build an altar. After conquering Jerusalem in 1187, Salah a-Din restores it as a Muslim site. The original dome built by al-Malik is of bronze. Later Arabs require the metal for weapons and replace the dome with lead sheets. The Dome collapses during the earthquake of 1016, restored in 1022, damaged again by an earthquake in 1033. In 1958 King Hussein of Jordan finances the renovation of the dome with gilded aluminum sheets, completed in 1964. A new gilded bronze dome is built in 1994 after rainwater penetrates the plates. Muslims pray on the Temple Mount southwards in the al-Aqsa Mosque, in the direction of Mecca, with their backs to The Dome of the Rock.

692   Counter-caliph Abdullah ibn al-Zubayr of Arabia dies. His empire falls under Sunni Umayyad Caliph Abed al-Malik of Damascus.

705   al-Walid ibn Abed Malik, 6th Umayyad Caliph in Damascus (705-715).

al-Walid ibn Abed Malik's influence

- The peak of the Umayyad Empire occurs during the his reign, rules from Kabul, Transoxia, Indus, North Africa to Spain.
- Builds many public and religious buildings and private palaces.
- Rebuilds a shrine over the ka'aba, the black stone in Mecca. Constructs the Tomb of Mohammed in Medina for pilgrims.
- Converts the Byzantine Church of St. John in Damascus into the Great Mosque.
- Constructs the **al-Aqsa Mosque** on the Temple Mount in Jerusalem to allow Muslim pilgrims visiting the Dome of the Rock an opportunity to pray inside a mosque.

710   Muslims convert Byzantine Church of St. John in Damascus into the Great Mosque.

711   al-Aqsa Mosque (Masjid al-Aqsa=the more distant/furthest). Umayyad Caliph al-Walid completes the al-Aqsa Mosque in Jerusalem allowing Muslim pilgrims visiting the Dome of the Rock a site to pray in a mosque on the Temple Mount. The al-Aqsa is the

oldest mosque in Israel. Only the southern wall remains from the original mosque. The mosque is destroyed by an earthquake in 749, rebuilt by 830. Finance for the restoration comes from the sale of the doors, which are stripped of their gold and silver decorations. During the Crusader period the al-Aqsa Mosque is converted into the Templar Knights Headquarters and transformed into a church, 'Templum Solomonis' (Solomon's Temple). In 1187 Salah a-Din restores the mosque. Earthquakes of 1927 and 1936 cause serious damage and extensive restoration takes place. Supporters of the Mufti, assassinate King Abdallah I of Transjordan at the entrance in 1951. A deranged Christian tourist damages the mosque by fire in 1969. Egyptian President Anwar Sadat prays here during his historic visit to Israel in 1977.

al-Aqsa Mosque, Jerusalem   Adrian Wolff

711   Jews are forced to live in ghettos called '*melah*' in Morocco, and called '*hara*' in Tunisia.

711   Jews living in Spain under Roman rule are merchants, craftsmen, artisans and farmers. Visigoth king, Reccared, a convert from Arianism to Christianity comes to power in Iberia in 586. Jews are now shunned, persecuted, deprived of rights to property and sometimes forcibly converted to Catholicism. Fearing extinction, the Iberian Jews provide intelligence information to the Moors thorough their co-religionists in North Africa.

711   Umayyad **Muslim forces** led by Tariq ibn Zayid (Berber) from North Africa **invade southern and central Spain,** defeating the Visigoths in Toledo in 714. Muslims will rule until their defeat by the

Christian '*Reconquista*' in 1492. Christian attitudes towards the Jews of Spain are not harmonious and subsequently the Jews welcome Muslim rule in Spain. The word 'Gibraltar' comes from Arabic Jabal (Mt.) Tarig. Cordova, the largest city west of Constantinople, becomes an intellectual center for philosophy and science. Modern mathematics and algebra is based on the Arabic system of notation.

716   In Palestine most Christians are town dwellers, Muslims are mainly basic farmers. West-East trade and commerce travels from Sinai along the 'Via Maris', a road parallel to the Mediterranean Sea to Damascus, Baghdad. Ramle the first Muslim town, capital of 'Jund Philistine' is constructed along the 'Via Maris' in the Coastal Plain.

716   Jewish lives are made difficult by both Muslims and Christians in Jerusalem, as Tiberias becomes a Jewish spiritual center,

717   'Umar II ibn Abel al-Aziz, 8th Umayyad Caliph (717–720). Muslim forces (717-718) unsuccessfully attempt to capture Constantinople.

720   Yazid II ibn Abel al-Malik, 9th Umayyad Caliph (720–724) during a period of sibling rivalry.

724   Hisham, brother of Yazid II, 10th Umayyad Caliph (724–743).

732   Zayd ibn Ali, father of nomadic Bedouin tribes in Arabia, dies.

Map 17. The Umayyad Empire early - mid 8th century

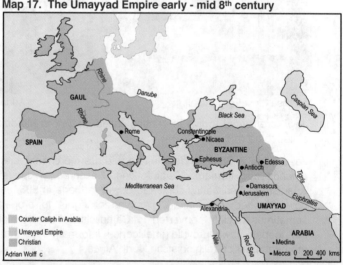

732   The **Battle of Tours (Poitiers) in Gaul**, Christian forces (Gauls) of Charles (Karl) Martel (688-741) halt Muslim invasion forces of Abd-ar-Rahman al-Ghafiqi of Cordoba. Christian troops approach

superior Muslim troops, unprepared for battle, choosing to defend their loot and war booty, subsequently defeated, ending Muslim incursion into Gaul. Umayyads remain in Spain and Portugal. "*The events that rescued our ancestors of Britain and our neighbors of Gaul from the civil and religious yoke of the Koran.*" Gibbon.

Mosaic Hisham's Palace, Jericho   National Parks Board

749   A severe earthquake causes serious destruction to many buildings in Palestine, including the Jordan Valley (Beit She'an) and Golan. Damage to the Dome of the Rock, the al-Aqsa Mosque and Church of the Holy Sepulchre in Jerusalem and buildings in Tiberias. The Caliph's winter palace, the Hisham's Palace in Jericho is destroyed.

Earthquake Damage, Beit She'an   Adrian Wolff

750   The 1st Abbasid Caliph Abu al-Abbas ibn Muhmad, defeats the Umayyad Caliph Ibrahim ibn al-Walid at the Battle of Abu Futrus (Petros) at Zab (Yarkon River). Establishes the Abbasid Caliphate from 750 until 1258. Abbasids quickly assassinate all members of the Umayyad leadership except Abd al-Rahman I who flees to Spain where the Umayyad dynasty is founded, continuing from 757 till 1031 in Cordoba (Cordova). Shi'ites and Kharijis are persecuted

Abbasid Caliphate 750 - 1258

- Abbasids, descendants of Abu al-Abbas, uncle of Mohammed.
- Abbasids assassinate all Umayyad leadership. Umayyads continue in Spain after 756, conquered in Cordoba in 1031.
- Abbasids are **Sunni** Muslim sect. Abbasids have a black banner
- Abbasid religious teachers are not bloodline successors of the Prophet Mohammed. Sunni authority on faith and practice.
- Abbasid Caliphate identifies with orthodox Muslim practices, failing to deliver social justice.
- New capital Baghdad in 762 along the Tigris River in Mesopotamia.
- Territories under Abbasid control become independent states.
- Teach math, arithmetic, geometry, algebra, astronomy, Persian numbers, zero. Astrolabe (Greek) determines hour of prayer.
- Road maps to Mecca.
- Music - guitar, lute.
- Economic and cultural stagnation in Palestine, not central to intellectual movements.
- Jerusalem is distant from the capital Baghdad, declines in importance, reduced size, smaller than during Byzantine Period.
- Ayyubids under Salah a-Din (1174-1193) unite with Abbasids.
- Mongols defeat Abbasids during their invasion.
- Many Greek and Latin texts are translated into Arabic.
- Jews are forced to wear a yellow badge.

762   al-Mansur ibn Muhmad establishes the new Abbasid capital in Baghdad on the Tigris River, near ancient Babylon. He rebuilds the al-Aqsa Mosque in Jerusalem damaged by the earthquake of 749.

786   Harun al-Rashid ibn al-Mahadi, brother of al-Ha'adi, 5th Abbasid Caliph (786–809). Abbasid power is at its zenith. Territorial control stretches from Mesopotamia to North Africa. The caliph creates independent vassal states in the frontier provinces. **Harun al-Rashid recognizes Charlemagne of Gaul as protector of all Christian Holy Sites in The Holy Land, in return, he pledges not to attack Muslim territory. This preference causes antagonism between the Eastern Orthodox Church in Constantinople and the Latin Catholic Church in Rome.**

Map 18. The Abbasid Empire 8th century

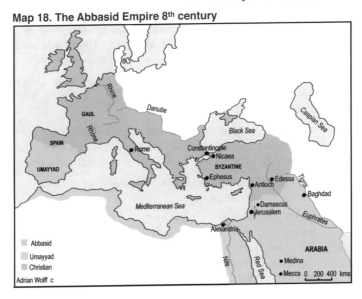

8th c   The **Karaite** Jewish sect is established in Babylon by Anan Ben David during the last decades of the 8th century. Karaites rigorously follow the Written Law (Tanach) rejecting the Oral Law of the sages and rabbis. Their customs include refraining from the use of phylacteries (tefilim), not celebrating the festival of Hanukah, forbidding intermarriage with a non-Karaite, and having their own religious courts. In the 13th and 14th centuries many Karaites immigrate to Crimea. During the 19th century the Karaites in Russia demand equal rights from the Tzar and several of their leading members claim their origins to be non-Jewish. This saves the community during the Nazi occupation and Karaites serve in the German Army. Community claims 40,000 Karaites live in Israel in the Ramle area, their headquarters at Moshav Mazliah.

789   Arched bridges are constructed over the Ayalon River at Ramle and the St. Helena water reservoir is built.

800   **The Holy Roman Empire.** Charlemagne/Karl der grosse, King of the Franks (France/Germany), grandson of Charles Martel (See 732) is crowned by Pope Leo III emperor on Christmas Day 800, rules until 814 uniting almost all Christian territory in Western Europe. He adds a word *'filioque'*- 'and the Son' to the Nicene Creed (See 325) giving Christ, the Son, the same importance as God, the Father. The unofficial beginning of the Holy Roman Empire, abolished by Napoleon in 1806. Crusaders use the term Sacrum Romanum Imperum.

813   al-Ma'amun ibn Harun, brother of al-Amin 7th Abbasid Caliph (813–833), a patron of learning establishes an Academy of Science. Scientific books are translated into Arabic. This period is marked by clashes between the caliph and various religious leaders.

831   The writings of sacred texts of the Muslim Holy Scripture, the Koran, are displayed on the walls of the Dome of the Rock in Jerusalem.

833   al-Mu'atzin bi-Allah ibn Harun, brother of al-Amin and al-Ma'amun, 8th Abbasid Caliph (833–842). Establishes a new elite guard for the caliph in Baghdad using Turkic slaves originating in Central Asia.

850   Babylonia Caliph al-Mutawakkil decrees *dhimmi* (Jews, Christians) wear a yellow badge.

878   Ahmed Abu-Tulon, 1st Fatimid Caliph in Egypt (878–905) usurps power from the Abbasids, annexes Palestine. The Tulonic Period in Palestine is noted for its social reform as farmers are allowed rights to their land and may purchase seeds. This denotes a change of agricultural policy as absentee landlords previously perpetuated a stagnant social and economic situation. Jews and Christians are persecuted, *dhimmi* laws enforced.

878   The port of Acre is reconstructed.

900   Beginning of the Hundred Years War between the Jewish convert king of the **Khazars** living in the Volga valley up to the Caspian Sea (Crimea) and the local pagan population, as mentioned by Yehuda Ha'levi and Chisdai Ibn Shaprut in 960. (See Adler). Shaprut, living in Spain, writes a letter inquiring whether the rumors of a Jewish Khazar Empire are accurate. The Khazar king, Yosef replies affirmatively. He describes the Khazar conversions to Judaism, names of Jewish kings, trade with the Arabs and battles with the Russians. Copies of these letters are found in the Cairo Genizah. Khazars are eventually defeated with the establishment of Islamic (Mongol) power in southern Russia (late 10th century).

905   Abbasids retake Palestine, killing Fatimid Ahmed Abu-Tulon.

909   Fatimids, founded by Ubayad Allah caliph of Tunisia, North Africa.

Fatimid Caliphate 909 - 1171
- Fatimids, **Shi'ite** Muslims (Ismailis) followers Ali ibn Abi-Talib and Mohammed's daughter, Fatima reject the Abbasids (Sunni) ruler in Baghdad as the leaders of the Muslim World.
- Fatimids, independent Muslim sect, rule from Egypt until 1171.
- Fatimid capital in Cairo founded 969, its influence is localized in North Africa, Palestine and Arabia.

- Fatimids persecute Sunni Muslims for not keeping Shi'ite customs.
- This period is characterized by fighting between Fatimids (Egypt), Abbasids (Baghdad), and Bedouin nomads.
- During the Fatimid Period non-Muslims (Jews and Christians) are forced to pay heavy taxes to the Muslim authorities while some are compelled to convert to Islam.
- Many churches and synagogues are destroyed, especially in Egypt 1011-1012.
- Persecution of Coptic Christians, previously the majority in Egypt.
- The theological university al-Ahzar in Cairo is founded.
- Salah a-Din and Ayyubids replace the Fatimids in 1171.
- Construct ports at Ashdod, Jaffa, Acre.

920 **Sa'adya Gaon** (ben Joseph 882-942) heads of the rabbinical academy in Sura (near Baghdad), translates into Arabic the Tanach together with its commentaries. He also writes on Hebrew grammar and philosophy in "Book of Beliefs and Opinions".

10th c During the 10th century many wealthy Jews flee the wars in Mesopotamia for Egypt, North Africa, and Aden. Jewish merchants trade in spices, medicinal herbs, dying materials, and iron.

938 Muslim residents of Jerusalem attack and burn the Church of the Holy Sepulchre. Christians constitute the majority in Jerusalem.

Map 19. The Fatimid Empire 11th century

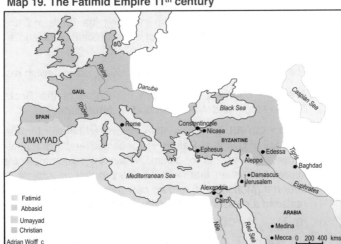

969 The 4th Fatimid Caliph al-Mu'izz conquers Egypt and constructs his new capital in Cairo. The Fatimids defeat all rivals.

976 Fatimids defeat the Abbasids in Palestine, murder the Christian Patriarch, burn the Church of the Holy Sepulchre and others.

996 **al-Hakim** ibn Amri, 6th Fatimid Caliph (996–1021). His persecution:
  • He also calls himself Imam.
  • Christians are banned from drinking wine.
  • Jews and Christians are persecuted, forced to wear distinguishing clothes such as a yellow cloth and a necklace.
  • Sunnis are persecuted, cursed and isolated by Fatimids for not keeping Shi'ite religious rules. Marked by religious intolerance.
  • Many synagogues and churches are destroyed.
  • Forced conversion of Jews and Christians to Islam.

1004 Fatimid Caliph al-Hakim attempts to become independent of some traditional Muslim traditions by forbidding Muslims under his control from making the haj to Mecca.

11thc Climatic changes in the Northern Hemisphere (950-1070). Cold conditions in Mesopotamia and Central Asia, drought in the Mid East, reduced flow of Nile River. Severe agricultural damage in North Africa.

1008 Christians Knights begin the '*Reconquista*' to regain all lands held by Muslims in Spain and Portugal. The area of Asturias in northern Spain fall to Christians in 1037. Increasing Jewish cultural activity in Spain, especially in the Cordova region.

1009 Caliph al-Hakim, launches a campaign of anti-Christian persecution in Palestine, destroys the reconstructed Church of the Holy Sepulchre in Jerusalem including the Tomb of Christ. Jews are forced to wear an amulet of a golden calf, bells, and a wooden block around their necks.

1012 The Jewish Quarter of Cairo is destroyed, killing Jewish residents.

1016 A severe earthquake damages the Dome of the Rock on the Temple Mount and Walls surrounding Jerusalem.

1016 **Hamza ibn Ali**, preaches Allah incarnated himself for last time in the body of Caliph **al-Hakim**. He becomes leader of a new religion, **Druze,** an offshoot of Islam. They are excommunicated from mainstream Islam that believes *"no prophet or apostle will come after me (Mohammed) and no new religion will be born." "Allah will not send a messenger after Him."* (Koran 40:34).

Druze
  ▪ Originally Fatimid Shi'ite Muslims in Cairo 1017 by Hamza ibn Ali ibn Ahmad who believes Allah incarnated himself the last and final time in al-Hakim ibn Amri Allah, the 6th Fatimid sultan.

- al-Hakim vanishes in the Egyptian desert in 1021.
- Name derived from Muhammad al-Darazi, a follower of al-Hakim, killed in 1019.
- Believe in Allah whose qualities cannot be understood or defined.
- Do not proselytize. A non-Druze cannot convert.
- Believe in transmigration of souls, reincarnation. When a Druze dies his soul will be incarnated in another Druze who is born - a male in a male, a female in a female.
- Druze do not believe in 'The Creation'. The world is created instantaneously, therefore no special day of the week that is 'different' or defined as a day of rest.
- Protect their religion and conceal its secret teachings, the *hikmah*.
- Druze are divided into two groups.
  - Religious sages, the *uqqal* follow Druze religious doctrines and keep Druze religious books containing the religious and philosophical expressions.
  - Non-religious *juhhal* Druze are ignorant of the *hikmah*, nor do they own a copy of their religious teachings.
- **Druze practice:**
  - Druze do not pray in mosques, meet in inconspicuous building called *hilweh*, usually on the village outskirts. They pray every Thursday evening, men and women sit in separate sections.
  - Final Day of Judgment will be in Egypt where the Druze religion began. Until such time, no religious Druze may travel to Egypt and their religious books will open to non-religious.
  - Religious Druze wear distinct clothing (*a'arkol*). Men wear baggy trousers and a white headscarf. Women cover their legs, arms and head with a white cloth (*nakab*).
  - No mixed marriages with non-Druze. If so, forced to leave.
  - Strict monogamy.
  - Divorce is permitted but may not remarry their former spouses.
  - Abstinence from alcohol, sexual modesty, non-smoking, and pork.
  - Burial on same day of death. No tombstones are erected since the soul is incarnated into another person.
  - Do not practice Ramadan fasting and the feast (id al-Fitr).
  - Druze have a religious duty to assist other Druze.
- Druze do not have nationalistic aspirations and are very loyal to the leaders of the country in which they reside.
- 1.5 million Druze reside in Southern Lebanon; Golan plateau in Syria and Israel; in the Galilee and Carmel in northern Israel.

- In 1860 Druze are in conflict with Maronite Christians in Lebanon cause French intervention forcing Druze to flee to Syria and the Galilee.
- Druze flag has five horizontal colors representing:
  green (earth), red (fire), yellow (sun), blue (water), white (spirit).
- Non-religious (80%) Druze males are conscripted into the IDF.

1017   Muhammed al-Darazi, formally a Shi'ite missionary, converts to, and preaches the new **Druze** religion that identifies with his name.

1019   The original preacher and missionary of the Druze, Muhammed al-Darazi, is killed in Lebanon, a Shi'ite populated area.

1021   al-Hakim vanishes in the Egyptian desert, apparently murdered. Many legends result from his disappearance. His followers believe he will reappear after one thousand years. Hamza ibn Ali continues preaching and writing of the sacred texts of the Druze religion.

1030   The 7th Fatimid Caliph al-Tahir (1021-1035) orders the rebuilding of the Walls of Jerusalem damaged in the earthquake in 1016.

1031   Umayyad Caliphate ends in Spain. Muslims remain in southern Spain and Portugal.

1033   Another severe earthquake in Palestine causes damage to the al-Aqsa Mosque, the Church of the Holy Sepulchre and other buildings, including damage to the recently repaired Jerusalem walls. Ramle and the coastal towns are also damaged.

1034   Fatimid caliph al-Tahir rebuilds the al-Aqsa Mosque and other sites damaged by the earthquake. Christian and Jewish pilgrims experience difficulties due to a lack of economic growth as Jerusalem's population and physical area decreases to less than during the Roman Period.

1035   Fatimid Caliph al-Dahrib (1035–1048) continues rebuilding the damaged walls of Jerusalem. Many buildings outside the walls remain destroyed from an earthquake.

1038   Peace Treaty between Fatimid Caliph al-Dahrib and Byzantine Emperor Basil II. Christians pilgrims may visit The Holy Land.

1039   Construction of the 'Monastery of the Holy Cross' in the Valley of the Cross where, according to Christian tradition and Queen (Saint) Helena, the original tree used for the Holy Cross, grew. The Monastery, built away from the walls of Jerusalem, is isolated, has thick defensive walls.

1040   Seljuks originating from Central Asia conquer Persia, embrace Islam.

Seljuks Sultanate 1040 - 1245

- Originates from (Oguz) Ghuzz, Turkomen tribe, Central Asia.
- Seljuks are converts to Islam.
- Seljuks are **Sunni** Muslims.
- Seljuks bring the Turkic language from Central Asia to Anatolia.
- Defeats the Byzantine Army at Manzikert, Anatolia in 1071.
- Harsh conditions for Jews and Christians under Seljuk rule.
- Seljuks conquer Persia (1040), Iraq (1055), Palestine (1071), Anatolia (1071).
- Sultan Togrul Bey originally makes Baghdad the Seljuk capital.
- Later Seljuks make their capital in Isfahan in Persia, constructing the Great Mosque of Isfahan (Masjed e-Jami).
- Establish Sunni madrassahs (religious teaching institutions).
- Mongols defeat the Seljuks, incorporated into Khorezmian Empire.
- Ottomans are the descendants of the Seljuks.

Map 20. The Seljuk Empire 11th century

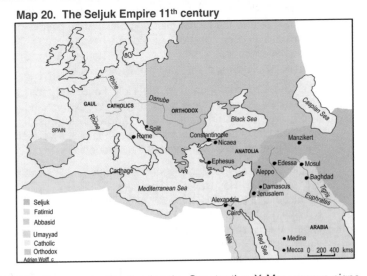

1048   The Emperor in Constantinople, Constantine X Monumecus signs an agreement with Fatimid Caliph al-Dhabi, Cairo for the rebuilding of The Church of the Resurrection, within the Church of the Holy Sepulchre.

1050   Italians from Amalfi establish a Christian Order dedicated to St. John the Baptist. **The Hospitallers Knights Order** gives services to pilgrims traveling around the Christian world by building hospices, offering food, medication, alms and protection. The monks join forces with the knights to receive weapons to protect the pilgrims. They wear a tunic with a white cross.

The Christians establish an armed force to protect the Christian pilgrims and traders from continuous Muslim attacks on their perilous journeys to the Holy Land. They treat the sick and are responsible for the safety of pilgrims and during the 1st Crusade, derive the name "Hospitaller". The Crusader Knight's Orders build hostels for pilgrims to provide services such as overnight accommodation, food and medical treatment, and in addition they are a source of information and engage in missionary activities. The monks who manage these hostels, receive access to weapons for the first time when they join forces with the Crusader Knights.

A **banking system** between Europe and the Holy Land is introduced to assist pilgrims from fear of losing their valuables on their journey. Before departing, a Crusader will sell his belongings to a Knight's Order, receiving a paper for an equivalent sum of money in the Holy Land. The various Orders become rich, powerful organizations, competing against each other and later become corrupt, looking for power and money. In Europe the Orders are often a threat to the feudal ruler and established clergy. Members of Knight's Orders construct and occupy many of the Crusader castles and fortresses in the Holy Land. The Hospitaller Cross has eight points, known as the "Maltese" Cross.

After the Crusader Period in the Holy Land ends in 1291, the Hospitallers transfer their headquarters to Cyprus and later in 1308, conquer the island of Rhodes, establishing their headquarters. After the abolition of the Templar Knights in 1312, the Hospitallers take over some of their properties.

Sultan Suleyman the Magnificent ousts them from Rhodes to Malta in 1522. The Hospitallers repossess Malta in 1530 on the instructions of Emperor Charles V of Germany (who is also Charles I of Spain) after he signs a Treaty with Sultan Suleyman. Napoleon expels the Hospitallers from Malta in 1798 for being pirates and slave traders. Today the European Knights of St. John in Britain belong to the Anglican Church and the German Johanniter Orden are Protestants. Both organizations have nothing in common with the original order except the name.

1054 The year 1000 marks the extensive expansion of authority of the Roman Church, gaining political power over kings, obtaining riches from the wealthy and fervent support from the masses.

The official schism in the Christian church between the Western Latin Catholic Church (Rome) and the Eastern Byzantine Orthodox Church (Constantinople). Pope Leo IX accuses the Byzantine Church of 'subtracting the "*filioque*" (and from the Son) from the original creed (Trinity), and making additional changes to minor theological subjects. Catholics view Christ as the Son of God, His representative on earth and equal to God. Orthodox revere The Virgin Mother. The Pope in Rome remains the head of the Catholic Church. The Emperor of the Orthodox Church remains in Constantinople with regional satellite churches in Antioch, Jerusalem, and Alexandria.

The Roman Patriarch in Rome considers itself a higher body of importance to Christians than the Orthodox Church in Constantinople.These differences are to become both incompatible and irreconcilable to each other, never to be bridged. Head of the Catholic Church the Pope resides in Rome, while the head of the Orthodox Church the Emperor in Constantinople (today in Jerusalem). The longitude at Split in Croatia is the dividing line between Eastern Orthodox in all areas east and Western Latins (Catholics) in areas to the west. Slavery has ended in Europe.

Differences in architectural design between Catholic and Orthodox churches

- Catholic churches have rows of seats, Orthodox stand during the service
- Catholic churches have statues of Christ, Orthodox icons of the Virgin.
- Catholic churches have symbols of the 14 Stations of the Cross, Orthodox none.
- Catholic churches have three apses, Orthodox a divider with doors after the pulpit.
- Orthodox churches face east, burn incense in overhead containers.

1055 Seljuks capture Baghdad, capital of the Abbasid Caliphate.

1055 Emperor Constantine IX in Constantinople obtains permission from the Fatimid caliph in Cairo to rebuild a separate wall around the Christian Quarter of Jerusalem.

1058 Seljuks continue their conquest westwards and capture Damascus, a Muslim city previously under Abbasid control.

1067 Civil war erupts in Egypt (1067–1074), during the reign of Caliph al-Mustansir, resulting in decline of Fatimid power and consequently their administrative control deteriorates in Palestine.

1067 Ramle is almost totally destroyed in an earthquake.

1071 Seljuks under Alp Arslan, seeking the wealth found in the Byzantine Empire, defeat them at the Battle of Manzikert (Erzurum today), north of Lake Van in Anatolia, capturing the Byzantine emperor Romanus IV Diogenes, who buys his freedom after signing a treaty, but is replaced in Constantinople by Michael VII. Seljuks control parts of Anatolia and continue to pressurize the

Byzantines from the east. **Seljuks Moslems** under Atsiz defeat the Fatimids in Palestine, **capture Jerusalem**.

1071 **Normans** defeat the Byzantines in Italy when their last stronghold at Bari, Italy, on the Adriatic coast, capitulates after a three-year siege. The Byzantines experience serious blows to their strength and influence.

1072 Seljuks rebuild the Muslim town of Ramle.

1073 Continuing civil war in Egypt. Seljuks Moslems expel the Fatimids from Palestine. The Seljuks establish Muslim religious learning institutes, called *madrassahs*. Christian pilgrims risk their lives in Jerusalem.

1076 Seljuks put down pro-Fatimid Muslim revolts in Palestine including massacre of 3000 Muslim inhabitants of Ramle. Other towns in Palestine are burnt and destroyed.

1081 Seljuks capture Nicaea, an important Byzantine commercial center in Anatolia, 200kms east of Constantinople. The defeated Byzantines request aid from Rome, giving rise to the subsequent Crusades.

1082 **Italian Venetians** capture Bari, forcing the Normans (see 1071) from the Adriatic Sea, now control the maritime routes to the east, especially to Constantinople. Consequently, the Byzantine Emperor Alexius I grants Venetians special trading privileges, developing the commercial importance and influence of Venice in the eastern Mediterranean.

1085 Seljuks capture Antioch gaining access to the Mediterranean Sea, but do not use this military success to their maritime advantage. Antioch (Turkish Province of Antakya today), originally founded by the Hellenic Seleucids, was an important Byzantine regional civil and military capital in southern Galatia, south-east Anatolia. Armenian Christians from the Tarsus Mountains travel south to establish in Cilicia, southeast Anatolia, called Lesser Armenia.

1089 Fatimids of Egypt begin to conquer the Seljuks in Palestine by capturing coastal towns.

Chapter 13. The First Crusade 1095 - 1099

11thc Increased religious renewal in feudal Europe during the 11th century. Construction of large religious buildings (abbeys and churches) having tall steeples pointing towards heaven at Cluny, Durham, Westminster, St. Mark's, and Pisa. (until this period there are no major churches in Europe). The structures are of Romanesque and later Gothic architectural design. Heretics are burnt at the stake in public, while the spiritual authority of the Papacy is extended to assume a more active role. A popular movement arises in Europe believing the 'Second Coming of Christ' will occur 1000 years after His Crucifixion. *"And they lived and reigned with Christ for a thousand years...This is the first resurrection."* (Revelation 20: 4, 5).

Many Christians become impatient in 1030 as no special event occurs. It will be the Crusaders' task to lead the faithful to Jerusalem to await the 'Second Coming of Christ'. There are similar thoughts 1000 years later when many faithful Christians, especially German Templars move to the Holy Land believing 'The Second Coming of Christ' will occur at the beginning of the 20th century. Such a belief arises again among some Christians as the beginning of the 21st century approaches.

Rome is the largest city in Western Europe with a population over 100,000 inhabitants while Cologne, the second largest city has 15,000 inhabitants. Both of these cities are small when compared to Byzantine Constantinople with over half a million inhabitants. Population growth and economic development in Western Europe during this period is concentrated mainly along the Trade Routes with the expansion of old towns and construction of new towns. In Europe, the majority live on the land controlled by feudal lords who are warriors; the clergy pray; and the peasants are bound 'to the soil' by rents and fees. Arable cultivated lands expand as irrigation canals are constructed. Nobles, bourgeoisie and peasants begin to seek new horizons in adventurous journeys as pilgrimage routes are established to the Holy Land.

The Jews, a minority are separated by religion and culture from Christian Europe. In the Islamic world Jews and Christians are a minority.

The political climate in Europe is:
- England - William of Normandy defeats the Saxons, establishes a new kingdom. The English kings will suppress independent

leaders in Wales and Scotland.
- Spain - Christians are occupied with the '*reconquista*' fighting the Muslim in Spain.
- France, Belgium and Germany - remain feudal.

Future trade between the East and West brings:
- From Byzantium: astronomical instruments to the east.
- From China: moveable-type printing, paper currency, compass, rudder, spinning-wheel, waterpower, and later gunpowder.

1095 Byzantine military power is in decline, pressurized on all of its borders. Byzantine Emperor, Alexius I Comnenus requests help from Rome to protect and assist the recovery of eastern Anatolia from invading Muslim forces. Rumors spread from Constantinople of Muslims desecrating Christ's grave in the Church of the Holy Sepulchre in Jerusalem, defiling other Christian Holy Sites in the Holy Land and attacking Christian pilgrims.

1095 The French Pope Urban II, sees himself as the leader of the western kings. On 18 November 1095, during a sermon in Clermont, France he calls for recruits to join a **Crusade** to fight in a Holy War to liberate Jerusalem from the 'infidel', and to protect Christian pilgrims traveling to the Holy Land. Crusader Knights' debts are cancelled, commonly owed to the Jews, who are the bankers and jewelers, not land-owners. Following this rally, barons, landowners and peasants are solidly behind the Pontiff and the Catholic Church.

1096 **The Crusades begin. The People's Crusade**
- Aim: To arrive in the Holy Land.
- End: Their annihilation in Anatolia.
- These Crusaders do not reach the Holy Land.
- Leader: Peter the Hermit, of Amiens, France.

The first Crusaders consist of disorganized thugs and hooligans led by Peter, a hermit of Amiens, Walter the Penniless and Gottschalk, a German monk, traveling along Danube River, rioting and plundering in Bavaria, Austria, Hungary and Bulgaria. The masses follow their feudal figureheads in the hope of adventure, battle, fame, wealth, exotic women, easy booty, new lands and redemption of their sins. The Pope pardons them, while their leaders promise loot. In the name of Christ, slaughter Jews in Verdun, Treves (Trier), Mainz, Speyer, Worms and Cologne, along the Rhine and Danube on their route eastwards, causing many Jews to flee northwards towards Slovakia, and later to Prussia, Poland and western Russia. Most of the estimated 40-50,000 who join the People's Crusade, fall victim to disease, hunger, thirst, or die in battle along the route.

Emperor Alexius I will not allow this unruly group of about 20,000 of the original participants into Constantinople fearing a festival of plunder. He compels them to continue into Anatolia, where at Nicaea, Anatolia the Seljuks slaughter and annihilate them. **End of the People's Crusade**.

1096   Participants in the 1st Crusade begin their journeys in August 1096 from Flanders in Belgium, France and Italy via land and sea to Constantinople where they assemble before the overland march southwards through Anatolia. Crusaders view themselves not as conquerors but as Christians returning to the Holy Land where Jesus preached and lived. English do not join as William the Conqueror (Duke of Normandy) recently installed a new regime. Tension will remain between England and France during the entire Crusader Period. The English fear a French invasion of English possessions in Normandy, northern France. Later, various English kings suppress Welsh and Scottish independent aspirations. The Spanish too, do not join the Crusades, absorbed in fighting Muslims in various '*reconquista*' campaigns to regain control of Spain. Crusaders originally set off with 60,000 participants including 5,000 knights (or cavalry), 30,000 foot soldiers, and countless civilians who assemble in Constantinople before continuing overland through Anatolia to the Holy Land and Jerusalem some 2000 kilometers away overland.

The First Crusade 1095 - 1099
- Aim: To control Jerusalem
- End: The only successful Crusader conquest of Jerusalem
- Majority return to Europe after the capture of Jerusalem
- The main leaders of the 1st Crusader leaders are:
  - Raymond of Toulouse, France
  - Godfrey of Bouillon, Belgium, and his brother Baldwin
  - Robert of Normandy (son of William the Conqueror)
  - Bohemond of Taranto, Italy and his nephew Tancred

1097   The Emperor Alexius I in Constantinople succeeds in obtaining an oath of loyalty from the Crusader leaders, apart from Tancred, to concede their conquests to the Byzantine Emperor and not grant them to Catholic Rome. In exchange for their loyalty, the Crusaders obtain guides, military escorts and logistic support (food, horses, wagons). The Crusaders first military success is a victory over the Seljuks at Nicaea, who under-estimate their military strength.

1098   The Egyptian Fatimids recapture Jerusalem from the Seljuks who retrace their steps towards Central Asia. The fighting causes a decline in the number of inhabitants in Jerusalem.

1098   Baldwin of Boulogne, brother of Godfrey de Bouillon, conquers the Armenian Christian region of Edessa (in eastern Anatolia and northern Syria of today) and takes the title of 'Baldwin of the County of Edessa' from 1100 until 1118. Baldwin of Boulogne will become King Baldwin II in 1118 until 1131. Edessa (Sanliurfa) is in southern Anatolia.

St.Peter's Crusader Castle, Bodrum, Anatolia, Turkey

1098   The main body of Crusaders continues southwards reaching Antioch (Antakya, today). Stephen of Blois (son-in-law of William the Conqueror) meets the Byzantine Emperor who informs him taking of Antioch is impossible. After a siege of seven months, the Crusaders eventually capture Antioch massacring the local Muslim population. Shortly afterwards, a relief force of 20,000 Muslim Seljuks arrive from Mosul under the leadership of Karbugah (Kerboga), encircling the Crusaders now trapped within the walled city suffering from dysentery and typhus. Crusaders defeat the Seljuks after receiving an inspiration that a 'Holy Lance' found below the cathedral in Antioch is the same that pierced the side of Christ on the Cross.

1098   A Crusader leader Bohemund of Taranto, Italy, refuses to turn over the town of Antioch to the Emperor's representative, setting up his own 'Principality of Antioch'. Subsequently the Crusaders decide not to grant the Emperor in Constantinople rights to any territory and towns they capture. The main body of Crusader soldiers become aware of their leaders' goals of personal gain and wealth, as now they decide to by-pass the coastal towns on their 'holy mission' and not interrupt their passage to loot before arriving at their final goal, Jerusalem. Soldiers are given a regular pay for each day served, with the potential of rich plunder to bring home.

Map 21. The First Crusade 1095 – 1099

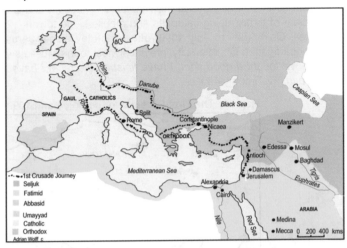

Crusader Crosses, Tyre, Lebanon   Mavis Wolff

1099   About 1200 to 1500 Crusader Knights and 12,000 foot soldiers, one-third of the original number assembled in Constantinople successfully cross Anatolia to arrive at the walls of Jerusalem. Camps are built outside the city walls on Mount of Olives and Mt. Zion. Godfrey de Bouillon sells most of his estates to payroll the 40,000 knights and infantry consisting of British, Flemish and German mercenaries.

The main Crusader attack led by **Godfrey de Bouillon** is made on the northern wall close to the Rockefeller Museum and Damascus Gate of today, using catapults and mobile siege towers 12 meters tall. On Friday 15 July 1099, after a 39-day siege, Jerusalem is once again a Christian city, previously lost to the Muslims in 638. *"I have fought a good fight, I have finished the race, I have kept the faith."* (2 Timothy 4:7).

Map 22. The First Crusade to the Holy Land 1099

The Crusaders massacre Muslims on the Temple Mount and many Jews in the shelter of the synagogues during the Friday Night's Services. The city is littered with stinking corpses. Over 40,000 Jews are reputed to be massacred in The Holy Land, including most of the remaining Jewish residents of Jerusalem. Some Jewish prisoners are taken from Jerusalem to Ashkelon where they are ransomed to the Jewish community in Egypt. Crusaders deny Jews and Muslims the right to pilgrimages and residence in Jerusalem (and in Hebron in 1119). Previously in 1094, Godfrey had declared at the Council of Claremont that he would avenge the blood of Christ, leaving no Jew alive if they would not convert to Christianity.

Crusader forces capture and restore the Byzantine Church of the Nativity in Bethlehem. **Jerusalem becomes the capital of Crusader Kingdom of Jerusalem (*Regnum Hierusalem* in Latin) from 1099 until 1187.**

Chapter 14. Crusader Kingdom of Jerusalem 1099 - 1187

The Crusader Kingdom of Jerusalem 1099 - 1187
- Aim: To conquer Jerusalem
- End: Salah a-Din's conquest of Jerusalem 1187
- Capital in Jerusalem
- Crusaders control Tyre, Coastal Plain, Galilee, Jerusalem, Northern Negev, Akaba

The Crusaders establish four states:
- Edessa - a county, ruled by Baldwin II of Boulogne 1100-1144
- Antioch - Principality of Antioch, ruled by Bohemond 1098-1268
- Tripoli - a county, ruled by Raymond of Toulouse 1109-1289
- Jerusalem - Kingdom, Godfrey de Bouillon, 'Guardian of the Holy Sepulchre', enduring 1099-1187

1099   After the conquest of Jerusalem, Crusaders request the Pope to settle in Jerusalem. Since the Pope shows no such interest, the Crusaders choose their own leader. **Godfrey de Bouillon**, (1060-1100) conqueror of Jerusalem. He does not wish to receive a crown where Jesus had a crown of thorns placed on His head ("*they had a crown of thorns, they put it on His head*" Matthew 27:29). He takes the title 'Guardian of the Holy Sepulchre'. Byzantine churches previously destroyed now begin to be reconstructed. Tancred captures Beit She'an, proclaims himself King of Tiberias.

1100   Godfrey de Bouillon, captures the port of Jaffa and Ramle, a Muslim town on the main route from the coast to Jerusalem. The Emir of Caesarea invites Godfrey to attend a banquet. On returning to Jaffa, Godfrey dies suddenly and very unexpectedly, probably from food poisoning. His brother Baldwin I de Bouillon, (1059-1118) is crowned the first Crusader King of Jerusalem (1100–1118). Both bodies of Godfrey and King Baldwin I are buried in The Church of the Holy Sepulchre, under the Golgotha. Their bones and tombstones disappear during inter-Christian rivalry.

1100   King Baldwin I controls:
- **'King's Highway'** from Damascus, Dead Sea, to the Red Sea.
- **'Via Maris'** the Coastal Route from Sinai to Damascus eastwards.
- **'Pilgrims Highway'** from Cairo to Medina and Mecca.

1100   Many Crusaders believe they have completed their vows of pilgrimage for the Christian cause and depart back to Europe, leaving a state of disunity and crusader chivalry to govern and protect the new Kingdom. Wealthy knights return to Europe, while the poor, who have little or no assets in Europe remain, given land, very similar to the feudal manor in Europe. Some Crusaders will take Orthodox wives. The majority of the population is Muslim except in Jerusalem, a Christian city of mostly Western European Latin Christians. The Eastern Orthodox - Syrians, Jacobites, Copts are the minority. **End of the 1st Crusade.**

1100 After success of the 1st Crusade, Jerusalem becomes a pilgrimage status for Western Catholic Christians in Europe, not for Eastern Orthodox Christians. Later Catholics will spread the word 'Jerusalem' to new converts in the Western Hemisphere.

Events that occur in Jerusalem during the Crusader Period:

1. Christian pilgrims visit Jerusalem, a minority will remain.
2. Construct the Citadel, *Turris David* (David's Tower), Jaffa Gate.
3. Convert the Dome of the Rock into a church, the 'Lord's Temple' (*Templum Domini*).
4. Templar Knights occupy the al-Aqsa Mosque, converted into a Christian religious building renamed Solomon's Temple (*Templum Solomonis*). They name the subterranean water cisterns Solomon's Stables that has nothing in common with the biblical King Solomon or his stables.
5. Reconstruction of the Church of St Anne on the via Dolorosa (the road of sorrow), the church on Mt. Zion and Mary's Tomb in Gethsemane.
6. Churches are erected to mark all sites of the Stations of the Cross along the via Dolorosa. In Europe 14 Stations of the Cross are a tradition, while only 9 are mentioned in the New Testament. The first two stations are located in the Antonia Fortress where the Trial and Judgment of Jesus takes place, seven sites along the road (via Dolorosa) leading from the Antonia Fortress to the Gate of Jerusalem. The last five Stations are inside the Church of the Holy Sepulchre.
7. Most of the Christian inhabitants of the Holy Land are European Christians (Latins or Catholics) while a minority of Christians are Orthodox (Greeks, Armenians, Syrians, Jacobites, and Copts).
8. The majority of Crusaders are of French descent.
9. Official documents are written in Latin in 12thc and in French in 13thc.
10. After the Jews flee from the Crusaders in Jerusalem, Christian Arabs tribes from Transjordan immigrate to the Jewish Quarter of Jerusalem.
11. Ancient Roman aqueducts, water storage pools and sewerage systems are operating, unlike European cities which rely on rivers.
12. Europeans are amazed by items found in the Orient - carpets, carved furniture, linen, gold, silver tableware, mosaic floors, ivory boxes, fruits, spices and fragrances.

1101   Phoenicians originally founded the port of Arsuf in the 6th century BCE, named after Reshef, the god of war and storms. During the Hellenic period, the name is changed to Apollonia producing a very valuable purple dye from sea-snails found in the area. In 1101 King Baldwin I, aided by the Genoese fleet conquers Apollonia renames it Arsour (Arsuf, later, an Arabic name), constructing a small port.

1102   King Baldwin I captures Caesarea. Crusaders massacre the Muslim population in revenge for the death of Godfrey de Bouillon. Crusaders find pepper and other spices in the port warehouses. These spices, new to the Europeans will become a future source of income, exported to Europe. Crusaders locate an emerald-green hexagonal glass goblet and decide it is the '*Holy Grail*', from which Jesus drinks wine during the Last Super and Joseph of Arimathae collects the blood from the wounds of Jesus on the Cross. It is displayed in the Cathedral of Saint Lorenzo in Genoa. The Genoese control Caesarea gaining authority over a third of the town including important income-generating facilities - bakeries, work-shops and ship repair yards.

1104   Despite his previous agreement with the Genoans, King Baldwin I signs the '*Pactum Varmundi*' with Venice. The agreement grants Venetians one-third of all towns under Crusader control (usually along the coast), whether royal or baronial, regulating Venetians extra-territorial jurisdiction and their exemption from local courts except in certain isolated cases. In addition to these general grants and privileges, the treaty records precise details Venetians rights in Acre the major Crusader port after 1105. The Venetians gain rights to establish an oven, a mill, a bath-house; to use weights and measures and bottles for liquid and dry measures. The Venetians are to regulate the very lucrative control of taxes, tolls, dry-dock port facilities, bakeries, metal works etc. This marks inter-Italian city-state rivalry for control of Trade and Ports in the Holy Land.

Italian Maritime Crusaders are closely associated with mother cities in Italy, Venice, Genoa and Pisa controlling all eastern Mediterranean maritime trade. Italians supply indispensable naval aid and shipping, essential to bring regular supplies from Europe to harbors in the eastern Mediterranean. For these services, Italians acquire exceptional port privileges to include:
• Control of one-third of the port and streets in key cities in an independent enclave include customs house, inns and hostels, stores, bazaars, bakery, grain silos, dry-dock ship repair facilities.
• Free access to Byzantine ports without paying customs and taxes.
• Tax collectors, moneychangers.

The Crusader Legal Structure

1. High Court - The King's Court, highest court of government, foreign and taxation policies.
2. Court of Burgesses - Office of records, transactions, civil litigation.
3. Court of Chains, the Maritime Court - A chain is stretched across a harbor entrance, enforcing payment of taxes.

Trade – Crusaders expand trade between Italy and the Levant

1. **Trade Route 1 - the northern route:** From Ceylon, India, Persian Gulf, Mesopotamia, Syria, Lebanon, Mediterranean.

   Trade Route 2 - the southern route: From Ceylon, India, Aden, Red Sea, Akaba, Negev Spice Route, Gaza, Suez, Alexandria. Route 2 requires fewer overland travel, therefore is less dangerous than #1.

   Overland: Beijing, Kashgar, Samarkand, Astrakhan or Persia, Baghdad, Constantinople, or Antioch, or Tyre.

   The **'Via Maris'** is the overland route in The Holy Land parallel to the coast from Sinai to Gaza, Ashkelon, Jaffa, Acre, Sephoris (Zippori), Tiberias, Golan, Damascus and onwards to Baghdad and the east.

2. **Trade from the East:**
   Shipping technology: stern rudder, compass.
   Glass, mirrors, porcelain.
   Paper, paper making, block printing.
   Spices: pepper, cloves, ginger, salt, nutmeg, cinnamon, incense.
   Foods: oranges, lemons, sugar cane, raisins, dates, sesame, wheat, olive oil, wine, honey, pistachio nuts, rice.
   Textiles: cotton, flax silks, dyes (indigo, saffron, henna), rugs, woven textiles, spinning-wheel.
   Medicines: camphor, cubeb, aloe, cosmetics, hygiene.
   Minerals, chemicals: copper, iron, tin, silver, potassium, silver nitrate, sulphuric acid.
   Gems, precious stones of high value: pearls, gold & silver, jewelry, porcelain.
   Sciences: medicine, mathematics (zero), astronomy, geography, physics.
   Gunpowder, windmills, slaves, stories of Sinbad the Sailor, Ali Baba and the Forty Thieves, Aladdin etc.

3. **Trade from the West:**
   Basic materials: wood, linen, iron, wheat, metal-ware, glass. The natural forests in the Holy Land are decimated as wood is used for war siege towers, ramps, lances, fences.
   Banking: moneychangers.
   Literature: Western historical literature, often translated by multilingual Jews.
   Padded horse-collar.
   Irrigation techniques for crops in Mediterranean areas.

Later: clocks, watches, eyeglasses, telescopes, tobacco, war weapons.

4. Landmark changes in East-West trade

1. In 1271 Marco Polo leaves Venice, leading his second journey to China and Far East, where Kublai Khan (Mongol) is seeking Christian allies in the 'west' against Muslims. He opens new Overland Trade Routes north of Muslim controlled territory.
2. In 1498 Vasco da Gama from Portugal discovers a sea route via Africa to India, opening a new Maritime Trade Route ending the Muslim Trade Route monopoly from Far East to Europe.
3. Wheeled transport disappears from the Middle East until the 19th century. Huge (1000) camel caravans remain.

1105   Muslims surrender the port of Acre to the Crusaders without a fight.

1115   Crusader forces add to their territorial control the Kingdom of Montreal, located east of the Jordan River and Dead Sea from Moab to Akaba on the Red Sea.

1118   King Baldwin I dies and Baldwin II de Boulogne, cousin of Baldwin I, former King of the County of Edessa, King of Jerusalem (1118-1131).

1119   **Templar Knights.** Hugh de Payens of France establishes The **Templar Christian Order** with its headquarters on the Temple Mount, hence named Templars. They are a military and religious order within the Catholic Church, whose monks carry weapons to protect pilgrims on their journeys to Jerusalem, devoting themselves to the "Defense of the Holy Sepulchre". Membership is first limited to nobles who take vows of poverty and obedience, wearing a white tunic with a red cross. King Baldwin II allows them to occupy the Dome of the Rock, renamed in Latin *'Templum Domini'*, and the al-Aqsa mosque, renamed *'Templum Solomonis'*. They use the subterranean Herodian Temple Mount cisterns as horse stables, now called Solomon's Stables, which has no connection with King Solomon's Temple or his stables.

St. Bernard of Clairvaux (1090-1153) assists Templar Knights members to promote their cause, adopting the Benedictine rule. Templars introduce a **banking system** between Europe and the Holy Land allowing pilgrims the convenience of not having to transport their valuables with them on their perilous journey to the Holy Land. A pilgrim can sell his possessions and receive a paper entitling him to receive a similar value of assets in the Holy Land. The Order adopts a pact of secrecy on all internal activities. Templar Knights are known for their bravery and also for their wealth. European rulers looking for way to obtain the Templar wealth and assets result in Pope Clement V and King Philip IV of

France to charge the Templars with bribery and heresy. The Pope abolishes the order in 1312, sharing their wealth and properties with the King of France and a minority share to the Hospitaller Knights. The Templar Knight Order has no connection with the German Protestant movement "Deutsche Templer" of the 19th and 20th century, whose members settle in Palestine.

1124   Crusaders, aided by Venetians, capture the port of Tyre.

Map 23. Crusader States early 12th century

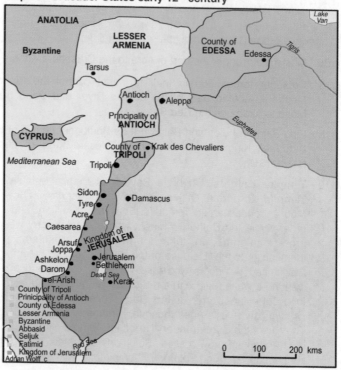

1126   The Banias Springs at the foothills of the northern Golan Heights is controlled by the Assassins, an Isma'ili (Muslim) sect known as Hashishiyun led by Hasan as-Sabah from Khorassan (in the Elburz Mountains in northern Persia). Bahram Isma'ili constructs a heavily fortified fortress at Banias to protect themselves from an attack by the Ayyubids. Invading Mongols annihilate them 13th century.

1128   Zengi (Zangi 1084–1146), a Turkic (Ayyubid) officer in the Seljuk army seizes Mosul in Mesopotamia and proclaims himself Emir of Mosul and Aleppo. He troops hastily defeat the Seljuks controlling Mesopotamia, Damascus, and Aleppo (Halab today).

1128   German Knights of the Hospitallers Order build St. Mary's Hospice (on Misgav Ladach Street today) to provide medical services to the Crusaders suffering from battle wounds as well as diseases (malaria, bilharzia, gonorrhea).

1129   Crusaders build forts in the Galilee at Beaufort, Hunin and Banias.

1129   Following the massacre of the Assassins in Damascus, Bahram Isma'ili offers the fortress of Banias to the Crusader King Baldwin II in exchange for protection and asylum. King Baldwin II's unsuccessful adventure to besiege Damascus causes his return to Banias. The Crusaders fortify and expand the fortress at Banias on the border with the Ayyubid Muslims (Zengi).

1131   Fulk V of Anjou (1092-1145), King of Jerusalem (1131–1145) He is husband of Melissande, the daughter of King Baldwin II.

1132   Shams el-Mulk, governor of Damascus attacks and captures the Crusader fortress at Banias, gaining entry to the Upper Galilee.

1134   The **Lazarite Christian Order** is established to assist lepers. This Order is named after an episode in the New Testament describing how Christ raised Lazarus from the dead after 4 days (John 11:1-44), and Christ's curing of a leper (Luke 5:12,13).

1136   Crusaders capture Beit Guvrin on the cross-roads controlling the route east-west between the Sinai Coast and Judean mountains, Jerusalem and Dead Sea; and the route north-south from the Coastal Plain to the Negev, Arava and Red Sea. A Crusaders township is constructed over the ruins of a Roman town that includes an amphitheater, and gladiator stadium seen today.

1139   Ayyubid leader Zengi, assisted by Ibrahim ibn-Turgut the ruler of Banias, threatens the Abbasids in Damascus.

1140   Abbasids in Damascus make a joint pact with Crusader King Fulk V to attack Zengi as Banias again, is under Crusader control.

1141   The Jewish doctor, philosopher and poet **Yehuda Ha'levi** (1075-1141) is born in Christian controlled Toledo, Spain. He professes Jewish festivals to be a major factor in keeping and identifying Jews together in the Diaspora. He moves to the Muslim controlled Cordoba (Cordova), to escape persecution. He is reputedly murdered while kissing the holy ground outside Jerusalem (Roth) before completing his pilgrimage. It is also claimed he dies in Egypt.

1142   Crusaders build Ibelin/Jabeneh (Yavne), along the 'via Maris'.

1142   King Fulk constructs Blanchegarde (Tel Zafit) (Kfar Menachem) a Crusader administrative center to control the Ashkelon-Ramle road

1144   Crusader 'County of Edessa' in southern Anatolia and northern Syria falls to Zengi. All their attempts to recapture Edessa fail. Europeans see this defeat as Crusaders' weakness.

1144   'Blood-libel' against the Jews of Norwich of falsely accused of killing a Christian boy for ritual purposes. (See Jews 1192, 1840).

1145   Following the death of her husband King Fulk V, Melissande is Queen of Jerusalem (1145–1148).

1147   Crusader fortress at Darom (Dir el-Ballah, Gaza) on the 'Via Maris'.

Crusader Fortress Krak des Chevaliers, Syria   Mavis Wolff

Krak des Chevaliers, Syria. Interior Courtyard   Mavis Wolff

1147   Following the fall of The County of Edessa, Queen Melissande in Jerusalem sends a letter to Pope Eugenius III who issues a formal crusade, freeing the participants from repaying any debts, including to Jews. King Louis VII of France and King Conrad III of Germany 'take the cross' to lead their armies in the **Second Crusade** to liberate County of Edessa from Muslim forces. Jews are massacred in the Rhineland by Crusaders passing on their way to the Holy Land.

The Second Crusade 1147 - 1149
- Aim: To liberate the County of Edessa
- End: Crusader forces attack their Abbasid ally in Damascus where they are surrounded and defeated by Nur a-Din
- The Crusaders never reach the Holy Land
- Leaders of the Second Crusade are:
  - King Conrad III of Germany
  - King Louis VII of France

1147   Nur a-Din, son and successor of Zengi, (assassinated by a servant in 1146), defeats Crusader forces of King Conrad III at Dorylaeum in Anatolia forcing him to retreat to Nicaea, Anatolia. Conrad III taken seriously ill returns to convalesce in Constantinople. On his recovery, he travels by ship to Acre then proceeds to Jerusalem. King Louis VII of France with his wife Eleanor of Aquitaine arrive in Nicaea one month after Conrad III's defeat. (Eleanor of Aquitaine later marries King Henry II of England, is the mother of Richard I).

1148   King Louis VII leaves Nicaea for Antioch where he is welcomed by Prince Raymond, Queen Eleanor's uncle. Raymond urges Louis VII to attack Aleppo the center of power of Nur a-Din. Louis VII disagrees, continuing to Jerusalem where he mets Queen Melissande, her son the future King Baldwin III, the barons of Jerusalem, and in addition the Crusader leader King Conrad III. They conclude the best method to proceed against Nur a-Din is to use a force of 50,000 men to attack Damascus, a city controlled by an Abbasid Muslim ally of the Crusaders. Nur a-Din's army approaches Damascus, laying siege and exposing weaknesses in Crusader planning and execution in battle. Louis VII is forced into a humiliating withdrawal from Damascus and Crusaders fail to re-conquer Edessa. **End of the 2nd Crusade.**

1148   Queen Melissande dies, buried on the Mount of Olives in the 'Church of the Tomb of the Virgin Mary' next to the Garden of Gethsemane. This orthodox site can be visited today. Her 17 year old son Baldwin III (1131-1162) King of Jerusalem (1148-1162), is known to be well educated, does not impose excessive taxation during his reign.

Crusader Church of the Holy Sepulchre, Jerusalem   Adrian Wolff

Golgotha, Station XII, Crucifixion Site, The Holy Sepulchre   Judy Romano

1149   Renovations to the Church of the Holy Sepulchre.

1154   Ashkelon (Ascalon), the last Muslim town (and port) on the coast of the Holy Land falls to Crusader and Templar Knights forces.

1154   Ayyubid leader Nur a-Din captures Damascus from the Abbasids.

Unction Stone, Church of the Holy Sepulchre, Jerusalem   Adrian Wolff

Tomb of Christ, Station XIV, Church of the Holy Sepulchre   Adrian Wolff

1155   Monk Berthold of Calabria founds the **Carmelite Catholic Order** of 'Our Lady of Mount Carmel'. The original monks are French and German and connect this site on Mount Carmel to the Jewish Prophet Elijah. The followers live a pious, ascetic hermit-like life. (This is not a Jewish pilgrimage site, not recognized by Jews).

1157   Facing the Ayyubid challenge, the Crusader governor Humphrey of Toron (Tibnin), the Lord of Banias offers half of his territory including Banias to the French Hospitallers who undertake to pay half of the cost of the defense and to maintain a garrison at Banias. Nur a-Din annihilates a Hospitaller convoy moving towards Banias. King Baldwin III moves reinforcements from Tripoli and Antioch towards Banias forcing Nur a-Din to retire towards Damascus.

1159   **Benjamin of Tudela** (Navarra), Spain, a gem dealer, travels for 13 years investigating Jewish communities in Italy, Greece, Eretz Israel, and Persia. He is one of the first Europeans to approach China, before he returns to Spain. *"In every place he entered he made a record of all that he saw or was told of by trustworthy persons - matters not previously heard of in the land of Sepharad (Spain)."* In Constantinople *"In the Jewish Quarter are about 2,000 Rabbanite Jews (merchant/traders) and about 500 Karaites."* *"..the Greeks (Orthodox) do not obey the Pope of Rome."* He describes the *"Wealth like that of Constantinople is not to be found in the whole world. Here are men learned in all the books of the Greeks, and they eat and drink, every man under his vine and his fig-tree."* *"No Jew is allowed to ride on horseback. The one exception is R. Solomon Hamitsri, who is the king's physician...There is much hatred against them (the Jews). The Greeks hate the Jews, good and bad alike, and subject them to great oppression, and beat them in the streets...Yet Jews are rich and good, kindly and charitable and bear their lot with cheerfulness.The district inhabited by the Jews is called Pera."*

Benjamin of Tudela arrives in *"Jerusalem (which) has four gates (Abraham, David, Zion and Jehoshafat) facing our ancient Temple now called Templum Domini. Upon the site of the sanctuary Omar ben al Kata'ab erected an edifice with a very large and magnificent cupola, into which the Gentiles do not bring any image or effigy, but merely come there to pray. In front of this place is the Western Wall which is one of the Walls of the Holy of Holies...come all Jews to pray before the Wall of the Court of the Temple."* He travels to Bethlehem, Hebron, Ashkelon, Tiberias, Damascus, Baalbek, Mamath, Aleppo, Kurdistan, Mesopotamia and Persia.

In *"Baghdad, the great city and the royal residence of the Caliph al-Abbasid...the head of the Mohammedan religion, and all the* kings of Islam obey him. He occupies a similar position to that held by the Pope over the Christians...He (the caliph al-Mustanjid) is kind unto Israel and many belonging to the people of Israel are his attendants...He reads and writes the holy language (Hebrew)." "He rides on a mule and is attired in the royal robes of gold and silver and fine linen; on his head is a turban adorned with precious stones of priceless value. Every sick man who comes is maintained at the Caliph's expense and is medically treated. In Baghdad there are about 40,000 Jews they dwell in security, prosperity and honor under the great Caliph." Benjamin of Tudela continues to Persia "to Hamadan the great city of Media...30,000 Israelites...to Isfahan...about 15,000...Shiraz...10,000 Jews live...to Ghaznah the great city on the River Gozan where there are about 80,000...to Samarkand...some 50,000 Israelites...to Tibet." He describes trade "Men from Shinar, El_Yemen and Persia bring all sorts of silk, purple and flax, cotton, hemp, worked wool, wheat, barley, millet rye, and all sorts of food, and lentils of every description, and they trade with one another, whilst the men from India bring great quantities of spices". "Thence (from Ibrig, Ceylon?) to cross over to the land of Zin (China) is a voyage of forty days. Zin is in the uttermost East and some say that there is the Sea of Nikpa (Ning-po) where the star Orion predominates and stormy winds prevail". He travels to "Jews living up the Nile River (Aswan, Helwan) and Mizrim...which is Pishon or Al-Nil.The number of Jewish inhabitants is about 7000. Two large synagogues, one belonging to the men of the land of Israel and one belonging to the men of the land of Babylon". (Adler. Jewish Travelers in the Middle Age).

1163   After the death of Baldwin III, his brother Amalric I is King of Jerusalem (1163–1174), protecting the rights of vassals under Crusader authority and prevents Muslim unity. Amalric marries Maria Comnena, grand-niece of the emperor in Constantinople. Crusader forces under King Amalric I invade Egypt for its refusal to pay the yearly tribute to the Kingdom of Jerusalem.

1164   Crusader forces are diluted in the Holy Land during their campaign in Egypt allowing Nur a-Din the opportunity to capture the Crusader fortress at Banias, then defeats the Crusaders in Egypt.

1168   Crusader fortresses, Belvoir, constructed by the Hospitaller Knights has a commanding view of the Beit She'an Valley to control traffic along the Jordan Valley, south of the Sea of Galilee. Also Mirabel-Migdal Afek is constructed on the Via Maris near the head waters of the Yarkon River. Crusaders build their castles and fortresses on hilltops within sight of each other.

1169   Salah a-Din defeats the Crusader army near Damietta, Egypt.

1169   Byzantine Emperor Manuel I Comnenus signs a treaty with the Principality of Genoa, and with Pisa in 1170, breaking Venetian maritime trade monopoly in the eastern Mediterranean.

Belvoir Hospitallers Crusader Fortress   Adrian Wolff

Mirabel-Migdal Afek, exterior   Adrian Wolff

1170c Chinese use gunpowder in battle, and have a magnetic compass, both are unknown in Europe and the Middle East.

1171   Anti-Latin Catholic demonstrations in Constantinople lead to the arrest of Venetians and confiscation of their property. These measures bring tension between Eastern and Western Christians climaxing in the disastrous 4th Crusade in 1204.

Mirabel-Migdal Afek, interior   Adrian Wolff

Map 24. Crusader Settlements 12th century

1171   On Nur a-Din's orders, **Salah a-Din** Yusuf ibn Ayyub (born 1138 in Taproot, Tigris River, dies in Damascus 1193), to mention during prayers the name of the Abbasid caliph in Baghdad in place of the

caliph of Cairo, replacing the ailing Fatimid ruler. Salah a-Din establishes Ayyubid Sultanate uniting Fatimid Shi'ites in Egypt with Abbasid Sunnis in Baghdad. The Ayyubid capital is **Damascus**. **End of the Fatimid Caliphate**.

Ayyubid Sultanate 1171 - 1250
- **Salah a-Din** establishes the Ayyubid Dynasty, capital in **Damascus,** uniting Fatimid and Abbasid Muslims (Cairo and Baghdad) to fight the invading Crusaders.
- The Ayyubids are **Sunni Muslims**.
- The Fatimid Shi'ite caliph in Egypt is replaced by Salah a-Din.
- Egypt is the most powerful state in Near East during this period.
- Ayyubids build *madrassahs* (religious teaching institutions).
- Ayyubids build a citadel in Cairo and defenses around Aleppo.
- Abbasids in Baghdad and Mamluks in Egypt (1250) replace the Ayyubid Dynasty after Salah a-Din death (1193).

1174   Nur a-Din the Ayyubid leader dies in Damascus. King Amalric I attacks Banias, receives this fortress after Nur a-din's widow pays a ransom. King Amalric I dies in Jerusalem, his son Baldwin IV (1161-1185) a leper king aged 13, king of Jerusalem (1174–1185).

1175   Salah a-Din becomes supreme Muslim leader (1175-1193).

1176   Seljuks defeat the Byzantine Army of Emperor Manuel I Comenus at Myriocephon in Anatolia, weakening the Byzantine Empire.

1176   Rabbi Moshe ben Maimon (**Maimonides** or the **Rambam**) 1138-1204, born in Cordoba, Spain, a Jewish philosopher, jurist, and physician is the leading Jewish intellectual dignitary figure of this period. He contributes to philosophy, science (logic, maths, optics) and jurisprudence. His medical texts include treatises on diet, drugs, toxicology and treatments (hemorrhoids, asthma) are standard teaching methods for generations and are translated into many languages. His family moves to Fez, Morocco but is forced to flee after publishing a letter commiserating with persecution of Moroccan and Tunisian Jewry. Arrives in the Holy Land 1165, moves to Cairo in 1165. He is physician to the court of Salah a-Din. Appointed *nagid* (grand rabbi) of Egypt in 1171.

The Rambam codifies all major Jewish law into a single readable work. His Commentaries are to the Mishna (Review of the Oral Law), the Torah and The Thirteen Principles of Faith. The principles are divided into:
1. The nature and belief in God.
2. The authenticity, validity and immutability of the Torah.
3. Man's responsibility and ultimate reward.

The 13 Articles of Faith.

1. In the existence of a Creator. Exodus 20:2
2. In God's Unity. Deuteronomy 6:4 There is one God. If there were many gods, they would have body, form, limitations and definitions.
3. That God is incorporeal. Deuteronomy 4:15. Not confined to a body, has no image or form which cannot be grasped or comprehended by human thought. Job 11:7-9.
4. That God is Eternal. Deuteronomy 33:27. (Has no beginning nor end).
5. To Him alone is it right to pray. Exodus 20:5.
6. That all the words of the Prophets are true.
7. That the prophesy of Moses our teacher is true and that there has never arisen a prophet like Moses. Numbers 16:28.
8. Moses received the Torah on Mt. Sinai. Deuteronomy 31:24.
9. God will not alter nor change his law. Jeremiah 32:19.
10. The Creator knows the deeds of men and their thoughts. Ecclesiastes 12:13.
11. Reward for the righteous and punishment for the wicked.
12. The Messiah will come at the end of days. Isaiah 2:2.
13. God will quicken the dead in His abundance of loving-kindness

In 1176 he commences his major work *'The Guide for the Perplexed'* on Jewish religious philosophy, explaining the fundamental theology and philosophy of Judaism. The laws as a whole aims at - the welfare of the soul (human intellect) and the welfare of the body (human relations). The Rambam dies in Egypt 1204, is buried in Tiberias.

1177 Crusader (Frankish) and Templar Knights forces under King Baldwin IV defeat Salah a-Din in the Battle of Montgisart at Gezer (Tel Jezer). Subsequently Salah a-Din learns to regard Crusader forces seriously.

1179 Ayyubid leader Salah a-Din captures the Crusader fortress Chastellet, at Jacob's Fjord (Ateret, Benot Yaakov) in the Upper Galilee, with ten meter high walls and an impregnable ramparts. This fortress controlled a major the Jordan River crossing between the port in Acre and the Golan onwards to Damascus. The 1500 Templar Crusaders of which 800 including 80 knights are killed and 700 are captured, taken to slavery. King Baldwin IV's troops stationed in Tiberias arrive too late to assist the Christians.

1182 King Philip II **expels the Jews from France,** expropriating their properties and turning synagogues into churches.

1182 Local Orthodox in Constantinople massacre Catholics, constituting a serious threat to the position of the papal legate in Rome.

1182   Renaud (Reynald) of Chatillon, Lord of Antioch is also Lord of Krak de Moab and Krak de Montreal, having previously spent 16 years in Muslim captivity in an Aleppo prison. He constructs a fleet of ships in the Crusader Castle in Moab (Krak de Moab) transporting them 200 kilometers through the Arava to the Red Sea. Renaud proceeds to attack the Muslim positions in the Gulf of Akaba, conquers the Coral Island (Jazirat Far'un) as his forces loot and sack ports in the Red Sea area. Egyptians, with the help of local Bedouins in Arabia finally locate the Crusaders in the Hejaz Desert, a short distance from Medina. Renaud withdraws as he has over-extended his supply lines.

Map 25. The Ayyubid Empire late 12th century

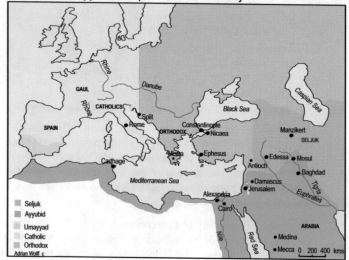

1183   Salah a-Din occupies Aleppo, now encircling the Crusaders.

1185   Baldwin V (1177-1186) son of Baldwin IV, aged 9, king of Jerusalem (1185–1186) is poisoned soon after ascending the throne.

1186   Guy de Lusignan (1129-1194), husband of Sibyl, (sister of Baldwin IV), king of Jerusalem.

Military Techniques

1. **Siege Towers**. Levels 15-20m high, several platforms, transported on wheels. Covered to protect soldiers from stones, missiles, arrows, burning cloth, etc.

2. **Battering Rams.** Iron-tipped, long, hanging from chains. The construction is covered to protect soldiers from stones, missiles, arrows,

burning cloth, flaming asphalt, etc.

3. **Ballista** 1. Giant bow, operated by cords.

2. Spoon-shaped catapults to project stones, rocks.

4. **Tunnels**. Remove outer wall stones. Tunnel under wall, burn timber props causing walls to collapse.

5. **Horses** Crusader - Two horses, one light for travel, one heavy for battle.
Muslim - Fast, mobile Arab horses. Change horses during battle.

6. **Battle Plans** Crusader - Prefer open ground battle plan for attack, heavily armored horsemen, infantry for defense, no mounted archers.
Muslim - Light armor and light horsemen, mounted archers, quick sudden attacks, do not meet Crusaders on open ground, would make a wedge between infantry and cavalry.

7. **Body Armor** Crusader - Metal scales, sewn or riveted to tunic, weigh 50 kgs, elbow length, falling below the knees.
Muslim - Mail chain, relatively light. Also use leather armor.

8. **Helmet** Crusader - Heavy flat top, full covered helmet.
Muslim - Elongated egg-shaped helmet.

9. **Shield** Crusader - Large shoulder height, heavy leather covered wooden frame. Muslim - Light round shield.

10. **Mace** Crusader - Spherical, fluted, hatched. Also double-edged axe.

11. **Bow** Crusader- Bow is used for hunting, only later used on foot by stationary archers.
Muslim - The bow in fighting is almost exclusively used by Muslims during this period. The mounted archers use the bow while riding.

12. **Sword** Crusader - Heavy, long. Muslim - Curved, two-sided.

13. **Soldier** accessories Crusader - Dagger, lance.

14. **Pikeman** Crusader - Not mounted

15. **Techniques** Crusader - Heavily armored knights charge on horseback in a tightly packed group, with lances pointing forward. At close quarters use axes and swords.
Muslim - Attempt to split the tightly knit Crusaders by feigning a retreat, wear light-weight leather armor, long-range bows and arrows, shoot from the saddle beyond the Crusader lances.

1187   **The Battle of the Horns of Hittin** 2 - 6 July 1187. A truce is drawn up between **King Guy** de Lusignan of Jerusalem and **Salah a-Din**, the Muslim leader, whereby each side will not attack each other's caravans. Crusader Knight Renaud (Reynald) of Chatillon annuls this truce by attacking a Muslim caravan in Transjordan, capturing Salah a-Din's sister, who immediately requests reparations and the release of all the Muslims and their captured goods. Renaud refuses. Consequently Salah a-Din on 1 July 1187, moves his troops from the Golan to the southern end of the Sea of Galilee (Zemach). King Guy does not wish to enter into battle. Raymond III of Tripoli, (also Lord of Tiberias through his wife Lady Eschive), forces the king's hand. He declares if King Guy refuses, it will be seen as a sign of weakness and he, King Guy will be deposed.

On 2 July 1187 Salah a-Din blocks the main road to Tiberias where Lady Eschive resides. On 3 July 1187 the Crusaders move their forces from the regional Crusader center of Sephoris (Zippori) towards Tiberias, a distance of about 25 kilometers - one day's journey. They wait and lure the Muslim forces into the open plain west of the **Horns of Hittin**, overlooking the Sea of Galilee. The march is exhausting due to the intense mid-summer heat. The Crusaders, together with their horses, spend the night without water. Muslims control all the wells in the immediate area. The heavily armored Crusaders prefer to meet their enemy face-to-face in a tight battle formation in an open plain. Salah a-Din does not take the bait, leaving the Crusaders to wait, without water. Crusader knights have two horses, one a lighter, faster horse used for transportation and a second heavy horse covered in armor, used in battle. A knight requires four foot-soldiers to supply him with his weapons and assist with his horse during battle. Forces of Salah a-Din now surround Crusader forces on the plateau.

The day 4 July 1187 is another hot, dry day. Crusaders, still in tight formation, fight off minor Muslim advances and harassment to their rear supply units, thereby holding up the advance of the Crusader cavalry in the front. Still no fresh water supplies are forthcoming to the Crusaders who cannot reach the wells and have not received fresh water supplies for two days. On 5 July 1187 Muslims open a gap near the Horns of Hittin allowing Crusader cavalry to descend the cliffs towards Tiberias to drink water. Muslims immediately close their ranks, preventing Crusader cavalry from ascending the 250-meter climb back to the plateau. Conditions for Crusader troops on the plateau become desperate from the lack of water being surrounded and attacked by Muslim horsemen firing arrows.

By 6 July 1187 the Crusaders are wilting as both men and horses have not received fresh water supplies for over three days. Crusaders remain completely surrounded by Muslims who exploit to their advantage the strong westerly wind blowing every afternoon in the summer months, by igniting the dry natural grass. Smoke blows into the Crusader faces unable to see the enemy. Foot-soldiers break rank and flee, discontinuing the essential coordination with the cavalry.

The 30-40,000 Muslim forces of Salah a-Din defeat the Crusader forces of King Guy de Lusignan comprising 22-27,000 men in addition to about 1,200 cavalry. King Guy's life is spared. Salah a-

Din offers the fallen king rose-water, with ice from Mt Hermon. Renaud of Chatillon is killed together with over 200 Templars and Hospitaller Knights. Most of the Crusader Knights are slain in the battle, while the remaining captive knights are treated honorably and later ransomed. Less fortunate are the foot-soldiers, most of who are sold into slavery. Virtually the entire military force of the Kingdom of Jerusalem has been destroyed. King Guy immediately makes his way to Jerusalem.

The Battle of the Horns of Hittin is the largest defeat of the Crusaders, never recovering their military power. From this date commences their expulsion from the Holy Land.

1187 Following his success at Battle of the Horns of Hittin, Salah a-Din captures Tiberias, Upper Galilee including Banias, continuing along the coast to Acre, Jaffa, Caesarea, Ashkelon and Gaza. Salah a-Din arrives (2 October 1187) at Jerusalem defended by a handful of men under command of Balian of Ibelin. The Crusader Army has previously been destroyed at Hittin, forcing King Guy de Lusignan to quickly capitulate in Jerusalem without any battle since no Christian reinforcements are available to assist him.

Wajeeh Nuseibeh, Custodian, at the doors of the Holy Sepulchre. Adrian Wolff

1187 Salah a-Din allows the inhabitants of Jerusalem to leave for Acre after paying a ransom. He is known to distribute half his spoils to his soldiers. No church is destroyed, no one is massacred and no looting occurs. Though Salah a-Din offers to release Crusader soldiers for a ransom, the king does not buy freedom for the local Christian inhabitants. Those unable to raise the amount are sold into slavery. *"Salah a-Din looked at two lines of defeated Crusaders as they left the City (Jerusalem), one going into slavery, the other - their ransom being paid - going to freedom."* [Anton Felton, Jewish Carpets, cited in A. Elon, Jerusalem, City of Mirrors]. King Guy prefers to retain his wealth for himself, becoming captive to Salah a-Din when in 1188 he is exiled to Acre.

1188　The Eastern Orthodox Christians (Syrian or Greek) elect to remain in Jerusalem, while the Latins (Catholic) Christians are temporally barred from entering Jerusalem. A few days after the Muslim conquest, Christian pilgrims are permitted to visit the Church of the Holy Sepulchre. **All churches, except the Church of the Holy Sepulchre are converted into mosques.** The Church of St. Anne, (on the via Dolorosa) near St. Stephen's Gate (Lions Gate) is converted into a Muslim religious college, a *madrassah*. Salah a-Din replaces the Latin Catholics authority inside the Church of the Holy Sepulchre to the Egyptian Christian Copt sect. Salah a-Din does not trust the various Christian sects, giving control of the key to the door of the Church of the Holy Sepulchre to a local Muslim family, Nuseibeh, who continue this obligation until today.

1188　**This signifies the End of Crusader Kingdom of Jerusalem. Christian Jerusalem is lost, including the most tangible symbol of Christian faith, the Church of the Holy Sepulchre. The Church of the Holy Sepulchre and The Temple Mount remains to this day under the control of the Wakf (Muslim Higher Religious authority).**

1188　Various Crusader Kings had severely limited Jewish presence in Jerusalem, now under Salah a-Din Jews may resettle in Jerusalem. All Muslim mosques and shrines are restored.

1188　Crusaders remain in Acre, Tyre, Antioch and Tripoli.

Chapter 15. Third to Sixth Crusades 1188 - 1229

1188 Safed, the regional Crusader center in the Upper Galilee falls as Salah a-Din releases King Guy de Lusignan from imprisonment in Nablus, who immediately repudiates his oath not to attack Muslims by making a siege around Acre. After a one-month siege, prisoners are exchanged as Christian forces enter Acre. Salah a-Din then assembles an additional siege around the Crusaders inside Acre who have no access to the hinterland, but control the naval passage. Sibyl, wife of King Guy dies during the siege

1188 Isobel, daughter of King Amalric I, a sibling of both King Baldwin IV and Sibyl. She is previously married to Humphrey, annuls her marriage so as to marry King Conrad I by means of royal intrigue.

St. Anne Crusader Church, Jerusalem   Adrian Wolff

1189 After an eighteen-month siege Salah a-Din captures Belvoir Castle controlling the main road in the Jordan Valley. Tyre and Acre ports are the only major towns remaining under Crusader control.

1189 Following the fall of Jerusalem and the total defeat of the Crusaders, Pope Gregory VIII calls for a new Crusade.

> **The Third Crusade 1189 - 1192**
> - Aim: To capture Jerusalem
> - End: Peace Treaty to allow Christian Pilgrims to enter Jerusalem
> - Does not capture Jerusalem
> - Leaders of the Third Crusade are:
>   - King Frederick I (Barbarosa) of Germany drowns in Anatolia at start of Crusade, depleted troops led by Leopold V of Austria.
>   - King Philip II (Augustus) of France
>   - King Richard I the Lion-Heart of England

1189   German Emperor **Frederick** I Barbarosa (red beard) of Swabia (1123-1190), a participant in the 2nd Crusade, fears once he embarks on a Crusade the French King Philip II (1165-1223, reigns 1179-1223) will attack his empire. Therefore Frederick requests from the Pope that King Philip II join the new Crusade. He sets out in May 1189 accompanied by the largest crusader army with about 100,000 troops. The Byzantine Emperor Isaac II Angelus persuades King Frederick I to by-pass Constantinople, crossing the Dardanelles into Anatolia.

1189   The English king, Henry II dies in 1189 succeeded by his son, **Richard I** (1157-1199). Both the French and Germans suspect Richard I, the Lion-Heart, will use this opportunity to increase his territory in Normandy. Subsequently the Pope orders Richard I to join the Crusade. The three kings agree to meet near Sidon in Lebanon before proceeding to The Holy Land. Kings Philip II of France and Richard I of England decide between themselves to meet at Messina, Sicily, where they sign an agreement outlining their mutual obligations and rights before proceeding to Sidon.

1190   King Frederick I defeats the Seljuk army in Anatolia and reaches Iconium (Konya today). He drowns while crossing the Kalykadnos River in Cilicia, Lesser Armenia. His troops are decimated by bubonic plague in Antioch. The remaining German forces, with low morale now under Leopold V (1159-1194) an Austrian Duke, continue to Tyre as only a few thousand enroll with the French and English Crusader forces. The majority return to Germany.

1191   King Philip II of France arrives at Acre on 20 April. The task begins in earnest to relieve the Muslim siege surrounding King Guy.

1191   King Richard I first sails to Cyprus where his sister Joan and fiancée Berengaria of Navarre are shipwrecked, held captive by the Byzantine governor of Cyprus, Isaac Comnenus. Richard I defeats the local Byzantines army, captures Isaac Comnenus and conquers the island of Cyprus. The Byzantines lose Cyprus, never to rule the island again. Richard I then sets sail for Acre arriving on

8 June 1191, where he gives new vigor to the break the Muslim siege on Acre. It has taken almost two years before all the Crusader forces reach the Holy Land. He successfully captures Acre on 12 July 1191, and when their ransom is not paid on time, massacres about 3000 prisoners-of-war. Immediately Philip II of France and Leopold V of Austria disapprove of Richard I on him taking the credit for capturing Acre.

Acre is renewed into an all-season port, unlike Jaffa port that contains treacherous rocks at its entrance limiting it to summer sailing only. The Acre port is extended, comprising a quay 325 meters long, the largest in the Holy Land.

1191   King Philip II leaves Acre for France in August 1191 with perhaps the intention to gain control of English possessions in Normandy, while Leopold V returns to Austria, leaving Richard I to control the outcome of the 3rd Crusade. Richard I, with the Templar Knights defeats Salah a-Din, capturing the Mediterranean ports of Asour (Arsuf/Apollonia) and Jaffa, slaughtering their prisoners.

1191   On the route from Jaffa to Jerusalem Richard I captures Ramle and is forced to winter at Latrun as his forces cannot, in the muddy winter rainy season, ascend the Judean Mountains to Jerusalem. He receives messages from England urging him to return home as his brother John is intent on usurping the throne.

1192   In the spring of 1192 Richard I leaves Latrun moving his forces towards Nevi Samuel, a Crusader fortress on the western hilltop from where he views Jerusalem. Byzantine writings from the 5th century designate Nevi Samuel as the burial place of the Jewish Prophet Samuel, constructing a large church above an enclosed tomb. Crusaders believe this the holy site of Shiloh and call the new church 'The Holy Church of Samuel of Shiloh'. The mountain Montjoie (mountain of joy) at Nevi Samuel is the spot pilgrims arriving from the foothills have their first sight of the walls and domes Jerusalem. Richard I realizes his Crusader forces are too small to conquer Jerusalem, does not attempt battle or capture Jerusalem from the Muslims. A legend states Richard I refuses to gaze upon the city he cannot conquer and covers his eyes with his shield. Richard I, The Lion Heart is never to enter Jerusalem.

1192   A Peace Treaty between Salah a-Din and Richard I (to last five years), allows Christian pilgrims free access to Christian holy places. They are permitted to pray at both the Church of the Holy Sepulchre and the Church of the Nativity in Bethlehem. Control of Jerusalem remains in Muslim hands. **The knights of the Third Crusade will reach Jerusalem as pilgrims, not as conquerors.**

1192   From Nevi Samuel Richard I returns to Acre for England without booty (he did not conquer). Before leaving the Holy Land he accedes to popular opinion deposing King Guy for failure of the 3rd Crusade, giving him (Guy) governorship of Cyprus where he resides until his death in 1194. Crusader control is now limited to towns along the coast from Tyre to Jaffa only. **The 3rd Crusade ends in failure to capture its major objective, Jerusalem.**

Map 26. The Third Crusader Period 1187 -1192

1192   Richard's fleet cannot travel through the Straits of Gibraltar as it remains in Muslim hands, forcing him to return to England overland. Both Philip II of France and Leopold V of Austrian remember the circumstances of their last meeting with Richard I in Acre and await his appearance in their home territory. Richard I is imprisoned in Wachau, near Vienna, Austria while his brother John usurps the throne in England. You already know the rest of the story - Robin Hood and all that! Richard I is eventually ransomed, returning a hero, to be crowned a second time and spends the remainder of his life in France until his death in 1199.

1192   England is bankrupt, while the Jews are expected to pay the debts accrued during Richard's Crusade including the substantial ransom paid for his freedom. Anti-Semitic outbursts in England follow the re-coronation of King Richard I in Westminster Cathedral culminating with the mass suicide of 150 Jews in the Tower of York.

The Second Kingdom of Jerusalem-Acre 1192 - 1291
- Capital in Acre

- No King resides in Jerusalem, remaining resident in Cyprus
- The Crusader Kings do not control Jerusalem
- Crusaders control part of the coastal area, from Tyre to Jaffa
- End: Expulsion of the Crusaders from the Holy Land in 1291

1192   During the **Second Crusader Kingdom of Jerusalem-Acre from 1192 to 1291, Acre is capital while all kings rule from Cyprus. Crusader Kings do not control Jerusalem.** The Kingdom of Cyprus lasts 1192 until 1570 when the Ottomans conquer Cyprus.

1192   King Conrad I, the 2nd husband of Isobel is immediately assassinated and his widow is persuaded to marry Henri de Champagne (King Richard's nephew) (1192-1194).

1193   Salah a-Din, the respected, honorable leader and professional soldier dies in Damascus. He is remembered as never going back on his word. Salah a-Din's death signals the **end of Muslim Ayyubid - Abbasid (Sunni-Shi'ite) unity.**

1194   King Henri de Champagne rules for two years until he is defenestrated. Isobel is now looking for a 4th husband to be king! She marries Amalric II de Lusignan, King of Acre (1194–1205) who is never to be crowned. He is the uncle of Guy de Lusignan.

1195   Byzantine Alexius III blinds, deposes his brother Emperor Isaac II.

1197   King Heinrich IV of Germany **organizes a new crusade** which disintegrates when a rebellion erupts against his rule in Sicily. He dies of malaria at Messina, Sicily. His father is King Frederick I Barbarosa (3rd Crusade), his son King Frederick II (4th Crusade).

1198   A Peace Treaty is negotiated between King Amalric II and al-Malik al-Adel of Egypt enabling the Crusaders to gain rights to the Galilee and southern Coastal Plain. al-Malik al-Adel is showing his independence from the Abbasids in Baghdad.

German Knights of the **Templar Order**, known as **Teutonic Knights**, ("Deutschritterorden" in German), had previously participated in the remainder of King Frederick I Barbarosa's army in the 3rd Crusade. The Pope and the German king recognize the Teutonic Knights as a Crusader Order in 1198.

Teutonic Knights construct fortresses in the Galilee at Montfort (Starkenberg) (1226), Judin (Yehiam), Mi'ilya (1220) and Safed (1240). They cooperate with King Frederick II of Hohenstaufen during the 6th Crusade in 1228, extending their control over the entire Galilee until the Mamluk invasion and conquest in 1260.

1198   Pope Innocent III encourages western Latin Christians (Catholics) to conquer the Orthodox capital Constantinople, to unify the church under the control of Rome and in addition to gain the benefits of trade. The Pope uses the pretext he needs to restore Isaac II to the throne in Constantinople and notes that Isaac's son Alexius IV had previously made lavish promises to the Crusaders as a reward they place him (Alexius) on the throne in Constantinople.

1201   **Earthquake** damage in Nablus area.

1202   Pope Innocent III proclaims the **Fourth Crusade** with the aim to control the Byzantine Empire by conquering their wealthy capital, Constantinople. He announces papal income tax on all clerical incomes to finance a new crusade.

> **The Fourth Crusade 1202 - 1204**
> - Aim: To conquer the Byzantine Empire
> - End:Venetian Crusaders attack, plunder, capture Constantinople
> - The Crusaders never reach the Holy Land
> - Leaders of the Fourth Crusade are:
>   - Doge Enrico Dandolo of Venice
>   - Boniface of Montferrat
>   - Philip of Swabia

1202   Venice has acquired considerable trading privileges within the Byzantine Empire especially during the Crusader Period by providing maritime transportation services for transporting troops, knights, their entourage and logistic material from Europe to the Holy Land. The Crusader Army of 10,000 troops arriving in Venice in the summer of 1202 is smaller than the anticipated 30,000 participants and in addition there are not sufficient funds to pay the Venetians for transporting the Crusaders to the Levant. In lieu of payment, the Doge of Venice, Enrico Dandolo, suggests the Crusaders attack the Hungarian Orthodox Christian town of Zara (Zadar in Croatia today) on the Adriatic Sea, which poses a threat to the Venetian ships. The result is Latin Christians battle Orthodox Christians in the Battle of Zara, with victory going to the Venetians. Leaders of the new 4th Crusade are Boniface of Montferrat and Philip of Swabia. Philip is the brother-in-law of Alexius IV, the son of the deposed Emperor Isaac II.

1204   Crusaders forces sail for Constantinople, viewed by Venice as an opportunity to dominate one of the greatest commercial centers of the world. Local Orthodox in Constantinople do not wish the Latins (Catholics) to influence their local politics and definitely have no interest in the Venetians taking over their city, its administration and its tax collection. The Crusaders depose the usurper Alexius III and install Alexius IV (the younger) as co-emperor together with his blinded father, Isaac II. The promised remuneration is not forthcoming, causing Latins (Catholics) to storm the city as Venetians battle Greek Orthodox Christians in Constantinople. On 13 April 1204 Constantinople falls to the Latins and with the permission of its Venetian leaders, this glorious, wealthy capital is subjected to pillage and massacre for three days. Many priceless icons, relics and other objects are taken to Venice during the rape and plunder of the Hagia Sophia Church in Constantinople.

1204 The Pope is unable to rectify the situation in Constantinople especially as he absolved the Crusaders from their debts and promised booty. The rift between the Eastern and Western churches widens as the relationship between the Pope in Rome and the Eastern Orthodox never normalizes, remaining formal and correct, even to this day (See Pope 2000). The Byzantine Empire is damaged beyond repair and awaits for its conquest, finally arriving with the Ottoman Sultan, Mehmed II in 1453. The 4th Crusade is a disaster ending with no impact on the Holy Land.

1204 Jews of Constantinople are not free from Christian violence. Crusaders plunder and burn the Jewish Quarter. Legend tells the Venetian Crusaders take the **Golden Menorah** as payment for their maritime services during the disastrous failed 4th Crusade of 1202-1204. The Menorah, with a considerable weight in gold, is melted down and consequently lost for eternity. (See 70, 324, 534).

1204 The Venetians impose their own order in Constantinople electing Baldwin of Flanders, Emperor and the Venetian Thomas Morosini, Patriarch. Venetian emperors reign in Constantinople until 1261.

1205 King Amalric II dies. Maria de Brienne, (daughter of Conrad I and Isobel), wife of Jean de Brienne, is Queen of the Kingdom of Acre (1205–1212). She rules from Cyprus.

1209 Jean de Brienne (future king of Acre) encourages French and English rabbis, with their congregations settle in Jerusalem.

1210 St. Francis of Assisi, Italy establishes the **Franciscan Order** of Friars promoting peace between humans and nature, especially animals. He emphasizes poverty and repentance. St. Francis preaches in the vernacular, bringing the Gospel to the faithful in local languages. He also preaches a fierce religiosity persuading the faithful to boycott Jews and their businesses. The Italian language develops during this period. Following the Crusader ouster in 1291, the Franciscans become responsible for 'Latin' Catholic Christian sites in 'The Holy Land'. They wear a white robe.

1212 Jean de Brienne king of Acre after the death of his wife Queen Maria. He rules from Cyprus from 1212 until 1225.

The Children's Crusade 1212
- Aim: To reach Jerusalem
- End: Miserable death, lucky ones sold into slavery
- Do not reach Constantinople or the Holy Land
- Leaders of the Children's Crusade are:
  - Stephen of Cloyes, near Orleans, France
  - Nicholas of Germany

The Children's Crusade begins when thousands of children in France and Germany assume they can find a dry passage to the Land of Israel like Moses who parted the Red Sea. They believe adults have sinned and therefore providence will be granted to them, the children, the symbols of innocence. A French shepherd Stephen of Noyes leads over 30,000 boys and girls, most below the age of twelve to embark on ships from Marseilles. These children are sold into slavery by unscrupulous mariners at the Muslim port of Bougie, Algeria in North Africa. Nicholas leads 20,000 children from Germany. They travel overland to Italy, lose their way (in Italy), are slaughtered, others die of hunger, thirst, and disease, while the lucky survivors are sold into slavery and never reach Constantinople. **End of the dreadful Children's Crusade**.

1215 The Bible clearly states human rights and duties. For example *"Laws of people who are entrusted to safeguard someone else's property."* (Exodus 22:6). *"You shall not show favoritism in judgment, small and great alike shall you hear, you shall not tremble before any man."* (Deuteronomy 1:17). King John I of England bows to pressure from the barons (also economic, military reasons) who force him to sign **The Magna Carta**. This is the first western document of human rights stating that *"no freemen shall be...imprisoned or diseased (dispossessed) ...except by the lawful judgment of his peers or by the law of the land."*

1215 Pope Innocent III approves a new Crusade to restore the Kingdom of Jerusalem. He decrees Jews are forced to wear a visible badge to distinguish themselves from Christians.

1216 The German Emperor King Frederick II (Hohenstaufen) (1194-1250) promises Pope Honorius III his cooperation in a new Crusade to regain lost territory in the Holy Land.

The Fifth Crusade 1218 - 1221
- Aim: To capture Egypt and barter it for Jerusalem
- End: Surrender and ransom in Egypt
- Never reaches The Holy Land
- The leaders of the Fifth Crusade are:
  - Jean de Breinne

The idea of the Crusader movement has lost its impetus in Europe. Large resources of available finance, the adventurism and enthusiasm have ceased. A successful attack on the Holy Land seems impossible inducing the Crusaders to attack Egypt, the wealthy gateway to the Orient. Therefore the Crusaders aim to conquer Egypt is not an objective, but is to be used to bargain, which, according to their reasoning, would cede Jerusalem from Muslims back to Christians.

1218   Forces of Duke of Austria and King of Hungary land in Acre in 1217 and together with King Jean de Brienne (of Acre) sail for Damietta in the Nile Delta in May 1218. During the lengthy siege of Damietta, the papal legate, Cardinal Pelagius arrives with French Crusaders in Acre. He regards all Crusaders to be under the jurisdiction of the church, refusing to accept the leadership of King Jean de Brienne.

Map 27. The Fifth Crusade 1218 – 1221

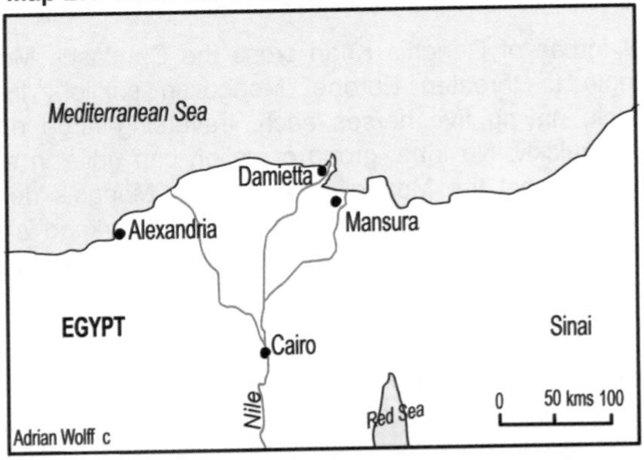

1219   Egyptian Abed el-Kamil requiring Crusader support, offers peace terms to King Jean de Brienne including cession of Jerusalem. The Ayyubids in Egypt are seeking independence from the Abbasids in Baghdad. Cardinal Pelagius, supported by Crusader Military Orders and the Italian States, stubbornly refuse, preferring a military solution. Following the spurning of his offer Abed el-Kamil begins to destroy many Christian sites in the Holy Land, dissolving the Peace Treaty of 1192 between Richard I and Salah a-Din.

1219   al-Aziz Othman, the Abbasid Governor of Damascus fears the Fifth Crusade and their military potential to attack Damascus, therefore he destroys the Crusader fortress at Banias.

1219   Crusaders finally capture Damietta on 5 November 1219. For the next year no progress is made, as the Crusaders are expecting

King Frederick II of Germany to join with fresh reinforcements of troops and materiel. He never arrives as he is forced to postpone his departure as he must firstly settle his affairs in Germany and difficulties in Sicily inherited from his father King Heinrich IV.

1220   German Teutonic knights construct the Mi'ilya fortress in the Western Galilee to protect the Trade Route to the Acre port.

1221   Cardinal Pelagius advances from Damietta towards Cairo without studying the level of the annual Nile floods, which together with the Egyptian Army and reinforcements from Syria, cut the Crusaders from their rear in Damietta and halt their movement southwards towards Cairo. The trapped Crusaders are unable to retreat, surrendering at Mansura where they sign a truce of eight years. King Jean is ransomed for a large sum. The Crusaders do not gain any territorial concessions, lose many lives, and do not recoup the cost of the disastrous expedition in Egypt. The Crusaders are becoming the objects of ridicule in Europe, as Crusading is no longer a popular cause. **End of the failed 5th Crusade.**

1221   Mongol forces of Genghis Khan cross the Caucasus Mountains and begin to threaten Europe. Mongolian soldiers travel on horseback, having five horses each, traversing large distances relatively quickly. No tribe, group or caliph can unite in sufficient numbers to repel the Mongolian army. The Mongols defeat the Khwarizm (Tartar) Empire at their capital, Samarkand along the 'Silk Road' forcing them to move both south and west, upsetting the balance of power.

1223   Mongols enter Anatolia and are joined by the Armenians in Lesser Armenia in their fight against the Seljuks.

Montfort Castle, Western Galilee   Adrian Wolff

1225 King Frederick II of Germany, also King of Acre (1225–1243) marries Isabel (Isabella/Yolonda), daughter of King Jean and Maria de Brienne. Known as 'Stupor Mundi' (Wonder of the World), being a warrior, scholar, poet, student of philosophy and an intellectual.

1226 Fearing a new Crusade of King Frederick II, al-Aziz Othman, the Abbasid governor in Damascus constructs **Nimrod** fortress on the passage above Banias controlling the road from the Galilee to the Golan and Damascus. German Teutonic Knights protect the Trade Route approaching the Crusader port of Acre by constructing the **Montfort** (Starkenberg) fortress in the Western Galilee.

Nimrod Fortress, Golan   Adrian Wolff

Nimrod Fortress, Water Cistern   Adrian Wolff

1227 King Frederick II returns to Germany from Brindisi, Italy abandoning his participation in a new crusade due to problems within his kingdom. The new Pope Gregory IX declares Frederick excommunicated for twice delaying his departure for the Holy Land. (Previously delayed his departure in 1219 to assist the 5th Crusade trapped in Egypt).

The Sixth Crusade 1228 - 1229
- Aim: To gain Christian control of Jerusalem.
- End: Peace Treaty between King Frederick II and Muslims allowing Christian control of Holy Sites in Jerusalem and Bethlehem.
- The leader of the Sixth Crusade is: King Frederick II of Germany

1228 Queen Isabel, wife of King Frederick II dies in 1228 and their son Conrad (future Conrad IV) becomes regent from Cyprus. When King Frederick arrives in Acre in 1228, the Hospitaller and Templar Knights refuse to cooperate with the excommunicated crusader leader. Only the German Teutonic Knights give support to King Frederick II who captures Acre and restores the walls of Caesarea.

1229 King Frederick II successfully negotiates a 10-year Peace Treaty with Egyptian Sultan al-Abel el-Kamil receiving without fighting, Christian control of their holy sites in Jerusalem, Bethlehem, Nazareth, with a corridor towards the sea, Western Galilee and Sidon. This treaty is widely denounced by devout Christians and Muslims, while Frederick II finds himself unpopular with Crusaders, clergy and aristocracy who all blame him for not regaining the entire Kingdom of Jerusalem. The excommunicated Frederick II crowns himself king in the Church of the Holy Sepulchre, Jerusalem without a priest present, as one of the Teutonic Knights reads the ceremony.

1229 Pope Gregory IX disapproves of the truce, severely disciplines Frederick II, giving an 'interdict' against Christian religious ceremonies in Jerusalem. Nevertheless, a limited number of Christians begin to resettle in the Christian quarter and once again the Church of the Holy Sepulchre is under Christian control. Muslims control the Temple Mount and the eastern quarters. Frederick II retains Acre as capital where he resides to enable him a quick escape to Cyprus. After learning papal troops are occupying his Kingdom of Sicily, Frederick II quickly returns to Europe, leaving Acre port ignobly as the city's butchers pelt him with scraps of meat. **End of the Sixth Crusade.**

Chapter 16. The End of the Crusades 1230-1291

1230 King Frederick II makes his peace with the Pope at San Germano, who lifts his interdict.

1240 Thibaut IV of Champagne's poorly organized Crusade ends in slaughter at Hirbia-Furbie, Beit Hanun in Gaza. He signs a short-lived treaty as Muslims allow Christian pilgrims to visit Jerusalem, Ramle and Hebron. **All Crusader towns will now fight independently without receiving reinforcements.** Richard of Cornwall (brother of King Henry III) re-fortifies Ashkelon. Local Crusaders loose interest in fighting after Ashkelon falls in 1247.

1240 Teutonic (Templar) Knights reconstruct the Safed Castle.

1241 General Batu leads Mongolian troops to reach Hungary, defeating the Christians. News of the death of Batu's uncle, Ogodei Khagan, the khan in Mongolia, halts the Mongol juggernaut in Central Europe near Vienna. Batu returns to their capital Karakorum in vain to become the next khan. A similar event will occur in 1259.

1242 King Louis IX of France forces the Jewish communities to give up their copies of the Talmud. 24 cartloads of Jewish books burned in the square in front of the Louvre in Paris.

1243 Conrad IV, son of King Frederick II and Queen Isabel, King of Acre (1243–1254), rules from Cyprus never arriving in the Holy Land. Alice, queen dowager is regent.

1244 Blanchegarde (Tel Zafit) captured by Salah a-Din in 1187, recaptured by the Crusaders in 1192, is destroyed by the Mamlukes in 1244.

1244 Egyptian Ayyubids invite and encourage Khwarizm Turks to attack the Crusaders despite the previously signed alliance between them and King Frederick II of 1229. Khwarizms with 10,000 cavalry capture parts of the Galilee including Tiberias, then conquer the Crusaders in Jerusalem, seriously damaging The Church of the Holy Sepulchre. Jewish life in Jerusalem ceases during this period. **Christian Jerusalem is lost, not to be administered by Christians again until its capture from the Ottomans in 1917 by British General Edmund Allenby.**

1245 Franciscan friar Giovanni de Piano Carpini (1182-1252) travels from Lyon to Mongolia bringing letters from Pope Innocent IV to Guyuk Khan (khan from 1246 until 1248).

1245 King Louis IX, the Pious, of France (1214-1270) prepares the 7th

Crusade. He ardently believes a Crusade under his leadership to be God's calling. He arranges a Peace Treaty with England obliging them not to invade France, the Genoese to provide maritime transport, and raises funds in his domain. Pope Innocent IV authorizes a customary levy on all clerical incomes.

The Seventh Crusade 1248 - 1254
- Aim: To capture Egypt and exchange it for Jerusalem
- End: Crusader leader is captured and ransomed in Egypt
- Crusaders never arrive in the Holy Land
- Leader of the 7th Crusade is: King Louis IX of France

1248   King Louis IX takes three years to begin his voyage, leaving France for Cyprus in September 1248 with an army of 15,000 where they spend the winter and plan to attack Egypt first before embarking on their aim to capture Jerusalem.

1249   Crusaders land in Egypt strengthened with the arrival of Louis IX's brother Alphonse of Poitiers bringing re-enforcements, capturing Diametta in the Nile Delta. End of Moslem Period in Portugal.

Map 28. The Seventh Crusade 1248 – 1254

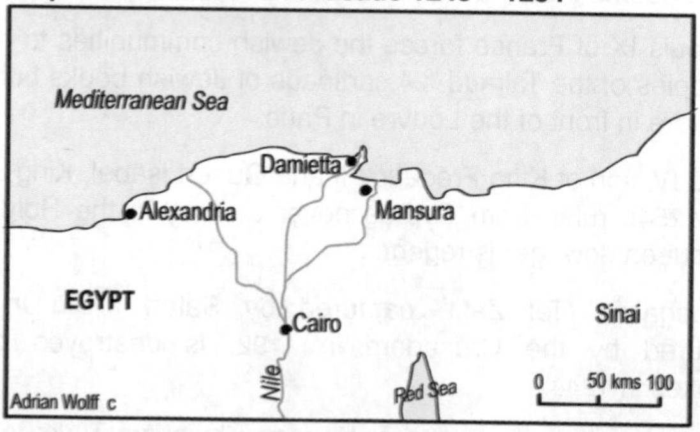

1250   Robert of Artois, a brother of King Louis IX, rejecting the advice of more experienced campaigners, leads a surprise attack on an Egyptian camp near Mansura, only to be trapped inside the city. Louis IX arrives with the main army to extricate the besieged Crusaders, eventually winning a costly battle, but becomes trapped inside the city. The Queen persuades the Genoese and Pisans to cede Damietta by arranging a considerable ransom for the king. He is released, Damietta surrenders, making no territorial gains and the entire episode is a financial disaster. **End of the disastrous 7th Crusade**.

1250   King Louis IX does not return to France immediately, moving his forces into The Holy Land strengthening Crusader fortifications. His influence on French Gothic style architectural projects are:

extension to the Church of the Holy Sepulchre, rebuilding of Caesarea (present walls 900 meters long, 13 metes high, gates, port, cathedral), Abu Gosh, Atlit, Safed, and Acre's port facilities.

Caesarea, Gothic Crusader Architecture Adrian Wolff

Architecture of Crusader Fortresses
1. **Ditch**. Dry moat 15 meters wide, 8-10 meters deep, with an inclined base
2. **Walls.** 15-18 meters high, 5 meters wide, defender's lodgings within the thick wall
3.**Towers.** Rising above walls. Round or square, overlooking the main gate
4. **Bridge.** May have arch or column in the ditch
5. **Gate.** Wooded pivots, strong locking beam inside, always L-shaped to force attackers to turn 90 degrees in a tight, closed space

Crusader Architecture in Jerusalem
 • Crusader King's Palace is built at David's Tower, including the moat
 • Church of the Holy Sepulchre, St. Anna, Mary's Tomb in Kidron Valley
 • Tower of David
 • Armenian Quarter
 • Markets in Jerusalem along the Cardo in the Jewish Quarter

Caesarea, Crusader Moat   Adrian Wolff

1250   Former Mamluk slave, rising to general al-Malik az-Assayer Rukn ad-Din **Beybars** (1223-1277) kills Turan the last Ayyubid Sultan, in Cairo.

Mamluk Sultanate 1250 - 1516 in Palestine (in Egypt till 1811)

- The Mamluks, originally **child slaves** brought from Central Asia to Egypt, converted to Islam and trained as military fighters known as *ahl as-sayf* (people of the sword).
- Only a Mamluk who has been brought up in the military career can become a leader. If a Mamluk marries a local Muslim, their son is not regarded as a Mamluk and cannot be a ruler or a dynasty.
- Mamluks take control Egypt from the Ayyubids. Muslim world is divided into Shi'ite east and Sunni west.
- Mamluks control from North Africa, Egypt, Palestine, Syria and southern Anatolia.
- The Mamluks are **Sunni Muslims,** their capital in **Cairo.**
- Bahri Mamluk Period 1250-1382 originating from Turkic peoples. Tugru Izadin Aibeck is proclaimed the First Mamluk Sultan.
- Burji Mamluk Period 1382-1517 originating from Circassians in the Caucasus.
- Mamluks build training colleges (madrassah), roads, bridges markets, mosques, and hospitals in Palestine. Domestic art flourishes.
- Believe in the separation between civil and military rule.
- Mamluks encourage, construct university in Cairo, further Islamic studies.

- Forced conversion of Egyptian Christian Copts to Islam, now become a minority.
- Mamluks capture Palestine divide into three provinces - Damascus, Safed, Gaza. Destroy the ports preventing Crusaders returning.
- Palestine is regarded as a 'passage' to Damascus, not developed economically or agriculturally.
- Mamluk towns built or resettled in Palestine: Beit She'an, Gesher, Jenin, Ikron, Jaljulia, Gaza, Khan Yunis.
- Bridges built in Palestine: Gengic (Ramle), Benot Ya'akov (Jordan River), Yavne, Damnia.
- Mosques built in Palestine: Hebron, Mar Musa, Lod, Ramle.
- Build khans-inns (Khan et-Tijjar, 'The Merchants Inn', near Ilania), hostels, bazaars.
- Jerusalem is not found on a Trade Route, remains a desolate town, not fortified, nor repopulated.
- Mamluks extort high taxes/tolls from non-Muslim pilgrims traveling to Jerusalem.
- *Dhimmi* laws enforced. Non-Muslims pay head tax (*jizya*); highway tax (*gafir*); inheritance tax; may not ride a horse, must wear distinctive clothing; forced to pay 'gifts' to Mamluk officials and administrators.
- Population of Jerusalem is estimated to shrink to 30,000 inhabitants.
- Building renovations in Jerusalem: al-Aqsa, Dome of the Rock, Khans, bazaars (*shuk*), water systems.
- Low-rank administrators are appointed in Palestine.
- During this period, Safed attracts many Jews.
- Mamluks defeat the Mongols at Battle of Ain Jalut (Harod) in 1260.
- Ottomans defeat the Mamluks in Palestine (1516), in Egypt (1517).
- After the Ottoman conquest of Egypt, Mamluks remain as Governors (Beys) as administrators for the Ottomans.
- Ottomans conquer all the Mamluk territory.
- Napoleon defeats the Mamluks at the Battle of the Pyramids (1798).
- Mamluk leaders are massacred by Muhammed Ali in Cairo in 1811 and survivors flee to Nubia in Sudan.

1250 **First Mamluk Period** in Egypt (1250–1382), known as Bahri or Turkic Period according to their ethnic origin.

1250 Founding of the **Alawite Muslim sect in Syria.** Alawis refuse to recognize the Assassin (Niziriyah) Imams. Alawis, originally Shi'ite followers of Ali ibn Abi-Talib recite the name of Ali in place of Mohammed in the '*Shahadah*' (first verse of the Koran). Alawis do not make a *haj* pilgrimage to Mecca, do not pray in a mosque, regard the Pillars of Islam as purely symbolic, do not fast during Ramadan. Some members of this sect celebrate Christmas and burn incense and believe in reincarnation. Today Alawis are a minority sect in Syria, rule the country by dictatorship.

1253 Hulagu, brother of Mongke Khagan conquers Persia eliminating the Assassins, violent extremist Islamics in the Elburz Mountains.

1254 King Louis IX, on learning of the death of his queen, leaves the Holy Land for France. Konradin, son of Conrad IV (1254–1269) rules from Cyprus, never arrives in the Holy Land.

1258 **Mongols** under General Hulagu, annihilate the Abbasid regime in Baghdad slaughtering 80,000 (of the 250,000 inhabitants) including the caliph and his sons. Mongols parade Abbasid Caliph al-Musta'sim naked on his horse through the streets of Baghdad and together with his sons, are sown into carpets to be trampled to death by horses. The Caliph's head is used as 'the ball' in polo. Christians and Jews are unharmed during the Mongol assault. *Dhimmi* status is abolished. **End of the Abbasid Caliphate.**

1259 Mongols continue to capture Muslim territory conquering Damascus, the former Ayyubid capital. The Mongol khan, Mongke Khagan dies (khan 1251-1259). His brother Hulagu, commander of the Mediterranean frontier hurries back to stake his claim as successor. Hulagu returns to Mongolia with over 100,000 troops making a 'show of force', leaving only 10,000 Mongolian troops to face the Mamluks.

1260 Mongols capture Nimrod fortress in the Northern Golan, allowing their easy entry in the Upper Galilee and areas west of the Jordan River. Sometimes there occurs a battle bringing about changes in the direction of history. Results of the Battle of Ain Jalut could have been totally different, affecting the future of the Middle East in particular, had the khan in Mongolia not died in 1259. Mongols are not (yet) Muslims and could have been victorious over the Mamluks having previously annihilated the Abbasids in Baghdad and captured Damascus. After Hulagu's return to Mongolia in 1259 the extremely depleted Mongolian troops approach the Holy Land. Mamluks request Crusaders' assistance against the invading Mongol forces. The Crusaders do not oblige, allowing Mamluk Sultan Qutuz to pass unmolested through their territory.

In the Battle of Ain Jalut in the Harod Valley, just north of the Gilboa Mountains and east of Beit She'an, Mamluks troops of Sultan Qutuz led by General Beybars (Baibars) defeat the Mongols. During this battle, Mongolian General Kitbuka is killed causing the troops to disperse and retreat towards the Euphrates River. Palestine is annexed. Mamluks gain admiration in the Muslim world. **End of Mongol presence in Palestine.**

A third brother Kublai proclaims himself khan, the first Yuan emperor in Shangdu, China, (1260-1294), unites the Mongols with China. Later Mongols embrace Islam as Emperor Ghazzan (1295-1304) converts.

1260 Mamluk military leader General Beybars murders all of his opponents including Sultan Qutuz, becoming Sultan in Cairo. His bloodthirstiness, ruthlessness and dishonesty follow him throughout his lifetime as sultan. He is poisoned in 1277.

Map 29. End of the Crusader Period late 13ᵗʰ century

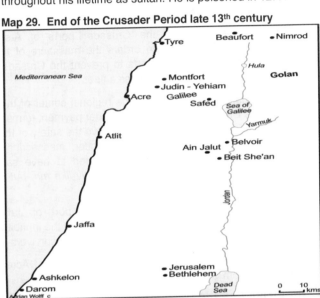

Mamluk Period in Palestine is marked by:

- Land of Israel divided into provinces – Safed, Damascus, Gaza.
- A corrupt administration.
- The post of Administrator is often sold to the highest bidder who oppresses the locals.
- Mamluks do not encourage trade, industry, agriculture, nor lower taxes.
- Destroy coastal cities and ports fearing European attack.
- Jews are forbidden to purchase land, ride a horse within city limits, forced to wear turban of a distinct color.
- Non-Muslim pilgrims make short visits to Jerusalem to escape paying the extortionate taxes.
- Jerusalem, not on a Trade Route, little commerce, stagnates economically.
- Mamluks promote religious importance of Islam constructing colleges (madrassah).
- Population of Jerusalem falls below 30,000 inhabitants.

- Towns built in Palestine: Beit She'an, Gesher, Jenin, Ikron, Jaljulia, Gaza, Khan Yunis.
- Construct roads and bridges in Palestine (Ramle, Bne'ot Ya'akov, Damiya).

1261 Byzantine Emperor Michael II, with support of French and Germans, defeats Emperor Baldwin II, the last of the Venetian emperors in Constantinople, who flees to Venice ending the lucrative Venetian monopoly of maritime trade between Constantinople and Venice.

1265 Sultan Beybars conquers the Crusader ports of Arsur/Arsuf (Apollonia) and Caesarea. He orders the massacre of the local population, destroying these ports to prevent the Crusaders from returning. Beybars does not possess a fleet.

1266 Sultan Beybars surrounds Safed the regional center of the Upper Galilee. The Crusaders negotiate surrender payment terms for safe passage to Acre. After the Crusaders leave the safety of the castle walls, Beybars suddenly rescinds his offer, massacring all the Crusaders, except two. Beybars is reputed to have said, '*You negotiated with some-one that looks exactly like me, but was not me.*' The Safed castle is destroyed.

1268 Sultan Beybars conquers the Crusader port of Jaffa. The Byzantine city of Antioch falls to Beybars and all the inhabitants are slaughtered in a festival of brutality. There are no survivors.

1269 Hugo I of Jerusalem = Hugo III of Cyprus King of Acre (1269–1284), rules from Cyprus.

1270 **The Eighth Crusade 1270**
- Aim: To capture Jerusalem via Egypt
- End: Crusader king dies in the North African desert
- Crusaders do not reach the Holy Land
- Leader of the Eighth Crusade is: King Louis IX of France

Europeans decide upon the 8th Crusade. Armies are no longer made up of unpaid conscripts volunteering their services hoping to find their fortunes in the Orient. Crusading has become more expensive with knights and conscripts now demanding pay, limiting the Pope's and European kings ability to embark on yet another Crusade. King Louis IX of France bears responsibility for the disaster and collapse of his 7th Crusade. In 1267 he begins preparations to lead an 8th Crusade.

1270 After three years of preparations, the Crusaders led by King Louis IX sail from France to Tunis in North Africa. Soon after their arrival dysentery strikes French troops claiming the lives of both Louis and his son Jean Tristan. Louis' brother Charles of Anjou arrives in Tunis with the Sicilian fleet to bargain with the Mamluks for indemnity to evacuate the remnants of the Crusader army. This Crusade like the previous 7th Crusade never materializes ending in tragedy on North African soil, never reaching the Holy Land, nor bringing any assistance to the Christians and Crusaders in the Holy Land. **The 8th Crusade ends the final organized Crusade by Christians to gain control Jerusalem and the Holy Land.**

Acre, Crusader Port   Adrian Wolff

1271   Mamluks capture the German Teutonic Knights' fortress of Montfort controlling the route in Western Galilee and hinterland to the port Acre. Sultan Beybars captures the Crusader castle at Krak de Moab in Jordan, increasing Mamluk influence east of Jordan River.

1271   English crown-prince Edward lands in North Africa with expeditionary troops, only to be badly defeated by Mamluk forces.

1271   **Marco Polo**, (1254–1324) born in Korcula, Croatia, leads his second journey to the Orient through Acre to China, returning in 1295. He receives approval from the khan, Kublai, in Mongolia. Polo returns with paper money, compass, explosives, coal and asbestos. He describes meeting Jewish traders in Beijing, China.

1277   After the Mamluks capture Damascus, Sultan Beybars dies in Egypt. He is rumored to have drunk from a poisoned cup, prepared for another person. His sons are quickly murdered by Mamluks destroying any chances of a dynasty. Sultan Qalawun succeeds.

1280   Only the coastal ports of Sidon, Tripoli, Acre and Atlit remain in Crusader hands. The Muslim noose is quickly closing on them.

1286   Henri (Hugo) II ruling from Cyprus, last King of Acre (1286–1291).

Acre, Crusader Halle des Chevaliers   Adrian Wolff

1287   Kublai Khan seeks Christian allies in the west against the Muslim threat. Rabban Sauma, a Turkic Nestorian Christian travels to Europe attempting to increase trade.

1289   Mamluks capture Tripoli (Lebanon), closing in on the Crusaders.

1289   **The infamous end of the Crusaders in the Holy Land**
  - Acre is the seat of government, the king rules from Cyprus.
  - Some barons reside in Cyprus, others are nominal lords in the Holy Land being fiefs of lands, actually under Muslim control.
  - Christians are a minority in the Holy Land. A serious immigration movement of Christians to settle permanently never materializes.
  - Crusaders and Knights Orders are divided amongst themselves.
  - French hegemony has given way to predominance of Italian States of the ports.
  - Genoese-Venetian rivalry has been extended to the Levant.
  - Many criminals and undesirables find their way into Acre.

1290   King Edward I (Longshanks) (1239-1307) forces the Jews of England to pay for his costly battles against the Welsh and for the construction of many of his castles. Jews must wear a distinctive yellow identification and when he depletes the **Jews** of their wealth, they **are expelled from England.** (See Henry VI 1442).

1291   Acre is besieged by Mamluk Sultan al-Malik Khalil, conquered after forty-four days. The carnage includes massacre of many Christians and Jewish residents. The survivors are enslaved. The largest Crusader port, Acre is destroyed preventing any attempt by the Crusaders to land reinforcements. Some Crusaders flee before the final assault, making their way south along the coast to Atlit port (The Pilgrim's Castle), departing together with Templars for Germany, and the Hospitallers Knights for Cyprus and Rhodes.

Map 30. Mamluk Empire late 13th century

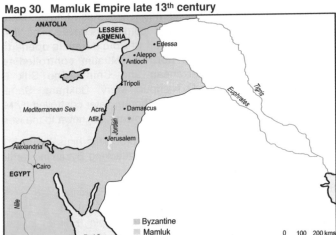

1291   **Thus ends the Crusader Period lasting 200 years, never to return to the Holy Land. Christians resume control during the British Mandate of Palestine (1918-1948).** Mamluks control the overland Trade Route from Egypt to Damascus and on to the Orient. The Crusaders never achieve their goals of conquering and controlling Jerusalem, other than a brief period from 1099 to 1187. From the Muslim point of view, the Crusades are a minor 200-year invasion, temporally upsetting the status quo between the various Muslim rulers of the time. The Crusaders had no influence whatsoever, making no impression on life in Muslim-controlled territory - they came, they were defeated, they left.

13thc   The Italian city-states make treaties with the Mamluks to maintain their control of maritime trade in the eastern Mediterranean.

Chapter 17. Mamluk and Early Ottoman 1291-1798

1291+ After the expulsion of the Crusaders, Jewish communities from Provence and Flanders are revived in Eretz Israel. Jews living in Europe and the Levant are known to be traders and merchants. The Jewish population in Eretz Israel is partially supported by donations made by Jews living in the Diaspora, linking them to 'The Land הארץ'.

1293 Mongols defeat the Seljuk Army in Anatolia, creating a vacuum filled by Osman I, Emir (prince) of northern Anatolia.

1295 Mongols welcome Christian missionaries and traders. Marco Polo returns to Venice from China, recording his travels titled 'Il millione', dies 1324 in Venice. **The result of Polo's travels opens the new Overland trade routes north of Muslim controlled territory between the Mediterranean and China, The Silk Road** - Damascus, Baghdad, Nishpur, Merv, Bukhara, Samarkand, Kashgar, Turfan, Apis, Khara, Khorum, later controlled by Muslims. He brings the compass and gunpowder, unknown to the west.

1299 Osman I (Othman I) (1259-1326) proclaims himself sultan in 1299 establishing the Ottoman Empire attacking Byzantine territories in Anatolia. Osmans = Ottomans.

Ottoman Empire 1299 - 1923 (1516 -1918 in Palestine)
- Ottomans are **Sunni Muslims,** established in Anatolia.
- Ottoman capital is Bursa in 1326, Adrianople (Edirne) in 1389, and finally Constantinople (**Istanbul**) from 1453 **after defeating the Byzantines**.
- At its zenith the Ottoman Empire territory extends from Hungary, Ukraine, Southern Russia, Algeria, N. Africa, Near East, Turkey, Persia. It controls many different people with different languages, cultures and religion. No independent territories or countries exist within the Empire.
- Ottoman Empire lasts for over 600 years, one of the longest.
- Turkey is named after Turkic peoples from Central Asia who invade Anatolia.
- Ottomans capture Christian youngsters, train as fighters 'kapikuli', making up special elite military forces as janissaries. The military has artillery and engineering corps.
- Ottomans defeat the Mamluks in Palestine 1516 at Khan Yunis, and in Egypt 1517. Mamluks remain administrators in Egypt until 1811.
- Ottomans administer Palestine from 1517 until their defeat by the British in 1917/8.
- Ottomans build roads, bridges, railways, and telegraphs.

- Administration - local officials appointed by the sultan. Religious officials are the intermediaries between government and people.
- A multi-cultural population within the empire is taxed to pay for:
  1. The Sultan's expensive, opulent life-style.
  2. Up-keep of a large military force.
  3. Maintaining an inflated and corrupt bureaucracy.
  4. Supporting Muslim religious institutions.
- The decline in power of the Ottoman Empire is caused by corruption, incompetent administration, over-spending, local nationalism, decline in military power. European influence, and internal reform, all bring about the fall of the Sultanate and creation of the Turkish Republic.
- Ottoman Empire disintegrates following their defeat in World War I. The Sultan is exiled and Mustafa Kemal (Ataturk) declares Turkey a secular, independent Republic in 1923. Ottoman territories are lost. Turkey controls only Anatolia in Asia Minor and Thrace in Europe, including Istanbul and Dardanelles, the maritime passage between the Black and Aegean Seas.
- During World War II, non-Muslims living in Turkey are forced to pay an asset 'varlik' tax. This tax is frequently based on a fictitious calculation of wealth and official receipts are hard to come by.
- Turkish language - Arabic vocabulary and Arabic script is used until it is changed in 1928 to Latin letters by Ataturk (Turkish Republic).
- Turkish music, literature, painting, architecture.
- Many sultans have Jewish physicians and financial advisors.
- Jews may own property, engage in commerce, professions, construct synagogues.
- Jews living in Eretz Israel are supported by donations from Jews living in the Diaspora, linking the donors spiritually to The Land.

1300+ European population and economy is in decline.

1300+ Mamluk authorities begin restoring the walls of the Temple Mount. These smaller stones at the uppermost level as seen today at the Western Wall. The Dome of the Rock roof is gilded and the roof of the al-Aqsa Mosque is repaired. Severe *dhimmi* laws enforced.

1301 Osman I usurps power after defeating the Byzantines in Anatolia.

1306 King Philip IV of **France expels the Jews** who had returned after previously being expelled by King Philip II in 1182.

> **Expulsion of Jews 1000-1600**
> Austria 1421
> Crimea 1016, 1350
> England 1290, 1442
> France 1182, 1306, 1321, 1394

Germany 12thc, 1348, 1510, 1551
Hungary 1349, 1360
Lithuania 1445, 1495
Naples 1541
Papal States 1584, 1595
Portugal 1497
Provence 1430
Sicily 1492
Silesia 1159, 1494
Spain 1492
Tunis 1535
Wales 1290

1308   Hospitaller Knights conquer the island of Rhodes, establishing their headquarters.

1310   Zenith of the Mamluk Empire during the reign of Sultan Kalaoun.

1312   Pope Clement V and French King Philip IV seeking money and wealth, level false charges against the Templar Knights arresting them, abolishing the order, dividing their wealth and properties, while a minority share is usurped by the Hospitaller Knights.

1331   Ottoman Sultan Orhan defeats Byzantines and captures Nicaea.

1337   The 100-Years War (1337-1453) between England and France. Both countries lose interest in crusading to Jerusalem, now need to maintain forces within their own territories.

1338   Restoration of water conduits built originally by King Herod (known as Solomon's Pools) to bring water from springs in the Bethlehem area to the Temple Mount.

1342   **Pope Clement VI entrusts Franciscans (Catholics) as Guardians of the Christian Shrines in the Holy Land.**

1347   Inflation, war, and crop failures in Europe create **The Great Famine** (1315–1317). **The Black Death** (1347-1352) caused by fleas from infected rats transmit plague bacteria to humans, kill 25-30% of European and Near East populations. Jews in Europe are erroneously blamed for causing the plague, (of poisoning wells), are persecuted, others burnt in pubic areas. German Jews are expelled, flee towards Italy and Poland. A shortage of both serfs to work the land and skilled artisans who now charge for their services. New opportunities open up for serfs beyond rural bondage, thereby **ending the Feudal System.**

1349   Ottomans establish the Sultanate of Rum in central and eastern Anatolia.

1354 Ottomans capture Ankara. Byzantine Emperor John VI is forced to cede control of Gallipoli on the European side of the Dardanelles, allowing the Ottomans complete control of the maritime passage from the Black to the Aegean Seas.

Map 31. The Byzantine Empire 14ᵗʰ century

1365 Christian knights besiege and ransack Alexandria, soon recovered by the Mamluks.

1361 Sultan Murad I, son of Orhan, (rules 1360-1389) conquers Adrianople. Byzantium is now reduced to Thrace (European Turkey), southern Greece and Constantinople.

1389 Sultan Murad I is killed defeating Christian Orthodox Serbs at the 1ˢᵗ Battle of Kosovo. His son Bayezid I sultan 1389-1403. Ottomans control Thrace, Macedonia, Bulgaria, and Serbia surrounding the Byzantine Empire. Adrianople in Thrace renamed Edirne is the new Ottoman capital. Serbian Christians are forced to pay a tribute to the Ottomans and serve in the Sultan's army. These Christian slaves convert to Islam, trained as fighters 'kapikuli' make up special elite military forces 'janissaries'. Byzantine control is now reduced to southern Greece, Thessalonica, Constantinople and Lesser Armenia.

1391 In Valencia, Spain Jews are forcibly converted to Catholicism. The Golden Age for Spanish Jews ends. During this pre-Inquisition period in Spain 100,000 Jews flee to Muslim lands, approximately 50,000 Jews convert to Christianity and about 100,000 Jews are murdered. Today nearly 20% of the population of Spain and Portugal have Jewish ancestry as seen in DNA testing (American Journal of Human Genetics, December 2008). Many great intellectual Jews originate in Spain include Rabbis Isaac Abrabanel, Yehuda Halevi, Rambam (Maimonides), Ibn Shiprut.

1440c Mamluks continue to impose heavy taxes on non-Muslims (Christians and Jews) living in Jerusalem, forcing many to emigrate

1442 King Henry VI **expels the Jews from England**. Very few Jews and crypto-Jews are living in England after being expelled by Edward I in 1290 until their return under Oliver Cromwell in 1650.

1450+ The beginning of the Renaissance Period of cultural secular revival in Europe. Rapid decline in serfdom in western and central Europe.

1453 Ottoman Sultan Fatih (conqueror) Mehmed II (sultan 1451-1481) defeats the last Byzantine Emperor Constantine XI capturing their capital Constantinople. **End of Eastern Christian and Byzantine Empire.** Greek inhabitants call Constantinople *Istenpolis* (in Greek) 'the city', and refer to Hagia Sophia Church as 'In the City'. Constantinople is renamed **Istanbul**, the new capital of the Ottoman Empire. (Muslims pronounce the letter "P" as "B"). The Orthodox Patriarch of Constantinople is designated Head of the Eastern Church and all Christian subjects of the Ottoman Empire are under his authority. Greek Orthodox headquarters are transferred to Jerusalem in 1845. **No new churches or synagogues are constructed (renovations are allowed) within the Ottoman Empire until the 18th century.**

1456 An **earthquake** damages The Church of the Holy Sepulchre and al-Aqsa Mosque.

1456 Johannes Gutenberg (1400–1468) taking an idea from Italian Jews, builds a printing press in Mainz, Germany. Books spread knowledge and ideas among the literate. Printing does not influence the Muslim world where only religious books almost exclusively are printed.

1450's All major Catholic churches in Europe have paintings of 14 **'Stations of the Cross'** depicting the stages from the Trial to the Crucifixion of Jesus though only 9 stages are mentioned in the New Testament. Christians construct a small church or chapel at each of the stations on the Holy Circuit, known as **Stations of the Cross** along the Via Dolorosa in Jerusalem, originally designated by Queen Helena in the 4th c. Byzantine and Crusader churches or chapels at each site were previously destroyed.

Station I   Judgement, Condemned to death - Matt. 27:37; Mark 14:61,62; Luke 13:3
Station II   Flagellation, Takes the Cross - John 19:1,2,3,13,16
Station III Falls for the First Time - Traditional site

Station IV Meets His Mother - Traditional Site
Station V Simon of Cyrene assists - Matthew 27:32; Luke 23:26,27
Station VI Veronica wipes His brow - Traditional Site
Station VII Falls a Second time - Traditional Site
Station VIII Addresses the women of Jerusalem - Luke 23:28
Station IX Falls a Third time - Traditional Site
Station X Stripped of His robes - Matthew 27:33,34; Luke 23:34; John
14:17, 18; 19:17,18
Station XI Nailed to The Cross -Matthew 16:24; John 19:19,25
Station XII Crucifixion - Matthew 27:38-46; Mark 15:34
Station XIII His body is handed to Mary - Traditional Site
Station XIV The Tomb of Christ - Sepulchre - Matthew 27:59-61; 28:2;
Mark 15:16; John 20:11-30; Luke 23:50-53

Via Dolorosa, Station V. Hands of St. Francis. Catholic site Adrian Wolff

1472 Mamluks repress Christians and Jews, destroying churches and synagogues.

1474 Muslims destroy the original Rambam Synagogue for late payment of the non-Muslim head tax, the *jizya*.

1483 Jerusalem has 1000 Christians and 100-150 Jewish families.

1488 The famous Mishna commentator Rabbi Obadiah ben Avraham Yare of Bertinoro, Italy, emigrates to Jerusalem where he finds the Jewish and Christian inhabitants living under Muslim oppression in conditions of poverty. As the spiritual head, he improves the intellectual level, encouraging in the younger generation to study the Talmud.

1490 **The Star of David** is carved on the frescos of the 4th century synagogue in Capernaum. The origins of 'the star' is the word

'David' written in paleo-Hebrew on the shield of David. The Jews of Prague establish a 'Star' on the window of the synagogue in the 13th century. King Charles IV in 1357 gives the Jewish community a banner with the Star as a sign of their status. This symbol is found in the windows of the Altneuschul (Old-New) Synagogue in Prague constructed in 1490. In the 15th century **The Star of David begins to have religious and national significance.** See 141BCE.

Star of David, Star of Solomon - Synagogue, Capernaum. Adrian Wolff

1492   Queen Isabella of Castile (rules 1474-1504) and King Ferdinand II of Aragon (rules 1479-1516, also known as Ferdinand V of Castile) complete the Reconquista in Spain, conquering the last Muslim controlled areas in Granada, Andalusia, **ending Muslim control in Spain. Jews constitute about 30% of the urban population of Spain, are merchants, involved in the growth of the textile and woolen industries, tailors, cobblers, tanners, smiths, weavers, financiers, lawyers, scientists, physicians and surgeons, skilled artisans (jewelers, enamelers, carpenters), scribes, rabbis, etc.**

1492   **Anti-Jewish measures in Spain**
The Jews of Spain are given two options
- leave - "*depart...not to return...confiscation of all their property.*"
- convert to Catholicism.

The **Spanish Inquisition of Jews** authenticated in 1484, is practiced in earnest in late 1492. If Crypto-Jews remaining in Spain or 'conversos' practice Judaism, he/she is tortured, martyred, and burnt to death. Jews would eat pork in public to prove their conversion to Catholicism. Hence they are known as '*Marranos*', meaning 'swine' in Spanish.

Between 150,000 to 250,000 (about a third of the total Jewish population) Jews flee Spain, causing a downturn in the Spanish economy. Many prefer Muslim-ruled areas finding less anti-Semitism until the Age of Enlightenment in Christian Europe. About 240,000 undergo conversion and stay, of which over 25,000 are later burnt in public. The relatively high proportion of Jews who convert is due their integration into Spanish culture, employment in government and their prominent roles in commerce and trade. Jews found within the borders of Aragon or Castile would be forced to convert or be killed.

Jews have difficulties disposing of their property, selecting a destination country and finding the means to travel. Jews are prohibited from leaving Spain with precious metals, coinage, or jewels. German-states, England, France and most of Italy are closed. Portugal is an option till 1497. North Africa, and the Balkans are chosen. Exiles are robbed and sometimes sold to slavery by ship-captains. Sephardi Jews rise to distinction in many of the countries where they settle.

1492 Sultan Bayezid II (born 1447, rules 1481-1512) warmly accepts Jewish refugees from Spain to settle in the Balkans, Greece and Turkey. The Jews are free to practice their religion, customs, language (Ladino) and professions. There is Jewish revival, tolerated and open to economic opportunities, establishing industries - firearms, gunpowder, artillery and textiles. The Jewish population of Istanbul multiples 5 times to be over 10% of the total.

1492 Jews emigrating from Spain to Eretz Israel find Jerusalem lacking in employment opportunities, preferring Safed having a rich hinterland of sheep for wool and cotton for local textile production.

1492 Cristobal Colon (Christopher Columbus, 1456-1506) seeks to find a new route to the Indies. According to his letters he also desires to assist thousands of Jews find a new home. He is assumed to be a Sephardic Jew (family flee to Italy after anti-Jewish massacres in Catalonia in 1392). His father is an Genovese merchant. He shows a strong interest in Jewish matters and his letters are filled with references to the Hebrew Bible. He travels with at least six *conversos* -Jewish cartographers, doctors and translators e.g. Luis de Torres. There was no priest on his voyage. King Ferdinand thinks the first country with direct western sea routes would become the richest in Christendom. Columbus's voyage was not funded by Queen Isabella, but by two Jewish Conversos Louis de Santangel and Gabriel Sanchez who advanced an interest free loan of 17,000 ducats to pay for the voyage, and by Don Isaac Abrabanel, rabbi and Jewish statesman.

His letters preserved in the Archives of the Indies in Seville, he writes, "*David, that most prudent king, was first a shepherd and afterward chosen King of Jerusalem, and I am a servant of that same Lord who raised him to such a dignity.*". His letters to his son Diego contains Hebrew H"B ב"ה (*b'ezrat haShem*, "with the help of God") commonly used in Jewish correspondence. A letter he requested Diego to show to Queen Isabella does not contain the mark. His letters and logs mention the words Jerusalem, Moses, David, Abraham, Sarah, and Isaac. He does not quote from the Christian Bible.

1497   Jews are exiled from Portugal by Queen Isabella, daughter of King Ferdinand II and Queen Isabella of Spain, when she marries Manuel, King of Portugal. A condition is made that he purifies the country of its Jews. Manuel allows Jewish emigration without their children. Many emigrate to Holland.

1498   Vasco da Gama, a Portuguese navigator is the first Western European to sail from Europe (Lisbon) round Africa to India and return to his homeport bringing luxurious goods and spices. The success of this voyage **opens a new maritime trade route between Europe and the treasures of Asia**, breaking the **Muslim Overland Trade Route monopoly. The Silk Road begins to decline in importance, trading towns fall into a recession and the population is forced to return to subsistence agriculture. Jewish inhabitants of the major towns along the Silk Road immigrate westwards, while some will remain in China.**

1512   Ottoman Sultan Selim I (born 1470, rules 1512-1520). Sephardic Jews of Istanbul assist Sultan Selim I to improve manufacturing techniques of firearms and artillery.

1514   Ottomans capture Muslim lands east and south of Turkey (Persia, Syria, Egypt) before attacking Christian Europe. After defeating Shah Ismail at the Battle of Chaldirin, occupying their capital Tabriz, Persia is no longer a threat to the Ottomans in the east. The Sultan is now free to turn his attention to the Mamluks in Egypt.

1516   Ottoman forces under General Pasha Sinan defeat Mamluks in Syria at the Battle of Marj Dabiq, north of Aleppo, moving their attention towards the Mamluk capital Cairo, in Egypt. At the Battle of Khan Yunis in Gaza in December 1516, Ottomans defeat the Mamluks led by Ghisbardi Bardi el-Azali. In this battle both sides use approximately 10,000-12,000 soldiers and one thousand cavalry. The Ottoman artillery-fire frightens the Mamluk cavalry who break rank and disperse. **Jerusalem now falls under Ottoman Imperial control from Istanbul. End of the Mamluk Period. The Beirut Vilayet (province) administers Palestine now divided into Sancak (districts) - Jerusalem, Gaza, Shehem (Nablus), Ajlun (Jordan), Safed. Christian control inside the Church of the Holy Sepulchre is divided between the Copts, Armenians, Greeks and Franciscans.** All Muslim opposition in the Eastern Mediterranean is neutralized, allowing the Ottomans to begin their unhindered conquest of Christian Europe north of the Balkans.

1517   After their defeat at Raydaniyah near Cairo, the Ottomans permit the Mamluks to administer Egypt as viceroys (*vali*) and collect taxes, transferred to Istanbul, lasting until in 1811 when Muhammed Ali Pasha ousts of the Mamluks from Egypt.

1522   Sultan Suleyman the Magnificent, the Lawgiver (Kanuni), (born 1494, sultan 1520–1566), conquers vast territorial areas in Central Europe up to Vienna where he is defeated. He expels the remnants of the Crusader Hospitaller Knights Order in Rhodes, forcing their retreat to Malta. Moses Hamon, a Jew, is his physician

Map 32. Ottoman Empire 16th century

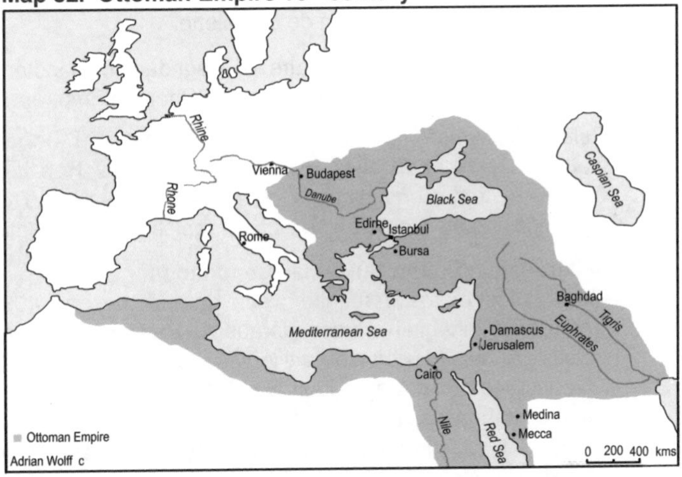

1523   Ottomans grant permission to reconstruct the Rambam Synagogue previously destroyed in 1474 for late payment of the non-Muslims head tax, the *jizya*.

1525   Census in Palestine 250,000. Data is used for taxation and land ownership.

1526 The various Sultans recognize Catholics (Franciscans) as 'guardians' of Christian Holy Sites in the Holy Land. King Charles V, (1500-1558) the Habsburg king (head of the Holy Roman Empire in 1519) is also known as King Carlos (Charles) I of Spain (son of Juana Loca, is grandson of King Ferdinand and Queen Isabella of Spain). At the Battle of Pavia in 1525 King Charles V defeats King Francis I (Francois) of France (1494-1547, king 1515-1547). Francis I signs a Treaty with the Turkish Sultan Suleyman, pledging not to attack Ottoman troops and their over-extended supply-lines during his second Austrian campaign, defeating the Habsburgs at the Battle of Mohasco, Hungary in 1526. Christian Europeans fear Muslim invasion and territorial conquest. King Francis I of France makes trade and diplomatic agreements with Sultan Suleyman ensuring Ottoman forces will keep Habsburg pressure away from France. The agreement allows French subjects freedom to travel within the Ottoman Empire, while other European Christian nationals require French permission to travel. **This accord lays the foundation of French predominance in the Levant and French Catholic (Franciscan) authority of Christian Holy Sites in the Holy Land**.

1530 Sultan Suleyman's failed attack with over 100 ships and 30,000 troops, cedes Malta to the Hospitaller Knights of St. John under Maltese Grand Master, Jean de La Valette.

1534 Ottomans complete the capture of Baghdad, Mesopotamia and Tunis incorporating these areas into the Ottoman Empire.

1538 Sultan Suleyman commands the construction of **Jerusalem's walls (1537-1541) as they stand today** to deter Habsburg King Charles V from considering a crusade to Jerusalem. The aging marble inside the Dome of the Rock is replaced with ceramic tiles.

In Jerusalem Sultan Suleyman commands:
- Rebuilding of the damaged **walls** around the city (1537-1541) protecting inhabitants from marauding Bedouin (falaheen). The walls are built to withstand artillery fire (stand up to the light arms fire in 1948 at the Mount Zion Gate), following topography similar to the Roman walls. **The present Old City walls**.
- Eight gates: Jaffa Gate (expanded 1898), Zion Gate, Dung Gate, Golden Gate, Lion's (St. Stephen's) Gate, Herod's Gate, Damascus Gate, New Gate (opened 1889). Golden Gate is sealed to prevent The Messiah's entrance.
- Damascus Gate is constructed over a previous Roman Gate.
- The mosaics covering the walls of the Dome of the Rock are replaced with marble tablets.

- Water system is improved, repaired and widened from Solomon's Pools in Bethlehem, (built by King Herod in the 1st century BCE). Patrols are made along the water canals to prevent and repair damage made by local Bedouin (falaheen).
- Tower of David is built with a dry moat and is a separate, fortified area, constructed to withstand a siege.
- Sultan's Pool constructed in the Hinnom Valley.
- Four new public fountains (*sabil*) are constructed, including the fountain near the Sultan's Pool at the foot of Mount Zion.
- Improvement in the water cisterns and sewers in Jerusalem.

Map 33. Ottoman Jerusalem 1541

Highlights of the Ottoman Administration in Jerusalem

- Jerusalem has a governor (*bey*) of the local district (*sancak*).
- Jerusalem is subordinate to the general governor (*wali*) of the province (*vilayet*) of Damascus, or Beirut or Sidon and has no contact with central authorities in Istanbul.
- Jerusalem has lower status than other administrative regions such as Safed, Nablus, and Gaza.
- Jews have a quota of 300 families to reside in Jerusalem. They bribe authorities not to expel any additional Jews.
- Franciscan Friars obtain the position of the '*Custodia Terra Sancta*' and are responsible for collecting taxes levied on Christian pilgrims. Christians pay a '*rusum*' or registration taxes and need to obtain permission from the governor before marrying
- Christians living in Jerusalem are mainly Orthodox-Syrian, speaking Arabic. Catholics are in a minority.

- Each of the Christian communities control a specific section of the Church of the Holy Sepulchre, leading to friction and frequent conflicts. The keys remain with a Muslim family (Nusseibeh).

Jerusalem, Ottoman Walls   Adrian Wolff

1543   Martin Luther (1483-1546) is a major contributor to European anti-Semitism when he writes '*On the Jews and their Lies*'.

1546   Widespread **earthquake** damage in Palestine.

1549   Sultan Suleyman orders the construction of sturdy walls around Safed, protecting the inhabitants from marauding robbers.

1551   Ottomans expel Franciscans from Mt Zion church and monastery.

1553   Census in Jerusalem. Jews 1000-1500 inhabitants, Christians about 1800. Muslims are the majority (number unknown).

1560   Sultan Suleyman the Magnificent grants a *ferman* (edict), officially recognizing the rights of Jews to pray at the Western Wall.

1560   Donna Gracia Mendes, a wealthy 'Marranos' originally from Spain, and her nephew Joseph Ha'Nasi, obtain Turkish permission to resettle Jewish refugees from Spain and Portugal in Tiberias, a walled town. Irrigation systems are dug around mulberry trees for silk production.

1561   First European Ghetto completed in Venice, forcing Jews to live within a defined area.

1564   Rabbi Joseph Ha'Nasi rebuilds Jewish communities in Tiberias.

1567   **Rabbi Joseph Caro** (1488-1575) completes the ***Shulhan Aruch*** or 'Prepared Table' in Safed, spreading the Jewish codex - the religious tradition and jurisprudence in a practical method to allow the reader to help himself. The Jewish laws, codified from its Talmudic sources is accepted by Jewish communities throughout the world as the method of Jewish customs and observance.

Safed, Grave of Rabbi Joseph Caro   Adrian Wolff

The *Shulhan Aruch* is divided into four parts.

Part 1 Laws concerning daily conduct, tzitzit, tefelin, mezuzah, prayer, minyan, reading of the law, kaddish, memorials, study of sacred books, repentance, charity, tale-bearing and slander, chalah, kashrut (preparation of foods), grace before and after meals.

Part 2 Laws concerning forbidden foods, benedictions, buying and selling, interest, business, prosecutor, defendant and evidence procedure, theft and robbery, monetary damages borrowing and hiring, trusts, things lost and found, unloading an loading. Rules regarding physical well-being, cruelty to animals, vows and oaths, prayer for the journey, afternoon and evening prayers, reading of the 'Shema' and regulations for the night. Honoring father and mother, circumcision, shaving, sickness and the physician, visiting the sick, one who is dying, rending the garment, mourning.

Part 3 Holiness, preparation, kindling candles for the Sabbath, service on Sabbath and Holidays, Weekday matters prohibited on Sabbath, Laws concerning New Moon, the month of Nisan, Matzot, Eve of Passover, Passover night, Counting of the Omer, Public Fasts, the ninth of the month of Av, new Year (Rosh Hashanna), Day of Atonement (Yom Kippur), Tabernacles, Hanukah and Purim.

Part 4 All laws appertaining to women, marriage, fasting on the wedding day, nuptial canopy (chuppah), seven Days of Banqueting, chastity, on the conduct of man and women, duty of the husband to his wife, duty of a wife to her husband, laws forbidding being alone with or familiarity towards women, menstruation, laws of a bride, women who have given birth after abortion, immersion.

Safed, Entrance to Ha'ari Synagogue   Adrian Wolff

Safed, Grave of Ha'ari, a pilgrimage site   Adrian Wolff

1570   **Rabbi Isaac ben Solomon Luria** (1534-1572) moves to Safed where he is known as **Ha'ari** (the lion). He writes only one book, a commentary on the Zohar, the Book of Concealment. After 1280 quotations of the Zohar (See 2nd century) circulate among Jewish thinkers and Kabbalists into the life of their communities. 'Kitvi (writings of) Ari' (כיתבי ארי) and its main work 'Tree of Life' עץ חיים is the theoretical foundation of Kabbalah, assisting the reader to understand the Zohar. 'The Ari' teaches his pupils the Kabbalah - meditation, concentration and symbolism based on Talmudic mysticism. At his grave in Safed the biblical quotation is written *"you shall love your fellow as yourself"* (Leviticus 19:18). His prominent pupil, Haim ben Joseph Vital (1542-1620) is the major interpreter of Ha'ari's Kabbalistic methods as written in *Sha'are Kedushah* (Gates of Holiness). This is the major work on Kabbalist meditation. Safed, a Jewish religious, kabalistic and intellectual center, attracts students from all corners of the Diaspora. In 1740 Italian Rabbi Moses Haim **Luzzatto**, the Ramhal (1707–1746) writes *Mesilat Yesharom* (The Path of the Upright) influencing Kabbalist thought.

Kabbalah

The word Kabbalah is used to describe the esoteric teachings of Jewish mysticism. It seeks to bring an awareness of God and Creation whose intrinsic elements are beyond basic understanding. The knowing of God is made through the belief of God, the Creator of the universe and the belief of God is beyond any speculation. The 'soul' fills the body, and Hashem fills the world. Therefore the 'soul' is our contact with Hashem, without which, we would be an empty shell.

Kabbalists follow a Jewish religious tradition, while study broadens understanding of Torah into inner secret law of revelations of the universe. Study of Kabbalah gives students methods to understand this symbolism within mystical theology of Judaism.

The *Sefirot* (Divine Emanations) use intellectual ladders to reach higher levels of understanding. Ten progressive Divine names (in Hebrew). *"Abraham said, 'My Lord, Hashem/Elohim* (Genesis 15:2). *"I prayed to Hashem and said 'My Lord, Elohim."* (Deuteronomy 9:26).

1571   At The Battle of Lepanto off Greece, European Catholic naval forces defeat the Ottoman fleet sailing from their naval base, loosing their experience commanders. The Ottomans will never be able to advance along the eastern Mediterranean in the future.

1576   Sultan Murad III (1546–1595) orders the deportation of 1000 Safed Jewish families to Cyprus, decreasing the production of Safed wool. He signs a *ferman* (edict) prohibiting Jews from wearing silk and forcing them to wear distinctive headgear.

1577   The first Jewish printing press in Eretz Israel founded in Safed by veteran printer from Prague, Eliezer bar Yitzhak, who together with Avraham Ashkenazi publish works of the local sages. Due to limited marketing success, closes down in 1587.

1582 **The Western Calendar**
Julius Caesar establishes the **Julian Calendar** in 46BCE on 1 January, named after the Roman god Janus who has two faces, one looking forward and one backwards. William became King of England on 25 December 1066, instates 1 January. During the early medieval period Christian Europe regarded Annunciation Day (25 March) as the beginning of the year.

Pope Gregory XIII proclaims a new calendar, the **Gregorian Calendar**, based on the Julian (Roman) Calendar, but restores the vernal equinox to 21 March 325, the date of the legitimizing of Christianity at the Council of Nicaea. The Gregorian Calendar has no century leap year unless it is divisible by 400. The Julian calendar is 13 days behind the Gregorian calendar. This calendar is widely accepted throughout the Christian world, introduced to Russia only after the October 1917 Revolution that actually took place at the beginning of November that year. Christians celebrate Easter on the first full-moon after the northern spring equinox.

1586 Ottoman Authorities force the closure of the Rambam Synagogue for late payment of the non-Muslim head tax, the *jizya*. Jews flee Jerusalem for Hebron and Tiberias.

1610 Sephardic Jews of Jerusalem are granted permission to construct the Ben Zakai Synagogue. During the Jordanian period (1948-1967) it is used as a donkey stable.

1625 Ottomans appoint Muhammad ibn Faruk governor in Palestine, notorious for his persecution of Jews.

1630's Kabbalist Rabbi Jacob Zemah settles in Jerusalem. Remembered for his Edit of the writings of the 'Harari' and Rabbi Haim Vital.

1648 Wars and unrest in The Pale of Settlement (western region of Imperial Russia to include Poland, Lithuania, Belarus, Bessarabia and Ukraine) results in massacres of Jews, as survivors are admitted into Western Europe. (See 1882, 1904).

1658 Rabbi Jacob Hagiz originally from the Maghreb in North Africa moves to Italy. Later he establishes Beit Ya'akov, a *beit midrash* for Torah study in Jerusalem.

1674 Completion of the 'Church of St. John the Baptist in the Desert' in Ein Kerem, over previously destroyed Crusader and Byzantine churches.

1683 Ottomans withdraw from Vienna in winter (previously defeated in 1529). Beginning of Ottoman gradual decline as Venetians transport European finished products and purchase Ottoman sourced raw materials, resulting in their scarcity, causing black markets, inflation and corruption over the next few centuries.

16thc + 17thc **Characteristics and Differences between Western Europe and Ottoman Turkey.**
Jerusalem is unique - has been conquered many times yet has continuous habitation for over 3000 years. Jerusalem has strategic religious importance to all three monotheistic religions. Jerusalem is not found on a trade route, no rivers nearby, no natural resources either agricultural or mineral and no wealthy hinterland. The architecture and ambience of Jerusalem within its present Walls is very similar to other Muslim cities found in the Orient.
The Jewish 'talmid' or **learned scholar** has a high position in Jewish society. Jews are disallowed to own property. Jews, being literate and multilingual, are more able than their usually illiterate and monolingual fellow citizens, both to gain and retain knowledge and experience. A rabbi is not a priest, he is a teacher, for there can never be an intermediary between man and Hashem.

Christian Europe towns do not have a bustling bazaar. Once a week European farmers bring their wares to a fair or market before moving on to another town, unlike a Muslim city that trades every day. **The heroes of the European city are the warrior/fighter.** Coffee drinking is popular in the Orient, arriving in Europe only in the 16th century. Economic and industrial strides made in Western Europe are not found within the realms of the Ottoman Empire noted by a lack of technological progress in most spheres of agriculture, industry and transportation. The Ottoman world prefers manual handicrafts to mechanized industry, as science stagnates.

Various Ottoman sultans tax the dominant low-productive agricultural sector to pay for their wars and opulent life-style, adversely affecting the majority of the population who are illiterate subsistence farmers, rural dwellers and nomads. The Ottoman Empire has limited attractive exports other than cotton, while Europeans export manufactured goods. Europeans are building ocean-going sea-worthy all-season ships capable of sailing to the New World and Pacific Ocean bringing valued raw materials to Europe. Ottoman ship-building is locally focused, limited to Mediterranean summer plodders incapable of exploring new continents.

Muslim cities are very different to European Christian cities of the same period. In the Muslim world the market place operates daily and is not only a place of commerce but also a meeting place in coffee shops for **traders and merchants** who have **a high position in the Muslim society.** Mohammed was a merchant. The sultan has a harem consisting of slaves and concubines. In the world of Islam, women are of an inferior status, especially in education and public life, quite different from the west where powerful queens rule empires - Isabella, Elizabeth, and Catherine.

Turks regularly use the facilities of their 'Turkish Public Baths' more than once a week. They view themselves much cleaner and hygienic than the European Christian world, where bathrooms are not found in the royal palaces and private baths in each home becomes the norm only after World War 2.

Printing facilities are limited within the Ottoman Empire. The Koran is written by hand and religious clerics fear any outside influence by reading non-religious books. The population within the Ottoman Empire remains virtually illiterate until the mid-20th century.

1695 Adrian Reland (1676-1718), is a Dutch professor of Oriental languages at Harderwijk (1699) and Utrecht (1701). His most important works are *Palaestina ex monumentis veteribus illustrata* (Utrecht, 1714), and *Antiquitates sacrae veterum Hebraeorum*.

"*Not one settlement in the Land of Israel has a name that is of Arabic origin. Most settlement names originate in the Hebrew, Greek, Latin or Roman languages. In fact, till today, except to Ramlah, not one Arabic settlement has an original Arabic name...most of the settlements names are of Hebrew or Greek origin, the names distorted to senseless Arabic names. There is no meaning in Arabic to names such as Acco (Acre), Haifa, Jaffa, Nablus, Gaza, or Jenin and towns named Ramallah, El Halil (Hebron) and El-Kuds (Jerusalem) lack historical roots or Arabic philology. In 1696, the year Relandi toured the land, Ramallah, for instance, was called Bet'allah (From the Hebrew name Beit El) and Hebron was called Hebron (Hevron) and the Arabs called Mearat HaMachpelah El Chalil, their name for the Forefather Abraham*".

"*Most of the land was empty, desolate, and the inhabitants few in number and mostly concentrate in the towns Jerusalem, Acco, Tzfat, Jaffa, Tiberius and Gaza. Most of the inhabitants were Jews and the rest Christians. There were few Muslims, mostly nomad Bedouins. Nablus, known as Shehem, was exceptional, where approximately 120 people, members of the Muslim Natsha family and approximately 70 Shomronites, lived. In the Galilee capital, Nazareth, lived approximately 700 Christians and in Jerusalem approximately 5000 people, mostly Jews and some Christians. The interesting part was that Reland mentioned the Muslims as nomad Bedouins who arrived in the area as construction and agriculture labor(ers), seasonal workers*".

"*In Gaza for example, lived approximately 550 people, fifty percent Jews and the rest mostly Christians. The Jews grew and worked in their flourishing vineyards, olive tree orchards and wheat fields (remember Gush Katif?) and the Christians worked in commerce*

and transportation of produce and goods. Tiberius and Tzfat were mostly Jewish and except of mentioning fishermen fishing in Lake Kinneret -- the Lake of Galilee -- a traditional Tiberius occupation, there is no mention of their occupations. A town like Um el-Phahem was a village where ten families, approximately fifty people in total, all Christian, lived and there was also a small Maronite church in the village (The Shehadah family)." Taken from Avi Goldreich's article 4 August 2007.
www.faz.co.il/story?id=4457&base=&NewOnly=1&LastView=2030-12-31

1705 Rabbi Yehuda the Hassid from Siedlec, Poland immigrates to Jerusalem with 1000 followers, constructing an Ashkenazi synagogue. In 1721 Muslims break into the synagogue due to late payment of non-Muslim head-tax, the *'jizya'*. The wooden benches are stolen and the 'Scrolls of the Law' are burned. (see **Hurva Synagogue** 1836, 1864, 1948, 2010).

1732 Jews are given limited civil rights in England by King George II.

1742 Following the death of Tzar Peter the Great, the Empress Elizabeth forbids Jews to enter Russian unless they convert to Russian orthodoxy. Over 35,000 Russian Jews are expelled by 1753.

1757 A **violent clash in Church of the Holy Sepulchre during Easter service** as to the 'right' to hold and ignite the candle inside the Tomb of Christ. Greek and Armenian Orthodox physically attack each other. In the ensuing conflict, candles fall and the church catches fire. The Sultan issues a *ferman* (edict) giving the Orthodox and Catholics specific and separate possession of defined areas within the church.

1759 Widespread **earthquake** damage in Palestine.

1768 **Dahr el-Omar** (Amr) (1690–1775). The Ottomans recognize him as Sheikh of Acre, Nazareth, Tiberias, Safed, and all Galilee. He founds Haifa and fortifies Tiberias and Acre (export of Galilee cotton to France). He pioneers Arab liberation from foreign occupation and shows tolerance towards Jews and Christians.

1772 Catherine the Great of Russia grants Jews freedom of movement, but bans Jewish emigration from the 'Pale of Settlement' into Russia (western Russian border with Prussia and Austria-Hungary)

1782 Jewish civil freedom in Europe emerges firstly in England in 1732 giving Jews legal protection; the Toleration Patent in Austria in 1782; Jewish emancipation in the USA in 1783; in 1784 France removes personal taxes on Jews, implied in the French 'Rights of Man' in 1789; Holland in 1796; Venice in 1797; Mainz in 1798; Rome in 1810; and Frankfurt in 1811.

1784 The Acre, Khan al-Umdan ("Caravanserai/Inn of Pillars" is constructed over the Crusader Royal Customs House. The lower floor is used as warehouses while the upper level as an Inn for traders and travelers visiting the local port and markets.

Acre, Khan al-Umdan   Adrian Wolff

1789 Ahmed el-Pasha (1760-1804) known as el-Jazzar (the butcher), born in Bosnia, a Christian convert to Islam, conquers Damascus province (vilayet) in 1783 and Acre in 1789, in addition is governor of Sidon vilayet. He invites Haim Farhi, a Jewish financier in Damascus to Acre.

1798 **Napoleon** occupies Malta, expels the Hospitaller Knights of St. John for practicing piracy, ending their active control in the slave trade. Previously Knights of Malta would capture trading ships and ransom Jewish passengers, knowing Jewish communities, especially those in Alexandria and Istanbul would pay for freedom of a fellow Jew. Piracy is very prevalent along the Barbary (Berber) coast (North Africa from Gibraltar to Libya). In 1805 The US President Thomas Jefferson refuses to negotiate for the freedom of captured Americans in captivity. He sends US Marines Corps, who are successful in their endeavors. This has become a precedent in US policy in 'hostage taking'. Early 19thc, Britain campaigns against Muslim pirates. Piracy ends when France occupies Algeria in 1830.

1798 Napoleon sails with 360 ships, 60 war-ships, 65,000 soldiers and auxiliaries and 260 scientists invading Alexandria in Egypt, gateway to the Orient – to Persia, India and China. At Cairo Murad Bey leads the Mamluk Army known for its bravery and excellent cavalry confronting their opposition with swords. They do not change their type of weapons as they prefer the saber, despising modem firearms as being unworthy and unchivalrous in battle. Outdated military techniques of the Mamluks are no competition against French troops equipped with musket rifles. Some 30,000 French troops face a similar number of Mamluk forces who are slaughtered at the Battle of the Pyramids. British Admiral Nelson defeats the French fleet in the Bay of Aboukir. Napoleon's army is now cut off from returning to France, advances to conquer Palestine. Napoleon's success in Italy and the subsequent introduction of democratic administration in Western Europe will change their political maps, cultural and economic climates.

Chapter 18. Emancipation 1799 - 1881

1799 **Napoleon** (1769-1821) convenes the 'Assembly of Jewish Sanhedrin (Notables)' granting Jews civil rights, issuing an edict declaring Judaism an 'official religion' in France. Jews living within Italian States proclaim Napoleon 'Emancipator of the Jews', calling him in Hebrew *helek tov'* = bona-parte (used in Pirkei Avot V:15) allowing residence out of the ghettos. Napoleon publishes a manifesto promising Jews freedom to return to their land.

1799 Following the Mamluk defeat in Egypt, Napoleon continues with 12-13,000 troops along the Sinai Peninsula conquering el-Arish, Gaza and Jaffa (on his fourth attempt) and orders the execution of around 3000 defenders before his troops loot the port. The Armenian Church of St. Nicolas in Jaffa is used as a hospital where about one-third of the French troops die from the Black Plague. Napoleon is known to disregard the lives of his soldiers. His army proceeds to Ramle. Napoleon refrains from making a pilgrimage to Jerusalem which has no strategic importance, intending to conquer it only after controlling the coast. "*Jerusalem is not in my line of operations. I do not wish to be assaulted by mountaineers in difficult roads.*" (Gichon). He attempts to convince local rulers to accept French rule while the Jews are promised independence after the restoration of Jerusalem under French rule. He encourages the one million Jews living in the Eastern Mediterranean basin to support him (Gichon). French troops defeat the Turks and local Bedouins near Mt. Tabor.

1799 French troops lay parallel siege ditches around Acre defended by local Turkish warlord Ahmed el-Pasha (1760-1804) nicknamed el-Jazzar, the butcher, assisted by French royalists. French ladders are 5 meters while Acre's walls are 10 meters high. English Navy (Admiral Sir Sidney Smith, an anti-slavery protagonist, with 600-700 Royal marines) prevents the French from receiving fresh supplies as only 12 French heavy guns arrive overland. Napoleon's troops cannot traverse the internal wall, withdrawing after eight failed attempts. el-Jazzar's financial advisor, Haim Farhi personally pays for additional mercenaries to defend Acre. Later Farhi displeases el-Jazzar who cuts off his ear and gouges an eye.

After the Acre failure, the local population no longer supports Napoleon's adventures. French troops retreat to Haifa (the wounded are treated at Stella Maris monastery) and leave by sea from the ancient Greek port of Dor, south of Atlit along the Carmel Coast. (Many abandoned French weapons, recovered from the sea are on exhibition in the Nautical Museum at Dor). Over one-quarter of 13,000 French troops fail to return to Egypt. Eighteen months later British troops completely oust the French from Egypt. Napoleon returns to France, stages a coup d'etat, is 'elected' First Consul of The Directory.

Acre Walls, Mamluk Period   Adrian Wolff

1800   The **population** of Eretz Israel is 250,000 inhabitants, Jerusalem 8,000 with 5,500 Muslims, 1,500 Jews, and 1,000 Christians. Jerusalem remains unimportant both economically and politically. The majority of the Jews are ultra-orthodox religious, mainly reside in four towns - Jerusalem, Hebron, Safed and Tiberias. The majority of Arabs are Bedouin nomadic herders, while the minority live in the towns of Jerusalem, Acre, Ramle, Hebron and Jaffa.

1800+ Jews of Eretz Israel are persecuted during the period from 1800 to 1831. Various sultans in Istanbul issue a *ferman* (edict) forbidding Jews to own land, build new synagogues, insist they wear special distinguishing clothes and a yellow scarf. Weak central administration leads semi-independent leaders to increase taxation

1804   Russian Czar, Alexander I forbids Jews to lease land, or operate taverns. Russian authorities expel Jews living in villages forcing them to move to larger towns within the Pale of Settlement region in Western Russia limiting their choice of occupations.

1805   After the English leave Egypt, retired French royalist officers appoint Muhammad (Mehmet) Ali Pasha (1769-1849) Governor 'Bey' of Egypt, approved by the Ottoman Authorities in Istanbul. Muhammed Ali, originally from Albania, is previously sent by the sultan to assist in the war against Greece and later to save Egypt and Sudan from rebels.

1808   Fire in the Church of the Holy Sepulchre destroys the rotunda and seven columns. Control of all internal and exterior areas of the church remains divided between six Christian sects with no co-ordination between themselves regarding new construction and maintenance. The keys remain with a Muslim family Nusseibeh. Christian sects are: Greek Orthodox, Armenian Orthodox, Franciscan Catholic, Jacobite (Syrian), Copt (Egyptian) and Ethiopian Orthodox.

1809   Perushim, Habad-Lubavitch Ashkenazi Jewish scholars emigrate from Lithuania to Safed, disciples of the Vilna Gaon, Rabbi Elijah ben Solomon Zalman (1745-1797), founder of Habad. (See 1823).

1810   Czar Alexander I finances the re-construction of the damaged Tomb of Christ Station XIV, site of the Burial and Resurrection inside the Church of the Holy Sepulchre. The Unction Stone is replaced at the entrance to the Church. This stone symbolizes the washing of the body of Christ before placing Him in the Sepulchre. The Stone and Tomb are seen in the church today.

1811   Muhammad Ali massacres remaining Mamluk military functionaries in Egypt, while others flee to Nubia in Sudan. **End of the Mamluk Period in Egypt.**

1812   Russia opens a Consulate in Jerusalem to serve the increasing numbers of Russian Orthodox pilgrims visiting Christian Holy Sites.

1813   Outbreak of cholera forces many Safed Jews to move to Jerusalem.

1817   At Wartburg, Thuringia, in Germany during the 300th anniversary of the publication of Martin Luther's Ninety-Five Theses that precipitates the Reformation, thousands of German intellectuals and students burn books they deem as not German. The German Jewish literary giant, Heinrich Heine writes Almansor in 1823 "*In a place where they burn books they will, in the end, also burn men.*" (See Germany 1933).

1818   Kaiser Frederich Wilhelm III of Prussia limits Jews from academic professions, excluding them from employment in state positions.

1821   Unsuccessful Greek Orthodox uprising against Ottomans in Greece leaves thousands killed. Jews, previously persecuted by the Orthodox side with Muslim Ottomans. Many Jews flee to Istanbul and Odessa.

19thc   Transport within the Ottoman Empire is mainly by pack animals or river boats, while wheeled transportation, railways and shipbuilding are very rudimentary. No permanent Ottoman ambassadors are appointed to the West as diplomats are temporary emissaries to meet with western rulers, before returning to Istanbul. Western empires appoint ambassadors who reside over consulates within the Ottoman Empire having important influential positions regarding diplomatic and economic ties with their country.

1822   The Rothschild banking family incorporates Star of David in their coat of arms. (See 1490).

1823   Bey of Tunisia forces his Jewish subjects to wear distinctive hats.

1823   The Hasidic Movement is founded in Poland by Rabbi Israel Ba'al Shem-Tov (1700-1760). (Hasid = singular; Hasidim = plural). Followers called **Habad Hasidim** immigrate to Hebron, stress intellectualism, wisdom, understanding and knowledge. They are religious, deeply faithful Jews, follow with devotion Jewish ritual practice - the *mitzvot* (blessings/good deeds). The Hasidic movement maintain traditional dress from 18th century Poland. Various branches of Hasidim follow their particular spiritual leader. Modern Lubavich Hasid proselytize among non-observant Jews to become newly-religious, traditional observant Jews. The Habad movement sends emissaries to out-reach Jews in many parts of the globe. They do **not** proselytize among non-Jews.

1827   The first of seven visits to Jerusalem by **Sir Moses Montefiore** (1784-1885) with his final trip in 1874, aged 91. Montefiore marries Judith Cohen in 1812 and is brother-in-law of Nathaniel Mayer Rothschild, of the Rothschild banking family. Appointed Sheriff of London in 1837, he is the first Jew in England to hold a municipal office. Various heads of state receive him graciously. Montefiore, who is childless, retires early to devote his life to assisting Jews emigrate from Eastern Europe and develop Eretz Israel.

1827   Czar Nicholas I issues anti-Jewish edicts in Russia conscripting all Jews aged 18 to serve in the Russian army for 25 years, avoided by a substantial payment or conversion to Christianity (reformed in 1874 to 'only' six years service). Other anti-Jewish statutes in Russia are: a Jew may not employ Christian domestic servants, prohibition from constructing a synagogue in the proximity of a church, censoring Jewish books, many books burnt and many Jewish printing presses forcibly closed. Over 90% of the Russian population are serfs, living in poverty with no personal freedom.

1831   Palestine is directly controlled from Istanbul, under two Provincial Districts (*Vilayet*).
   • The Vilayet of Damascus administers Nablus, Jerusalem, Hebron and Eastern Mountain areas.
   • The Vilayet of Acre administers the Galilee and Coastal Plain.

1831 Muhammed Ali attempts to modernize the traditional Ottoman regime in Egypt, breaking from the central Ottoman Authority, placing himself as the independent governor of Egypt, residing in Cairo. Ibrahim Ali Pasha (1789-1848) the eldest step-son of Muhammed Ali of Egypt leads an army, conquering Palestine (Acre in 1832) and Syria, defeating the Ottomans at the Battle of Konya, forcing the cessation of Syria, Adana and Palestine to Egypt. (Konya in Anatolia, is the ancient city of Iconium). Both Palestine and Syria come under direct Egyptian control as Ottoman influence from Istanbul declines. He replaces many separate administrators with a single governor Ibrahim Ali Pasha. Palestine is part of the Administrative District (*Vilayet*) of Damascus. European Powers recognize Muhammed Ali rule in Palestine and Syria.

The nine-year period of Muhammed Ali rule in Palestine (1831-1840) is acknowledged by the previously persecuted non-Muslims as an improvement in economic conditions and personal safety. The *dhimmi* laws are repelled. Both Christians and Jews note his reign as being less oppressive, more efficient public administration and collection of taxes, with less open corruption. Ibrahim Ali Pasha cancels the special road-tolls paid by non-Muslims while the head-tax (*jizya*) payable by all non-Muslims remains in force. Modernization of civil liberties include the freedom of non-Muslims to ride a horse, choice of clothing previously forbidden, building of synagogues and churches, and Jews and Christians are allowed to immigrate to Palestine.

Reforms are instigated in agriculture allowing ownership of land, and new irrigation techniques are adopted. Progress is made in industry, commerce, judicial system, public health and education. Both Jews and Christians are active in commerce. A new legal system of civil courts is introduced to circumvent *qadis* (Muslim religious judges).

1831 King Louis-Philippe of France grants Jews official legal status as equal citizens.

1832 Israel Bak (1797-1874) immigrates from Berdichev in Russia to Safed where he opens a Hebrew printing press.

1833 Education Act in France makes education and literacy more available to the population. Most French citizens are illiterate. Literacy, (being able to read Hebrew) amongst Jewish males has always been almost 100% as Torah study is obligatory. "*You shall teach them thoroughly to your children*" (Deuteronomy 6:7).

1834 Bedouin living in the Safed area riot in protest against Muhammed Ali's order to conscript them into the Egyptian Army. Bedouin kill

Jews forcing many to flee to Jerusalem. Jews are also murdered in Hebron and Jerusalem.

1834 European Powers of Great Britain, France, Russia, and Austro-Hungary take a greater interest in Eretz Israel and open consulate offices in Jerusalem and in Jaffa, a port having no quay (pier) making any approach, especially in winter, treacherous. Ocean-going vessels are forced to anchor in the open sea while small rowboats transfer both people and materiel to shore. Jaffa, the main port for Jerusalem, is used for import and export, as the Acre port remains a fishing harbor with no hinterland. Volume of trade with Europe increases while various European representatives provide postal services. A fire breaks out in the Church of the Holy Sepulchre during the Orthodox Easter service. Dozens are killed during the stampede towards the single exit of the church.

1835 Ibrahim Ali Pasha grants permission to Jews of Jerusalem to repair the four ancient synagogues (Ben Zakkai, Prophet Eliyahu, Middle and Stambuli synagogues).

1836 Muhammed Ali publishes an edict allowing European Jewish immigration to Eretz Israel and Jewish habitation in Jerusalem.

1836 Bribes are paid to Ibrahim Ali to allow reconstruction of the **Hurva Synagogue** previously damaged by Arabs in 1721 for late payment of non-Muslim head-tax (*jizya*). See 1864. The synagogue is destroyed by Jordanians in 1948, reconstructed 2010.

1837 An **earthquake** damages many areas in the Galilee including Tiberias, killing Jews in Safed as survivors who move to Jerusalem

1838 The local political influence in Eretz Israel of Great Britain becomes more dominant than both France and Russia. Great Britain opens a consulate office in Jerusalem and interests of non-Ottoman Jews now fall under British jurisdiction, giving them official representation in Eretz Israel. During this period the number of western European Christian pilgrims visiting Jerusalem increases. The first pharmacy opens in Jerusalem owned by the Anglican Church of England, indicating an improvement in the very rudimentary public-health conditions. Anglicans open a school in Jerusalem, also offering food and clothing to the local population who live in poverty. Anglican Church attempts, with little success, to convert Jews to Christianity.

1838 William Young, the British consul in Jerusalem describes the local Ottoman rule as treating Jews with a value not higher than a dog. Dutch and German (HOD–Holland and Germany) Jews living in Jerusalem opt out of the pool fund agreement distributing donations, preferring to receive donations directly by Jewish communities living in the Netherlands and Germany. **Population** of Jerusalem is 10,000, including 5,000 Jews, the majority.

1838 Galilee Bedouins attack the remaining Jews in Safed forcing many to flee to Jerusalem.

1839 Sultan Mahmud II (rules 1808-1839) issues a *ferman* guaranteeing all Ottoman Empire subjects personal safety and security of their wealth and assets regardless of religion. This edict will include property, no longer expropriated by corrupt Ottoman officials. He is known as a reformer of civil liberties and introduces the fez, a new style of headgear to become a Muslim symbol. The situation does not endure as he dies during this year.

1839 Muslims in Persia forcibly convert the entire 2000 Jewish community of Meshed to Islam after murdering between 30 to 49 (no exact number available). Jews secretly keep their Judaism. Many members immigrate to Israel 100 years later.

1840 Muhammed Ali of Egypt cancels previous debts of the Jewish community's head-tax (*jizya*) to the local Ottoman Authorities and makes civil reforms, now finds himself in conflict with the new Sultan Abdulmecid I in Istanbul, (1839-1861). Britain and Austro-Hungary assist Abdulmecid I to replace Muhammed Ali in Egypt fearing he (Ali) will become sultan in Egypt, resulting in diminished Ottoman control from Istanbul. In a twist of fate, France refuses to join, displaying European disunity. In 1827 British fleet destroys Ottoman fleet of Ibrahim Ali Pasha near Beirut and shell the port of Acre in one of the first uses of artillery explosives in battle (not simply weighted balls) successfully destroying part of Acre's walls. Following Ibrahim Ali's defeat, forcing his return to Egypt, Muhammed Ali relinquishes his power in Palestine and Syria in 1841, is retained governor (*suzerain*) of Egypt until his death in 1849. His descendants are hereditary rulers of Egypt. Sultan Abdulmecid I grants Europeans concessions in Palestine following their assistance to defeat Muhammed Ali. Ottoman Administrative control returns to Istanbul, condition of Jews and Christians in Palestine worsens revoking the brief period of civil liberties. Local administration becomes chaotic, noted for bribery and corruption of local officials.

1840 The French Consul in Damascus publishes a blood-libel against the Jewish community. Anti-Semitic rioting breaks out falsely accusing Jews of the ritual murder of a Franciscan Superior and the use of Christian blood for the Passover preparation. Jews are arrested, tortured, and some forcibly converted to Islam. Sir Moses Montefiore, together with Adolphe-Isaac Cremieux, (future French

Jewish deputy in 1842; Minister of Justice in 1848; founder of the influential Alliance Israelite Universalle in 1860); and Salomon Munk, a well-known Orientalist, campaign for the freedom and release of Jews in Damascus. Sultan Abdulmecid I receives the delegation in Istanbul and issues a *ferman* acquitting the unfortunate innocent Jews accused in Damascus, canceling the libel and protecting Jewish rights. **This is the first time in modern history Jews obtain a successful state order on behalf of a Jew falsely accused of libel.** British foreign secretary, Lord Palmerston, strongly recommends the Ottomans should encourage the Jews of Europe to return to Palestine.

1840   A Chief Rabbi (hakham bashi) is appointed in Jerusalem.

1840   Population of Palestine is approximately 250,000.

1841   European powers force Sultan Abdulmecid I to issue a *ferman* continuing civil reforms previously initiated by Ibrahim Ali to Jews and Christians in Palestine.

1841   Israel Bak moves from Safed to Jerusalem opening a printing house and establishing the only Hebrew printing press.

1841   First **Anglican** Bishop officially resides in Jerusalem, increasing English influence in Jerusalem. Protestants are recognized by a *ferman* as an independent '*millet*' (nation). (See 1849).

Entrance to Rachel's Tomb – a fortress   Adrian Wolff

1841   Sir Moses Montefiore finances the reconstruction and refurbishing of the Jewish Matriarch, **Rachel's Tomb** on the northern outskirts of Bethlehem. Today Rachel's Tomb is fortified, able to withstand attacks by Arabs intent on destroying the site.

1842   Russia, Austria and Spain open **consulate offices** in Jerusalem.

1843 Prussian and French consulates are established in Jerusalem advancing and reviving European influence in the region. Ottoman Authorities regard France as protector of Roman Catholic and Holy Sites in the Holy Land as a result of agreement in 1536 by King Francis I to Sultan Suleyman, renewed again in 1740.

1843 Sir Moses Montefiore travels with his personal physician Dr. Thomas Hodgkin (1798-1866) who identifies the malignant disease of the lymph tissue known as Hodgkin's disease. Hodgkin dies in 1866, is buried in the Christian cemetery, Jaffa. Sir Moses Montefiore instructs Dr. Simon Frankel to open a medical clinic in Jerusalem. Jews request additional finance for Torah studies.

1843 In Sarajevo, Rabbi Yehuda Alkalai (1798-1878) announces Jews should, without waiting for Divine Redemption return to Eretz Israel with the purpose of building a Jewish nation.He immigrates in 1874

1844 Siyyid Ali Mohammed (1819-1850), known as **Bab** proclaims himself 'messiah', risen 1000 years after Mohammed's birth, believing himself, not Mohammed to be the last prophet. **Bahai'i's** are not accepted by mainstream Muslims. In 1850 he is executed in Tabriz, Persia for his religious beliefs and teachings. Later his body is brought to Haifa.

1844 Russian authorities force Jews to pay a tax for the wearing of distinctive clothing.

1845 **Greek Orthodox Patriarch** officially moves from Istanbul to new headquarters in Jerusalem.

1845 **Population** census of Jerusalem is 15,000, includes 7,100 Jews, 5,000 Muslims, 3,000 Christians.

1846 Jews of Sana'a in Yemen are forced to clean the town's sewers. This edict remains in force when they immigrate to Israel in 1950.

1847 The Latin Patriarchate (Catholic) opens its offices in Jerusalem.

1848 The Armenian Orthodox Patriarchate opens a Printing Press in Jerusalem. The Valero family opens the **first bank** in Jaffa Road, Jerusalem. Increased European interest and pilgrimages result in Austria (Austro-Hungarians) opening in 1853 the first Post Office in Jerusalem (opposite the Citadel). Postal Offices representing Italy, Prussia, France and Great Britain will follow shortly afterwards in the Jaffa road.

1849 The first **Protestant** church in Jerusalem, Christ's Church, is constructed opposite the Tower of David.

1849 Sultan Abdulmecid I grants official status to Christians and Jews, ending their dhimmi status in 1856.

Austrian Post Box, Israel Philatelic Bureau

1852   Turkish Authorities in Jerusalem proclaim a 'Declaration of the Status Quo' between all Christian sects vying for control of the Church of the Holy Sepulchre. Specific areas within the Church are defined regarding ownership and upkeep of the various chapels, altars and common areas. The Greek Orthodox the dominant sect, controls the majority of area. Muslims occasionally attack Christians for being infidels (*dhimmi*) who suffer less than the Jews as Christians have European government protection.

1853   The Crimean War from 1853 to 1856 has ramifications for Christian control of their Holy Sites in the Holy Land. During this period the Russian Orthodox Church purchases property, encouraging pilgrimages to the Holy Land. Russia demands to exercise their protection over Russian Orthodox Christian subjects within the Ottoman Empire and claim the control of the Christian Holy Sites in Palestine. The Ottomans do not preserve the '*status quo*' promised by the Sultan to the Orthodox, allowing the transfer of the keys to the Church of Nativity in Bethlehem to the Catholics who replace the 'silver star' in the grotto over the spot where Christ was born establishing Catholic rights to the property and their exclusive possession of the grotto and the church. The Russians plan to 'emancipate' the church from the Catholics. Concurrently French Catholics also wish to maintain control of the Christian Holy Sites. The Russian Orthodox church demands the Ottomans controlling Palestine replace the Star of Bethlehem, which is later returned.

Hostilities begin when Russian troops assemble in Crimea. Ottomans seek aid from Britain and France (according to their joint military pact), to halt Russian influence and expansion from the

Black Sea to the Mediterranean Sea. Over 500,000 soldiers die in this war in Crimea, mostly from disease and poor medical aid. Russian support of the armies of Great Britain and France in Crimea result in Austria-Hungary loosing Italy, united in 1861 and Germany in 1871. Russian expansion is terminated thereby allowing French Catholics control over some Christian Holy Sites in Eretz Israel. A Jewish banker I. Camondo & Cie. of Istanbul provides finance to the Sultan during the war in Crimea. The family moves to Paris. The last family members are murdered in Auschwitz in 1944.

1853   **Avraham Mapu** (1808-1867) Russia, publishes a book titled '*Love of Zion*' in Hebrew, termed the creator of the Modern Hebrew novel

1854   The Rothschild Banking family donate the first Jewish hospital and school for girls on Misgav Ladach Street, Jewish Quarter, Jerusalem, administered by Dr. Albert Cohen.

1855   Frequently Jewish assets are confiscated by corrupt Ottoman officials. The head-tax (*jizya*) is replaced by '*bedel*' tax, an exemption from military service. Jews may not ride a horse, carry a fire-arm, must wear a different shaped collar, head-dressing and shoes, nor build a house without permission. Jewish religious buildings have to be lower in height than mosques. Blood libels will breakout in Damascus 1840, Beirut 1862, Istanbul 1864-5, Edirne 1872, Aleppo 1875.

1855   Sir Moses Montefiore visits Eretz Israel, receives a *ferman* from Kamil Pasha, governor of Jerusalem to purchases and plant citrus groves near Jaffa, known as the Montefiore Quarter of modern day Tel Aviv. He also purchases a plot of land opposite Jaffa Gate in Jerusalem. Until this date Jews living in Eretz Israel are mostly traditional ultra-orthodox Jews intent in serious Torah study, now become more exposed to secular occupations.

1856   Sultan Abdulmecid I gives France control of the Church of St. Anne on via Dolorosa, previously converted into a Muslim madrassah (religious training school). **Bells are restored in Monastery of the Cross.** Sound of Christian prayer is heard in Jerusalem.

1857   The Stambouli Synagogue is dedicated in the Jewish Quarter. (See Ibrahim Ali 1835). Perushim (disciples of Elijah, the Gaon of Vilna) establish the Bikur Holim Hospital in the Jewish Quarter of Jerusalem. Later the hospital will be rebuilt and expanded at a new location at the corner of Strauss and Ha'neve'im Streets.

1858   Austrian Hospice is completed on via Dolorosa, providing medical and hospitality services to European pilgrims visiting Jerusalem. Hotels do not exist during this period.

1859　Due to overcrowding inside the Jewish Quarter, Jewish immigrants originally from Holland and Germany (HOD) purchase a plot of land on Mt Zion, situated outside the city walls. Grand Duke Constantine Nicholaevitch acquires land to the west of the walls of the Jerusalem City, the Russian Compound. On this site, Russians construct a consulate building, cathedral, monastery, hospital and hospice. In front of this cathedral, a Herodian column is found in situ. It is assumed this stone cracked during quarrying and is left in the bedrock. Its importance is evidence of quarrying and stone-cutting techniques used in the Herodian Period. Later, following Russian Revolution in 1917 and demise of the church's patron, the Czar, Russian Orthodox sites in Israel will lack finance for maintenance. Royalist White Russians will be persecuted by Red Russian Orthodox Church which side with Communist Russians.

1860　Maronites, an eastern church in Lebanon are neither Eastern Orthodox nor Catholic, originating in the 4th and 5th centuries. In 1182 seek unison with the Latin Patriarch of Antioch, consummated by the pope in the 16th century. Maronite Christians of Lebanon, historically protected by France (many of the Crusaders are French) persecute local Druze. Druze do not have nationalist aspirations are supported by British and Ottomans. Both sides accuse the other of massacre as many Druze flee to Syria and northern Carmel Mountains area of Eretz Israel.

Mishkenot Ha'shananim-Yemin Moshe, Jerusalem.　　　Adrian Wolff

1860　Most streets within the Jerusalem city walls are narrow, impossible for two heavily laden donkeys to pass one another. There are no drains. The streets are dirty, filled with garbage and dust. Serious overcrowding within the walls of the city of Jerusalem. Concurrently it is dangerous to live unguarded outside a walled city because of the threat from marauding Bedouin. **Sir Moses Montefiore** promotes construction of the **First Jewish suburb outside the city walls**, *Mishkenot Ha'shananim* quarter opposite the Jaffa Gate, financed by an American Jew, Judah Touro (1775-1854) whose legacy is administered by Montefiore, donating money to both Jewish and non-Jewish institutions. Residential construction begins outside the Jerusalem city walls as Jews build westwards, Christians southwards towards Bethlehem, and Muslims northwards towards Ramallah.

1860   **Population** of Jerusalem reaches 18,000 inhabitants, about 44% are Jews. Jewish inhabitants in Eretz Israel is approximately 13,000-2100 in Safed; 1500 in Tiberias; 400 in Hebron; 400 in Jaffa; 120 in Acre; 100 in Haifa, and 8,000 in Jerusalem.

1860   Adolphe-Isaac Cremieux (French statesman) and Karl Netter establish Alliance Israelite Universalle (Kol Yisrael Haverim) in Paris to defend Jewish Civil Rights and religious freedom. In addition, they assist Jewish immigration and education in Eretz Israel by building schools and trade schools.

1862   Sultan Abdulaziz decrees Palestine must no longer be controlled under the provincial district *'Vilayet'* of Beirut. **A representative of the sultan is appointed in each** *vilayet* **under direct authority from Istanbul.** Palestine is divided into separate districts, the *Vilayet* of Acre and of Nablus. Each *vilayet* is divided into sub-districts or *sancak*. Jerusalem, a separate *sancak* under *Vilayet* of Damascus. Later Jerusalem will revert to control from the *Vilayet* of Beirut. The Ottoman Administration orders all arable land or *'min'* not cultivated for three consecutive years, to revert to Ottoman ownership. Local nomadic Felaheen and Bedouin in Palestine lose rights to land-ownership and land is sold to absentee owners or *effendis* who then lease the land to the local Arabs. Ottoman Administration headquarters in Jerusalem is located in the Kishle, next to the Tower of David, at the Jaffa Gate, later a Police Station.

1862   Rabbi **Zvi Hirsch Kalicher** (1795-1874). In 1862 Kalischer writes in *'Drishat Zion'* stating that settling in Eretz Israel is the first step towards the promised redemption.

1863   **Moshe (Moritz) Hes**s, born in Bonn 1812, dies in Paris in 1875, an important German socialist thinker, promotes workers be organized. Forced to flee Germany for Paris during the revolution of 1848, Hess publishes *'Rome and Jerusalem'* proposing national

Jewish consciousness and could be called the 'father of Zionist socialism' where Jews are a separate nationality in their own land. His remains brought to Israel in 1961, buried at Kvutzat Kinneret.

Hurva Synagogue, Jewish Quarter, reconstructed in 2010. Adrian Wolff

1864 Over the ruins of the **Hurva**, the magnificent Beit Ya'akov Synagogue is completed after seven years of construction, with a stone dome 24 meters high. This building is the largest structure within the Jewish Quarter and will be destroyed again, by the Jordanians in 1948 after the Jordanian Arab Legion's conquest of the Jewish Quarter. Restoration is completed in 2010.

1864 First Jewish school for girls is opened on Misgav Ladach Street in the Jewish Quarter named after its patron Baroness Evelina de Rothschild. Ultra-orthodox Jews protest at the opening of this school. No separate sewerage system exists within the walls of the Old City causing contamination of drinking water. Pollution causes an epidemic of dysentery forcing the inhabitants of Jerusalem to be quarantined. The **Yemin Moshe (Moses) quarter**, named after the benefactor Sir Moses and Judith Montefiore is constructed adjacent to Mishkenot Ha'shananim opposite the Jaffa Gate.

1865 Telegraphic services are opened linking Jerusalem to the coast and other towns.

1865 Palestine Exploration Fund (PEF) is founded in Britain to conduct surveys of the topography and ethnography in the Ottoman province of Palestine. Notable founders are Arthur P. Stanley and Sir George Grove. The society promotes studies by (amongst others) Charles Warren, Horatio Kitchener, Edward Henry Palmer, TE Lawrence, Kathleen Kenyon, Conrad Schick, Charles Wilson.

Few examples of excavations undertaken are:
Jerusalem (1867-1870) - Warren
Western Palestine (1872-1877) - Wilson, Kitchener
Sinai (1872) - Palmer
Jerusalem (1897-1899) - Bliss and Macalister
Gezer (1902-1908) - Macalister
Zin (1913-1914) - Wooley, Lawrence
Ashkelon (1920's)- Garstang
Mt. Carmel (1925)- Garrod
Gaza, Beth Pelet (1929-1933) - Petrie
Samaria (1931-1933) - Crowfoot
Tel el-Duweir (1934-1938) - Starkey

1865 Captain **Sir Charles Wilson** (1830-1905), a British Officer and topographer conducts the first professional topographical Survey of Palestine, the Survey of Jerusalem (1864-1866), and the Survey of Sinai (1868-1869), leading to an improvement in the water supply to Jerusalem. He identifies the Herodian Bridge (Wilson's Arch) connecting the Temple Mount with the Upper City.

1866 Increased European presence in Palestine, especially at the port of Jaffa and Jerusalem. Sir Moses Montefiore helps finance the improvement of the supply of water to Jerusalem. The local Jews and Ashkenazi (non-Ottoman) Jews are represented by various foreign consulates and not solely by the British consul.

German Templer Building, Tel Aviv.   Adrian Wolff

1866 Christians build churches with steeples to been seen from afar, as some await the Second Coming of Christ believing it will take place at the beginning of the 20th century. A Protestant German Christian sect, The **Templers** (Templgesellschaft) led by Christoph Hoffmann, immigrate to await the expected Second Coming of Christ. They establish agricultural and trade colonies in Haifa, Jaffa, Emek Refaim in Jerusalem, Sarona (now in Tel Aviv), Waldheim, Bethlehem-in-the-North, and Wilhelima near Ramle. *"And they lived and reigned with Christ for a thousand years. But the rest of the dead did not live again until the thousand years were finished. This is the first resurrection."* (Revelations 20:4,5).

1867   British archaeologist **Sir Charles Warren** discovers a shaft (*tzinor*) in David's City, the Ophel, allowing buckets to be lowered into the Gihon Spring to collect water without leaving the city walls.

1867   Non-Muslims (Christians or Jews) have tribulations purchasing land within the Ottoman Empire as bribes need to be paid. The Ottomans begin to relax these rulings due to the general financial failure of the Empire. Ottoman Authorities give permission to **restore bells in the Church of the Holy Sepulchre**. See Monastery of the Cross 1856.

1868   A new Jewish suburb at Mahane Israel is constructed outside of the walls as Jews continue to move outside the over-crowded Jewish Quarter. The first modern bakery in Jerusalem is opened.

1868   A new religion independent of Islam the **Bahai'i** is founded in Persia by Mizra Husayn Ali (1817-1892), known as the **Baha'ullah** or The Glory of Allah (God). Bahai'is are followers of the **Bab** (Siyyid Ali Mohammed) (See 1844). Persians force Baha'ullah to flee to Acre, is imprisoned for 24 years, dies in 1892. This site contains his shrine, manicured gardens, his house and a museum.

Bahai'i Gardens, Acre   Adrian Wolff

1868 Construction of a German school for Arab Girls, Talita Kumi (in King George Street today). French Sisters of Zion Convent is built on the via Dolorosa by Alphonse Ratisbonne, an apostate Jew from Strasbourg, living in Jerusalem until his death in 1884. A road and water cistern from the Herodian period is found beneath the convent including squares carved on the floor used by Roman soldiers to place objects for games. At this site the arch of the basilica Ecce Homo commemorates Hadrian's victory over the Jews following the Bar Kochba revolt in 135. Crusaders term the arch Gate of Dolorus (the Gate of Sorrow) where Christians claim, Jesus passes on His journey to the Golgotha-the Crucifixion site. Latin Patriarchate is constructed near the Jaffa Gate, increasing Catholic influence and control of Christian Holy Sites.

1869 The road is completed allowing wheeled carriages from Jaffa, the port on the Mediterranean coast to Jerusalem, making the route safer and physically less tiresome for travelers. Khans or inns and 17 fortresses are constructed to house Ottoman soldiers for the protection of travelers. The number of pilgrims and tourists visiting the Holy Sites of the three monotheistic religions increases.

1869 The Suez Canal 160 kilometers long connecting the Mediterranean Sea with the Red Sea and Indian Ocean is opened. The sea route from Europe to India and Far East substantially shortens sailing time, resulting in increased trade passing through the area and advancing European Power interest in the Middle East. The Suez Canal is constructed with French engineering. The British prime minister, of Jewish origin, Benjamin Disraeli (1804-1881, PM 1868, 1874-1880) promotes gains obtained from the Suez Canal, as Britain becomes more active in Middle East. (See 1875, 1882).

1869 Construction of a new Jewish suburb Nahlat Shiva outside the Old City of Jerusalem. Emperor Franz Joseph of Austria visits Jerusalem. Sultan Abdulhamid II gives Germany the Muristan plot, previously site of the Crusader Knights of St. John hospital.

1870 Karl (Charles) Netter (born Strasbourg 1826, dies at Mikve Israel in 1882) establishes Mikve Israel, a Jewish Agricultural College, providing Jewish immigrant pioneers training in secular vocations. Previously in 1851, Netter establishes Jewish vocational schools in Paris and together with Adolphe-Isaac Cremieux a leading French politician, founds Alliance Israelite Universalle. (See 1860). Later schools are built in Jerusalem, Tel Aviv, Haifa, Tiberius and Safed.

1870 The compulsory Education Act is passed in England. Previously illiteracy is very common. The British PM, Benjamin Disraeli states in the House of Commons 15 June 1874, "*Upon the education of the people of this country the fate of this country depends.*"

1870 Social integration begins between Sephardic and Ashkenazi Jews who have similar traditions, but slightly different customs.

1870's Russians murder non-Arab Sunni Muslim Circassians in the Caucasus. Turkish Authorities allow their immigration to the Galilee, settling in Kfar Kama and Rehania, numbering 4500 today. Males serve in the Israeli Army. They do not pray in mosques.

1870 Turkish Authorities are not satisfied with the productivity of the local Arab workers and transfer Nubians from Sudan to drain the swamps along the Carmel coast near Caesarea. Today they populate the village of Jezr a-Zarka opposite the town of Or Akiva.

1870 Germans are victorious over the French Army in Alsace allowing Germany to achieve influential status in the Ottoman Empire, receiving special rights and benefits in Palestine such as land to construct churches and easing of German pilgrimage tolls.

1870 Jerusalem population. Jews 8000, Muslims 4000, Christians 2200, Armenians 1800. (William H Seward, Travels Around the World).

1871 The German Chancellor Otto von Bismarck (1815-1898) unifies the agricultural-based principalities into modern industrial-based German nation promoting the development of railways, roads, canals, workers-rights, national social welfare system, expanding the educational system, which is now available to the middle-class.

1872 The large, impressive **Nesim Bek** or **Tiferet Israel Synagogue** is completed in the Jewish Quarter of the Old City. The Jordanians destroy the synagogue in 1948.

1872 The Russian Orthodox Church purchases land in Ein Kerem.

1873 Road construction within Jerusalem onto Bethlehem and Hebron.

1873 German Templers construction in Emek Refaim, Jerusalem.

1874 Construction of Ratisbonne Monastery in Shmuel Ha'Nagid Street. Jewish expansion to the west in the **Mea She'arim** quarter, built as a walled suburb with many gates. Today Mea Sha'arirm is home to ultra-Orthodox Jews. Sir Moses Montefiore's final visit to Eretz Israel. He encourages, finances the development of Jewish printing press, textile factories and Jewish agricultural colonies.

1875 Ottoman Empire, unable to pay interest on its foreign loans raised in British banks and is declared bankrupt by European Powers. Britain purchases Ottoman shares of the Suez Canal Company borrowing money in London from Lord Rothschild, ensuring British control of the Canal and its income from shipping tolls until 1956.

1875 Another Jewish suburb Even Israel is constructed in Jerusalem. An Arab suburb, Abu Tor is constructed to the southeast of Jerusalem.

1875   First Jewish agricultural settlement in modern Eretz Israel when Safed Jews purchase land at Ja'uni, (Gai-Oni), later renamed **Rosh Pina** in the Hula Valley, Upper Galilee. This settlement, abandoned after crop failures and malaria, is resettled in 1882.

1876   Sultan Abdulaziz (1861–1876) dies. His rule is noted for the further disintegration of the Ottoman Empire. Sultan Murad V the new sultan brings new ideas of liberalization and civil liberties, is quickly deposed and replaced by Sultan Abdulhamid II (1876-1909). The First Ottoman Constitution is written during his reign. Continuing decline in Ottoman Empire power, financial instability, together with an increase in local nationalist movements seeking independence.

1876   Construction in Jerusalem of the Peres Blancs (White Fathers) Monastery, St. John's Eye Hospital on Mt of Olives and roads built from the Old City walls to the Mt. of Olives.

1877   A Jerusalem municipal council known as the *'majlis baladia'* is established to administer the increased development of Jerusalem.

1877   Jews living in Russia are prohibited from sending money to Jews within the Ottoman Empire and particularly to Jews in Eretz Israel.

1878   The Hejaz Railway is constructed from Damascus to Medina affording Muslim pilgrims an easier route to the *haj* holy sites in Arabia. Many trees are cut down in Eretz Israel.

1878   The first Jewish urban colony in modern Eretz Israel is founded at Petach Tikva east of Jaffa. The settlement initially abandoned due to malaria, is resettled again in 1882.

1878   British FM Lord Salisbury recognizes French interests in Lebanon/ Syrian in return for French reciprocating their interests in Cyprus.

1880   French Catholics construct the Convent of the Soeurs du Sainte Rosaire in Mamilla, opposite the Jaffa Gate, Jerusalem.

1880   **Population** of Eretz Israel increases rapidly from about 250,000 in 1800 to approximately 450,000 inhabitants in 1880, mainly due to Arabs moving from the surrounding territories. The total Jewish population is about 26,000. Jerusalem has about 30,000 inhabitants, Jews make up the majority with 18,000 (60%).

1881   Armenian Catholic Church of Our Lady in Spasm is constructed on via Dolorosa at Station IV.

1881   Rabbi **Samuel Mohilever** (1824-1898) a religious Zionist leader appeals to rabbis to promote Aliyah (immigration) to Eretz Israel and to support ICA (Jewish Colonial Association). In 1882 he requests financial assistance from the Rothschild Bankers in

Frankfurt to purchase land for Jewish settlement in Eretz Israel, founding Ekron (Mazkeret Batya) in 1882. As honorary president of 'Hovevei Zion' in 1884, he stresses the need to instruct Jewish agriculturalists and to urgency for Jewish watchmen to protect their fields from marauding Arabs.

1881 **Avraham Menachem Mendel Ussishkin** (1863-1942) establishes in Odessa, 'The Society of Pioneers to Eretz Israel'.

1881 **Eliezer Ben-Yehuda** (Perleman) (1859-1922), founder of the Modern Hebrew language emigrates from Lithuania to Eretz Israel. Up to this date, Hebrew is used almost totally as a language of prayer, constructed with Biblical, Mishnaic and Medieval Hebrew words. His vision of the revival of Jewish national aspirations includes a modernization of the Hebrew language to be spoken, written and read by Jews. Ben-Yehuda believes Jews who immigrate to Eretz Israel from many countries will be united when they speak one language, Hebrew. His family is known as the first Hebrew speaking family in Eretz Israel, using Sephardic pronunciation, which he believes is closest to the original Hebrew. Hebrew is the official language (together with Arabic) of Israel.

1881 Ottomans are unable to pay their foreign creditors. European powers gain financial control of Ottoman assets and debts in Europe through a Council of the Administration of the Public Debt. France occupies Ottoman Tunisia.

1881 Czar Alexander II (1855-1881) abolishes compulsory military service for Jews. Conditions for serfs and Jews improve temporarily. He is assassinated by conservatives (1881). Widespread pogroms (anti-Jews riots) follow.

19thc+ Ottomans allow Jews to gather at the Western Wall only on the Sabbath.

1881 **The Russian Ecclesiastical Mission** built in Dabgha Street next to the Church of the Holy Sepulchre, headed by Archimandrite Antonin Kapoustin following the visit to Jerusalem of Grand Duke Sergei Alexandrovitch. The building complex incorporates The Russian Orthodox Church and the St. Alexander Nevsky chapel, completed in 1896. This is the headquarters in Israel for the Royalist (white) Russian Orthodox Church, and had little or no contact with the Red Russian Orthodox in Russia, who they claim, sided with the Communist regimes' participation in the execution of their patron, the Czar Nicholas II and his family. This complex houses one of the most exciting archaeological sites for Christians in Jerusalem, including a gate from the period of King Herod.

- The Church (Basilica) is constructed over the ruins of the original Byzantine Church of Holy Sepulchre built by Queen Helena in the 4th century. A visitor can view the columns, mosaics and steps leading up to the original church entrance (as shown on the Madaba mosaic map).
- The original Herodian City Gate, known by Christians as Judgment Gate. Here they claim Jesus passed through with His Cross on His way to the hill of Golgotha situated outside of the city walls, a few meters from this church. **The Eye of the Needle** (Matthew 19:24; Mark 10:25) is adjacent to this gate.
- An arch and two columns are part of a Roman Temple to Jovian built over the Crucifixion site by Hadrian in 2ndc CE.

The Eye of The Needle, Russian Orthodox Church, Jerusalem.   Adrian Wolff

Matthew 19:24 Mark 10:25 (The New Testament, The Holy Bible, New King James version) "*It is easier for a camel to go through the eye of needle than for a rich man to enter the kingdom of God.*"

The original New Testament is written Greek "πάλιν δὲ λέγω ὑμῖν, εὐκοπώτερόν ἐστιν κάμηλον διὰ τρυπήματος ῥαφίδος διελθεῖν ἢ πλούσιον εἰσελθεῖν εἰς τὴν βασιλείαν τοῦ θεοῦ".

The quotation in modern Greek confirms the word 'camel', nevertheless some Greek scholars tend to interpret the word as "rope" κάμιλο

The ancient Greek word *kamêlos*, means 'cable, large rope' may have been misused/mistranslated as *kamilos,* a camel.

The Aramaic word *gamla* means a camel (also in Hebrew and Arabic) or 'a large rope', possibly because the ropes were made from camel hair.

Chapter 19. First Immigration till Eve WW I 1882 - 1913

1882 The Ottoman Empire remains unable to pay its foreign debts. British troops land in Egypt to secure the Suez Canal Zone (See 1875), defeating Egyptian nationalist forces led by Arabi Pasha. Egypt becomes a British Protectorate from 1914 until 1922.

1882 The Greek Catholic 'Church of the Holy Face and St Veronica' is built on via Dolorosa at Station VI. Jerusalem-based Italian architect Antonio Barluzzi restores the church in 1953. The Ethiopian Church, Bond of Mercy (in Ge'ez), is completed in 1893. Ethiopians, early converts to Christianity, believe the Queen of Sheba came from Ethiopia to visit King Solomon in Jerusalem where she received the emblem of the Lion of Judah. This emblem is carved on the church gate. *"The queen of Sheba heard of Solomon's fame...She arrived in Jerusalem with a large entourage."* (I Kings 10:1,2).

1882 Following the 1878 Berlin Conference, soldiers of the Austro-Hungarian Empire invade Bosnia and Herzegovina as local Christians mistreat Bosnian Muslims. Some settle in the Ottoman empire. In 1882 a group seeks refuge in Caesarea building homes and construct a mosque still standing today.

1882 From this date until the Russian Revolution in 1917, many pogroms (anti-Jewish riots) take place in Russia, initially inspired by Russian Interior Minister, Ignatiev and partially by the Russian Orthodox Church. A pogrom offers considerable profit. If the family flees or are killed, not only might the debtor never have to pay back his debt but the Jew's house, chattels, land and stock are possessed. Hundreds of thousands of Jews will emigrate to the west, the majority to America, Great Britain, Australia, Argentina and South Africa and a minority to Eretz Israel. Founding of the **'Hibbat Zion'** (Love of Zion) Zionist Movement in Odessa whose members are **Hovevei Zion** (Lovers of Zion). Many prominent Zionist thinkers are members of this organization including **Leon Pinsker, Ahad Ha'am, Lilienblum, Smolenskin, Levanda**. (See 1862 Kalisher, 1881 Mohilewer). The Hibbat Zion Movement opens branches to encourage Jews to immigrate to Eretz Israel and receives financial aid from the Rothschild banking family. *"By the rivers of Babylon, there we sat and also wept when we remembered Zion."* (Psalms 137:1).

1882 As a direct reaction to the pogroms in Russia, **Israel Belkind** establishes the **BILU** movement in Odessa, promoting secular

Jewish immigration to Eretz Israel. BILU = (acronym in Hebrew) *"The House of Jacob, come and let us go"* (Isaiah 2:5). Many young Jews join the BILU as Jewish nationalism presents the alternative of assimilation.

1882   The beginning of increased Jewish Immigration to Eretz Israel **The First Immigration, *Aliyah Alef*** (1882-1903). Secular young Jews in central and southern Europe inspired by the BILU and Hibbat Zion movements flee the pogroms and continual anti-Semitism making their way to Eretz Israel. Over 25,000 immigrate. The bond between Jews and the Land of Israel is never severed.

1882   Hibbat Zion in Odessa appoints **Dr. Leon Pinsker** (1821-1891) as its leader. Following the pogroms in Russia, Pinsker doubts the success of the emancipation of European Jewry and promotes immigration to Eretz Israel. His book *'Auto-Emancipation'* analyzes the psychological and social roots of anti-Semitism. He concludes assimilation to be impossible because anti-Semitism is so deeply rooted in society that regards Jews as foreigners, proclaiming Jews have no future living outside their spiritual Jewish homeland in Israel.

1882   **Ahad Ha'am** (1856-1927), (Asher Ginzberg), joins Hovevei Zion, settles in Eretz Israel in 1922, is an influential author and thinker, grounded in Jewish values and heritage. He writes of a 'new type of Jew in Eretz Israel', proud of his Jewish traditional heritage, rooted in his education. The continuation of Jewish spiritual creativity and the continuation of the Jewish people's (Am Israel עם ישראל) national identity in 'a Jewish state, not a state of Jews'.

Zichron Ya'akov. Children's graves. Many die from malaria.   Adrian Wolff

1882   Almost all the natural forests from Biblical times are destroyed. Wood is used for fuel (charcoal), and the village of Umm al-Fahm (mother of the coals) indicates the main vocation of its inhabitants. Trees are also used as railway sleepers for the Hejaz Railway line. The Romans are reputed to plant trees in the Carmel Mountains.

1882   The young Jewish new immigrants find Eretz Israel predominantly an impoverished parched desert; with marshy pools, home to malaria carrying mosquitoes. Definitely not *"a land of wheat, barley, grape, fig and pomegranate. A land of oil-olives and date-honey."* (Deuteronomy 8:8). (**Seven Species שיבעת המינים** in the Bible). The pomegranate symbolizes beauty, fertility and abundance. The agricultural techniques practiced by the local population have not changed for centuries. The early pioneers establish new secular urban areas in **Rosh Pina, Rishon Le'Zion, Zichron Ya'akov, Mazkeret Batya**. *"Your land it will no longer be said 'Desolate Place'... your land will become inhabited."* (Isaiah 62:4) *"...and return them to the land that You gave to them and their forefathers."* (2 Chronicles 6:25). **There is little direct communication between the existing veteran ultra-orthodox urban Jewish population and the mainly secular and culturally more emancipated new immigrants**.

1882   Arabs in Palestine use primitive agricultural techniques, not producing food surpluses for export, nor create a market for industrialized goods. Terraced walls are neglected or in ruin. Trees felled for fuel and rain has removed fertile soil.*"...[a] desolate country whose soil is rich enough, but is given over wholly to weeds-a silent mournful expanse....A desolation...There was hardly a tree or a shrub anywhere...the olive and the cactus had almost deserted the country."* Mark Twain, The Innocents Abroad, 1867.

1882   **The Jews begin legitimately to purchase land from absentee landlords, dig water-wells, plant fields.** Arab squatters are evicted and the Jews clash with the nomadic Bedouin preventing them from watering and feeding their herds on newly cultivated Jewish-owned lands and developed wells. Local Arab marauders will attack the new Jewish settlements at: Kinneret, Degania, Yavniel, Sejara, Merhavia, Hadera, Jaffa, Petach Tikva, Ben Shemen, Nes Ziona, Rehovot, Gedera and also in Jerusalem.

1882   **Naftali Hertz Imber**, born in Romania in 1856 immigrates to Eretz Israel. He meets **Sir Laurence Oliphant**, a Christian Zionist and lives in Oliphant's Haifa residence. Inspired by Pioneers in Rishon Le'Zion, Imber writes a poem called *Tikvateunu* (Our Hope), later be set to music by Samuel Cohen based on a Moldavian melody, now known as *Ha'tikva* (The Hope) is sung by the participants at the Sixth Zionist Congress in Basle in 1903, becoming the unofficial Anthem of the **Yishuv** (the Hebrew term to describe pre-State Jewish settlement and its institutions). On 14 May 1948 '*Hatikva*' becomes the Israeli national anthem, sung by the National Assembly on completion of the signing of the Declaration of Independence of the State of Israel. Imber settles in America in 1892, dies a pauper in 1909, unable to eke out a living from poetry.

As long as deep in the heart	כל עוד בלבב פנימה
The soul of a Jew yearns	נפש יהודי הומיה
And towards the East	ולפאתי מזרח קדימה
An eye looks to Zion	עין לציון צופיה
Our hope is not yet lost	עוד לא אבדה תקותנו
The hope of 2000 years	התקוה בת שנות אלפים
To be a free people in our own land	להיות עם חופשי בארצנו
The land of Zion and Jerusalem	ארץ ציון ירושלים

Wheat fields, Be'eri, NW Negev. Note: poor soil quality.   Adrian Wolff

1883   The BILU immigrants establish new urban settlements in **Yesod Hama'ala,** Upper Galilee, and **Nes Ziona** in the Coastal Plain.

1883   The Ohel Moshe and Mazkeret Moshe (Agrippas Street) suburbs in Jerusalem are constructed, expanding Jewish settlement in the western part of the city.

1883   **Baron Edmond de Rothschild** (1845–1934). Following pogroms in Russia, the Paris branch of the Rothschild banking family becomes politically active in Jewish and Zionist affairs. He visits five times (1887,1893,1899,1914,1920) purchasing land, boosting the local economy and creating sources of livelihood. Rothschild supports the establishment of settlements in Eretz Israel, especially involved in the development of the new towns Zichron Ya'akov and Rishon Le'Zion where wineries are established. His remains, together with those of his wife Adelaide (1853-1935) are interred in Zichron Ya'akov in 1954. Rothschild desires to be anonymous as his backing and activities are made in the name of 'hanadiv ha'yadu'a' (the well-known benefactor). His personal financial contributions to the early settlements prevent a financial collapse. Local Ottoman authorities do not invest in any new Jewish development in agricultural or urban settlements. Eretz Israel is devoid of infra-structure (irrigation systems, industry, port with a pier) and natural resources. The Rothschild Foundation purchases many thousands of acres in Eretz Israel and all activities under Rothschild's support are subject to accountability. Jewish settlers are unaware of the importance of financial accountability.

Yesod Hama'ala, Pioneer home   Maya Wolff

1883 **Moshe Leib Lilienblum** (1843-1910) a Hibbat Zion leader in Odessa calls for normalization of Jewish life in Eretz Israel through participation in agriculture, commerce and industry. After the pogroms of 1881 he sees no solution to anti-Semitism and concludes Jews should immigrate to Eretz Israel. **Dr. Max Nordau** (1849-1923), a physician, psychiatrist and philosopher publishes 'The Conventional Lies of Civilization', attacking the hypocrisy and intellectual dishonesty of many social norms.

1883 During his visit to Jerusalem **General Charles Gordon** of Khartoum identifies the site of the Crucifixion of Jesus in the **Garden Tomb** outside the Damascus Gate. This site is purchased by British Protestants in 1895 and developed into a pilgrimage site.

1884 French Catholics construct St. Vincent de Paul monastery in Mamilla, near the Jaffa Gate.

1885 BILU immigrants establish the new urban settlement in **Gedera** in the Ayalon District. **Menachem Ussishkin** is appointed secretary of Hovevei Zion. Nathan Birnbaum uses the term, "Zionism".

1885 Ahmed, (born 1835 in Pakistan dies in India 1908) leader of Ahmedi Muslims claims to be called upon by Allah as a new prophet. His followers believe the body of Jesus was brought to India. Ahmeds, like Bahai'is, are excommunicated from Islam. Ahmedi headquarters in London has over 15 million followers worldwide. Ahmedis in Haifa establish a small community who pray in a mosque, unique for its two tall minarets.

1886 Schmidt's German College is built opposite Damascus Gate. In addition a German Catholic Hospice is constructed in today's Hillel Street. This building is later used as the British General Allenby's temporary headquarters during WW I.

1886 Karl Benz develops and patents the first internal combustion petrol-engine in Germany. The petrol engine will enable the production of self-propelled vehicles, radically increasing the demand for petroleum, found in large quantities in the Middle East. European interests suddenly takes on a new proportion.

1887 **The Ottoman authorities change the status of Jerusalem to an independent** *sancak* **(district)** ruled by a governor titled *mutasarrif*, directly responsible to Istanbul.

1887 Construction in Jerusalem of Beit Ya'akov and Mahane Yehuda suburbs, Notre Dame Monastery opposite the New Gate, the American Colony east of Damascus Gate, Sheik Jarrah and Wadi Joz for Arabs and Christians in the east, and Katamon close to the summer residence of the Greek Patriarch at Saint Simon in south-west Jerusalem. Germans finance a hospital for lepers in Talbieh.

1887 On the initiative of **Shimon Rokach**, Jews move to the sand-dunes north of Jaffa into new suburbs **Neve Shalom** and **Neve Zedek**. **Aaron Chelouche** previously in 1883 purchased the area of 800 dunams. Finance is obtained from **Zerach Barnet**, a London fur dealer. These suburbs, originally of Jaffa will become part of the new city of Tel Aviv after 1909.

1887 Mordechai Lubowsky establishes Mishmar Hayarden east of Rosh Pina opposite the Benot Ya'akov Bridge over the Jordan River. This isolated village is later abandoned, resettled in 1949.

1887 Baron Edmond de Rothschild visits new agricultural settlements in Eretz Israel and continues to invest in their infrastructure.

1887   Russian schools and universities restrict Jewish entry with quotas.

1888   Russian Orthodox Christians build the Church of Mary Magdalene on the Mt. of Olives, noted for its five onion-shaped gold-plated towers. French Catholics build the convent of the Soeurs de Reparatrice (near the New Gate) in Jerusalem. Opening of the new Rothschild Hospital on the Prophets (Ha'nevi'im) Street, the first Jewish hospital outside the walls of Jerusalem. Today this building, owned by the Hadassah Organization, is used as a training and educational center for teaching of nursing subjects, public health and optometry.

Map 34. Jewish settlements 1880+

1888   Pioneering Jews, assisted by the Rothschild Foundation purchase land in 1888 in the **Golan Heights**. In 1891 on their third attempt, they establish a settlement, **Bnei Yehuda**. After continual terror attacks by Arabs and the murder of two of their members (a mother and her child), the Jewish pioneers are forced to abandon in 1920 due to its isolation. Following the Six-Day War, a new Israeli settlement is established in 1972, near the original site.

1889   The French Catholics construct the St. Louis Hospital on the Prophets (Ha'nevi'im) Street. The New Gate (Herod's Gate) in the west of the Christian Quarter facilitates entry and exit of the expanding commerce and population in the Old City. Over 2000

Yemenite Jews begin their immigration to Eretz Israel by walking across the Arabian Desert. Some settle in the Shiloah Valley (**Siloan/Silwan**) and **Ophel**. They will be forced to evacuate during the anti-Jewish riots in 1936. Sha'are Zedek suburb is built west of Mahane Yehuda in Jerusalem. A 'Hebrew School' is established in Jaffa. In 1890 French Catholics construct the Church of St. Etienne, (the Biblical Institute) in Emile Botta Street of today.

1890   Jews in Odessa, members of the Hibbat Zion movement, continue to encourage and assist Jews to settle in Eretz Israel, especially in agricultural settlements. A large number of their members emigrate from Lithuania to the new urban settlements of **Hadera** and **Rehovot**, near the ancient Philistine town Ekron. The Rehovot settlers have previous experience in agricultural training. The Hadera settlers receive finance from Baron de Rothschild to plant eucalyptus groves in an attempt to drain the malaria-filled swamps. Opening of the modern winery, the **Carmel Winery** in Rishon Ya'akov in 1890 and another at Zichron Yaakov in 1892. The wineries are established by Baron Edmond de Rothschild, owner of Chateau Laftie in France.

1891   The Shimon Ha'Zadek suburb is constructed in West Jerusalem.

1891   Sultan Abdulhamid II publishes a *ferman* forbidding any Jew, even a Jew of Turkish citizenship, from purchasing arable land in Palestine. Jews are restricted to purchasing land in urban areas only and are forbidden to purchase state lands '*miri*'. Jews pay bribes to Turkish officials to immigrate and remain in Eretz Israel.

1891   Various guilds in Moscow expel Jewish craftsmen as Jewish artisans and their families emigrate. Czar Alexander III orders Jews into compulsory military service. Concurrently, local illiterate hoodlums perpetrate many anti-Semitic pogroms (killing of Jews).

1891   **Baron Maurice de Hirsch** (1831-1896), a German financier and philanthropist, is concerned about the plight of Jews living in Eastern Europe and Oriental Countries. He creates the **Jewish Colonization Association (ICA)** in London to finance Jewish immigration to agricultural settlements in Argentina and Brazil, where the fund acquires land. He also donates to Alliance Israelite Universalle for the establishment of Jewish schools.

1892   Opening of the **railway line** connecting Jaffa with Lod and Jerusalem, now becoming less isolated and more accessible for pilgrims. The railway also eases the transportation of goods into the hinterland, especially of imported items brought through the port of Jaffa. Josef Navon originally obtained the concession to build the railway in 1888, but is unable to make the financial commitment and transfers his rights to a French consortium. Architect Conrad Schick designs The German Catholic Hospital of St. Paul opposite the Damascus Gate, and the Bukharian Quarter for Jewish immigrants from Bukhara in the Caucasus, noted as a very wealthy suburb.

1893 **Max Bodenheimer** (1865-1940) and **David Wolffsohn** (1856-1914) establish the Hibbat Zion society in Cologne, Germany.

1894 **Yemin Moshe** suburb is constructed adjoining the Mishkenot Hasha'anan'im suburb, opposite the Jaffa Gate. Beit Israel Quarter is constructed in West Jerusalem. Jewish workers from Rehovot establish Motza on the western approach to Jerusalem.

1894 Christians (Armenian Orthodox) are massacred in Damascus as many flee to Jerusalem. A German Protestant priest, Ludwig Schneller constructs for the Armenians a school and orphanage, in the 'Schneller Complex' near the western entrance to Jerusalem.

Dr. Benjamin Theodor Herzl, Israel Philatelic Bureau

1894 In France, the European pillar of democracy and culture, a French Jewish Army Officer, Captain Alfred Dreyfus is unjustly accused of treason and espionage, based on forgeries in incriminating documents. Anti-Semitism spreads in French society. Dreyfus is courtmartialed, sent to solitary confinement on Devil's Island in 1895. A public outcry results in Dreyfus being pardoned by the French president in 1899, proclaimed innocent in 1906, re-instated by the French Army and awarded the French Legion of Honour. The open anti-Semitic aspects of the **Dreyfus Trial** influence **Dr. Theodor (Benjamin Ze'ev) Herzl** (1860-1904), Paris correspondent of a Viennese newspaper, to become the leading mouthpiece for the Zionist cause. Dr. Theodor Herzl meets **Dr. Max Nordau** in France during the Dreyfus trial, discussing the ideals of a future Jewish State.

1896　The English Hospital is opened in Ha'nevi'im Street in the Mea She'arim Quarter, Jerusalem by the 'London Society for Promoting Christianity Among Jews'. This Society is unsuccessful.

1896　Herzl publishes '*Judenstaat*', 'The Jewish State, or State of the Jews: An Attempt at a Modern Solution of the Jewish Question'. He claims anti-Semitism will never disappear and a solution for Jews is to create their own independent State.

1896　The Rothschild Foundation purchases land in the Upper Galilee. A new settlement, **Metula** is founded and will define the northern border in the Upper Galilee with Lebanon, in an area is suitable for deciduous fruit. The new settlement of **Be'er Tuvia**, south of Gedera is founded to accommodate the new immigrants.

1897　The First Zionist Congress opens in Basel under the leadership of Theodor Herzl, comprising 197 representatives from 17 countries. Herzl is elected President of the **World Zionist Federation,** Dr. Max Nordau is elected vice-president, and co-founder of the World Zionist Organization. Representatives from various Jewish communities gather discussing problems of the Jewish people. This congress is a landmark for Jewish consciousness with an overwhelming consensus for the need to establish an independent Jewish state in Eretz Israel. The Zionist solution is the redemption and ingathering of the exiles from the Diaspora to a politically independent state. **Prof. Zvi Hermann Schapira**, a founding father of the 'Hovevei Zion' movement in Russia, recommends the establishment of a 'national fund' for purchasing land in Eretz Israel. **Nahum Sokolov** (1859-1936) also attends the Congress.

1898　The Second Zionist Congress in Basel decides to actively promote Jewish settlement in Eretz Israel. **David Wolffsohn** (1856-1914) director of The Jewish Colonial Trust will financially assist settlement activities in Eretz Israel. Wolffsohn received religious Jewish education, teaches Herzl Jewish tradition and values. Born in Lithuania, flees to Germany to avoid Russian military conscription. Menachem Ussishkin is elected to the Zionist General Council.

1898　The Ottomans refuse permission for foreign Jews to purchase land in Eretz Israel.

1898　German Emperor Kaiser Wilhelm II (1859-1941) visits Palestine. He very briefly meets Dr. Theodor Herzl outside Mikve Israel on his journey to Jerusalem. Impending news of his visit stimulates improvement in the roads. The Jaffa Gate in Jerusalem is widened to enable the Kaiser to enter the Old City while sitting in his carriage. The Kaiser dedicates the Lutheran Church of the Redeemer (Erloser Kirche) constructed on Muristan, near Church of the Holy Sepulchre. Herzl is unsuccessful in meeting the Kaiser in Jerusalem whose anti-Semitic feelings are well-known.

The Jaffa Gate prior to 1898   Silver Print Gallery, Ein Hod

Jaffa Gate, Jerusalem   Adrian Wolff

1898 Establishment of a new settlement **Mahanai'im**, near Rosh Pina. Lack of fresh water sources and malaria cause many deaths, forcing abandonment of this settlement until 1920.

1899   Baron Edmond de Rothschild disposes of his financial interests in settlements in Eretz Israel transferring them to the ICA (Jewish Colonization Association) of Baron de Hirsch. The **Rothschild Foundation** will continue to finance projects in Eretz Israel - the development of the wine-making industry, co-sponsor of the Palestine Electric Corporation, the Hebrew University, the Knesset Building, and the Supreme Court building in Jerusalem. ICA continues to support educational and research facilities in Israel, the Faculty of Agriculture of the Hebrew University in Rehovot, the Volcani Institute and other regional agricultural research and teaching facilities, assisting over 100 settlements, mainly in the Galilee and Negev.

1900   In Jerusalem 60 separate Jewish neighborhoods exist west of the Old City. The Prophets Street becomes a main artery location of the English Hospital, German Hospital, French St. Joseph Monastery, Rothschild Hospital, Italian Hospital. French Catholics construct St. Stephen's Church in the American Colony.

1900   To celebrate 25 years rule of Sultan AbdulHamid II, over 100 clock towers are erected throughout the Ottoman Empire in city centers, adjacent to government buildings. Six are constructed in Eretz Israel–in Safed, Acre, Haifa, Jerusalem, Jaffa and Nablus.

1900   Founding of the first co-operative, the 'Pardes' in Petach Tikva to market citrus products.

1900   The **population** of Jerusalem is 45,000 with 28,200 Jews (63%).

1901   The 5th Zionist Congress in Basel, Switzerland the **Jewish National Fund** (JNF), (Keren Kayemet Le'Israel KKL in Hebrew) dedicates finance for Jewish settlement in Eretz Israel.

The JNF will finance the purchase of land in Eretz Israel for:
- the establishment of settlements and their infrastructure
- to assist the cultivation by financing the purchase of tractors, other machinery and irrigation equipment
- initiate afforestation projects, etc.

After the establishment of the State of Israel in 1948, all JNF-owned land will become 'state-owned'. The JNF will be responsible for land development and afforestation, Zionist education, and assistance of immigrants. The JNF finances the building of water reservoirs at Sapir in the Arava, Reshafim in Beit She'an Valley, Kedma near Kiryat Gat, Timna Lake in the Arava. The JNF sponsors major archaeological projects at Beit She'an, Caesarea and Shuni; constructs major recreational sites in the Negev at Mitzpe Ramon, Eshkol, Golda near Mashabe Sadeh, Yeruham, Dimona, Nitzanim etc. *"When you come to the land you shall plant trees."* (Leviticus 19:23).

1901   David Wolffsohn together with Menachem Ussishkin, combine all the small, weak, separate groups of Jewish organizations and societies into one body, the **World Zionist Organization**, now transformed into a political body with Ussishkin as president. This movement will gain impetus leading to the Balfour Declaration in 1917 and the founding of the independent Jewish State in 1948. Ussishkin also establishes the Anglo-Palestine Company (APEC) in Eretz Israel as part of the Jewish Colonial Trust (ICA).

1901   Paul Nathan (1857-1927) representative of the Rothschild Bank in Berlin establishes Hilsverein der deutschen Juden (Aid Society for German Jews - Ezra) and are benefactors of the Laemel school in Jerusalem after 1910.

1901   The Ottoman Administration rebuilds Be'er Sheva, the administrative capital of the Negev.

1901   Founding of **Yavniel** and **Kfar Tabor** in the Lower Galilee, and **Menahamia** in the Jordan Valley. The architectural style of the villages and the houses is similar to the Templer homes, with stone walls, red roof tiles, having a main street and a row of houses on each side, a walled yard in the rear with fields for agriculture.

Kfar Tabor, Galilee, Pioneer Settlement   Adrian Wolff

1902   Herzl publishes **"*Alte-Neuland*" (Old-New Land)** expressing the yearning for a Jewish State based on social solidarity, civic equality and the role of religion in society, including the use of science and technology for its development. Herzl's expression **"*if you will it, it*** *is no dream*" will become the motto of the Zionist movements. The Hebrew translation of Herzl's book is titled 'Tel Aviv', from Ezekiel 3:15 "*I came to the exiles to Tel Aviv (hill of spring)*".

1902 The Jewish Colonial Trust, a subsidiary, the Anglo-Palestine Company (APEC) Bank, channels finance for settlement activities, will become Bank Le'umi Le'Israel (owned by the Jewish Agency). The first branch is opened in Jaffa in 1903. England exports iron and cotton to Eretz Israel, importing the local citrus, and barley.

1902 In Vienna, the chairman of the Jewish National Fund, Johann Kremenetzky begins the system of donations - The Blue Box, the Golden Book, and JNF stamps.

1903 Jewish National Fund purchases land at **Kfar Hittin, Hulda, Ben Shemen, Kinneret and Degania.**

1903 Herzl rejects the offer of British Colonial Secretary Joseph Chamberlain (1836–1914) to establish an autonomous Jewish settlement in Uganda.

1903 Following the pogrom in Kishinev, **Vladimir Ze'ev Jabotinsky** (1880-1940) will immerse himself in Zionist activities. Rumors of a pogrom become imminent in Odessa encouraging Jabotinsky to organize Jewish self-defense groups.

1904 Dr. Theodor Herzl, born in Budapest in 1860, dies aged 44 at a spa in Austria from complications of pneumonia and a weak heart condition. Nevertheless his Zionist ideals and encouragement of settlement activities in Eretz Israel will continue.

1904 The murder of 49 Jews in 1903 and damage to over 1,300 Jewish homes and businesses in Kishinev. Over 3000 Jews are murdered in the 1905 Revolution. The continuing Anti-Semitic fervor in Russia, promotes large-scale emigration of Jews to the United States, Argentina, South Africa, Australia and Eretz Israel.

1904 **The Second Immigration, *Aliyah Bet*** (1904-1914) movement is a direct result of the continual pogroms in Russia (Kishinev, Kiev, Odessa) and the disillusionment of the results of the 1905 Revolution. During the years 1904 until 1914 over 40,000 mainly secular Jews will immigrate to Eretz Israel including future Jewish Labor and Social Zionist leaders.

1904 **Aaron David Gordon** (1856-1922), member of Hibbat Zion immigrates, establishing **HaPoel HaTzair** Labor Movement, believes the redemption of the land by physical means as a goal, that without Jewish labor there can be no Hebrew culture.

1905 Founding of **Ha'poal**, the Jewish Labor Organization in Eretz

Israel. Ber Borochov (1881-1917) is appointed Secretary-General. **Menachem Ussishkin** proposes practical Zionist activities entitled 'Our Program' comprising political action, acquisition of land, Aliyah (immigration), settlement, education and organization. Jewish workers should cultivate their lands without hired labor.

1905 Ottomans construct The 'Hejaz (Hijaz) railway' from Damascus to Dara'a and Mecca completed in 1908, to transport Muslim pilgrims making the *haj* to Mecca and Medina. Many trees are felled in Palestine for railway sleepers. The 'coastal branch' of the line is from Haifa-Afula-Beit She'an-Zemach-Dara'a (Deraa). Circassians from Central Asia are settled along the line to protect it.

1906 German Catholics finance the construction of Dormition Abbey on Mt. Zion, dedicated in 1910. This church is built over the ruins of the previous Byzantine Basilica and Crusader church. According to Catholics, this site is where the Virgin Mother, St. Mary takes her final breath before ascending to heaven. *'Dormi'* is Latin for sleep.

1906 The Bezalel School of Arts and Crafts is established in Jerusalem by Boris Schatz (1866-1932), financed by the Jewish National Fund

1905 **Meir Dizengoff** (1861-1937), an engineer and active member of Hovevei Zion is sent by Baron de Rothschild in 1892 to Eretz Israel to establish a glass factory in Tantura (Dor) for the production of wine bottles for the fledgling wine industry in Zichron Ya'akov. The color of the sand in this area is unsuitable for wine bottles and the factory is closed in 1894. In 1905 Dizengoff returns, settles in Jaffa, the main port and entry of new Jewish immigrants to Eretz Israel.

1906 Great Britain threatens the Ottomans with force to cede the Sinai Peninsula to Egypt. The Negev/Sinai border is drawn as a straight line between Taba on the Gulf of Akaba, Red Sea and Rafiah (Rafah) on the Gaza Mediterranean Coast.

1906 **David Ben-Gurion** (1886-1973) immigrates to Eretz Israel from Russia. His father Avigdor Gruen is a member of Hovevei Zion. In 1903 Ben-Gurion joins the Po'alei Zion movement in Russia, traveling, giving lectures to Jews encouraging the members to settle in Eretz Israel, and demands Hebrew be spoken. During his first years in Eretz Israel he performs various manual jobs in agriculture in Petach Tikva, in the wine-cellars at Rishon Le'Zion, and as a watchman at Sejara (Ilania) in the Lower Galilee. He becomes the leader of the labor movement and heads the struggle for Jewish independence in Eretz Israel. Appointed 1st Prime Minister of Israel in 1948.

1906 **Nahum Sokolov** General-Secretary of World Zionist Organization.

1907 **Arthur Ruppin** (1876-1943) 'the father of Zionist settlement' purchases land in Eretz Israel for the The **Jewish National Fund (JNF)** from Arab land-owners, increasing the quantity of land available for Jewish immigrants in both urban and rural areas. He also makes purchases in the Jezreel Valley, Haifa, Rehavia and Mt. Scopus in Jerusalem. His policy emphasizes the settlement organization must take into account the needs of the settlers.

1907 Following many anti-Semitic pogroms in Russia, **Itzhak Ben-Zvi** (1884-1963), an active member of Poalei Zion becomes involved in Jewish self-defense. His parents' home is searched in 1906 and weapons found. His father is exiled to Siberia for 16 years and after his release, settles in Eretz Israel. Ben-Zvi escapes to Vilna and settles in Eretz Israel in 1907. Itzhak Ben-Zvi will become the 2nd President of the State of Israel 1952-1963.

RISCHON LE ZION: KOLONISTENFAMILIE UNTERWEGS.

Jewish Travelers   Silver Print Gallery, Ein Hod. www.viviennesilver-brody.com

1907 **Israel Shochat** (1886-1961) immigrates in 1904 during the Second Aliyah, is a member of Hovevei Zion, influenced by his wife Mania Wilbuschewitch Shochat (1880-1961), a spiritual leader of Hashomer. In 1907 Shochat, Itzhak Ben-Zvi, Mendel Portugali , Zvi Beker, Israel Giladi, Alexander Zaid, Yehezkiel Hankin, Yehezkiel Nissanov, Moshe Givoni, and Meirka Heznovitz, establish the Jewish Defense Organization **'Bar Giora'** initially around the Sejara (Ilania) area near Mt.Tabor, Lower Galilee, to protect Jewish travelers and settlements from marauding Arab killers. The name is taken from Simon Bar Giora, a leader of the Jewish Revolt in

Jerusalem against the Romans in 70. Many founding members are from the Po'alei Zion movement in Russia who attempted to protect Jews during the various pogroms. This organization grows into 'Ha'shomer', The Watchman in 1909, developing into the Hagana - the pre-State Jewish Defense Organization in 1920. (See 1909 Hashomer, 1920 Hagana).

1907 **Alexander Zaid** (1886-1938) is one of the original members of Bar Giora and Hashomer, rides his horse while dressed as an Arab. Zaid, born in Siberia immigrates to Eretz Israel in 1904, dedicates his life to the defense of Jewish settlement. He is one of the founders of Kibbutz Kfar Giladi in the Upper Galilee. Bedouin murder Zaid in 1938.

1908 **Rachel Yannit Ben-Zvi** (1886-1979) immigrates to Eretz Israel, a founding member of Hashomer, encourages the creation of the Jewish Legion to serve with the British Army in World War I. She marries Itzhak Ben-Zvi in 1918, is active in the Israel Labor Party.

1908 Dr. Arthur Ruppin purchases land for the Jewish National Fund (JNF) on southwestern corner of the Sea of Galilee (Kinneret) for the establishment of a 'workers farm'.

1908 During the late Ottoman period most Arabs fellaheen tenants are permanently in debt to the land-owners and merchants who charge 20-100% interest. The Jewish demand for land increases its value enticing landlords to sell, foreclosing Arab settlements based on primitive agricultural methods of a single annual crop of grain, usually of poor quality. The Arabs have little income from the land after paying the landlord, money lender and tax-collector. Jews use scientific agricultural methods, replacing miserable crops for luxuriant orange orchards. The Bedouin have no legal title to the land which they do not register, fearing military service to the Ottomans. Heavy taxes are imposed on local Jews.

1909 The Bar Giora organization is limited in manpower and operational ability. The leaders Israel Shochat and Itzhak Ben-Zvi decide to expand the involvement of Jewish Defense to protect Jewish settlements, now increasing in number in Eretz Israel. They found settlements at Tel Adashim, Tel Hai and Kfar Giladi.

They are appointed chairmen of **Hashomer, 'The Watchmen'** for the defense of Jewish settlements often in isolated areas, surrounded by Arab villages. (shomrim=plural השומרים). The original leaders also include **Israel Giladi, Zvi Becker, Yehezkiel Nissanov, Alexander Zaid, and Mendel Portugali.**

1909 The Jewish National Fund continues to purchase land in the Jezreel and Harod Valleys. Crops fail due to the scarcity of water.

The cemetery in Gidona gives evidence to the heavy toll paid by the early settlers and their children, many succumb to malaria.

1909   Jews in Jaffa, despondent with the continual persecution and anti-Semitic violence resolve to move northward on the sand dunes to establish the first modern Jewish City in Eretz Israel. **Akiva Arye Weiss,** a founder of the **Ahuzat Bayit Company** establishes a new Jewish Quarter, distributing 66 lots in a lottery (see photo below) **Aaron Chelouche** previously in 1883 purchased the area of 800 dunams of land of Nave Shalom and Nave Zedek (Kerem Djebali) in 1890. Finance is obtained from **Zerach Barnet.** (see 1887).

Lottery for the plots of Ahuzat Bayit - the future Tel Aviv, 1909
Silver Print Gallery, Ein Hod. www.viviennesilver-brody.com

Tel Aviv is named after the Hebrew name of Herzl's book 'AltNeuland'. The 'Herzlia Gymnasia' Hebrew High School is established on the site of the present Shalom Tower. Meir Dizengoff is elected the first mayor of Tel Aviv in 1921, which will quickly expand to become the commercial center of Israel. A small industrial zone is developed in Givat Herzl. Dizengoff's home in Rothschild Boulevard will become a museum and is where the Jewish leadership proclaims the Independent State of Israel on the evening of 14 May 1948.

1909   **Rachel** (Bluwstein) (1890-1931) arrives in Eretz Israel in 1909 moves to an agricultural school for girls at the Kinneret until 1913. She studies agronomy and drawing in France returning in 1919 to Kibbutz Degania. She lives in Tel Aviv for the final five years of her life, buried on the shore of the Kinneret. All her poetry is published under her first name only. Her prose remains the country's momentous bestsellers of popular Israeli folk-songs, expressing love for Eretz Israel and a nostalgia for the Kinneret.

1909 The remains of Mizra Husayn Ali founder of the Bahai'i religion are transferred from Persia to Haifa by Abdul Baha, the son and successor of Baha'u'llah.

1909 Aref al-Dajani mayor of Jerusalem from 1909-1918.

1910 The Augusta Victoria Hospital and convalescent home is completed on Mt. Scopus, including a tower 60 meters high. Designed by Robert Leibniz to resemble a German castle. The hospital includes a malarial convalescent ward, and a German pilgrim hostel. The Givat Shmuel suburb is constructed in the west.

1910 **Dr. Aaron Aaronsohn** (1876-1919) an agronomist, receives international recognition. He discovers wild 'emmer' wheat (See 8000BCE). He establishes an agricultural college at Atlit. He plants a double row of palm trees at the entrance, seen today. He is a passenger in an airplane that falls into the English Channel in 1919

1910 **Degania**, the first collective communal settlement or **kibbutz** (kibbutzim = plural) is founded on the southern shore of the Kinneret (Sea of Galilee) where the Jordan River exits towards the Dead Sea. Finance for purchasing the land and infrastructure is provided by the Jewish National Fund by Arthur Ruppin. The kibbutz movement is very successful in rural development and absorbing immigrants (young orphans and teenagers), and in the defense of the Yishuv.

The kibbutz originally has no private property or private ownership. All facilities and profits are shared equally amongst the kibbutz members. Initially all income is obtained from agricultural production. Later other sources of employment and income will result from investment in industry (metal, plastics, electro-mechanical etc.) research and development, textiles, tourism, etc. Children sleep in 'children's quarters', kibbutz members eat all their meals in the communal dinning-room, laundry done communally, visits outside the kibbutz and use off the kibbutz vehicles required an advance request. Committee meetings and guard duty occupied many evenings a week. This lifestyle will change drastically in the 1980's.

1910 Baron Edmond de Rothschild purchases the Ophel, site of the original City of David, settled by Yemenite immigrants.

1911 The Hebrew language is used during the 10th Zionist Congress in Basel, Switzerland.

1911 A Jewish settlement **Merhavia** is founded in the Jezreel Valley.

1911 David Ben-Gurion moves to Turkey to study law.

1912 The Ottomans suppress Arab nationalist movements in Syrian and Palestine causing the Arabs to view the Turks as 'oppressors'. The Ottomans disallow attempts to replace Turkish as the official language with the use Arabic language. (Arab Congress in Beirut).

1912 The Blau-Weiss (Blue-White) Jewish youth movement is established in Germany and Czechoslovakia to assist Jewish youth to immigrate to Eretz Israel. Pinchas Rosen (Rosenblueth) (1887-1978) is a co-founder of this organization and is the first Minister of Justice.

1912 **Henrietta Szold** (1860-1945) establishes the 'Women's Organization of America-WIZO', **Hadassah**, to raise funds for medical and health care services and education in Eretz Israel. Hadassah is the largest Jewish organization in the United States.

1912 The Turkish Authorities imprison two 'Hashomer' members, Haim Sturman (1891-1938) and Zvi Nisanov for illegal weapons possession. Sturman, a member of the SNS is killed by a land mine in 1938. Sturman's son Moshe, is killed during the War of Independence (1948) and grandson Haim, killed in the War of Attrition (1969).

1912 **Joseph Trumpeldor** (1880-1920) immigrates to Eretz Israel. He had previously served in 1904 as an captain in the Russian Army loosing an arm during the Russo-Japanese war, nevertheless, he requests to be sent back to the battlefront. Trumpeldor's concept of Zionism is the establishment of agricultural communes in Eretz Israel and the creation of Jewish self-defense units to protect the settlements. He befriends Vladimir Ze'ev Jabotinsky.

1912 **Population** of Jerusalem is 70,000 including 45,000 Jews (64%).

1913 Founding of **Kvutzat Kinneret** in the SW corner of the Sea of Galilee (Kinneret).

Chapter 20. WW I and British Mandate 1914 - 1928

1914   Prior to WW I, Ottoman Administration headquarters in Palestine are found in Jerusalem, Acre, Jaffa, and Gaza. Arab rioters attack Jews in Jerusalem, Jaffa, Jewish rural settlements and Jewish travelers. The Ottoman Authorities collect taxes from local fiefdoms and toll-taxes '*darbia*'. Jews and Christians are treated as second-class citizens. Payment of '*bakshish*' or graft, is a way of life.

Europeans had previously assisted the ailing Ottoman Empire, relinquishing the power of Muhammed Ali in Egypt in 1841, later supporting in the Balkan crises in 1870's and 1912/1913. The Triple Entente advise the Ottomans in 1914 to remain neutral. The Ottoman administration are convinced of the future German victory.

Map 35. Ottoman Empire 1914

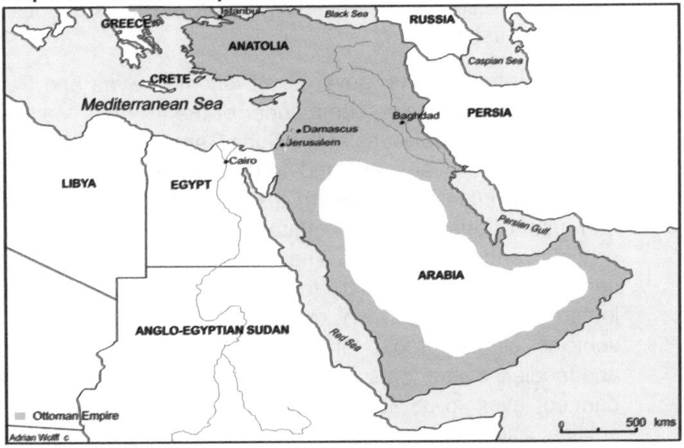

1914   Outbreak of **World War I**. During a visit to Sarajevo Archduke Ferdinand, heir to the Austro-Hungarian throne is assassinated 28 June 1914 by a Serbian nationalist Gavrilo Princip. World War I is mainly fought in Europe, by European countries over disputed European issues. The participants are: **The Triple Entente** consisting of Great Britain and its Commonwealth, France, Belgium, Italy, Greece, Serbia, Russia, the US and Japan, against The **Central Powers** of Germany, Austro-Hungary, Bulgaria and Ottomans. Great Britain and France declare war against the Ottomans 28 October 1914 when they give shelter to a German warship after it shells Russian Black Sea ports. The United States enters the war only in 1917 supporting Britain and France. Additional American troops and war materiel will accomplish an overpowering strategic advantage to the war effort, breaking the deadlock, defeating the Central Powers. Local **Arabs refuse to be conscripted into Ottoman Army claiming they are not Palestinians.** Enver Pasha, the Ottoman Minister of War will become responsible for the destruction of the Ottoman Empire.

1914   All foreign post offices are closed, while Turkish post offices are opened. Misgav Ladakh Hospital suspends operations due to lack of available foreign funds. Hebrew road signs are removed, Jewish immigration curtailed and prohibition of Jewish land purchases,

1914   Following anti-Jewish riots in Jaffa on 17 December 1914, Hassan Bek, Turkish administrator of Jaffa exiles all non-Ottoman Jewish males living in Jaffa to Egypt which is under British Administration. He also forces Jews to pay for their own passage. Jamal Pasha declares he is expelling the Jews for their own good. Over 12,000 Jews flee Eretz Israel to escape the oppressive Ottoman rule. (By 1917 over 10,000 Jews flee Tel Aviv northwards as about 1500 die during this upheaval).

1915   **Ahmad Jamal Pasha**, governor of Ottoman Syria and Palestine, stationed in Damascus, commander of the 4th Army leads a failed attack on British positions at the Suez Canal (3 February 1915). He orders sanctions against, and terrorizes the non-Turkish Jewish population, imposing a 'wealth tax', the *'varlık vergisi'*. Ottomans ban use of the Hebrew language, close APEC Bank, Jewish schools, and newspapers. The Turks begin to 'appropriate' any items they deem necessary for the war effort. Jewish homes are looted, confiscate Jewish owned crops, horses, cattle, wood, vehicles, clothing, tools, fence-posts, barbed wire, irrigation pipes and medical instruments. There is starvation. Jewish immigration is banned, even to Jewish Ottoman citizens. The Ottomans recruit soldiers and workers, impose heavy taxes on residents, crops and animals, forests are cut down for fuel and railway sleepers.

1915   The Turkish authorities arrest Zionist leaders including David Ben-Gurion and Itzhak Ben-Zvi for demonstrating against oppressive policies in Palestine, then, they are exiled to Egypt where they meet Vladimir Ze'ev **Jabotinsky** (1880-1940). Turks exile Joseph Trumpeldor to Egypt where he too meets Jabotinsky. After seeing Jewish deportees in Egypt, Jabotinsky collaborates with Trumpeldor to create a Jewish Legion within the British Army. They conclude that Jews from the **Yishuv** (term used by the Jews for Eretz Israel) should volunteer to fight in the British Army for the liberation of Eretz Israel from the Ottoman Turkish regime. Trumpeldor sees the establishment of a Jewish Army essential for the protection of Jews in Eretz Israel. Their request is initially refused, as British do not wish them to be part of a 'fighting unit'. Trumpeldor eventually convinces the British to create a Jewish regiment (Legion). During WW I over 10,000 Jews living in Eretz Israel volunteer to enlist into the British Army. (See 1916, 1917).

1915 **Dr. Aaron Aaronsohn**, an agricultural scientist establishes an 'Agricultural Station' at Atlit to make the 'desert bloom'. A plague of locusts causes heavy crop losses in Eretz Israel, Lebanon and Syria. Ahmad Jamal Pasha appoints Aaronsohn as chief inspector to combat this plague, famine and increase in food prices.

1915 Aaronsohn travels through Palestine and Syria to view the locust plague situation. He witnesses evidence of the Armenian genocide and fears the Jews would be next on the Ottoman slaughter list of non-Muslims. He is outraged, influencing him to establish in Zichron Ya'akov a pro-British spy-ring, נצח ישאל לא ישקר **NILI** ניל"י *the Eternal One of Israel does not lie"* (1 Samuel 15:29). On his journeys he notes the size and location of Turkish Army camps, supply depots, gasoline storage sites and includes the political and economic situation. NILI members have knowledge of wells in Sinai and Negev. This information assists the British and Commonwealth troops stationed in Egypt to invade and conquer Palestine. Eitan Belkind serves in the Ottoman Army under Jamal Pasha, witnesses the killing of over 5000 Armenians. Aaronsohn promotes the 'Zionist cause' in Europe, calls on the Diaspora to return to their ancestral home in Eretz Israel. Anti-Zionist Jews answer to Zionism is not immigration, but assimilation.

Summary of NILI
- To assist the Yishuv in a period of famine and disease
- To draw attention to the situation in Eretz Israel
- To fulfill the Zionist dream of establishing a Jewish State
Founders: Aaron, Sarah and Alexander Aaronsohn, Avshalom Feinberg, Na'aman and Eitan Belkind, Yosef Lishansky, operating from the Agricultural Experimental Station in Atlit.
In September 1917 a pigeon fails to complete its flight, landing in the governor's yard in Caesarea; Na'aman Belkind in captured.

1915 US Ambassador Henry Morgenthau and German Ambassador Hans Wangeheim approach Ottoman Authorities, are successful in interceding on behalf of the Jews living in Eretz Israel to obtain relief from anti-Jewish measures. Sir Herbert Samuel presents a plan for British control of Palestine and Jewish autonomy.

1915 German officers led by General Otto Liman von Sander advise the Ottoman Army in Palestine and Sinai. General Friedrich Kress von Kressenstein leads the Ottoman Army across the Sinai desert.

1915   Ottomans, with over 20,000 troops in Palestine wish to support pro-Ottoman Egyptians to attack British garrisons along the Suez Canal. A railway line is constructed inland out of range of British naval vessels and commandos, extending from Beit She'an, Tulkarem, Lod, Be'er Sheva, Nitzana, Keseima, entering about 10 kilometers into Sinai.

Turkish railway bridge arches, Be'erotai'im, NW Negev.   Adrian Wolff

1915   Emir Hussein believes the British would assist him to create an independent Arab nation to include Arabia, Persia, Anatolia, and Palestine up to the Suez Canal. The British High Commissioner in Egypt Sir Henry McMahon informs Hussein that Great Britain, together with their ally France recognize Arab independence. Following World War 1 new countries are created in 'Greater Syria'

1915   British Home Secretary Sir Herbert Samuel suggests Palestine be made into a British Protectorate after the war, with the encouragement of Jewish immigration. The Cabinet rejects it.

1916   Jews living within Turkish Administrative areas in Eretz Israel are forced to enlist into the Ottoman Army. Some Jews flee to the Galilee already stricken by famine, while others flee to Egypt. Ottoman rulers in Palestine are prevented by German General Erich **von Falkenhayn,** (1861-1922) from persecuting Jews and Christians and from the forced evacuation of Jews from Palestine.

1916   The ANZAC, (Australian and New Zealand Army Corps) are composed in Egypt from the 1st Australian Imperial Force and the 1st New Zealand Expeditionary Force. British Army with 30,000 troops, cross the Suez Canal at Kantara, entering Sinai to halt the continuing construction of the German/Turkish railway line. They continue very slowly from the Sweet Water Canal in Egypt to construct a railway and water pipeline in Sinai to ensure continual water supplies for troops and horses, taking two years to complete. This pipeline and railway will eventually reach Deir al-Balah in Gaza. Thousands of workers from the Egyptian Labour Corps construct the railway line. Later these Egyptian laborers will construct British Army bases in Palestine (Sarafand, etc.).

1916 The Sykes-Picot Agreement
Before WW I Palestine, Lebanon, Syria and Iraq do not exist as independent, separate countries, are Provincial Administrative Districts (Vilayet) of the Ottoman Empire. The Vilayet of Beirut, Sidon and Tyre; the Vilayet of Damascus; while Iraq is composed of three districts - Mosul, Baghdad, and Basra. Palestine is ruled under a separate Vilayet of Jerusalem.

Britain represented by **Sir Mark Sykes** and France by **Georges F. Picot** sign on 9 May 1916 the Anglo-French Accord, designated to divide the spoils of war in the Middle East after the impending disintegration of the Ottoman Empire. Two new states are to be established under British rule - Palestine and Transjordan; and two under French rule - Syria and Lebanon. The border between the British and French territory is based on the Ottoman Districts of the time - the *Vilayet* (province), *Sancak* (district) and *Kaza* (sub-district). The Hashemites of Arabia, allies of the British will be appointed kings in new countries, Jordan and Iraq.

The Sykes-Picot Agreement is abandoned at the Paris Peace Conference of 1919. Great Britain, with Commonwealth forces conquer Palestine, the Golan Heights, Transjordan and Mesopotamia during WW I and thus in 1920 the British demand changes in the border. They see Golan Heights (source of over 30% of Israel's fresh water) as an integral part of Palestine, especially since the Jordan River (Dan and Banias rivers) originate at the foothills of Mt. Hermon and rain waters falling on the Golan flow to the Sea of Galilee (Kinneret) (See Aryeh Shalev, page 28). The third source of Jordan River, the Hitzbani (Snir) originates in Lebanon. In March 1920 representatives of both Great Britain and France sign a mutual agreement concerning the Golan Heights defining the border between British controlled Palestine and French controlled Syria. The border runs from the foothills of Mt. Hermon, west of the Hejaz Railway Line in a straight line to the Yarmuk River. The Banias Springs are included into Palestine. The western sector of the Golan Heights is included into British Palestine. The French capture Damascus July 1920, deposing King Feisal I (installed by the British). See Hussein 1917,1919; Feisal I 1918,1919,1920,1921,1923; GB1920,1922,1923; France 1920,1922.

Border changes are made again in December 1920 to include Banias into Syria. Western Golan remains included into British Palestine. The border reaches the outskirts of Kuneitra, then westwards to include half of the Sea of Galilee. This border allows British control of the watershed on the Golan and railway line from the Yarmuk Valley to Samakh (Zemach) at the southern shore of the Sea of Galilee (Kinneret). The final international border is finally established 7 March 1923 after the British and French Mandates are officially created. The border is defined being from the foothills of the Golan; Banias in Palestine; to the contour 100 meters above Lake Hula and the Hula Valley; along the east bank of the Jordan River; to the Sea of Galilee 10 meters east of the high water mark until Sussita; the border moves up to the Golan Plateau to the Yarmuk Valley, including el-Hamam (Hamat Gader) into Palestine. Syria has no rights to the waters of the Jordan River, Lake Hula and Sea of Galilee. (See Aryeh Shalev). British construct pill-box fortresses in south-east Golan slopes to maintain their presence (see photograph) and control the Yarmuk Valley, includes the Railway Bridge over the Yarmuk River near el-Hamam (Hamat Gader). League of Nations Treaty #1324 of 2 February 1926 is signed by F.M. Plumer High Commissioner for Palestine and Henry de Jouvenel, Le Haut Commissaire de la Republique Francaise en Syrie et au Liban, defines *"Agreement of good neighbourly Relations concluded on behalf of the Territories of Palestine, on the one part, and on behalf of Syria and Great Lebanon,...other part."* Professor Norman Bentwich's book 'Palestine' published in 1934 shows a map with Banias, the Golan slopes and Hamat Gader clearly to be part of British Palestine.

In 1920 the Ottoman Empire is divided by the Treaty of Sèvres. The League of Nation defines Iraq's borders under the British Mandate of Mesopotamia, under King Faisal in 1921, gaining independence from Britain in 1932.

1916   Jews may not establish settlements in the Golan even though previously the Rothschild Fund legally bought large tracts of land.

1916   **Dr. Chaim Weizmann** (1874-1952), president of the World Zionist Organization moves to Great Britain in 1904 to further his scientific and Zionist life, first visits Eretz Israel in 1907. During World War I at Manchester University in Britain, he successfully assists the British war effort by discovering a method to extract acetone from maize. Acetone is used in the manufacture of the explosive compound, cordite. Dr. Chaim Weizmann will be appointed 1st President of the State of Israel 1948-1952.

British Pill-Box on southern Golan overlooking Hamat Gader. Adrian Wolff

Roman Baths at Hamat Gader Thermal Springs.   Adrian Wolff

1916 A Jewish Regiment of 650 volunteers from the Yishuv are conscripted into the British Army, serving in The **Zion Mule Corps** a transportation unit with distinction at Gallipoli in the Dardanelles under Lt. Col. John Henry Patterson DSO, with Trumpeldor as his second-in-command. After service in Gallipoli, the Zion Mule Corps is disbanded, sent to Britain where they serve as the core of the newly formed 38th Battalion of the Royal Fusiliers.

1916 Following the Allies defeat and retreat at Gallipoli, the Turkish Army threatens British interests in the Suez Canal and oil fields in the Persian Gulf. Great Britain enters the war theater in the Middle East to change the potential post-war situation. The British open a route to Russia through Turkish held Mesopotamia (Vilayet of

Mosul, Baghdad and Basra). TE Lawrence arrives at Kibbutz Ruhama (the first kibbutz in the NW Negev founded in 1911), approaches Zvi Herschfield, an agronomist, for assistance to gather intelligence about the Turkish Army in the area. He refuses citing the potential of Ottoman reprisals against the isolated Jewish settlers. The Ottomans destroy the Kibbutz in 1917 regardless.

1916 Many Turkish soldiers are brought to Jerusalem from Sinai and Gaza with typhus and cholera. Typhus epidemic in Jerusalem.

1916 **Kfar Giladi** is founded in the Upper Galilee, near Metula.

1917 Joseph Trumpeldor and Vladimir Ze'ev Jabotinsky again submit a proposal to the British government, now accepted. The **Jewish Legion**, designated the 38th British Battalion of the Royal Fusiliers in 1917 is transferred to Eretz Israel in 1918. The 39th Battalion incorporates Jewish American volunteers into the 40th Battalion of the Royal Fusiliers. At the end of the British Palestine Campaign in 1918 the battalion name is changed to the Judean Regiment with a '*menorah*' as the official ensign and the word '*kadima*', (forward). All Jewish Legion soldiers previously have a Magen David ensign.

Grave of Sarah Aaronsohn, Zichron Ya'akov. Adrian Wolff

1917 A note found on a carrier pigeon in Bosnian Muslim village, Caesarea (See Bosnians 1882) leads the Turks to Zichron Yaakov, to capture and torture (in public) **Sarah Aaronsohn** (1890-1917), sister of NILI founder Dr. Aharon Aaronsohn. She commits suicide in prison. A note is found in her hand saying, "*I did not betray*". Turkish police torture Ephraim and Zvi Aaronsohn (father and son), hound NILI members in Zichron Ya'akov and Hadera forcing Jews to betray their neighbors. NILI member, Joseph Lishansky flees Turkish police, arriving in Hadera where Hashomer members hand him over to Turkish authorities to be hanged in Damascus. Na'aman Belkind another NILI member is caught for anti-Turkish activities, brought to Damascus where he too is tried and hanged.

Avshalom Feinberg (1889-1917, Aaronsohn's deputy and fiancee of Sarah Aaronsohn), is shot near Rafah while traveling on foot towards British positions in Sinai. His fate is unknown until after the 6 Day-War in 1967 when his remains are found under a palm tree that had grown from dates in his pocket.

British Liaison officer in Cairo, Captain Ian Smith does not take Aaronsohn's exceptional information seriously until February 1917. The Jews have little influence or importance in Britain's conquest of Eretz Israel other than the NILI information of numbers and positions of the Turkish Army.

Aaronsohn hopes the British will accept Jewish autonomy in Palestine. His mentors are Sir Mark Sykes and William Ormsby-Gore, MP, a recent convert to Judaism.

1917   Jaffa Road, the first **tarred road**, is laid in Jerusalem.

1917   David Ben-Gurion marries Paula Munweiss (1892-1968), a nurse and devoted member of Poalei Zion.

1917   In April 1917 the USA (President Woodrow Wilson) enters World War I, without involving itself in areas under Ottoman control.

1917   Hussein ibn Ali, the Grand Sharif (religious leader) of Hejaz and Mecca is in contempt of the liberalization in Istanbul, religious autonomy, women's rights and abolishment of slavery. Hussein sees the construction of a railway to Mecca as an attempt to exert greater Ottoman control. His sons Feisal, Abdullah, Ali and Zeid are pro-British who led them believe in Arab independence.

British Intelligence Officer Major **TE Lawrence** (1888-1935), with 2500 Bedouin led by Feisal defeat Ottoman Turkish troops in Syria, Transjordan and Arabia including at Akaba on the Red Sea. **Lawrence sees himself fighting primary for Arab independence and secondary for British colonial power,** imposing his personal vision of Arab independent rule in Ottoman provinces. He is against the Agreement promising both Syria and Lebanon to France, signed at the Paris Peace Conference in 1919.

Hussein, leader of the Arab world during World War I does not object to Jewish immigration into Eretz Israel.

1917   Ottoman Turks build defenses along the Gaza-Be'er Sheva Road.

British POW's Second Gaza Operation   Courtesy Lt. E. Noel Symonds

Be'er Sheva 1917   Courtesy Lt. E. Noel Symonds

1917   British and Commonwealth (Egyptian Expeditionary Force-E.E.F.) forces approach Gaza City through wadis and cactus fences used to enclose sheep and goats. In 'Operation Gaza 1' E.E.F. attack Gaza outnumber Turkish troops by 2 to 1, fail to hold a hill, Ali el-Mukhtar at the entrance to Gaza City. Over 500 Allied and 301

Turkish troops are killed in this operation (25 March 1917). British forces withdraw due to lack of water. British General Murray remains in el-Arish not commanding from the battle area. Austrian officers and NCO's reinforce Turkish troops. In 'Operation Gaza 2' Allied troops attempt to march over sand dunes west of the main Gaza-Rafiah Road, once again outnumbering Ottoman troops by 2 to 1, fail to capture Gaza. Over 2000 Allied troops lose their lives. (17 April 1917). British POW's are paraded in Jerusalem.

ANZAC Memorial, Be'eri   Adrian Wolff

1917   Aaronsohn meets with France's Georges F. Picot in Cairo (8 July 1917) and tells of his reservations of creating a new country Syria, comprising many different religions and sects. Aaronsohn meets with TE Lawrence (12 August 1917). Lawrence tells him Jews will be killed if they do not co-exist with the Arab majority. Aaronsohn wishes for a Jewish nation without integrating the local Arabs and will not assist the Arab Revolt for independence, but would assist British forces against the Ottomans. Britain views the Jews as allies, wants to secure Palestine to control Sinai, the Suez Canal and Persian Gulf oil.

1917   General Murray is replaced by **General Edmund Allenby** (1861-1936), commander of E.E.F. After his predecessor's two earlier unsuccessful attempts to capture Gaza, he makes use of aerial reconnaissance for intelligence gathering, (use of aircraft in warfare is still in its infant stages and is hardly utilized in the European war-theater. The Italians use strategic bombing campaign against Austrians). General Allenby successfully deceives Ottomans into thinking the Allies are about to attempt a third assault on Gaza. He sends **Captain Richard Meinertzhagen** on horseback towards Turkish lines, when confronted by an imminent attack, feigns injury leaving a blood-stained cloth on the sand and a bag containing apocryphal maps of a supposed British attack on Gaza, preferable to an attack on Be'er Sheba. Instead, on 31 October 1917 the Allies with 40,000 troops attack Be'er Sheva (with 5000 inhabitants, commanded by General Ismet), comprising British, Commonwealth and ANZAC (Australia and New Zealand Army Corps) cavalry and mounted infantry (Imperial Light Horse Cavalry) for transporting infantry into the battle zone to fight hand-to-hand with sword and pistol. Allenby's troops, the 20th British Infantry Corps and Yeomanry Division, together with 800 bayonet-wielding horsemen of the Australian Light Horse Brigade begin at Halutza (oasis) before moving along the Be'er Sheva-Nitzana railway line, attacking from the east, charging against the afternoon setting sun. Many exposed horses (nearly 2000) are killed by Turkish machine guns and artillery as they are unable to jump across the wadis or traverse the barbed wire. Gaza is now isolated from railway lines to the north and west.

Be'er Sheva, British and Commonwealth War Cemetery   Adrian Wolff

Allied troops are lucky to succeed in surprising and defeating Turkish forces at Be'er Sheva capturing the wells, as no water sources are available before troops arrive at their final goal. Had the Allied troops not succeeded in a quick, swift battle, both men and horses would have been severely put to the test having been on the move for three days. Turks retreat northwards as their columns are attacked by British aircraft. There are 1241 British and Commonwealth graves (67 unidentified) in the British Military cemetery in Be'er Sheva - result of a 30-hour operation. This is one of the last successful cavalry battles to take place as horses and frontal attacks become outdated when facing modern machine guns and tanks. British WW I cemeteries are also found in Haifa, Jerusalem, Ramle, Be'er Sheva and Dir el-Balah. General Allenby captures Gaza, finding Turkish troops have looted the town before their withdrawal. General Allenby's troops then continue northwards through the Judean Hills to Hebron and Jerusalem. Another column heads along the coast towards the railway junction at Lod. Jews are forced to evacuate Tel Aviv, head for Petah Tikva.

1917   British Foreign Minister, **Lord Arthur Balfour** (1848-1930) on 2 November 1917 in his letter to Lord Lionel Walter Rothschild supports rights to a **Jewish National Homeland in Palestine**. This document known as the **'The Balfour Declaration'** states **the British Government views** *"with favour the establishment in Palestine of a national home for the Jewish people, and will use their best endeavours to facilitate the achievement of this object"*. Nahum Sokolov assists Dr. Chaim Weizmann to prepare the Declaration. *"You will return to the land of your inheritance and posses it."* (Joshua 1:15).

1917   During the Russian Revolution, White Russians and nationalist Ukrainians murder over 150,000 Jews, about 1/3 of the Ukrainian Jewish population, causing many Jewish survivors to emigrate, including to Palestine. Stalin erroneously blames Jews for causing the 'Great Famine' in 1930's, resulting in more anti-Jewish killings.

1917   New Zealand troops capture Jaffa. General Allenby using British and Colonial troops capture the Arab towns of Ramle and Lod on the main road connecting Jaffa with Jerusalem, now changes his transportation method from camels to donkeys for the final slow climb up the Jerusalem Hills since camels cannot manage the rocky, steep climb in rainy wintery conditions. He marches towards Jerusalem with three infantry brigades from the west with a brigade through Beit Horin and also through Shaar Hagai, Another southern artillery brigade from Hebron pounds villages in the hills south and west of Jerusalem while Turkish troops flee towards Jericho. Before Christmas on 9 December, two Commonwealth cooks, sergeants Sedwick and Hurcomb of the London Regiment are looking for eggs in Lifta, a village on the western outskirts of Jerusalem. A group of Muslim dignitaries including the Mayor of Jerusalem approach them carrying 'the keys to the Holy City' and a white flag. The sergeants bring the keys to their officer, who makes the dignitaries repeat the surrender, repeated a third time to the commander of the forces in the area.

British General John French (1852-1925) captures a barren hill, French Hill, named after him, on the northern approaches to Jerusalem, west of Mount Scopus. Jerusalem officially surrenders to Major-General John Shea on 11 December 1917. General Allenby enters the Old City on foot through the Jaffa Gate, is welcomed by the local population, as no flags are raised. Muslim Indian troops secure the Temple Mount including Muslin holy sites. Jerusalem is conquered without gunfire, saving the walls and holy sites from destruction. He declares *"every building will be...protected according to the existing customs and beliefs."*

1917 Turkish military leader Enver Pasha removes Jamal Pasha, following over one million deaths from disease and starvation in Syria, the slaughter of Armenians and persecution of Jews.

General Erich von Falkenhayn is the German chief military commander in Palestine. Previously at The Battle at **Verdun** in 1916 he commanded the German Fifth Army with 1,100,000 soldiers and 1,200 artillery pieces. Following the German success, he is appointed chief military commander in Palestine. He is reputed to have prevented Ottoman persecution of Jews in Palestine during a period of anti-Armenia phobia. His biographer Holger Afflerbach claims, *"An inhuman excess against the Jews in Palestine was only prevented by Falkenhayn's conduct, which against the background of the German history of the 20th century has a special meaning, and one that distinguishes Falkenhayn."*

Summary of Battles in Palestine during World War 1

1. **Asluj (Telalim)**, site of ancient wells. British and Commonwealth Forces assemble Desert Mule Corps (DMC).
2. **el-Bugger Ridge**, 16km west of Be'er Sheva. On 25 October 1917. ANZAC 3rd Light-Horse and 8th Light-Horse Brigades.
3. **Tel el-Saba (Tel Sheva)** 5kms east of Be'er Sheva. Australian 4th Light-Horse Brigade led by Australian General Sir Harry Chauvel (1865-1945) charge from 4kms SE of Be'er Sheva, capturing its vital water supply and junction.
4. **Khnweilfe** 17kms NE of Be'er Sheva (Lehavim). Rear guard action by Turkish 7th Army allow soldiers to escape northwards.
5. **Jemmameh and Huj** (Sederot). Rear guard action by Turkish 8th Army allow their retreat northwards.
6. **Megido.** General Chauvel defeats Turkish forces at Megido, establishing head-quarters of the Desert Mule Corps.
7. **Jenin.** Australian 3rd Light-Horse Brigade intercepts retreating Turkish troops taking over 8000 prisoners.
8. **el-Afule (Afula)** captured by Indian 4th Cavalry Division.
9. **Beisan (Beit She'an)**, key junction for south (Jordan Valley, Dead Sea, Akaba) and east (Dara'a, Damascus) taken by Indian 4th Cavalry Division.
10. **Semalch (Zemach)** captured by Brig-Gen. William Grant leading the Australian 4th Light Brigade.

11. **Esdod (Ashdod).** Mounted ANZAC troops first break to coastal road.

12. **Ramelah (Ramla) and Ludd (Lod, Lydda)** are captured by ANZAC Light-Horse Brigades together with by two armored cars on 16 November 1917, severing rail communications between Turkish 8th Army and Jerusalem. Jewish settlers warmly welcome the Light-Horse Brigades.

13. New Zealand cavalry capture **Jaffa** on 16 November 1917.

14. **Jerusalem** capitulates without fire on 11 December 1917.

15. **British aircraft** bomb the railway station in Tulkarem, an airfield in Ramle, and German military headquarters at Augusta Victoria on Mt. of Olives, Jerusalem.

16. **Musallebeh (el-Aija and Abu Tellal),** 8kms west of Jordan River, 22kms north of the Dead Sea. On 14 July 1918 German army is defeated by Australian Light Horse.

1918 British warplanes drop bombs on an Ottoman-German military column traveling between Tulkarem and Nablus, in addition destroy the German airfield at Jenin (20 September). Allied troops capture the Afula area on the Haifa-Damascus railway line. Allied troops turn westwards and capture Megido. The title Viscount Allenby of Megido and Felixstowe is bestowed on General Allenby, British High Commissioner for Egypt (1919-1925). According to Christians, Megido is the site of the final battle between the forces of good and evil that will occur at Armageddon (Tel (Har) Megido). *"And they gathered them at a place called in Hebrew, Armageddon."* (Revelation 16:16). Allied troops capture the Christian-Arab town of Nazareth (21 September), establishing their regional headquarters. British and Australian planes (22 September) bomb Turkish columns east of Nablus in wadi Fara attempting to reach the Jordan River. The 38th Battalion (Jewish Legion) engage the Ottomans in the Jordan Valley. Haifa and Acre, both small ports on the Mediterranean Sea are captured (23 September). British and Commonwealth Forces horse mounted cavalry cover 400 kms in 12 days to complete their conquest of Palestine. Turks surrender at Halab (Aleppo) in Syria. Allied troops capture Amman on 25 September.

British and Commonwealth War Cemeteries, graves
Haifa, 302
Ramle, 3576
Jerusalem, 5889
Be'er Sheva, 1173
Deir el Balah (Gaza) 719
Gaza, 2643

Museums
The Jewish Legion, Avihail
Turkish Memorial, Be'er Sheva

British Mandate Period in Palestine **1918 - 1948**
- British Administration replaces the Ottoman rule.
- Jerusalem Municipal Ordinance orders all new public and private buildings be faced with Jerusalem stone.
- The Jews greet the British conquerers as liberating heroes.
- Cessation of graft and bribery of officials, nepotism, inefficient administration, exploitation of a government posts.
- Arab rioting, terrorism and murder of Jews continues.
- Era of expansion of Jewish towns and building new settlements.
- Jewish immigration to Palestine is restricted after 1930.
- The British depart Palestine on 14 May 1948.

1918 Sir Ronald Storrs, Oriental Secretary in Cairo is appointed Military Governor of Jerusalem. Great Britain merges the Mesopotamian provinces of Mosul, Baghdad and Basra into a single country, Iraq.

1918 Jews return to Tel Aviv following their expulsion by the Ottomans.

1918 **Population** of Jerusalem drops to 55,000 due to epidemics, famine, and starvation.

1918 British appoint, Musa Qassem al-Husseini, a Muslim, mayor of Jerusalem 1918-1920.

1918 The new post-Ottoman situation allows the British colonialists to bring outsiders from the Hejaz (Arabia) to become 'kings' in new countries - Transjordan, Iraq and Lebanon. They are not accepted by the 'local tribes' who have different tribal and ethnic ideals. Feisal arrives in Damascus on 3 October 1918 assuming to be the ruler of Syria/Lebanon according to the Sykes-Picot Agreement. The French have other ideas offering him land-locked areas of Syria with a French liaison officer. Feisal refuses, resulting in the British to grant him a new country, Iraq (see 1921).

1918 Baron Edmond de Rothschild donates the Meyer de Rothschild building in Jerusalem to The Hadassah Organization of America.

1918 The Zionist Organization elects 'community representatives' or *Va'ad Ha'Kehillah*, to administer Jewish religious affairs, representing both Ashkenazi and Sephardics. Britain appoints Dr. Chaim Weizmann, member of the 'Young Committee' or *Va'ad Hatzerim*, to lead Zionist Commission on the future development and settlement in Eretz Israel. He is the liaison between Zionist leadership and British authorities. His charm and strong personality opens political doors of British Foreign Office, American Presidents and global Jewish leaders. TE Lawrence sets up and translates the meeting in Akaba (June 1918) between Emir Feisal I, son of Hussein ibn Ali and Weizmann who offers to support the Zionist cause in Eretz Israel on condition Britain will support his claims in Syria/Iraq.

1918 **World War I ends** on 11 November 1918. An estimated nine million servicemen are killed during the four years of fighting and an additional five million civilians are thought to have died from friction, hunger and disease. Over one million Jewish soldiers serve in the armies of both sides with over 30,000 Jewish soldiers killed. WW I shatters existing empires - Ottoman, Austro-Hungarian and Russian. New countries are established in the Middle East, where no independent country had previously existed, as this area was previously under direct control from Ottoman Istanbul.

1919 TE Lawrence is instrumental in arranging (and translating), signing of the Emir Feisal - Dr. Chaim Weizmann agreement in London on 3 January 1919.
"**Article 2.** *Definite boundaries between the Arab States and (Jewish) Palestine shall be determined.* **Article 4.** *All necessary measures shall be taken to encourage and stimulate immigration of Jews into Palestine on a large scale, and as quickly as possible.*" Through TE Lawrence, Feisal abandons his father Hussein's claim on Palestine in return for Arab sovereignty in Baghdad and Amman. France claims Damascus. On 1 March 1919 Feisal writes (through TE Lawrence) to American Zionist Leader Felix Frankfurter "*We Arabs, especially the educated amongst us, look with deepest sympathy on the Zionist movement.*" (Lawrence, The Changing East). On 17 January 1921 Lawrence writes to British Colonial secretary Winston Churchill, Feisal "*agreed to abandon all claims of his father to Palestine*" (Churchill Papers 17/14). Lawrence is soon forgotten by the desert Bedouin.

1919 Dr. Aaron Aaronsohn flies from London to attend the Paris Conference. His planes crashes in heavy fog over the English Channel. His body is never recovered.

1919 Completion of the new Italian Hospital on Shivtei Israel Street, designed by Antonio Barluzzi. The Israeli Government purchases this building in 1963 to house the Ministry of Education.

1919 Following cancellation of Sykes-Picot Agreement at the Paris Peace Conference, Hussein ibn Ali refuses to accept British proposals to transfer Syria and Lebanon to France. In 1924 Hussein is deposed in Arabia by the Wahhabi sect led by Ibn-Saud proclaiming himself king in 1926. He dies in Amman, 1931. Britain installs his son Feisal I (Faysal) (1885–1933) as ruler in Lebanon.

1919   Joseph Trumpeldor returns to Eretz Israel, organizes the **Gedud Ha'avoda**, a Jewish Battalion for the defense of Jewish settlements in remote areas of Upper Galilee.

1919   Chaotic conditions follow the Bolshevik Revolution in Russia of 1917. Violent confrontations between opposing Red and White factions result in an unstable and unsafe situation, with increased anti-Semitism. Following numerous pogroms in Russia, Dr. Max Nordau calls without success, for the immediate immigration of 600,000 Jews to Eretz Israel. **The British government allows unlimited Jewish immigration into Eretz Israel.**

1919   David Ben-Gurion calls upon all Jews, both in Eretz Israel and abroad to unite in a political Zionist force to establish an independent Jewish state in Eretz Israel.

1919   **The Third Immigration or Aliyah Gimmel** (1919-1923). Over 34,000 Jews immigrate, fleeing chaos, starvation, unruliness, anti-Semitism, and increased number of pogroms in Russia. Most new immigrants are young 'pioneers' (*halutzim* in Hebrew), arriving without possessions, making a personal commitment to the settlement and pioneering spirit of Eretz Israel. They drain the swamps, pave the roads, establishing communal settlements (kibbutzim) in many parts of the country, including over 20 new settlements in the Jezreel Valley. Moshavim (moshav = singular) are founded, financially assisted by the Jewish National Fund.

1919   Menachem Ussishkin settles in Eretz Israel, is elected head of the Zionist Commission, playing an important role in the practical development of settlement activities, organizing a network of Hebrew language schools and is also active in the establishment of the future Hebrew University. Eliezer Ben Yehuda and Ussishkin successfully request the British Authorities to add Hebrew to the two other official languages (English and Arabic) in Eretz Israel.

1919   The Zionist Socialist **Labor Party, (Mapai)** is founded. Most Jewish workers become members of this political party.

1920   Jewish National Fund (JNF) through **Yehoshua Hankin** (1864-1945) implements a policy of Land Purchases for future settlements. He is instrumental in establishing and/or expanding Jewish settlements in Rehovot, Hadera, Merhavia, Jezreel, Zebulun and Hefer Valleys for growing citrus.

1920   At the **San Remo Conference, The League of Nations grants Great Britain a Mandate for Palestine** to include Trans-Jordan and Palestine (west of the Jordan River) and a mandate for Iraq. The British government's pro-Zionist policies are evident by the appointment of **Sir Herbert Samuel,** (1870–1963) the First British High Commissioner in Palestine (1920-1925). Samuel, a Jew and former cabinet minister, identifies with the Zionist movement and will welcome the creation of the State of Israel. Government House, the official residence is built in Talpiot, Jerusalem. The Arab population in Palestine is opposed to the Zionist program. Arab violent resistance and non-cooperation results in British appeasement in 1923. French President Alexandre Millerand opposes Zionism citing it will disturb the Arab world. (See 1922).

Map 36. The Middle East 1920

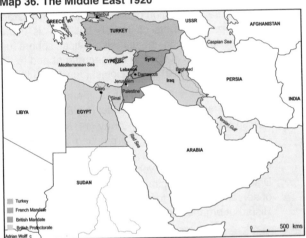

1920 **The League of Nations grants France a Mandate for Lebanon and Syria.** These provinces were previously controlled before WW I from Istanbul. King Feisal I mistrusts the French Colonel Edouard Bremen (from their earlier meetings) and does not accept the French Mandate in Lebanon. Feisal is deposed to become king of a new kingdom in Mesopotamia, Iraq. (See 1916, 1921). French Catholic allies, the Maronites, are the dominant force in Lebanon.

1920 The first **moshav** (moshavim = plural) a small-holder agricultural settlement is founded at **Nahalal** in the Jezreel Valley. The Jewish National Fund purchases land and develops the infrastructure. Each family is allocated a parcel of land, leased at a nominal rent. Purchases of raw materials and sales of the produce are made on a co-operative basis. During a visit to Nahalal Lord Balfour remarks *"This prosperous community, only three years ago, was settled on* *land so fever-stricken that neither Arab nor German nor any other population had dared to settle on it, and those who had made the endeavour had to give it up under disastrous conditions. It is wonderful to reflect that this center of disease has now become a center of health and prosperity and is going to be an example to all other settlements in the district, and to all other settlements within the area of Palestine."* (JNF).

1920   Britain appoints Ragheb Nashashibi, a Muslim, mayor of Jerusalem (1920–1934).

1920   Dr. Max Nordau again calls at the Zionist Conference in London for the immediate immigration of Jews to Eretz Israel.

1920   The General Federation of Jewish Labor, the **Histadrut** is founded to organize the rights of Jewish Labor. This unified labor union remains powerful in the Israeli political sphere until the 1990's. Itzhak Ben-Zvi is elected to the secretariat and to the Va'ad Le'umi (National Committee) of the Zionist (Jewish) Authority.

1920   **Berl Katznelson** (1887-1944), a member of the Hibbat Zion in Russia, immigrates to Eretz Israel (1908), volunteers to serve in the Jewish Legion of the British Army (1918). He is a Zionist and labor leader of the Histadrut, promoting working class unity and establishes the Workers Sick Fund (**Kupat Holim**). He initiates joint relationships between labor movements in the Yishuv and Diaspora. He champions Jewish values and instigates Sabbath observance, Jewish festivals, and dietary laws (kashrut) within the Histadrut organization.

1920   The **Keren Hayesod** is founded to promote and give financial assistance to:
- Immigration (Aliyah)
- Immigrant Absorption (Klita)
- Settlement (Hit'yash'vut).

1920   **Itzhak Sadeh**, (1890-1952) a former soldier in the Russian Army during WW I, immigrates to Eretz Israel. He trains militants and is appointed the Deputy-Commander to Joseph Trumpeldor of the Gedud Ha'avoda (Labor Battalion).

1920   Spontaneous **Arabs riots** against Jews in Ayelet Hashahar, Mishmar Hayarden, Mahanai'im, Rosh Pina, Sharona, Kfar Tabor, Degania and Menahemia. In Jerusalem 5 Jews and 4 Muslims are killed; 211 Jews, 21 Muslims and 3 Christians wounded and 2 Jewish girls raped. Jerusalem is placed out of bounds to ex-Jewish Legion soldiers. Jabotinsky organizes former members of the Jewish Legion to confront the Arab rioters in Tel Aviv and

Jerusalem as they march towards the Jaffa and Damascus Gates. British arrest Jabotinsky and 19 others sentencing him to 15 years imprisonment in Acre, is freed in 1921 during the general amnesty granted by the new British High Commissioner Sir Herbert Samuel. Jabotinsky leaves for London, joining the Board of Directors of the Keren Hayesod.

1920　In the Upper Galilee, Arabs from Jabal Amil offer to negotiate peaceful co-existence with local Jewish settlements. Under false pretenses, enter the fortified settlement of Tel Hai. Once inside they open fire killing Joseph **Trumpeldor** and seven other Jewish defenders of Tel Hai. Trumpeldor legendary last words are *"it is good to die for one's country"*. The town of Kiryat Shmona is named after the eight.

Memorial and Graves of Tel Hai Defenders, Kfar Giladi　Adrian Wolff

1920　**Eliyahu Golumb** (1893-1945) previously volunteers for the Turkish Army but is forced to flee to Egypt in 1915 where he enlists in the Jewish Legion of the British Army. **Dov Hoz** (1894-1940) immigrates to Eretz Israel in 1906 following the anti-Jewish pogroms in Russia. During World War I he too volunteers for the Turkish Army, but also is forced to flee to Egypt in 1915, joins the Jewish Legion. Hoz is active in the Histadrut and Hagana. He, together with his wife and daughter are killed in a motor accident in the Sharon Region in 1940. Golumb marries Ada, and Hoz marries

Rivka, sisters of Moshe Sharett-Shertok. (See Sharett 1933).

Following anti-Jewish riots, the fall of Tel Hai and numerous attacks by Arabs in March and April of this year, demobilized soldiers of the Jewish Legion recognize the British authority will not come to Jewish aid. **Eliyahu Golomb (in his home) and Dov Hoz establish the Jewish Defense Organization, the Hagana, to defend Jewish settlements and protect Jews living in the Yishuv.** Other leaders include Israel and Manya Schohat, Itzhak and Rachel Ben-Zvi. The Hagana, considered illegal by the British mandatory authorities, is an independent, non-political defense organization under the control of the Jewish leadership. They make strategic changes in the concept of Jewish defense that began as a local militia system of Hashomrim (watchmen) in 1909, now replaced by the larger unified national defense organization. A local commander is appointed in each city and region and volunteers train in weaponry and field-craft. Each settlement is responsible for its own defense. A local committee collects money for defense purposes. Workshops (Taas) are established to produce hand grenades and military equipment stored in sliks. An army comprising untrained militia is transformed into a capable force.

1920   Itzhak Sadeh is appointed Second-in-Command and Chief of Operations of Hagana. Many Hagana members had served in the British Army during WW I. The Hagana uses British Army training techniques and battle procedures, as they recognize the British as having successful training methods of Colonial Armies consisting people of different educational and cultural backgrounds.

1920   Nahum Zemach, Menachem Gnessin and Hanna Robinah establish the Habimah or Jewish National Theater in Tel Aviv.

1920   The Women's International Zionist Organization (**WIZO**) is founded in London by Rebecca Sieff, Romana Goodman, Edith Eder and Henrietta Irwell. This international organization is active today in professional and vocational training and education of women; care and education of children.

1920   British begin various public works programs creating jobs for many Jewish immigrants. Many Arabs from surrounding territories move to Palestine in search of work. A pumping station is built at Solomon's Pools near Bethlehem to ensure constant water supply to Jerusalem. New Jewish suburb in Atarot is constructed north of Jerusalem, abandoned after being totally surrounded by Arabs in 1948. Resettled after the Six-Day War in 1967.

1921   British establish The Supreme Muslim Council (**WAKF**) to appease

Arab nationalism and preserve the balance of power between inter-Arab clan rivalries. They appoint **Haj Amin al-Husseini** (1893-1974), an Arab nationalist, as Grand Mufti/Supreme Muslim Leader, heading the Muslim Religious Council in 1923. The British are hoping, without any success, that he will moderate his violent anti-Jewish feelings and assassination of Arab moderates.

1921   The Romema suburb is constructed at the entrance to Jerusalem.

1921   David Ben-Gurion is elected Secretary-General of the **Histadrut,** Israel General Federation of Labor, co-headed with Berl Katznelson. Ben-Gurion uses the Histadrut as a means to undertake agricultural settlement, development of industry and building construction in Eretz Israel. The Histadrut establishes Bank Ha'poalim (The Workers Bank).

1921   **Mr. Winston Churchill** visits Palestine, tells an Arab delegation *"the manifest right that the Jews, who are scattered over the world, should have a national centre where some of them may be re-united; and that centre must be in the Land of Palestine, with which over more than 3000 years they have been intimately associated."* At Hebrew U he states *"My heart is full of sympathy for Zionism."*

1921   France deposes Feisal I in Lebanon (1920). Britain installs him king in Iraq. He writes to Felix Frankfurter (USA Zionist leader) *"We Arabs...look with the deepest sympathy on the Zionist movement."* Feisal I dies (1933) from cardiac complications during anti-monarchy riots. His son Ghazi (1912-1939) is king.

1921   On May Day **Arabs begin rioting** killing 13 Jews in Jaffa, continuing in Petach Tikva, Rehovot, Jerusalem, Hadera and Haifa. The British High Commissioner orders temporary closing of ports to Jewish immigration, even to those Jews in possession of valid visas. Jewish communities of Kfar Saba and Kfar Malal are evacuated to Petach Tikva preventing their slaughter by rioting Arabs. Tel Aviv separates its municipal services from Jaffa until 1950. Ex-members of the Jewish Legion, now of the Hagana, move into defensive positions, prevent slaughter of Jews in Tel Aviv. Arab non-co-operation with the British Authorities.

1921   Jewish leadership promotes the large-scale establishment of new settlements in the Jezreel Valley (1921–1925). Jewish population increases to 2500 inhabitants in new settlements of Nahalal, Ginegar, Tel Adashim, Balfouria, Kfar Yehezkiel, Geva, Ein Harod, Tel Yosef, Heftzibah, and Beit Alpha. Many will perish from malaria.

1921   Dr. Chaim Weizmann is elected leader of the World Zionist Organization at the World Zionist Congress in Carlsbad.

1921   All Jewish orphans living in Yemen who are minors, are forced to convert to Islam.

1921   Public Works Department (Ma'atz) is established for construction of roads, tunnels, ports.

1922   A military takeover in Turkey led by **Mustafa Kemal (Ataturk)**. Sultan Mehmet VI is forced to flee. The sultan previously held the title of the caliph, the spiritual and political leader of all followers of Islam. Turkish Assembly abolishes the sultanate in 1924. **End of the Ottoman Empire.**

1922   Great Britain grants independence to Egypt.

1922   Menachem Ussishkin is elected President of the Jewish National Fund (JNF) whose headquarters move to Jerusalem.

1922   The **League of Nations** formally approves Mandates to both Great Britain and France. **Britain separates Palestine into two areas -** all the territory east of the Jordan River, called Transjordan, covering 80% of the Mandate area is immediately closed to Jewish immigration and settlement. In 1945 Transjordan becomes independent, the Hashemite Kingdom of Jordan, the Emir Abdullah (1881-1951) king in 1946, advised and protected by Britain.

Great Britain retains full administrative control of all Palestine west of the Jordan River up to the Mediterranean Sea and does not grant the Jews a "*national homeland in Palestine*" in the remaining 20% of Palestine as defined in the Balfour Declaration of 1917. Britain wishes to appease the Arabs who control both the Suez Canal and Persian Gulf Oil.

Mr. Winston Churchill, British Colonial Secretary issues a 'White Paper' confirming Jewish rights to a homeland in Palestine, while limiting Jewish immigration to its economic capacity. He states that Jews may not exercise any political domination over the non-Jewish population and does not share in the government. "*The existence of a Jewish National Home in Palestine should be internationally guaranteed.*" His opinion is based upon a letter of 24 October 1915 by **Sir Henry McMahon**, the British High Commissioner in Egypt written to King Hussein of the Kingdom of the Hejaz, conveying the promise to the Sherif of Mecca to recognize and support the independence of the Arabs within the territories proposed by him, **ex**cluding the Vilayet of Beirut and the independent Sanjak of Jerusalem. All of Palestine west of the Jordan is excluded from McMahon's pledge. (British White Paper 1922). In a 1922 letter to Sir John Shuckburgh of the British Colonial Office, McMahon wrote "*It was my intention to exclude*

Palestine from independent Arabia." Sir Henry McMahon writes to The Times of London 23 July 1937 *"I feel it my duty to state, and I do so definitely and emphatically, that it was not intended by me in giving this pledge to King Hussein, to include Palestine in the area in which Arab independence was promised. I also had every reason to believe at the time that the fact that Palestine was not included in my pledge was well understood by King Hussein."*

Map 37. British and French Mandates 1922

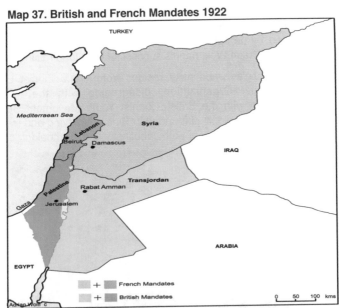

1922 Vladimir Ze'ev Jabotinsky opposes the Partition of Transjordan and Palestine. **Jews call Palestine by its biblical name, 'The Land of Israel', or 'Eretz Israel' ארץ ישראל in Hebrew.**

1922 Britain conducts a **census** in Palestine. Total population 752,000. Jews 84,000 (11%) and Arabs 664,000 (89%). Arab population has increased from about 450,000 in 1880. **Population** of Jerusalem 62,000; Jews 34,000 (54%) the majority; 15,000 Christians and 13,000 Muslims. British Mandate authorities always appoint a Muslim mayor of Jerusalem, not allowing democratic elections because a Jewish majority would have elected a Jewish mayor.

1923 Baron Edmund de Rothschild establishes PICA (Palestine Jewish Colonization Association) to finance settlement activity. Benjamina near Zichron Ya'akov in the Carmel is named after him.

1923 The Beit Hakerem suburb is constructed in west Jerusalem.

1923 Lt.-Col.**Frederick Hermann Kisch** (1888-1943), British Army World War I, heads the British Military Intelligence Section to the Paris Peace Conference in 1919. He accepts Dr. Chaim Weizmann's proposal to immigrate to Eretz Israel where he is appointed a member of the Zionist Executive, responsible for defense topics. Brigadier-General Kisch is killed in Tunisia in 1943 in active service of the British Army.

1923 Many Jews are unemployed due to economic stagnation, limiting industrial investment in Eretz Israel, while famine is partially caused by drought. Zionist Leadership's finances are diminishing until Dr. Chaim Weizmann's successful USA fund raising mission.

1923 Vladimir Ze'ev Jabotinsky resigns from World Zionist Executive and Zionist Organization, disagreeing with the method of negotiation with the British. Zionist Youth Movement **Betar** (Brit Joseph Trumpeldor) is founded in Riga, identifying and inspired by the national ideology of both Jabotinsky and Trumpeldor.

Reading Power Station, Tel Aviv   Adrian Wolff

1923 **Pinchas Rutenberg**, (1879-1942) an electrical engineer, reputedly assists in the assassination of the assumed White Russian Czarist spy Father Gapon, who infiltrates the red Russian Socialist organization after the uprising of 1905. After the communists come to power, he becomes disillusioned and leaves Russia for Italy. During WW I Rutenberg is instrumental in conscripting Jewish American volunteers into the Royal Fusiliers. He arrives in Eretz Israel in 1919. In 1923 he establishes the Jewish-owned Palestine Electrical Corporation and builds the first Power Station (Reading) just north of Tel Aviv, on the northern bank of the Yarkon River where it enters the Mediterranean Sea. Within two years, another two Power Stations are established. *"...and night shines like the day, darkness and light are the same."* (Psalms 139:12). The Palestine Electrical Company receives permission to supply the entire country with electrical power, except for Jerusalem, where a separate corporation is founded. In 1954, the Government of Israel becomes the majority shareholder in the Israel Electricity Corporation. Israel has no energy sources, importing coal, gas and oil from non-Arab states due to the Arab economic boycott. Egypt supplies oil to Israel after 1979 and gas from Sinai, discontinued in 2012, due to terror attacks. Israeli Gas comes on stream in 2017.

1924   The first political murder in the Yishuv when a Dutch Rabbi Jacob Israel de Haan is killed due to his anti-Zionist, pro-orthodox views.

1924   The British continue a policy of unrestricted Jewish immigration.

1924   **The Fourth Immigration or Aliyah Daled** (1924-1929). Over 70,000 Jews arrive in Eretz Israel, mainly from Poland escaping increased anti-Jewish economic policies. Jews fleeing Eastern Europe prefer Eretz Israel to other destinations, but not all Jews are to remain due to the economic woes in the Yishuv. Many educational and cultural institutions are established.

Many immigrants are older people, arriving with their families preferring urban life-style, settling in towns, with 40% choosing Tel Aviv. Population of Tel Aviv doubles within two years from 16,000 in 1923 to 34,000 in 1925, as the town expands northwards.

1924   **Chaim Nahman Bialik**, (1873-1944), a Jewish poet, storyteller, editor, member of the Odessa Jewish Hovevei Zion group immigrates. His writings influence Modern Hebrew and Jewish culture becoming the Hebrew National Poet, studied in all Israeli Jewish schools. The words of his poems will be put to music, becoming popular Hebrew songs.

1924   **Zalman Shazar** (1899-1974) an active member in the Poalei Zion movement in Russia immigrates to Eretz Israel, becomes a member of the Histadrut Secretariat. Shazar is appointed the 3rd President of the State of Israel (1963-1973).

1924   **Rabbi Abraham Isaac Kook** (1865-1935) immigrates to Eretz Israel in 1904. In 1921 is appointed Chief Ashkenazi Rabbi. He identifies with the Zionist movement, establishing a 'yeshiva' (The Rabbi Kook Institute) combining religion with Zionism.

1924   **Haim Arlozorov** (1899-1933) immigrates to Eretz Israel, joins the Zionist Labor Party in 1918 and soon becomes a leader of the organization. See Arlozorov 1930,1931,1933.

1924 Mekor Baruch, Mekor Haim, Rehavia, Kiryat Moshe, Talbiah and Geula suburbs are constructed in western Jerusalem. Neve Ya'akov suburb is constructed north of Jerusalem, abandoned in 1947 following Arab attacks, resettled after 1967.

1924 **The Israel Institute of Technology, the Technion** is founded in Haifa, moving to a larger campus on Mt. Carmel in 1953. This scientific academic institution will maintain the highest academic standards and will become world renowned, producing Nobel Prize winners. Technion graduates comprise:
• Over 70% of the founders, managers of Israel's hi-tech industries.
• Over 74% of Israel managers in the electronic industries.

1924 **Lord Alfred Mond** (Lord Melchett) visits Eretz Israel in 1921 with Dr. Chaim Weizmann, contributes to the Jewish Colonization Corporation, writes for Zionist publications. He is elected the first President of the Technion in 1925. He founds the town Tel Mond.

1924 The modern Church of All Nations (Gethsemane = Gat Shmanim, Hebrew for olive press) church is built over ruins of Crusader and Byzantine churches on the lower slopes of the Mt. of Olives. Antonio Barluzzi is the architect. Christians believe after partaking in the Last Supper, Jesus and His followers wander into the Kidron Valley to the olive grove where Jesus receives the kiss of betrayal and is taken prisoner by the Roman troops. They also believe on this rock, Jesus prays during His Agony. (See Jesus 30CE).

1924 British Authorities appoint a new Jerusalem municipal council with six members - three from each community (Arab and Jewish), under a Muslim mayor.

1924 The Supreme Moslem Council in Jerusalem publishes 'A Brief Guide to al-Haram al-Sharif (Temple Mount) "*Its identity with the site of Solomon's Temple is beyond dispute. This too is the spot, according to universal belief on which 'David built there an altar unto the Lord, and offered burnt offerings and peace offerings'*".

1924 Beit Ve'Gan, Mahanayim, Sanhedria suburbs are constructed in west Jerusalem. Kibbutz Ramat Rachel, established on Jerusalem's southern outskirts overlooking Bethlehem, combines agriculture (fruit growing) with urban services (laundry, bakery, hotel). Founding of **Afula**, to become the capital and urban center for the Jewish settlements in the Jezreel (Yisreel) Valley. Limitations on available urban land surrounding the town, its proximity to the Haifa Bay area, and hot climate hinder its growth.

1924 Colonel George Stewart Symes, Acting British High Commissioner (1925-1928).

1924 Vladimir Ze'ev Jabotinsky establishes Federation of **Revisionist** Zionists in opposition to the World Zionist Organization. He believes in the establishment of the Jewish State in historical Eretz Israel, to include areas in Transjordan.

1924 Polish Jews are amongst the 35,000 immigrants, many settling in Tel Aviv.

1925 Field Marshal Lord Herbert Plumer British High Commissioner (1925-1928).

1925 The **Hebrew University** is dedicated on Mt. Scopus in East Jerusalem, initiated by Dr. Chaim Weizmann with finance received from the **Rothschild family, Sir Ellis Kadoorie Foundation** (1865-1922) and **Felix Warburg** (1871–1937). Jews are previously excluded from academic positions in Russia, Germany, Austria and USA, now have their own university, will achieve international academic standards. Albert Einstein supports the Zionist cause, is involved in establishing the Hebrew University, serving on the Board of Governors and Chairman of its Academic Council. He writes "*The Zionist cause is very close to my heart...I am glad that there should be a little patch of earth on which our kindred brethren are not considered aliens.*" He adds "*I have always felt an obligation to stand up for my persecuted and morally oppressed tribal companions...The prospect of establishing a Jewish university fills me with particular joy, having seen countless instances of perfidious and uncharitable treatment of splendid young Jews with attempts to deny their chances of education.*" (Einstein's letters to Paul Epstein 1919 and Fritz Haber 1921). He bequeaths his papers to the Hebrew University. During the War of Independence in 1948 Jordanian forces surround the campus, necessitating the construction of a new campus in Givat Ram, west Jerusalem. Mt. Scopus campus, is reopened in 1981 following the unification Jerusalem.

1926 General Strike by Arabs in Palestine, against a visit to Jerusalem of the French High Commissioner to Syria.

1926 Pinchas Rutenberg receives British approval for a 70-year concession to utilize the Jordan and Yarmuk rivers at Naharai'im for a hydroelectric power station, completed in 1932. This structure is destroyed by Jordanians in 1948, never re-built.

1926 Tnuva, a kibbutz marketing cooperative is established for the distribution of diary products.

1926   The British cease all public works programs, causing a severe economic depression in Eretz Israel. Harsh economic conditions cause many Jews to be unemployed. In 1927 only 2700 Jews immigrate to Eretz Israel, over 5000 emigrate to western countries.

1927   A severe **earthquake** (11 July) destroys many buildings, damaging the Church of the Holy Sepulchre, al-Aqsa Mosque, Augusta Victoria Hospital on Mt. Scopus and old town in Lydda (Lod). The Terra Sancta complex, owned by the Franciscan Order (Catholics) is completed corner of Keren Ha'yesod and Ben Maimon Streets, architect Antonio Barluzzi. Pontifical Jesuit Biblical Institute is established in Jerusalem. St. Andrew's Scots Memorial Church and Hospice is constructed to commemorate Britain's victory in WW I and its conquest of the Holy Land. Before his death in 1329, King Robert Bruce of Scotland requests Sir James Douglas brings his heart to Jerusalem carrying out his unfilled wish to visit Jerusalem. He sets out from Scotland with 'the heart', to be killed fighting Moors in Spain. The 'heart' is buried at Melrose and body in Dunfermline, Scotland.

1928   YMCA building is constructed on King David Street. Architect Arthur L. Harmon, also designs the Empire State Building, NY. James Jarvie donates $1million for construction, dedicated in 1933. Concession to supply **electricity** in Jerusalem is given to Jerusalem Electric and Public Services Corporation Ltd., financed by both British and Jewish capital. Water pumping stations are built at Ein Fara in the Wadi Kelt area to increase the water supplies to Jerusalem. Kiryat Shmuel suburb is constructed in western Jerusalem. Nathan Strauss Health Center is established, later to become Bikur Holim Hospital in Jerusalem. Chapel of the Flagellation on via Dolorosa is reconstructed at Station II, architect Antonio Barluzzi.

1928   After four months of interim administration under Sir Harry Luke, Sir John Chancellor is appointed High Commissioner until 1931. His administration is noted for initially condemning Arab attacks. He assists Lord Passfield's White Paper in 1930 which retreats from the commitment of the Balfour Declaration for creating a Jewish state.

Chapter 21. Arab Disturbances 1929 - 1938

1929 Rockefeller Museum is constructed on Sultan Suleyman Street, East Jerusalem opposite Herod's Gate (Gate of Flowers), exhibiting archaeological finds from the American School of Oriental Research in Jerusalem. Construction of Geula and Kerem Avraham suburbs adjoining the Me'a Sharim in Jerusalem.

1929 The **Jewish Agency** is founded by Felix Warburg and Louis Marshall, with Dr. Chaim Weizmann elected as president and Nahum Sokolov as chairman. It centrally administers Jewish interests of the Yishuv (pre-State Jewish settlement and institutions in Israel), controlling activities of the Jewish National Fund and Keren Hayesod. The leadership is elected under regulations issued by 'Knesset Israel' known as the **'Zionist Executive'**.

The activities of the Jewish Agency will include:
- Purchase of land
- Finance of infrastructure development
- Construction of Jewish settlements in various locations
- Assistance and education of immigrants

The Jews' Wailing Wall, 1890's.   Silver Print Gallery, Ein Hod

1929 All Hagana leaders and its activities are transferred from the Histadrut and placed under the direct responsibility of the Zionist Executive. Colonel Frederick Kisch, an ex-British officer is appointed to oversee Hagana activities. See Kisch 1923.

1929   During the years 1918 to 1929 of open Jewish immigration to Eretz Israel, the number of Jews choosing Israel as their final destination is relatively small when compared to Jewish emigration from Eastern Europe to other countries such as the United States.

1929   The **Mufti of Jerusalem, Haj Amin al-Husseini** incites Muslims to attack Jews praying at Western Wall on Yom Kippur (Day of Atonement) on the pretext Jews wish to take over the al-Aqsa Mosque. In addition Arabs spread rumors Jews intend to pray as a group (*minyan*) at the Western Wall rather than individually. Arab homes are built almost up to The Western Wall exposing a narrow alley 4-meters wide accommodating only a few Jewish pilgrims. In the Jewish Quarter, Jewish merchants are forced to abandon their stores. The British ban blowing the shofar and reading from the Torah at the Western Wall. The local Jews note the pro-Arab reactions of the British administration and police.

1929   The Mufti of Jerusalem, al-Husseini **incites Arabs to riot against Jewish immigration**. Ultra-Orthodox Jews living in **Hebron** refuse a Hagana offer to reinforce their security arrangements. After Arabs massacre 63 Jews in Hebron and desecrate their bodies, the remainder of the Jewish residents leave. The British Medical official statement of District Surgeon Dr. John MacQueen and District Superintendent Raymond Cafferata withhold information of the unspeakable savagery and mutilation of Hebron's Jewish community. Nineteen local Arab families protect and save Jews in Hebron. Following the Israeli Army victory in the West Bank in the 6-Day War Jewish settlement is renewed in 1968.

In **Safed** ultra-Orthodox Jews also refuse a Hagana request to reinforce their security arrangements. Arab riots in Safed 5 Jews, mostly children and old people. Only direct intervention by British Police (absent in the Hebron instance) prevents further bloodshed by allowing Jewish residents safety inside the British Police Station compound, the 'seraya'. During Arab riots of 1929, Jews are killed in: Hebron (63), Safed (5), Haifa (6), Tel Aviv (6), Be'er Tuvia, Jerusalem and Motza (30), Atarot, Mishmar Ha'emek, Beit She'an, Ekron, Hulda, and Ramat Rachel. Jewish communities temporarily fall to the Arabs in: Lower Motza, Hulda, Be'er Tuvia, Mishmar Ha'emek, Mahanai'im and Hebron. **Following these Arab riots, British policy shifts away from being sympathetic towards Zionist cause to a new position supporting Arabs, viewing Palestine as a colonial province, not as an independent Jewish State. Jews in the Yishuv mistrust the British.**

1929   As a result of previous Arab anti-Jewish riots in 1921, the Hagana has become more active to protect and defend Jewish lives by training volunteers in cities and regional areas, each with a local commander. During the 1929 riots, 119 Jews are killed.

1929   Religious Zionist youth movement **Bnei Akiva** is founded with Rabbi Kook their spiritual leader. Meir (Berlin) Bar Ilan (1880-1953), president of World Mizrahi Association and member of the Zionist Executive promotes Bnei Akiva, youth movement.

1929   The British construct a deep-water port in Haifa, completed in 1933, designed by British engineer Sir Frederick Palmer.

1929   The 'Geddes Plan', commissioned from Scottish town planner Patrick Geddes is approved, designating the image of Tel Aviv during the British Mandate period.

1929   The economy of the Yishuv is growing faster than surrounding Arab territories. Arabs migrate into Palestine in search of work.

1929   The Jewish **population** increases from 85,000 in 1917 to 170,000 by 1929, Arabs increase from 664,000 in 1922 to one million.

The King David Hotel   Adrian Wolff

1930   The Jewish National and University Library is constructed within the Hebrew University campus on Mt. Scopus, designed by Eric Mendelsohn. (See Mendelssohn 1937). The King David Hotel is constructed on King David Street. This hotel has a special ambience of the Orient. Government House, the British High Commissioner's official residence is built in Arnona, Jerusalem.

1930   **In an effort to quell riots and appease Arabs, the British decide to halt land purchases by Jews, publish an edict, the Passfield White Paper recommending a cessation of Jewish** immigration to Eretz Israel at a time of continual pogroms in Eastern Europe and the rise of fascism in Germany. The British ignore all evidence that both the Arab executive and Supreme Muslim Council organize and incite the local Arab population to riot. A reminder of the British 'Aliens Act of 1907, to limit Jewish immigration to Britain.

From 1930 until the end of the British Mandate (1948), Jewish immigration is restricted and many Jewish immigrants enter illegally. Arab immigration into Palestine is never restricted during the British Mandate 1918-1948.

1930 **Felix Warburg**, (1871–1937), an American Jewish leader (together with Jacob Schiff establish the American Jewish Joint Distribution Committee-**The Joint**, in October 1914) feels deceived by Lord Passfield who previously assured him all Jewish immigration would be permitted. In their reports, British authorities refer ambiguously to over 100,000 Arab immigrants into Palestine from surrounding territories. So-called 'landless' Arabs claim to be displaced by Jews, now receive state lands from the British authorities. In 1931 Felix Warburg personally lobbies the British Prime Minister, Ramsay MacDonald (1931-1935) to renounce the White Paper. He allows limited Jewish immigration and acquisition of land.

1930 **Magen David Adom (MDA)** Jewish ambulance and first-aid services is established. Red Cross International will not recognize Magen David Adom as an equal member with its own symbol, a red 'Star of David' due to anti-Semitism of its various members and power of Muslim Red Crescent Society. In 2002 head of USA Red Cross Association resigns over these reasons.

1930 Haim Arlozorov, is leader, spokesman of Mapai, the Israel Labor Party, calls for a bi-national political solution.

1931 The first English newspaper The Palestine Post is established, later renamed in December 1949, The Jerusalem Post.

1931 Construction of the Church of St. Peter in Gallicàntu on Mt. Zion on the remains of a Byzantine structure. At this traditional site St. Peter hears a cockcrow (gallicantu) in the morning after he attends the Last Supper. Matthew 26:35; John 18:27. Rebuilt in 1997.

1931 Nahum Sokolov replaces Dr. Chaim Weizmann as leader of World Zionist Congress. During the congress, participants criticize British immigration policies and express their lack of trust of the British Administration. Ya'akov Dori (1899-1973) appointed Haifa District Commander of the Hagana, initiates training and para-military exercises for the defense of Jews. He immigrates to Eretz Israel in

1906 after anti-Semitic riots in Russia and joins Jewish Legion of the British Army during World War I.

1931 At Danzig, the Betar Zionist Revisionist Youth Movement elects Vladimir Ze'ev Jabotinsky its leader. Avraham Tehomi, a former Hagana head in Jerusalem, together with about 2000 Hagana Betar members establish a new military organization Organization B, the National Military Organization, Irgun Zeva Le'umi - the **Irgun or Etzel**. They object to the official policy of 'havlagah' (restraint). They retaliate against anti-Jewish terrorist activities and protest British White Paper restrictions on Jewish immigration.

1931 Jewish Agency Executive elects Haim Arlozorov as Head of the Political Department. He loses confidence in his previous belief in cooperation between Arab and Jewish national movements and also changes his view on Great Britain's commitment to Zionism now limiting Jewish immigration into Eretz Israel.

1931 **Census.** 1,036,000. About 175,000 Jews, 762,000 Muslims, 89,000 Christians (40,000 Orthodox, 35,000 Catholics, 26,000 others), and 10,000 Druze. Jerusalem has 90,500 inhabitants including 51,200 Jews (56%), 19,900 Muslims and 19,300 Christians.
Source: Statistical Abstract of Palestine GB Government Office of Statistics

Literacy	Males	Females
Jews	90%	80%
Muslims	25%	10%
Christians	70%	40%

1932 With the rise of fascism in Germany, **Rachel (Recha) Freier** (1892-1984) inaugurates the **Youth Aliyah** program to assist immigration of Jewish youth to Eretz Israel. Freier immigrates in 1941 and establishes an Agricultural Training Center for education of under-privileged children in kibbutz boarding schools. In 1958, Freier initiates the Israeli Composers Fund for promoting original Israeli musical compositions. In 1966, she will establish the Testament Scheme to record major Jewish historical events.

1932 **Henrietta Szold** (1860-1945) director of **Youth Aliyah** department of the Jewish Agency institutes many large-scale immigration projects. Until 1948 over 30,000 Jewish children are brought to Eretz Israel through this program.

1932 Opening of the Tel Aviv Museum of Art, exhibiting examples of Israeli art. The first Maccabi Games is held in Tel Aviv, staged in Israel every 4 years since 1952. Jewish athletes from all over the world compete and many immigrate to Israel.

1932 The Jewish Agency Building is constructed in Jerusalem.

1933   General Strike by Arabs against Jewish immigration.

1933   Fascist political parties in Germany obtain a majority of votes in a general election. Adolf Hitler becomes Chancellor of Germany, immediately bans any opposition, freedom of speech and civil rights. The Nazis declare themselves the sole political party. Hitler believes in racial superiority of Germanic people, and inferiority of other races – Jews, Slavs, Gypsies and Blacks. Nazis will enact various anti-Jewish decrees, limiting Jewish participation in various professions, educational positions, commercial enterprises and employment in public administration. Nazis call for a one-day boycott of Jewish-owned shops and businesses. Books by authors whom the Nazis dislike are burned (See Heine 1817). **Jews begin to leave Germany and Eastern Europe** to US, Eretz Israel, Great Britain and over 25,000 find refuge in Shanghai. Jews fleeing Germany include 14 Nobel Prize laureates and 26 of the 60 professors of theoretical physics.

1933   **Fifth Immigration or Aliyah Hey** (1933-1939). Despite restrictive immigration policies, over 280,000 Jews, many entering illegally, arrive in Eretz Israel during the six-years before WW II. Majority originate from Germany and Poland and many are educated. Industrial production increases substantially in Eretz Israel.
   • Electricity - Rutenberg
   • Citrus - Packaging and Marketing (Jaffa brand)
   • Cement - Nesher
   • Vegetable Oils - Shemen
   • Wineries - Carmel
   • Dairy and Milk products - Tnuva
   • Dead Sea Works - potash, bromine
   • Hebrew Printing Press

1933   Haim Arlozorov, Head of the Political Department, Jewish Agency is murdered in Tel Aviv. His assassination shocks Jews of the Yishuv. Although it is thought the Revisionists are behind the murder, this case is never solved. Previous to his death, Arlozorov had dedicated himself to immediate immigration of Jews from Nazi Germany, making an agreement known as *ha'avara*, or transfer. German Jews could block their assets in Germany in deutche marks at a discounted rate and after 12 months purchase German manufactured goods, up to the maximum value of their discounted assets in Germany. Almost 140 million DM are transferred before outbreak of the war. Some 52,000 Jews use this conduit transferring their assets from abroad. Moshe Sharett-Shertok (1894-1965) fills Arlozorov's position. Sharett immigrates in 1906. During WW I he is active in recruiting members for the Jewish

Brigade of the British Army. He is Israel's 1st Foreign Minister and 2nd Prime Minister 1953-1955.

1933 Vladimir Ze'ev Jabotinsky takes a separate political path when disagreeing with Labor Party (Mapai) leader David Ben-Gurion's approach of using the Labor Union, Histadrut as comprehensive socialist workers organization- being both employer and employee.

1933 Sir Elly Silas Kadoorie (1867-1944) provides funds to establish an agricultural school at Sejera (Ilania) in Lower Galilee near Mt. Tabor. Graduates who join the Palmach include Itzhak Rabin, Yigal Allon and Haim Guri. Sir Elly and his brother Sir Ellis (1865-1922), born in Baghdad, settle in Hong Kong where they develop very successful business interests in both Hong Kong and Shanghai. Sir Elly is active in Jewish community affairs, elected President of the Palestine Foundation Fund in Shanghai. He contributed for the establishment of Hebrew University in Jerusalem 1925, Jewish schools in Eretz Israel, an Arab school in Tulkarem and educational institutions in Iraq.

1933 The Egged Bus Co-operative, the National Public Transport system is created from an amalgamation of the Jerusalem, Haifa, Central and Southern bus routes.

1934 The Daniel Sieff Institute opens in Rehovot, established with financial support from Israel and Rebecca Sieff of Great Britain, in memory of their son Daniel. Dr. Chaim Weizmann is appointed head this scientific institute, renamed **The Weizmann Institute of Science** in 1949, maintaining high academic standards of research and post-graduate study, including a Nobel Prize winner.

1934 The Zionist Executive establishes a new organization of Clandestine Immigration Operations (**Ha'apala**) of Jews. Between 1934 until statehood in 1948, Ha'apala will assist 122,000 Jews to enter Eretz Israel, including 22,000 clandestine immigrants who arrive between 1934 and 1939. (See Ha'apala 1945, 1946).

1934 The Yerushun Synagogue on King George Street, Jerusalem is inaugurated.

1934 Hussein Fakhri al-Khalildi is appointed Muslim mayor of Jerusalem (1934–1937). The British always appoint a Muslim mayor even though over 75% of taxpayers are Jewish.

1934 Naharia is established as a farming village on the coast, north of Acre, settled by many German Jews fleeing Nazi persecution, becoming a seaside resort with an industrial base (dairy, metal industries). Naharia is completely surrounded by Arabs during the War of Independence before its liberation by the IDF in 1948.

1934 Over 30,000 Arabs from Hauran (SW Syria/NW Jordan) move unrestricted into Palestine, attracted by work in and around the new British port in Haifa and construction of other infrastructure projects. They call Haifa '*Um el-Amal*' (the city of work).

1935 Water pumping stations built at Rosh Ha'ayin supply Jerusalem.

1935 Completion of Mosul-Haifa Pipeline from Iraq to Haifa, by-passing the Suez Canal. Local Arabs will frequently attack this pipeline, forcing the British to dispatch more troops. (See Wingate 1938).

1935 The Hagana begins to illegally manufacture arms (hand grenades) in **Mikve Israel**. Hagana creates a unit to deal with Arab terrorism.

Tel Aviv Kiosk in Rothschild Boulevard   Adrian Wolff

1935 The Nuremberg Laws are passed in Germany denying Jews all civil rights. Jewish educational facilities are closed; Jews are denied entry into Germany and encouraged to emigrate; marriage between Jews and non-Jewish Germans is prohibited. Jews are forbidden to employ a non-Jewish maid in their homes; and later, Jews are forced to wear an identifying yellow patch on their clothing. German Jews are banned from academic and professional positions in the fields of medicine, law, accounting, education, etc. German academics and churches are largely silent while protestors are unable to gather popular support as the majority of Germans embrace Hitler's racist measures. Many German and Polish Jewish immigrant families arrive in Eretz Israel during the 5th Immigration or Aliyah Hey, settling in Tel Aviv increasing the population in 1935 to over 120,000 inhabitants (all Jewish). In Tel Aviv there is an atmosphere of 'Europe in the Levant' with sidewalk cafes and boulevards.

Bauhaus Building, Rothschild Boulevard, Tel Aviv   Adrian Wolff

1935 **Bauhaus Architecture.** The Bauhaus school is founded by Walter Gropius in Weimar, Germany to create a comprehensive style in all arts including architecture."*Study its nature, then design to function properly. Fill its function in a practical way, be durable, inexpensive and beautiful.*" (Walter Gropius 1919). The Bauhaus style becomes influential in Modernist architecture and modern design. The school exists in three German cities (Weimar 1919-1925, Dessau 1925-1932, Berlin 1932-1933), under Walter Gropius (1919-1928), Hannes Mayer (1928-1930) and Ludwig Mies van der Rohe (1930-1933), when the school is closed under pressure from the Nazi regime. Many architects, now living in Tel Aviv had acquired training in architecture during the 1920's in the Bauhaus School in Germany. These principles of modernism or the '**International Style**' are applied to new building construction in Tel Aviv which has the largest concentration (4000) of Bauhaus buildings in the world and in 2003 is approved a UNESCO Heritage site 'The White City'. The municipality has designated over 1500 for preservation and restoration and many have been refurbished. Between 1931 and 1937 over 2700 new buildings are constructed in Tel Aviv using simple lines, high ceilings and smaller picture windows with cement overhangs to provide shade. Long narrow balconies, each shaded by the balcony above it, allow residents to catch the breeze blowing in from the sea to the west. Slanted roofs were replaced with flat ones, providing a common area where residents can socialize in the cool of the evening. Excellent examples of

Bauhaus architecture can be found at 29 Idelson and 3 Strauss streets, Tel Aviv. Buildings are raised on pillars to allow the wind to blow beneath to cool the apartments, also providing a play area for children. In the warm summer Tel Aviv as residents take to the streets to enjoy the evening air, frequenting the numerous small parks and coffee shops. This tradition continues in the café society and nightlife of the city today. Dizengoff Circle, planned by Jenia Averbouch is constructed in 1934.

1935   The 19th Zionist Congress at Lucerne led by Nahum Sokolov, elects Dr. Chaim Weizmann president and David Ben-Gurion Chairman of the Jewish Agency Executive.

1935   The poetess **Lea Goldberg**,(1911-1970) born Königsberg, Prussia 1911, immigrates in 1935 after having received her doctorate at the University of Bonn. She is a prolific Hebrew poet, author, playwright, translator, and researcher of Hebrew literature.

1935   James Grover McDonald (1886-1964) in 1933 is appointed High Commissioner for Refugees, affiliated to the League of Nations. He supports the emigration of German Jews, appealing to the US government and Vatican. President Roosevelt tells McDonald he would assist with a donation from Congress, however, few of his commitments ever become a reality, are at best, only partially or never implemented: e.g. *MS St. Louis* a passenger liner carrying 937, mostly German Jewish refugees, sailing from Hamburg 13 May 1939, is NOT permitted to dock in the USA. In addition the USA convinces Cuba to disallow embarkation, as did Canada.

In 1943 Roosevelt rejects Churchill's proposal to settle European Jews fleeing the Holocaust in recently liberated North Africa. He suggests arming Arabs to gain their support in the war effort.

McDonald is a member of The Anglo-American Committee of Inquiry on Palestine (1945) to examine the possibilities for mass settlement of European Jews in Palestine. Its final report 30 April 1946, calls for the immediate admission into Palestine of 100,000 Jewish Displaced Persons, rejected by British PM Attlee, also seen very negatively by British Foreign Minister Bevin. "*I had to tell myself that this was not Hitler seated before me*". McDonald is appointed the first US Ambassador to Israel.

1936   The British protects the TAPLINE (Trans-Arabian Oil Line) passing through British territory from Persian Gulf to Haifa (after 1948 to Sidon). Due to harsh desert climate, Britain build airfields for reconnaissance flights along the pipeline, H1, H2 etc. in Iraq.

1936   Britain construct about 15 airfields in Palestine and an international

Airport outside Lod.

1936 British High Commissioner in Palestine Lt.-Gen. Sir Arthur Wauchope (1931-1938), an Anglo-Boer War and WW I veteran, promises Arabs to examine their complaints of continuing Jewish immigration.

1936 The Supreme Muslim Council, (WAKF) later known as the Arab Higher Committee headed by the Mufti of Jerusalem, al-Husseini, **declares a General Strike and boycott of taxes. Arab riots and anti-British activities** begin in Jaffa on 15 April demanding 'The British stop all Jewish immigration' and 'Halt the sale of land to Jews'. After 16 Jews and 6 Arabs are killed in Jaffa, the British declare on 20 April a night curfew including closure of the port. British troops fire live ammunition at Arab rioters and close Arab newspapers for incitement, demolish Arab homes in the *casbah* on the hill overlooking the port, a source of terror organizations. Arab rioters are forced to sweep streets of debris. Jaffa is quiet after the operation. A road 10 meters wide is constructed through the *casbah* area of Old Jaffa today, to allow quick movement to and from the port and British Police Station opposite the Clock-Tower. Under British Mandatory Law, rioters can be detained and expelled without trial, and homes destroyed. British House of Commons criticizes the military for use of excessive force.

1936 From April to September 1936, 70 Jews are murdered by Arabs. Jewish homes and businesses looted, set ablaze, busses attacked, fields burnt, crops destroyed, and forests torched. Incited by the Arab Higher Committee, riots continue for three years until the outbreak of WW II in 1939. Violence against Jews takes place within the background of anti-Jewish persecution, laws and anti-Jewish economic measures in Germany in Poland.

1936 The Arabs persist in a campaign of sabotage, intimidation and murder against Jews and moderate Arabs. The British Administration continues to channel money to the Mufti, al-Husseini encouraging him to cease the violence. His anti-British propaganda and leading anti-Jewish riots continues as he receives funds from Nazi Germany. Arabs led by Izadin el-Khassam kill numerous British Policemen stationed in Palestine. During anti-Jewish riots Yemenite Jews living in Silwan (Siloan) in East Jerusalem, abandon their homes. In Safed, Muslim leader publicly calls for slaughter of Jews *'itbach al-Yehud'* murdering the Unger family - father and his three children aged 9,7,6.

1936 Zionist Executive gains permission to build a separate port in Tel Aviv. After statehood, Tel Aviv port will fall into disuse, especially after a new port is opened at Ashdod in 1966. From 2000 the Tel Aviv port will become a successful entertainment center.

Tower and Stockade, Sha'ar Hagolan, re-enactment   Adrian Wolff

1936   Hagana decides on a policy of restraint or *havlaga* following the Arab riots and does not retaliate or revenge the various Arab atrocities. All Jewish rural settlements are instructed to be surrounded by a defense system comprising fences, watchtowers and trenches under a policy of **Tower and Stockade**. New settlements are completed very rapidly, located in isolated, uninhabited, outlying areas. The first settlement is Tel Amal/Nir David (Gan Hashlosha) in the Jezreel Valley. From 1936 to 1939, 58 settlements are established and in the future, determine the boundaries of the State of Israel. Arab marauders are repulsed, no Jewish settlements are over-run during the riots 1936 to 1939, due to protection offered to settlers inside the Tower and Stockade structures, different to 1929 when certain Jewish settlements are captured. Many new Jewish immigrants move to rural settlements.

1936   Eliyahu Golumb initiates an active Jewish defense by creating *'plugot sadeh'* **(special operational field units).** Itzhak Sadeh, appointed commander of the *'plugot sadeh'*, is considered the father of the modern Israeli Defense Force and establishes the Palmach (strike force) in 1941. The *'plugot sadeh'* train for defense against Arab terrorist gangs and will gain further experience in Wingate's 'Special Night Squads' (see Wingate 1938). Operational techniques previously used to defend static settlements now change as these units attack Arab terrorists in their villages. During World War II Sadeh encourages Jews of the Yishuv to volunteer for active service in the British Army. The Hagana duplicates British Army training methods of field-craft and battle-procedure employing field-training in rural areas (not on the parade ground) and uses live ammunition, when available. The Hagana initiates new training methods. Soldiers must complete a training course before promotion, as seniority is not sufficient to rise in rank. Corporal, sergeant and officer courses are established.

1936 Arabs persist in a campaign of sabotage, intimidation, assassination of moderate Arabs who oppose the Mufti and anti-British riots. The British declare the Arab Higher Committee an illegal organization and the mufti, al-Husseini is removed as president of the Supreme Muslim Council. Consequently the British deport him to Lebanon for publishing anti-British propaganda, he moves to Damascus continuing his call for anti-Jewish rebellion. He visits Hitler in Berlin 28 November, 1941. The British appointed a Muslim Mayor of Jerusalem Hussein Fakhri al-Khalidi is deported to Seychelles for anti-British propaganda.

1936 Hagana establishes a committee to rescue European Jewry and assist their illegal entry and absorption into Eretz Israel.

1936 Vladimir Ze'ev Jabotinsky, the Betar leader is appointed head of the Etzel (Irgun Zeva Le'umi) National Military Organization. One of the policies of Etzel (also know as the Irgun) is reprisals against continual Arab terrorism and to revenge Jewish deaths.

1936 Construction of the Church of the Beatitudes overlooking Tabgha, where Jesus preached to the multitudes, **Antonio Barzluzzi** is the architect. (See 28CE).

1936 British construct a new road outside of the Old City walls to the Western Wall and Dung Gate, avoiding Arab quarters.

1936 Opening in Ramallah of the Palestine Broadcasting Station, later to become Israel Broadcasting Station. (Ramallah is situated at a higher altitude than Jerusalem)

1936 Bronislav Huberman (1882-1947) establishes the Palestine Symphony Orchestra, comprising top Jewish musicians he brought from Europe. The first concert is performed in Tel Aviv under the baton of maestro Arturo Toscanini. Later renamed the **Israel Philharmonic Orchestra** achieving international standards. The world-renown pianist Artur Rubinstein (1887–1982) is a regular performer in Tel Aviv with the IPO. He is reputed to say *'when people are sick they go to a doctor, in Tel Aviv they come to a concert'*. Rubinstein International Piano Competition is regularly held in Tel Aviv. He requested his ashes be strewn in Jerusalem.

1936 Jews living in the United States establish a central method to collect and transfer donations to Eretz Israel through the establishment of the 'United Jewish Appeal', UJA.

1936 Dr. Chaim Weizmann moves to his home in the grounds of Daniel Sieff Institute in Rehovot. Weizmann House is designed by Bauhaus architect Erich Mendelsohn, who also designs Hebrew University and Hadassah Hospital buildings on Mt. Scopus, Jerusalem; Hebrew University Agricultural Facility in Rehovot and Haifa Government Hospital. Before fleeing Nazi-Germany, Mendelsohn designs Einstein Tower at Potsdam, Germany in 1919, an outstanding example of Expressionist Architecture.

1936 Riots this year. Arabs murder 44 Jews in: Rosh Pina, Tiberias, Yavniel, Haifa, Kfar Horesh, Afula, Beit She'an, Karkur, Tel Aviv, Nes Ziona, Kiryat Anavim, Motza, Jerusalem and Beit Ha'arava.

1936 **Population** of Jerusalem is 125,000 including 76,000 Jews (61%).

Map 38. The Peel Commission Partition Plan, 1937

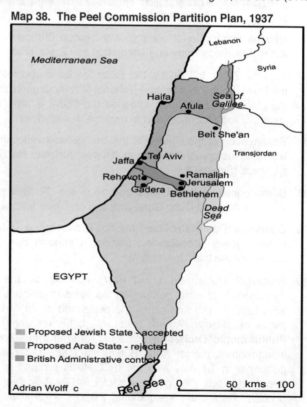

Proposed Jewish State - accepted
Proposed Arab State - rejected
British Administrative control

Adrian Wolff c

1937 **British Peel Commission calls for limiting Jewish immigration and physical Partition of Palestine between Jews and Arabs.** The Peel Commission proposes:

* A small Jewish state in the Coastal Plain and parts of the Galilee.
* An Arab state in Samaria, Judea, and the Negev.
* British control Jerusalem, Bethlehem, a corridor to Jaffa.

The Peel Commission signifies a change in official British policy towards Jews in Eretz Israel from a "national homeland" as written in the Balfour Declaration to 'A Jewish State' with defined borders. The Zionist Executive (Chaim Weizmann and David Ben Gurion) accepts the Peel Partition. **Arabs are offered statehood, reject these proposals outright and continue to riot and kill both Jews and British troops and police. Arabs oppose a Jewish State between the Jordan River and the Mediterranean Sea.**

1938 **Kibbutz Hanita** is founded near the Lebanese border, continuing the policy of establishing new settlements in outlying areas. This kibbutz will define the border with Lebanon in the Western Galilee.

1938 German Army invades Austria, known as 'Anschluss' or annexation. Austrians are ever willing to initiate new anti-Semitic laws and terror campaigns against Jews. At the **Evian Congress** delegates excuse their countries from accepting additional refugees. Britain excludes Palestine from the Evian discussion entirely. Australia could not accept refugees immigrating because, "*as we have no real racial problem, we are not desirous of importing one.*" **Britain pressurizes Greece, Yugoslavia, Bulgaria, Roumania and Turkey to disallow Jewish refugees from passing through their territories. The world's democracies made it clear that they were willing to do next to nothing for the Jews of Europe.**

1938 Arabs in Palestine continue rioting against Jewish immigration and settlements killing 59 Jews between May to July 1938. In Tiberias Arabs murder 19 Jews.

1938 British construct around Palestine 52 reinforced concrete defensive Police Stations designed by **Sir Charles Tegart,** previously British Commissioner of Police in Calcutta, India. These fortresses often at crossroads, provide protection to British Police and military operations and used as maintenance centers. A similar method is employed by the British in India during this period. Tegart also constructs a frontier fence along the northern border of Palestine with Lebanon to control movement of Arab insurgents smuggling goods and weapons into Palestine used in anti-British riots.

1938   Duties of British Army stationed in Palestine are primarily that of an Imperial Police Force - to maintain law and order between the local Arabs and Jews. British troops are almost totally indifferent to and ignorant of local political affairs, not familiar with background to the political situation and uninvolved in the emerging Zionist nationalism in Eretz Israel. The aim of the Jews is to establish their national homeland Eretz Israel as Britain had committed itself in the Balfour Declaration of 1917. Absentee landlords are selling their lands to Jews. Arab nationalism is also emerging concurrently and is violently opposed to any Jewish presence in Eretz Israel whose growth is seen as a territorial threat to Arabs. The ex-Mufti of Jerusalem, al-Husseini, now living in Damascus actively encourages Arabs to riot. Local Arabs volunteer for the armed forces by providing lines of communication, secure bases and safe houses for terrorists who are targeting Jews and Jewish settlements (villages, kibbutzim and moshavim) in outlying areas and Jewish Quarters of the various towns. **It never occurs to Arabs, nor would the Mufti of Jerusalem ever allow possibility of any peace talks or co-existence with the Jews.**

1938   British Army Captain, **Orde Wingate** (1903-1944), has a *"formidable willpower and determination"* (King-Clark), is regarded as one of the founders of modern guerrilla warfare, became an ardent Zionist. He is a deeply religious Christian having a thorough knowledge of the Bible serving him as a spiritual, historical and geographical guide. He learns Arabic during his tour of duty with the Sudan Defense Force (1928-1933), explores remote parts of Abyssinia and leads an expedition deep into Libyan Desert. Wingate learns to speak Hebrew and constantly refers to passages from the Bible, which impresses Jewish soldiers, many of them immigrants who have little knowledge of the language. Wingate, an artillery officer, is posted to Palestine as an Intelligence Corps Officer from 1936 until 1939. He writes *"Principles Governing the Employment of Special Night Squads"* and *"Training of Jewish Supernumeraries"*, ignoring traditional British 'spit and polish' while stressing importance of thorough training (field-craft). In 1941, during WW II, Wingate, together with support from Haile Selassie's Ethiopian Forces, capture Addis Ababa from the Italians. In 1944, he successfully severs the important Mandalay-Myitkyina railway line in Burma. Shortly afterwards Major-General Orde Charles Wingate is killed in an airplane crash in Burma, aged 41. He is buried, together with the American aircrew in Arlington Cemetery, Washington DC.

Lieutenant Robert (Rex) King-Clark, 1st Manchester's Regiment, is redeployed from Ismalia to Palestine in 1937, posted to Mount

Canaan, outside Safed. The unit commands a motorized machine-gun regiment to provide military escorts to the supply-convoys between Nazareth, Safed and Tiberias. Captain Orde Wingate informs King-Clark to report together with a NCO and ten men with two 15-cwt trucks and drivers for a secret position of special duty at Ayelet Hashahar in the Hula Valley, joined by Corporal Fred Howbrook. King-Clark then moves to Kibbutz Afikim until September 1938. Wingate establishes two other squads, at Kibbutz Hanita under Lt. Mike Grove and at Kibbutz Ein Harod under Lt. 'Bala' Bredin, where Captain Wingate establishes his headquarters. During WW II Lt.- Col. R King-Clark, Lt.- Col. M.R.L Grove, Maj.-Gen. H.E.N Bredin. These officers do not have any prior or special feeling for Jews or the Zionist Cause.

On instructions from Wingate, British troops train Hagana 'plugot sadeh' members in basic military skills - drill, weapon-handling, field-craft and battle-drill tactics. At night, they operate to prevent terrorist activity by searching for and eliminating Arab terrorists. Operations are between the Lebanon border in the north; Transjordan frontier in the East; Jezreel Valley in the south and Meron road in the west. Wingate calls the unit "**Special Night Squads**" since they would mainly operate at night. It is assumed Wingate chose to establish his squads without the prior knowledge of the British Military headquarters in Palestine. Arab terrorists ignite the Mosul-Haifa Oil pipeline by placing an oil-soaked rag beneath it, piercing the pipeline with rifle-fire, resulting in a conflagration seen for many miles around. The policy of the Oil Company is against retaliation, which they thought would encourage further sabotage.

Rather than operate from British Army bases, Wingate uses kibbutzim to provide complete security of operational planning and preparation on a highly confidential level, receiving reliable information on terrorist movements from Jewish sources. Trucks transport the squads fifteen kilometers from their goal and the remaining distance is covered on foot to achieve surprise. Squads walk at night 20-30 kilometers in silence in single file over trackless hilly country, with the possibility of meeting armed terrorists at any moment. The countryside is very stony with waist-high thorns. The squads enter Arab villages without warning and without a British Police escort. The Night Raids last from 1938 to 1939 performing two long patrols and one short patrol each week during the eighteen months period. In over 20 operations more than 100 terrorists are killed. The SNS consists of 5 British officers and 36 soldiers together with 80 'Israelis'. The Hagana learns from Wingate's theory and operational methods. In 1939 all the British

Officers are transferred to the Far East to assist with build up of British Forces before World War II. The Night Raids are successful in containing Arab terrorism.

1938   British Army and Police quell Arab riots in the north and then move southwards. They apply force and sometimes use of artillery fire on civilian areas (Jenin). British Military Governors are appointed in the Galilee, Jerusalem, Hebron. Arabs continue their anti-British and anti-Jewish campaign of murder, intimidation and sabotage, including attacks on Jews traveling towards Jerusalem.

1938   Completion of the Romanian Orthodox Church on Shivtei Israel Street, Jerusalem, with its double domes and gilded ceilings. Construction in Ein Kerem of a Catholic Church, The Shrine of the Visitation. Antonio Barluzzi is the architect.

1938   Germany annexes Sudetenland in Czechoslovakia. Many residents of Sudetenland are of German descent. Prior to WW I, Sudetenland is part of Austro-Hungary. Germans perpetrate **Kristallnacht** (The Night of Broken Glass) when frenzied anti-Semitic mobs burn nearly half of the synagogues in Germany, murder nearly 100 Jews and arrest over 30,000 Jews (10% of Germany's Jewish population) who are sent to concentration camps. Jewish religious objects are desecrated or destroyed while the police stand by. Afterwards the Jewish community is fined one billion Reichsmarks to pay for the damage.

1938   British hang Betar member Shlomo Ben-Yosef (born Tabachnik in 1913, Poland) in Acre prison after finding him guilty of a failed attempt to retaliate against an Arab bus traveling from Rosh Pina to Safed and Acre following the murder of Jews by Arabs. Hagana member Mordechai Shwartz, (1914-1938), is hanged by the British in Acre prison for possession of weapons.

1938   The Arab campaign of hostility and inflexibility to the partition plan, together with widespread campaign of murder and intimidation, compels the British **Woodhead Commission** to revise the Peel Commission Plan of 1937, limiting Jewish immigration. Jews are to control Galilee, retain Jezreel and Hula Valleys and Metula. British appoint Muslim Mustafa al-Khalidi Jerusalem mayor 1938-1944.

1938   Opening of the **Hadassah Hospital** on Mt. Scopus, Jerusalem, deigned by Erich Mendelsohn. (See Hadassah 1948; 1961; 1962; 1975). Jews in the Diaspora, mainly in the USA contribute through donations for the construction and running of the hospital. Hadassah Hospital treats both Arab and Jew alike and will become world renown for its standard of excellence in teaching, training, diagnosis, rehabilitation, research and development, and caring for the sick. The Hadassah Organization sponsors teaching facilities in nursing, public health, optometry etc.

Hadassah Nursing School 1918, Tipat Halav for the well-baby mother and child clinics, Technological education in youth villages and Hadassah College of Technology 1930's, Hadassah Medical School 1949, Hadassah Dental School 1953, Hadassah Community Services 1953, Hadassah Occupational Therapy School 1978, Hadassah Public Health School 1980. "*For I will cure you and heal you from your wounds.*" (Jeremiah 30:17).

1938 Central Post Office Building is constructed in Jaffa Road, Jerusalem.

1938 During 1938, 94 Jews are killed by Arab terrorists.

Summary Arab Riots 1936 – 1939, estimates (Dr. Yigal Eyal)
Arabs killed = 5000, injured = 14,000, expelled = 5600, homes destroyed = 2000

Jews killed = 300–400

The British execute about 140 Arabs prisoners in Acre during the 1936-1939 Arab Strikes.

The British never bombed or used artillery on Jewish civilian areas.

Chapter 22. WW II until UN Partition 1939 - 1947

1939 **Sixth Immigration or Aliyah Vav** (1939-1945). On the eve of World War II, Central and Eastern European Jews are desperate to emigrate. Five refugee ships bringing immigrants to Eretz Israel are sunk, resulting in 3000 Jewish deaths.

1939 Britain desires stability and non-violence in Palestine, allowing their troops to enter the impending European war theater. British Colonial Secretary Malcolm MacDonald wishes to appease the Arabs and issues a **White Paper** permitting Jewish immigration to Eretz Israel only with Arab consent.

The White Paper, Palestine, Statement of Policy, May 1939

3. *After a period of 5 years no further Jewish immigration (total 75,000) will be permitted unless the Arabs of Palestine are prepared to acquiesce in it.*

16. *Sale of Arab land to Jews must be restricted...Arab(s)...are to maintain the existing standard of life...High Commissioner will be given...powers to prohibit and regulate transfer of land.*

Arabs entry is not restricted between 1922 to 1939 as more Arabs enter Palestine than Jews. This edict will severely limit Jewish immigration to 1500 a month in the face of the continuing anti-Jewish policy of Nazi Germany and the imminent outbreak of a World War. The White Paper bans the sale of more than 5% of the land to Jews. Jews in the Yishuv regard the White Paper as a British plan to establish an Arab Palestinian State without an independent Jewish state. This policy is not fully implemented, opposed by PM Sir Winston Churchill. The cabinet postpones this subject until the end of the War.

1939 The **Kindertransports** (Children) rescue operation begins after a violent pogrom of 9 November 1938, **Kristallnacht**. The Jewish community in Palestine requests to accept 10,000 Jewish children from the German Reich. However, the British in Palestine are unwilling to accept the children owing to the very restrictive immigration policy. The British government allows the children into Great Britain. From December 1938 until the outbreak of World War II, organized groups of 9354 children and youth, 70% of them Jewish, reach Great Britain. (Yad Vashem).

1939 WW II is a continuation of the unfinished economic, social and political changes that followed WW I. On 1 September 1939 German troops invade Poland. On 3 September Great Britain evokes its Peace Agreement with Poland, entering into war with

Germany, as **World War II begins. The Mufti and Arabs side with Nazi Germany.** *"Co-operation with Nazi Germany is meant to give a free hand to destroy all Jews in Arab countries and in Palestine".* (Mufti). **During the darkest hours of Jewish history, the Holocaust, the British break their previous promises to the Jews - the Balfour Declaration - to allow Jewish immigration into Palestine.** Jews of the Yishuv view British government policies as decidedly anti-Zionist.

1939   The Jews in the Yishuv support the British during the period of the war, while the Jewish Resistance Movements Etzel, Lehi (אצ"ל-האירגון הצבא הלאומי בארץ ישראל, לח"י-לוחמי חירות ישראל) operate underground. The Zionist Executive leadership, under David Ben-Gurion, begin a non-cooperation policy with British authorities and concurrently cease anti-British activities during the War. The Jewish leadership promotes illegal immigration of Jews. The Jewish Agency finances the Zionist Executive's activities.
Leaders are:
Hagana - Moshe Sneh, Yisrael Galli
Etzel - Menachem Begin, Natan Yellin-Mor
Lehi - Avraham (Yair) Stern

1939   **Abraham Yair Stern** (1907-1942) immigrates in 1925. He resigns from the Etzel/Irgun in 1939, establishing a separate organization to achieve Jewish sovereignty in Eretz Israel. They regard Britain as an enemy, using armed revolt to force their withdrawal. (See Stern, Lehi 1942). Etzel (Revisionists) torch the British Department of Migration building in Jerusalem. Menachem Begin is appointed head of the Betar organization in Poland.

1939   British Authorities do not have legal authority to conscript Palestinian civilians into the British Army. About 30,000 Jews from Eretz Israel volunteer to fight in the British Army, positioned in logistics and communications units. Their knowledge of war operations and methods will assist the Hagana to establish the Israel Defense Force after the war. Jewish soldiers from Eretz Israel operate in Greece, Crete, France, Malta and Italy and 700 volunteers are killed in action serving in the British Army. Their names are engraved on the wall beneath the memorial at Yad Vashem, Jerusalem. Towards the war end, the **Jewish Brigade** consisting of 5000 volunteers are active in Northern Italy under their own flag. (See Jewish Brigade 1944, 1945). Only a few score of Arabs volunteer to serve while many Arabs continue their anti-Jewish policies. General Archibald Wavell, British C-O-C of Middle East Command is strongly pro-Arab and against providing the Jews with defensive weapons. Despite British official anti-Zionist position, Jews of the Yishuv are not hostile to British soldiers stationed in Palestine. Britain views Jews in Palestine as their most pro-British allies in the Middle East, constructing British Army camps (Tel Hashomer, Saraband, Ras el Ain (Rosh Ha'ayin)), for training, Rest and Recreation centers, and a center for treating and rehabilitating the sick and wounded. Local industry and agriculture expands to supply the British war effort.

1939 The Zionist Executive appoints Ya'akov Dori first Chief of Staff of Hagana (Jewish Defense Organization), later of the IDF.

1940 Hagana sabotages the *Patria* in Haifa with over 5000 immigrants, attempting to force the British to accept their entry. The ship sinks, 260 are drowned. British transfer 1600 immigrants to Mauritius.

1940 **British restrict Jewish land purchases** in the Galilee, Carmel, Samaria, Judea, Southern Coastal Plain and Negev enacting Land Transfer Regulations and begin a policy of harassment of Hagana members. Ben-Gurion declares the British as 'bad faith'.

1940 The Citrus Marketing Board is established, export under the brand name '*Jaffa*', are internationally known for their high quality.

1940 Revisionist leader Vladimir Ze'ev Jabotinsky dies suddenly during a mission to New York. In 1965, his remains together with his wife Johanna are reburied in a state ceremony on Mt. Herzl.

1940 Italian bombers flying from pro-Vichy Syria, drop bombs on Tel Aviv, killing 17 and again in 1941 (12 July), killing 22 civilians.

1940 German aircraft accidentally drop bombs on London, leading to a British retaliatory strike on Berlin.

1940 Germany shelves '*Operation Sea Lion*' (invasion of Britain), prepares to capture Gibraltar, North Africa, Suez Canal and Middle East.

1940 About 100,000 Jews are murdered in Europe from 1933 until 1940.

1940 During 1940, 137 Jews are killed in Arab terrorist attacks in Israel.

1941 An estimated 30% of the local Templer inhabitants of various German Colonies in Palestine (See Templers 1866) are interned or expelled (to Australia), for having pro-Nazi sympathies and for flying Nazi flags. Some volunteer to serve in the Wehrmacht and Gestapo. In 1952 the German government compensates Israel and Jewish Holocaust survivors for Nazi atrocities, reducing from the final sum the value of German (Templer) properties in Israel.

1941 Jewish youth volunteer for active military training in the Yishuv. The Hagana establishes a special commando operations unit the

Palmach (*plugot mahatz* = strike force) with 1000 initial volunteers, ensuring all have a high standard of physical fitness and ability. Over 7000 will volunteer to serve, and over 1000 killed. The Palmach combines 14 days military training with agricultural work for 16 days a month. The kibbutz movement pays their monthly stipend and provides training facilities on their lands. **Itzhak Sadeh commands the Palmach with Yigal Allon as his deputy.** Sadeh already has an extensive military career during WW I in the Russian Army; deputy commander of Trumpeldor's Gedud Ha'avoda; commander of Hagana special field units (plugot sadeh); participates in Wingate's SNS; Second-in-Command of the Hagana. All Hagana and Palmach operations are clandestine, termed illegal by the British.

1941 Following continual British Army defeats in North Africa, the German Army is now positioned in Libya, Greece, Crete and the Caucasus causing Britain to be concerned Turkey will enter the war, siding with Nazi Germany. Fearing an invasion from Vichy Lebanon, the British Army erects anti-tank boulders in the Carmel Mountains near Beit Oren. The British Army finances and trains the Palmach as a guerrilla unit to operate against the Germans/Turks should the British evacuate Palestine. They promote Jewish Arabic-speaking agents to enter Arab areas gaining information. The British term this operation PPOF (Palestine Post-Occupation Force). This support of the Palmach ends when the British Army has military gains in North Africa.

1941 The Jewish leadership fear a British defeat, now voice the subject of a second mass suicide. The Palmach (Yigal Allon (1918-1980) and Moshe Dayan (1915-1981 who is shot in the eye) assist the British in reconnaissance. The British invasion of Lebanon and Syria (before WW II is under French control) successfully expels the pro-Nazi Vichy-French provisional governments.

1941 A naval commando unit, **Palyam** (Palmach sailors) is established to assist illegal immigrants arrive in Eretz Israel. British recruit 23 Palyam naval and Hagana commandos ("*Yordei Ha'sira*") led by a British officer Major Sir Anthony Palmer to sabotage the Oil Refineries in Tripoli, Lebanon (18 May 1941) serving the German Air Force. All members and their vessel the '*Sea Lion*' disappear before arriving at their goal. There is no knowledge of their fate.

1941 Rashid Ali al-Khilani is a follower and admirer of Hitler. Promising oil, he leads a rebellion to establish a Nazi-style regime in Iraq. The deposed Mufti of Jerusalem al-Husseini participates in this pro-German coup in Iraq, issuing a '***fatwa***' against British interests in Iraq. "*I invite all my Muslim brothers throughout the whole world to* *join in a holy war for Allah....Proud Iraq has placed herself in the vanguard of this holy struggle."* (Yad Vashem). Arabs kill 179 Jews during riots in Baghdad, Basra and other towns in Iraq. Over 5000 Jewish homes and businesses are looted or destroyed. Local police make no effort to protect the Jews. On a pro-British mission to bomb the oil fields controlled by the pro-Nazi regime in Iraq, Etzel commander David Raziel, (1910-1941) is killed outside Baghdad when his vehicle is strafed by a German fighter. Ya'akov Meridor (1913–1995) is appointed Etzel commander. The British defeat the pro-German revolt in Iraq, as their leaders including Haj Amin al-Husseini flee Iraq to Nazi Germany where he meets Adolf Hitler. He pledges full Arab cooperation with the Nazi regime, including the recruitment of Arab soldiers to fight the British, espionage, propaganda and the training of Arabs (include Anwar Sadat) as Nazi agents. (See Husseini 1944).

1941   The Ba'ath Party is founded in Damascus by Michel Aflaq and Salah al-Din Bitar. Its aim is to unify the whole Arab world including Palestine into one Arab country.

1941   **Moshe Sneh** (1909-1972) a medical doctor from Poland immigrates to Eretz Israel in 1939, is appointed the political head of the National Command of the Hagana.

1941   During 1941, Nazis murder over 1,100,000 Jews.

1942   The British permit the Palmach to establish an air-wing to train pilots in light aircraft. Over 2500 Hagana volunteers serve in various administrative positions in Royal Air Force. Less than 10 will have actual battle combat experience by end of WW II.

1942   The Zionist Executive denounces all anti-British actions of Avraham Yair Stern and his Lehi splinter group. A Lehi representative, sent to meet with the German Nazi consul in Beirut, is caught by the British. Later the British capture another representative Nathan Yellin-Friedman (Mor) in Halab (Aleppo), Syria, on his way to meet with the German Nazi consul in Ankara, Turkey. The British decide to silence Stern who is captured in the Florentine Quarter of Tel Aviv, killing him, reputedly while handcuffed. Only after Stern is killed, do his followers take on the name **Lehi** - Lochomei Herut Israel (Fighters for the Freedom of Israel) and sometimes are also known as 'The Stern Gang'. Itzhak Shamir becomes a member of the tripartite Lehi leadership together with Israel Eldad (Scheib) and Nathan Yellin-Friedman (Mor). Many Lehi members are exiled to camps in Africa, while others are jailed and a few killed in operations. After the end of WW II the Lehi and Etzel attack the British Mandatory Authorities for their continued refusal to allow unlimited entry of Jewish immigrants into Eretz Israel. In 1948 Lehi and Etzel are absorbed into the Israel Defense Force on the establishment of the State.

1942   In the Black Sea, a Soviet submarine torpedoes and sinks the Jewish refugee ship, the **Struma** holding 769 Romanian Jews. The ship had previously been refused disembarkation by both Turkish and British authorities. There are only two survivors.

1942   Representatives of Jewish Agency locate nearly 1000 orphaned Jewish children in Poland. They travel through Russia, Persia, Iraq sail to Suez, reach Eretz Israel by train on 18 February 1943 known as the 'Teheran Children'. British Authorities allow their entry.

1942   **Menachem Begin** (born Brisk, Lithuania 1913, dies Jerusalem 1992) previously a leader of Betar in Poland arrives in Eretz Israel with the Polish Army of General Wladyslaw Anders. In 1943 he is appointed leader of Etzel (Irgun Zeva Le'umi - National Military Organization) which will fight the British for Jewish Independence. Begin is influenced by the teachings of Vladimir Ze'ev Jabotinsky. He encourages debating and is elected 7th Prime Minister of the State of Israel from 1977 to 1983, is the first Israeli Prime Minister to sign a Peace Treaty with an Arab country, Egypt, in 1979.

1942   During 1942, Nazis massacre over 2,700,000 Jews.

1943   The Jewish Agency Zionist Executive establishes Kibbutz Revivim, the southernmost of the first of three *"mitzpim"* **outposts**, (Revivim, Gevulot and Beit Eshel) in the Negev. Their existence influences the United Nations' 1947 decision to include the Negev into the borders of the soon to be established State of Israel. Mitzpe Revivim is built like a castle with an internal courtyard surrounded by a stone wall for protection against Arab marauders. The roof is used as a watchtower. Revivim loses many of its members, immigrants from Italy in Arab raids and acts of terrorism before Independence in 1948. Members of Revivim participate in the battle for Bir Asluj (Nitzana) temporarily halting the advance of the Egyptian Army in 1948.

1943   The reconstruction is completed of al-Aqsa Mosque on the Temple Mount, Jerusalem previously damaged in the earthquake of 1927.

1943   **The British Government will not allow unlimited Jewish immigration from Nazi Europe into Eretz Israel, especially as the British FM Anthony Eden tells his private secretary Oliver Harvey that he *"loves Arabs and hates Jews"*.** (See Harvey, Oliver. *"The Diplomatic Diaries of Oliver Harvey 1941-1945"*).

1943   **Lebanon** achieves independence from the French mandate.

1943   During 1943, the Nazis murder over 500,000 Jews.

Map 39. Jewish Settlements in the Negev 1941 – 1946

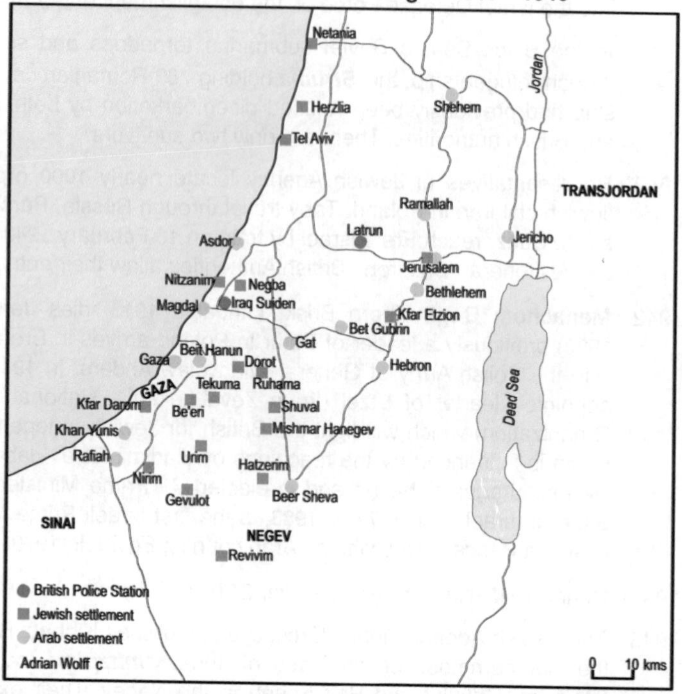

1944   Haj Amin al-Husseini broadcasts on German radio 1 March 1944:
        "***Arabs arise as one man and fight for your sacred rights. Kill
        the Jews where ever you find them.***" (Yad Vashem).

1944   Prime Minister of Great Britain Sir Winston Churchill suggests the
        establishment of a Jewish State in Eretz Israel. The British High
        Commissioner Sir Harold MacMichael (1938-1944) approves the
        proposal. **The British War Office does not carry out Churchill's
        order to bomb the Auschwitz Death Camp in Poland. The US
        Air Force bombs the factory area of Auschwitz but not the gas
        chambers or railway line. On average 20,000 Jews are killed
        every day in each of the larger Death Camps of Auschwitz and
        Treblinka in Poland.** Churchill permits the formation of the **Jewish
        Brigade** in the British Army, with volunteers from Eretz Israel.
        British War Office objects to Jewish Brigade serving the in Middle
        East and is against a Jewish insignia.

1944   A group of 37 volunteers are trained as parachutists, while 27 are
        dropped into Europe to organize Jewish resistance and rescue

schemes in Hungary to thwart deportation to the Death Camps. Germans capture 12. Yoel Palgi survives his capture and torture. Seven including the poetess **Hannah Szenes, Enzo Sereni, Haviva (Emma) Reik, Rafael Reiss and Zvi Ben Ya'akov** are caught and executed by the Nazis. Their remains are returned to Israel in 1950 for burial in the Military Cemetery on Mt. Herzl, Jerusalem. The Hebrew poem '*Marching to Caesarea*' (*Eli, Eli* in Hebrew) by Hannah Szenes is preserved in Israeli culture and sung by every generation.

My God, my God	אלי, אלי
May these things never end,	שלא יגמר לעולם
The sand and the sea,	החול והים
The patter of the water,	רשרוש של המים
The lightening of the sky,	ברק בשמים
And prayer of man.	תפלת האדם

1944   The British policy to restrict Jewish immigration causes two Jewish resistance movements the Etzel and Lehi to join forces in a campaign of terror to pressurize the British to leave. Even though they will carry out over 300 operations, the actions of the Etzel and Lehi are disputed to have none or little influence on hastening the British withdrawal. The Etzel attack three British police stations (Jerusalem, Jaffa, Haifa) killing six British policemen. Later they raid the British radio station at Ramallah. The Zionist Executive disassociates itself from Jewish counter reactions. The Lehi/Stern Gang, a splinter group, makes an unsuccessful attempt to assassinate the British High Commissioner Sir Harold MacMichael. In Cairo, the Lehi assassinate Lord Moyne (Walter Edward Guinness, 1880-1944), the British Minister of State in the Middle East. This action has wide repercussions as the British Administration takes a severe anti-Zionist line. Two Lehi members Eliyahu Hankin and Eliyahu Tzuri who perpetrate the assassination are caught and hanged in Acre prison. Etzel raids British Police headquarters in Tel Aviv-Jaffa, Beit Dagan, Haifa, and Kalkilia.

1944   The ex-Mufti of Jerusalem al-Husseini plans to poison the water systems of Tel Aviv in **'Operation Atlas.'** On 5 November 1944, three Germans and two Arabs parachute southeast of Jericho. The head of the operation Kurt Wieland is a resident of the German Colony in Jerusalem and Hassan Salame a leader of the Palestinian Revolutionists against the British. They carry 10 containers with a deadly arsenic poison. Bedouins witness the parachuting and inform the British police. Four are located while Hassan Salame, escapes (later killed at Castel by the IDF in the War of Independence). Separately the Electricity structure and the main gasoline pipe from Iraq to Haifa are damaged.

1944   Hagana remains officially against anti-British activities during wartime capturing Etzel and Lehi fighters in the **'Small Season'** Operation (December 1944 to March 1945) handing them to the British, creating ill-feeling among Jews. Incarceration of Jewish underground leaders is to be for a 'season', a short while.

1944   In 1944 Nazis murder over 600,000 Jews, many are Hungarian Jews

1945   The **Jewish Brigade** with 5000 soldiers is formed within the British 8th Army with its own emblem, a Magen David on a background of blue and white, commanded by General Ernest Benjamin (1900-1969), a Canadian serving in the Royal Engineers. During the war 30,000 Palestine Jews volunteer to serve in the British forces, over 700 are killed in action. The Jewish Brigade serves with distinction in Egypt, North Africa and on the Senio River front in Italy. They assist Jewish Displaced Persons to Immigrate to Israel. Military experience and battle-procedure methods acquired by members of the Jewish Brigade have a very significant and positive value in the formation of the infant Israel Defense Force that will be forced to fight for the survival of the Jewish State, when upon gaining its independence in 1948, five Arab armies invade.

1945   An underground munitions factory producing bullets is located on a hill in Rehovot, called the **'Ayalon Institute'**. This 'illegal operation' operated by 45 men and women in 2 daily shifts, is hidden from the British underneath a kibbutz 24-hour daily laundry service. The noise from the factory is absorbed by the washing machines. Over 2 million 9mm bullets are transported in milk cartons, and in fuel trucks. The factory operated until Independence in 1948 when the workers establish Kibbutz Ma'agan Michael. Hand grenades and mortars are illegally manufactured from 1935 at the **Mikve Israel Agricultural School**.

1945   **The Arab League** founded in Cairo, is a confederation of Arab states to further unify Arab decisions, "*to strengthen the ties between the participants, to coordinate their political program...and to consider in general the affairs and interests of Arab countries*". A permanent secretary resides at Arab League headquarters in Cairo. **The Arab League propaganda attempts to prevent the creation of a Jewish State in Palestine**.

1945   Great Britain grants **Transjordan** independence on 23 March 1945.

1945   On 12 April 1945 France terminates its mandate for **Syria**, now an independent country. Syria, previously part of the Ottoman Empire, became a French Mandate from 1922 until the British invaded and expelled the pro-Vichy French Administration in 1941.

1945 Following unconditional surrender of German Forces, **WW II ends in Europe on 8 May 1945.** After the second atomic bomb is dropped on Japan on 14 August 1945, Japan will surrender on 2 September. **Six million Jews including 1.5 million Jewish children are killed during the Holocaust 1933-1945. About 250,000 Jews remain in Displacement Camps. Over 40% will immigrate to Israel.**

Following the horror and treatment of civilians in both World Wars, The Fourth Geneva Convention of 1949 declares 'the Protection of Civilians in Time of War.' The Book of Deuteronomy 20:10,13, written 3000 years earlier describes *"When you draw near to a city to wage war against it, you shall call out to it for peace...But if it does not make peace with you...You shall smite all its males.* (not the women and children)". Post WW II era brings the disintegration of the British Empire, with two new superpowers - USA and Soviet Union and the rise of China and Japanese economic power.

1945 During WW II over 1,500,000 Jewish soldiers serve in Allied Armies, including 550,000 in US Army, and 500,000 in Red Army. Over 30,000 Jewish volunteers from Palestine serve with British Army. Over 200,000 Jewish soldiers are killed in service in Red Army. Another 80,000 Jewish soldiers (over 50,000 U.S.) are killed while serving in various Allied Armies. Thousands of Jewish Partisans in Nazi-occupied territory attack German communication and transportation facilities.

1945 After the cessation of hostilities, members of the Jewish Brigade enter Concentration and Displaced Persons Camps. The mere presence of these Jewish soldiers in the camps, with a Star of David insignia on their sleeves, together with their assistance and care for the Holocaust survivors, encourage many to immigrate to Eretz Israel and help fight for its survival. Many Eastern European Holocaust survivors, now stateless refugees are uncomfortable and insecure returning to their homes; or to live under Communist regimes now reaching Berlin. Representatives of the Jewish Agency assist Jewish refugees to trek towards the Mediterranean Sea ports in France and Italy where they embark on illegal immigrant transport ships (usually very over-crowded, old vessel, not meant for this purpose) and sail for Eretz Israel. *"I am opening your graves and raising you up...My people, and I will bring you to the soil of Israel."* (Ezekiel 37:12,14).

1945 After World War II until statehood in 1948 over 85,000 clandestine illegal Jewish immigrants, mainly Holocaust survivors enter through *Ha'apala* operations (See Ha'apala 1934, 1946).

1945 British Prime Minister Sir Winston Churchill rejects a plea from Dr.

Chaim Weizmann for the creation of a Jewish State in Eretz Israel. British Labour Party's Clement Atlee (1883-1967) is elected Prime Minister, continuing anti-Zionist, pro-Arab British foreign policies of the pre-war White Paper restricting immigration of Jews to Eretz Israel. (The British Labour Party platform of 1944 is against the White Paper, favoring a Jewish State, mentions transferring the Arab population to Transjordan. The Labour Party, once in power in 1945, ignores these statements in its party manifesto. See Peters.) An Anglo-American committee begins its inquiries into Jewish refugees in Europe. (See James Grover McDonald 1935).

1945   Itzhak Sadeh is appointed to the Hagana General Staff. He influences training, tactics and strategy including reconnaissance, field engineering, naval and air operations. Yigal Allon is head of Palmach special operations battalions, replaces Itzhak Sadeh.

1945   Following cessation of hostilities in Europe, the Zionist Executive instructs Hagana and Palmach to begin anti-British operations hastening them to leave Eretz Israel. Hagana ship *Berl Katznelson* bringing Jewish refugees is intercepted by British troops after most passengers land on the coast fleeing into awaiting Hagana trucks.

Hagana ship 'Dov Hoz' arrives legally with 1014 passengers after hunger strike at La Spezia, Italy.   Ha'mapalim Museum, Atlit

1945   The Zionist Executive appoints Moshe Sneh as the representative in Paris. He will be instrumental in convincing Russia (Soviet Union) to support the establishment of the Jewish State.

1945   Anti-Jewish rioters loot Jewish-owned business and kill 130 Jews in Cairo and Alexandria in Egypt and another 140 in Tripoli, Libya.

1945 British Foreign Minister **Ernest Bevin** (1881-1951) **announces Britain never promised to create a Jewish State, but only a homeland for Jews.** Jews riot in Tel Aviv. British troops open fire, killing six. **The British continue the White Paper policy of restricting Jewish immigration and land purchases.** Following the Bevin statement, the Etzel attack British Police Stations in Jerusalem and Jaffa, killing 10 soldiers and policemen.

1945 The Zionist Executive follows a 'struggle policy' *'ma'avak'* to promote immigration and settlement of Jews. Palmach soldiers cut the fence of the British Detention Camp (for illegal immigrants) at **Atlit**. Over 200 interned illegal immigrants, previously from the Displaced Persons Camps in Europe, walk to freedom towards Beit Oren, to be dispersed among the Jewish population of Haifa. No lives either British or Jewish are lost in this operation. During *The Night of the Coastal Police Stations*, the Hagana blowup British Police Stations at Givat Olga near Hadera and Sidna-Ali in Herzlia used for surveying the coast for illegal immigrants vessels. The Hagana continues its anti-British policies sabotaging 153 different locations on the railway lines in *The Night of the Trains*.

Atlit Detention Center Barracks   Adrian Wolff

1945 **Census** 445,000 Jews and 927,000 Arabs, total 1,502,000.

1946 British PM **Attlee** rejects the immediate transfer of 100,000 Jewish refugees from Displacement Camps in Europe to Eretz Israel as agreed in the Anglo-American Committee of Inquiry of 1945. The Zionist Executive considers influencing the PM Attlee through diplomatic channels of US President Truman who sends his personal representative to London, to be rejected by Attlee. Jews attempting to immigrate are sent to Detention Camps in Cyprus.

1946 **Seventh Immigration or Aliyah Zayin** movement from 1946 till Independence in May 1948. Over 50,000 illegal immigrants, mostly Holocaust survivors from Europe evade the British, entering Eretz Israel. The British detain Jewish immigrants (at Atlit), survivors of the Nazi Holocaust on their arrival at Haifa; 52,000 (over 80% in the 13-25 age-bracket), are deported and transferred to 12 Detention Camps in Cyprus, released only in 1949.

1946 The Hagana carries out *The Night of the Radar Stations* blowing up British Radar Stations at Stella Maris on the Carmel Mountain overlooking the Haifa Bay, to hinder British coastal surveillance of illegal immigration. The Hagana continues its anti-British policies in an operation *The Night of the Bridges*, destroying all the railway bridges connecting Eretz Israel with its neighboring territory. All these operations are successful except at Achziv south of Rosh Hanikra where 14 Hagana members are killed. The British previously in 1942, built a railway tunnel at Rosh Hanikra to connect the railway line from Beirut to Haifa joining with Cairo.

1946 The Etzel explode a bomb in the British Army Headquarters in the King David Hotel, Jerusalem. Despite the Etzel warnings of evacuation, 91 Britons, Arabs and Jews are killed. The Zionist Executive and Dr. Chaim Weizmann condemn the timing and location of this attack. This attack is seen very negatively in the Western capitals. Following the explosion in the King David Hotel, the British arrest nearly 2800 Jewish leaders in the two-week *Black Sabbath* operation, called by the British as *Operation Agatha* in an effort to reduce the activities of the Jewish leadership in Eretz Israel. The British also attempt to arrest the Etzel and Lehi leadership and operatives, as Menachem Begin the leader, remains undercover. Itzhak Shamir (1915-2012) a Lehi commander is arrested, exiled to Eritrea. Shamir will become the 8th Prime Minister of the State of Israel (1983-1984 and again 1986-1992). Sir Alan Cunningham, High Commissioner for Palestine issues a statement saying, "*It is, therefore, my duty to give solemn warning that it is firmly resolved to root out terrorism and violence. Lawlessness, from whatever source it may arise, will in future be dealt with with the utmost vigour and determination...They are not directed against the Jewish community as a whole but solely against those few who are taking an active part in the present campaign of violence and those who are responsible for instigating and directing it.*" British PM Attlee' private message to US

President Truman states "*The (Jewish) weapons were considered quite adequate for defence against Arab marauders.*" A communiqué issued by Jewish Agency states "*The Jewish community of Palestine cannot give up its right to self-defence; it cannot entrust its fate into the hands of the administration which according to the Royal Commission for Palestine has failed to discharge 'the elementary duty of providing public safety'.*" All quotations The Observer, London 30 June 1946.

1946   The British enact Emergency Regulations in Eretz Israel stationing 100,000 British troops to control both the Arab anti-Jewish rioting and killing, and Jewish efforts to force the British out.

1946   Britain appoints Abdullah I (son of Hussein ibn Ali) as Hashemite king of Transjordan, known as Jordan. Abdullah is assassinated in 1951. Great Britain signs a military treaty with Jordan. Officially all Palestinians except Jews are entitled to citizenship of Jordan.

1946   A commission is headed by Herbert Morrison (Britain) and Henry Grady (USA) to deal with the post–World War II problem of Jewish refugees wanting to immigrate to Palestine. They suggest the partition of Palestine into semi-autonomous Arab and Jewish regions under the British High Commissioner authority. Both Arabs and Jews reject this proposal. Britain refers the issue to the UN.

1946   In the summer of 1946 the Zionist Executive concentrates its efforts to assist Jewish immigration (**Ha'apala**) and their settlement in Eretz Israel. (See Ha'apala 1934, 1945). All Hagana activities remain underground, hidden from the British since possession of weapons is punishable by death. The Hagana executes a successful operation against the British Naval Station at Bat Galim in Haifa, capturing many light-weapons and ammunition.

1946   Etzel and Lehi continue an anti-British policy killing seven British soldiers in Tel Aviv. Etzel members enter RAF airbase at Hazor, destroying 21 RAF 4-engine Liberator bombers. Two Etzel members sabotage the Jerusalem Railway Station killing an Arab and a British sapper. The British take severe measures against Jewish and Arab terrorists. Moshe Barzani and Meir Feinstein are captured and sentenced to death, blowing themselves up when a grenade is smuggled in an orange into the Jerusalem prison.

1946   Virtually no Jews live in the western Negev besides three outposts (mitzpim) established in 1943. Immediately following completion of Yom Kippur fast, Jewish Agency simultaneously establishes 11 new settlements within 24 hours defining the future border in the south. New settlements are: Kedma and Gal-On near Kfar Menachem and Kiryat Gat of today; Shuval and Mishmar Hanegev further south; Nevatim and Hatzerim near Be'er Sheva; Urim in western Negev and 'four points' - Be'eri, Tekuma, Nirim bordering the Gaza Strip close to Khan Yunis, and Kfar Darom in Gaza. Major C S Jarvis (Governor-General of Sinai) in 1938 writes *"look at the barren sand-hills and malarious marshes that the Jews have won back to cultivation...to realize...the pioneers...eke out a living in the most unpropitious circumstances."*

1946 **Cameri Theater** established in Tel Aviv by Yossi Yadin, Hanna Merom, and Yosef Milo.

1946 **David Ben-Gurion, re-elected Jewish Agency Chairman, is also responsible for the defense. He dedicates himself tirelessly to strengthen the security situation of Jews living in Eretz Israel foreseeing the impending withdrawal of Great Britain's Police and Army from Palestine. He instructs Hagana to change from a partisan organization defending the Yishuv from Arab terrorism, into a national army capable once the British depart, of resisting the expected invasion by the armies of various Arab countries. This is one of Ben Gurion's greatest actions as a statesman since without a strong army and preparations for the impending invasion, the Yishuv could not have survived the war.**

1946 Czech Foreign Minister Jan Masaryk (1886-1948) convinces his Prime Minister to allow displaced Jews to pass through Czechoslovakia on their way to Eretz Israel. The Hagana purchase with Soviet approval, Czech surplus arms. Following constant Allied bombing of aircraft production facilities in Germany during WW II, German aircraft production is transferred to Czechoslovakia, manufactured in the Avia factory. The Hagana will pay well over market prices for this World War II military surplus, (Europe is no longer at war). An international boycott exists against selling arms to the Hagana, desperately in need of arms as war with the Arabs appears imminent. After Independence May 1948 these arms are shipped and Messerschmitt fighter planes for the infant Israel Air Force.

1946 No USA military equipment is officially sold to the Hagana.

1947 In an Etzel counter-reaction in Haifa 17 Arabs are killed.

1947 Continuing Arab violence and inability of Britain to fulfill its objectives prompts British Foreign Minister, Ernest Bevin in February 1947 to attempt to satisfy both Arab and Jew by referring the British Mandate for Palestine to United Nations. Following World War II there is a change in British world-wide political, diplomatic and economic strategy and position. The British

Government promotes a withdrawal from both Palestine and in Indian sub-continent. In this post-war period Britain makes a strategic decision to assist US to encircle Soviet Communist influence. United States sends troops to Europe; while Britain maintains troops Malaya and Burma in Southeast Asia. Britain assists Greece in its civil war against communists, maintaining military bases and an airfield in Cyprus.

British opinion is: Jews, even though outnumbered 2:1 will be able to repulse local Arab attacks, but after the British withdrawal, they will not succeed in defending themselves against invading Arab Armies, who will defeat them. King Abdullah I will then transfer his capital from Amman to Jerusalem, inviting the British to return to Palestine.

1947 UN establishes UNSCOP (United Nations Special Committee on Palestine) May 1947 to prepare a solution for Palestine. In August 1947 the UNSCOP report unanimously recommends partition of Palestine into an Arab and a separate Jewish state.

1947 Etzel attack a British Officer's Club in Jerusalem, killing twelve. Consequently British hang four Etzel members, Dov Gruner, Mordechai Alkachi, Yehiel Dov Drezner and Eliezer Kashani in Acre prison. Etzel successfully blows a hole in the wall of Acre prison, freeing 41 Jews and in addition 214 Arab prisoners use this opportunity to escape. British hang three Etzel members Ya'akov Weiss, Avshalom Haviv and Meir Nakar for their roles in the Acre prison breakout. Etzel then hangs two British sergeants, abducted in an effort to thwart the hangings of their members.

1947 Hagana ship **Yehuda Halevi** brings 400 Moroccan Jewish Immigrants to Eretz Israel. The British authorities decide to send the ships back to the ports of embarkation in Europe. The Hagana ship **Exodus 1947** overfilled with 4530 Jewish immigrants including 655 children, all Holocaust survivors from Concentration Camps and Displacement Camps in Europe, is denied entry into Haifa port. During the British attack on the vessel two immigrants and one American volunteer are killed, with over 200 immigrants wounded. The British force the ship back to France from where the ship departed, and then to Hamburg from where the vessel originally embarked. Most of the passengers will make their way back to Eretz Israel, some are captured and deported to British Detention Camps in Cyprus. *Exodus 1947* raises the Jewish Question in the international arena, forcing a solution for an independent Jewish State.

1947 **Dead Sea Scrolls** (over 900 fragments) are found in eleven caves at Qumran along the northwestern shore of the Dead Sea. These are the oldest written copies of the Bible that has not been changed in any way in the 2000 years since these particular scrolls were written. They are permanently displayed in the Shrine of the Book, the Israel Museum, Jerusalem to include The Book of Isaiah, The Habakkuk Commentary, The Thanksgiving Scroll, The Community Rule, The War Rule (The War of the Sons of Light against the Sons of Darkness), The Genesis Apocryhon (in Aramaic), The Copper Scroll, Psalms Scroll, The Temple Scroll, and Leviticus Scroll. Additional manuscripts and fragments are housed in the Rockefeller Museum, Jerusalem. Other texts are The Book of Jubilee, Enoch, Tobit, Ben Sira and Damascus Document.

1947   Zionist Executive orders the arrest of Etzel members in the **Large Season** Operation aiming to cease their anti-British activities. Many members of the Palmach disagree with this policy and are excused from participating. The capture of Jews by Jews causes much resentment within the Yishuv. No weapons or violence is used. The captured Etzel members are handed to the British not put on trial and are incarcerated for a short period only. Many Etzel leaders are exiled, while Menachem Begin, Shmuel Katz and Haim Landau successfully escape the British dragnet.

1947   An airport is established at Sde Dov, north Tel Aviv. In October 1947 the Zionist Executive convinces the British to establish an Air Wing – the beginning of the Israel Air Force (IAF). Eleven light planes are purchased. Approximately 25 pilots join the fledging Air Force, about 20 with operational experience during WW II. The more veteran pilots instruct Israeli volunteers flying techniques.

1947   **The British Cabinet decides on 28 October 1947 to ends its Mandate and leave Palestine on 15 May 1948.** They view a Jewish state to be a pro-British state in the future.

1947   **On 29 November 1947 the General Assembly of the United Nations passes Resolution 181.** *"Independent Arab and Jewish States and the Special International Regime for the City of Jerusalem, set forth in part III of this plan, shall come into existence in Palestine."* **Palestine is partitioned into two separate states, a Jewish and an Arab state.** The West Bank is referred as Judea and Samaria.

> - The Jewish state established along the coast, Upper Galilee, Beit She'an and Jezreel valleys, and the Negev.
> - The Palestinian State in Judea and Samaria, Jaffa and Gaza.
> - Jerusalem and Bethlehem are to be held as international territory.
> - *"Free access to the Holy Places".*

The Jewish leadership accepts the United Nations resolution while Arabs reject it outright as it does not grant them the whole of Palestine and they refuse to establish their own state. Arab rioting and murder follows.

Map 40. UN Resolution Partition Plan 1947

The Palestinian National Covenant, written in 1964 states: "Article 19. *The partition of Palestine in 1947 and the establishment of the State of Israel is entirely illegal.*" "Article 20. *The Balfour Declaration...(is) deemed null and void.*"

Chapter 23. Israel's War of Independence 1947 - 1949

1947   The very day after United Nations partition resolution (29 November 1947) local Arabs begin rioting and killing Jews. A bus traveling from Netania to Jerusalem is attacked outside Petach Tikva, killing 5 Jews. Thus begins **Israel's War of Independence**.

1947   After the UN Resolution, Etzel emerges from the underground, openly attacks British forces attempting to hasten their departure. In a counter-reaction to Arab rioting, Etzel places a bomb at the Damascus Gate Bus Station in Jerusalem, killing 5 Arabs, also in Haifa, Tel Aviv and Jerusalem. In a reprisal against Etzel activities, Arabs place a bomb killing Jews 39 at Haifa Petroleum Refineries.

1947   The Palmach brings 65 ships with illegal immigrants, also assist Jews from Syria and Lebanon to enter Eretz Israel on foot. By end December Hagana volunteers reach 15,000 soldiers including 3,000 infantry, many with WW II experience. Palmach 3000; Etzel 4000 including 1000 soldiers; Lehi 750 with 150 soldiers.

1947   Muslims attack Jews in Aden, killing 82 of this small community, plundering 106 of the 170 Jewish-owned stores. Four synagogues and 230 Jewish homes are burnt. In Aleppo (Halab), Syria, Arabs destroy Jewish houses, shops, schools and synagogues damaging the Aleppo Codex. Anti-Jewish riots in Iraq, plunder Jewish-owned businesses and kill Jews. Jewish leaders including Shlomo Hillel emigrate preparing for the evacuation of Iraqi Jewry.

1947   Total **population** 1,845,000; Jews 630,000, Muslims 1,097,000. Christians 140,000. Jerusalem has 157,000 inhabitants including 97,000 Jews (62%) and about 60,000 Arabs. During 1947, 152 Jewish civilians are killed by Arab terrorists.

1948   Almost every Arab town and village has a weapons depot. Local scouts, *najada* and *futuwa,* and an alarm system *faza'a* quickly mobilize the population to defend the village or attack Jewish travelers. Occasionally Arabs use services of British Army deserters together with their equipment and vehicles. The Arab League in Cairo declares its armies will occupy Palestine to '*drive the Jews into the sea*'.

1948   **British Army trains two Arab military units, without preventing Arab armies from invading Israel before the Mandate ends.** Maj.-Gen. Sir John Bagot (Glubb Pasha 1897-1986) leads the **Jordanian Arab Legion** with 8000 soldiers. British Brigadiers Lash and Arthur; Colonels Ashton, Goldie, and Newman. **The Transjordan Frontier Force** has 3000 troops.

1948   The Arab Liberation Army led by Fauzi el-Kaukji attack Kfar Szold before the British depart. Jewish defenders and a few Hagana soldiers repulse the attacks.

1948   **Golda Meir** (1898-1978), born in Kiev, senior Jewish Agency representative visits the USA requesting financial aid from US Jewry. She will be appointed the 5th Prime Minister of Israel (1969-1974) during the Yom Kippur War of 1973.

1948   Pro-Arab British Army deserters using their military vehicles, bomb the Palestine (Jerusalem) Post building, the only English language newspaper. With immense effort, the paper is printed the next morning. In a counter-reaction Etzel kills 20 Arabs. British Army deserters using a British military vehicle place a car bomb in Ben Yehuda Street, Jerusalem, killing 50 Jews. In the month of January 1948, 117 Jews are killed.

1948   In February 1948 an estimated 100,000 Jews reside in Jerusalem, of which 1500-2000 in the Old City and an estimated 40,000 Arabs. During February 107 Jews are killed.

1948   Etzel blows up a train near Rehovot, killing 28 British soldiers and later, another train near Benjamina, killing 40.

1948   The Arab Liberation Army ambushes a Hagana convoy near Cabri in the western Galilee carrying supplies and troop reinforcement to Yehiam, killing 42 Jewish soldiers, both male and female. Yehiam is situated adjacent to Crusader fortress Judin captured by Muslims in 1187. The fortress gives protection to the kibbutz defenders and is not overrun by Arab fighters.

Road bloc near Cabri   Courtesy of Zofim, Israel

1948   The Mufti's Arab Army of Salvation operates in Jerusalem and Gush Etzion, captures Bab el-Wad/Sha'ar Ha'gai the main road from Lod to Jerusalem, causing food shortages. Water is scarce after Arabs destroy water pipes leading to the city. Arabs place bombs in a stolen British Army car, park at Jewish Agency Jewish headquarters on King George Street, Jerusalem, killing 12.

1948 In March 1948, 161 Jews are killed, including 70 in Jerusalem.

1948 Givati Brigade led by Lt. Col. Shimon Avidan begins 'Operation Nachshon' 3-13 April to open the road to Jerusalem transporting supplies to the beleaguered population. This signals a change in Hagana techniques from guerrilla-style to a full-scale military operation. In Lod, the Hagana kill 10 Iraqi soldiers.

1948 On 4 April The Arab Liberation Army led by Fauzi el-Kaukji leaves Jenin in Samaria, entering the Jezreel Valley to attack Kibbutz Mishmar Ha'emek. Hagana forces led by Itzhak Sadeh repulse the Arab Liberation Army after five days of hand-to-hand fighting.

1948 Arab forces led by Muslim Brotherhood (الإخوان المسلمون al-Ikhwān al-Muslimūn) capture the Crusader Fortress of Castel, a strategic location overlooking the main road from the coast to Jerusalem. They use this base to attack convoys traveling slowly up the hill from Bab el-Wad/Sha'ar Hagai to Jerusalem. Hagana soldiers capture the Castel, but are immediately attacked by Arab forces forcing them to withdraw, leaving behind their wounded and dead. The next day the Hagana successfully recapture this site, finding all wounded soldiers left behind in their retreat, killed and their corpses mutilated. Abd Ghader el-Husseini is killed in an Arab counter-attack on the Castel as morale of Arab fighters drops considerably after the death of their leader.

1948 Etzel troops (5 killed) enter Deir Yessin killing Arab fighters which stimulates the population to flee. The Jewish leadership and Hagana condemn this action. Many contradictory statements are made of the numbers killed. The massacre and rapes was fabricated by Hazem Nusseibeh, editor of the Palestine Broadcast Service in 1948. He is instructed by Hussein Khalidi "*We must make the most of this...So the Arab armies will come to liberate Palestine from the Jews*". Arabs never cease to remind the world of this incident. www.2nd-thoughts.org/id38.html

Jews have witnessed many 'Deir Yassin' attacks on their communities in the Arab world and on Jewish settlements in Eretz Israel (for example the Etzion Bloc, Hebron). (See Joan Peters, From Time Immemorial page 175.) "*In towns where Jews lived for hundreds of years, those Jews were periodically robbed, raped and in some places massacred, and in many instances, the survivors were obliged to abandon their possessions and run.*"

Also see Sir Martin Gilbert "In Ishmael's House."

1948   On 13 April, in **Sheik Jarrah**, East Jerusalem, Arab mobs attack a convoy of 110 Jewish doctors and nurses traveling to Hadassah Hospital, Mount Scopus, killing 77, only 8 are unharmed. British forces make no serious attempt to save the civilians ambushed other than a very brave personal effort by Major John (Jack) Churchill. The British Army does not explain how one British officer (Churchill), with one vehicle, (APC) and 12 soldiers could save 110 civilians ambushed by hundreds of Arab rioters. The official British position of Gen. Gordon MacMillan displays apathy towards Jews in his letter to the Palestine Post, 23 April 1948 to Dr Judah Magnes, President, Hebrew University and Chairman of Hadassah. (See King-Clark, *Jack Churchill, Unlimited Boldness*).

Hadassah Convoy   Courtesy of Mynet.co.il

1948   On 16 April, one month before their scheduled departure, British troops suddenly evacuate **Safed** without informing Jewish leadership. They permit 4000-4500 Iraqi and Lebanese troops under the command of Fauzi el-Kaukji into the citadel, the British Police Station, the Jewish School (turned into a British Army complex) and other key positions overlooking the Jewish Quarter in Safed. Less than 1200 of the 12,000 inhabitants of Safed are Jewish, living in a narrow quarter together with 222 defenders. Arabs kidnap a young 19 year old Jew, Menachem Mizrahi. His screams are heard throughout the Jewish Quarter as they torture him to death. This is the reason behind the decision of Safed Jews to plan a mass suicide if their situation becomes desperate, and for local Jews to reject residence to any Arab in Safed following Independence in 1948. In 1993 Abu Mazen (Mohammed

Abbas) a Palestinian future prime minister and president born in Safed in 1936, requests permission to visit. Safed Municipal leaders refuse. The Mufti of Jerusalem and Fauzi el-Kaukji encourage Arabs living in Safed to temporarily leave, promising after the conquer, to settle in the Jewish Quarter. Palmach soldiers under Yigal Allon climb up the western mountain slope at night to reinforce the local defenders. The Arab population flee Safed hearing the sound of a solitary Davidka mortar, fearing Israeli troops possess many heavy artillery weapons. 52 Jewish defenders and civilians are killed.

Davidka Mortar, Safed   Mavis Wolff

1948 Palmach (Harel Brigade) kill Iraqi soldiers and capture the Arab village Sari, used to attack convoys traveling to Jerusalem. They destroy buildings in Biddu and Beir Surik at Sha'ar Hagai. On 20 April 1948 Arabs once again successfully block the main road to Jerusalem killing six Jews in a convoy near Deir Ayub at **Sha'ar Hagai**. Arab snipers target the convoys moving slowly up the hill as drivers and passengers pay with their lives. The overweight armored vehicles called 'sandwiches' are constructed with a wooden board between two metal plates to protect driver and passengers. Jerusalem again is besieged resulting in food and water shortages. Burnt-out skeletons of armored vehicles remain at the road side as a monument to memorialize the battles to keep the road open to Jerusalem.

1948 The Palmach immediately initiates **Operation Harel** to open the road to Jerusalem. 10th Harel Brigade led by (later Brigadier-

General) Uri Ben-Ari make 61 nightly operations during 89 consecutive days. They open the route to Jerusalem by counter-attacking Arab positions in the hilltops overlooking the road. Operating at night, their daylight hours are spent sleeping, cleaning their equipment and attending the funerals of their fallen comrades from the previous night's operation. Arabs capture Nave Ya'akov and Atarot in northern Jerusalem forcing Jewish civilians to flee towards central Jerusalem, resettled after victory in Six-Day War. In Operation Jibes the Palmach attack at Nevi Samuel northwest of Jerusalem used to assault convoys to Jerusalem. Palmach fighters are unable to hold their territorial gains nor to secure the Jewish suburbs of Nave Ya'akov and Atarot.

1948   Jewish leadership in Haifa makes public appeals to Arab residents not to close their shops and businesses. Arab leadership reiterate their decision to evacuate the entire Haifa Arab population. (See 'The Economist' 2 October 1948). *"The mass evacuation, prompted partly by fear, partly by order of Arab leaders, left the Arab quarter of Haifa a ghost city...By withdrawing Arab workers, their leaders hoped to paralyse Haifa."* (Time, May 3, 1948). *"...the Jewish Haganah asked (using loudspeakers) Arabs to remain at their homes but most of the Arab population followed their leaders who asked them to leave the country"* (Times of London, reporting events of 22.4.1948). In **Operation Scissors** (Misporai'im) the Hagana captures Haifa and Acre. Over 65,000 Arabs flee to Lebanon. As a continuation of Operation Scissors, the Carmeli Brigade begins Operation Ben Ami to capture Yehiam and Hanita in the Western Galilee, named after Ben-Ami Pechter, a Hagana leader previously killed in the Yehiam convoy. Hagana capture Tiberias causing the local Arab population flee.

1948   In early May, Golda Meir and Ezra Danin travel to meet King Abdullah I of Jordan, failing to dissuade him from joining the war about to begin.

1948   Newly established Hagana Air Wing (Israel Air Force-**IAF**) sends representatives abroad to purchase British Norseman aircraft, USA ex-WW II surplus transport aircraft and B-17 bombers, to be delivered after Independence. Czech-made Messerschmitt fighters (from the Avia factory) are flown to Israel end-May after external fuel tanks are designed and assembled on the aircraft. British Spitfire fighters are purchased arriving in December 1948.

1948   The British withdraw on 9 May 1948 from the Police Station at **Gesher** in the Jordan Valley allowing the **Iraqi Army** to cross over the Jordan River, capturing of the hydro-electric power station at Naharai'im built by the Palestine Electric Company (a Jewish-

British company). (This site is never returned to Israel). The night before the invasion all children and non-combatant women of Kibbutz Gesher are escorted on foot to the safety of Kibbutz Afikim, 10-kilometers in the north. Hagana and Kibbutz Gesher fighters attack the Iraqi army camp pitched on a field opposite the kibbutz which goes up in flame, forcing their withdrawal. The Iraqi Army re-enters the Adam (Damiya) Bridge, conquering Samaria almost reaching the Mediterranean Sea (which would split Israel into two), capturing the Jewish settlements of Kfar Yona and Ein Vered. The Hagana halts the Iraqi forces in the Hefer Region (Emek Hefer), 10 kilometers east of Netania on the coast. A War Memorial at the tank junction near Kabatia, south of Jenin commemorates the 700 Iraqi soldiers killed in this area.

1948 Etzel fighters blow-up the Arab Headquarters opposite the Jaffa Clock Tower used as a munitions storage facility. 41 Etzel fighters are killed in Jaffa. Operation Hametz on 12 May 1948 Hagana surround Jaffa as 50,000 Arab residents flee towards Gaza.

1948 The Jordanian Arab Legion destroys the water pumping station at Rosh Ha'ayin, disrupting regular supplies of water to Jerusalem, forcing water rationing.

1948 On 12 May 1948 Arabs attack the Jewish civilian settlement Ein Zurim and Kfar Etzion in the **Etzion Bloc** near Hebron (previously settled in three waves 1927-1929, 1935-1936, 1943-1945). 240 Jewish civilians defenders and soldiers fall, including 15 who are killed after they surrender, their bodies are desecrated and dismembered. Only four Jews survive the massacre. All 35 members of a Palmach relief unit are slaughtered attempting to reinforce the Jewish civilians under siege "...*I know of no battle more glorious, tragic or heroic...than the battle in the Etzion Bloc.*" David Ben-Gurion. In 1949 demobilized Palmach soldiers establish Kibbutz Netiv Ha'Lamed Hey (Hebrew for '35') to commemorate the fallen Palmach soldiers. Israelis resettle Etzion Bloc after 1967, with over 70,000 residents now living in 14 communities of Gush Etzion, Efrat and Betar Ilit.

1948 The British depart from various locations before 14 May 1948 without informing the Jewish leadership thus allowing Arabs to take over strategic sites and installations at:
• Nebi Yusha fortress in Upper Galilee
• Safed and Mt Canaan police buildings, Shalva House
• Rosh Pina Police Station
• Latrun Police Station
• Iraq-Suidan Police Station in Lachish (Metzudat Yoav)

1948   **British troops transfer the Latrun Police Station to the Jordanian Arab Legion**, a strategic site commanding the main road from the coast to Jerusalem. In Operation Maccabi, the Hagana is unsuccessful at opening the road to Jerusalem. Hagana tries again, unsuccessfully, to capture Latrun in Operation Bin Nun A. The Jordanian Arab Legion repulses the repeated Hagana attacks (six times) on Latrun. IDF captures Latrun in 1967

Latrun Police Station   Adrian Wolff

1948   The Hagana, in Operation Kilshon 14 May 1948 captures all vacated British positions on the watershed of Jerusalem, surrounded with barbed wire, known as 'Bevingrad'.

1948   As Britain prepares to pull out their forces, Hagana fervently and intensely assembles and organizes an army to await the impending war. **Continuous pressure on Zionist Executive to assist the immediate immigration of hundreds of thousands of displaced Jewish refugees living in Displacement Centers in Europe. Concurrently Arabs apply pressure on Jews living in Arab countries to emigrate pennilessly. Before Israel's Independence, an international embargo exists against selling and supplying the Hagana with weapons creating a serious shortage of arms and ammunition. Hagana soldiers are supplied with locally manufactured Sten-guns of dubious quality and rifles 'taken' from British bases. Until Independence both the Hagana and the Palmach military units are without heavy machine-guns, anti-tank guns, artillery, tanks and military aircraft.**

1948   **Concurrently Arab countries are purchasing weapons and munitions.** Following the cessation of fighting in World War II,

Egypt becomes a depot for weapons and army surplus. Britain signs a military pact for the defense of Egypt.

1948   Britain evacuates its troops 14 May 1948. Sir Alan Cunningham British High Commissioner and General Gordon MacMillan fly from Atarot airport Jerusalem to Haifa, depart by sea. British troops remain in Haifa and Ramat David airfield before departing end June 1948, **ending the British Mandate since 1918.**

1948   On the Eve of Independence, the US Secretary of State, General George Marshall sends an ultimatum to Ben-Gurion to postpone declaring independence, warning of an imminent war, fearing the war will interrupt oil supplies to the USA. Ben-Gurion responds that *"Israel must reserve the right of self-defense even if it goes down fighting"*. USA declares a military embargo on the Middle East. Britain continues to supply the Arab with weapons.

1948   On the Sabbath Eve 14 May 1948 the Jewish leadership, under **David Ben-Gurion**, declares an independent Jewish country, **The State of Israel, a homeland for the Jewish People.** The ceremony takes place at the Dizengoff House (home of the Tel Aviv Museum) in Rothschild Boulevard, Tel Aviv, signed by the 37 representatives of the General Council of Jews (Va'ad Leumi), the Jewish Agency and other bodies. ***"In the land of Israel the Jewish people came into being. In this Land...shaped their spiritual, religious and national character...gave to the world the eternal Book of Books...The State of Israel will open to Jewish immigration and the ingathering of exiles...devote itself to developing the land for the good of all its inhabitants...rest upon the foundations of liberty, justice and peace, as envisioned by the Prophets of Israel...complete equality of creed or race or sex. It will guarantee freedom of religion and conscience, of language, education and culture. It will safeguard the Holy Places of all religions...."***

"I will return the captivity of My people Israel...they will rebuild desolate cities and settle them...will plant vineyards and drink their wine; they will cultivate gardens and eat their fruits". (Amos 9:14).

On 15 May 1948 (5708 ה' באייר) Jews have their own independent country after nearly 2000 years since the Destruction of the Second Temple in 70CE. *"...**to live as a free people in their own country**"* (Hatikva-The National Anthem). Jews begin to immigrate freely into Israel. *"I have returned to Zion...and the streets of the city will be filled with boys and girls playing."* (Zechariah 8:3,4).

The State of Israel 1948 onwards
- The Arabs attack Israel in numerous wars.

- The Arab armies are always defeated.
- Arabs civilians flee from battle areas.
- Israel opens its borders to Jewish immigration.
- Israel grows economically, Arab neighbors stagnate economically and culturally.
- Jerusalem the capital is divided 1948 until Israel victory in the Six-Day War in 1967.
- In the Jordanian Period 1948-1967, Palestinians do not call for an independent Palestinian State in the West Bank and Gaza.
- Within four years, Israel will absorb more than a million mainly penniless Jewish refugees, its Jewish population will triple.

The **Israeli flag** combines the 'Star of David' and two blue stripes on a white background. The blue color originates in *"...they shall place upon...each corner a thread of turquoise wool."* (Numbers 15:38). The white and blue, together with gold and purple are the colors of the High Priest and the colors of the Tabernacle hangings. *"You shall make the Tabernacle of ten curtains – twisted linen with turquoise, purple and scarlet wool."* (Exodus 26:1). Blue symbolizes the infinite sky, representing the Eternal.

The **National Emblem,** a seven-branched candelabra, the Menorah. *"A menorah (made entirely) of gold with its bowl on its top; seven lamps are upon it, and there are seven ducts for (each of) the lamps on its top."* (Zechariah 4:2).

1948   On Independence, the Hagana has 32,000 troops. During the War of Independence 6200 Jews are killed including 1200 civilians.

1948   **Before Independence, attacks upon Jews are performed by local Arabs assisted by outside armies. After Independence the balance will change as armies of five Arab countries immediately invade and attack the infant Jewish state. Arab Armies invade from five Arab countries – Lebanon, Syria, Iraq, Jordan, and Egypt including additional troops from Saudi Arabia and Algeria.**

- **Lebanon** - invade the Western Galilee
- **Iraq -** invade the West Bank (Samaria)
- **Syria -** invade the Upper Galilee
- **Jordan -** invade the West Bank and Jerusalem
- **Egypt -** invade the coast (assisted by **Saudi Arabia and Algeria**) and West Bank (Judah) up to Jerusalem

Arab countries' forces total 39,500 troops in mid-May 1948. This number denotes only those participating in the invasion forces, not including a much larger number of military personal found at headquarters, in various logistics corps and command forces remaining in Arab countries to support troops fighting in Palestine.

1948 Secretary-General of the Arab League Azzam Pasha tells a press conference "*This will be a war of extermination and a momentous massacre.*" (NY Times 16 May 1948). "*We will smash the country with our guns and obliterate every place the Jews seek shelter in.*" Iraqi Prime Minister Nuri Said, quoted in 'Sir Am Nakbah' ("The Secret Behind the Disaster") by Nimr el Hawari, Nazareth, 1952.

The Middle East Military Balance, mid-May 1948				
Country	Troops	Tanks	Artillery	Air Force
Iraq	5,000	40	20	28
Syria	4,000	10	12	16
Egypt	5,500	60	25	44
Jordan	10,000	120	12	0
Saudi	2,000	35	26	0
Lebanon	2,000	12	16	16
Other	11,000 (1)	8	10	0
Total Arab	**39,500**	**285**	**121**	**104**
Israel	**32,000** (2)	**3** (3)	**28**(4)	**4**(5)

(1) Including Arab Liberation Army 8,000; others 3,000.
(2) Less than 50% of IDF troops are field combatants.
(3) Stolen from British forces.
(4) All captured from Arab forces.
(5) 1of the 4 Messerschmitts are downed in first operation at Ad-Holom 30 May 1948. The IAF has 16 additional non-combat aircraft.
Source: Meir Pa'il Emergence of Zahal.1979. Zmora, Bitan, Moadan Tel Aviv

Hagana ההגנה

- Golani Brigade in Jordan Valley, Eastern Galilee. Col. Nahum (Speigel) Golan
- Carmeli Brigade in Haifa,Western Galilee.Col.Moshe (Zalitsky)Carmeli
- Alexandroni Brigade in the Sharon District. Col. Dan (Epstein) Even
- Etzioni Brigade in Jerusalem. Col. David Shaltiel
- Kiryati Brigade in the Tel Aviv area. Col. Michael (Rabinowitz) Bengal
- Givati Brigade in the South. Col. Shimon Avidan

Palmach (strike force) פלמ"ח- פלוגות מחץ

- Yiftach Brigade in the Galilee. Gen.Yigal Allon, Col. Mula Cohen
- Harel Brigade in Jerusalem. Col. Itzhak Rabin, Col. Joseph Tabenkin
- Negev Brigade of 800 troops in the south. Col. Nahum Sarig

1948 Many Hagana and Palmach members previously served in the British Army during WW II in field units, logistics, communications and transportation positions, obtaining battle knowledge and methodology. They now make a special contribution to train the newly founded national Israeli Army.

1948   Most Palmach volunteers are kibbutz members. From 1946 to 1948 800 officers graduate from Palmach Officers courses. Over 1000 Palmach members are killed in action, including 400 from the Harel Brigade opening the Jerusalem Corridor. Palmach commanders become Chief of Staff of the IDF are: Moshe Dayan, Itzhak Rabin, Haim Bar-Lev, David Elazar, Mordechai Gur and Rafael Eitan.

1948   **Mahal,** מתנדבי חוץ לארץ מח"ל- About 4400 overseas volunteers from 56 countries (See IAF below). 122 Mahal (118 men and 4 women) are killed in action during the war. Israeli PM Itzhak Rabin said at a memorial service *"They came to us when we needed them most." "The Mahal forces were the Diaspora's most important contribution."* David Ben-Gurion. Mahal manufactures radar equipment (Morris Ostroff).

1948   **Gahal** גיוש חוץ לארץ גח"ל- (WW II veterans, now immigrants) 16,000 troops. They are ex-partisans and/or previously members of the East European Armies during WW II. Known as 'The Last of Kin' 275 Holocaust survivors, the last remnants of their families who immigrate to Israel, are killed during their military service in War of Independence.

1948   In the **Israel Air Force (IAF)** 90% of the pilots and navigators, most with combat experience in World War II are volunteers (Mahal) from abroad. They previously flew fighters, bombers and transport planes and are radio-operators. The veteran pilots train new Israeli pilots. Ground forces comprise many Israelis, quickly trained in technical skills needed to support the aircraft.

1948   **The Lebanon Army** invades Israel, conquering most of the western and central Galilee, before Hagana victories, forcing their withdrawal.

1948   On 18 May Palmach enters Zion Gate to defend the Jewish Quarter, Old City, but reinforcements fail to arrive. A British soldier (Sir John Glubb Pasha) leads Jordanian Arab Legion capturing the Jewish Quarter. Jews surrender Saturday 28 May 1948 after 150 days of fighting, losing access to Western Wall and Jewish Holy Sites. About 350 Jews are taken prisoner, released after cease-fire agreement on 3 April 1949. Israeli losses are 39 fighters, including a 10-year old runner Nesim Gini, and 29 civilians. Arabs loot and plunder the Jewish Quarter destroying synagogues including the Hurva and Nesim Bek Synagogues, many yeshivot (religious study centers) including Yeshivat Yosef Porat. The Four Sephardic Synagogues are converted to donkey stables. Jewish graves desecrated and tombstones used to build walls of the Arab Legion barracks in al-Azzariya, also as curbstones on Jericho Road constructed through the Jewish cemetery on Mt. of Olives. See Hurva 2010.

1948 The **Egyptian Army** invades from the south. One column proceeds through the Hebron Hills towards Jerusalem, arriving at Kibbutz Ramat Rachel on the southern border of Jerusalem, overlooking Bethlehem. The kibbutz is overrun by Egyptian forces, changes hands three times before the defenders including Etzel fighters, reinforced by the Etzioni Brigade halt the Egyptians in hand-to-hand fighting, forcing their withdrawal to the Faluga Salient in the northern Negev.

1948 The Egyptian Air Force has two squadrons, each has 24 Spitfire aircraft and additional usable bombers. On 15 May 1948 Egyptian aircraft take off from the el-Arish airfield to bomb **Tel Aviv** and Sde Dov airport, damaging the runway and aircraft. On 17 May 1948 the Egyptian Army attacks Kibbutz **Nirim** situated on the border between the Western Negev and Gaza. The kibbutz, built as a fortress, resists the initial attack while every building above ground is destroyed and eight young defenders are killed. The Egyptians withdraw. Nirim is rebuilt several kilometers to the north.

1948 The **IAF** transports light weapons from Czechoslovakia in 'Operation Balak' (May–August), including 24,000 rifles, 4200 mortars and 40 million bullets. These weapons replace ex-British weapons 'acquired' during the Mandate. Hence the word *'Chechi'* is used for the original service rifle in the IDF. The IAF receives three separate orders of Messerschmitt fighter aircraft consisting of 9, 5 and 10 aircraft, arriving in the third week of May 1948. The IAF bombs and strafes the Iraqi Army stationed at Tulkarem.

1948 **Druze** communities living in the Carmel Mountains (See Druze 1860) are constantly suffering from marauding Arabs who pillage their crops and pressurize them to attack Jews. Druze have no nationalistic goals, resist Arab advances. After establishment of the state, Druze elders insist on all non-religious Druze males conscription into the IDF.

1948 An Egyptian column exits Gaza captures various Jewish settlements. **Yad Mordecai** holds out for six days, Egyptians are about to capture Kibbutz **Nitzanim**, north of Ashkelon (7 June) defended by 140 members, reinforced by Givati Brigade soldiers. They decide to surrender after 33 fighters are killed and raise a white flag. Twice Egyptians kill the flag bearer. A third time **Mira (Miriam) Ben Ari** (1926-1948) carries the flag and shoots the approaching Egyptian officer dead, before she too, is shot. The remaining 105 defenders are paraded in Gaza, held in captivity until the Armistice Agreement, April 1949. The Egyptian advance along the coast with infantry and 500 vehicles encamp at Asdor (Ashdod), the **Ad-Holom** Bridge. No Jewish settlements are located along the coast between this Egyptian military camp and Tel Aviv. Two newly acquired Messerschmitts on 30 May attack at the Ad-Halom bridge. One piloted by Ezer Weizman (1924–2005) future Israel Air Force commander and President of Israel, the other piloted by Eddie Cohen, crashes on landing, killing the pilot. IDF Givati soldiers blow-up the coastal railway line and the bridge over the wadi (2 June 1948). The Egyptian Army retreats towards Gaza realizing its supply lines are over-extended.

1948   On 18 May 1948, the **Syrian Army** invades the south of the Kinneret (Sea of Galilee) at Zemach. All residents of Kibbutz Sha'ar Hagolan and Masada evacuate towards Kibbutz **Degania**. Syrians totally destroy the two Kibbutzim. On 20 May 1948 Syrians advance to Degania defended by kibbutz fighters, assisted by a handful of Hagana fighters. Defenders climb on the tanks, throw hand grenades inside the hatch, stopping them at the entrance to the kibbutz. The Syrians withdraw.

Syrian Tank, halted at the gates of Kibbutz Degania   Adrian Wolff

1948   The Syrian Army re-enters Israel at the Benot Ya'akov Bridge, over the Jordan River north of the Kinneret capturing Mishmar Hayarden and the Jordan River Delta.

1948   On 19 May 1948 Jewish residents and workers avoid slaughter at Beit Ha'arava at the northern end of the Dead Sea by evacuating by boat for Sodom rebuilt at the southwest end of the Dead Sea. Beit Ha'arava is resettled following Israel's victory in Six-Day War.

1948   On 22 May 1948 Egyptian aircraft bomb the airfield at Ramat David (named after David Lloyd George, British PM) still occupied by the British (RAF) damaging four RAF Spitfire aircraft. During the second Egyptian bombing operation, British fighters down two planes. British send stern messages to the Egyptian government.

1948   Palmach, in Operation Yiftach recapture Malkia and Kadesh Naftali in the Upper Galilee. The Golani Brigade capture Megido, forcing the Arab Liberation Army of Kaukji to withdraw as many local Arabs flee towards neighboring Arab countries.

1948   The **Israel Defense Forces** (**IDF**)(26 May 1948), is officially established, disbanding all militias (Hagana/Palmach) and armed groups (Etzel/Lehi), incorporated into one fighting force, signed by Menachem Begin representing the Etzel and Lehi and Israel Galili representing the Defense Ministry. Etzel/Lehi troops using stolen British weapons cannot obtain sufficient ammunition as Czech weapons now available in IDF, have metric caliber. *"He neither slumbers nor sleeps, the Guardian of Israel."* (Psalms 121:4).

> **Zionist Leader: David Ben-Gurion.**
> IDF (Israel Defense Force)
> • Chief of Staff: Major-General Ya'akov Dori
> • Deputy Chief of Staff: Brigadier-General Yigal Yadin*
> • Northern Command: Brigadier-General Moshe Carmeli
> • Central Command: Brigadier-General Dan Even
> • Jerusalem Command: Colonel David Shaltiel
> • Southern Command: Brigadier-General Yigal Allon
> • Air Force: Brigadier-General Aharon Remez
> • Navy: Brigadier-General Nachman (Paul) Shulman
> • *Due to illness of M-G Dori, B-G Yadin is Acting Chief of Staff

1948   Invading Arab Armies overrun Jewish settlements during May-Malkia, Kadesh, Mishmar Ha'ayarden, Naharai'im, Atarot, Nave Ya'akov, Jewish Quarter, Old City, Etzion Bloc, Hartuv, Yad Mordecai, Nitzanim,

1948   On 30 May 1948 Hagana troops of Gahal (survivors of the war in Europe) and the 7th Givati Brigade attack on Latrun fails to remove the Jordanians from the fortified British Police Station. Ben-Gurion wishes to keep the road open to Jerusalem.

1948   The IAF bombs Rabat Amman in Jordan. The British government warns the Israelis not to repeat this action, threatening to attack Israel using the British-Jordanian Military Pact Agreement as a pretext. The IAF does not bomb targets in Jordan again during the War of Independence. On 10 June IAF bombs Damascus.

1948 During two Egyptian attacks on Kibbutz Negba on 21 May and 2 June 1948, the 150 local fighters, reinforced by a handful of IDF troops armed with only light weapons, repulse over 1000 Egyptian troops assisted with tanks. There are 21 Israel casualties.

1948 The Egyptian Navy shells Caesarea, inflicting very limited damage. Four Egyptian Dakota aircraft bomb Tel Aviv. Two Egyptian aircraft are downed by Col. Modi Alon. The Israel Air Force attacks Egyptian war ships approaching the Israeli coast.

1948 Gadna troops capture Hirbet ei-Namane and Beit Masil, southwest of Jerusalem.

1948 Kibbutz Hulda, established in 1931 east of Ramle, serves as a base for convoys leaving for the Jerusalem. The IDF recruits port workers from Tel Aviv port to hastily construct a road, the **Burma Road**, to bypass Sha'ar Hagai enabling truck convoys to bring food and supplies to the besieged town. The road from Beir Muheis into Bab el-Wad is opened. IDF attack on Latrun fails during Operation Yoram.

1948 The Yiftach Brigade captures the British Police Station at Nebi Yusa in the Upper Galilee, previously handed to the Arabs. This fortress in the Naftali Mountains has a commanding view over the Hula Valley. The Lebanese Army captures Malkia and Kadesh Naftali. The Yiftach Brigade retakes these positions the next day.

1948 The **First Truce is declared** on 11 June 1948 of between Israel and the invading Arab armies. This cease-fire gives the IDF and Arab armies time to regroup. IDF begins Operation Betzer conscripting additional soldiers, growing from 32,000 on 15 May to 35,000 troops on 11 June, to 59,000 by the end of the truce on 8 July 1948. UN mediator Count Berndotte of Sweden proposes a formula for peace, rejected by both the Arabs and Jews.

1948 Ben-Gurion had appointed American WW II Army officer Colonel David Marcus (aka General Mickey Stone) as Hagana Jerusalem Front Commander in charge of the Etzioni, Harel and 7th Brigades. He is accidentally killed by a sentry at the Abu Gosh IDF camp. Arab residents of Abu Gosh do not participate in the fighting, their village is undamaged and after the war, flourishes economically.

1948 The Etzel and Lehi arms supply ship the **Altelena** lands at Kfar Vitkin on 20 June. The IDF off-loads most of the arms and ammunition. Eliyahu Lankin and Shmuel Katz order it to sail. The Altelena is grounded off Frishman beach in Tel Aviv on 22 June, as the Etzel refuses to hand over the remaining arms to the IDF. The Etzel ignites the ship as weapons, ammunition and the ship are lost. 16 Etzel and 3 Hagana soldiers die during this controversial episode, influencing the relationships between Ben-Gurion and Begin – one of mistrust. The IDF lost the use of the sorely needed ship.

1948   After being under continual attacks for months, Jewish defenders of Kfar Darom, a lone settlement inside Gaza originally established in 1946 are evacuated. Resettled after the Six-Day War in 1967, evacuated during the 2005 Gaza Disengagement.

1948   At the beginning of the First Truce the IDF was on the defense. **This Truce ends on 8 July 1948. The IDF changes its tactics on 9 July initiating ten days of intensive offensive attacks lasting until 18 July 1948, changing the course of the war.**

1948   On 9 July 1948 the Givati and Negev Brigades begin Operation An-Far (anti-Farouk) to cut the Egyptian supply lines in the Negev and capture the Tel a-Zafi area. At Gal-On the IDF uses one of the only two tanks in its possession, both stolen from the British. The tank moves forwards towards the Egyptian lines, breaking down after traveling only about 100 meters.

1948   The Egyptian Air Force attempts to bomb Hadassah Hospital in Tel Aviv. The bombs land near-by causing civilian casualties.

1948   Operations from 9 until 19 July. The Carmeli Brigade in Operation Brosh is unsuccessful in recapturing Mishmar Hayarden from the invading Syria Army now positioned west of the Jordan River. controlling the Benot Ya'akov Bridge over the Jordan River. The terrain in this area is very steep. The Syrians will withdraw from this area as part of the Armistice Agreement of July 1949 to the International Border east of the Jordan River, but in 1951 enter No Man's Land and remain until 1967. The Golani Brigade in Operation Dekel takes control of the road north of Haifa to Naharia and then turns southeast towards Zippori and Nazareth.

1948   Hassan Salameh, wounded at Rosh Ha'ayin is brought to the 'Egyptian' hospital in Ramle, where he dies. In **Operation Dani** (LRLR = Lod/Ramle, Latrun/Ramallah) the Yiftach Brigade, led by **General Yigal Allon**, successfully capture Lod (Lydda) and the Kiryati Brigade captures Ramle. The Hagana destroys the Mufti's Arab Army of Salvation headquarters in Ramle used by Arabs to attack the Jerusalem convoys. 600 Arab fighters flee to Latrun. Most of the local Muslim population flees to Judea. The Yiftach Brigade is unable to capture Latrun and Ramallah. Gadna troops capture Ein Kerem to the west of Jerusalem.

1948   The Egyptians fail to capture Be'erot Itzhak near the Gazan border. The Israeli defenders pay a heavy price with 33 casualties, both civilians and soldiers. The Negev Brigade in Operation 'Death to the Invader' cuts through Egyptian lines, surround Majdal (Ashkelon), isolating the **Faluga Salient** and Beit Guvrin from the sea.

1948   Three newly acquired IAF B-17 Flying Fortresses bomb Cairo, Gaza and el-Arish.

1948   The IDF captures Malha, a village in the southern Jerusalem. **Etzel** leader Menachem Begin via Shmuel (Muki) Katz requests from Jerusalem commander David Shaltiel to capture the Jewish Quarter of the Old City. On 16 July in Operation Kedem, Etzel forces enter through the New Gate, are forced to withdraw when confronted by superior numbers of Arab troops and weapon power. An ammunition truck bringing weapons and bullets to Etzel fighters is blown-up in Jerusalem before arriving at the New Gate.

1948   The Arab Liberation Army is driven out of Sejera and Afula regions in Lower Galilee.

1948   Israeli Naval commandos sink the Egyptian flagship, the *'Emir Farouk'* off the Gaza coast by steering an explosive laden speedboat towards the Egyptian vessel.

1948   **The Second Truce** is declared on 18 July 1948 with no time limit. The UN threatens sanctions on any side if the truce is broken. IDF troops now reach 63,000 soldiers with new recruits, many of them new immigrants recently arriving in Israel.

1948   Israel Navy in 'Operation Pirate' sabotages an Italian freighter the *Lino* in the open sea off Italy carrying arms (rifles, ammunition and spare parts) to Alexandria, Egypt. The damaged *Lino* sails for Bari, an Italian port, where the arms are transferred to another vessel, the *Argero*. Israel Navy commandos using an Italian fishing trawler capture the *Argero* in the open sea, transferring all the weapons to the Israeli INS Haifa, which sails for Haifa together with the Italian crew. The *Argero* is scuttled.

1948   Naval Cadets from the Naval School in Acre reinforce the IDF at Beit Affa in the Faluga Salient. The Egyptians capture 22 cadets, most under 18 years old, murder them in captivity and place their bodies in a mass grave. Their remains are returned 10 months later, buried in the Nahalat Itzhak Military cemetery in Givata'im.

1948   At end of July 1948 the Jordanian Arab Legion bombards Jerusalem breaking the cease-fire. In Mamilla, Jerusalem 34 Jews are killed. IDF now moves its troops to the north and south.

1948   Operation Gis and Dust on 31 July to supply IDF forces and materiel in remote Negev settlements. Equipment is airlifted at night to new makeshift airstrips.

Small section graves from 1948. Nahlat Itzhak Military Cemetery. Adrian Wolff

1948   Dov Joseph, Military Commander of Jerusalem, mayor August 1948 until January 1949.

1948   Lehi members assassinate UN mediator, Swedish Count Folke Bernadotte in Jerusalem. He proposed to give areas already captured by the IDF in Lod, Ramle, and Negev to the Arabs. The Western Galilee will be included in Israel. Israelis and Arabs reject this proposal. Dr. Ralph Bunche, (USA) is appointed UN mediator.

1948   On 15 October 1948 the IDF begins Operation Yoav (10 Plagues) to capture **Be'er Sheva**, force Egyptian troops out of the Negev, including from Majdal (**Ashkelon**) on the coast and cut the Egyptian supply lines originating from Sinai into Gaza.

1948   The acting Chief-of-Staff Yigal Yadin and senior IDF leaders disagree with General Yigal Allon's plan to pursue the Egyptians in the Negev, citing insufficient forces and lack of heavy weapons. Nevertheless Allon, a 30-year old general will be successful. Allon writes "*A nation that does not respect its past is condemned to a barren present and a future that is shrouded in uncertainty.*"

1948   By October 1948 the IDF consists of 95,000 troops. Nearly 4,000 IDF soldiers and over 1,000 civilians have been killed and 15,000 wounded during this war. Arab invasion troops has grown to 53,000 soldiers. An estimated 15,000 Arabs soldiers are killed and 25,000 wounded. **The numbers of Arab Armed Forces** participating in the invasion of Israel do not include additional Arab logistics and command forces remaining in their home territories.

The Middle East Military Balance, October 1948				
Country	Troops	Tanks	Artillery	Aircraft
Iraq	10,000	40	60	16
Syria	8,000			
Egypt	15,000	40(2)	40	18
Jordan	9,000(1)	100	12	0
Saudi	6,000	30	76	12
Lebanon	2,000	10	16	16
Other	3,000	8	10	0
Total Arab	**53,000**	228	214	46
Israel	**95,000**	120	240	24(3)

(1) Including 6,000 local Palestinian volunteers.
(2) Locust tanks made in USA, WW II surplus left in Egypt.
(3) Fighter planes and an additional 55 planes.
Source: Meir Pa'il Emergence of Zahal.1979. Zmora, Bitan, Moadan.Tel Aviv

1948 The Givati Brigade successfully creates a wedge in the Egyptian Army at Iraq el-Manshiyeh, between Faluga and Beit Guvrin cutting their supplies from the coast in the west. The IDF infantry, without armor, fail to defeat the Egyptians holding the British Police station at Iraq Suedan (Metzudat Yoav) at the crossroad to the Negev in the south and from Majdal to Beit Guvrin and Hebron in the east. In hand-to-hand combat at Plugot, the Givati Infantry capture Hill 100 and Hill 113. In another hand-to-hand combat, the Givati Infantry defeats Saudi infantry on six hills at Huleigat. The Negev Brigade captures Beer Sheva, capital of the Negev, populated by about 1000 Arabs.

1948 On 22 October 1948, the IAF presents a plan (of Colonel Cecil Margo DSO, DFC) to David Ben-Gurion to reorganize the Israel Air Force into a modern Air Force, accepted one week later. Ben-Gurion proposes Col. Margo to become the head of the Israel Air Force. He declines feeling it is more suitable for an 'Israeli'.

1948 Operation Yiftach, the Oded Brigade captures Tarshiha, Sas, Malkia, and Kadesh along the Lebanon border. Operation Hiram, IDF defeats the Arab Liberation Army which retreats and leaves the war theater. IDF controls the Upper Galilee by 28 October.

1948 The IDF enters Majdal (Ashkelon) and the remaining Egyptian troops flee towards Gaza as some are evacuated by boat. The IDF continues southwards recapturing Kibbutz Yad Mordechai on

5 November 1948. On 9 November, the Police Station at Iraq Suedan (Metzudat Yoav) is finally captured on the 8th attempt by the 8th Armor Brigade. The IDF enters Beit Hanun in Gaza surrounding the Egyptian troops. Egyptians fearing their forces are overextended, withdraw all troops from positions along the Israeli coast. On 22 November 1948 in Operation Horev the IDF enters Sinai to secure the Negev and move towards el-Arish in Sinai, thereby forcing King Farouk of Egypt to negotiate a truce. The Alexandroni Brigade fails to capture the Egyptian emplacements at Faluga in the northern Negev. The Negev Brigade captures Nitzana (el-Auja/Bir Asluj) on the Negev-Sinai border reaching the outskirts of el-Arish. The Harel Brigade arrives at Kusseima in the central Negev-Sinai border.

1948   The United Nations on 29 December 1948 calls for an Egyptian initiated cease-fire. **The United Nations has not called for a cease-fire before this date during the period when the Arab Armies had invaded and attacked Israel.**

1948   In aerial combat operations during the war, 21 enemy aircraft are downed without Israeli loss. All IAF losses are from AA (anti-aircraft) fire, technical problems or human error. IAF operations make only a marginal influence to the final outcome of the war.

1948   **Jews defeat the Arab armies. About 600,000 Arabs flee the war theater created by the invading Arab armies and subsequent Jewish offensive. Arabs flee believing the Jews will take retribution against them with similar vengeance as they claimed they would have persecuted the residing Jews in their defeat. These Arabs are not absorbed into the host countries and are to remain in refugee camps. Arabs living in Palestine had regarded themselves as 'southern Syrians or Arabs', but never as 'Palestinians'. Many Arabs return to the Arab lands they had emigrated from in previous decades** (see previous chapters).

"The Arab civilians panicked and fled ignominiously. Villages were frequently abandoned before they were threatened by the progress of the war". Glubb Pasha London Daily Mail 12 August, 1948. *"The Arab states encouraged the Palestine Arabs to leave their homes temporarily in order to be out of the way of the Arab invasion armies"*. Jordanian Falastin, 19 February, 1949. *"These refugees is the direct result of the action of the Arab states in opposing the partition and the Jewish State. The Arab states agreed on this policy unanimously and they must share in the solution of the problem."* Emil Ghoury, Secretary, Arab Higher Committee, Beirut Daily Telegraph, 6 September, 1948.

Sixty years later, Palestinians define the Jewish defense against the Arab invasion, terror and violence in 1948 as the '*nakba* '- the catastrophe.

1948 **Displaced Jewish civilians in Israel. The Arabs attack Jewish civilian areas.** Over 10% of the total Jewish population became displaced inside Israel during the war, having lost their homes or agricultural fields due to war damage, or proximity to the fighting. They move into every available building, sometime living in stairwells.

Jerusalem = 35,000
Tel Aviv = 18,000
Haifa = 6,000
Other outlying areas = 11,000
Total Jewish refugees inside Israel=60,000 (10% of total population)

Summary of the War of Independence.
Jews, outnumbered and under-armed repulse the invasion armies of five Arab countries, succeed in retaining control of the territory granted to them by the United National Resolution of 29 November 1947, and capture additional parts of the Galilee and Negev to Eilat on the Red Sea. The Western Wall, Jewish Quarter, Atarot, and Etzion Bloc are lost. Israel survives. According to British statistics, more than 70 percent of the land in what would become Israel was not owned by Arabs. It belonged to the mandatory government.

Museums
Hagana Museum, Rothschild Boulevard, Tel Aviv
Palmach Museum, Levanon Street, Tel Aviv
Etzel Museum, Sir Charles Clore Park, Tel Aviv

1948 **Jews find refuge in Israel as the 'Doors of Zion' are opened. Over 250,000 Jews are displaced in war-torn Europe. Persecution of the Jewish populations in all Muslim countries.** Many are killed, Jewish businesses and property confiscated forcing over 800,000 Jews to flee penniless to Israel and other western countries. Jewish communities 2500 years old are ethnically cleansed. This is the Jewish '*nakba*' or catastrophe. The value of Jewish assets confiscated from Jews fleeing Arab states are much greater than the value of the assets left behind by the Arabs fleeing Palestine. The United Nations has failed to discuss the plight of the Jewish refugees, terrorized and expelled from Arab countries. The new immigrants to Israel are housed in temporary tent-camps *(ma'abarot)* in very primitive conditions before their transfer into newly constructed housing developments all over the country. Many new immigrants are directed to new or existing kibbutzim, moshavim and new 'development towns'.

1948   In **Operation Magic Carpet** December 1948-September 1949, the Israeli government airlifts over 50,000 Jews from Yemen and Aden to Israel. Most passengers have never seen an airplane before, let alone have flown in one!

1948   During 1948, 379 civilians are killed by Arab terrorists.

1948   **Population** end 1948 = 873,700, Jews= 686,701 (78%). (CBS)

Jewish immigrants to Israel 1948 - 1951
1948 = 101,814
1949 = 239,576
1950 = 170,215
1951 = 175,129
Total = 689,739

See Appendix Table 6.8. Central Bureau of Statistics. www.cbs.gov.il

1949   On 1 January 1949, Great Britain calls for Israel to withdraw all forces from inside Sinai, threatening war with Israel using the the 1936 Anglo-Egyptian Defense Treaty. Egypt requests a cease-fire. David Ben-Gurion bows to pressure and orders General Yigal Allon to withdraw all IDF troops to the International Border. Egypt has over 4000 troops in the Negev in the Faluga Salient inside Israel and additional 22,000 in Gaza. Britain does not pressure Egypt to withdraw these troops. On 6 January 1949 the IDF surrounds the Egyptian Army headquarters in Rafiah, forcing Egypt to request an armistice.

1949   On 7 January 1949 near Nirim in the western Negev, IAF Spitfire aircraft shoot down two RAF Spitfires and subsequently another three RAF planes with the loss of two RAF pilots, without any IAF loss. RAF planes fly from air bases in Egypt, entered Israeli airspace, into a war zone. The RAF ends Negev incursions.

1949   First elections are held in January 1949, the government installed in March 1949. The Israel Labor Party (Mapai) captures 46 of the 120 seats. Daniel Auster is appointed mayor of Jerusalem (1949-1950). On 14 February 1949 the first session of the newly elected Knesset (Parliament) takes place in the hall at the Jewish Agency Headquarters in Jerusalem. Dr. Chaim Weizmann is elected the first president and David Ben-Gurion first prime minister.

1949   Major-General **Yigal Yadin** (1917–1984), appointed Chief of Staff (1949–1952), plays an important role in the foundation of the

Israel Defense Forces (IDF) unifying the Air Force, Navy and Ground Forces into one central command; creating the standing army, supported by reserve forces. Upon his retirement, he is appointed professor of Archaeology, Hebrew University leading the excavations at Masada, Hazor, and Judean Desert Caves.

1949   On 24 February 1949 the **Israel-Egypt** Armistice Agreement is signed at Rhodes (UN mediator Dr. Ralph Bunche). Egypt withdraws troops currently in Faluga Salient and Iraq Manshiyeh (Kiryat Gat today). Egypt continues the administration of Gaza allowing terrorists to infiltrate into Israel causing murder, sabotage and damage.

1949   **Operation Uvda** begins 3 March comprising both Negev Brigade in the Central Negev and Golani Infantry Brigade in the Arava to occupy the Negev and reach the Gulf of Akaba. Both brigades reach Eilat on 10 March 1949. Soldiers improvise a flag on the beach at Um Rashrash using ink on a white cloth. Israel now has territorial control of a small strip 12 kilometers along the Red Sea coast from the British-established Sinai-Negev border at Taba towards Akaba.

Botanical Gardens at Kibbutz Ein Gedi   Adrian Wolff

1949   On 10 March 1949 in an amphibious landing from Sodom, Alexandroni Brigade captures the **Ein Gedi** on the western shore of the Dead Sea. In 1953 some brigade members establish a Nahal settlement at Ein Gedi, almost 400 meters below sea level. The Kibbutz established in 1956, is a tourist attraction famous for its lush sub-tropical botanical gardens, a wonder in the desert; a hotel and a hostel; field school and Nature Reserve. *"Like a cluster of henna in Ein-gedi vineyards."* (Song of Solomon 1:14).

1949   The **Israel-Lebanon** Armistice Agreement is signed on 23 March at Rosh Hanikra.

1949   The **Israel-Jordan** Armistice Agreement is signed in Rhodes on 3 April 1949. Jordan maintains control of the West Bank (Judah and Samaria) which it formally (illegally) annexes, fearing local Palestinians will take control. Only Great Britain, Iraq and Pakistan recognize this move. Article 8, paragraph 2 of the Israel-Jordan Armistice states Jordan will assure *"free access to the holy places and cultural institutions."* Jordan refuses to honor its commitments. Israeli Jews and Christians are barred from entering East Jerusalem and access to their holy sites. No new Christian church is permitted to be constructed during the Jordanian period (1948-1967). The Jewish Quarter is destroyed, including the synagogues and yeshivot (Jewish learning centers). Jordan does not relinquish the area it captured at Naharai'im in the Jordan Valley. During the years 1948-1994, Jordan never entertains the idea of an independent Palestine in the West Bank fearing Palestinians will usurp the rule in Jordan.

1949   Only on 13 May 1949 does Britain recognize the State of Israel de facto and 28 April 1950 de jure. In May 1949, Israel is admitted as a member of the United Nations.

1949   In July 1949, the UN sponsored Palestinian Conciliation Commission meets in Lausanne, Switzerland. **Israel offers to grant 100,000 Arab refugees entry into Israel on condition it is part of a peace agreement. The Arabs reject the offer.**

1949   On 20 July 1949 signing of the **Israel-Syria** Armistice Agreement at Mahanai'im in the Upper Galilee. Syria withdraws it troops from positions it holds west of the Jordan River at Mishmar Hayarden and in the Jordan River Delta area. Both Israel and Syria withdraw their troops to new positions along each side of the Demilitarized Zone equidistant from International Border of 1923. (See Sykes-Picot 1916). Within two years (May 1951) Syria will move its forces to the western side of the Demilitarized Zone, placing its troops on the eastern bank of the Jordan River; the northeastern shore of the Kinneret (Sea of Galilee), capturing the southeastern Golan slopes including el-Hamam (Hamat Gader). (See Syrians 1951).

1949   **Iraq,** having sent its forces to invade and destroy the infant State of Israel, never signs any Armistice Agreement and to this day is still formally in a State of War against Israel.

1949 **The Arab States regard these Armistice Agreements as temporary and not binding upon them to recognize or accept Israel or its borders.** Lebanon is the only country to recognize the common international border. No Arab state makes peace with Israel; on the contrary, they promote an economic and political anti-Israel boycott, close all airspace and sea-lanes to Israeli vessels or any foreign carrier flying or sailing to or from Israel. Arab countries prepare their armies for their next attack while assisting terrorists and other non-regular fighters to attack Israeli civilians and settlements.

1949-1967 Jordanian illegal Occupation of the West Bank and Jerusalem

The first Palestine Congress (30 September 1948) views Palestine as part of Syria. Jordan maintains control of the West Bank (Judah and Samaria) and East Jerusalem which it formally (illegally) annexes, fearing local Palestinians will take control, recognized only by Britain, Iraq and Pakistan. This action is regarded as illegal by the Arab League. All residents automaticaly gain Jordanian citizenship (24 April 1950) The Jordanians immediately expel all the Jewish residents of East Jerusalem. All but one of the 35 synagogues in the Old City are destroyed or used as stables and chicken coops. The ancient Jewish cemetery on Mount of Olives is desecrated, tombstones used for construction, paving roads and lining latrines. Access to the Holy Places is denied to Israeli Jews who are barred from visiting their holy site, The Western Wall. Tourists entering East Jerusalem have to present proof they are not Jewish.

In East Jerusalem, Arab Christian rights are curtailed as the Christian population declines from over 25,000 in 1947 to 12,646 in 1967. The Christian population of Bethlehemn 1948 is approximately 85% of its total, declining to 46% in 1967 to less than 15% of its 35,000 inhabitants today.

Agriculture remains the primary activity of the West Bank. Electricity and water supplies to Jerusalem and the West Bank remain erratic or non-existent. During this period only 4 out of 708 towns and villages have 24-hour running water. No foreign Arab leader visits Jerusalem during the nineteen years when Jordan controlled East Jerusalem.

Map 41. The State of Israel 1949

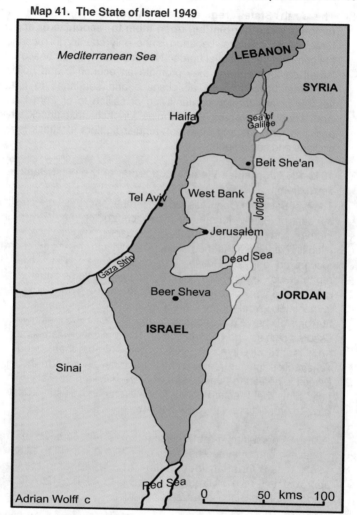

Adrian Wolff c

Chapter 24. State Building 1949 - 1966

1949   The remains of Zionist leader Dr. Theodor Herzl are interred in a state funeral in Mt. Herzl Military Cemetery. Railway line from the coast to Jerusalem is reinstated. Jerusalem Electricity Company in west Jerusalem is connected to the Israeli National Grid. Most of the 65,000 Arab inhabitants in east Jerusalem have no electricity during the early years of the Jordanian Period (1948-1967).

1949   The Daniel Sieff Institute in Rehovot, is renamed 'The Weizmann Institute', a post-graduate institute maintaining the highest international standards of academic research in science and technology in five faculties: biology, biochemistry, chemistry, physics, and mathematical sciences. It has produced a Nobel Prize winner. Yeda Research & Development Co. Ltd. promotes commercial development of research undertaken in the Institute.

1949   **Jerusalem** is declared capital of Israel (13 December 1949). A unique situation as international communities appease Arabs by failing to recognize Jerusalem as the capital of Israel and continue to locate their embassies in Tel Aviv to this day. Israeli government rations food due to pressure of extraordinary population increases, lack of sufficient agricultural infrastructure and foreign exchange.

1949   IDF reduces its troops from 110,000 to 47,000, with 12,000 permanent soldiers and 35,000 conscripts. Veterans are placed in reserve units after completing their compulsory 3-year service.

1949   In 1949, 239,954 Jewish immigrants settle in Israel. www.cbs.gov.il

1950   Israeli Parliament, the Knesset passes 'The Law of Return' giving every Jew the right to immigrate and receive Israeli citizenship.

1950   The two-year **Operations Ezra and Nehamia** (the air operation is known as Operation Ali Baba), airlifts 120,000 Jews from Iraq to Israel, ending the vibrant, successful and continuous Jewish life in Babylonia/Iraq for over 2500 years. Iraqi government expropriates all Jewish-owned property. A few thousand Jews wish to remain.

1950   The United Nations Refugee Works Administration **(UNWRA)** Mandate *"Anyone whose normal place of residence was in Mandate Palestine...from 1 June 1946 to 15 May 1948...lost both home and...livelihood...is eligible for UNRWA registration...descendants...of...Palestine refugees are also eligible."* (for eternity!). Jews who flee their homes in the Jewish Quarter of the Old City Jerusalem, Atarot, Neve Ya'akov, Etzion Bloc and other areas are never compensated. **UN does not assist**

Israel to absorb the over 800,000 penniless Jews who flee from Arab lands to Israel, nor the many thousands of displaced Jewish survivors of the Holocaust who immigrate during the same period. Arab countries reject any resettlement of Palestinian refugees who may not become citizens of the host countries.

1950 **The Arab League** in Cairo adopts a motion forbidding any of its members having any political or economic ties with Israel, nor is any member allowed to make peace with Israel. Egypt bans any Israeli or foreign vessels bound or originating from Israel or any commerce to or from Israel to pass through the Suez Canal.

1950 Israel is open to any Jewish refugee, as Jewish population increases from from 630,000 end 1947; 686,000 end 1948; 1,203,000 end 1950; to 1,591,000 end 1955. (See Appendix 6.7).

1950 The Israeli government through fiscal policy, pursues a **Decentralization Policy** to encourage both the growing population and developing industry to locate outside the Tel Aviv area. Government laws establish new Development Towns in the north and south, granting entrepreneurs financial incentives to establish businesses in these areas. Examples of this policy are:

1. Population dispersal plans 1948 - 1967.
2. Subsidize low-cost housing.
3. Preferential taxation rates.
4. Directing new immigrants to Absorption Centers located in new Development Towns.
5. The Law to Encourage Investments in Development Areas.
6. The government finances a high proportion of the infrastructure investment of Development Areas to facilitate low-cost land purchases by homeowners.

New Development Towns and year established.

North	South
Kiryat Shmona, 1949	Ashdod, 1957
Hazor, 1953	Ashkelon, 1950
Beit She'an, repopulated 1949	Kiryat Malachi, 1951
Migdal Ha'emek, 1953	Kiryat Gat, 1954
Nazareth Ilit, 1957	Sderot, 1951
Ma'alot, 1957	Ofakim, 1955
Karmiel, 1964	Netivot, 1956
	Be'er Sheva, repopulated 1948
	Arad, 1961
	Dimona, 1955
	Yeruham, 1951
	Mitzpe Ramon, 1954
	Eilat, 1951

1950   Israeli Government buildings are constructed in the Kirya area of Jerusalem's Givat Ram quarter. These buildings cannot be described as 'an architectural esthetic success'. Israeli Government functions are transferred from Tel Aviv to Jerusalem. The first municipal elections are held. Shlomo Zalman Shragai mayor (1950-1952).

1950   Population is 1,370,100 including 1,203,000 (88%) Jews, 170,563 Jewish immigrants this year, 52 civilians killed by Arab terrorists.

1951   In May 1951 Syrians troops move westwards on the Golan Heights across the Demilitarized Zone, now stationed in new positions along the east bank of the Jordan River, the northeastern shore of the Kinneret (Sea of Galilee) and the southeastern slopes of the Golan including Hamat Gader in the Yarmuk Valley. Syria ignores its signature to the Israeli-Syrian General Armistice Agreement 1353 of 20 July 1949. *"Article 1:2 No aggressive action by the armed forces. Article 2:1 No military or political advantage should be gained. Article 3:3 No element of land, sea or air...shall advance beyond or pass over for any purpose whatsoever the Armistice demarcation Line".* Israel, tired of war, involved in absorbing hundreds of thousand immigrants, developing infrastructure and industry, does not engage this Syrian aggression.

1951   Syrian soldiers situated in new positions on Golan Heights overlook Kibbutz Ein Gev on the Kinneret eastern shore, continue to shoot at the Israeli farmers and fishermen below. IDF Golani Infantry troops in a retaliatory operation 'Mislat Ha'damut' attack Syrian Army positions just north of Ein Gev. IDF is very dissatisfied with co-ordination in this operation, which leaves 41 Golani troops dead, half from 'friendly fire'.

1951   Egypt finances and encourages Fedayeen terrorist raids from Gaza into Israel. Terrorists have an advantage of not retracing their steps and can continue to freedom in the West Bank, before returning to Gaza via Egypt. During 1951, 111 Israelis (soldiers and civilians) are murdered from attacks originating from Jordan, and another 26 Israelis in attacks originating from Gaza.

1951   After Friday morning prayers Muslim Fundamentalist supporters of the Mufti assassinate King Abdullah I of Jordan as he exits al-Aqsa Mosque in Jerusalem (20 July), due to his previous contacts with Israeli officials. Abdullah's son Talal is incapable of governing. His grandson Hussein is appointed King of Jordan within two years.

1951   A section of **Hula Valley swamps** (wetlands) is drained (completed 1957), increasing cultivated areas and reducing sources of malaria. Environmentalists protest as some 500 million birds rest here during their bi-annual migration between Europe and Africa. Birdlife and many rare species of flora and fauna are found. After the drainage many migratory birds cease to nest and feed in the Hula. In 1971, parts of Hula areas are re-flooded.

Hula Valley, Golan Heights in background   Adrian Wolff

1951   During 1951, 175,279 Jewish immigrants settle in Israel.

1952   The austerity economic program continues. PM Ben-Gurion emphasizes the importance of Israeli foreign policy encouraging friendship with countries beyond the immediate circle of Israeli's neighbors - Iran, Turkey and Ethiopia.

1952   General Mohammed Naguib and Colonel Gamal Abdul Nasser stage a military coup seizing power in Egypt forcing King Farouk to abdicate in favor of a Revolutionary Council, that exiles him. General Naguib is both President and Prime Minister.

1952   The Middle East is divided with the USA supporting conservative monarchies, the USSR supporting socialist, secular dictatorships.

1952   Yitzhak Kariv is elected mayor of Jerusalem from 1952 until 1955.

1952   '**Reparations Agreement**' to compensate Jewish Holocaust survivors is negotiated by Dr. Nahum Goldman, chairman the Zionist Federation, signed by West German Chancellor Konrad Adenauer and Israeli PM David Ben-Gurion. After very stormy debates and passionate discussions, the Knesset finally approves. A very positive economic revival follows in Israel from the flow of German money.

1952   **Arab States reject** as completely unacceptable UN Special Political Committee proposal 11 December 1952 that Israel and Arab countries should begin direct Peace Talks aimed at a final peace in Palestine. **Israeli government agrees to the proposal.**

1952 Fedayeen terrorists attacks originating from Jordan and Gaza murder 114 Israelis (soldiers and civilians) and 48 respectively.

1953 **Bahai'i Shrine** of the Bab is completed in Haifa. The Baha'ullah, Mizra Husayn Ali (1817-1892), founder of the Bahai'i religion together with the remains of his son Abdul (Abbas) Baha (dies 1924) are brought from Acre, interred in the golden-domed Shrine.

Haifa, Bahai'i Gardens, view from lower entrance   Adrian Wolff

1953 Between 1950 and 1953 IDF learns from its failures and trains new operational regiments. A specialized paratrooper commando unit, number 101, commanded by **Major Ariel Sharon** is created. The IDF enforces a policy of 'after me' - troops follow the officer into battle. Wounded comrades are never left in a battle zone. IDF devises a concept of strategic depth, built on infantry with armor and air force assistance. Fighting must be brought into enemy territory as existing armistice lines are too close to the Mediterranean Sea and the country can be split in two. Regular fighting units are trained for general operations (*batash*), canceling the need to use specialized forces.

1953 The Heichal Shlomo, the Center of the Chief Rabbinate of Israel, is constructed in Jerusalem to include the Great Synagogue and Wolfsohn Museum of Jewish Culture. Fire erupts in Church of the Holy Sepulchre, Jerusalem, under Jordanian control.

1953 On 2 May 1953, on his 18th birthday, **Hussein** (1935-1999) is crowned king of the Hashemite Kingdom of Jordan.

1953 Egypt continues to encourage anti-Israel terrorism by providing finance and training camps in Gaza. Arab terrorists murder an Israeli mother and her children in Yehud. IDF commanded by Major Ariel Sharon raids Kibya in West Bank from where the terrorists originate, killing the perpetrators and villagers. In August, five Israeli civilians are murdered in the Negev. This year, Arab terrorists murder 124 Israelis (soldiers and civilians) in attacks originating from Jordan and 38 Israelis in attacks from Gaza.

1954 Colonel Gamal Abdul Nasser places General Mohammed Naguib under house arrest, eliminates all opposition and proclaims himself President of the Republic of Egypt. He bans the Muslim Brotherhood and encourages Palestinian fedayeen ("*those who sacrifice themselves*") raids from Gaza into Israel. A Joint Egypt-USSR Military Agreement. Russia will engineer, finance and build the Aswan Dam on the Nile River in return for influence and military bases in Egypt, much to USA and British aversion.

1954 Israeli Secret Service (Mossad) sets up a spy ring in Egypt to sabotage US and British buildings, hoping to distance them from President Nasser. Egyptians capture Israeli agents. Max Meir Binet (1917-1954) commits suicide in prison, and two others (Moshe Marzouk and Shmuel Azar) are hanged. Others receive long prison terms, released following the Six-Day War in 1967. Israeli Defense Minister, Pinchas Lavon denying any knowledge of their presence in Egypt, is forced to resign. Israel's reputation is damaged. This episode is known as the Lavon Affair or *Esek Bish* – the mishap.

1954 The Retaliation Policy on Arab military targets is begun due to continual terrorism originating from Israel's Arab neighbors. About 80% of these IDF raids are unsuccessful. Syrians snipers kill two Israeli policemen in a patrol boat in the Kinneret. Terrorists originating from the West Bank murder three Israeli civilians, members of Kibbutz Mevo'ot Betar in the Jerusalem Hills. Arab terrorists ambush a bus traveling up the Scorpion Pass in the Negev, massacring 11 Israeli civilians. Jordanian troops standing on the ramparts of Old City Wall fire at Jews in Mamila in Israeli controlled West Jerusalem, killing three Jewish civilians. During 1954 Arab terrorists murder 117 Israelis in attacks originating from Jordan and 50 Israelis from Gaza.

1955 Opening of **Bar Ilan University** in Ramat Gan taking an example from Pirkei Avot 2:2 "*Torah study is best with worldly knowledge*". Also "*All study of the Torah without work must in the end be futile.*" The university is named after Rabbi Meir Bar-Ilan (Berlin), a pre-state religious Zionist leader. Bar-Ilan University houses Israel's largest schools of education, social work, Jewish studies, prominent scientific research institutes, strategic studies, Land of Israel studies, Jewish Law and Philosophy. The university has many community outreach programs for both Israelis and Diaspora Jewry, including programs for the elderly, disadvantaged youth, gifted youth, Jewish communities and educational institutions abroad. The Mizrahi movement in America gives financial support.

1955 Construction of Dominus Flevit Church on Mt. of Olives over ruins of a previous Byzantine Church, Antonio Barluzzi is the architect. Christian tradition states Jesus stops here on His final visit to Jerusalem as He weeps foreseeing the destruction of Jerusalem. Dominus Flevit = The Lord wept. (Luke 19:41; 21:20; Mark 13:2.)

Mt. of Olives, Dominus Flevit Catholic Church   Adrian Wolff

1955 Gershon Agron is elected mayor of Jerusalem 1955 until 1959.

1955 The Joint Egyptian-Syrian Military Command, unites both armies.

1955 IDF attacks terrorist camps and training facilities in Gaza in Operations Black Arrow, Elkayam and Volcano killing over 180 Egyptian soldiers. These reprisal raids are in retaliation for continual terrorist infiltrations and attacks against Israeli settlements and civilians. IDF attacks Syrian positions northeast of Kibbutz Ein Gev on the Kinneret in a reprisal for continual Syrian shooting at Israeli fishermen.

1955 **Population** is 1,789,100 including 1,590,500 (89%) Jews.

1956 Construction of the **National Water Carrier** (completed in 1964) to bring water from the Kinneret (Sea of Galilee) in the north to reach the Negev in the south, some 350 kilometers. See: Water 1964.

1956 The opening of the **Tel Aviv University**.

1956 Jordanian troops kill four Israeli archeologists investigating antiquities near Kibbutz Ramat Rachel outside Jerusalem. Terrorists originating from Gaza attack settlements in the Western Negev at Gevulot, Nirim and Kisufim. IDF makes a retaliatory raid against continual terrorist activity originating from Kalkilia, just inside the West Bank, east of Kfar Saba. After 17 IDF soldiers are killed, IDF leadership is dissatisfied with the effectiveness, discontinuing the retaliatory raids.

1956 A parcel bomb explodes in Gaza, killing Egyptian Colonel Mustafa Hafez Hayeli. Egypt receives pledges for loans from USA, Great Britain and World Bank to construct the Aswan Dam. Simultaneously Nasser receives arms and loans from Soviets causing USA, Great Britain and World Bank to cancel their support. Egypt nationalizes Suez Canal Company (26 July) now coming under Soviet influence, forcing Britain to relinquish control, without granting any compensation, as Egypt begins to collect all toll fees. Britain begins to consider a military operation against Egypt

1956 Jordan joins Egyptian-Syrian Military Command, isolating and surrounding Israel. Egypt places two 155mm artillery guns (again in 1967) thereby closing Tiran Straits at the entrance to Gulf of Akaba to all shipping to or from Israeli Red Sea port, Eilat.

1956 On 27 October 1956 Israel reaches an agreement with Great Britain and France in Sevres to attack Egypt in the wake of its continual financing and encouragement of terrorist activities originating from Egyptian-controlled territory and closing of the Red Sea to Israeli shipping. Israel prepares battle plans taking into account the possibility of British and French withdrawal from the war theater and leaving them as the lone combatants.

1956 From 29 October to 5 November 1956 Israeli troops enter Sinai in **Operation Kadesh - the Sinai Campaign**.

The Israeli aims of this operation are to:
- Reopen the Tiran Straits and allow shipping to and from Eilat.
- Destroy the Egyptian Army in Sinai.
- Destroy terrorist bases in Gaza and Sinai.

Prime Minister of Israel: David Ben-Gurion
- Chief of Staff: Lieutenant-General Moshe Dayan
- Northern Command: Major-General Itzhak Rabin
- Central Command: Major-General Zvi Tzur
- Southern Command: Major-General Asaf Shimhoni
- Air Force: Major-General Dan Tolkovsky
- Navy: Major-General: Shmuel Tankus

1956 All IAF pilots are Israelis trained to operational proficiency. Israel Air Force consists of US manufactured P-51 Mustangs, Harvards, B-17 bombers, and French Meteors, Ouragans and a few months prior to the war, Mystere fighters are delivered. IAF Ouragans and Mysteres bomb Egyptian positions and airfields proving their operational success in war conditions.

1956 Egyptian forces ambush IDF paratroopers approaching Abu Ageila in Sinai, attempting to capture the main road from Nitzana to Suez. IDF Armored Infantry captures Abu Ageila, Rafiah, Gaza Strip, el-Arish on northern Sinai coast and Egyptian Sinai Headquarters at Um-Katef. Egyptian troops flee towards the Suez Canal. IDF takes three days to reach the Suez Canal and Sharm el-Sheik, breaking the naval blockade on the Gulf of Akaba and Israeli Red Sea port of Eilat. Another three days of mopping-up isolated Egyptian forces. The IAF proves its operational ability in war conditions to transport troops, weapons, ammunition, evacuate wounded, destroy enemy forces, positions, materiel and convoys.

1956 An Egyptian destroyer Ibrahim al-Awal shells the Israeli port of Haifa. The Israeli Navy captures this vessel in the open sea and is renamed INS Haifa. British RAF planes flying from Cyprus and Malta bomb Egyptian Air Bases.

1956 On the night 31 October/1 November, two days after the Israeli attack, British paratroopers in Operation Musketeer, land and capture Port Said at western entrance to the Suez Canal. French paratroopers in Operation Omelette, land and capture Port Fuad on the eastern entrance. There are serious misunderstandings and lack of co-ordination between British and French forces in planning and execution of this operation. Problems are measurements (metric or British), types of equipment, even agreement of the name of the operation (Hamilcar or Amilcar), etc. The Joint Anglo-French operation lasts 44 hours, resulting in a complete political failure, with political maneuvering, indecisiveness and constant change of military plans. US President Dwight Eisenhower (1890–1969, president 1953-1961) forces a cease-fire and withdrawal of all British and French troops without any political gains despite their military success, removing British influence in the Middle East

1956 **The Sinai Campaign - Operation Kadesh Summary**
The Israeli Army:
- Defeats the Egyptian Army. Captures Sinai Peninsula and Gaza Strip, a hotbed of anti-Israel terrorist activity
- The Straits of Tiran at the entrance to the Gulf of Akaba are opened to Israeli shipping
- Operation Kadesh 189 Israeli troops are killed and 899 wounded

1956 President Nasser boasts of Egypt's ability to repel the British, French and Israeli forces. **Egypt expels the Jewish community of over 25,000, confiscating their property.** Jewish citizens of Egypt now become penniless, stateless refugees. Many immigrate to Israel. The Suez Canal Zone and Suez Canal Company remain nationalized, closed to Israeli shipping.

1957 The United States forces Israel to withdraw its troops from Sinai and Gaza. UNTSO (United Nations Truce Supervising Organization) posts 3,300 troops along Israeli-Egyptian border from Mediterranean Sea to Taba on the Red Sea and also at Sharm el-Sheik to ensue the Straits of Tiran remains open to Israeli shipping. (See Nasser 1967). Suez Canal remains closed to Israeli shipping. Gaza remains a hotbed of terrorism.

1957 Fredric Mann Auditorium opens in Tel Aviv, home to the Israel Philharmonic Orchestra. Renamed Charles Bronfman in 2013.

1957 **Yad Vashem, the Holocaust Memorial is opened in Jerusalem.** World War II began when the Allies fought to destroy Nazi German expansion, not because of the Holocaust. The Holocaust is the sad story of the genocide of Jews during the period 1933–1945.

Yad Vashem, Jerusalem. Children's Memorial   Adrian Wolff

A Knesset Law is passed in 1953 to:
- commemorate the six million Jews murdered in the Holocaust.
- preserve the heritage of the thousands of destroyed Jewish communities
- pay tribute to the heroic stand of the fighters and ghetto inmates.
- honor Righteous Among the Nations who risked their lives to save Jews.
"Was there such a thing in your days or in the days of your forefathers? Tell your children about it, and your children to their

children, and their children to another generation." (Joel 1:2,3).
"Lest you forget the things that you saw with your own eyes." (Deuteronomy 4:9). *"In My house and within My walls I will give them a place of honor and renown* (יד ושם)*"* (Isaiah 56:5.). The site includes a Memorial Hall, Children's Memorial, Historical Museum, Hall of Names, Avenue of the Righteous Gentiles, Valley of the Dead Communities, Pillar of Heroism, Library and Archives. A new museum is opened in 2005.

1957   At Mt. Scopus Jordanian soldiers kill four Israeli policemen and a UN truce supervisor. 19 Israeli are killed in terror attacks during this year, including 5 Yeshiva students at Kfar Chabad.

1958   United Arab Republic unites Egypt and Syria, disbanded in 1961.

1958   Israeli Foreign Ministry opens **Mashav, Center for International Development Cooperation**, to provide guidance and training in Israel and abroad. *"The State of Israel is committed to fulfilling its responsibility to contribute to the fight against poverty and global efforts to achieve sustainable development"*. Assistance is provided in agriculture, public health, education, medicine, community development, and advancement the status of women. Over 250,000 from developing countries benefit from this program.

1959   All Christian sects finally agree on restoration of the Church of Holy Sepulchre to repair damage sustained in the 1927 earthquake

1959   Egypt's Nasser (26 July) *"In the next battle we shall erase Israel."*

1959   The Eilat-Ashkelon Pipeline Company constructs a 16-inch pipeline between Eilat on Red Sea and Ashkelon on Mediterranean Sea continuing to the Petroleum Refineries in Haifa. Petroleum is imported from Iran, transferred to Oil Tankers in the Mediterranean Sea, bypassing the Suez Canal. After the Islamic Revolution in 1979, Iran ceases petroleum supplies to Israel.

1959   Mordechai Ish-shalom is elected mayor of Jerusalem (1959-1965).

1960   **Settlements are established in the Arava desert** producing over 60% of Israel's vegetable exports, dates, dairy, field crops, 10% of the country's cut flowers, 90% ornamental fish. All agriculture is Hi-Tech using advanced, innovative techniques. The region has Agricultural R&D centers, agricultural packing houses, telecommunications, tourism services, industry and solar energy. Ketura Suntech photovoltaic (PV) solar-panel technology produces noiseless electricity without emissions or smoke, and uses no water. (See Water 1960). Algatechologies cultivates microalgae, to produce a natural astaxanthin, a powerful antioxidant.

1960   Israel Security Service (Mossad) captures Nazi functionary Adolf Eichmann in Argentina and spirits him to Israel. Eichmann's public trial takes place in 1961 at Beit Ha'am in Jerusalem where he is accused of crimes against humanity and the Jewish people. Found guilty, hanged and cremated in 1962. His ashes are dispersed at sea, beyond Israeli territorial waters.

1960   **Population** 2,150,400 including 1,911,300 (89%) Jews.

1961   The **Hebrew University** Mount Scopus campus is not operational after 1948 due to personal security danger to staff members and students. A new campus is officially inaugurated on Givat Ram, Jerusalem, to incorporate the **National Library**. The university has produced a Nobel prize winner for economics. *"Through wisdom a house is built, and it is established through understanding; and through knowledge, its chambers become filled with all dear and pleasant treasures."* (Proverbs 24:3,4).

1961   Opening of the largest hospital in the Middle East, the **new Hadassah Hospital in Ein Kerem**, West Jerusalem. The modern state-of-the-art facilities become world renowned and thousands of students from all over the world are given an opportunity to study at this hospital. The original Hadassah Hospital on Mt. Scopus is closed to the public in 1948, as the journey is too dangerous.

1962   During Hadassah Jubilee celebrations, the synagogue in the Hadassah Hospital, Ein Kerem is dedicated containing Jerusalem stone floors and walls. The twelve windows display Marc Chagall's stained-glass paintings of the 12 Sons of the Patriarch, Jacob.

1962   Following continual Syrian shelling of Kibbutz Ein Gev farmers and fishermen in the Kinneret, the IDF attack the Syrian army position at Nukeib, on the northern border of Ein Gev. 8 IDF soldiers are killed in this operation. The UN censors Israel.

1962   **From 1962 to 1964 Syria begins to construct a 73 kilometer canal along Golan Heights from Mt. Hermon in the north to the southern Golan to prevent rain and melting snow water from reaching Kinneret (Sea of Galilee), Israel's largest reservoir of fresh water.** Original plans also include boring a 200-meter vertical shaft in the Southern Golan (near Kibbutz Afik today) using the gravitational force to drive hydroelectric turbines. Water will exit though a tunnel to the Yarmuk River where they begin to construct a dam wall. Evidence of the canal, the shaft and dam wall can still be seen today. Israeli tanks and aircraft attack the construction equipment. Pressure from the USA and threat of war force the Syrians to halt construction in 1964. If this project continued to its completion, Israel would have been deprived of 30% of its fresh water sources and the Kinneret would have dried up.

1963   Opening of Hebrew Union College in King David Street, Jerusalem including the World Union of Progressive Judaism and Nelson Glueck School of Biblical Archaeology. Opening of Haifa University contributing to the Israel IBM Research Center, one of the very few IBM Research centers located outside of the USA.

1963   Ba'athist military coups in Iraq and Syria both ruled by totalitarian dictators, replace established families that previously ruled Syria.

1964   Israeli economy is in a recession from 1964 till 1967.

1964   **Completion of the construction of the National Water Carrier.** Israel has reached a serious consumption level of its water resources, utilizing almost all of its natural water from underground aquifers, the Jordan River, springs and streams. Any expansion of water resources can only be marginal under conventional methods and any future growth necessitates substantial capital investment. The rains fall in winter mainly in the north and central parts of the country while evaporation is high due to the long hot summers. Rainwater runs into the sea or into large drainage depressions situated below sea level, the fresh water Kinneret (Sea of Galilee) and very salty Dead Sea, making it essential to pump the water from one region to another. Capital investment is made available to supply the growing population and increased consumption per capita utilizing floodwater, recycling and desalination and the strategic need to become self-sufficient in agricultural production. See Appendix 6.2.5

The three sources of the Jordan River are:
1. Dan in the northeast corner of Israel.
2. Banias emerging from springs at the foothills of Mt. Hermon.
3. Hetzbani (Snir) River originating in Lebanon.

Israel is unique whereby most of the land is owned by the State. In addition **ALL water resources are State-owned**, controlling the distribution and consumption of water through **The Water Law.** A legal framework and administrative system is required for its implementation as norms are defined for agriculture, industrial and domestic consumption.

Water Law. "*Israel's Water sources are public property, controlled by the State, and devoted to the needs of its residents and country's development. A person's right in land does not grant him rights in a water source located on that land or passing through it or within its boundaries.*" "*Every person is entitled to receive and use water, subject to the provision of this law*". "***No person shall***

draw water - be it for his personal use or for supply to others...Unless licensed to do so by the Water Commissioner."

Water Quotas. The Israeli Ministry of Agriculture lays down policy for overall agricultural planning based upon demand for crops and water consumption necessary for its production, to obtain the greatest efficiency in water allocation. **The system operates through allocation of quotas to agricultural producers depending on regional-ecological considerations.** The state encourages agricultural development in semi-arid areas having a lack of infrastructure (including water pipes, pumps, canals, dams, etc.). National-scale infrastructure projects must be financed by government sources as the full cost of water development cannot be borne by the farmers themselves. Government intervention takes the form of micro-economic farm planning, together with administrative system of marketing. Cotton is grown locally using recycled (grey) water, an increased source of usable water. Water intensive crops - fodder grains, barley, sorghum, corn, sugar and rice are also imported.

Desert Agriculture, Planting area-no top soil. Neot Hakikar. Adrian Wolff

Kibbutzim have diversified to combine agricultural and industrial production. Today their income from non-agricultural sources exceeds agricultural output. The moshav (smallholding) movement is restricted by the small size of each unit and the ability to adjust crop mix, causing a shift away from the small-scale single-crop single-family production output. The moshav is forced to develop and expand its production units by arranging for cooperative cultivation of orchards, vegetables and field crops, adjusting economies of scale.

Results of the Water Policy. *"I will turn the desert into a pond of water and a parched land into sources of water."* (Isaiah 41:18). Experience gained in Israel has proved semi-arid regions can support a high level of modern agriculture and sometimes higher than countries with temperate climate. It is essential to combine advanced technology with appropriate institutional planning and organizational framework. A substantial capital investment together with gene research and improved strains will give the desired results. The economic and social cost of agricultural contribution to the Gross National Product and the Settlement Policy makes rural settlement more attractive.

Water Technology. *"I constructed pools from which to irrigate a grove of young trees"*. (Ecclesiastes 2:6). Inter-regional water is transferred from a water surplus areas in the north to water deficit areas in the south. Transporting water from one region to another will not solve problems of semi-arid zones, as flexibility in existing institutional framework must adjust to new realities. Not only laying of pipes and pumping water, but it also entails technological, sociological, judicial, and organizational administration. Over 70% of water consumed in urban areas is desalinized.

Desert Vegetables (eggplant) - no soil. Neot Hakikar.   Adrian Wolff

The Israeli National Water Company (Mekorot) has the technology to efficiently transport and use all water resources. Construction of the **National Water Carrier** between 1956 to 1964 traverses mountains, gullies (wadis) and rocky terrain by the construction of inverse siphons. Due to budgetary restrictions, water flows through the first 35 kilometers in open canals using gravity. Water is chlorinated and filtered in reservoirs at Tsalmon and Eshkol making it fit for drinking before entering closed pipes. Mitzpe Ramon is the southernmost point some 350 kilometers from the Kinneret. Regions further south receive water from local brackish wells and from desalination plants. Water is pumped at around 4 atmospheric pressures making National Water Carrier the largest single consumer of electricity.

The National Water Carrier pumps surplus water from Kinneret during winter into the aquifers to recharge the groundwater and avoid evaporation in surface reservoirs. It is essential to obtain information on physical quantity of water required for optimal water input to agricultural output. Water consumption combined with genus of plants and climatic conditions have to be studied. The methods of bringing the water to the plant is improved by introducing a wide range of irrigation innovations such as the drip system and include the technical adjustment of irrigation systems to particular crops leading to a physical decrease in the quantity of water consumed per unit of produce. Crop structure finds a suitable mix to meet domestic and export demand while using the optimum usage of available water resources. Solutions are not easily found when the time factor of agriculture production is taken into account, and adjustment plans do not always coincide with market or climatic variables.

Crops. *"Everything has its season...a time to plant and a time to uproot the planted."* (Ecclesiastes 3:1,2). *"He who works his soil will be sated with bread."* (Proverbs 12:11). Israeli Agricultural policy is to increase crop-yields, food preservation and increased shelf life. Greenhouses create an artificial climatic situation to grow vegetables and flowers. Compatible investment funds are also essential to make this operation sustain itself and become profitable. Israeli farmers revolutionize watering of agricultural crops through the **drip irrigation system** which is adopted worldwide. Water is flows directly to the roots of the plant through tiny holes in small tubes, easily redeployed according to need. The system is set on a timer, reducing evaporation and eliminating run-off. The water is delivered directly to the roots of the crop resulting in is less moisture on the leaves and surrounding soil, suppressing mould and weeds, reducing the need for chemicals and pesticides. Israel recycles over 75% of its waste-water (reclaimed/recycled) used for agriculture, waste management and fish farms in the desert. Vegetables, olive groves and dates orchards are irrigated with saline water in the Arava region yielding high-quality produce for export. Netafim and Dan markets the technology in over 110 countries creating self-sustaining agricultural communities in drought-stricken areas.

Desert Agriculture, Drip Irrigation no top-soil, Kadesh Barnea. Adrian Wolff

Plantations in the desert, Ashlim   Adrian Wolff

Methods of improving the quality of water in Israel.
1. Prevention of the pollution of the mountain and coastal aquifers.
2. Regular checking chemical composition, microbiological quality.
3. Regular checking pollution of Kinneret, taking preventive measures
4. Treating the water of the National Water Carrier.
5. Biological treatment with the introduction of fish.
6. Water treatment by filtration.
7. Maintaining Quality Standards and Testing of drinking water.

Desert Agriculture - Drip Irrigation - no top soil, Kadesh Barnea. Adrian Wolff

Israel's Agricultural Success. Israel's agricultural production has increased several times over since 1948. Advisory services cover all crop and animal production, including crop protection, irrigation and soil analysis, farm machinery and farm management. Successful desalinization, reuse and water consumption control has decrease Israel's dependency on rainfall.

The Ministry of Agriculture, through its advisors reaches out to the farmers through intelligent one-to-one field visits, group activities, seminars, courses, R&D and technology dissemination:

- Promote agriculture and rural development by raising production and managerial capabilities.
- Provide information, knowledge and agricultural technological developments.
- Promote water saving, correct the use of effluents, reducing pollution and pesticide contamination.

Examples of Israel's excellence in agricultural technology:
- Arava desert region produces 40% of Israel's vegetable exports and 10% of the cut flowers.
- Average Israeli Holstein dairy cow yields over 13,000 liters/year.

Forests. "*When you come to the land you shall plant any food tree.*" (Leviticus 19:23). "*In the wilderness I will set cedar, acacia, myrtle and pine tree; I will place cypress, fir and box tree together in the desert.*" (Isaiah 41:19). In 1960 the Knesset passes the Basic Lands Law. The Jewish National Fund (JNF)=(KKL) is responsible for land development and afforestation. In Biblical times Eretz

Israel had many natural forests, but over time, with numerous wars (trees used for making of war machinery – walls, catapults, bows, arrows etc), and construction of railway, decimating the natural forests by the early 20th century, other than in Northern Galilee and Mt. Carmel areas. The JNF undertakes a national tree planting policy (including national tree planting day tu b'shvat in February). Afforestation has become more sophisticated with new tree varieties and a greater integration between natural scrub and planted forests, with use of landscape architects. A few varieties trees are planted in forests. Forests are successful especially in the arid (less than 200mm) Lahav region of Northern Negev. Israeli research shows trees consume more carbon dioxide in low rainfall areas. Jewish National Fund directs water conservation methods, creating reservoirs, improving underground water table, preventing erosion and flooding and reclaiming land. Reservoirs are often built in parks to double as recreation areas.

Afforestation in the Negev Desert   Adrian Wolff

1964   Pope Paul VI makes an official visit to Nazareth, the Galilee, East Jerusalem, while refraining from entering Israeli West Jerusalem.

1964   Palestinian national interests are headed from 1921 to 1964 by the ex-Mufti of Jerusalem, Haj Amin al-Husseini (1895-1974). **The Palestinian Liberation Organization (PLO=Fatah)** is established in Cairo with Ahmad al-Shakairy (1908-1980) as president. An independent Palestinian State is not created in the West Bank or in Gaza. The PLO Charter states their aim is to wipe out the Jewish state, Israel, promoting violence such as hijackings, suicide bombings and assaults on Jews and Israelis, while the words 'negotiations' and 'compromise' are not found in the PLO vocabulary. They operate in Gaza with complete Egyptian permission, encouragement and finance. **The word 'Jerusalem' is not found in any of the 33 Articles, nor in the 'State of Palestine Declaration' of Independence 15th November 1988.**

The Palestinian National Covenant, published in 1968 states:
Article 1: "*Palestine is the homeland of the Palestinian Arab people and an integral part of the Great Arab Homeland.*"
Article 2: "*Palestine, with the boundaries it had during the British mandate, is an indivisible territorial unit.*" (State of Israel does not exist).
Article 9: "***Armed struggle is the only way to liberate Palestine** and is a strategy and not tactics. The Palestinian Arab people affirm its absolute resolution and abiding determination to pursue the armed struggle and march toward the armed popular revolution, to liberate its homeland*".
Article 19: "*The partitioning of Palestine in 1947 and the establishment of Israel is fundamentally null and void, whatever time has elapsed.*"

PLO founder Yasser Arafat (1929-2004) is born in Cairo as Abel-Raof Arafat al-Qudwa al-Husseini, also known as Abu Omar. He believes terror the prime means to obtain a Palestinian homeland. (See Intifada 2000). During the 1950's Arafat joins the Muslim Brotherhood in Egypt and heads Palestinian Student Union at Cairo University. The Palestinian National Covenant Article 7: "*It is the national duty to bring up individual Palestinians in an Arab revolutionary manner.*" PLO place a bomb on the Israeli National Water Carrier on 1 January 1965.

Palestinian Arabs do not consider themselves Palestinians prior to World War I, though the Jews did refer to themselves by that name. At no time has there ever been an Arab state in Palestine. Jordan never considers the West Bank to be Palestine.

1965 **Wolfgang Lotz** (1921-1993), born in Germany to a Jewish mother. He is not circumcised. He and his mother immigrate to Palestine in 1933, changing his name to Ze'ev Gur-Aryeh. At 15 he joins the Haganah, joins the British Army in World War II, serving in Egypt. In 1960, posing as an ex-Nazi, Lotz is sent by the Israeli Mossad to Egypt to collect information on the supply of Soviet arms, the growing influence of German advisers and scientists working on Egyptian rocket production. He is set-up as a horse breeder, and frequents horse riding clubs where he befriends Brig.-Gen. Fouad Osman, head of security for rocket bases and military factories. Lotz is caught in 1965, sentenced to 25 years in jail, released after the 1967 Six-Day War with other Israeli spies and soldiers.

1965 Egyptian-born Israeli spy, **Eli Cohen** (1924-1965) infiltrates Syrian political and military circles. Cohen's largest contribution is details of the Syrian project to divert the Hetzbani River in Lebanon towards Syria, and the Syria water canal on the Golan to prevent the rainwater descending to the Jordan. After bowing to international pressure, Syria halts the project on 30 July 1965. He encourages planting eucalyptus trees around their military camps on the Golan, making them easily visible to Israeli Intelligence. This knowledge will assist Israeli troops during the 1967 Six-Day War to by-pass the military camps. He is captured and publicly hanged in Damascus. His remains are never returned to Israel.

1965 **Teddy Kollek** (1911–2007) immigrates in 1933 to Kibbutz Ein Gev. Shortly before WWII he organizes a rescue mission to bring Jews from Austria to England. He acquires arms and ammunition for the Hagana. During Kollek's terms as Mayor of Jerusalem (1965-1993), the town will grow physically, culturally and be beautified, seen in new suburbs, increased walkways, landscaping, public parks, statues, public buildings (Israel Museum, Jerusalem Theater, Biblical Zoo), development of the Jewish Quarter, Old City.

Shrine of the Book, Israel Museum, Jerusalem   Adrian Wolff

1965 **Israel Museum** in Jerusalem, contains the largest permanent exhibition of antiquities, Judaica and Jewish folklore. The campus houses the Shrine of the Book, Model of Herodian Jerusalem, Billy Rose Garden, a large sculpture exhibition. Renovated and renewed in 2010. The **Dead Sea Scrolls**, found in caves at Qumran at the Dead Sea in 1947 are exhibited in the **Shrine of the Book,** a white circular building. (See Essenes -150, 68). The **Aleppo Codex** is the earliest known manuscript comprising the full text of the Tanach (Bible). This Codex, written in Eretz Israel in the 10th century, transferred to Egypt in the 11th century to protect it from the Crusaders, is deposited with the Aleppo Jewish community in the 14th century. In 1947, during riots in Aleppo against Jewish property, the community's synagogue is torched and the Codex is damaged. Smuggled out of Syria in 1958, only 295 of the original 495 pages survive.

1965 The computerized, container port of Ashdod is opened.

1965 **Population** 2,598,400 including 2,299,100 (89%) Jews.

Knesset, Jerusalem   Adrian Wolff

1966 The **Knesset** (parliament) building is completed above the Kirya in Jerusalem. The Rothschild Foundation provides finance.

1966 Syrians using the territorial advantage of the Golan Heights, repeatedly fire artillery, mortars and machine-guns on Israeli villages, farmers, fishermen and fields in the Upper Galilee and Kinneret areas. Following regular terrorist infiltrations from the Hebron Hills, the IDF enters Samoa, killing 18 Jordanian soldiers.

1966 The **Church of the Annunciation** in Nazareth (began in 1955, consecrated 1969) designed by Giovanni Muzio of Milan is completed, built over ruins of previously destroyed Byzantine and Crusader churches and another small church built in 1730 by Franciscan Catholic Fathers. The original church is where according to Christian tradition, the angel Gabriel appears before the Virgin Mary to announce She will give birth to the Messiah. In the grotto, a granite stone marks this spot. This very imposing and striking church is the largest in the Middle East, designed in modern Italian style with elaborate mosaic murals donated by various Catholic communities all over the world. The Church rotunda is built to resemble a lighthouse. The church is 65 meters long, 27 wide and 55 high. "*A light to bring revelation to the Gentiles.*" (Luke 2:32); "*Then Jesus spoke to them again saying 'I am the light of the world.*" (John 8:12).

"*Now in the sixth month the angel Gabriel was sent by God to a city in the Galilee named Nazareth, to a virgin betrothed to a man whose name was Joseph of the house of David. The virgin's name was Mary...the angel said to her, 'Rejoice...the Lord is with you, blessed are you among women...And behold you will conceive in your womb and bring forth a Son, and shall call his name Jesus.*" (Luke 1:26-31).

Church of the Annunciation, Nazareth   Adrian Wolff

The Latin quotation above the entrance is "*And the Word became flesh and dwelt amongst us'* (John 1:14).

Chapter 25. Six-Day and Yom Kippur Wars 1967 - 1973

1967   January to April 1967, Syrians regularly fire artillery, mortar and machine-guns at Israeli villages, farmers, fishermen and fields in Upper Galilee and Kinneret areas. Syria plans, without an operational date, Operation Amalita Saddam to capture the Upper Galilee. Syrians open fire 12 May on Israeli tractors in fields of Kibbutz Tel Katzir, Ha'on and Ein Gev. Later that day an aerial combat results in Syrian aircraft losses 6, Israeli 0

Southern Kinneret and Golan. Syrian artillery emplacements on Golan fire at Israeli civilian targets below.   Adrian Wolff

1967   Russia informs Syria of an Israeli Army buildup in the Upper Galilee opposite the Golan Heights. This fallacious misinformation provokes the Syrians into a war footing.

1967   The Egyptian economy is in a recession, while president Nasser has a low esteem with other Arab leaders. He orders the mobilization of over 100,000 troops, 1000 tanks in 7 divisions towards the Israel-Egypt border without confirming battle plans to attack Israel. The IDF surmises the Egyptian Army is not ready for war against Israel, lacking equipment, an operational program and has committed troops to Yemen. Nasser publicly encourages the need to annihilate Israel. Egyptian Government controlled radio announces "*This is our chance Arabs, to deal Israel a mortal blow of annihilation, to blot out its presence in our holy land.*" The Palestinian Liberation Army of Ahmed Shukairy in Gaza is placed on full alert.

1967   The IDF begins to mobilize its reserve soldiers (16–19 May), sent to positions in the north, center and south of the country.

1967 On 22 May **Egypt closes Tiran Straits** at the entrance to Gulf of Akaba blocking all Israeli and foreign shipping sailing to and from Eilat. Egyptian radio announces *"The Arab people is firmly resolved to wipe Israel off the map."*

1967 On 23 May the Israeli government votes against war with her Arab neighbors, ordering the Foreign Ministry to initiate serious consultations to prevent war from breaking out. Foreign Minister Abba Eban and General Meir Amit fly to Washington DC. They are unsuccessful to influence the USA to stop Egyptian war preparations.

1967 On 24 May French President Charles de Gaulle threatens Israel with an embargo should it attack any Arab country. (See De Gaulle 3 June 1967). Israel Defense Forces are supplied with French aircraft and helicopters (Mirage, Mystere, Super Mystere, Vautour and Ouragan) and in addition, Israel has ordered and paid for five missile boats manufactured in French shipyards in Cherbourg, which have not been released. (See Cherbourg 1969).

1967 President Nasser announces 27 May *"Our basic objective will be the destruction of Israel. The Arab people want to fight...The mining of Sharm el-Sheik (Straits of Tiran) is a confrontation with Israel. Adopting this measure obligates us to be ready to embark on a general war with Israel."* Egypt orders all UN troops to withdraw immediately from positions in Sinai along the Egypt-Israel border. UN Secretary-General U'Thant immediately accedes to Nasser's demands without any discussion at UN Security Council, a move that does not comply with the UN Charter.

1967 On 28 May Israel forms a National Unity Government to include Minister of Defense **Moshe Dayan,** raising morale in Israel. Dayan has little influence in the operations and planning.

1967 On 30 May Jordan's **King Hussein** flies to Cairo, signing a Joint Military Pact. Egyptian General Abdal Muneim Riad is appointed joint-commander of Jordanian Army. Iraqi President Aref announces 31 May *"The existence of Israel is an error...Our goal is clear-to wipe Israel off the map."* Ahmed Shukairy, Chairman, Palestine Liberation Organization (PLO) states 1 June *"This is a fight for the homeland - it is either us or the Israelis. There is no middle road. The Jews of Palestine will have to leave. We will facilitate their departure...it is my impression that none of them will survive."* **Armies of Egypt, Syria, Jordan, Iraq and Saudi Arabia on high alert, moving their troops towards the Israeli border.**

1967 On 3 June before hostilities begin, France imposes a military embargo on Israel. This is not surprising in the light of de Gaulle's previous lobbying of Petain's deputy, the anti-British Admiral Francois Darlan and other high ranking Vichy officers (Operation Torch 1942). US General Eisenhower never trusted de Gaulle.

1967 IDF is surrounded by superior numbers of forces and weapons. IDF operations are offensive, all taking place inside enemy territory

The Six-Day War 5 - 10 June 1967.
Prime Minister of Israel: Levi Eshkol
- Minister of Defense: Moshe Dayan
- Chief of Staff: Lieutenant-General Itzhak Rabin
- Northern Command: Major-General David Elazar
- Central Command: Major-General Uzzi Narkiss
- Southern Command: Major-General Yeshayahu Gavish
- Air Force: Major-General Motti Hod
- Navy: Major-General Shlomo Erel

The Middle East Military Balance, June 1967

Country	Population	GNI/capita	Troops	Tanks	Aircraft	Bombers
Egypt	32 million	$170	250,000	1,300	242	57
Syria	6.5 million	$280	50,000	450	95	2
Jordan	2.2 million		45,000	200	24	-
Iraq	7.5 million		70,000	400	130	31
Total Arab	48.2 million		415,000	2,350	491	90
Israel	2.8 million	$1,460	260,000	900	203	

Source: Lt.-Col (Res.) Yossi Abboudi, IAF Historian. The World Bank

1967 The Israel Air Force begins **Operation Moked** on 5 June using preemptive air strikes against Arab airfields and aircraft. Israel has every combat fighter plane operational including 44 Fougas. Only four Mirage planes are kept in reserve.
07.45 First Wave. Israeli aircraft have complete radio 'black-out', flying low towards their targets destroying Egyptian airfields and 189 Egyptian Aircraft. 17 IAF aircraft are lost during this assault.
09.34 Second Wave, bomb Egyptian airfields.
12.15 Third Wave, bomb Egyptian, Syrian and Jordanian airfields.
14.00 Fourth Wave, bomb Syrian and Iraqi (in H3) airfields.
The initial IAF bombing controls the final outcome of the Six-Day War. Nearly 90% of all IAF operations are against enemy ground forces. The first bombing wave on Egypt is a surprise while aerial attacks on Jordan, Syria and Iraq occur after war has begun.

1967 **The Southern Front.** As the initial IAF air attacks begin, IDF armor and infantry advances on Egyptian positions in Operation Sadin Adom (Red Sheet). In three days IDF Armor and infantry reach Suez Canal capturing the entire Sinai Peninsula, opening the

Straits of Tiran. IAF Fougas give Israeli armor support in the conquest of el-Arish. 550 Egyptian tanks are destroyed in Sinai.

1967 **The Central Front.** At 10.00 Israeli PM Levi Eshkol sends Jordan's King Hussein a message (through the US) stating Israel will not initiate any attack against Jordanian positions. King Hussein receives a message from President Nasser claiming Egyptian imminent capture of Be'er Sheva. Jordanian artillery opens fire against Israeli positions in Jerusalem and capture Government House, on Armon Hanatziv in East Talbot, the UN Headquarters of UNTSO (United Nations Truce Supervising Organization). Jordanian troops move over Allenby Bridge towards Jerusalem intending to ultimately join up with Egyptian troops, which he assumes to be near Be'er Sheva. Jordanian artillery attacks occur on Kfar Saba. Jordanian aircraft bomb Kfar Sirkin and the industrial area of Netania. The IDF retaliates.

1967 **The Israel Air Force.** End of Day One, enemy losses are 376 aircraft of the total 451 enemy aircraft lost during the six days of operations. Egypt 327, Syria 65, Jordan 30, Iraq 28, Lebanon 1. Israeli total losses are 46 planes and 24 pilots. Helicopters are used extensively to transport infantry capturing Sharm el-Sheik, Bir Gafgafa, and Southern Golan. (Lt-Col. (res.) Yossi Abboudi).

1967 An Iraqi armored brigade in Jordan is prevented from crossing into West Bank being decimated by IAF before arriving at the Damiya Bridge over Jordan River. IAF Fougas destroy Jordanian troops and vehicles between Jericho and Jerusalem.

1967 By 7 June, IDF captures the road to the Hadassah Hospital and Hebrew University on Mt. Scopus. Defense Minster Moshe Dayan is initially against capturing the Old City and Western Wall, but circumstances override his personal opinion. Eastern Jerusalem including the Western Wall and Jewish Quarter of the Old City is now in Jewish hands for the first time since its destruction by the Romans in 70CE. **Jerusalem is reunited.**

1967 The IDF begins Operation Pargol to capture the **West Bank** - Judea and Samaria in a two-day operation. Israeli forces led by colonels Moshe Brill and Uri Ben-Ari capture the Adam and Allenby Bridges over the Jordan River and cross inside Jordanian territory. The Israeli government orders their immediate withdrawal.

1967 When Israel entered the West Bank and Jerusalem in 1967 it did not occupy territory to which any other party had title. While Jerusalem and the West Bank, (Judea and Samaria), are **illegally occupied by Jordan in 1948,** they remained in effect part of 'the Jewish National Home' that had been created at San Remo in 1920 (www.2nd-thoughts.org/id350.html). In the 1967 6-Day War, Israel in effect recovered territory that legally belonged to it.

1967   **The Northern Front.** For 19 years, Syria shelled Israeli settlements in the Upper Galilee and Kinneret (Sea of Galilee) regions. During the first three days, Syria embarks upon heavy unabated shelling of Israeli settlements - at Kfar Szold, Gonen, Gadot, Dan and other Israeli civilian locations. Since the start of the war Israeli Defense Minister Moshe Dayan refuses to allow IDF Northern Command (Maj.-Gen. David Elazar) to attack Syria. A delegation of Upper Galilee leaders appeal to PM Levi Eshkol to use the current opportunity to remove the source of Syrian shelling of their homes and fields. Only on Day 5, PM Eshkol orders Dayan to allow an IDF attack on Syrian positions.

1967   On 10 June the IDF in Operation Makefet Katan captures Banias, a source of the Jordan River and in Operation Makefet Gadol captures all the areas between Banias and Kinneret. The Israeli attack is made during day-light, uphill, against superior numbers of manpower and weapons. On the same day the IDF conquers Mt. Hermon, a strategic mountain commanding an excellent view of Upper Galilee and the Golan plateau up to Damascus. IDF conquers the entire Golan Heights including Kuneitra within 18 hours. Israeli total losses are about 700 soldiers killed.

Map 42. Israel After Six-Day War Victories 1967

The results of the Six-Day War are:

- Israel defeats the armies of Egypt, Syria, Jordan and Iraqi armor.
- Israel expands its borders to include the Golan Heights, the West Bank (Judea and Samaria), the Sinai Peninsula up to the Suez Canal.
- Jerusalem is united. Jews pray at the Western Wall, their holiest site.
- The Gulf of Akaba is reopened to Israeli shipping to and from Eilat.
- Syrians are pushed behind the international border, halting the threat against Israeli water sources, and incessant Syrian shelling of settlements in the Upper Galilee. Israel now has tactical and strategic parity and can easily identify a Syrian buildup of forces on the Golan.
- The various holy sites are now open to all religious denominations.

1967   Due to losses incurred in the Six-Day War, IAF is at 75% its pre-war size. Additional operational fighter/bombers cannot be replaced subject to French arms embargo withholding 55 pre-ordered Mirage aircraft. Only in 1969 Israel begins to receive additional aircraft when A-4 Skyhawks and F-4 Phantom jets arrive from United States.

Jerusalem Old City, from Mt. of Olives.   Adrian Wolff

1967   The Israeli government does not intend to permanently expand the borders. On 19 June **the Government unanimously votes to withdraw from Sinai and Golan** in return for a peace treaty. In addition the government approves of negotiating a satisfactory border with Jordan. **Arab states refuse the Israeli offer, rejecting the creation of an independent Palestinian state a third time.**

1967   **Israeli government expands the municipal the borders** of Jerusalem, incorporating 28 small Arab villages and constructs new Jewish suburbs to the north, south and east. New underground infrastructure systems are installed in the Old City.

1967   The popular Hebrew song, Jerusalem the Golden 'Yerusahla'im shel Zahav', composed by Naomi Shemer (1930-2004), commemorates the unification of Jerusalem.

1967   **Population** of Jerusalem: 261,000 including 119,600 Jews (75%).

1967   Immediately after the war Russia begins to supply Egypt and Syria with its latest fighter/bomber, the MiG 21. By October Egyptian Air Force is 80% its pre-war size.

1967   On 1 September 1967, the Arab Summit meeting in Khartoum pass a resolution to be known as "the three noes". **NO negotiations, NO recognition, NO peace with Israel. Arabs renounce the talk-negotiation-compromise option and remain firmly against the Jewish state. Arabs believe any recognition and acceptance of Israel would contradict Muslim belief of Jewish inferiority, as Jews cannot be allowed to defeat the Arabs in battle. Peace will not be forthcoming.** Ahmad al-Shukairy, the PLO president encourages Arabs to use their resources and production of petroleum as a weapon against the 'Imperialist West'.

Map 43. Jerusalem 1967

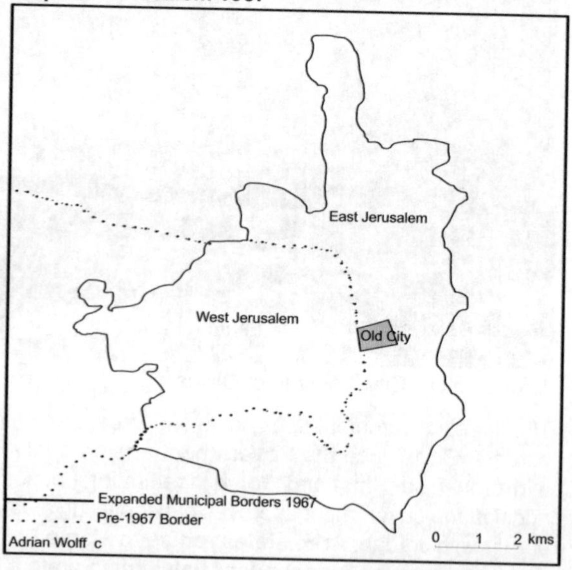

East Jerusalem

West Jerusalem

Old City

——— Expanded Municipal Borders 1967
. . . . Pre-1967 Border
Adrian Wolff c

0   1   2 kms

1967   The IDF establishes military governments in West Bank and Gaza. No democratic electoral system had previously existed as mayors were appointed. Israel assists with the Development Budgets.

1967   Egypt did not develop the Gazan infrastructure 1948 to 1967. In Gaza City, the Israelis find no electricity network other than three generators; no running water; no underground sewerage system. In the next few years the Israeli Electricity Company will erect an infrastructure. Their teams are attacked by terrorists forcing the IDF to send troops to protect the workers. Due to the danger to inspectors who read the electricity meters, a meter is placed at the entrance to Gaza. The Israel Electricity Corporation sells electrical current to the local authority, similarly priced as Israeli municipal consumers. The Gaza municipality sells the electricity at three times its cost price and continues to make a loss. Locals 'steal' electricity by creating by-passes, or drill a hole in the meter glass to prevent the disc from rotating. Only 12 tractors exist in Gaza. Citrus is exported, unsorted in bulk, to Eastern Europe. Israel will introduce citrus packing-houses and Gazan produce is graded and exported (at higher prices) through Israeli ports.

1967   In November 1967 the UN Security Council passes **Resolution 242. "(i) Israel will withdraw from territories occupied in the recent conflict.** (ii) *Termination of all claims or states of belligerency and respect for and acknowledgment of the sovereignty, territorial integrity and political independence of every State in the area and their right to live in peace within secure and recognized boundaries free from threats or acts of force."* **This resolution omits the words "the" and "all" when referring to territories. It clearly states an end of a state of belligerency and the right of every sovereign state to exist within defined borders. 'Palestine' is not mentioned**.

1967   In October, three Styx surface-to-surface missiles fired from an Egyptian Russian-made missile boat inside Port Said harbor sink the Israeli flagship, the destroyer INS Eilat killing 47 crew. This incident causes the Israeli Navy to change its strategic thinking. Missile boats will become the chief operational vessel.

1967   Despite IDF presence, Gaza is used as a base for recruiting terrorists for anti-Israeli operations both inside Israel and abroad. Palestinian terrorists trained in Lebanon, carry out hundreds of sorties against Israeli settlements in the northern Galilee and against Israelis abroad. The Lebanese government is helpless in administering control over the terrorist activity, encouraged and receiving financial support and weapons supplied by Syria. Palestinian terrorists trained in Syria pass through Jordan to infiltrate the West Bank. Many activities are initiated by Egypt. From 1967 until 1970 the Jordanian government fails to rein in terrorist activity on their border with Israel. Over 1000 terrorist raids result in 47 Israeli civilians and 234 Israeli soldiers killed.

1967 Prior to the Six-Day War a simple wire fence designates the border between Israel and Lebanon. Due to increased terrorist activity originating in southern Lebanon, Israel constructs a fortified border with electronic fences, mines and a sand road (to recognize infiltrators foot-prints). All Israeli settlements close to the border are enclosed within a fence. IDF increases its presence in the region.

1968 The INS submarine Dakar, formally HMS Totem, originally launched in 1943, is renewed and refitted. After sea and dive trials, INS Dakar leaves Portsmouth in England entering the Straits of Gibraltar. Disappears. An International Search and Rescue Operation is launched. Two days later a SOS signal from the emergency buoy is received near Cyprus. All 69 crew-members are lost. A memorial is erected in the military cemetery at Mt. Herzl, Jerusalem. INS Dakar is discovered in 2001, 3-kilometers deep, midway between Crete and Israeli coastline.

1968 Hahya Hamoda President of the Palestinian Liberation Organization (PLO) following the resignation of Ahmad al-Shakily.

1968 The economic situation in Egypt is desperate as villagers move to Cairo, pressurizing the government for housing and employment. President Nasser breaks the Cease-Fire Agreement by moving anti-aircraft batteries towards the Suez Canal. War against Israeli positions will draw attention away from internal Egyptian conditions towards an external scapegoat, Israel.

1968 **The War of Attrition**
Egypt aims to force an Israeli withdrawal in Sinai by inflicting as many casualties as possible. Israeli increased military presence along the Suez Canal causes strains on Israeli society and economy. Egypt's endeavor from 1968 to 1970 is unsuccessful.

1968 The Egyptian Army opens fire at Israeli Army positions on the Suez Canal, killing 10 IDF soldiers. Egyptian commandos attack Israeli fortifications and patrols. IDF does not possess superior artillery fire. IAF aircraft bomb Egyptian electrical sub-stations, bridges. IDF helicopters transport commandos into Egypt for lightening raids.

1968 Russia begins intensive three-year arms supply to Egypt and Syria replacing the weapons destroyed in the 1967 Six-Day War, also furbishing and improving these two armies with weapons of the latest technology, not seen in member Soviet Bloc countries, including latest models SAM 6 and Strela (surface-air-missiles) and anti-tank missiles. Israel does not attack Soviet positions in Egypt.

1968   Terrorists place a mine near Eilat blowing-up a school bus, killing 2 children and 3 escorts. Following this incident, IDF enters Karameh in Jordan, a training center for Palestinian terrorists. Over 150 terrorists and 27 IDF soldiers are killed. Terrorists hijack an EL AL flight from Rome to Israel, forcing it to fly to Algeria. Israeli passengers are freed two months later following the release of 16 Palestinians in Israel. During the Succot holiday, terrorists toss a hand grenade at Israelis rejoicing at the Tomb of the Patriarchs, Hebron injuring 47. Terrorists place a bomb at the Tel Aviv Central Bus Station, killing 1, injuring over 50. A bomb in the Mahane Yehuda open market in Jerusalem, kills 12 Jews and 2 Arabs. Terrorist activity in the West Bank. Terrorists kill 55 Israelis in 1968. The IDF creates techniques for Reprisal Raids (pe'ulot tagmul) across enemy lines. Preventative operations (pe'ulot mena) are performed with impunity, almost without causalities.

1969   Yasser Arafat is Palestinian Liberation Organization (PLO) leader.

1969   The IDF constructs a series of 16 fortified positions along the Suez Canal, the **Bar Lev Line**, named after a previous Chief of Staff, Haim Bar Lev. The well-protected bunkers are bases to patrol the canal, maintaining a minimum number of troops, not designed to withstand a full Egyptian Army invasion across the Suez Canal.

1969   Israeli Naval commandos are successful in innovative operations inside Egyptian territory capturing Green Island in the Red Sea.

1969   On 20 July in Operation Boxer, IAF begins to bomb Egyptian artillery and tank positions on a daily basis. In various aerial dogfights in the Suez Canal area, Egyptian MiG fighter planes are downed without Israeli loss. In September 1969 US manufactured F4 Phantom fighter/bombers are integrated into the IAF, improving Israel's strategical advantage and its ability to bomb targets deep inside Egypt. The IAF expands and improves its airfields in Sinai.

1969   Egyptian Air Force is unable to respond to the IAF resulting in Egyptian President Nasser requesting Soviet intervention. Russia supplies Egypt with SAM (surface-air-missiles) and Russian MiG fighter planes with Russian pilots who do not fly over Sinai.

1969   Palestinian Terrorism. Attack on an aircraft engine plant in Germany, an EL AL plane at Zurich, a female Palestinian terrorist places a bomb in a supermarket, in the Hebrew University campus, in Haifa, outside the EL AL offices and EL AL passengers in Athens.

1969   The al-Aqsa mosque in Jerusalem is damaged by fire ignited by a Christian tourist.

1969   Completion of the pipeline between Eilat and Ashkelon to transport Iranian oil to consumers in Europe. Iran halts these operations following the fall of the Shah in 1978.

1969   France had previously refused to allow Israel to receive the missile boats it had already paid for in advance. On Christmas Eve 1969, the Israeli Navy breaks the French military blockade and embargo by sailing its five missile boats from Cherbourg.

Cherbourg Missile boat, Israel Navy Museum, Haifa.   Adrian Wolff

1970   Four IAF jets are downed over the Suez Canal area by SAM (surface-air-missiles) missiles. An aerial dogfight on 31 July, IAF pilots down nine Egyptian MiG's, five reputedly flown by Soviets.

1970   Egypt agrees to a US-brokered 90-day ceasefire on 7 August, using the truce to move missiles towards the Suez Canal. Nasser intends to renew the War of Attrition after the truce. In this static war, Egypt with a large population, fully supported by the Soviets, is able to replace its fallen soldiers and equipment.

1970   Palestinian terrorism. Attack at Munich Airport, a Jewish Old Aged Home in Munich. A Swissair plane heading for Tel Aviv explodes shortly after take-off in Zurich killing all passengers and crew. Fire rockets at a school bus near Avivim, a moshav close to Lebanese border, killing nine school children, the bus driver and two teachers. Place a bomb at Tel Aviv Central Bus Station, killing two.

1970 Ba'athist General Hafez al-Assad (1928-2000), member of the minority Alawite sect, head of Syrian Air Force, ousts Prime Minister Nureddin Atassi in a military coup, appoints himself president in 1971. Syria is never to experience a democratic society. Assad favors a policy of rhetoric militarist hostility towards Israel. He announces on 17 March 1971 "*We have never committed ourselves, nor shall we ever do so, to restrict terrorist activities. Syria is the lung through which terrorist activity breathes*". The President/Dictator Assad does not allow terrorists to attack Israel directly from Syrian territory but supports the terrorist movement and its operations inside Lebanon and gives safe haven to various terrorist organizations establishing their headquarters in Damascus – Popular Front for the Liberation of Palestine, Islamic Jihad, Hamas, etc. Syria provides the terrorists training camps, finance, and weapons to Hezbollah in Lebanon.

1970 President Nasser of Egypt dies before the end of the 90-day cease-fire. Nasser is regarded as an independent pan-Arabic leader of the Arab world controlling the Arab League, a hero, bringing honor despite Egypt's defeat in the Six-Day War. Vice-president, **Anwar Sadat** is president of Egypt. Previously during WW II era Sadat was a local agent of the pro-Nazi German SS in Egypt and later a Muslim Brotherhood activist. He does not follow Nasser's pro-Arab nationalism and permits religious publications in Egypt. His speeches encourage hatred of Israel and begins planning a military assault on Israeli-controlled Sinai.

1970 During the War of Attrition 115 Egyptian aircraft are downed. IAF loses 17 planes and 8 pilots killed. 1425 Israeli soldiers are killed.

1970 Opening of **the Ben-Gurion University of the Negev in Be'er Sheva**. This university boasts excellent Desert Research faculties.

1970 Palestinian terrorists based in Jordan plan to infiltrate Israel, demand complete freedom of movement and arms, posing a threat to the monarchy. From September 1970 to July 1971 King Hussein acts against Palestinian terrorists who are trying to overthrow his regime. Known as the **'Black September'**, Jordanian forces attack and expel Palestinian terrorists. Some try to find refuge in Israel, while most flee to Syria. Syria threatens Jordan while Israel warns Syria not to invade Jordan.

1970 **Population** 3,022,100 including 2,582,000 (85%) Jews.

1971 Palestinian terrorists assassinate Prime Minister of Jordan Wasfi Tal visiting Cairo. A terrorist throws a hand grenade into an Israeli-licensed car traveling in Gaza City, killing two children.

1972 **Israeli Government settlement policy in Judah and Samaria (West Bank) and Gaza.** Before 1948 Jews had lived on privately owned lands in West Bank (Etzion Bloc, Hebron, Nave Ya'akov, Atarot) and Gaza (Gaza City, Kfar Darom), were either displaced in the 1929 riots or conquered in 1948, then barred from these areas.

New settlements are established in East Jerusalem in Ramat Eshkol (1968), French Hill, and East Talpiot (1970); Hebron at Kiryat Arba; the Etzion Bloc; and in the Jordan Valley. Jews move into 250 housing units at Kiryat Arba, outside Hebron (1972).

The Legal position. Many feel the existence of these settlements is a violation of International Law. Nevertheless, since an independent Palestinian State never existed, the Israeli Administration simply replaces the previous illegal Jordanian control in the West Bank and the Egyptian control in Gaza. Many 'new' Jewish settlements are previously pre-1948 settlements destroyed by the Arab onslaughts, for example: at Nave Ya'akov, Atarot, Kfar Darom, Gush Etzion, Hebron.

In 1922, the League of Nations Mandate grants Great Britain, Palestine as part its victory over the Ottoman Turks in 1917/1918. Egypt never claims legal sovereignty over Gaza. No country other than Great Britain, Iraq and Pakistan officially recognize illegal Jordanian control over the West Bank.

Israel does not 'occupy' (annex) but takes over the administrative control of these areas, awaiting a final peace settlement. An 'occupying' state is entitled to reap benefits from state lands but is prohibited from selling them. The state may lease the land to 'settlers'. Opponents regard the settlements as a violation of Fourth Geneva Convention *"The occupying power shall not deport or transfer parts of its own civilian population into the territory it occupies."* Most new settlements are constructed on vacant, unexploited, derelict lands. The Israeli government claims settlers have moved voluntarily. Jews had owned private lands in the West Bank and Gaza prior to 1948.

Palestinian mouthpieces claim Arab terrorism to be a result of Israeli settlement policy, concealing the fact that before 1967, cemeteries in Israel contain evidence of hundreds of Israelis killed by Arab terrorists originating from the West Bank and Gaza. (see 1947-1967).

1972 Palestinian terrorism. Sabotage Dutch and Italian oil refineries. Force a Belgium Sabena airliner to land at Lod Airport. Israeli paratroopers raid the plane, free the hostages and kill the terrorists. Japanese terrorists, in an operation for PLO, kill 25 in the arrivals hall at Lod Airport. Attack Israeli athletes participating in the Olympic Games in Munich. In the shoot out, 11 Israeli athletes, two Germans and 5 terrorists are killed. In response to rising terrorism during September and October, the IDF attacks various Palestinian terrorist sites in Lebanon. The long arm of the Israeli security forces will ensure all terrorists involved are assassinated.

1972 Egyptian President Anwar Sadat sends a 'peace proposal' with his emissary Foreign Minister Ismail Fahmi to US Secretary of State (Kissinger). Egypt demands complete Israeli withdrawal from Sinai and Palestinian 'Right of Return'. PM Golda Meir rejects this 'offer' as she did not want to link the situation in Sinai with Gaza, the West Bank, Golan or Jerusalem.

1973 Libyan Airlines plane enters Sinai airspace, refuses to respond, is shot down. In Beirut IDF commandos assassinate 3 Palestinian leaders involved in planning the massacre of the Israeli athletes at the Munich Olympic Games. Italian police arrest five Arabs near Rome airport in possession of a SAM (surface-air-missile) missile.

1973 In April, IDF obtains intelligence the Egyptian Army is preparing to attack Israel. In Operation Blue and White, Israeli Army Reservists are called to military duty. No confrontation ensures. This is an Egyptian ploy designed to test IDF reaction to its maneuvers.

1973 On 13 September, in two dogfights, the IAF downs 12 Syrian planes while losing only I aircraft. On 25 September King Hussein of Jordan initiates a secret meeting with Israeli PM Golda Meir. King Hussein informs Israel of Egyptian and Syrian serious intentions to immediately go to war. This information is reputed to have come from a pro-Jordanian spy in the Syrian Military Headquarters. PM Meir does not inform the IDF of this meeting. The Israeli political leadership is thereby also responsible for Israel's lack of preparedness of the forthcoming war.

1973 In reaction to increased Syrian troop reinforcements on the Golan, on 27 September the 77th Oz Battalion (Lt.-Col. Avigdor Kahalani) is moved from Sinai to the northern Golan.

1973 On 1 October, Israeli Intelligence units receive a serious warning of an imminent war to commence with simultaneous attacks by both Egyptian and Syrian Armies. This information is obtained from a reliable sources (reputedly Ashraf Marwyan, Pres. Nasser's son-in-law and others) but is not taken seriously by the head of Israeli Military Intelligence Major-General Eli Zeira or by Defense Minister Moshe Dayan. At a meeting with Knesset Foreign Affairs Committee and IDF High Command, Dayan prefers to read the newspaper. (Arie Shalev).

1973 On 4 and 5 October Russia evacuates its troops and their families from Egypt and Syria. Israeli Intelligence community sees this as a ominous sign that war is imminent. Once again head of Israel Intelligence Zeira and Defense Minister Dayan claim there is a low probability of war. They do not act or take these signals seriously against the objections of Chief of Staff, Lt.-Gen. David **Elazar**.

1973 The same day, Arab terrorists seize Soviet Jewish émigrés on a train bound for Vienna. The Austrian government closes the transit camp. Israeli Cabinet discusses this event without reacting to the growing military threat on its borders. PM Golda Meir flies to Vienna asking Austrian Chancellor Kreisky to reopen the facilities.

1973 *"From mid-July until October 6...Mossad...provided 23 unequivocal early warnings, primarily citing Egypt and Syria's complete and detailed war plans"*. (Shabtai Shavit). Sadat is determined to use military force to capture Sinai, believing Egypt cannot repair and regain its honor lost in the 1967 Six-Day War through a negotiated peace agreement, leaving only the military option viable.

1973 IDF thinking, *'conceptzia'* (reasoning) assumes Egypt and Syria will not go to war if:

1. Arabs do not have the ability to contain Israel's aerial superiority.
2. Arabs do not have missiles or bombers capable of attacking Israeli cities and bases.
3. Arabs cannot achieve their goal of capturing all Sinai and the Golan and can conquer only a limited area.

IDF predict war unlikely until 1975 when the Arab countries are due to receive long-range bombers. Events of the next few days will show the fallacies and narrow mindedness of this strategy.

1973 Early October, IAF reconnaissance photos display Egyptian and Syrian troop build-ups on the borders. On 5 October both Egyptian and Syria armies remove the tarpaulin covers from their forward deployed artillery and tanks, now reinforced with bridge-laying tanks. The IDF 7th Reserve Tank Brigade (Col. Avigdor 'Yanush' Ben-Gal) is transferred from Sinai to the Golan, fearing the Syrians may try to capture an Israeli military position or a civilian settlement

1973 5 October, Prime Minister Golda Meir receives a briefing at the IDF GHQ. Notwithstanding the warnings that war is imminent, Israeli Defense Minister Dayan and Head of Military Intelligence Meir Zeira continue to claim the probability of war with Egypt and Syria is low. Israeli Chief of Staff David Elazar asks for the immediate mobilization of five reservist divisions. Although Dayan approves only one division, PM Meir gives her approval for three. However, these divisions will not be in position before the war begins 24 hours later. Fearing that any military move will adversely affect Israel's political image, PM Meir and Dayan contend that the standing Israeli army has sufficient strategic depth (different from pre-1967 ideology) to absorb an initial Arab offensive and to quickly counterattack once the reserves are deployed. With elections coming up, Meir is reluctant to call up the reservists at a time when Zeira does not predict war. The IDF is not prepared for a war.

1973 **Israel Air Force** has plans for a pre-emptive attack against Egyptian (at 10.00) and Syrian (at 12.00) missile sites, agreed by the Chief of Staff, Elazar. PM Meir refuses permission for this operations since the USA Secretary of State Henry Kissinger warns Israel, 'don't preempt'.

1973 **Israel Navy** views Egyptian/Syrian build-up seriously. It is on full war footing, moving its vessels into operational positions before hostilities begin. The Arab navies are neutralized for the entire war.

1973 IDF predicts Syria will try to seize an Israeli military position and settlement - not initiate full-scale war. On the morning of 6 October, IDF GHQ informs Northern commander Maj-Gen. Itzhak Hoffi, that war will to break out at 18.00. Both Dayan and Zeira claim the chances of a full-scale war to be 'high' only as war begins at 14.00. Only two Israeli tank divisions are in position on the Golan Heights. Israeli tanks enter their forward positions, without artillery support, lacking enough time to load supplies for a multi-day battle. Tanks also do not have the necessary communications network or 'night vision' equipment. Various IDF units are told to respond only if the enemy initiates contact. It will take over 12 hours before the first reserve tanks move towards the Golan. IAF Commander Maj-Gen. Benny Peled predicts war will begin before 15.00 reasoning that enemy planes would not want to operate after dark.

The Yom Kippur War, 6 October 1973
Prime Minister of Israel: Golda Meir
- Minister of Defense: Moshe Dayan
- Chief of Staff: Lieutenant-General David Elazar
- Northern Command: Major-General Itzhak Hoffi
- Central Command: Major-General Yona Efrat
- Southern Com: Major-General Shmuel Gonen (Ariel Sharon)
- Air Force: Major-General Benyamin Peled
- Navy: Major-General Benyamin Telem

1973 Armies of Egypt and Syria simultaneously open fire on Israeli positions at 14.00 on 6 October 1973, **Yom Kippur,** Day of Atonement, the holiest day of the Jewish calendar.

The goals of both Egypt and Syria are:
- to regain the honor lost in the 1967 war
- to attempt to capture territory Israel conquered in 1967
- to force Israel's withdrawal

The Middle East Military Balance, October 1973							
Country	Population	GNI/capita	Troops	Tanks	Aircraft	Bombers	Sam's
Egypt	34 million	$260	550,000	2,500	403	55	146
Syria	7 million	$500	150,000	2,000	292	-	36
Total Arab	41 million		700,000	4,500	695	55	182
Israel	3.5 million	$2,570	320,000	1,700	391	-	5
UK (1971)	54 million		372,000	1,013	464		

Source: Lt.-Col (Res.) Yossi Abboudi, IAF Historian. The World Bank.
Note: The Egyptian Armed Force is larger than the UK.

1973 **Day 1. 6 October 1973**

Golan Heights. All tank commanders are unaware this is not a 'day of shelling' but reality of war as the Syrians open their continuos salvos and enter the northern and central Israeli Golan. The Syrian Army has 150,000 troops with nearly 2000 tanks, most latest model Russian T-62 tanks with infra-red night vision equipment, 1200 artillery pieces and 7 Infantry divisions reinforced with tanks. On Day 1 along, the 120-kilometer Golan border, Israel has 177 tanks in position. Syrian commandos have anti-tank rockets. In the Northern Golan border Israel has relatively limited strategic depth (compared to the Sinai Peninsula) and therefore the IDF High Command will firstly reinforce (with reservists) the Golan fighters. Syrian commandos flown by helicopters capture Israeli positions on Mt. Hermon.

The Valley of Tears, Northern Golan   Adrian Wolff

1973 **Northern Golan.** Facing the Syrians in the small funnel-shaped area of the Valley of Tears at Mt. Hermonit (next to the Druze village of Bukhata) the 7th Armored Brigade has 113 tanks facing

450

over 570 Syrian tanks and 360 artillery guns. (An additional 500 Syrian tanks are brought into position on the second day). Battle lasts four days and three nights. Outnumbered and out-gunned Israeli armor face two-three attacks during daylight hours each day and another two attacks at night. A tank officer radios his battalion commander saying *"I have 6 tank shells and have 12 Syrian tanks opposite me"*. He could not answer. The tank crew survives. In the Valley of Tears, after four days every Israeli tank is hit and only 17 remain operational, 62 totally destroyed tanks. 131 Israeli soldiers killed, 12 missing in action. Over 500 Syrian tanks and armored vehicles are destroyed and hundreds are captured. This classic battle in which a military force in a defensive position defeats an invading armored force. At Prokhorovka in the Battle of Kursk, July 1943, the greatest clash of armored forces in history, Soviet armored forces suffered a human casualty rate of over 50%.

1973 **Central Golan.** The 188th Armored Brigade in the central Golan has 57 tanks facing over 600 Syrians tanks and artillery. Within 24 hours 90% of the armored officers are either killed or wounded including the 188th Armored Brigade commander, his deputy and operations chief. The main Syrian break through is in the central region. IDF tanks lack night vision equipment. Every Israeli tank is hit at least once during the war. IDF Infantry are without anti-tank rockets and do not take part in the fighting during the first days. It is every soldier's nightmare to participate in a battle lasting four days without let-up as earthshaking shells fall continuously. The sound of tons of explosions and pungent smell of chemicals remain impregnated in the memory of the survivors. Any unprotected soldier will die. They are all heroes.

1973 **Suez Canal.** Hostilities break out along the Bar-Lev Line, an early-warning line with 16 outposts, is not fully manned, since non–essential soldiers are allowed to go home for Yom Kippur. Along the 170km Suez Canal IDF has 266 tanks in position. The Egyptian Army, totaling 550,000 troops is comprised of nearly 2500 Russian T-62 and T-55 tanks, 1500 artillery guns, Frog and SCUD missiles, armored infantry brigades and commandos. The Egyptians successfully cross the Suez Canal and construct 5 bridgeheads within 12 hours. Egyptian infantry initially ignore the 16 Israeli fortresses on the Bar-Lev Line and go around them. Within 48 hours Egypt captures all the Israeli fortifications except 'Budapest' in the north. In the skies over Sinai, the IAF downs 20 Egyptian helicopters containing commandos planning to ambush IDF reinforcements moving towards the Canal. Also 12 Egyptian fighter planes are downed.

1973   **Arab Reinforcements.** Arab countries of Morocco, Iraq, Tunisia, Algeria, Sudan and Jordan send troops to the battlefront.

1973   **Day 2. 7 October 1973**
Central Golan. By the second day of the war only 18 British Centurion and 12 M4 Sherman tanks of the original 57 tanks in the IDF 188th Armored Brigade in the central Golan remain operational. The old Sherman tanks are without night vision. Tank battles are fought within 20-40 meter range from the enemy. Syrian tanks reach outskirts of IDF Golan command headquarters at Nafah. On Day Two, due to the critical situation in the north, the IAF scraps plans to attack Egyptian positions in Sinai, and all IAF operations on this day are concentrated in the Golan. Six IAF planes are lost and only one SAM site is destroyed. During the first days of the war, efficient enemy anti-aircraft fire (SAM surface-to-air missiles, etc) hinders the IAF in-depth bombing and limits the IAF ability to assist front line ground troops.

Sinai - By the second day of the war, only 100 of the original 266 IDF tanks in Sinai remain operational. About 15% of IDF tanks are hit by Egyptian RPG's (rocket propelled grenades).

1973   **Day 3. 8 October 1973**
Golan. Israeli artillery is in position to defuse the enemy anti-aircraft batteries. Syrians achieve their furthest penetration, running out of fuel a few kilometers before Benot Ya'akov Bridge over Jordan River. The Israeli offensive begins.

Sinai. Egypt gains their furthest penetration eastwards in Sinai forced into a defensive position east of the Suez Canal. Egypt operational plans call for establishing a bridgehead inside Sinai.

1973   **Day 4. 9 October 1973**
In the Golan the remaining Israel tank crews have lost many senior officers, either killed or wounded. 8 IDF tanks remain operational in the central Golan. Artillery support and 11 tanks will arrive.

1973   **Day 5. 10 October 1973**
Golan. Large tank battle in central Golan south of Kuinetra. None of the 800 Syrian tanks that crossed the border ever return.
Russia signs a Joint Military Aid Agreement with Egypt.

1973   **Day 6. 11 October 1973**
Golan. Israeli troops cross the 1967 Cease-Fire Line (Purple Line) and enter Syrian territory in the northern Golan. Over 900 Syrian tanks are captured. The IAF disables 8 Syrian airfields, effectively grounding Syrian aircraft. The IAF attack Syrian infrastructure –

electric power stations, water pumps, army camps, Syrian Military and Air Force GHQ.

1973 **Day 7. 12 October 1973**
Golan. Israeli troops decimate an Iraqi Armored force destroying over 200 Iraqi armor (Lt.-Col. Avraham Zohar). 28 Jordanian tanks are also destroyed by Israeli armor on the Golan. Only 13 IDF tanks remain operational at the Valley of Tears. On the Golan, Israeli losses are 780 killed and over 2200 wounded

Sinai. IAF attacks Egyptian SAM missile sites in the Suez Canal area. Within two weeks all Egyptian SAM sites are damaged. The IAF seriously disrupts supply routes in Egypt, delaying vital logistics supplies reaching the 2nd and 3rd Egyptian Armies in Sinai.

1973 After Egypt refuses a US brokered cease-fire, the USA begins Operation Gross Marshal sending urgently needed weapons and ammunition to Israel as stocks are running very low. One-third of the total aid is air-lifted and the remainder is sent by sea.

1973 **Day 9. 14 October 1973**
Sinai. In the largest armored battle of the war, nearly 400 Israeli tanks (17 destroyed) go into action against about 450 Egyptians tanks (180-240 destroyed), halting the Egyptian military advances.

1973 **Day 11. 16 October 1973**
Sinai. IDF creates a bridgehead over the Suez Canal, as Israeli troops enter the African side. Designed by Col. David Laskow.

1973 Russia prepares to move its fleet from the Black Sea into the Mediterranean Sea. The United States reacts by moving its 6th Fleet out of Naples towards the Israeli coast.

1973 **Day 16 and 17. 21-22 October 1973**
The IDF successfully recaptures Mount Hermon. Israeli troops are 44 kilometers from Damascus.

1973 **Egypt rejects the 1st UN sponsored Cease-Fire on 22 October 1973. The UN does not sponsor a cease-fire before this date and does not censure either Egypt or Syria for launching a premeditated war against Israel. While the 'going is good' for both Egypt and Syria, the UN remains silent.**

1973 **Day 19. 24 October 1973** US political pressure, fighting stops.
Golan. Israeli troops are east of the 1967 border, the Purple Line, within artillery range of Damascus, not shelled for political reasons.

Sinai. Israeli troops are situated west of the Suez Canal on African soil. The Egyptian Second Army is isolated on the east bank of Suez Canal, north of Bitter Lakes up to Mediterranean Sea. The

Egyptian Third Army is completely encircled east of the Suez Canal south of the Bitter Lakes.

1973 **Day 20. 25 October 1973**
The Israeli-Egyptian disengagement negotiations begin at kilometer 101 on the road from Port Suez to Cairo.

1973 Israeli losses in the Yom Kippur War are over 2800 dead and 8800 wounded. This is a very high proportion of the total number of soldiers and as a percentage of the total population.

1973 The tenacity, leadership and military common sense of Israeli Chief-of-Staff, Lt.-Gen. David Elazar, and the professionalism of the field officers and soldiers saves the IDF from total collapse. He dies in 1976, aged 51.

1973 Over 100 Syrian aircraft are downed during the war, preventing the Syrian Air Force from assisting ground forces. Numerous Syrian aircraft are destroyed on various airfields before take-off. IAF losses in Golan are 27 aircraft and an additional 6 inside Syria.

1973 Nearly 450 Egyptian and Syrian aircraft are destroyed. IAF losses total 102 fighter planes, 17 helicopters and light planes. 53 IAF pilots are killed, 40 captured as POW's. Over 50 IAF pilots are rescued after bailing out. About 10% of IAF losses are from SAM missiles, the remainder by ground fire.

Map 44. The Yom Kippur War 1973

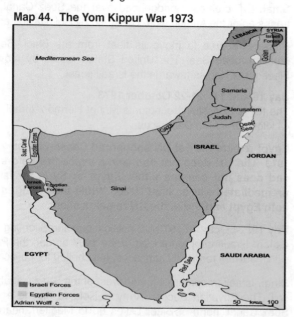

454

The Military and Political Results of the Yom Kippur War are:
- Israel displays its military superiority, defeats all the Arab armies.
- Israeli troops conquer territory within Syria towards Damascus.
- Israeli Army is on the western side of the Suez Canal on African soil.
- Egyptian Second Army holds a bridgehead on the east bank of the Suez Canal, failing to make a strategic penetration inside Sinai.
- Egyptian Third Army is surrounded on southeastern bank of Suez Canal
- **Israeli Navy** destroys 44 ships of the superior Arab fleets without loss, is in complete control of the Eastern Mediterranean opposite both Egypt and Syria.
- After Cease-Fire Agreements are signed with Egypt and Syria, Israeli troops withdraw in 1974.
- Only the USA gains political advantage from the war as Egypt moves away from its Russian allies and begin to receive aid from the US.
- The war results in no political, social or economic changes in Syria. Assad's position remains unchallenged.

1973 The Israeli government establishes a commission under retired Israeli Supreme Court of Justice Head Simon Agranat (1906–1992) to examine events preceding the outbreak of hostilities and during the first three days of fighting. This very partial examination published in 1974 does not address the failings of the political echelons and their personal responsibility in refusing to accept the professional considerations of the Chief of Staff. Prime Minister Golda Meir resigns in 1974 while Defense Minister Moshe Dayan emerges from the report unscathed, remains in government and subsequently appointed Foreign Minister. Public sympathizes with Chief of Staff David Elazar. Many public demonstrations follow.

1973 Arab Oil Producers (OPEC) impose an oil embargo against the west, protesting Israel's existence. Petroleum prices rise steeply and an oil shortage is felt in some countries.

1973 After his retirement from government in 1963 David Ben-Gurion moves to Kibbutz Sde Boker in the Central Negev to carry out his conviction of 'pioneering the desert'. He dies in 1973 aged 87, buried next to his wife Paula at a gravesite overlooking Nahal Zin.

David Ben-Gurion quotations about the Negev in January 1955.
"It is in the Negev that the youth will be tested - its pioneer strength, vigor of spirit, and creative and conquering initiative...we accomplish the great mission of populating the wilderness and bringing it to flourish...It has the potential to be densely populated.. (to) be settled there with agriculture and... with industry."

"It is in the Negev that the creativity and pioneer vigor of Israel will be tested...and (its) capacity for science and research...research to

desalinate seawater with inexpensive processes; to exploit solar energy;...to use wind power to generate electric power; to prevent the wastage of scarce rain water; to investigate the vegetation found in the Negev."

Other quotations

"May every Jewish mother know that she has put her son under the care of commanders who are up to the task."

"In Israel, in order to be a realist you must believe in miracles."

Ben Gurion's Hut, Sde Boker, Negev.   Adrian Wolff

Ben Gurion's Grave, Sde Boker, overlooking Nahal Zin.   Adrian Wolff

Chapter 26. Israel's Development 1974 - 2000

1974   Israel and Egypt sign a 'Disengagement Agreement of Forces'. Israeli troops withdraw from positions in Africa, west of Suez Canal back into Sinai. Egyptian troops remain along the east bank of Suez Canal. Later this year Egypt is forced to remove artillery from Sinai in excess of the Disengagement Agreement.

1974   Beginning of Religious-Zionist settlement movement, Gush Emunim, constructing settlements in Judah, Samaria and Gaza. Settlers arrive at Sebastia near Shehem. Jordan invaded Palestine in 1948 illegally occupying a part of the Jewish National Home that had been created at San Remo in 1920. Israel in the 1967 6-Day War recovered territory that legally belonged to it, where the UN pledged that the Jews should be settled. It was never sovereign land belonging to any other state. Before 1967 the Arab war of extermination against Israel had already gone on for decades.

1974   On 31 May, Israel and Syria sign a Disengagement Agreement. Israel withdraws from areas it conquered beyond the Purple Line (the post Six-Day War border), including Kuneitra where Syria agrees to resettle as a civilian town. This never happens.

1974   Yasser Arafat is the first non-governmental organization head to address the United Nations General Assembly in New York. He has a gun holster strapped to his side.

Safed cemetery. Graves of murdered school-children   Adrian Wolff

1974   Palestinian terrorists exiting bases in Lebanon enter a Kiryat Shmona school building taking hostages, killing 16 schoolchildren and 2 IDF soldiers. Palestinian terrorists enter a school in Ma'alot taking Safed schoolchildren and their teachers hostage. 22 schoolchildren (including a brother and sister) and 4 adults are killed. Terrorists enter the fields of Kibbutz Shamir in the Upper Galilee, killing three women volunteers from abroad. Arab terrorists kill 33 airline passengers during a hijacking at Rome. A TWA airliner explodes over the Ionian Sea after taking off from Athens, on a flight from Tel Aviv to New York killing all 88 on board. Terrorists from Jordan enter Beit She'an, murdering 4 Israelis. A terrorist throws a hand grenade at a cinema audience in Tel Aviv, killing two Israelis. 67 are killed in terror attacks in 1974.

1975   The United Nations General Assembly adopts resolution 3379 which "*determines that Zionism is a form of racism and racial discrimination*". This racist resolution is revoked only in 1991.

1975   The rededication of the Hadassah Hospital on Mt. Scopus, closed since 1948, is completely restored and reopened in 1978.

1975   The PLO together with Lebanese Muslims attack Christians and their property, to overthrow the Christian-dominated Lebanese government. A Civil War erupts (1975-1990) allowing Syrian troops to invade and control the political arena of Lebanon.

1975   Palestinian terrorists using a speedboat released from a mother ship, raid Tel Aviv beach taking hostages in the Savoy Hotel. The IDF storm, killing seven terrorists. Three IDF soldiers are killed including Colonel Uzi Ya'ari, commander of the operation. Palestinian terrorists from Lebanon infiltrate into the fields of Kibbutz Kfar Yuval on the northern border, killing two. Terrorists place a bomb in Zion Square, Jerusalem, killing 14 and again in a second attack 7 are killed. In 1975 39 are killed in terror attacks.

1975   **Population** 3,493,200 including 2,959,400 (85%) Jews.

1976   Ma'ale Adumim, a satellite town is established east of Jerusalem, offers low cost housing.

1976   Israeli Police kill six Arabs during riots following a government decision to confiscate 100,000 dunam (10,000 acres) of Arab lands. Each year thereafter Israeli Arabs protest on 'Land Day', 30 March. In 1976 14 are killed in terror attacks.

1976   An Air France aircraft leaves Tel Aviv, lands at Athens where Palestinian terrorists board the flight to Paris. They hijack and force it to fly to **Entebbe**, Uganda. Terrorists release non-Israeli hostages, while both the pilot and co-pilot chose to remain with the captives. The French government (PM Jacques Chirac) sends an aircraft to collect the passengers – but it is too small to carry all of the passengers on the ill-fated Air France flight!!! The IDF dispatches commandos to Entebbe, led by Col. Dan Shomron and Lt.-Col. Yonathan Netanyahu (killed during the operation) where on 4 July 1976 they kill the hijackers and rescue the hostages who are flown back to Israel, to be welcomed in jubilation. This operation displays the courage of the Israeli government to attack terrorists in a third country. A passenger Dora Bloch is taken to hospital (before the rescue operation) is apparently murdered.

1976 The Arab League grants Palestinian Liberation Organization (PLO) full membership status.

1976 al-Jazeera TV station opens in Qatar. This is the first non-official TV station available in the Arab world other than BBC World service. al-Jazzer is the mouthpiece of the Muslim Brotherhood (Hamas), promoting their ideology.

1976 South Lebanon Army commander Major Saad Hadad requests humanitarian aid from Israel. Border gates open known as 'The Good Fence'. Lebanese produce and workers enter Israel. The border closes in 2000 following Israel's withdrawal from Lebanon.

The Good Fence' near Metula - closed in 2000   Adrian Wolff

1977 A new town, Katzrin is established on Golan Heights near the site of an ancient synagogue. Katzrin, the regional capital of Jewish settlements on the Golan Heights boasts a regional high school, college for higher education, a law court, and a museum.

1977 The Likud, right-wing political party led by Menachem Begin gains the highest number of votes in the Israeli election. For the first time since 1948, the left-wing socialists are not in government. Many new economic laws are enacted including a more liberal exchange rate policy, introduction of competition for traditional Histadrut and government corporations. The Israeli economy will grow rapidly, leading to hyperinflation during the early/mid 1980's.

1977 An Israeli merchant vessel saves 66 Vietnamese refugees floating in a small boat off the Asian coast. They, and a subsequent group, are given refugees status in Israel.

1977 Egyptian President, Anwar Sadat visits Jerusalem, addresses Israeli Parliament (Knesset), warmly welcomed by all political parties and public. Arab countries Libya, Syria, Iraq, Algeria, South Yemen and the PLO accuse Sadat of treason. Egypt breaks off diplomatic relations. PLO leader Ahmad Shukairy is exiled from Egypt to Tunisia, dies in Jordan (1980).

1978 Continual firing of katyusha rockets and terror attacks from Lebanon on Israeli settlements in Upper Galilee. The IDF invades Lebanon in **Operation Litani** to destroy PLO sites situated between the border up to the Litani River. The Lebanese government 'invites' Syria to seize control of the ongoing civil war.

1978 Palestinian terrorists launch a boat from a mother ship off Kibbutz Ma'agan Michael, hijack an Egged bus on the Haifa Road, forcing the driver towards Tel Aviv, firing sporadically at passing cars, killing passengers. The hijacked bus is eventually stopped at Glilot Junction, north Tel Aviv, 35 Israelis die. 57 are killed in terror attacks in 1978.

1979 IDF commandos land in Beirut, killing Ali Hassan Salameh, mastermind of the Munich Olympic attack in 1972. He is the son of Hassan Salameh, leader of the Army of Salvation killed by the Hagana in Ramle in 1948.

1979 Terrorists from Lebanon raid Naharia from the sea, four Israeli civilians including a father and his two infants are killed. One of the terrorists, Samir Kuntar, repatriated in 2008, assassinated in 2015. From this date until printing this book there has been no successful terrorist attacks on Israel originating from the sea. (See 1985).

1979 Israeli PM Menachem Begin and Egyptian President Anwar Sadat sign the **Egypt-Israel Peace Treaty**, in Washington DC in the presence of the US President Jimmy Carter. This treaty is guaranteed by the USA government. Egypt becomes the first Arab country to sign a Peace Agreement with Israel. Israel withdrawals its entire military and civilian personnel from Sinai by 1982.

1979 Iranian religious leader Ayatollah Khomeini (1902-1989) returns from exile in Paris forcing the Shah of Persia, Mohammed Reza

Pahlevi (1919-1980) into exile in Egypt. Muslim Fundamentalists receive a large majority in a national referendum proclaiming the "*first day of Allah's government*" on 1 April 1979 establishing "*The Islamic Republic of Iran*", severing its ties with Israel. Khomeini gains the title of Iman, the highest position a Muslim Shi'ite and is the supreme leader (*Vali-e-Faqeeh*). Muslim religious revolution in Iran enforces stringent Muslim orthodox way of life - separation of sexes and Islamic code of dress. The newly established Islamic Religious Judiciary eradicates opposition by sentencing to death or long-term imprisonment any dissident leader opposed to these radical fundamentalist changes in every-day life.

1980   The European Economic Community (EEC) adopts the Venice Declaration acknowledging Israel's right to exist and the Palestinian people to self-determination.

1980   Palestinian terrorists, originating in Lebanon enter Kibbutz Misgav Am in the Upper Galilee taking children and adults hostage. Terrorists place a bomb on an EL AL plane in Zurich, found and neutralized by EL AL security officers. Palestinian terrorists kill 6 Israeli civilians in an attack on Beit Hadassah in Hebron.

1980   **Population** 3,921,700 including 3,282,700 (84%) Jews.

1981   **Destruction of the Iraqi Nuclear facilities outside Baghdad.**
Iraqi dictator Saddam Hussein previously visits France as guest of PM Jacques Chirac to obtain nuclear technology needed for construction of nuclear facilities at Osirak, outside Baghdad. (This may explain Chirac's policy of not actively joining the American-led coalition invasion of Iraq in 1991). France desires to obtain long-term Iraqi-petroleum supplies, and to sell military weapons. Israel fears Iraqi intentions to produce nuclear weapons. Saddam Hussein tells Iraqi paper al-Thawra "*The Iranians need not fear our nuclear reactor, we have no plans to use it against Iran, only against the Zionist enemy*".

Iraq desires to upgrade its standing in the Arab world to become the second Muslim-country after Pakistan, to obtain nuclear power. Before 25-kilograms of French enriched uranium is due to arrive in Iraq making the Osirak (Tamuz) facility operational, Israeli PM Menachem Begin orders on 8 June 1981 the Israel Air Force (IAF) to fly 1000 kilometers in each direction to **destroy the Iraqi nuclear facilities outside Baghdad**. All IAF aircraft return safely despite the extreme danger and difficulty of the operation. The IAF planes (six F-15 escort fighters and eight F-16 bombers) fly over hostile territory (Jordan and Saudi Arabia). The planes do not refuel in the air before returning to base. One of the pilots, Col. Ilan

Ramon is the Israeli astronaut, killed in 2003 in the ill-fated US Shuttle Columbia disaster. The Iraqi nuclear program is set back indefinitely to the relief of all of its neighbors, especially Iran that had previously attacked this facility twice during the Iran-Iraq War.

1981   Rededication of the Hebrew University campus on Mount Scopus closed since 1948.

1981   Muslim Fundamentalists assassinate Egyptian President Anwar Sadat attending a parade to commemorate the anniversary of Egyptian military achievements against Israel in the October (Yom Kippur) War. Sadat is remembered by his people not as a hero of the war, but for his corrupt nepotism having sold out to the United States and not designating Egypt's pan-Arabism his first priority. Revitalization of Nasser's charisma in Egypt after Sadat's death.

1981   Israeli law, jurisdiction and administration is extended on Golan Heights. Officially, the Israeli Government does not use the word "annexation". Israel offers the Golan Druze citizenship.

1981   During 10 days in June, Palestinian terrorists fire over 1100 katyusha rockets on 33 towns and villages in the Upper Galilee. In retaliation the IAF bombs the PLO headquarters in Beirut.

1982   Syrian President Hafez al-Assad orders the slaughter of 10-20,000 Sunni and Moslem Brotherhood civilians in Hamah, Syria to eradicate any opposition to his dictatorial rule.

Map 45. The State of Israel 1982

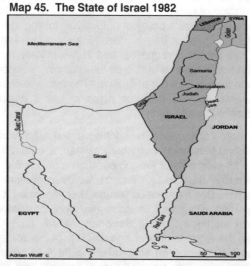

1982   **All Israeli military installations and civilian settlements are withdrawn from Sinai in accordance with the Peace**

Agreement. The withdrawal includes the Oil Fields of Abu-Rodis, developed by Israel after 1967. Israel dismantles the town of Yamit and numerous agricultural settlements situated in Sinai, resettling the population inside Israel. Following the Six-Day War in 1967, the Israeli government permits the overcrowded Rafiah Refugee Camp (called Canada, from bags of food supplies) to expand across the border into Sinai. Egypt is adamant the border will follow the original International Border from Rafiah to Taba (See 1906 British Sinai). Israel offers to release control over the entire Rafiah Refugee Camp. The Egyptians are inflexible, unmoved by the human suffering as the new fence/wall traverses through homes, splitting families, dividing the community.

1982   Palestinian terrorists wound Israeli UK Ambassador Shlomo Argov in London who never recovers and dies 20 years later. Following the attempt on Argov's life, the Israeli Army invades Lebanon in **'Operation Peace for the Galilee'**.

The aim of this operation is:
- To remove the persistent terror threat and continuous shelling of Jewish towns and settlements of Northern Israel perpetrated by the PLO controlling southern Lebanon.

The results are:
- Israel expels the PLO from Lebanon. The PLO leadership, including Yasser Arafat are exiled to Tunisia.
- Israel, unable to make 'peace' with Lebanon, remains in southern Lebanon', cannot prevent Hezbollah shelling of Israeli settlements.

1982   On 9 June 1982, the IAF destroys 19 Syrian SAM anti-aircraft batteries without loss. One of the largest aerial battles in the Middle East comprises over 100 aircraft, resulting in 29 Syrian planes shot down without Israeli losses. Another dogfight 23 Syrian MiG's are downed without Israeli loss. During the war in Lebanon, the Syrians lose 99 aircraft, 82 in dogfights (44% of Syrian planes engaged in aerial combat are shot down), with only a single IAF loss. Four IAF aircraft are downed by ground fire. The Israeli-designed Merkava tank is operational.

1982   Palestinians assassinate Lebanese Phalange Christian leader Pierre Gemayel in Beirut. In retaliation, Phalangist Christians massacre Palestinians refugees in Sabra and Shatila camps in Beirut. President of Lebanon Amin Gemayel is assassinated by the Syrian Army now stationed in Lebanon. Syrian troops massacre hundreds of Christian inhabitants of the towns of Damur and Zahlah (Zahle) in Lebanon.

1982 Radical Lebanese Shiites establish **Hezbollah** (Party of God), with the aim of an Iranian-style Islamic regime, is supported by Iranian revolutionary guards. This Islamic terrorist organization sends a suicide bomber into the US Marines base in Beirut, killing 237 American soldiers. In November 1982, 76 IDF soldiers and 27 security personnel are killed when a gas leakage causes an explosion in the IDF Headquarters in Tyre, Lebanon. A Hezbollah suicide bomber explodes at a Israel military compound in Tyre, killing 28 Israeli soldiers and personnel and 32 local detainees.

1983 Yasser Arafat and 15,000 PLO members are expelled from Beirut by boat for Tunis. Israel is unable to sign a Peace Agreement with Lebanon, controlled by Syria which regards it as a Syrian province.

1983 The IDF withdraws to a 10-kilometer strip in Southern Lebanon.

1983 21 are killed in terror attacks in 1983.

1984 Palestinian terrorists hijack a bus traveling from Tel Aviv to Ashkelon. IDF halt the bus, freeing the hostages killing all the terrorists. 9 are killed in terror attacks in 1984.

1985 In Operation Moses, 6000 Ethiopian Falasha Jews fly to Israel.

1985 A mega-terrorist attack is planned by PLO leader Abu Jihad (Khalil al-Wazir, assassinated in Tunis in 1988), originating from the sea. In 'Operation The Way of the Hawk' the Israeli Navy destroys the PLO ship 'Moonlight' in an Algerian Port. A second vessel the 'Ataviros' sails from Port Said towards the Israeli coast. It too is sunk by Israeli Naval vessels sabotaging this attack on Tel Aviv.

1985 IAF planes bomb the PLO Headquarters in Tunis, killing 50.

1985 An Egyptian soldier fires on a group of Israeli holiday makers at Ras Burka, near the Coral Island, south of Taba in Sinai killing seven Israeli civilians, including four children. Hezbollah suicide bomber detonates his vehicle adjacent to a IDF convoy traveling in southern Lebanon, killing 12 IDF soldiers.

1985 IDF experts search for survivors of the Mexico City earthquake.

1985 **Population** 4,266,200 including 3,517,200 (82%) Jews.

1986 An IAF F-4 Phantom is downed over Lebanon during the war. The pilot is collected by an IAF helicopter, while the navigator, Captain Ron Arad is captured by Hezbollah, reputedly handed over to Iran. IDF capture two senior Hezbollah leaders, Sheikh Abdel Karim Obeid and Mustafa Dirani as bargaining chips for knowledge and return of Ron Arad, returned to Lebanon in 2004. Arad's fate remains unknown.

1986   Terrorists attack Israelis in Cairo, killing four including the wife of an Israeli diplomat. 14 are killed in terror attacks in 1986.

1987   Muslim terrorists kidnap westerners in Beirut.

1987   An Arab uprising, the **Intifada** against Israeli Occupation of the West Bank and Gaza begins in Gaza and quickly spreads to the West Bank. Violence continues until 1993, signing of the Israel-PLO Peace Accord. 11 are killed in terror attacks in 1987.

From the Six-Day War 1967 until the outbreak of the Intifada in December 1987 no roadblocks exist between Israel with the West Bank and Gaza. Palestinians are allowed to move freely without any permits, working in Israel having full labor rights. Freedom of movement of Palestinians into Israel ends due to continual knifings and attacks upon Israelis. Their work places in Israel are permanently lost. Palestinians make no political or economic gains during this Intifada-Arab uprising.

1988   The Palestine branch of the Muslim Brotherhood, **Hamas** حماس an acronym of حركة المقاومة الاسلامية *Ḥarakat al-Muqāwamah al-'Islāmiyyah* 'The Islamic Resistance Movement' is established. They introduce Islamic rule, to liberate Palestine through *jihad*, holy war. Hamas believes the land of Palestine is an Islamic *wakf* throughout the generations *'until the Day of Resurrection', no one can rename it or part of it; or abandon it or part of it'*. The Hamas Movement in Gaza issues a Charter stating *'Israel will rise and remain erect until Islam eliminates it'*. Hamas organization is extremely violent, murdering local opposition, Israeli civilians and soldiers, without any regard to various agreements between the Palestinian Authority and Israel. They do not see themselves as part of any peace or cease-fire agreement.

1988   King Hussein ceases Jordanian administration in the West Bank.

1988   IDF commandos assassinate Khalil al-Wazir (Abu Jihad) Yasser Arafat's deputy in Tunis, was personally responsible for planning of many terror attacks. 14 are killed in terror attacks this year.

1989   In USSR President Mikhial Gorbachev (1931-) supports reform in the Soviet-bloc countries, whose regimes collapse within 12 months. He allows Russian Jews to immigrate to Israel.

1989   A terrorist on an Egged bus towards Jerusalem forces it into an abyss killing 16 passengers. 40 are killed in terror attacks in 1989.

1990   Muslim Fundamentalists kill 11 Israeli tourists on a bus in Egypt.

1990   A new wave of immigration of Russian Jews arrives in Israel, over one million within the next ten years.

1990 During the Succot pilgrimage festival Arabs riot on the Temple Mount in Jerusalem throwing stones down at the thousands of Jews praying at the Western Wall plaza. In an effort to protect the worshippers at the Jewish Holiest Site and halt the stone throwing, Israeli Police open fire, killing 21 Palestinian rioters. The Israeli government appoints a commission to investigate the events which finds the Muslim clerics had incited the Palestinians, and justifies Israel Police response with the use of force.

1990 Iraqi troops invade Kuwait, which is quickly conquered. The West suddenly fears Iraqi control over the wealthy Kuwaiti petroleum and gas fields. Yasser Arafat supports Saddam Hussein. Palestinians are expelled from Kuwait.

1990 23 Israeli civilians are killed in terror attacks during 1990.

1990 **Population** 4,821,700 including 3,946,700 (82%) Jews.

1991 **The Gulf War 1, Operation Desert Storm.** Many countries join the coalition by sending troops to the Persian Gulf area to invade Iraqi-captured Kuwait. The only troops that actively take part in any operation during the Gulf War are the USA, UK and Australia. Iraq fires 38 SCUD missiles from area H3 in western Iraq towards Israel. The US forbids Israel to retaliate. In Israel, only one death results directly from the SCUD missile attacks and about another 20 others die indirectly. This result is due to 'chance' and the discipline of the Israeli population who enter their bomb-shelters during each air-raid siren warning. Extensive damage to residential areas in Tel Aviv, Ramat Gan and also in the Haifa Bay area.

USAF bombs various sites in western Iraq from a high-altitude, with very limited success. USA refuses Israeli requests for low-level attacks using helicopters, which they expect to prove to be more effective. USAF replies they do not have helicopters in western Iraq. (US helicopters are under the command of the army, navy or marines). US Army does not have operational missions to destroy the SCUD missile launching sites in western Iraq as they are fighting in south-eastern Iraq. Iraq fires SCUD missiles at US Army bases in Saudi Arabia killing 28 US servicemen.

1991 In **Operation Solomon** over 14,000 Falasha Ethiopia Jews are airlifted to Israel within 36 hours. Over 1000 passengers fly in one EL AL Boeing 747 jumbo jet, a world record!

1991 101 are killed in terror attacks during 1991.

1992 Completion of the New **Supreme Court** Building opposite the Knesset, designed by architects Rami Karmi and Ada Karmi-Melamed. The investment is made available by the Rothschild

Foundation. The building, a popular tourist site, houses courtrooms, judges' chambers, boardrooms, library and an administrative wing. Previously the Supreme Court is located in the Russian Compound in Jerusalem. *"Speak the truth with one another; and in your gates judges with truth, justice and peace."* (Zechariah 8:16).

1992   Thirty-nine are killed in terror attacks during 1992.

1993   The **Israel-Palestinian** (Palestinian Authority) **Peace Treaty** is signed between Israeli Prime Minister Itzhak Rabin and Palestinian Authority President Yasser Arafat at the White House, Washington DC, in presence of US President Bill Clinton. Israel withdraws from Jericho, and later from Palestinian towns and villages in the West Bank. Israeli settlements in the Gaza Strip remain. Terrorism does not stop. This agreement is known as the **Oslo Accords** since the secret process of discussions leading up to this agreement is held in Oslo, Norway. Yasser Arafat, the Palestinian Authority leader is given the chance to become an international statesman, but chooses to remain a financier, supporter and supplier of terrorism. He gladly hands out weapons to individuals and groups who desire to kill Israelis. Arafat frequently flies to world centers and on his return brings weapons in his aircraft.

Yassar Arafat supports terror. Ha'aretz Israeli Newspaper, 7 March 2003 by Uzi Benziman. *"In August 1995, Israel learns that Awad Silmi is planning to carry out a car bomb attack. Israel asks the Palestinian Authority to arrest him. The Palestinian Preventative Security Forces...arrest Silmi...In fact, the(y)...provide Silmi with an apartment and a gun and explain to him that this is how they are protecting him from the long arm of the IDF. They tell Israel that Silmi has been tried and imprisoned. Arafat never intended to adhere to the spirit of the Oslo Accords by renouncing terror and settling disputes with Israel through dialogue."*

1993   Islamic terror attack on 'the west'- The first NY towers bombing.

1993   Ehud Olmert is elected mayor of Jerusalem 1993-2003. 62 Israelis including security forces are killed in terror attacks during 1993.

1994   Jewish settler Baruch Goldstein enters the Cave of Machpaleh (Patriarchs) in Hebron perpetrating the Third Hebron Massacre, murdering 29 Arabs before he is killed. (The First Hebron Massacre in 1929 when Arabs massacres 67 Jews. In 1968 Arabs throw hand grenades at Jews celebrating at this site, injuring 47).

1994   During a visit to Johannesburg Yasser Arafat publicly states the peace agreement he signed with Israel has the same value as the agreement Mohammed made with the Quraysh tribe of Mecca. (See Mohammed 622 and 630).

1994 The **Israel-Jordan Peace Treaty** is signed by Prime Minister of Israel Itzhak Rabin and King Hussein of Jordan at the Arava, in presence of US President Bill Clinton. The Israeli population warmly receives King Hussein during his various visits to Israel. Jordan makes no territorial claims over the West Bank it had administered from 1948 until 1967. Israel does not cede any territory except small areas in the Arava. Israel does not regain Nahrai'im in the Beit She'an Valley, lost in 1948.

1994 A team of IDF medics travels to Rwanda erecting a field hospital to assist survivors of the carnage and massacre during ethnic rivalry.

1994 A suicide bomber kills five bus passengers in Hadera. A Palestinian suicide bomber blows himself up together with 22 passengers on a Dan Bus in Dizengoff Street, Tel Aviv. 72 Israelis including security forces are killed in terror attacks during 1994.

1995 Signing on 28 September of **Oslo II Israel-Palestinian Authority Peace Accord**. Israel commits to withdrawal from areas in the West Bank including Hebron. Further Israeli withdrawal in 1996.

1995 A Jewish fanatic assassinates Israeli Prime Minister Itzhak Rabin (1922-1995) as he leaves a Peace Rally in Tel Aviv.

1995 In a double suicide bombing at the Beit Lid Junction, 21 IDF soldiers are killed while waiting to travel to their bases. 52 Israelis, including security forces are killed in terror attacks during 1995.

1995 **Population** of Israel is 5,612,300 including 4,544,300 (81%) Jews. Jerusalem has 602,700 inhabitants, with 425,600 Jews (71%) and 177,100 non-Jews.

1996 Yehya Ayyash, master-mind behind many suicide bombs is blown-up in Gaza when answering his cellular telephone. Ayyash is given a state funeral, eulogized by Arafat. Addressing a rally in Bethlehem Arafat calls "*Jihad, Jihad, Jihad*" for a holy war against Israel. Arafat addresses Arab diplomats in Stockholm. "*We plan to eliminate the State of Israel and establish a purely Palestinian state. We will make life unbearable for Jews by psychological warfare and population explosion.*" (Honestreporting).

1996 **Operation Grapes of Wrath in Lebanon**. Following continual Hezbollah shelling and terrorist attacks against the IDF in southern Lebanon and Israeli civilian settlements in Northern Galilee, the IDF attacks numerous terrorist sites in southern Lebanon.

1996 Commemorations for **Jerusalem 3000** years. Hasmonean Tunnel is opened, excavated outside the Temple Mount exiting in the via Dolorosa. Arabs falsely claim this tunnel passes under the Western Wall towards the Dome of the Rock. Arab riots result in the death of 21 Jews, including 14 IDF soldiers and 69 Palestinians. Opening of the Western Wall Tunnel is made in agreement with the WAKF, who are allowed to clean out 'Solomon's Stables' under the Temple Mount, creating the largest mosque on the country.

1996 A Hamas terrorist bomber blows up an Egged bus in Jerusalem, killing 27, then another killing 18. A Hamas suicide bomber blows himself up in Dizengoff Street, Tel Aviv, killing 14 as they cross the intersection at King George Street. Eighty-seven Israelis including security forces are killed in terror attacks during 1996.

1997 The French Catholic Church of St. Peter in Gallicantu on the slopes of Mount Zion in Jerusalem is completely rebuilt.

1997 Two IAF transport helicopters collide over Sha'ar Hayeshuv while waiting for permission to enter Lebanon, killing 73 soldiers.

1997 A bomb in a restaurant near Dizengoff Street, Tel Aviv, kills three Israeli women and an infant. Bombing attacks in Ben Yehuda Street and Mahane Yehuda Market in Jerusalem, killing four and fifteen respectively. 41 are killed in terrorist attacks during 1997.

1998 The **Wye Agreement** brokered by the United States between Israel and Palestinians results in further Israeli withdrawals from additional Palestinian areas in the West Bank.

1998 The IDF sends a specialized team to **Yerevan**, Armenia to locate survivors in devastated buildings caused by the earthquake. The IDF sends a team to Nairobi, Kenya to locate survivors in the wreckage of the public buildings destroyed in terrorist bombing. The US Embassy building is also bombed and damaged.

1998 Terrorists throw hand grenades in Be'er Sheva wounding 63 Israelis. Suicide Hamas bombers in Gaza drive a car ready to explode next to an Israeli bus carrying Israeli school children. An IDF jeep patrol intercepts the terrorists' vehicle that explodes, killing one IDF soldier. Two suicide car bombers attack at Mahane Yehuda Market, injure 25, killing the bombers. 16 Israelis are killed and 398 injured in 434 Arab terror attacks during 1998.

1999 King Hussein of Jordan dies. His eldest son King Abdullah I is king. Israeli population remembers King Hussein with warm affection.

1999 The IDF sends teams to **Golcuk,** Turkey, to locate survivors of the earthquake. Israel will assist construction of housing for survivors.

1999   Eight are killed in 219 Arab terror attacks during 1999.

2000   Israeli PM, Ehud Barak without any agreement with Lebanon, unilaterally withdraws all troops from southern Lebanon. The Hezbollah leadership celebrates 'victory' against the 'Zionist'. Since 1982 over 800 IDF soldiers die in Lebanon. Lebanese troops do not enter the area vacated by the IDF allowing Hezbollah terrorists to immediately occupy all previous IDF positions. Hezbollah closes **'The Good Fence'** between Israel and southern Lebanon. Peaceful neighbor relationships are not forthcoming.

The area of Har Dov or Mt. Dov (Jabel Rus/Shaba'a Farms) is part of Lebanon until 1965 when the local Alawis population, aided by Syria, declare themselves and this area as Syrian. This area now becomes under Israeli control after the 6-Day in 1967. After the withdrawal of Israeli troops from southern Lebanon in 2000, IDF troops remain on **Har Dov** and **Ghajar**, officially part of Syrian Golan. In Ghajar, an Alawis chapel has a statues of the Virgin Mother, St. Maria. The Hezbollah fire rockets at Israeli positions on Har Dov and at Israeli settlements. UN officially recognizes the Border and **Har Dov** to be Syrian Golan and not Lebanon.

Har Dov, with Mt Hermon in background   Adrian Wolff

2000   President Hafez al-Assad of Syria dies. His son Bashir al-Assad, an ophthalmologist by profession, steps into his late father's position. Dictatorial rule continues in Syria.

Chapter 27. The Intifada 2000 - 2016

Note. Only major terror attacks are mentioned.

2000 **Pope** John Paul II makes an official pilgrimage to Jerusalem and other Holy Christian sites in Israel, paying an official visit to Yad Vashem, the Holocaust Memorial. He is warmly received by all Israelis. At the Western Wall, Jerusalem he places this prayer.

Pope John Paul II   Israel Philatelic Bureau

> *God of our fathers.*
> *You chose Abraham and his descendants*
> *to bring your name to the nations.*
> *We are deeply saddened*
> *by the behavior of those*
> *who in the course of history*
> *have caused those children of yours to suffer,*
> *and asking your forgiveness.*
> *We wish to commit ourselves*
> *to genuine brotherhood*
> *with the people of the Covenant.*
> Joannes Paulus II (1920–2005)

During meetings with Greek Orthodox leaders, the Pope is unable to bridge the gap between Catholic and Orthodox churches. He is curtly received by local Muslim leaders.

2000   The **Birthright** program's aim are to strengthen participants' personal connection to Jewish and Israeli history and culture during a subsidized 14-day tour of Israel. Over 250,000 individuals have participated since 2000. Eligibility ages are 18 to 26 having at least one grandparent of recognized Jewish descent and who do not actively practice another religion. The program initiated by Dr. Yossi Beilin in 1994 is supported by Charles Bronfman, Michael Steinhardt, Lynn Schusterman, Miriam and Sheldon Adelson, the Jewish Agency and Israeli government.

2000   International recession and stock market decline adversely affects Israeli Hi-Tech sector (25% of total exports) and international investments. Lower levels of investment and economic activity increase Israel's unemployment rates.

2000   US President Bill Clinton invites leaders of Israel and Palestinian Authority (PA) to **Camp David** to negotiate permanent peace. Israeli Prime Minister **Ehud Barak offers Palestinians over 90% of West Bank, 100% of Gaza and Arab East Jerusalem**. Talks end in failure. PA leader Yasser Arafat refuses to negotiate, therefore, no compromise is possible, as nothing has been finalized at these talks. This the fourth time the Palestinians refuse an offer by international community and/or Israel of an Independent Palestinian State. (See 1937, 1947, 1967).

2000   Dennis Ross, President Clinton's chief negotiator at Camp David writes ('The Missing Peace'): *"If there had been any hope for an agreement, it was gone now...Arafat was not going to say yes under any circumstances...Arafat was seeking to have it both ways, creating the illusion of being positive by accepting the ideas, but practically rejecting"*.

2000   On 28 September Israeli opposition leader Ariel Sharon, with authorization by the government and WAKF visits the Temple Mount in Jerusalem. Sharon does not enter al-Aqsa Mosque nor Dome of the Rock. Palestinians use this visit to begin the new violent uprising, the **al-Aqsa Intifada** knowing IDF will react to Palestinian terror. Arafat is fully aware United Nations, Arab world and EU sympathizers will condemn any Israeli action. Palestinian National Covenant Article 15: *"...it aims at the elimination of Zionism in Palestine."* A frenzied Arab mob destroys a Jewish Holy site, Joseph's Tomb in Shehem (Nablus).

PA Communications Minister Imad Al-Faluji, Al-Safir, 3 March 2001. *"Whoever thinks that the Intifada broke out because of the despised Sharon's visit to the Al-Aqsa Mosque is wrong...This Intifada was planned in advance, ever since President Arafat's return from the Camp David negotiations".* (MEMRI). Yasser Arafat's wife Suha said *"Arafat sent us away...He said: 'You have to leave Palestine, because I want to carry out an Intifada. He had already decided to carry out an Intifada after the Oslo Accords and after the failure of Camp David ".*(Palestinian Media Watch).

2000   Israeli Arabs riot, encouraged by Israeli Arab MK's (members of Israel's parliament) and Muslim religious leaders. Israeli Police kill 12 rioting Israeli Arabs and 1 Palestinian. At Umm al-Fahm, Israeli Arabs block the main road through Wadi Ara'a, throw rocks at passing cars killing one Israeli, destroy the local police station, post office, petrol station, bank and road safety signs. A government commission meets in Haifa. Israeli Arabs boycott it. Israel Police is criticized for unpreparedness. (Orr Commission 2003).

2000   Palestinians gain sympathy from Arab States and various left-wing movements in the West, voicing their anti-Israel stance in the international political arena. Anti-Israel positions become anti-Semitic with boycotts of Jews, Jewish-owned businesses and Jewish academics. Violent attacks against Jews increase, as Jews are physically attacked, synagogues vandalized and torched. Borders between Israel, the West Bank and Gaza are closed due to the security risk posed by Palestinian suicide bombers. Palestinians are barred from entering Israel in search of work as living conditions in West Bank and Gaza decline dramatically. Insufficient investment is made in West Bank and Gaza to provide new sources of employment. International grants are siphoned, virtually cease due to a lack of accountability and transparency. Palestinian leadership under Arafat makes no attempt to co-operate with various International Peace efforts (Mitchell Plan, Tennet Plan), as every public statement is apocryphal. Arafat continues to encourage, support, finance and plan Palestinian terrorist activities. (See 2002 Ramallah). The Palestinians continue violence with mortar shelling from Gaza, shooting attacks at Israelis and suicide bombing missions. IDF enter Palestinian towns in search of arms, suicide bombers, terrorist organizations and its infrastructure. A lack of trust grows between both Israelis and Palestinians and the chance of a peaceful settlement diminishes.

2000   Hezbollah terrorists from southern Lebanon infiltrate and kidnap 3 Israeli soldiers patrolling along the northern border. (See 2004).

2000   Two IDF reserve soldiers lose their way entering Ramallah, are captured and publicly slaughtered in cold blood. The horrifying scene is shown on TV. The IDF begins a policy of assassination. In 2000, 139 Israelis, civilians and security forces are killed and 125 injured in 2,728 terror attacks.

2000 The **population** of Israel is 6,369,300 with 4,955,400 (78%) Jews. Jerusalem has 657,500 inhabitants, 448,800 (68%) Jews; 159,000 Muslim; 50,000 Christian, mainly Orthodox - Greek or Armenian.

2001 Opening of the eighteen terraces of the Bahai'i gardens in Haifa.

2001 **UNESCO Heritage Sites in Israel**. Acre (Old City) 2001, Masada 2001, Tel Aviv (White City) 2003, Biblical Tels 2005 (Hazor, Megido, Be'er Sheva), Spice Route 2005 (Nabatean cities in the Negev - Avdat, Mamshit, Halutza, Shivta), Bahai'i Gardens Haifa 2008, Yad Vashem (Pages of Testimony) 2013, Beit Guvrin Cave City 2014, Beit She'arim 2015.

2001 Palestinians dance for joy in Gaza and Ramallah on 9/11 after watching on TV the hijacked airliner attacks on the Twin Towers, NY. An AP cameraman is kidnapped in the West Bank, threatened with his life if pictures of Palestinian celebrations are broadcast.

2001 Muslims attack and kill Christians in Gaza, Sudan, Nigeria, India, Philippines, Indonesia, Thailand, and Hindus in Kashmir, India.

2001 Hamas terrorists assassinate Israeli Minister, Rehav'am Ze'evi (1926-2001) in Jerusalem. They flee to Jericho, placed under 'house arrest'. A suicide-bomber explodes outside the Dolphinarium discotheque on the Tel Aviv beachfront, a killing 20 teenagers and one passerby. The Israeli government expels all Palestinian Authority offices from Jerusalem. A suicide attack on a Jerusalem restaurant kills 15, including 7 children. IDF informed Arafat of the names of the bombers 4 days before the attack - he did not take any action. During 2001, 208 Israeli civilians and security forces are killed and 1525 injured in 1794 terror attacks.

2002 Off the Gazan coast the Israel navy apprehends a freighter (Karin A) purchased by Yasser Arafat, financed by Iran. Documents pertaining to Arafat's personal involvement are found in the Mukhata, Ramallah. The boat's cargo has 50 tons of military hardware - mortars, mines, rifles, ammunition and missiles. The IDF enters the Refugee Camps in Shehem, and Jenin, finding rockets, mortars, armaments and suicide belts. A terrorist suicide bomber enters the Park Hotel in Netania on Passover Eve during Seder Service killing 30 Israelis and wounding another 35. Following this massacre, 30,000 IDF soldiers embark on Operation **Defensive Shield**, entering Palestinian towns to destroy terrorist infrastructure. Israeli PM Sharon refuses all foreign demands to withdraw IDF troops from the PA controlled towns. The IDF forcibly isolates Arafat in his headquarters (Muka'ata) in Ramallah, where he remains until his death in 2004. Documents found in Muka'ata connect Arafat directly to financing and promotion of acts of terror, including his signature on the weapons budget. He personally finances, encourages and supplies weapons to various militias to kill Jews, led by groups (Hamas, al-Aqsa Brigade) or individuals. Marwan Barghouti, Arafat's military Chief of Operations is captured. Arafat is completely indifferent to the suffering of the Palestinian people and publicly announces there "*will be one million Palestinian martyrs on their victory towards Jerusalem*".

2002 Palestinian terrorists take over the Church of the Nativity in Bethlehem before being exiled to Europe. Later one joins the Real IRA in Eire while another is caught robbing banks in Belgium. The IAF destroys the home of Gaza Hamas leader Salah Shehedah killing him, his wife, assistant and 13 others. The IAF is criticized for excessive fire-power. A bomber in a Jerusalem bus, kills 19 mostly schoolchildren. An Egyptian living in LA kills 3 Jews at the airport, before he is shot by EL AL security personnel. In 2002 456 Israelis are killed, 2,300 injured in 1,781 Arab terror attacks.

Memorial with names of Terror Victims at Jerusalem Bus Stop. Adrian Wolff

2002 **Israel begins to construct a fence/wall between Israeli and Palestinian areas**. Suicide bombing is reduced.

2002 al-Qaeda suicide-bomber drives a bomb-laden jeep into a hotel Mombassa, Kenya lobby, killing 3 Israelis and 12 Kenyans. That day, al-Qaeda terrorists fire a shoulder-held missile at an Israeli airliner as it takes off from Mombassa airport, missing its target.

2003 An Israeli Air Force Colonel, Ilan Ramon (1954–2003) is one of the seven astronauts aboard the ill-fated US Shuttle, Columbia that disintegrates on its return to earth. His remains are buried at Nahalal, overlooking the Jezreel Valley. One of the planned scientific experiments in space was prepared by Israeli schoolchildren for the research into the differences between growth of crystals on earth and in space. Ramon's son, Captain Asaf Ramon is killed in an IAF flight training exercise in 2009.

2003 Uri Lupoliansky, an ultra-orthodox Jew, is elected mayor of Jerusalem from 2003 to 2008.

2003 In Akaba, Jordan talks are held between the Palestinian PM Mahmoud Abbas (Abu Mazen) and Israeli PM Ariel Sharon together with US President, George W. Bush jr. and King Abdullah II of Jordan. Abbas pledges to halt terror attacks, Sharon to dismantle all illegal settlements. Palestinians decide on a *'hudna'* (a temporary cease-fire). Israel releases 323 Palestinian prisoners as a sign of good-will. The various terrorist organizations - Hamas, Islamic Jihad, Fatah do not stop their terrorist activities, continue to reinforce and regroup their cells. They threaten to *'continue until the last Zionist is either dead or pushed into the sea.'* Terrorists continue to strike at Israeli civilians. *"IDF sources said...Yasser Arafat is encouraging Fatah cells...to commit attacks...(he) recently sent money to the Fatah cell in Balata (Nablus) refugee camp that carried out Tuesday's suicide bombing in Rosh Ha'ayin."* (Ha'aretz 15 August 2003). **Israel ceases all contact with the Palestinian Authority, and halts IDF withdrawal from Palestinian areas.**

2003 The Palestinian (PA) Prime Minister Mahmoud Abbas (Abu Mazen) resigns due to lack of popular support. Abbas does not make any serious effort to collect weapons in terrorist hands and stop terrorism. His replacement is Ahmed Qureia (Abu Ala). Forbes magazine's annual 'Rich List' cites Yasser Arafat personal wealth to be at least $300 million.

2003 Knesset member Yossi Beilin and Palestinian Yasser Abed Rabbo sign the **Geneva Accord,** constituting an end to all claims on both sides. Palestinians recognize the Jewish people's right to a state, and Israel recognizes Palestine as their national homeland. The words "return" or "right of return" do not appear in the document. Israel will pay an agreed sum in compensation to refugees (Arabs will not pay any compensation to Jews who fled penniless from Arab states). This document has no legal standing, is not signed by any government representative–not Israeli nor Palestinian.

2003 During 2003 214 Israelis are killed and 1004 wounded in 3838 terrorist attacks. The reduction compared to the previous year is attributed to Shin Bet's success in thwarting anticipated attacks and the construction of the 'separation fence' requiring Palestinians to cross the Green Line at specified points.

2004 Hezbollah return the remains of three Israeli soldiers kidnapped while patrolling along the northern border 1210 days after their capture in 2000. One of the soldiers is an Israeli Arab. The German government assists with the exchange to include 430 Palestinians, and 35 'internationals' including Sheikh Abed Karim Obeid and Mustafa Dirani, captured by IDF in Lebanon and held as bargaining chips for the return of the IAF navigator, Captain Ron Arad whose whereabouts remain unknown. (See Arad 1982). An Israeli, Elhanan Tannenbaum, is also released.

2004 Israeli Air Force assassinates Hamas leader Sheikh Ahmed Yassin in Gaza. Yassin always called for the destruction of Israel and supported violence. Dialogue and negotiations with Israel were not in his vocabulary. New Hamas leader Abdel Azziz Rantisi is known for his virulent anti-Israel stance and public statements calling for the destruction of the state. He is assassinated shortly. (14 March).

2004 An IDF APC (armored personnel carrier) is blown-up by a mine in Gaza City (the soldiers are searching for weapons production facilities) killing all six IDF soldiers. Palestinians desecrate the soldier's bodies. A large contingent of weapons is waiting in Sinai for a suitable tunnel to be built. In a preemptive action the IDF enters the Philadelphi Route between Gaza and Sinai searching for tunnels when one APC is blown-up, killing 5 IDF soldiers.

2004 Palestinian PM Ahmed Qurei (Abu Ala) openly acknowledges *"We have clearly declared that the Aqsa Martyrs Brigades are part of Fatah. We are committed to them and **Fatah bears full responsibility**."* (London-based *Asharq al-Awsat* 20 June).

2004 US President George W. Bush jr. describes 'new realities on the ground' to include some Jewish settlement concentrations when defining the new border beyond the 'Green Line'. President Bush states Palestinian refugees "right of return will be to Palestine, not Israel". PM Sharon publicly calls for disengagement and removal of Israeli civilian population and army out of Gaza. His political party, the Likud votes against this proposal.

2004 **The Security Barrier.** UN General Assembly adopts a Palestinian-initiated request from the International Court of Justice (ICJ) in The Hague regarding Israel's security barrier. *"What are the legal consequences arising from the construction of the wall being built by Israel...in the Occupied Palestinian territory."* The ICJ decides Israel violates international law routing of the security fence and calls on Israel to dismantle sections built in West Bank and East Jerusalem, dismissing Israel's security arguments. The US, EU and Russia declare the case outside ICJ jurisdiction. *"You set a boundary they cannot overstep."* (Psalms 104:9).

The **Israel Supreme Court** states:

- The ICJ shows disregard of the reasons for the fence's construction.
- The ICJ ruling on the fence is not binding on Israel, based on partial facts only, not taking into consideration Israel's need to protect itself.
- The State has authority to build the fence on the West Bank, and is under no obligation to move it within the Green Line. The fence can protect settlements and not just the area within the Green Line and can serve to connect settlements to Israel.
- The Israel Supreme Court orders a small section of the barrier outside Jerusalem to be re-routed to reduce economic and social hardships caused to local Palestinians.

Examples of modern security barriers.
1. Unilaterally built fences
Africa
Botswana - Zimbabwe
Egypt - Gaza; Egypt – Libya
Morocco - Algeria
Nigeria – Cameroon
South Africa – Swaziland; South Africa – Mozambique
Spanish Morocco – Morocco, 2700 kms

Americas
USA – Mexico

Asia
Afghanistan - Pakistan 2400 kms
China – Hong Kong; China – Macau
India- Bangladesh
Israel - Sinai (Egypt) 240 kms
Kuwait – Iraq 215 kms
Saudi Arabia - Iraq, 900 kms; Saudi Arabia - Yemen
United Arab Emirates - Oman
Uzbekistan – Tajikistan, 215 kms

Europe
EU (Poland) – Ukraine
Portuguese coast
Spain – Gibraltar;   Spanish coast at Ceuta and Melilla

2. Common built fences
Malaysia - Thailand, 75 kms
North Korea – South Korea

3. Fences built on disputed territory
India – Pakistan (Kashmir), 3300 kms
Israel - Palestine, 700 kms
Western Sahara – Mauritania (Polisario)

4. Fences built within towns

Belfast, Northern Ireland 1969 - present.
Berlin 1961 – 1990 (West and East Berlin)
Jerusalem 1948- 1967 (West and East Jerusalem)
Nicosia 1974 – 2003 (Greek and Turkish sections)
Rafiah 1978 - present (Gaza – Sinai)

Security Wall between Jerusalem and Bethlehem   Adrian Wolff

2004   The well-loved Israeli composer Naomi Shemer (1930–2004) dies. Known for her children's 'The Land of Israel' songs and music composed to poems of Rachel and Natan Alterman. Her song, '*Jerusalem of Gold*' becomes popular following the Six-Day War in 1967. Shemer is awarded Israel Prize in 1983 for her contribution to Israeli music. Her songs are identified and loved by all generations of Israelis. Uzzi Hitman (1949–2004) a songwriter and Arik Lavie (1927-2004) a singer, pass away.

2004   Yasser Arafat remains in the *muka'ata* in Ramallah. He is taken ill. A French military jet flies him to a Paris military hospital. Arafat dies and is buried in Ramallah. In Gaza, various imams publicly blame 'the Zionist entity' (Israel) for poisoning Yasser Arafat. Arabic TV al-Jezeera reports tension between various Palestinian leaders for control of Arafat's fortune, estimated at between $4.2 and $6.5 billion. www.aljazeera.com/cgi-bin/review/article_full_story

It is rumored Suha, Arafat's wife, will inherit his fortune, while Palestinian leaders claim this lucre belongs to '*beit al-mal'* (the Palestinian Treasury) and should be transferred to the Palestinian Authority. Uzi Benziman, Ha'aretz 12 November 2004. "*Israel was released...from the punishment of the most treacherous...of its enemies...Arafat...who eight months after he signed the Oslo Accords (in 1993)...(said) that the agreement was equivalent to the one between Mohammed and the Qureish...that the Prophet Mohammed broke...and is considered a paragon of Muslim cunning and tactics....It will remember him as the person who gave the green light for the continuation of cruel terrorist acts while he was still conducting truce negotiations with Israel's leaders....In Israel's eyes, Yasser Arafat was a primitive individual who played in the territories that were given to his rule by corrupt and unbridled rules that faithfully reflected his conceptual world".*

2004   Following the tsunami devastation in SE Asia, the IDF sends 50 medical trauma specialists and erect a field hospital in Sri Lanka.

2004   During 2004, 3956 Terrorist attacks. Shootings 1621; Qassam rockets 309; Mortar shells 1231; Explosives 592. (Source: Israel Government Press Office). 117 Israelis are killed and 589 wounded. 15 suicide attacks during the year. **Israel Police state - areas where the security fence/wall has been constructed, theft rates are reduced by 12%.**

2005   **Mahmoud Abbas**, (Abu Mazen) is elected president of the Palestinian Authority. During his election campaign, Abbas appears on the shoulders of wanted terrorists; denounces 'the Zionist enemy'; promises the Palestinians 'right of return'. His doctoral thesis denies the Holocaust and he publishes a book '*The Other Side:The Secret Relationship Between Nazism and Zionism.*'

2005   Egyptian President Mubarak, Israeli PM Sharon; King Abdullah II of Jordan and Mahmoud Abbas of PA meet at Sharm el-Shiek.
   1. Israeli and Palestinian delegations declare a truce. Palestinians to end violent attacks (Hamas claim temporary *hudna).*
   2. Israel will cease attacks on Hamas leaders and begin withdrawing from Palestinian cities.
   3. Egypt and Jordan announce return of their ambassadors to Israel (after 4-year hiatus).
   4. Israel announces release of 900 Palestinian prisoners.
   5. Mahmoud Abbas announces cessation of anti-Israeli and anti-Semitic propaganda and rhetoric on Palestinian TV and Radio. Does not occur. Claims political violence is completely legitimate. Text books continue to have inciting material, non-recognition of Israel, glorification of terror attacks and terrorists.

2005   The Israel government votes in 2004 (67 to 45) for a disengagement, withdrawing all Israeli settlers and army from Gaza and Northern Samaria. Settlers demonstrate and demand a referendum. PM Ariel Sharon proclaims that in a final settlement Gaza will never be included into the State of Israel. An anti-Disengagement movement, led by West Bank and Gush Katif leaders begin national wide protests.

2005 President **Ezer Weizman** (1924–2005) dies. During WW II, he volunteers in the RAF as a fighter pilot. A founder of Israel Air Force (squadron 101). Head of the Air Force. Head of IDF Operations during the Six-Day War in 1967. On retiring from the military, he enters politics becoming a cabinet minister. In 1993 appointed president. He is involved in the Israel negotiation team that signed the Peace Agreement with Egypt in 1979. All sections of the population remember him warmly for his down-to-earth speech and lack of snobbism. President Weizman and his wife would pay a condolence call to the home of every bereaved family of an IDF fatality in action.

2005 Rafik Hariri, PM of Lebanon, is assassinated in Beirut. He had called for withdrawal of Syria troops and influence in Lebanese political affairs. The US accuses Syria of instigating the murder. A UN investigation implicates Syrian government members and Hezbollah. Syria had previously eradicated elected Lebanese leaders - Phalangist Christian Pierre Gemayel and Amin Gemayel in 1982, and the Lebanese Druze leader Kamal Jumblatt in 1977. UN Security Council Resolution 1559 - Never accomplished.
1. Strict respect of the sovereignty, territorial integrity, unity, and political independence of Lebanon under the sole and exclusive authority of the Government of Lebanon throughout Lebanon.
2. Calls all remaining foreign forces to withdraw from Lebanon.
3. Calls for the disbanding and disarmament of all Lebanese and non-Lebanese militias;
4. Supports the extension of the control of the Government of Lebanon over all Lebanese territory.

2005 Egyptians authorities refuse to allow a local writer, Ali Salem to accept an award from the University of Be'er Sheva in Israel. In Beirut anti-Syrian journalist, Samir Kassir is assassinated.

2005 IDF and Israel Police implement **the Disengagement policy in Gaza and Northern Samaria** assembling 55,000 officers, soldiers, Border and Israel Police to remove all 7000 settlers from 21 Gaza settlements and a few hundred from 4 in northern Samaria. Protestors harass the evacuation procedures. Evacuation of Gaza takes six days, Samaria, one day. From 1967 until Disengagement 230 Israeli soldiers and civilians are killed in Gaza. Since the Intifada in 2000, over 500 rockets and an additional 6000 mortar shells were directed at Israeli civilians and IDF bases within and outside the Gaza border, continuing after Disengagement.

- On the soft sand dunes of Gaza, Israelis produced export quality lettuce, peppers, spices, flowers, etc. Over 4000 Gazans were employed. Palestinians destroy these hot-houses within six months.

- A high number of Gazans are unemployed (40-60%).
- Immediately after entering Gush Katif, burn the synagogues.

2005   During military parade in Jabalya Camp in Gaza, Hamas shows 'strength' by publicly displaying their weapons. An explosion caused by mishandling explosives kills 17. Hamas respond by firing 44 Qassam rockets into Sderot and Western Negev communities. IAF responds. IDF arrest over 200 Hamas members in the West Bank.

2005   In 2005 popular Israeli artists pass away,
Ehud Manor 1941–2005, songwriter, translator
Ephraim Kishon 1924–2005, satirist, author, film script writer.
Batya Gur 1948–2005, author of detective Michael Ohayon.
Gary Bertini 1928–2005, conductor
Dalia Rabikovitch 1934-2005, poetess

2005   A young Gazan woman Wafa al-Biss receives medical treatment at Soroka Hospital, Be'er Sheva (for burns), is found at Erez Crossing wearing an explosive belt planning to explode herself in a crowded area of the hospital. Upon her release from Israeli prison in the 2011 Shalit exchange, she tells cheering schoolchildren "*I hope you will walk the same path we took and God willing, we will see some of you as martyrs*".

A suicide bomber from Jenin explodes outside the Netania Mall, killing five. Immediately thousands of Palestinians in Jenin take to the streets in happiness, firing their weapons into the air, with jubilant smiles of victory over the Zionists. The Palestinian daily, al Hayat al Jaded, reports Abbas signs a new law to support the families of suicide bombers. Almost daily firing of Qassam rockets from Gaza into the Negev, causing material damage while residents suffer psychological trauma. During 2005, 45 Israelis are killed in terror attacks. 5 suicide bombings; explosives 199; mortar shells 848; shooting 1133; Qassam rocket attacks 377.

2006   Hamas wins the only Gazan Parliamentary elections, ousting Fatah, killing over 5000. Hamas derives tax income from the over 900 smuggling tunnels constructed between Gaza into Egypt. Hamas neglects general infrastructure and civilian services. UNWRA continues to support 80% of the population with schools and food. Unemployment is above 40%. Over 50% of the population is under 18 years old.

2006   Terrorists tunnel under the border at Kerem Shalom, enter an IDF camp, kill two soldiers and take a third (Gilad Shalit) captive in Gaza. Without Red Cross visits, Shalit is released in 2011 after 1941 days of captivity, in exchange for 1027 terrorists.

2006   **The Second Lebanese War.** Hezbollah terrorists fire into northern Galilee, cross the border, killing 8 soldiers and taking 2 hostage (Ehud Goldwasser and Eldad Regev–their bodies are returned 2008). Firing erupts immediately on a broad front. IAF attempts, with limited success, to bomb the rocket launches, depots, Hezbollah sites, including their headquarters in Beirut and villages in southern Lebanon, inflicting heavy material damage. Hezbollah rockets and ammunition are stored in civilian areas using 'human shields'. IAF bomb daily and after seven days 30,000 IDF soldiers enter. 1.5 million Israelis remain in shelters and others move to the center and south of the country. The IDF is unable until the cease-fire after 34 days to halt guerrilla-style firing of rockets at civilian targets in Israel. 45 Israeli civilians and 121 IDF soldiers are killed. The IDF's performance is disappointing.

Templer Building damage in Haifa.   Adrian Wolff

Hezbollah claim victory as Israel is incapable of silencing the rockets. Israeli still elusive goals include the return of the two kidnapped soldiers. Israeli Chief–of-Staff Lt.-Gen. Dan Halutz and Defense Minister Amir Peretz resign. (See Winograd 2008). Hezbollah fire 3970 rockets damaging over 600 buildings. 1012 rockets land in Kiryat Shemona, 808 in Naharia, 642 in Ma'alot, 471 in Safed, 181 in Tiberias, 176 in Carmiel. UN resolution 1701 calls for disarmament of Hezbollah (doesn't occur), sending 15,000 foreign troops to assist Lebanese army control southern Lebanon.

Examples of failure of aerial bombing to force a defeat and demoralize the enemy.
• WW II German bombing of towns in England - London, Coventry etc.
• WW II Allied bombing of German towns, factories and infrastructure.

- USA bombing of Tokyo during 1945.
- USA bombing of North Viet Nam in the 1960's.
- USA carpet bombing in Iraq during Gulf War 1 in 1991.
- Israeli bombing of Hezbollah areas in Beirut 2006.

2006 The government of Iran organizes a conference of Holocaust Deniers in Teheran. The US, UK, EU and other countries condemn the sponsors as Iranian president Mahmoud Ahmadinejad and leaders continue their call for the destruction of Israel.

2006 Songwriters Yossi Banai (1932-2006) and Shoshana Damari (1923-2006) pass away.

2006 During 2006, 30 Israelis are killed in terror attacks. Over 1700 Qassam rockets are fired from Gaza into Israel killing 2 civilians.

Exhibition of Qassam rockets fired into Sderot area in 2007. Adrian Wolff

2007 Israeli president Moshe Katzav is indicted for rape and jailed. Shimon Peres the veteran, well-respected politician is president 2007-2014. He tells *"when there is nothing, you can create anything. If you say no to every suggestion, you will pay dearly."*

2007 IAF bombs a nuclear site in Syria. Syrians firstly deny any bombing took place, then claim the site is an agricultural center, later an abandoned military camp, and finally an active military facility. UN inspectors find weapons-grade uranium in the rubble.

2007 A civil war erupts in Gaza as Hamas violently ousts the Fatah administration. Poverty continues in Gaza as the border crossings with Israel are frequently closed due to terror threats. Hamas controls the tunnels dug from Rafiah into Sinai, a lucrative source of income. The USA, EU, UN and Russia define Hamas as a terrorist organization until it recognizes Israel, renounces violence and accepts previously signed agreements between Israel and PA.

2007 **International Demonization and Delegitimization of Israel**

Arabs states, institutions and individuals continue to deny Jewish history and any Jewish connection with The Land of Israel or even the Holocaust. (Yasser Arafat informs President Clinton in 2000 that a Jewish Temple never existed on the Temple Mount.) Following the infamous 2001 NGO Forum in Durban, Israel is demonized equating it with the Nazis, accusing Israel's so-called disregard of international law and abuse of human rights. These attacks (BDS - Boycott, Divestment, Sanctions), often led by government-funded groups, mushroom, publicizing boycotting Israeli lecturers, performers, products and sporting performances. This campaign includes inviting the public to join a demonstration or physically disturbing an Israeli invitee. Israelis abroad can be at risk and in some European countries, be threatened of prosecution as war criminals. The 2010 Vatican Synod criticizes Israel, the only country in the Middle East where the Christian population is increasing. The British University and College Union proposes a boycott of Israeli universities and academics, later rescinded.

The UN demands investigations of Israel, not of Hamas despite the thousands of Hamas and Hezbollah rockets, funded by Iran, fired into Israeli towns. At the UN:
• Each year, there are 20 times more UN General Assembly resolutions condemning Israel than any other country.
• The UN Human Rights Commission has never adopted a single resolution critical of China, Iran, Sudan, Syria, Saudi Arabia or Zimbabwe; one-third of its condemnations were directed at Israel.
• The UN was silent while after 1948 the Jordanians destroyed 58 Jerusalem synagogues, systematically desecrated the ancient Jewish cemetery on the Mount of Olives and prevented Jews from visiting the Temple Mount and the Western Wall.

Former British PM Tony Blair said at the Interdisciplinary Center in Herzlia, Israel, 24 August 2010 "*In any of our nations, if there were people firing rockets, committing acts of terrorism and living next door to us, our public opinion would go crazy. And any political leader who took the line that we shouldn't get too excited about it wouldn't last long as a political leader.*"

Omar Bargouti, head of the anti-Israel Apartheid week and BDS (Boycott, Divestment, Sanctions) opposes the two state solution, doesn't recognize Israel's right to exist. He declares *"The two-state solution for the Palestinian-Israeli conflict is really dead".* There is only one state to which all Palestinian refugees and their descendants will "return".

2007 **Continuation of international anti-Israel coverage.** BBC virtually ceases reporting on rocket attacks from Gaza publishing only six instances during the entire year while detailing 56 Israeli military operations. Stories never directly name Palestinian attacks as the aggressors. Images of Israelis tend to be of soldiers and armored units. Images of Palestinians are mostly wounded civilians, funerals, or debris from Israeli strikes. In 2012, only 2 of the 20 New York Times Op-Ed columns written about Israel were positive. In 2015 UN's Annual Commission on the Status of Women report, only Israel is mentioned infringing women's rights, regarding the situation of women in Palestine and Gaza. *"Not Syria where government forces routinely employ rape and other sexual violence and torture against women as a tactic of war. Not Saudi Arabia. Where women are physically punished if not wearing compulsory clothing. Not Sudan. Where domestic violence is not prohibited. There is no minimum age for "consensual" sex. Not Iran. Where every woman who registered as a presidential candidate in the last election was disqualified."* Anne Bayefsky USA

Matti Friedman, former AP reporter tells *"Vandalism of Palestinian property is a story. Neo-Nazi rallies at Palestinian universities or in Palestinian cities are not...Jewish hatred of Arabs is a story. Arab hatred of Jews is not. Our policy...was not to mention...the Hamas founding charter that Jews were responsible for engineering both world wars...100 houses in a West Bank settlement are a story. 100 rockets smuggled into Gaza are not. The Hamas military build-up amid and under the civilian population of Gaza is not a story. But Israeli military action responding to that threat – that is a story...Israel's responsibility for the deaths of civilians as a result – that's a story. Hamas's responsibility for those deaths is not."* A photo-journalist explains: *"...the riots are nothing more than groups of young Palestinian kids who with their face covered, who throw rocks and disperse, after the first tear gas is shot or go home if no soldier comes."* (IDF spokesman).

http://blogs.jpost.com/content/what-bds-organizers-should-have-told-us-didnt

2007 During 2007, Gazans fire 1263 Qassam rockets and 1511 mortars from Gaza into the NW Negev, Sderot and Ashkelon. The Hamas administration makes no effort to halt the firing. Smuggling of ammunition continues from Sinai into Gaza though underground tunnels. 13 Israelis are killed in various terror attacks during 2007.

2008 The Winograd Commission publishes its report on the political and military performance during the Second Lebanese War. The IDF professionalism is severely criticized. The new Chief of Staff, Lt.-Gen. Gaby Ashkenazi makes operational changes. The political power structure remains unchanged.

2008 **Israeli Achievements. Highest percentage per capita in the world, See Appendix 6:2.**
- Scientific papers
- Venture capital
- Patents for medical equipment
- Start-up companies
- Usage of recycled water
- Population with post high-school education
- Newspaper readership
- 95% of households use solar energy to heat hot water
- More books and articles are translated annually to and from Hebrew than Arabic

2008 Nir Barkat (1959-) is elected mayor of Jerusalem.

2008 Islamic terrorists attack sites in Mumbai, India killing 173, including the Habad Center, murdering the rabbi, his wife and 4 other Jews.

2008 In 2008 over 3600 rockets and mortars are fired from Gaza into Israel, including 40 long-range Grad missiles. Terror attacks kill 36.

2009 Israeli PM Netanyahu pronounces the acceptance of a two-state solution, Israel and Palestine, on condition of Arab recognition of Israel as '**The Jewish State**'. Arabs reject outright any such a concept. Palestinians wish as stage one, to have sovereignty over the entire area of the West Bank based on the pre-1967 lines without compromise, **which they never recognized beforehand**.

Muslims regard Judaism a religion only and not a nationality. Muslim Brotherhood, Hamas and Islamic Movement in Israel state
1. There is NO Jewish 'people' or nation. The Land of Israel, conquered by Islam (in 638) is part of the Ummah (Muslim land) and therefore must always under Muslim rule. Muslims fear that if Jews rebuild The Temple they will become a 'relevant' religion.
2. Remove foreign authority, law and culture from Arab lands.
3. Live according to Sharia Law. *"Religion with Allah."* (Koran 3:19).

2009 Following the continual firing of rockets and mortars from Gaza, the IDF retaliates in **Operation Cast Iron – Gaza War I**. The IDF pages Gaza civilians to leave areas where Hamas operate, to include booby-trapped houses, schools, mosques and welfare institutions converted into weapons warehouses. The IAF destroy weapons manufacturing or storing facilities. UNRWA schools are a hotbed of anti-Semitic indoctrination (in their text-books). During

22-day operation, Hamas fires into Israeli civilians areas over 1200 rockets smuggled into Gaza from Egypt. 10 IDF and 3 Israeli civilians are killed. Hamas continue to attack relief-aid convoys and plunder the goods. After the fighting stops, Khaled Meshal admits he thought Israel would attack for only three days, did not expect the scale of the operation and the damage in Gaza.

2009   The UN Human Rights Commission Fact-Finding Mission led by Judge Richard Goldstone investigates *"all violations of International Human Rights Law and..Humanitarian Law...committed at any time in the...military operations...in Gaza from 27 December 2008–18 January 2009"*. The UN report (September 2009) rebukes both Israel and Hamas with war-crime violations. The report fails to take into account rocket firing from Gaza into Israeli civilian areas in the six years prior to the Israeli operation and omits, without explanation, highly relevant, credible information (e.g. Hamas' use of Human Shields, Incitement etc). The report misguidedly applied rules of war that were designed for conventional warfare, where armies of both sides are clearly identifiable, to guerrilla warfare where the combatants cannot be distinguished from the civilian population. Judge Goldstone later (2011) at Stanford University said the UNHRC *"repeatedly rush to pass condemnatory resolutions in the face of alleged violations of human rights law by Israel but...have failed to take similar action...of even more serious violations by other States...they failed to condemn the firing of rockets and mortars at Israeli civilian centers"*. Goldstone wrote (April 2011 Washington Post) the report would have been different if he had been aware of information that has become known since its issuance. He approved Israel's subsequent internal investigations, contrasting Israel's reaction with the failure of Hamas to investigate or modify their methods.

2009   The Knesset approves a bill stating any withdrawal from Israeli territorial sovereignty requires approval of a minimum of 61 of the 120 Knesset members and a majority in a referendum.

2009   Natural gas fields are discovered in the Mediterranean Sea off the coast of Haifa. 'Tamar' fields come on stream in 2017 to supply all of Israel's needs plus export natural gas.

2009   Iran sends a weapon-laden ship, the Francop, to the Hezbollah in Lebanon, intercepted by the Israel Navy (off Cyprus) and brought to Ashdod port, Israel. The 36 containers include a cargo of 690 122mm Grad missiles; over 5,000 107 and 106 mm Katyusha rockets; 20,000 hand grenades; 9,000 mortars and ½ million rifle bullets. **These rockets are intended to be fired at civilian targets as their military efficiency in battle is very limited. The**

Syrian Foreign Minister denies the ship contains any weapons. During 2009, 566 rockets are fired from Gaza into Israel (406 during Operation Cast Iron). 15 deaths in 1354 terrorist attacks. No suicide bombings occur in 2009.

2010   IDF sends Home-Front Officers to assist with locating and treating survivors of the earthquake in Haiti. A mobile field-hospital is erected, together with operation and diagnostic equipment. The IDF treats thousands of civilians in this disaster area. An Israeli company Teva Pharmaceutical Industries is the top International corporate donor to Haiti victims. Israeli medical teams assist burn victims in the Congo. Their expertise is in 'speed to arrive', 'useful equipment' and 'ability to improvise in difficult situations'. Israel sends a field hospital doctors and staff to Japan following the tsunami in 2011, to Philippines in 2013 and Nepal in 2015.

2010   Hamas terrorist arms smuggler Mahmoud al-Mabhouh is assassinated in Dubai. His son, Abdel-Rauf told he *"fought the Jews, hit the Jews, kidnapped and killed Israelis. He outfitted and dispatched suicide bombers."* Israeli Mossad makes no comment.

2010   Syria, with Iranian aid, continues to arm the Hezbollah who store over 40,000 (100,000 by 2016) missiles in southern Lebanese villages, often next to public buildings and schools. Iranian leaders continue threatening using their nuclear capability to destroy Israel.

2010   Dedication of the Hurva Synagogue, Jewish Quarter, Jerusalem completely rebuilt after its destruction by Jordan in 1948.

2010   Israel is accepted to OECD (Organization for Economic Cooperation and Development). Membership shows strength of Israel economic standing, improving its credit rating and economic ties with foreign investors, thereby expanding trade and growth. **Partial list of Israeli inventions and products. see Appendix 6.2**

2010   During 2010, 437 rockets and mortars are fired from Gaza into Israel. Eleven deaths (civilians and soldiers) in 798 terror incidents. No suicide bombings occur in 2010.

2011   Saudi daily, 'Okaz 7 June 2011 Khalif Al-Harbi writes *"The secret to Israel's survival...lies in democracy and respect for the worth of the individual...The collapse of the Arab countries,..., lies in dictatorship and...oppression...while denying dignity to individuals."*

2011   Israeli constructs a physical barrier 240 kilometers long between Israel and Sinai, to keep terrorists and illegal immigrants from attempting to enter Israel.

2011   PA President Abbas requests UN recognize an independent country Palestine according to the 4 June 1967 borders, (Arabs never recognized). He denies Jewish presence in Israel. "(Jews) *claim that 2,000 years ago they had a Temple. I challenge the(m)"*. *"When he (Netanyahu) claims that they (the Jews) have a historical right dating back to 3000 years BC—we say that the nation of Palestine upon the land of Canaan had a 7,000-year history BC"*. No ancient references exist to any 'Palestinians' 9000 years ago. A Palestinian official states *"no Jews will remain in Palestine"* ignoring UN resolution on 29 November 1947, to partition British-controlled Palestine into two states, one Arab and one Jewish. At UN General Assembly Israeli PM Netanyahu calls for 'direct negations'. Abbas ignores his plea.

2011 **Water.** Continuous drought years in the Middle East from 2004 until 2011. Severe water consumption controls are enacted in Israel. Fresh water quotas to agriculture are reduced by one third. Expansion of 'Recycled Water Facilities' and increase in the use of 'Desalinized Water Production' and 'Saline Water'. **Agricultural production in Israel increases 5 times during this period** (www.cbs.gov.il 19:17). Israeli **fruit farmers** increase production by 42% in the last decade by the use of treated waste water and drip irrigation. The drought also causes the destruction of crops in Syria, causing a consequent migration of many thousands of destitute rural inhabitants to flock to the towns.

2012 Wolfson Hospital in Holon performs, free of charge, lifesaving heart surgery treating over 2900 children, including Gaza.

2012 Syrian Major-General Adnan Sillu tells the London Times 19 September of the existence of chemical weapons and their supply to the Lebanon-based terrorists, Hezbollah. *"They wanted to place warheads with the chemical weapons on missiles - to transfer them this way to Hezbollah. It was for use against Israel, of course"*.

2012 Frequent attacks on the gas pipeline near al-Arish in Sinai permanently halt supplies from Egypt to Jordan and Israel. Egypt exported nearly half its gas production to Israel.

2012 The **'Arab Spring'** begins in Tunisia in 2010 spreading to Bahrain, Egypt, Libya, Syria and Yemen. Dictators in Tunisia, Libya, Egypt and Yemen are removed. Demonstrations proclaim the lack of work places, opportunities, corruption and alienation of the leadership/dictatorship from the population. Demonstrators use electronic unofficial communications (al-Jazeera TV, Facebook, Twitter) to update the population. Israel is concerned with the influence of the Islamic regimes that become more hostile towards Israel. All the *'isms'* such as liberalism, socialism, do not succeed in the Arab world due to the numerous ethnic divisions and sub-religions. There is a lack of 'social stability'. (See Overlords 2010).

2012   After 1697 rockets and mortars are fired from Gaza towards Israel from January to October 2012 (more than 12,800 since 2001), IDF launches **Operation Pillar of Defense** against terror sites in Gaza. Ahmed Jabari, head of Hamas' military wing in the Gaza is killed. Hamas command centers, underground rocket launchers, smuggling and storage centers are hit. During this operation Hamas fires 1506 rockets towards Israeli urban centers. The Israel anti-missile **'Iron Dome' defense system** intercepts 421 missiles (84%) heading towards urban centers. Six Israelis are killed.

Khaled Meshal, Hamas ideological head visits Gaza, declares *"Palestine is ours from the river to the sea and from the south to the north...no concession on an inch of the land. We will never recognize the legitimacy of the Israeli occupation...no matter how long it will take."* Hamas deputy, Mahmoud Zahar adds Hamas will continue getting arms in preparation for the next battle. He calls on Muslim nations to provide Gaza with money and weapons.

In spite of the anti-Israel venom, Ismail Haniyeh, Hamas Prime Minister in Gaza, allows his daughter, grand-daughter, mother-in-law and brother-in-law to receive medical assistance in Israeli hospitals in 2013 and 2014.

2012   Social protest in Israel against high housing prices and income inequality resulting in the high tax burden of the working-poor.

2012   On 29 November UN votes to recognize Palestine as 'non-member observer status'. **Abbas does not agree for direct negotiations**, nor ever recognize Israel as a Jewish State. *"No trace of Jewish history in 'our land'...Temple exists on the minds of radical organizations."* (Official Palestinian TV). *"We do not recognize Israel, nor the partition of Palestine, and Israel has no rights in Palestine"*, Hamas spokesman (Salah al-Bardaweel). For Arab countries to acknowledge a Jewish state would require them to acknowledge Jews as 'a people'. Abbas states that a future Palestinian state would not permit a single Israeli settler to live within its borders (ethnic cleansing?).
https://www.foreignaffairs.com/articles/israel/2016-12-12/how-build-middle-east-peace Article in Foreign Affairs by Moshe Yaalon.

2013   IDF Maj.-Gen. Yossi Baidatz, tells of *"The nature of the wars does not change, but the character of the enemy does." "We must separate from what characterized combat doctrine in recent years and understand that asymmetrical conflict is the main type of conflict". "The adversary is of an entirely different sort from that of the past. Since the 1970s unconventional warfare has been the primary military threat to Israel – expressed by conflict with terror organizations and not with states".*

2013 Israeli hospitals treat hundreds of wounded from the Civil War in Syria regardless of their affiliation.

2013 The Palestinian Authority makes large monthly payments to Israeli Arabs and Palestinians remaining in jail for terrorism offenses.

2014 Ariel Sharon, former Israeli PM passes away having been comatose since 2007. A controversial figure according to both his supporters and detractors. One of the great field commanders of the IDF, warmly revered by all who served under him.

2014 The **Arab Spring** which began in 2010 as popular social protests against lack of economic possibilities and political tyranny, unfold into internal battles and civil wars. This has led to chaos (فـوضـى *fauda*), conflict and factionalism, civil strife (فـتـن *fitnah*) between Muslims. (See Overlords 2104).
Jordan, Syrian and Egypt would clash over control of Palestine, even if Israel would cease to exist as each country claims Palestine to belong to it.

2014 Palestinian PM Mahmoud al Habbash demands the Western Wall be returned to the Palestinian Authority. PA President Mohammed Abbas states Jews should be prevented from entry to "our Noble Sanctuary" (Temple Mount).

2014 Israel Navy captures a vessel Klos C off the Sudanese Red Sea coast, containing long-range missiles, mortar shells and bullets destined for either terrorists in Sinai or the Hamas in Gaza. These weapons originate in Syria, transported and paid for by Iran.

2014 Israeli ex-PM Ehud Olmert (2006-2009) is sentenced to 6 years imprisonment, found guilty of accepting bribes, perjury and corruption during his tenure as mayor of Jerusalem (1993-2003). He allowed the HolyLand Building Project to blight the Jerusalem skyline despite the many petitions. During his tenure the Israeli economy grew and its international standing improved. He appointed a corrupt finance minster (who also served a jail sentence). He allowed the then Chief of the Israeli Air Force to be appointed the IDF Chief of Staff, a faulty decision as seen by its poor performance during the 2nd Lebanon War in 2006.

2014 Pope Francis visits Bethlehem and Jerusalem. He invites the Orthodox Patriarch Bartholomew I to a joint prayer inside the Church of the Holy Sepulchre, where they sign a pledge to work towards unity between the Eastern and Western Churches who have been at loggerheads since 1054. At the Western Wall he leaves a note in his native Spanish, the text of the Christian daily prayer (Luke 11:2-4). In his speech before the two chief rabbis of

Israel he says *"Together, we can make a great contribution to the cause of Peace. Together, we can firmly oppose every form of anti-Semitism and all other forms of discrimination."* The Pontiff prays and urges 'peace'. He places a wreath on the grave of the Zionist leader Theodore Herzl.

2014   The newly elected president of Egypt Abdel Fattah Saeed Hussein Khalil el-Sisi (1954-) bans the Moslem Brotherhood organization. Egypt closes the tunnels connecting Gaza into Sinai, removing a major source of Hamas income collected from tunnel taxes. Hamas fails to pay monthly salaries to their 40,000 officials. (Since the violent ouster of the PA from Gaza in 2007, the PA continues to pay their 70,000 PA Gaza officials a monthly salary).

2014   In the West Bank (Etzion Bloc) Hamas operatives kidnap and murder three Jewish yeshiva students, hitch-hiking home. In unity, Hamas in Gaza begin to fire mortars into Israel. During **Operation Brother's Keeper** the IDF captures Hamas leaders in the West Bank and 51 terrorists previously released following the release of the Israeli soldier Gilad Shalit. Tens of tunnels are located in the Hebron area. After three months, the two murderers are located and killed in Hebron. *"I pursued my enemies and overtook them, and not returned until they were destroyed. I struck them down and they could not rise, they fell beneath my feet."* (Psalms 18:37, 38).

Hamas fire over 450 rockets at Israel from the beginning of this year. Since Israel withdrew from Gaza in 2005, over 8,000 rockets have been fired into Israel. A Jewish extremist captures and murders a Palestinian youth in East Jerusalem, leaving the burnt body in the Jerusalem forest (the perpetrator is caught and jailed).

2014   **Operation Protective Edge** begins with the aim to disarm Hamas and destroy its ability to fire rockets into Israel. The IAF attacks Hamas rocket launching sites, munition factories and storage sites, all found embedded in highly densely populated areas in Gaza. During this operation, Hamas fighters exit a tunnel inside Israel near Ein Hashlosha forcing the IDF to immediately change its main target, sending ground forces to locate and destroy 32 Hamas tunnels leading and entering Israel, some 30 meters below ground, all provided with water, electricity, air vets, ammunition, sewerage. Tunnels are interconnecting. The IDF warns Gazans prior to IAF strikes. During the operation, the IDF also facilitates the transfer of medical supplies in the Gaza Strip. The IDF permits Gazans with medical emergencies to enter Israel to receive care. Israel continues to supply water and electricity to Gaza. Hamas continues firing rockets from inside a hospital compound.

All the Israeli settlements (kibbutzim and moshavim) around Gaza have tens of rockets fall in their area. They encourage all the children and non-essential staff to leave, to be warmly received by host kibbutzim in the center/north of the country. All Hamas attempts to surprise Israel by launching a cell from the sea, using drones, kidnapping soldiers for bargaining purposes, etc., fail with no exception. After 50 days, Israeli losses are 66 soldiers and 6 civilians killed. IDF reports "*this operation led to severe damage to infrastructure and manufacturing capabilities. Fighting was complex in residential areas with a wide underground network in-between. We found homes and street booby-trapped, encountered anti-tank missiles, mortar and sniper fire at close quarter combat*".

Iron Dome rocket approaching incoming rocket (dot).
Photograph Adrian Wolff sitting on the sidewalk, against a wall

Summary of Operation Protective Edge

Rockets fired from Gaza 4,382, 86% intercepted. Rockets fired - Ashdod 302, Ashkelon 371, Be'er Sheva 302

Ratio of IDF casualties to number of soldiers: 1948 = 46%; 1973 = 29%; Lebanese War 1 = 14%; Lebanese War 2 = 13%; Protective Edge = 7.7%. Source: IDF

Hamas violates 11 agreements, firing at Israeli civilians and forces during ceasefires and UN-declared humanitarian windows. Both Egypt and Israel reject Hamas' demand to open an air and sea-port. The Rafah crossing is under Egyptian control. The IDF estimate 1768 Gazans die, including 750-1000 armed terrorists. Hamas is insensitive about their own lives as they see death as part of their ideology, expressing their faith in Allah. Hamas leader Khaled Hamiyeh states *"We won the military victory by the resistance and the legendary strength of our people will lead us to a lifting of the blockade".*

Beit Hanun from Netiv Ha'asara. Damage to high-rise buildings. Adrian Wolff

2014   Five killed in 80 terror attacks, 66 soldiers and 6 civilians killed in the Gaza Operation in 2014.

2015   Israel offers to allow the 18,000+ Palestinian refugees trapped in the Yarmouk camp near Damascus to resettle in the West Bank and Gaza. Palestinian PM Abbas states *"we rejected that and it's better they die in Syria than give up their right of return."* His wife receives medical treatment in Israel.

2015   IAF strike on Syrian nuclear facility, firstly claimed to be an field, then an abandoned facility. UN inspectors find nuclear chemicals.

Summary of Sponteneous Arab Riots.
1. 1839 Safed
2. 1920's, 1930's Izza Din el-Kasam
3. 1926 Husseini, Mufti of Jerusalem
4. 1929 Husseini, Mufti of Jerusalem
5. 1936 Husseini, Mufti of Jerusalem
6. 1947 UN decision to create two seperate states in Palestine.
7. 1987 Intifada I. Yasser Arafat. Use of stones, rocks.
8. 2000 Intifada 2. Yasser Arafat. Shootings and suicide bombings. Israel closes the borders with the West Bank and Gaza, builds a 8-meter high concrete seperation fence in urban areas and a metal fence in rural areas.
9. 2015 Intifada 3, sponteneous knifings, by Arab teenagers, young adults and women. Cars ram into civilians and soldiers.

2015 A new Arab Uprising, **the Third Intifada** begins with the excuse that Jews are praying on the Temple Mount, desecrating the Islamic Holy ground. This uprising is fueled by the media, through Facebook, radio and TV together with the various Imans, Hamas and political leaders encouraging the Arab population to kill Jews, using knives or ram them with cars. Most of the violence is performed by teen-agers and young adults, causing the IDF to enter the Palestinian towns. 17 killed in 155 terror attacks in 2015.

Economic comparisons – Gross Domestic Product 2015				
Country	GDP	Population	GDP/capita	Unemployment
Israel	$296	8.3	$35,393	6.1%
Egypt	$331	91	$3,614	13.2%
Jordan	$37	7.6	$4,940	11.1%
Lebanon	$47	5.8	$8,050	6.4%
Syria	$25	18.5	$1,351	11.2%+
West Bank & Gaza	$12	4.2	$2,868	26.2%
Spain	$1199	46	$25,831	24.7%
UK	$2849	65	$43,737	6.2%
USA	$17,947	321	$55,836	6.3%
www.worldbank.org; Syria 2014 www.cia.gov; GDP=billion, population=million				

2016 **Continued Israel bashing**

- **UNWRA** United Nations Relief Works Agency. Their schools and children's summer camps teach children all of Israel is "occupied Palestine," and must to be retaken by jihad.
- **UNHRC** United Nations Human Rights Council. Israel is the only nation on their permanent agenda, ignoring other states violations.
- **UNESCO** UN Educational, Scientific and Cultural Organization adopts a resolution removing Jewish and Christian presence in Jerusalem and Judea in ancient times. The Temple Mount is never mentioned, only called by the name al-Aqsa Mosque/Haram al Sharif. Countries support this resolution by abstaining include France, Spain, Sweden, Russia and Slovenia. Christians are silent. **Jesus' parents** "...found Him in the temple." (Luke 2:46). "Jesus went into the temple of God and drove out all of those who bought and sold in the temple." (Matthew 20:12,14). The Koran does NOT state the word 'Jerusalem' within its texts.
- **Christ at the Checkpoint Conference, Bethlehem Bible College.** Jesus is portrayed as a "Palestinian," who would stand with them against Israel.
- **Israel Apartheid Week.** An annual global series of events held in cities and on campuses, seeking to vilify Israel as a racist state.
- **World Council of Churches** Delegitimize Israel's right to exist.

- **Palestinian mythology.** Delegitimizing documented historical evidence of Jews presence in Israel.
- **Iran, Hamas, Hezbollah, PLO charters**. Call for the destruction of the State of Israel, to be replaced by a Muslim state of "Palestine."
- **BDS** Boycotts, Divestments and Sanctions is an international movement to cripple Israel's economy by "boycotting" its products, "divesting" financial interests, and implementing "sanctions" against Israel. The BDS begins in 2005, is a global campaign "*to impose embargoes and sanctions against Israel*" by banning all dealings with Israeli institutions, products and academics. Their leaders Omar Barghouti and Ali Abunumah have openly stated "*Definitely we oppose a Jewish state in any part of Palestine.*" "*The idea of two states was unacceptable from the beginning.*" And "*to bring down the state of Israel...Justice and freedom for the Palestinians are incompatible with the existence of the state of Israel*" (As'ad AbuKhalil, California State University Stanislaus).

BDS activists on campuses create a hostile atmosphere that makes Jewish students feel unsafe and threatened as a result of their professor's anti-Israel advocacy. Their goal is to deny Jews their human rights and are openly anti-Semitic. The BDS ignores Palestinian suffering in Syria, where they are killed or starved by the regime and IS (ISIL/ISIS), or in Lebanon and Jordan where they have no rights to employment or citizenship.

BDS pressure forces the Soda Stream factory to relocate from Ma'ale Adumim to the Negev laying off 800 Palestinian workers. BDS makes no attempt to find them new employment.

2016   The highly internationally respected and loved former president and prime minister Shimon Peres passes away (1923-2016). He told visitors "*not all miracles are in the Bible. The whole country is a miracle. We have no oil, no water, but look what Israel has accomplished. If this would have happened in the time of the Bible it would have been included as one of the great miracles.*"

2016   UN resolution 2334 (2016) does "*...not recognize any changes to the 4 June 1967 lines, including with regard to Jerusalem*". This includes the Jewish Holiest site, The Western Wall and the Jewish Quarter of the Old City, Jerusalem. This resolution does not take into account new realities on the ground. (See San Remo 1920, League of Nations 1922).

2016   In 2016, 17 civilians and soldiers are killed in terror attacks.

6. Appendix

6. 1 Leaders of the State of Israel

6. 1. 1 Presidents of the State of Israel

1.	1948 - 1952	Chaim Weizmann	1874 - 1952
2.	1952 - 1963	Itzhak ben Zvi	1884 - 1963
3.	1963 - 1973	Zalman Shazar	1889 - 1974
4.	1973 - 1978	Ephraim Katzir	1916 - 2009
5.	1978 - 1983	Itzhak Navon	1921 - 2015
6.	1983 - 1993	Chaim Herzog	1918 - 1997
7.	1993 - 2000	Ezer Weizman	1924 - 2005
8.	2000 - 2007	Moshe Katzav	1946 -
9.	2007 - 2014	Shimon Peres	1923 - 2016
10.	2014 -	Reuven Rivlin	1939 -

6. 1. 2 Prime Ministers of the State of Israel

1.	1948 - 1953	David Ben Gurion	1886 - 1973
2.	1953 - 1955	Moshe Sharett	1894 - 1965
3.	1955 - 1963	David Ben Gurion	1886 - 1973
4.	1963 - 1969	Levi Eshkol	1895 - 1969
5.	1969 - 1974	Golda Meir	1898 - 1978
6.	1974 - 1977	Itzhak Rabin	1922 - 1995
7.	1977 - 1983	Menachem Begin	1913 - 1992
8.	1983 - 1984	Itzhak Shamir	1915 - 2012
9.	1984 - 1986	Shimon Peres	1923 - 2016
10.	1986 - 1992	Itzhak Shamir	1915 - 2012
11.	1992 - 1995	Itzhak Rabin	1922 - 1995 assassinated
12.	1995 - 1996	Shimon Peres	1923 - 2016
13.	1996 - 1999	Benyamin Netanyahu	1948 -
14.	1999 - 2000	Ehud Barak	1942 -
15.	2000 - 2006	Ariel Sharon	1928 - 2014
16.	2006 - 2009	Ehud Olmert	1945 -
17.	2009 -	Benyamin Netanyahu	1948 -

6. 2 Israel's Economic Progress

- The population has the highest ratio of university degrees in the world.
- Produces more scientific papers per capita than any other nation.
- Highest number of startup companies per rata and ratio of patents filed.
- Israel is ranked #2 in the world for venture capital funds, behind USA.
- Israel has the second highest publication of new books per capita.
- Israel has the most museums per capita.
- Israel has 9 universities and 66 higher education institutes.
- In Israel 135 of every 10,000 workers are scientists and engineers.
- Over 50% of Israel's industrial exports are Hi-Tech
- Hi-tech comprises over 25% of Israel's total exports
- Highest concentration of Hi-Tech start-ups outside Silicon Valley.

6. 2. 1 Israeli Nobel Prize winners

- Shmuel Yosef Agnon, Literature, 1966
- Menachem Begin, Peace 1978
- Shimon Peres, Peace, 1994
- Yitzhak Rabin, Peace, 1994
- Daniel Kahneman, Economics, 2002 for *'having integrated insights from psychological research into economic science, especially concerning human judgment and decision-making under uncertainty'*.
- Avram Hershko, Chemistry, 2004 (Technion) and jointly
- Aaron Ciechanover, Chemistry, 2004 (Technion) for *'discovering one of the human cells most important cyclical processes to repair DNA, control newly produced proteins, and immune defense systems'*.
- Robert Aumann, Economics, 2005 (Hebrew Univ.) for *'understanding of conflict and cooperation through game-theory analysis'*.
- Ada E. Yonath, Chemistry, 2009 (Weizmann Institute) *'for studies of the structure and function of the ribosome'*.
- Daniel Shechtman, Chemistry 2011 (Technion), *'discovering quasicrystal in which atomic patterns show a more subtle kind of repetition.'*

6. 2. 2 Medical Inventions in Israel

- Israeli scientists are for decades **at the forefront of oncology**.
- Israel's Teva Pharmaceuticals, the largest generic drugs company in the world. Develops a simple blood test distinguishing between mild and more severe cases of Multiple Sclerosis.
- A device helps restore use of paralyzed limbs, providing hope to stroke sufferers and victims of spinal injuries.
- Young children with breathing problems sleep with 'Child Hood', replacing the inhalation mask with an improved drug delivery system.
- Neuroscience Center at Sheba Medical Center focuses on brain research of depression and **Alzheimer**'s disease.

* Research creates human monoclonal antibodies to neutralize highly contagious smallpox virus without inducing the dangerous side effects.
* Movement Disorder Surgery program successfully eliminated physical manifestations of Parkinson's disease with a brain pacemaker to stop tremors. Israeli researchers identify a protein that protects brain cells from medication to reduce motor disturbances.
* Israel is developing a nose drop that will provide a five-year flu vaccine.
* Women who undergo hysterectomies are treated with uterine fibroids developed in a noninvasive alternative to surgery. A product to enhance the use of real-time ultrasound guidance during intrauterine procedures.
* A capsule containing a miniature camera transmits high-quality images of the digestive system.
* Instruments replace traditional surgery by non-invasive outpatient procedures. Invention of the first medical imaging simulator in performing sonographic examinations and assessments.
* Researchers at The Hebrew University developed in laboratory cultures a treatment that completely destroys HIV-infected human cells.
* The commercial cultivation of microalgae to produce natural astaxanthin, a powerful antioxidants.
* Transcatheter aortic valve replacement (TAVR) utilizing a catheter.
* Catheter inserts a **'Stent'** to support the arterial walls.
* A **defibrillator** is implanted to treat arrhythmia.
* **Pressure Bandages** prevents infection and bleeding, saving lives.
* The **ReWalk Brace** uses motors to enable paraplegics to walk.
* An **Artificial Pancreas** for Diabetics patients.
* **OrCam** camera is attached to eyeglasses, wired to a portable computer in the wearer's pocket. It "speaks" text and objects that the user points to. It also recognizes faces and monitor traffic lights.
* Israeli medical teams treat children in Cambodia, Rwanda, South Africa, Kosovo, Turkey, Sri Lanka, Haiti, Philippines, also infected with AIDS.
* MicroRNA-based test for the tumor type in primary and metastatic (secondary) cancer, identifies the tumor origin allowing physicians to select the best treatment options for the patient. Cancer-fighting Doxil is used to treat certain types of cancer. Israel's NaNose breath detector gave an 80% accurate diagnosis detecting pre-cancerous growths, matching far more expensive, slower and invasive alternatives,. A Myeloma drug is developed by scientists at Haifa.
* Motor skills games for developmentally disabled and autistic children. Israeli Internet-based reading system for Dyslexics.
* iExelon Rivastigmine, improving the function of brain nerve cells.
* Diabetes Insulin medications products developed by Israeli scientists.
* Epileptics-Israeli discovery of the underlying mutant gene and the bracelet sends out an alert when a person goes into seizure.

- Liver disease. Israeli-developed antibody immunotherapy treatments.
- Emphysema-Protein replacement therapy.
- Hospital catheters are protected from infection using the new plastic from Israel that disables micro-organisms. Throat surgery utilizes Israeli surgical lasers.
- New methods allow donors from other blood groups.
- Spinal implant products are developed. Skin non-steroid alternative.
- Researchers from Tel Aviv University (TAU) discover the mechanism by which melanoma, the most aggressive and deadly form of skin cancer, spreads in the body. They also discovered a way to halt its spreading to other parts of the body.

6.2.3 Virtual Communications Inventions in Israel

- Microsoft, IBM, Intel, Motorola, Google, Apple, Cisco, Hewlett-Packard, Oracle, AOL and Samsung all have R&D facilities in Israel employing many thousands of engineers and technicians. Part of Windows and Apple operating systems are developed in Israel.
- Pentium NMX Chip technology is designed at Intel in Israel. Pentium 4 microprocessor and the Centrum processor are entirely designed, developed, and produced in Israel.
- Voice over Internet Protocol VoIP mail technology is developed in Israel (1995), transmits telephone calls via the internet greatly reducing the cost of the call, changing the way the world's systems currently operate.
- AOL Instant Messenger ICQ software is developed in Israel (1996).
- Cell phone technology is developed in Israel by MOTOROLA.
- **Flash Drive** device to upload, reliably store and transfer data using a standard USB connection. Apple Inc. uses an Israeli-made (Anobit) flash storage technology for their iPad, iPhone, iMac products.

6.2.4 Israeli Technology (Hi-Tech)

- Israeli companies are leaders in software, semi-conductors, web analysis, internet and security.
- Israel is second only to Silicon Valley in total investment by Samsung.
- Harness solar power for clean electricity production without fossil fuels.
- In 1970 Israeli Hi-tech Scitex integrates a **digital** computer into the **printing process** for the first time, revolutionizing printing.
- In 1993 Indigo revolutionizes the printing industry with the world's first high-quality **digital print**, enabling a small number of copies or different images to be printed easily and economically from a digital home printer.
- Developing miniature laser projectors for cellular telephones.
- Innowattech is developing a system to generate electricity from the pressure of traffic driving along roads. Piezo-electric generators are installed beneath the upper layer of asphalt converting mechanical energy of traffic passing over them into electrical energy.

- Ormat, an Israeli company is a pioneer in geothermal and solar energy harnessing Earth's heat to generate electricity. For decades solar heating panels are used for heating water in private homes.
- The world's first all-electric car network of re-charging points and battery changing stations is set up in Israel, Denmark, Hawaii, California, Canada and Australia, initiated by an Israeli, Shay Agassi.
- Photovoltaic technology used, without emissions, smoke, noise or water, producing electricity from organic waste-cattle manure and garbage.
- Scientists at Tel Aviv University are exploring the use of ultra-violet (UV) light to purify and desalinize water.
- Israeli teens win "robotics Olympics" 1st prize for its Dalek firefighter and Israelis came 1st and 2nd in both individual and team Olympiad exams.
- MobilEye detects vehicles using only a camera and software algorithms for collision avoidance technology to 'interpret' a scene in real-time
- **Waze** is a GPS-based navigation application program for smartphones and tablets displaying travel times and route details, acquired by Google in 2013 for $1.1 billion.
- M-Systems invented the USB Flash Drive (DiskOnKey), the FlashDisk (DiskOnChip) in 2006, acquired by SanDisk Corp.
- Mazor surgical robotics such as SpineAssist the first commercially available mechanical guidance system for spine surgery.
- Firewall. Check Point provides hardware and software products for IT security. Verint technology for banking and finance institutions. Provides 'Intelligence' to governments and enterprises to fight terror and crime.
- The algorithm (code) for sending e-mails is from Ben-Gurion Univ 1980.
- All mobile phone technology **SMS** (Texting), was developed in Israel, 4G devices can be used, as is the chipset, is Israeli. Voice-mail service and recorded messages invented in Israel and call-centre technology.
- Facebook has many Israeli-developed in-built and add-on applications. Israeli-developed search engines.

6.2.5 Agriculture

- In 1950 agricultural exports are 49% of the Israel's total exports, in 2015 agricultural export are only 2% of total exports.
- **Water.** Continuous drought years in the Middle East from 2004 until 2011. Severe water consumption controls are enacted in Israel as agricultural fresh water quotas are reduced by one third. Expansion of 'Recycled Water Facilities', increase in the use of 'Desalinized Water Production' and 'Saline Water'. **Agricultural production in Israel increases from $1464 million in 2004 to over $8000 million in 2016** (www.cbs.gov.il,19:17). The drought also causes the destruction of crops in Lebanon, Syria and Jordan.
- **Reclaimed Water.** Over 94% of all sewerage is treated, more than 80% of all treated waste-water is provide to agriculture irrigation without

adversely affecting the quality and quantity of crop yields. Sewerage is treated firstly using bar screens to block the large particles. Oxygen, micro-organisms and bacteria are added to create biological reactions purifying the water, to break down organic materials and separation into sludge. Finally the treated wastewater is filtered through sand. It takes about 400 days in a purification facility. Monitoring technologies are developed for drinking water and water control.

- **Growing Crops with Saline Water.** Olive groves in Negev irrigated with saline water, yield high quality oil. In the Arava, greenhouse vegetable and dates are grown using saline water, yield sweet crops for export.

- **Drip irrigation** revolutionizes the combination of irrigation with fertilizer directly to the plant roots with a slow, balanced drip and micro-irrigation solution yielding increased growth and higher quality while conserving water and energy. They are self-cleaning and maintain uniform flow-rate regardless of water quality and pressure. Israeli agricultural techniques are applied to the constant monitoring of roots has reduced water, fertilizer consumption and growing time by half.

- **Squeezing every drop of water from the air** with reusable plastic trays, made from non-PET recycled, recyclable plastic with UV filters and a limestone additive. The trays surround each plant or tree, collecting dew from the air, reducing the water needed by crops or trees by up to 50% percent. The trays block the sun reducing weeds and protect the plants from extreme temperature changes.

- Israeli **fruit farmers** increase production by 42% in the last decade by the use of treated waste water and drip irrigation while fresh water quotas are reduced by one third. Improved picking baskets and collection trolleys save 30% on manpower costs.

- **Tailor-made farm solutions** use software to help producers grow fruits and vegetables, raise poultry and dairy cows, manage vineyards and make olive oil. Farmers are advised on when to plant, irrigate, harvest, how to cope with drought; how to choose the crops best for their specific area; how to implement ideal storage and temperature control procedures based on climate; and how to track the growth of chickens, livestock and fruit, all required for running a modern, professional, efficient, profitable farm.

- Breeding beneficial insects and mites for **biological pest control** and bumblebees for natural pollination in greenhouses and open fields. Habitat for Barn Owls for the control rodent population. Crop protection using a slow-release herbicides and a targeted insecticide.

- Algae ponds nourished by power-plant effluent, generate 30 times more feedstock for **biofuel** than do land-based crop alternatives.

- **Potatoes** thrive in hot, dry climates, irrigated by saline water. New **vegetables** grown in the Arava region. Chocolate-colored cherry tomatoes better tasting, having higher levels of anti-oxidants and vitamins. Peppers and purple beans having higher nutritional value with no fibers and can be eaten raw. Seedless eggplant absorbing less oil. Dwarf watermelons grown above ground ripen in winter, weigh 2.5 kgs.

- Hardier **seeds** for better crops introduce genetic materials into seeds without modifying their DNA. This method immediately and efficiently improves plants before they are sowed, curing fruit-tree diseases in orchards and groves, and for seedling treatment in the nursery.
- **Seedless** very tasty peppers, melons, watermelons and papayas.
- **Dairy farming.** Manufacturing advanced systems for dairy herd management, monitoring and feeding.
- **Fishing in the desert.** Specially developed microbes purify fish waste byproducts in the tank, with no need for spillage and refilling. A 'zero-discharge' system eliminates environmental problems in conventional fish farming, not dependent on electricity or proximity to a body of water.
- **Grain cocoons** provide a simple and cheap way for farmers to keep their grain market-fresh keeping water, air, bugs and micro-contaminants out, even in extreme heat and humidity conditions.
- Cherry and cluster **tomatoes** developed in Israel have a longer shelf life, improved taste and tolerate diseases. Over 40% of hothouse tomato crops in Europe and North America originate from Israeli seeds.
- Israeli grown **seedless grapes** are harvested all year round, use special pruning techniques and plastic sheeting to cover the vineyards.
- Israel is the only country to begin the 21st century with more trees than it had 100 years earlier. **Jewish National Fund (KKL)** JNF has planted over 240 million trees, maintains natural woodland, redeemed and reclaimed land for farming, prepared infrastructure for thousands of new homes, developed over 600 recreation areas, built over 200 reservoirs, rehabilitates rivers, streams and springs; restores archaeological and historical sites, educates and supports R&D projects.
- Developed technology to extend the shelf life of popular flowers.
- **Food for the needy.** Leket Israel collects surplus food from restaurants, banquet halls, caterers and food courts which is transferred to local food assistance agencies for distribution to soup kitchens, shelters and non-profit organizations. This organization also prepares sandwiches for underprivileged school children and hot meals for the needy.

6. 2. 6 Israeli Aid and Co-operation

- Recuse operations in earthquake devastated areas include erection of 'field hospitals' with operating theaters.
- Train both agriculturists and medical doctors who are invited to Israel.
- Agricultural and water technology advise to many Third World countries.
- Boosting milk production.
- Solar power and internet availability for African countries.

6.3 Summary of The Crusades

Crusade 1 1095 - 1099

Aim: To free Christian Holy Sites in The Holy Land from 'the infidel', and protect Christian pilgrims.

End: Most Crusaders return for Europe.
Not sufficient numbers of Crusaders remain in The Holy Land.

1096 Godfrey from Bouillon (1060-1100), Flanders. Crowned Guardian of Holy Sepulchre.

1096 Baldwin II from Boulogne, Flanders. Godfrey's cousin. County of Edessa. King 1118-1131.

1096 Bohemond from Taranto, Italy. Principality of Antioch.

1096 Tancred from Taranto, Italy. King of Tiberias.

1096 Raymond from Toulouse (main leader) France. County of Tripoli.

1096 Robert from Normandy.

1096 Peter the Hermit, leader of 'The Peasants Crusade'. Annihilated in Anatolia.

1097 Baldwin I from Bouillon (1058-1118), Flanders. Godfrey's brother. Later crowned King of Kingdom of Jerusalem (1100-1118).

1097 Assemble in Constantinople.

1099 Godfrey of Bouillon, captures Jerusalem, crowned 'Guardian of The Holy Sepulchre' 1099-1100.

First Crusader Kingdom of Jerusalem 1099 - 1187

Crusade II 1147 - 1148

Aim: To free Edessa, previously captured in 1144 by Muslims (Zengi).

End: Crusaders are defeated in 1148 near Damascus by Nur a-Din, the Ayyubid leader from Mosul.

1147 Conrad III, King of Germany. Defeated by Nur a-Din at Nicaea in 1147. Retreats from Damascus in 1148.

1147 Louis VII, King of France. Arrives after Conrad's defeat at Nicaea. Retreats from Damascus in 1148.

Crusade II never arrives in The Holy Land.

Crusade III 1189 - 1192

Aim: To re-capture Jerusalem from Salah a-Din.

End: Crusaders re-establish control of Coastal Plain (Tyre to Jaffa).

1189 Frederick I (Barbarosa), (1123-1190), King of Germany (drowns in Cilicia, Anatolia at start of Crusade).

1190 Leopold V (1159-1194) Duke of Austria, returns after capture of Acre.

1191 Philip II Augustus (1165-1223), France, returns after capture of Acre.

1191 Richard I the Lion-Heart, (1157-1199) King of England.

Richard I does not capture Jerusalem. Signs a Peace Treaty to gain Christian pilgrimage rights to Jerusalem and Bethlehem.

Crusade IV 1202 - 1204

Aim: Pope Innocent III in 1198 initiates new Crusade. Venetians against the new Byzantine (Orthodox) Emperor.

End: Venetian Crusaders attack, plunder and capture Constantinople. Collect booty. Do not arrive in The Holy Land.

1182 Local Orthodox Christians massacre Latins in Constantinople.

1195 Alexius III dethrones Isaac II Angelus. Isaac's II son Alexius IV asks Venetians for help.

1202 Doge Enrico Dandolo in Venice, Italy.

1202 Boniface of Montferrat, France; Philip of Swabia, Germany.

1204 Alexius IV, Venetians un-paid, sack Constantinople

Crusade IV never arrives in The Holy Land. Schism between Orthodox and Catholic Christians.

Children's Crusade 1212

Aim: To reach the Holy Land.

End: Thousands of children sold into slavery, others slaughtered, or die of hunger, thirst, and disease.

1212 Stephen of Cloyes, France.

1212 Nicholas, Germany.

The Children's Crusade never arrives in The Holy Land.

Crusade V 1218 - 1221

Aim: To conquer Egypt and exchange it for Jerusalem.

End: Surrender and ransomed at Mansura, in Nile Delta.

1218 Jean de Brienne, Germany, King of Acre.

1219 Cardinal Pelagius, France.

Crusade V never arrives in The Holy Land.

Crusade VI 1228 - 1229

Aim: To capture Jerusalem from Muslims.

End: Negotiate a Treaty with al-Abel al-Kamil of Egypt for Christian rights in Jerusalem and Bethlehem.

1228 Frederick II (1194-1250) King of Germany, also King of Acre.

1229 Self-coronation in Jerusalem.

King Frederick II gains without military confrontation, the right for Christian pilgrims to ascend to Jerusalem and Bethlehem. The Crusaders control Nazareth, the central and northern Coastal Plain.

Crusade VII 1248 - 1254

Aim: To acquire Jerusalem from the Muslims by first attacking Egypt to bargain for the Kingdom of Jerusalem.

End: King Louis IX captured and ransomed in Egypt.

1249 Louis IX (1214-1270) King of France.

Crusade VII never arrives in the Holy Land.

Crusade VIII 1267 - 1270

Aim: To capture Jerusalem via Egypt.

End: Armies reach Tunis. Disease and plague afflict the army. Louis IX dies in the Tunisian Desert and expedition ends in failure.

1270 Louis IX, King of France.

Crusade VIII never arrives in The Holy Land.

The final Christian Crusade attempt to control the Holy Land.

6. 3 Crusader Kings of Jerusalem
Kingdom of Jerusalem 1100 - 1187

1099-1100 Godfrey of Bouillon, (1060-1100) from Flanders, crowned 'Guardian of Holy Sepulchre'.

1100-1118 Baldwin I of Bouillon (1058-1118), brother of Godfrey of Bouillon. 1st crowned King of Jerusalem.

1118-1131 Baldwin II of Boulogne, cousin of Baldwin I. Count of Edessa 1100-1118.

1131-1145 Fulk V of Anjou (1092-1143). Joint ruler with his wife, Queen Melissande.

1131-1148 Queen Melissande, daughter of Baldwin II. Rules together with Fulk V. Queen Regent (1145-1148).

1148-1162 Baldwin III (1131-1162), son of Queen Melissande. Known to be well educated. Does not impose excessive taxation.

1162-1174 Amalric I, brother of Baldwin III. Protects rights of vassals, prevents Muslim unity.

1174-1185 Baldwin IV (1161-1185), son of Amalric I. Leper king, at 13.

1185-1186 Baldwin V (1177-1186), son of Baldwin IV. Child king, poisoned

1186-1192 Guy de Lusignan (1129-1194), husband of Sibyl, sister of Baldwin IV. Exiled from Jerusalem in 1187.

Kingdom of Acre 1192 - 1291

1192-1192 Conrad I, 2nd husband of Isobel (sister of Sibyl). Assassinated immediately.

1192-1194 Henri de Champagne. (grandson of Eleanor of Aquitaine). 3rd husband of Isobel, daughter of King Amalric I. Thrown from window.

1194–1205 Amalric II de Lusigan (1155-1205), uncle of Guy de Lusignan, 4th husband of Isobel. Never crowned.

1205-1212 Maria de Brienne, daughter of Conrad I and Isobel de Brienne

1212-1225 Jean de Brienne, king regent.

1225-1243 Frederick II (of Germany 1194-1250), Self-coronation 1229.
Husband of Isabel(Yolanda),daughter of Jean and Maria de Brienne

1243-1254 Conrad IV, son of Frederick II. Never arrives in The Holy Land

1254-1269 Konradin, son of Conrad IV. Never arrives in The Holy Land.

1269-1284 Hugo I of Acre = Hugo III of Cyprus.

1286-1291 Henri (Hugo) II of Cyprus and Acre.

6. 4 Islam - Muslims Empires - Summaries

6. 4. 1 Rashidun Caliphate 632 - 661

1. Based in **Mecca**.
2. Rashidun means the 'righteous, guided ones'.
3. Capture: Arabia, Palestine, Alexandria, Damascus.
4. Defeat Byzantines in Palestine in 636 and capture Jerusalem in 638.
5. Nabatean traders convert to Islam.
6. Koran written and finalized in 651 (after Mohammed's death).
7. Three of the four 'Rashidun' caliphs do not die from natural causes.

6. 4. 2 Umayyad Caliphate 661 - 750

1. The Umayyad capital in **Damascus,** rivals the caliph in Mecca.
2. Umayyads are Sunni Muslims.
3. Expansion of Muslim Empire from Persia to Spain.
4. Rivalry for the 'rights' to the leadership of Islam between blood-relations of Mohammed (Shi'a) and other Muslim leaders originating from the converts of the Quraysh tribe, (Sunni).
5. Split between Sunni and Shi'ite (Shi'a) Muslims during the Umayyad Caliphate. Sunni Umayyads defeat Shi'ites at Battle of Kufah in 661.
6. Umayyads collect taxes (*jizya*) from non-Muslims (*dhimmi*).
7. Building in Palestine: Dome of the Rock (Caliph Abed al-Malik 691), al-Aqsa Mosque (Caliph al-Walid 711), Hisham's Palace in Jericho destroyed by earthquake 749, establish the first Arab town Ramle on the Via Maris in 716.
8. Inaugurate: Writing of the Koran, Arabic language for administrative purposes, Muslim coinage - dinar
9. Known as tyrannical rulers.
10. Abbasids defeat the Umayyads.

6. 4. 3 Abbasid Caliphate 750 - 1258

1. Descendants of Abbas, uncle of Mohammed, of Quraysh tribe in Mecca.
2. Capital in Baghdad, founded 762.
3. Abbasids are Sunni Muslims.
4. Develop philosophy, science, and medicine.
5. Translate Greek and Latin texts into Arabic.
6. Abbasid territorial control disintegrates in various independent states.
7. The Mongols defeat the Abbasids in Baghdad in 1258.

6. 4. 4 Fatimid Caliphate 909 - 1171

1. Descendants of Mohammed's daughter Fatima and husband Ali ibn Abi-Talib.
2. Founded in 909 by Ubayad Allah, caliph of Tunisia, ascends to power in Egypt in 969, rejects Abbasid ruler.

3. Capital in Cairo, founded 969.
4. Fatimids are Shi'ite Muslims.
5. Administer territory from North Africa to Arabia.
6. Reject the Abbasid regime in Baghdad.
7. Persecute Sunni Muslims for not keeping Shi'ite customs.
8. The Druze sect splits from the Fatimids in 1017.
9. Salah a-Din ousts the Fatimids in 1171.

6. 4. 5 Seljuk Sultanate 1040 - 1245

1. Originate from (Oguz) Ghuzz, a Turkomen tribe in Central Asia.
2. Seljuks are converts to Islam.
3. Seljuks are Sunni Muslims.
4. Seljuks bring the Turkic language from Central Asia, becomes the 'lingua franca' in Turkey.
5. Sultan Togrul Bey originally makes Baghdad the Seljuk capital.
6. Later the Seljuks make their capital in Isfahan in Persia, build the Great Mosque of Isfahan (Masjed e-Jami).
7. Seljuks conquer Persia (1040), Iraq (1055), Palestine (1071) and Anatolia (1071).
8. The Seljuks defeat the Byzantine Army at Manzikert, Anatolia in 1071.
9. Establish *madrassahs* (religious teaching institutions) to train Sunnis.
10. The Ottomans are the descendants of the Seljuks.
11. The Seljuks are incorporated into the Khorezmian Empire who in turn are defeated by the Mongols.

6. 4. 6 Ayyubid Sultanate 1171 - 1250

1. Salah a-Din the Kurdish leader, unites the Ayyubid and Abbasid Muslims to fight the invading Crusaders.
2. Salah a-Din ousts the Fatimids from Egypt.
3. The Ayyubids are Sunni Muslims.
4. Egypt is the most powerful 'state' in Near East during this period.
5. Decentralization of the Ayyubids after the death of Salah a-Din.
6. Continue *madrassah* (religious teaching institutions).
7. Build a citadel in Cairo and defenses of Aleppo.
8. Ayyubids end with the Mamluk accession to power in 1250 in Egypt.

6. 4. 7 Mamluk Sultanate 1250 - 1516 in Palestine, till 1811 in Egypt

1. Originate from Central Asia.
2. Freed ex-slave soldiers, converts to Islam.
3. Mamluks are Sunni Muslims.
4. Bahri Period 1250-1382 Turkic and Mongols.
5. Burji Period 1382-1517 Circassian from Caucasus.
6. The Mamluks defeat the Mongols at Battle of Ain Jalut in 1260.

7. Build khans (inns), hostels, bazaars, *madrassah*, teaching institutions.
8. Ottoman Sultan, Selim I in 1516 defeats the Mamluks in Palestine and 1517 in Egypt.
9 After Ottoman conquest of Egypt, Mamluks remain as Governors (Beys) to administer Egypt for the Sultan.
10. Napoleon defeats the Mamluks at the Battle of the Pyramids in 1798.
11. Mamluk leaders are massacred by Mohammed Ali in Cairo in 1811, surviving leaders flee to Nubia, Sudan.
12. Mamluk towns built in Palestine: Beit She'an, Gesher, Jenin, Ikron, Jaljulia, Gaza, Khan Yunis.
13. Bridges construction in Palestine: Gengic (Ramle), Benot Ya'akov (Jordan River), Yavne, Damnia.
14. Mosques construction in Palestine: Hebron, Mar Musa, Lod, Ramle.
15. Building renovations in Jerusalem: al-Aqsa, Dome of the Rock, khans, bazaars (*shuk*), water system.

6. 4. 8 Ottoman Empire 1299 - 1922

1. Originate from Seljuks in Anatolia.
2. Ottomans are Sunni Muslims.
3. Capitals - Bursa in 1325, Edirne (Adrianople) in 1389, Istanbul (Constantinople) in 1453.
4. Ottomans defeat Mamluks in Palestine at Khan Yunis 1516 ending Mamluk Period in Palestine and conquer Egypt 1517.
5. Ottoman territory extends from Hungary, Ukraine, Southern Russia, Algeria, North Africa, Near East, Turkey, Persia.
6. The Ottoman Empire lasts over 600 years.
7. Tax the population to pay for: Sultan's opulent life style, keeping a large military force, maintain an inflated and corrupt bureaucracy, support Muslim religious institutions.
8. Military: Salaried troops - mercenaries, ex-slaves, prisoner of war, including *'kapikulli'* Christian or non-Muslim converts to Islam comprise special elite military forces called 'janissaries', artillery and engineering corps, build roads, bridges, railway, and telegraph.
9. Turkish language - Arabic vocabulary and Arabic script. Turkish music, literature, painting, architecture.
10. Administration - local officials appointed by the sultan. Religious officials are the intermediaries between government and people.
11. Control many peoples with different languages, cultures and religion.
12. Ottoman Empire disintegrates: Local nationalism, overspending, decline in military power, European influence, internal reform provokes the establishment of the Turkish Republic.
13. Many sultans have Jewish physicians and financial advisors.

6. 5 Arab Uprisings

Also see 'Arab Spring' in 6. 6 Overlords 2010

1844 Mohammed Ahmed, known as the Ha'ma'adi, the messiah begins an uprising in Sudan against English colonialism and other foreigners such as the Ottomans. They propose a world comprising only of the Islamic religion.

1883 Colonel Hicks leads 10,000 Egyptian troops to their slaughter in the Sudanese desert.

1885 General Charles George Gordon (See The Garden Tomb, 1883) is defeated at Khartoum.

1898 General Herbert Kitchener defeats the Ma'adists in the Battle of Omdurman, Khartoum in Sudan.

1915 **Ahmad Jamal Pasha,** governor of Ottoman Syria and Palestine, stationed in Damascus, commander of the 4th Army leads a failed attack on British positions at the Suez Canal (3 February 1915).

1929 The **Mufti of Jerusalem, Haj Amin al-Husseini** incites Muslims to attack Jews praying at Western Wall on Yom Kippur (Day of Atonement) on the pretext Jews wish to take over the al-Aqsa Mosque. al-Husseini **incites Arabs to riot against Jewish immigration.** Arabs massacre 67 Jews in Hebron. Arab riots in Safed kill 20 Jews, mostly children and elderly.

1930 In an effort to quell riots and appease Arabs, the British decide to halt land purchases by Jews, publish an edict, the Passfield 'White Paper' recommending a cessation of Jewish immigration to Eretz Israel at a time of continual pogroms in Eastern Europe and rise of fascism in Germany. The British ignore all evidence that both the Arab Executive and Supreme Muslim Council organized and incited the local Arab population to riot.

From 1930 until the end of the British Mandate (1948), Jewish immigration is restricted as many Jewish immigrants enter illegally. Arab immigration into Palestine is never restricted during the British Mandate Period 1918-1948.

1936 The Supreme Muslim Council, (WAKF) later known as the Arab Higher Committee headed by the Mufti of Jerusalem, al-Husseini, **declares a General Strike and boycott of taxes. Arab riots and anti-British activities** begins in Jaffa on 15 April 1936 demanding that 'The British stop all Jewish immigration' and 'Halt the sale of land to Jews'.

1947 The very day after United Nations partition resolution (29

November 1947) local Arabs begin rioting and killing Jews. A bus traveling from Netania to Jerusalem is attacked outside Petach Tikva, killing 5 Jews. Thus begins **Israel's War of Independence**.

1948+ Arab terrorism as infiltrators cross the border from the West Bank and Gaza, killing Jewish civilians and soldiers.

1967-1970 Arabs smuggle weapons from Jordan into the West Bank and train terrorists. King Hussein clamps down in the Black September Operation.

1970's Terror attacks originating from the West Bank continue - see text.

1974 Terrorist cross the border from Lebanon and attack school children in Ma'alot. The Israeli government creates new military and para-military units - Civil Defense Volunteers in the Local Authorities, Special Operational Forces in the IDF, Police, Border Police.

1980's The number of terrorist activities decline.

1987 In December the **First Intifada** (Arab Uprising) begins, characterized by the use of stones against IDF forces. The Intifada ends with the signing of the Oslo Accords in 1993.

2000 The **Second Intifada** is characterized by suicide bombings and random attacks against Israelis, both civilians and soldiers. The Israeli government decides to construct a Wall/Fence between Palestinian and Israeli areas. The Palestinians do not achieve their goals of cessation of Settlement Construction. Their economic conditions worsen. The 'Uprising' quietens after 2005.

2015 The Muslim population has become more traditional/religious. They claim Israelis are praying on the Temple Mount as a pretext to begin a **Third Intifada**. The youth are influenced by anti-Israel propaganda in their schools, radio, TV and social media (Facebook). The Imans encourage Muslims to knife Jews.

2015 The rise of ISIS or IS (Islamic State in Iraq and Syria) gives hope to Muslims of their potential strength of an Islamic caliphate based upon basic Islamic principles. The Islamic State begins to control large areas of both Iraq ands Syria. The radicals act against practical Islam who, to their thinking, have western values. They slaughter to gain power, money and territory.

Arab discrimination and abuse against Palestinians since 1948

All Arab counties do not allow Palestinians to become citizens in accordance with Arab League Decree 1547 from 1959, "*in order to preserve the Palestinian entity and Palestinian identity.*" (exceptions: Palestinian Christians in Lebanon in the 1950's, Palestinians born from

Egyptian mothers in 2011). Palestinians face severe travel restrictions throughout the Arab world. They do not receive passports and their travel documents are only accepted by a few countries.

Palestinians cannot vote or run for office in national elections.
Children born to Palestinians do not get citizenship in their host countries.

Jordan
1948 Jordan illegally occupies The West Bank fearing Palestinians will take control of The West Bank and The Hashemite Kingdom of Jordan.

1967 Jordan refuses to allow Gazans who arrive after the Six-Day War to become Jordanian citizens, nor receive government services.

1970 During in the Black September riots 3500-5000 Palestinians are killed and 20,000 expelled, their camps demolished.

1988 Jordan revokes citizenship for millions of West Bank Palestinians as they declared "independence".

2012 Jordan passes an electoral law limiting the number of Palestinian members of Parliament to less than 10%.

2013 Jordan places Palestinian refugees from Syria in camps from which they cannot leave, refusing entry to thousands of others.

2014 Palestinian citizens of Jordan are denied civil rights in the military, college scholarships and admittance to public administrations.

Egypt
1948 Palestine refugees reaching Egypt are forced into camps.
1949 Expel all Palestinians from Egyptian camps into Gaza.
1950 Egypt refuses UNRWA in its territory, relegating it to Gaza.
1949-1956 Palestinians barred from schooling and employment.
2013 Palestinian refugees from Syria are jailed as they try to enter Egypt.
2013 Egypt closes the Rafah border with Gaza.
2015 Egypt refuses to allow Syrian Palestinians to register with UNHCR, for services or residency permits. Some are deported.

Lebanon
1950-58 Only issue one-way travel documents for Palestinians to leave.
1962 Palestinians classified as 'foreigners'. Banned from working as physicians, journalists, pharmacists or lawyers. Not permitted to build new houses or own property, or to repair their homes.

Many not live outside refugee camps, which are not allowed to physically grow. Population of camps has now triple capacity.

1975-78 At least 5000 Palestinians killed in Lebanese civil war.
1985-88 Thousands killed in 'War of the Camps' during the Lebanese Civil War. Palestinians are banned from working as taxi drivers.

1995 Those expelled from Gulf states could not return. (repealed in 1999.)
2005 Palestinians may not own property, nor inherit a home.

2007 Lebanese Army destroy Nahr el Bared camp leaving 31,000 Palestinians homeless.

2013 Lebanon refuses Palestinian Syrian refugees entry.

Kuwait

1991 Gulf War I, 400,000 Palestinians expelled.

Libya

1994-5 Expel 30,000 Palestinians confiscating their houses. Arab countries do not accept them.

2011 Palestinians are forced to pay a special tax.

2012 Palestinians loose their properties during the revolution and the collapse of the judicial system.

Iraq

1950's Expel striking Palestinian workers.

2005 After Saddam Hussein lost power, Palestinians in Iraq are abducted and killed by armed groups. About 15,000 are forced to leave Iraq. Thousands are stranded in camps in the desert between Iraq and Syria, when no Arab country would allow them to enter.

2015: Shiites in Iraq torture Palestinians.

Qatar

1994 Refuse to grant Palestinians work visas.

Syria

1970 Palestinians may not vote, run for office, own farmland, own more than one property.

2005-2008 Syria does not allow thousands of Palestinian Arab refugees fleeing from Iraq to enter the country.

2012 Palestinians are killed in the civil war, some starve to death as forces cut off all food and water to the Yarmouk camp. Israel offers to allow the 18,000+ Palestinian refugees trapped in the Yarmouk camp near Damascus to resettle in the West Bank and Gaza. Palestinian PM Abbas states *"we rejected that and it's better they die in Syria than give up their right of return."* Abbas' wife receives medical treatment in Israel.

6. 6 Overlords of the Middle East

Throughout history Judea, being at the axel between Africa, Asia and Europe, has been a disputed area as various powers fought to control the Trade Route from the Mediterranean Sea to Asia. If Israel would cease to exist, Jordan, Syria and Egypt would clash, all claiming Palestine.

BCE/BC

-1750 The Jewish Patriarch Abraham and his family *"departed from Ur Kasdim to go to Canaan"* (Genesis 11:31).

-13th c Joshua, leader of the Children of Israel, conquers Canaan from *"Mt. Hermon...to...Edom...Zin...Dead Sea...Ma'aleh Akrabim, Zin...Kadesh-Barnea...Kedesh in the Galilee...Shehem...Kiryat Arba...Bezer...Ramot...and Golan."* (Joshua 11:17; 15:1-3; 20:7,8).

-1006 King David unites the northern Ten Tribes of Israel and the southern Two Tribes of Judah into one kingdom. *"All the tribes of Israel came to David...ruler over Israel...sealed a covenant...in Hebron before Hashem, and...anointed David as king over Israel."* (II Samuel 5:1,3). David makes a population census in his realm. *"Go count the people of Israel and Judah...'Travel around among all the tribes of Israel, from Dan to Be'er Sheva...so that I may know the number of the people."* (II Samuel 24:1,2). An inscription uncovered at Tel Dan in 1993, bears the words *'House of David,* and *'King of Israel'.*

- 745 Tiglat-pilesar III (rules 744-727BCE) unifies Assyria with Babylonia, conquering and subjugating all kingdoms surrounding his territory. Assyrians conquer 'The Kingdom of Israel' in 722BCE, continue to capture Egypt, and control the west-east Trade Route.

-722 *"(Sargon II) captured Samaria and exiled Israel to Assyria... settled them in Halah, in Habor...the cities of Media."* (II Kings 17:6). *"none remained except the tribe of Judah"* (II Kings 17:18).

-315 Eretz Israel, once again a disputed area, will become a war zone. **Ioudaia** in Greek, or Judah in Hebrew is overrun by the new Seleucid king, Antigonus I (382–301). He collects taxes along the west-east Trade Routes including the 'Via Maris' in the Coastal Plain on Judea. Ptolemy I retreats southwards to Sinai and Egypt.

-312 Ptolemy I (Egypt) conquers the Seleucids in Jerusalem and Judah.

CE/AD

70 Romans defeats the Jews, capture Jerusalem, destroy Temple.

135 The Romans crush the Jewish 'Bar Kochba Revolt'. Emperor Hadrian passes laws to obliterate the memory of the Jews. Names

previously used for the territory, Judea and Samaria are abolished, now called Syria/**Palestina** (Palestine), after the Philistines who disappeared 800 years earlier when conquered by the Babylonians, later taken by Christian literature. Hadrian rebuilds Jerusalem into a pagan Roman citadel. Jewish minority in Judah.

651 Koran states The Land of Israel is given by God to the Children of Israel. God (Allah) tells Moses *"Oh my people, go into the Land (Eretz Israel) which Allah (God) has assigned for you."* (Koran 5:21)

683 Mu'awiya II ibn Yazid, 3rd Umayyad Caliph (683-684) in Damascus. Anarchy and violence between Shi'ite and Sunni Muslims continues. Invades Mecca.

930 Qaratians from eastern Arabia destroy the Ka'aba, steal the 'Black Stone, returned 22 years later, also desecrate the Zamzam Well.

1016 **Hamza ibn Ali**, preaches Allah incarnated himself for last time in the body of Caliph **al-Hakim**. He becomes leader of a new religion, an offshoot of Islam, the **Druze**. They are excommunicated from mainstream Islam that believes *"no prophet or apostle will come after me (Mohammed) and no new religion will be born".* *"Allah will not send a messenger after Him".* (Koran 40:34).

16th c The Ottomans under Sultan Selim I (1512-1520) conquer Persia (1514), Damascus (1516), Egypt (1517) ending the Mamluk Empire. Sultan Suleyman the Magnificent (1520-1566) conquers Belgrade (1521), Rhodes (1522), Hungary (1526), Algiers (1529), Tunis (1534), Baghdad (1535), Aden (1538), Sana'a (Yemen) (1547), Tripoli (1551), Mesopotamia (1566) reaching Persian Gulf. All areas conquered by the Ottomans become part of its empire, controlled directly from Istanbul. The Sultan appoints a governor (Bey) to rule in each province (vilayet), including collection of taxes and administration. A independent vilayet 'Palestine' **DOES NOT EXIST**, neither as a country, nor as a province.

1695 Adrian Reland (1676-1718), a Dutch professor visits the Middle East. *"Most settlement names originate in the Hebrew, Greek, Latin or Roman languages, except to Ramlah, not one Arabic settlement has an original Arabic name. There is no meaning in Arabic to names such as Acco (Acre), Haifa, Jaffa, Nablus, Gaza, or Jenin and towns named Ramallah, El Halil and El-Kuds (Jerusalem) lack historical roots or Arabic philology. Ramallah, was called Bet'allah (Hebrew name Beit El). Hebron...called Mearat HaMachpelah El Chalil".* *"Most of the land was empty, desolate, and the inhabitants few in number and mostly concentrate in the towns Jerusalem, Acco, Tzfat, Jaffa, Tiberius and Gaza. Most of the inhabitants were Jews and the rest Christians. There were few*

Muslims, mostly nomad Bedouins. Nablus, known as Shechem...and approximately 70 Shomronites...In Gaza lived...fifty percent Jews and...Christians. The Jews grew and worked in...vineyards, olive tree orchards and wheat fields and the Christians worked in commerce and transportation of produce and goods. Tiberius and Tzfat were mostly Jewish and except of fishermen fishing in Lake Kinneret - the Lake of Galilee."

1805 Muhammed (Mehmet) Ali Pasha, an Albanian Turk, modernizes the traditional Ottoman regime in Egypt, breaks from the central authority, placing himself the independent governor (bey) of Egypt.

1811 Muhammed Ali massacres Mamluk functionaries in Egypt.

1813 Muhammed Ali conquers Arabia, expels the Wahhabis from Hejaz.

1818 Ibrahim Ali Pasha (1789-1848), eldest step-son of Muhammed Ali of Egypt places Arabia under Egyptian control.

1820 Britain proclaims Abu Dhabi and Dubai, the seven pearl-fishing emirates ('Trucial States') as independent countries.

1822 Muhammed Ali conquers Sudan, and in 1823, Crete. In 1827 British destroys Ottoman fleet, halting Muhammed Ali's expansion.

1830 France occupies Algiers, and by 1847 controls all Algeria.

1832 Ibrahim Ali Pasha of Egypt defeats the Ottomans at the Battle of Konya, forcing the cessation of Syria, Adana and Palestine to Egypt, while Ottoman influence from Istanbul declines.

1839 The British occupy the port of Aden in Arabia.

1840 Population of Palestine is approximately 250,000.

1840 Britain and Austro-Hungary assist Sultan Abdulmecid I to replace Muhammed Ali in Egypt fearing he (Ali) will become sultan, resulting in diminished Ottoman control from Istanbul. Syria returns to the Ottomans. Muhammed Ali's dynasty continues in Egypt.

1844 In Persia, Siyyid Ali Mohammed (1819-1850), known as Bab proclaims himself 'messiah', risen 1000 years after Mohammed's birth, believing himself, not Mohammed to be the last prophet. He is executed in Tabriz, Persia in 1850 for his religious beliefs.

1860 Spain invades Morocco.

1860 Muslims in Syria and Lebanon ruled by a Christian governor (bey) riot against the wealthier Maronite Christians.

1867 Arabs in Palestine use primitive agricultural techniques, do not produce food surpluses for export, nor create a market for industrialized goods. Terraced walls are neglected or in ruin. Trees are felled for fuel and rain has removed fertile soil. "...*[a] desolate country whose soil is rich enough, but is given over wholly to weeds-a silent mournful expanse....A desolation...There was hardly a tree or a shrub anywhere. Even the olive and the cactus had almost deserted the country.*" Mark Twain. 'The Innocents Abroad'.

1868   A new religion Bahai'i, independent of Islam, is founded in Persia by Mizra Husayn Ali (1817-1892), known as the Baha'ullah or The Glory of Allah (God), followers of the Bab (Siyyid Ali Mohammed). They are not accepted by Muslims. Persians force Baha'ullah to flee to Acre, where he is imprisoned for 24 years, dies in 1892.

1869   Egypt opens the Suez Canal, constructed according to French design and engineering. In 1875 Britain purchases Ottoman shares in the Canal, borrowing money in London from Lord Rothschild.

1871   Iranian-Shiite Jamal al-Din al-Afghani, moves to Egypt, preaches Pan-Islamic nationalism.

1875   Ottoman Empire declared bankrupt

1876   Egypt is officially declared bankrupt.

1877   Russia declares war against Ottomans, enters Balkans, Caucasus, Anatolia.

1879   Sultan Abdulhamud II deposes Ismail, (son of Ibrahim Ali) in Egypt. Ahmed Urabi (Arabi) founds the Egyptian Nationalist party, leading a revolt against Ottoman and European interference.

1880   Population of Palestine is approximately 450,000.

1881   Ottomans are unable to pay their foreign creditors. European powers gain financial control of Ottoman assets and debts in Europe through a Council of the Administration of the Public Debt. France occupies Ottoman Tunisia.

Summary of the Disintegration of the Ottoman Empire
1829 Greece, independent 1830
1878 Cyprus, Romania, Serbia, Montenegro, Caucasus (Armenia)
1881 Tunisia
1882 Egypt
1908 Crete unites with Greece
1908 Bulgaria, Bosnia, Herzegovina
Assistance and Support to the Ottomans
1830 Europeans against Muhammed Ali's independence in Egypt.
1870's and 1912/3 Support Ottomans in the Balkan crises.
1914 Recommend Ottomans remain neutral during World War 1.
Ottomans are convinced of German ultimate victory.

1882 British troops invade Egypt, occupy Cairo, restore order, prevent further massacre of Copts, defeat and exile Ahmed Urabi. Britain initiates political, military, economic and judicial reforms, result in increased cotton production and exports.

1882 Beginning of the Immigration Movements of Jews returning to The Land of Israel. Jews begin to legitimately purchase land from absentee landlords. Arabs squatters are evicted. Jews dig wells, plant fields and clash with the nomadic Bedouin preventing them from watering and feeding their herds on these newly developed cultivated lands. Local Arabs attack the new Jewish settlements.

1887 The Ottoman authorities change the status of Jerusalem to an separate *sancak* (district) ruled by a governor titled *mutasarrif*, directly responsible to Istanbul.

1888 The Convention of Istanbul declares the Suez Canal neutral and guarantees passage to all vessels during war or peace.

1894 Turkish and Kurdish Muslims in 1894 and again in 1896 slaughter over 50,000 Armenian Christians living in Anatolia.

1898 Kaiser Wilhelm II travels to Istanbul to gain Ottoman support to challenge the British monopoly in the Persian Gulf.

1902 Abdul al-Aziz ibn Saud (1876-1953), a clan leader in Kuwait, together with Bedouin fighters, conquer Riyad, in 1902, Najd in 1922 and Hejaz in 1925, uniting them into the Kingdom of Saudi Arabia in 1932 under the puritanical Wahhabi Islamic order.

1905 Ottomans construct the coastal branch of the railway line from Haifa-Afula-Beit She'an-Zemach-Dara'a (Deraa) settling Circassians from Central Asia along the line to protect it. The Hejaz (Hijaz) railway runs from Damascus to Dara'a and on to Mecca. This railway completed in 1908, transports Muslim pilgrims making the *haj* to Mecca and Medina. Many trees felled in Palestine are used for railway sleepers. Hussein ibn Ali of Arabia objects to the Ottoman railway construction to Mecca and Medina which would deprive income to local camel owners transporting Muslim pilgrims

1907 The Jewish National Fund (JNF) is established to purchase land, increasing the quantity of land available for Jewish settlements.

1908 'Young Turks' begin a reformist coup (CUP) forcing the sultan to reinstate parliamentary constitution. Abdulhamid II remains sultan.

1909 Pogrom against Armenian Christians in Adana, Anatolia.

1909 British companies begin extracting oil in Iran. In 1911 British forces occupy southern Iran to protect the oil fields.

1909 Austria-Hungary annexes Bosnia-Herzegovina from Turkey.

1911 Italy invades Libya.

1912 The Turkish Petroleum Company (later Iraq Petroleum Company) is established by Germany, Holland and Britain to exploit the Ottoman oil fields of Mosul in northern Mesopotamia.

1913 'Young Turks' 2nd coup separatist rebellion.

1913 Second Balkan War. Bulgaria attacks Serbia and Greece, loosing territory to Ottomans. Turkey requests German military assistance. Prussian Field Marshall Otto Liman von Sanders is commissioned.

1914 Population of Palestine is approximately 700,000.

1914 Arabia is totally dependent on income from Haj pilgrimages, importing wheat from Sudan and Egypt. Hussein ibn Ali of Arabia (1853-1931) wishes to have control of an Arab kingdom independent from the Ottomans. He requires support from the Entente countries (France, Great Britain, Russia). His son Feisal ibn Hussein (1885-1933) expresses his loyalty to the Ottoman Empire and to the Pan-Islamic jihad cause.

1914 Outbreak of World War I. The participants are: (The Entente) Great Britain and its Commonwealth, France, Belgium, Italy, Greece, Serbia, Russia, the US and Japan, against; The Central Powers of Germany, Austro-Hungary, Bulgaria and Ottomans. Local Arabs refuse to be conscripted into Ottoman Army claiming they are not Palestinians. The majority of Arabs in Palestine are also against the British. Many young Jews in Eretz Israel travel to Egypt volunteering to be conscripted into British Army, but are initially rejected until 1917. Egyptians are not conscripted remain loyal to the sultan, who appoints the khedive (viceroy).

1915 The 'Young Turk' authorities arrest hundreds of Armenian civic leaders. Tens of thousands of Armenians are marched to 'relocation sites' as many are butchered. The Ottomans exile Arab Christians from Palestine who are protected by Russia (Orthodox) and France (Catholic) and also exile Jews.

1916 Before WW I Palestine, Lebanon, Syria and Iraq do not exist as independent countries, are Administrative Provincial Districts (Vilayet) of the Ottoman Empire - the Vilayet of Beirut, Sidon and Tyre; and the Vilayet of Damascus. Iraq is composed of three districts - Mosul, Baghdad, and Basra. Palestine is ruled under a separate Vilayet. Britain wants to secure Palestine, Mesopotamia (oil) and the Suez Canal. France is supported by Britain and Russia in its desire to annex Syria, hence King Feisal is removed in 1921 from Lebanon-Syria to become king in Iraq.

The Anglo-French Accord, known as the Sykes-Picot Agreement is signed to divide the spoils of war in the Middle East after the impending disintegration of the Ottoman Empire. Two new states are established under British rule - Palestine and Transjordan; and two under French rule - Syria and Lebanon. The border between the British and French territory is based on the Ottoman Districts of the time. The Hashemites of Arabia, allies of the British are to be kings in new countries, Jordan and Iraq. The Sykes-Picot Agreement is abandoned at the Paris Peace Conference of 1919.

1916 British troops in Arabia observe the various Arab tribal forces to be lacking conventional military discipline and are terrorized by the sound of artillery and airplanes. The Arabs welcome the weapons and payment (gold sovereigns) from 'Christian infidel' advisors, but do not accept them as conquerors.

1917 British Intelligence Officer Major TE Lawrence (1888-1935), with 2500 Bedouin, defeat the Ottoman Turkish troops in Syria, Transjordan and Arabia including those stationed at Akaba, on the Red Sea. Hussein ibn Ali, the Grand Sharif of Hejaz (Arabia) and Mecca and his sons Feisal, Abdullah, Ali and Zeid assist Lawrence. Local tribesmen join their forces with promise of regular pay and guns provided by the British. Hussein becomes the leader of the Arab world during World War I and does not object to Jewish immigration into Eretz Israel.

1917 British government's **Balfour Declaration** supports a Jewish National Homeland in Palestine.

1918 Great Britain and Commonwealth forces successfully defeat the Ottomans in Palestine, Golan Heights, Mesopotamia and Transjordan. The British view the Golan Heights as an integral part of Palestine. Turkey capitulates signing the 'Armistice of Madras'. The three Pashas escape - Jamal, Enver and Talaat in a German torpedo-boat across the Black Sea.

1918 World War I ends, shattering existing empires - Ottoman, Austria-Hungarian and Russian. New countries are established, especially in Middle East, where previously no independent countries existed.

1919 France claims both Syria and Lebanon, with French Mandate rule installed in 1920. Maronite Christians, traditional allies of France, become the dominant force in Lebanon.

1919 Britain installs Feisal Ibn Hussein (1885–1933) king in Lebanon. The joint Feisal-Weizmann agreement is signed in London. "**Article 2.** *Definite boundaries between the Arab States and*

(Jewish) Palestine shall be determined. **Article 4.** *All necessary measures shall be taken to encourage and stimulate immigration of Jews into Palestine on a large scale, as quickly as possible."*

1920 The San Remo conference grants Britain a Mandate over Palestine and Iraq. Arabs riot in both Palestine and in Iraq.

1920 Great Britain and France sign a mutual agreement regarding the Golan Heights defining the border between British controlled Palestine and French controlled Syria. The border is from the foothills of Mt. Hermon, west of the Hejaz Railway Line straight to the Yarmuk River. Banias Springs and the western sector of the Golan Heights is included into British Palestine. Syria has no rights to the waters of the Jordan River, Lake Hula and Sea of Galilee.

1921 British install Hashemite Abdullah ibn Hussein, king of Transjordan.

1921 British transfer Hashemite Feisal I Ibn Hussein from Lebanon to the newly created state, Iraq. Population of Iraq comprises 80% Muslim Arabs (majority Shi'ite, with Sunnis dominating government and army), 15% Kurdish (Sunni) and 5% Assyrian (Christian).

1921 Britain establishes the Supreme Muslim Council (WAKF) of Palestine, headed by Haj Amin al-Husseini who promotes a violent anti-Semitic campaign and to assassinate Arab moderates.

1922 Lebanon and Syria become French protectorates. Syria sees itself as ruler of both Trans-Jordan and Palestine.

1922 Despotic, corrupt, inefficient political rule by Wafd in Egypt, ruled by King Fuad I, gains independence from Britain.

1922 The League of Nations grants Great Britain the mandate to govern Palestine. Britain separates Palestine into two areas - all territory east of the Jordan River, called Transjordan, covering 80% of the Mandate area is given to Emir Abdullah. Transjordan is immediately closed to Jewish immigration and settlement.

1922 Increased Jewish immigration into Palestine.

1922 Jamal Pasha is assassinated in Tbilisi, Georgia by an Armenian for his part in the Armenian Genocide.

1924 Wahhabi sect led by Abdul al-Aziz Ibn-Saud conquer Arabia deposing Hussein ibn Ali proclaiming himself king in 1926, adding the name Saudi to Arabia. Hussein ibn Ali dies in Amman, 1931. Begin to destroy tombs and domes in Medina.

1925 Riots in Lebanon and Syria against French rule.

1927 Oil fields are discovered near Karkuk, northern Iraq. Britain is granted exploration and exploitation rights.

1928   Unilateral Disarmament policy signed by US Secretary of State Frank Kellogg and French Minister Arestide Briand to outlaw war and call on all nations to settle disputes by peaceful means. In a few years Japan will invade Manchuria (1931), Italy into Abyssinia (1936), Germany rearms, invades Austria and Czechoslovakia (1938) and Poland in 1939, Russian invades Finland in 1940.

1928   Hassan Al-Banna establishes "Al-Ikhwan Al-Moslemoon" (Muslim Brotherhood) in Egypt advocating a fundamentalist Islamic society.

1929   The Mufti of Jerusalem, Haj Amin al-Husseini incites Arabs to riot against Jewish immigration.

1930   In an effort to quell riots and appease Arabs, the British decide to halt land purchases by Jews in Eretz Israel. Jewish immigration is restricted as many Jewish immigrants enter illegally. Arab immigration into British Palestine is never restricted.

1931   Population of Palestine is 1,036,000, including 175,000 Jews.

1931   Italy conquers Libya.

1932   King Abdul al-Aziz Ibn-Saud controls the Kingdom of Saudi Arabia.

1932   King Feisal gains independence for Iraq, joins the League of Nations. He dies suddenly in 1933.

1932   Iraqi army troops massacre over 3000 Aramaic-speaking Assyrian Christians in Simele, Iraq, destroying their villages.

1935   The inauguration of TAP (Trans-Arabian Pipeline) pipeline from Iraq to Haifa, Palestine.

1936   Palestinians strike and riot against British rule demanding the British stop all Jewish immigration and halt the sale of land to Jews. Arabs persist in a campaign of sabotage, intimidation and murder against Jews and moderate Arabs.

1939   Population of Palestine is 1,500,000, including 445,000 Jews.

1939   World War II begins. The Mufti and many Arabs side with Nazi Germany. The British expel Mufti Haj Amin al-Husseini from Palestine. He moves to Damascus, then to Baghdad.

1941   Crown Prince Abdul Ilah's returns to Baghdad as an anti-British uprising begins, shutting off the TAP oil pipeline from Mesopotamia to Haifa on the Mediterranean Sea. Rashid Ali al-Kailani allies with Nazi Germany staging a coup, In addition, in Baghdad 179 Jews are murdered, 896 houses and 583 shops looted, leaving 2400 families homeless. The British defeat Rashid Ali who with the Mufti flee to Germany. Britain installs Nuri al-Said as prime minister.

1941 The Ba'ath Party is founded in Damascus by Michel Aflaq and Salah al-Din Bitar. Their aim is to unify the whole Arab world including Palestine into one Arab country.

1943 France officially terminates its Mandate granting Lebanon independence.

1945 Great Britain recognizes Transjordan as an independent country on 23 March 1945.

1945 France terminates its mandate for Syria on 12 April 1945. Syria regards Lebanon, Palestine and Jordan as Syrian territory and is against independence granted to these countries.

1945 **The Arab League** founded in Cairo, is a confederation of Arab states to unify Arab decisions, "*to strengthen the ties between the participants, to coordinate their political program...the affairs and interests of Arab countries*". Permanent secretary resides at the headquarters in Cairo. The Arab League's propaganda attempts to prevent the creation of a Jewish State in Palestine.

1945 WW II ends following unconditional surrender of German and Japanese Forces.

1946 Britain appoints Abdullah I ibn Hussein (1882-1951), as Hashemite king of Transjordan, to be known as Jordan. Officially all Palestinians except Jews are entitled to citizenship of Jordan.

1946 The British with about 100,000 troops, enact Emergency Regulations in Palestine to control both the Arab anti-Jewish rioting and killing, and simultaneous Jewish efforts to force the British out.

1947 Population of Palestine is 1,845,000, including 630,000 Jews.

1947 The United Nations grants the partition of Palestine into a Jewish state (Israel), an Arab state and an international zone around Jerusalem. The Jews accept it, the Arabs reject it as it does not allow them control of all Palestine. Arab rioting and murder follows.

1948 Five Arab countries attack Israel before the British evacuation of Palestine - Egypt, Jordan, Syria, Lebanon, Iraq and additional troops from Saudi Arabia and Algeria. Jordan illegally annexes the West Bank. The Jews defeat the Arab armies. Israel declares its Independence. Jews begin to immigrate freely into Israel.

1948 About 600,000 Palestinian Arabs flee the war theater created by the invading Arab armies and subsequent Jewish offensive, believing the Jews will take retribution against them with similar vengeance as they claimed they would have persecuted the Jews in their defeat. These Arabs are not absorbed into the host countries, remaining in refugee camps. Arabs living in Palestine had regarded themselves as 'southern Syrians or Arabs', but never as Palestinians. Many Arabs return to Arab lands their families had emigrated from in previous decades. Sixty years later Palestinians define the Jewish defense against the Arab invasion, terror and violence in 1948 as the 'nakba'- the catastrophe. Palestinians are supported by UNWRA.

Palestinians are not allowed to become citizens in any Arab country in accordance with Arab League Decree 1547, "*in order to preserve the Palestinian entity and Palestinian identity.*" (except Palestinian Christians in Lebanon in the 1950's). Children born to Palestinians do not obtain citizenship in their host countries.

1948   Persecution of the Jewish population in all Muslim countries, killing hundreds. Jewish businesses and property is confiscated forcing over 800,000 Jews to flee penniless to Israel and other western countries. (See Appendix 6.10) Jewish communities 2500 years old are ethnically cleansed. This is the Jewish 'nakba' or catastrophe. The value of Jewish assets confiscated is considerably greater than the value of the assets left behind by the Arabs fleeing Palestine. The United Nations has failed to deliberate the plight of the Jewish refugees, terrorized and expelled from Arab countries.

Over 250,000 Jews, displaced in war-torn Europe, find refuge in Israel as the 'Gates of Zion' are opened, housed in temporary tent-camps *(ma'abarot)* in very primitive conditions before their transfer into newly constructed housing developments all over the country.

1948   During the years 1948-1994, Jordan never entertains the idea of an independent Palestine in the West Bank with Jerusalem as its capital, fearing the majority of the population, the Palestinians, will usurp the rule in Jordan. Only Great Britain, Iraq and Pakistan recognize the illegal Jordanian control in the West Bank.

1948   Egypt does not recognize the inclusion of Gaza into Palestine claiming it to be part of 'greater Egypt', expelling all Palestinian from Egyptian camps into Gaza on 1949.

1949   The Arab States regard Armistice Agreements as temporary, not to recognize or accept its borders, nor make peace with Israel. On the contrary, they promote an economic and political anti-Israel boycott, close all airspace and sea-lanes to Israeli vessels or any foreign carrier flying or sailing to or from Israel. Arab countries prepare their armies for their next attack while assisting terrorists to attack Israeli civilians and settlements.

1949   Population of Israel is 1,174,000, including 1,034,000 Jews.

1950   Striking Palestinian workers are expelled in Iraq, Saudi Arabia, and Libya. Lebanon issues one-way travel documents for Palestinians.

1951   Muslim Brotherhood assassinates Hashemite King Abdullah I in Jerusalem. His son Talal is the new king of Jordan.

1952   General Mohammed Naguib and Colonel Gamal Abdul Nasser stage a military coup seizing power in Egypt. King Farouk is forced to abdicate in favor of a Revolutionary Council, that exiles him. General Naguib is both President and Prime Minister.

1952   Middle East is divided with the USA supporting the conservative monarchies (Saudi Arabia, Jordan, Iraq), while the Soviet Union supports the socialist, secular dictatorships (Syria, Egypt).

1953   King Talal of Jordan is forced to abdicate in favor of his 18-year old son Hussein.

1954   President Nasser bans the Muslim Brotherhood and encourages Palestinian fedayeen raids originating from Gaza into Israel.

1956   President Nasser the leader of Arab nationalism, now nationalizes the Suez Canal, and comes under Soviet influence.

1956   In retaliation for terror attacks, Israel attacks Egypt, invades the Gaza Strip and Sinai. France and Britain seize the Suez Canal, nationalized by Egypt earlier that year. USA forces their withdrawal

1956   France withdraws from Morocco, King Mohammed V, (1955-1961) and from Tunisia, Habib Bourguiba, president (1957-1987).

1958   Nasser unites Egypt and Syria (United Arab Republic - UAR) into a secular, socialist republic (dictatorship), intended to include all of Palestine. Egypt, backed by the USSR (Russia), intends to overthrow USA-backed religious, conservative Arab monarchies.

1958   The UAR is a threat to the monarchy in Jordan. King Hussein of Jordan hastily creates 'The Arab Union or Arab Federation' with his cousin the Hashemite King Feisal II of Iraq. This treaty is dissolved in the same year when Iraqi nationalists stage a coup d'teat.

1961   The UAR (Egypt and Syria) dissolves, damaging Nasser's prestige.

1962   Egypt sends over 70,000 troops to support the coup in Yemen.

1962   In Lebanon, Palestinians classified as 'foreigners', may not live outside refugee camps. Population of camps is now triple capacity.

1963   The Ba'ath Party in Syria consisting mainly of Alawis, seizes power in a military coup. The Ba'ath Party in Iraq seizes power, also in a military coup. Abdul Arif, president.

1964 The Palestine Liberation Organization (Fatah) is established in Cairo. Its aim is to destroy Israel and liberate Palestine. The PLO is a challenge to both Syria and Egypt who also wish to control territorial Palestine, both nations claiming it to belong to them.

1965 PLO, operating from neighboring Arab countries, launches terror attacks against Israel.

1966 Jordanian tanks and troops fire at civilian protesters in Nablus.

1967 The Egyptian economy is in distress. President Nasser publicly extolls the population of the need to annihilate Israel. Jordan's King Hussein and Egypt sign a mutual defense pact. In the Six-Day War, the Israel Defense Forces capture Jerusalem, the West Bank, the Sinai Peninsula up to the Suez Canal, and the Golan Heights.

1967 Jordan refuses to allow Gazans who arrive after the Six-Day War to become Jordanian citizens, nor to receive government services.

1967 Great Britain withdraws from Aden, including South Yemen. In 1968 withdraws from Persian Gulf, creating the United Arab Emirates.

1968 The Ba'ath Party in Iraq, led by Ahmed Hassan al-Bakr seizes power. Saddam Hussein controls internal security, removing Shi'ites (the majority) from any position of power.

1968 Palestinians in Lebanon launch attacks against Israel.

1968 Israel begins a settlement policy in Judea & Samaria (West Bank).

1969 Successful coup in Libya led by Colonel Muhammar Ghaddafi.

1970 Economic crises in Egypt stimulates President Nasser to shell Israeli positions on eastern bank of the Suez Canal. Egypt opens a static war with Israel along the Suez Canal.

1970 President Nasser dies, succeeded by his deputy Anwar Sadat.

1970 Hafez al-Assad, an Alawi from the Ba'ath Party, overthrows the president of Syria.

1970 Following assassination attempts on King Hussein of Jordan, Palestinians are expelled after ten days of civil war, known as 'the Black September.' Syrian tanks invade Jordan (temporarily). Jordan expels over 20,000 Palestinians and demolishes their camps. Many Palestinians flee to the refugee camps in Lebanon. The Palestinians and Jordanians dispute the numbers of casualties between hundreds to several thousands.

1970 Yasser Arafat is appointed supreme commander of the Palestine Liberation Army (PLA) the military arm of the PLO (Palestine Liberation Organization).

1973 The October, or Yom Kippur War. Egypt and Syria invade Israel simultaneously to regain Arab honor and territory lost during the Six-Day War in 1967. OPEC Oil producing countries impose an oil embargo on the western world.

1974 The United Nations recognizes the right of the Palestinian people to sovereignty, with Yasser Arafat as their leader.

1975 Christian and Muslim sects begin a 16-year civil war in Lebanon.

1975 French PM Chirac sells a nuclear reactor and jet fighters to Iraq.

1976 Syrian troops slaughter Palestinians in the Tel al-Za'atar refugee in Lebanon.

1977 Egyptian President Anwar Sadat is the first Arab leader to visit Israel.

1978 The PLO situated in southern Lebanon continue to shell the Galilee. Israel invades Lebanon to expel the PLO.

1979 Egypt (Sadat) becomes the first Arab country to sign a Peace Agreement (honored by the USA) with Israel (PM Begin), in the presence of the US President Jimmy Carter. Israel withdraws its entire military and civilian personnel from Sinai Peninsula by 1982. Egypt begins to receive substantial American Aid.

1981 Egyptian president Anwar Sadat is assassinated by the Egyptian Islamic Jihad. He is succeeded by vice-president Hosni Mubarak.

1982 Saudi Arabia and Yemen formally abolish slavery.

1982 Syrian president Hafez al-Assad orders the shelling of Hama, in Syria killing over 20,000 people - Sunnis and Moslem Brotherhood. In Lebanon radical Shi'ites establish Hezbollah (Party of God), supported by Iranian revolutionary guards. Bashir Gemayel, a moderate Christian, is elected president of Lebanon, shortly to be assassinated by Syrian agents. In retaliation Christian Phalange militiamen under Elie Hobeika kill Palestinian and Lebanese civilians in west Beirut refugee camps of Sabra and Shatila. Syrian troops massacre hundreds of Christian inhabitants of the towns of Damur and Zahlah (Zahle) in Lebanon.

1983 Hezbollah suicide bombers blow up the US and French barracks killing marines and French soldiers. A suicide bomber in Tyre kills Israelis and Lebanese prisoners in a compound.

1985 Israel withdraws to a buffer zone in southern Lebanon, ceded to friendly Christian militias.

1987 Palestinians begin an uprising (Intifada) against Israeli forces. In Gaza, Sheikh Ahmed Yassin establishes Hamas, the Palestinian wing of the Muslim Brotherhood, whose aim is to destroy Israel and establish an Islamic state.

1988 King Hussein declares cessation of official Jordanian administration in the West Bank. West Bank Palestinians can no longer receive Jordanian citizenship.

1990 Saddam Hussein declares Israel to be 'the enemy' and contributes money to the family of every Palestinian suicide bomber.

1991 Kuwait expels 200,000 Palestinian residents following the PLO's support of Iraqi dictator Saddam Hussein's brutal occupation of Kuwait, (August 1990-February 1991). PLO chairman Yasser Arafat declares "*what Kuwait did to the Palestinian people is worse than what has been done by Israel to Palestinians.*"

1993 The Israel-Palestinian (Palestinian Authority) Peace Treaty is signed between PM Rabin and PA President Arafat at the White House, in presence of US President Clinton. Israel withdraws from Jericho, and later from Palestinian towns and villages in the West Bank. Israeli settlements in the Gaza Strip remain. Terrorism does not stop. Syria does not accept Palestinian statehood, as it sees Palestine as being part of greater Syrian territory that also includes Lebanon. Egypt does not accept Palestinian statehood, as it sees Gaza as being part of greater Egyptian territory.

1994 Libya expels 30,000 long-term Palestinian residents in response to the Oslo process (The Israel-Palestinian Treaty), confiscating their properties. Arab countries do not accept them. Qatar refuses to grant Palestinians work visas.

1994 The Israel-Jordan Peace Treaty is signed by PM Itzhak Rabin and King Hussein of Jordan at the Arava, in presence of US President Bill Clinton. The Israeli population warmly receives King Hussein during his various visits to Israel. Jordan makes no territorial claims over the West Bank it had administered from 1948 until 1967.

1999 King Hussein of Jordan dies, is succeeded by his son Abdullah II.

2000 Israel unilaterally withdraws from southern Lebanon. Hezbollah leadership in Lebanon celebrates 'victory' against the 'Zionist'. Peaceful neighbor relationships are not forthcoming.

2000 Syrian president Hafez al-Assad dies, succeeded by his son Bashir

2000 At talks sponsored by US President Clinton at Camp David, Palestinian leader Yasser Arafat and Israeli Prime Minister Ehud Barak fail to reach a 'Peace Accord' as Arafat refuses to negotiate any compromise. After the talks break down, Palestinians begin widespread violence, as the new, 'Second Intifada' (Arab uprising) rapidly escalates.

2001 Muslims kill Christians in Gaza, Sudan, Nigeria, India, Philippines, Indonesia, Thailand, Pakistan; and Hindus in Kashmir, India.

2001 Palestinians dance for joy in Gaza and Ramallah on 9/11 when the hijacked airliners attack the Twin Towers, NY. The USA looses its influence in the Middle East. US President Bush encourages democracy. Arab states will collapse during 'the Arab Spring'.

2002 Israel starts to construct a fence/wall between Israel and Palestinian areas to combat suicide bombings and murders.

2005 After Saddam Hussein lost power, Palestinians in Iraq are abducted and killed by armed groups. About 15,000 are forced to leave. Thousands were stranded in camps in the desert between Iraq and Syria, when no Arab country would allow them to enter.

2005 The Israeli government implements the Disengagement policy in Gaza and Northern Samaria to remove all 7000 settlers from 21 Gaza settlements and settlers from 4 northern Samaria. Hamas leadership in Gaza view this as a 'victory' against the Zionists, as the first stage of removing the Jews from Palestine. The extremist leadership encourage all violent acts from Gaza against Israelis and Jews in the form of rockets, suicide bombers, shootings, knifing and hostage taking. *"He it is who has sent His messenger with the guidance and the religion of truth...He may cause it to prevail over all religion."* (Koran 48:28). *"And fight them until persecution is no more, and religion is all for Allah."* (Koran 8:39).

2007 Lebanese army fighting the militant Fatal al-Islam group displaces 31,400 Palestinians from the Nahr el-Bared refugee camp.

2009 Continual firing of rockets and mortars from Gaza. Operation Cast Iron–Gaza War I. UNRWA schools are a hotbed of anti-Western and anti-Semitic indoctrination (their text-books). Hamas continues to attack relief-aid convoys and plunder the goods.

2010 Palestinian leaders refuse to enter into any negotiations with Israeli leaders unless Israel ceases ALL settlement construction.

2010 Prior to World War 1 the Ottoman provinces 'vilayet' are created according to ethnic and sub-religious sects. Great Britain combines three Ottoman Vilayet (provinces) into one country, Iraq which has no 'common denominator', without previous 'nationalism'. In the 1970's Pan-Arabism declines in favor of 'local power' and independence, ruled by corrupt dictators. Development of the internet and social media allows more awareness of their 'suffering' compared to Western countries. Improvement in education levels has led to increased desperation of their socio-economic situation. Demonstrators remove the existing leaders. Arab religiosity increases their political power as 'Islam is the solution' gains momentum.

The **'Arab Spring'** unfolds differently in each country due to tribalism. Tunisian and Egyptian leaders fall quickly because they had no claim to tribal loyalty. In Libya Ghaddafi has the support of his tribe and its allies. In Syria, President Bashar Assad's Alawi minority has long been at odds with the Sunni majority.

The original slogan 'the people want to bring down the regime' striving for freedom/democracy, siting lack of work opportunities, economic decline, persistent corruption, the leadership/dictatorship alienation from the population. Protestors effectively use social media to organize/communicate, while the authorities attempt internet censorship. Protests involve strikes, demonstrations, marches, and rallies. Many demonstrations meet violent responses from authorities, pro-government militias and counter-demonstrators. The situation deteriorates into a civil war between ethnic and religious groups.

'The Arab Spring' begins in **Tunisia** in 2010, quickly spreads in 2011 to Bahrain, Egypt, Libya, Syria and Yemen. Tunisian president Ben Ali is exiled. Libya's Ghaddafi is killed during the civil war in which rebels are supported by NATO air strikes. Rebels then fight each other. Weapons find their way into the Hamas' hands in Gaza

Egypt's Mubarak wishes to pass the leadership to his son. A military coup, together with civil protests, depose him. Islamic parties (Muslim Brotherhood) gain the majority of the votes, electing Mohammed Morsi as president, who passes an Islamic constitution, oppressing the legal system, academia and media. The economy plummets, unemployment skyrockets, public order collapses and crime rises. Coptic Churches are destroyed and Christians are murdered in Egypt. Iran supports the Shi'ites against the Sunni leaders in Bahrain, Yemen and eastern Saudi Arabia.

Syrian protestors demand reforms. Shi'ite Iranian Revolutionary Guards and Lebanese Hezbollah fighters support the Alawi dictatorship against the Sunni majority, supported by Turkey and Saudi Arabia. Over 500,000 are killed by 2016. Syria is suspected to possess one of the largest stockpiles of chemical weapons in the world, allegedly holding supplies of sarin, mustard and VX gases, all banned under international law. The Syrian government is accused of using chemicals against civilians.

Examples of Muslims killing Muslims; Afghanistan, Pakistan, Iraq, Syria, Yemen, Gaza, Egypt, Libya.

2010 Morsi on Lebanon's Al-Quds TV (20 March) "*The Zionists have no right to the land of Palestine...(it) belongs to the Palestinians...to confront this Zionist entity*" to severe "*all ties*" including a total boycott of Israel and the avoidance of "*normalization of relations with it*" to "*nurse our children and our grandchildren on hatred*" for Jews and Zionists. The Muslim Brotherhood remains a most dangerous, anti-Semitic organization.

2010 All Christian communities living in the Arab world decline due to a combination of death threats, acts of violence and desecration of holy places. Christian communities living in Israel are larger (in 2016) than in 1948. During Israeli control, the Christian population of Bethlehem rose, now drops to 25% under Palestinian control.

2012 On 29 November 2012 The UN General Assembly votes to recognize Palestine as 'non-member observer status'. PM President Abbas declares "*This application for membership is...submitted on the Palestinian people's natural legal and historic rights and based on UN GA resolution 181 (II) of 29 November 1947...*", 65 years after Arabs reject the original partition resolution. Abbas does not state or agree for direct negotiations, nor does he ever recognize Israel as a Jewish State. Abbas publicly states there will be no Israeli settlers in the future Palestine. Official Palestinian TV airs "*No trace of Jewish history in 'our land'... Temple exists on the minds of radical organizations.*" A Hamas spokesman (Salah al-Bardaweel) states "*We do not recognize Israel, nor the partition of Palestine, and Israel has no rights in Palestine*". Israel does not appear in their maps, anti-Semitism continues in school textbooks and sermons. Arab countries do not permit or encourage their citizens to visit or trade with Israel.

2012 After 1697 rockets are fired in 2012 IDF launches Operation Pillar of Defense against terror sites in Gaza. Khaled Meshal, Hamas ideological head declares "*Palestine is ours from the river to the sea...south to the north. There will be no concession...never recognize the legitimacy of the Israeli...no matter how long it will take.*" A Hamas deputy, Mahmoud Zahar, adds that Hamas would continue preparing for the next battle and calls on Arab and Muslim nations to provide Gaza with money and weapons.

2012 On 18 December the UN General Assembly passes nine resolutions condemning Israel. The UN fails to condemn Syria for the murder of over 500,000 (and rising) during the civil war as over

5 million (and rising) flee to refugee camps in Turkey, Lebanon, Jordan, Iraq and Egypt, with over 6 million displaced inside Syria.

2013 Egypt closes the Rafah border with Gaza.

2014 IS, ISIL, ISIS The Islamic State of Iraq and Sham (Levant) 'Daesh' in Arabic, (داعش) are Sunni jihadist militants following Islamic fundamentalism, attempting to become a worldwide caliphate. The group capture territory in Iraq and Syria, enforcing strict interpretation of Sharia law. They also operate in Afghanistan, Libya and Nigeria. They spread terror targeting civilians to include forced conversion, rape and slavery. Foreign Islamic volunteers are estimate to account for over half of their forces. The West declares IS to be a terrorist organization. They inspire Muslims to murder civilians in France, Belgium, Germany, Spain, Turkey, Bangladesh, UK and USA. IS executioner's ideology and inspiration comes from the Koran to justify their barbarism. *"...they will be killed or crucified, or have their hands and feet ...cut off...".* (Koran 5:33). *"I will throw fear into...those who disbelieve. Then smite their necks."* (Koran 8:12) (also see Koran 47:4).

These 'Islamic fanatics' use violence to pursue 'purity over stability', throw out democracy and economic progress. They view secular states as being illegitimate as they fight brutal operations, discarding human rights as existing Muslim states disintegrate and cease to be governed from within their borders, collapsing into tribal enclaves used as bases for terrorism, exterminating civilians and opposing soldiers according to their sectarian affiliation.

Syria. al-Qaida and Salafi fighting the rebels and Syrian regime.
Egypt. Elected Muslim Brotherhood begins to create an Islamic state. Deteriorates into chaos and civil violence. Military coup.
Lebanon. Terror attacks, car bombs, assassinations.
Iraq. Civil war between Sunni and Shi'ites.
Yemen. al-Qaida supported Sunnis against Shi'ites
Libya and **Tunisia.** Anarchy.

2014 USA using drones, bomb IS (Islamic State) sites in Syria and Iraq.

2014 Shi'ites supported by Iran capture Sa'ana, capital of Yemen. The Bab al Mandab Straits at the entrance to the Red Sea is now under Iran's influence.

2015 Israel offers to allow the 18,000+ Palestinian refugees trapped in the Yarmouk camp near Damascus to resettle in the West Bank and Gaza. Palestinian PM Abbas states *"we rejected that and it's better they die in Syria than give up their right of return."*

2016 Muslim suicide bomber outside tomb of Mohammed in Medina.

6. 7 Population Statistics (1000's)

Year	Israel	Total					Total	Jerusalem				Tel Aviv
		Jews	% Jews	Moslems	Christians	Druze		Jews	% Jews	Muslims	Christians	
1800	250	15	6%		25		8	1.5	19%	5.5	1	
1840	250	20	8%				13	5	38%	5	3	
1845							15	7	47%	5	3	
1850							15	6	40%	4	4	
1870							16	8	50%	4	4	
1880	450	26	6%	370	45		30	18	60%	6	9	
1893				414			45	28	62%	8	9	
1914	700	85	12%	595	70	6	70	47	67%	10	15	0.1
1917	706	85	12%	589	71	7						0.2
1922	752	84	11%	643	76	8	63	34	54%	13	15	15
1926	877	150	17%	683	80	9						
1928	924	152	16%	762	89	10						
1931	1,036	175	17%	927	101	12	91	51	56%	20	19	46
1939	1,502	445	30%	1035	139	14	134					135
1945	1,743	554	32%	1,097	140							190
1947	1,845	630	34%				157	97	62%	60		210
1948	873	686	79%	112	30	14	84	83	99%	1		248
1949	1,174	1,034	88%	115	34	14	104					331
1950	1,370	1,203	88%	116	36	15	123	120	98%	3		335
1955	1,789	1,591	89%	136	43	19	146	144	99%	2		363
1960	2,150	1,911	89%	166	50	23	165					385
1961	2,234	1,911	86%	175	51	26	167	165	99%	2		386
1967	2,776	2,383	86%	289	71	32	261	196	75%	2,338	5,344	389
1970	3,022	2,582	85%	329	76	38	292	230	73%	66	51	384
1972	3,225	2,752	85%	360	74	38	314	292	72%	85	61	363
1980	3,921	3,282	84%	499	90	51	407	327	71%	96	68	334
1985	4,331	3,517	81%	577	99	74	458	378	72%	110	60	323
1990	4,821	3,946	82%	678	115	83	524	421	70%	127	60	340
1995	5,612	4,522	81%	811	120	92	603	449	68%	138	65	349
2000	6,369	4,955	78%	970	135	104	658	465	65%	151	71	354
2005	6,991	5,314	76%	1,141	146	115	719	492	63%	163	77	376
2010	7,695	5,803	75%	1,321	153	128	778	528	61%	182		404
2015	8,463	6,334	75%	1,471	165	136	866					433

Source: Statistical Abstract of Israel, Central Bureau of Statistics www.cbs.gov.il   Statistical Abstract of Palestine GB Government Office of Statistics
up to 1948, population of Palestine   until 1882 Jews also live in Safed, Tiberias, Hebron   1893 Census
after 1948, population State of Israel only   1931 Christians = 40,000 Orthodox, 35,000 Catholics, 26,000 Copts, Ethiopians, Anglicans, Presbyterians, Lutherans. Druze = 10,000
after 1948, West Jerusalem only   1945 GB, GHQ Palestine Nov 1945   1947 UNSCOP Report 1 Sep 1947

6. 8 Jewish Population

2015 (1000's)

Total	**13,900**
Israel	6,377
USA	5,700
France	475
Canada	385
UK	290
Russia	186
Argentina	181
Germany	118
Australia	113
Brazil	95
South Africa	67
Ukraine	63
Hungary	48
Mexico	39
Belgium	30
Netherlands	30
Italy	28
Switzerland	19
Chile	18
Uruguay	18
Sweden	15

Jewish Virtual Library

Jerusalem Population
1 May 2016 in 1000's
Total = 870
Jews = 534 - 61%
Ultra-orthodox = 34%
Religious = 30%
Traditional = 36%

6. 9 Immigration Statistics

Year	Total	Europe - American	% Europe - American	Asia - African	% Asia - African
1882 - 1903	20 - 30,000				
1904 - 1914	35 - 40,000				
1919 - 1923	35,183	31,524	89.6%	3,659	10.4%
1924 - 1931	81,613	77,777	95.3%	3,836	4.7%
1932 - 1938	197,235	172,778	87.6%	24,457	12.4%
1939 - 1945	81,808	74,445	91.0%	7,363	9.0%
1946 - 14.V. 1945	56,467	46,077	81.6%	10,390	18.4%
15.V.1945 - 31.XII.1948	101,828	97,755	96.0%	4,073	4.0%
1949	239,954	205,401	85.6%	34,553	14.4%
1950	170,563	89,887	52.7%	80,676	47.3%
1951	175,279	87,289	49.8%	87,990	50.2%
1952	24,610	6,915	28.1%	17,695	71.9%
1953	11,575	2,732	23.6%	8,843	76.4%
1955	37,528	3,227	8.6%	34,301	91.4%
1960	24,692	17,482	70.8%	7,210	29.2%
1965	31,115	17,175	55.2%	13,940	44.8%
1970	36,750	25,982	70.7%	10,768	29.3%
1975	20,028	18,406	91.9%	1,622	8.1%
1980	20,428	16,199	79.3%	4,229	20.7%
1985	10,642	7,715	72.5%	2,927	27.5%
1990	199,516	175,774	88.1%	23,742	11.9%
1995	76,361	73,307	96.0%	3,054	4.0%
2000	60,192	56,718	94.2%	3,474	5.8%
2005	21,180	14,422	68.1%	6,758	31.9%
2010	16,633	13,281	79.8%	3,352	20.2%
2015	27,908	26,662	95.5%	1,246	4.5%

Source: Statistical Abstract of Israel, Central Bureau of Statistics www.cbs.gov.il

6. 10 Jews in Muslim Countries

Country	1948	1958	1968	2014
Aden	8000	800	800	0
Afghanistan*	5,000	300	800	1
Algeria	140,000	75,000	3,000	>50
Bahrain	600		150	>40
Egypt	75,000	40,000	2,200	>40
Iran* , **	140,000		75,000	10,000
Iraq	135,000	6,000	2,500	>10
Jordan	0	0	0	0
Kuwait		0	0	0
Lebanon	20,000	6,000	7,000	>200
Libya	38,000	3,750	3,000	0
Morocco	265,000	200,000	55,000	2,000
Qatar		0	0	0
Saudi Arabia	0	0	0	0
Sudan	350	340	0	0
Syria	30,000	5,000	4,000	0
Turkey*, **	57,000		39,000	21,000
Tunisia	105,000	80,000	1,000	1,000
Yemen	55,000	3,500	1,000	>40
Total	1,073,950	420,690	194,450	34,381

*Muslim non-Arab country. ** estimate
Source: World Jewish Congress www.worldjewishcongress.org www.jewishdatabank.org Jewish Virtual Library
Source: Jewish Demography and Statistics, Israel Central Bureau of Statistics
Jewish YearBook 1968

6. 11 Terror Deaths in Israel

Civilians (not including security forces) killed in Arab terror attacks.

Year	Number killed	Year	Number killed	Year	Number killed
1920	9	1948	379	1976	14
1921	24	1949	37	1977	9
1922	5	1950	52	1978	57
1923	0	1951	41	1979	10
1924	4	1952	40	1980	16
1925	1	1953	46	1981	14
1926	1	1954	41	1982	6
1927	1	1955	30	1983	21
1928	0	1956	53	1984	9
1929	119	1957	19	1985	27
1930	0	1958	15	1986	14
1931	2	1959	10	1987	11
1932	4	1960	11	1988	16
1933	0	1961	8	1989	40
1934	0	1962	10	1990	33
1935	1	1963	7	1991	101
1936	44	1964	9	1992	34
1937	10	1965	10	1993	45
1938	94	1966	10	1994	65
1939	26	1967	16	1995	29
1940	137	1968	55	1996	56
1941	14	1969	33	1997	41
1942	4	1970	74	1998	16
1943	1	1971	18	1999	8
1944	3	1972	46		
1945	1	1973	27		
1946	28	1974	67		
1947	152	1975	39		

Source: The National Insurance Institute
Israel Ministry of Foreign Affairs. www.mfa.gov.il

Civilians and security forces killed in Arab terror attacks

2000	139	2010	11
2001	208	2011	22
2002	456	2012	10
2003	214	2013	6
2004	117	2014	5
2005	45	2015	13
2006	30	2016	17
2007	13	2017	
2008	36	2018	
2009	15	2019	

Source: Israel Ministry of Defense www.mod.gov.il, Shin Bet

Israel Foreign Ministry www.mfa.gov.il

Total number of civilians killed in Arab terror attacks in Israel
1948 - 1967 = 844   Independence until Six-Day War
1968 - 1993 = 836   Six-Day War - Israel-Palestinian Peace Accord

6. 12 Geographical Zones in Israel

	Region	Geology	Climate	Vegetation	Agriculture
1	Coastal Plain	Dunes, alluvium, travertine	Mediterranean	Sand dunes, intensive farms	Citrus, fish, vegetables, cotton
2	Upper Galilee	Turonian, cenomanian	Mediterranean	Natural forests	Deciduous fruits, olives
3	Lower Galilee	Volcanic, eocene, cenomanian, alluvian	Mediterranean	Natural forests	Deciduous fruits, olives, wheat, cotton, bananas
4	Northern Valleys	Volcanic, eocene, alluvian	Mediterranean	Grassland	Wheat, cotton, maize, barley
5	Carmel Range	Cenomanian, volcanic	Mediterranean	Natural forests	Olives, forests, bananas
6	Menashe Plateau	Eocene	Mediterranean	Grassland	Wheat, barley, rye
7	Gilboa Mountains	Eocene	Mediterranean	Natural forests	Forrested
8	Shomron (Samaria)	Eocene, cenomanian	Semi-desert	De-forested	Deciduous fruits, olives, wheat in valleys
9	Judah	Cenomanian	Semi/desert	De-forested, desert in south	Deciduous fruits, olives, wheat, grapes
10	Negev	Eocene, cenomanian	Semi/desert	Semi-desert, desert	Wheat, vegetables, flowers, dates, diary, spices
11	Eilat	Volcanic neogene, cretacous, jurassic, precamb	Desert	Rock desert	Vegetables, flowers, dates, diary
12	Jordan Valley	Eocene, alluvian	Desert	Oasis	Vegetables, flowers, dates, diary
13	Golan Heights	Cretacous volcanic	Mediterranean	Steppe natural grassland	Deciduous fruits, olives, maize, diary, berries
14	Mt. Hermon	Cretacous volcanic	Mediterranean	Natural grassland	Deciduous fruits, olives, cherries

6. 13 Level of the Kinneret (Sea of Galilee) and Dead Sea, May of each year   Area of Israel

	Kinneret	Dead Sea	Area of Israel	sq.kms
1930	-209.87	-389.55	Israel	22,072
1940	-209.96	-392.23	Land Area	21,643
1950	-209.63	-391.96	Jerusalem District	653
1960	-209.52	-394.59	Northern District	4,473
1970	-208.78	-395.77	Tel Aviv District	172
1980	-208.84	-399.66	Haifa District	866
1990	-211.25	-406.91	Central District	1,294
2000	-211.92	-413.53	Southern District	14,185
2010	-212.65	-423.19	Kinneret	164
2015	-211.79	-429.00	Dead Sea	265

Source: Central Bureau of Statistics www.cbs.gov.il

6. 14 Israel's Economic Growth

Year	GDP $ (1)	Pop (2)	GDP/capita $	Total Exports $ (3)	Agricultural Exports		Manufacturing (4)			% Hi Tech of total exports
					Total $	% of total	Exports $	Tech Exports $	% Hi Tech	
1950	12,851	1,370	9,380	35	17	49%				
1960	24,611	2,150	11,447	215	62	29%				
1970	31,519	3,022	10,430	776	157	20%				
1980	51,336	3,921	13,092	8,674	558	6%				
1990	68,106	4,821	14,170	17,312	657	4%	7,697	2,278	30%	13%
1995	124,227	5,612	22,135	19,046	741	4%	12,302	4,549	37%	24%
2000	163,875	6,399	25,610	46,296	702	2%	21,005	11,188	53%	24%
2005	184,699	6,991	26,420	57,286	1,027	2%	25,566	11,767	46%	21%
2010	205,000	7,695	27,433	80,326	1,327	2%	40,607	20,128	50%	25%
2015	296,825	8,463	35,603	91,636	1,392	2%	45,019	36,515	50%	25%

Source: Central Bureau of Statistics www.cbs.gov.il

(1) GDP $1,000
(2) Population in thousands
(3) Exports in $ Million
(4) Manufacturing sector, excluding diamonds, in $ Million

Economic Comparisons GDP/Capita and GDP in US$

	1967	1973	1980	1990	2000	2005	2010	2015	GDP	Patent Fillings 2015
Israel	1,460	2,570	5,350	10,860	17,830	20,180	27,270	35,393	296	14,470
Egypt	170	260	480	750	1,440	1,250	2,420	3,614	331	0
Jordan			2,000	1,390	1,790	2,490	4,140	4,940	37	169
Lebanon				1,240	4,730	5,710	8,580	8,050	47	145
Syria	280	500	1,570	920	990	1,500	2,750	1,351	25	224
West Bank Gaza								2,868	12	

Source: www.worldbank.org GDP US$ billions Source: World Intellectual Property Organization (WIPO) www.wipo.int

2014 National Expenditure on Civilian R&D.

	% of GDP		% of GDP		% of GDP
Israel	4.3	Greece	0.8	Portugal	1.3
Australia	2.1	Ireland	1.5	Spain	1.2
Austria	3.0	Italy	1.3	Sweden	3.1
Belgium	2.4	Japan	3.6	Switzerland	2.9
Czech Rep	3.0	Korea	4.2	UK	1.7
France	2.3	Netherlands	2.0	USA	2.7
Finland	3.2	New Zealand	2.0		
Germany	2.8	Norway	1.7		

Source: OECD

9. Bibliography and Selected Reading

Adler, A. (1927) ed. *The Itinerary of Benjamin of Tudela*. Reprint NY.

Adler, Elkan Nathan. ed. (1987) *Jewish Travelers in the Middle Ages*. Dover Publications Inc. NY ISBN 0 486 25397 X.

Agus, Irving. A. (1965) *Urban Civilization in Pre-Crusade Europe*. Yeshiva University Press. NY.

Aharoni, Yohanan; Avi-Yonah, Michael; Rainey, Anson; Safrai, Ze'ev. (1963, 1993). *The Macmillan Bible Atlas*. Macmillan, NY.

Albright, W.F. (1942) *Archaeology and the Religion of Israel*. The Ayer Lectures, Baltimore.

Albright W.F. (1946) *From the Stone Age to Christianity*. The John Hopkins Press. Baltimore.

Allon, Yigal. (1970) *Shield of David. The Story of Israel's Army*. Vallentine, Mitchell, London. Random House, NY.

Alt. A (1968) *Essays on Old Testament History and Religion*. Doubleday. NY.

Avi-Yonah, Michael. (1973) *Jerusalem The Holy*. Sadan Publishing House, Tel Aviv.

Bachi, Roberto. (1974) *The Population of Israel*. Jerusalem.

Bacon, J. and Gilbert M; (1990) Cons. ed *The Illustrated Atlas of Jewish Civilization*. Andre Deutsch, London.

Barnett, Corelli, (1991) ed. *Hitler's Generals*. Phoenix Giants. ISBN 1 85 799 2857

Barnett, R.D. (1966) *Illustrations of Old Testament History*. The British Museum, London.

Baron, Salo Wittmayer. (1952) *Social and Religious History of the Jews*. Columbia University Press, NY.

Baron, Salo Wittmayer. (1972) *Ancient and Medieval Jewish History*. Rutgers University Press, USA.

Baron, J.B. (1922) *Report and General Abstracts of the Census of Palestine*. Jerusalem.

Bar-Zohar, Michael. (1978) *Ben Gurion: A Biography*. Arthur Baker, London.

Bauer, Yehuda. (1970) *Flight and Rescue*. Random House, NY.

Begin, Menachem. (1977) *The Revolt*. Steimatzky's Agency Ltd, Tel Aviv.

Begin, Menachem. (1977) *White Knights*. HarperCollins, NY.

Bein, Alex. (1971) ed. *Arthur Ruppin: Memoirs, Diaries, Letters*. Herzl Press, NY.

Ben-Gurion, David (1964) *Israel: Years of Challenge*. Blond, London.

Ben-Sasson, H.H. Ed. (1976) *A History of the Jewish People*. Harvard University Press, Cambridge. Massachusetts.

Bentwich, Norman (1934) *The Modern World, Palestine*. Ernest Benn Ltd, London.

Benvenisti, Meron. (1970, 1976) *The Crusaders in the Holy Land*. Israel Universities Press. IUP cat 262155

Ben-Zvi, Itzhak (1957) *The Exiled and the Redeemed*. Jewish Publication Society of America, Philadelphia.

Bergman, Ronen. (2002) *Authority Granted: Corruption and Terrorism in the Palestinian Authority*. Yedioth Ahronot. Sifrei Hemed.

Bethell, Nicholas. (1979) *The Palestine Triangle*. Putnam Publishing Press, London.

Bible, *The MacArthur Study Bible*, New King James Version, John MacArthur (1997) Word Publishing. ISBN 0-8499-1222-9

Biger, Dr. Gideon. (1981) *The Birth of the Border* (Hebrew). Ha'aretz newspaper 20 December 1981.

Biger, Dr. Gideon. (1994) *An Empire in the Holy Land; Historical Geography in Palestine, 1917-1929* (Hebrew). Magnes, Tel Aviv.

Brandon, S.G.F. (1957) *The Fall of Jerusalem and the Christian Church.* S.P.C.K. London.

Bright, John. (1960, 1977) *A History of Israel.* SCM Press Ltd, London.

Bronowski, Jacob. (1973) *The Ascent of Man.* Little, Brown and Company. Boston/Toronto ISBN 0-316-10930-4

Bruce. F.F. (1963, 1975) *Israel and the Nations.* William B. Eerdmans Publishing Company, MI, USA. ISBN 85364 093 9

Burns, M (1992). *Dreyfus, a Family Affair.* Chatto and Windus, London.

Carta. (1983, 1986). *Carta's Official Guide to Israel.* The Israel Map & Publishing ISBN 965-220-089-1

Cavenagh, Sandy (1965) *Airborne to Suez.* Kimber, London.

Chernow, Ron. *The Warburgs, A Family Saga.* Pimlico. ISBN 0 7126 6210 3

Clarke, Thurston. (1981) *By Blood and Fire.* Putnam Publishing Group, London.

Cohen, Michael. J. (1982) *Palestine and the Great Powers.* Princeton University Press.

Collins, L. and Lapierre, D. (1972) *O Jerusalem!* Simon and Schuster, NY.

Comay, Joan. (1975) *The Temple of Jerusalem, with the History of the Temple Mount.* Henry Holt & Co. Ltd., London.

Cornfeld, G. and Freedman, D.N. (1976) *Archaeology of the Bible: Book by Book.* Harper & Row, San Francisco.

Creasy, Sir Edward. (1851, 1996) *The Fifteen Decisive Battles of the World.* Oracle Publishing Ltd.UK.ISBN 1 861 96001 8

Crossman, Richard. (1947) *Palestine Mission.* Harper & Brothers Publishers, London.

Cunningham, Sir Alan. (1948) *Palestine - The Last Days of the Mandate.* International Affairs. October edition.

De Vaux, Roland. (1961, 1978) *Ancient Israel, Its Life and Times.* Darton, Longman & Todd, London. ISBN 0 232 51219 1

Dubnow, Simon. (1925) *An Outline of Jewish History.* Max N. Maisel Publisher. NY.

Durant, Will (1944) *Caesar and Christ.* Simon and Schuster, NY.

Eban, Abba. (1977) *Abba Eban: An Autobiography.* Weidenfeld & Nicholson, London.

Eban, Abba. (1984) *Heritage: Civilization and the Jews.* Weidenfeld & Nicholson, London.

Eden, Sir Anthony. (1960) *Full Circle: The Memoirs of Anthony Eden.* Cassell, London.

Ellenbaum, Ronnie. (2012) *The Collapse of the Eastern Mediterranean: Climate Change. 950-1072.* Cambridge University Press.

Elon, Amos. (2002). *The Pity of It All. A Portrait of the German-Jewish Epoch 1743-1933.* Picador, NY.

Eissenfedt, Otto. (1965) *The Old Testament, an Introduction.* London.

Encyclopaedia Britannica. (1768, 1977) William Benton. Publisher. London

Encyclopaedia, The Jewish. (1916) Ed Singer. Funk and Wagnalls.

Encyclopaedia of Jewish History. Masada Publications, Israel.

Encyclopaedia Judaica. (1971, 1978) Keter Publishing, Jerusalem. MacMillan Publishing Company, NY.

Felton, Anton. (1997). *Jewish Carpets, A History and Guide.* Antique Collectors' Club. Woodbridge, Suffolk. ISBN 185149593

Felton, Anton. (2012) *Jewish Symbols and Secrets.* Vallentine Mitchell, London. ISBN 978 0 853038344

Frankenstein, Ernst. (1943) *Justice for My People.* Dial Press, NY.

Gibbon, Edward. (1960, 1968) *The Decline and Fall of the Roman Empire.* Penguin Books.

Gilbert, Martin. (2007) *Churchill & The Jews.* Simon & Schuster

Gilbert, Martin. (1978) *Exile and Return: The Struggle for a Jewish Homeland.* J.B. Lippincott Co. NY.

Gilbert, Martin. (1994, 1995). *First World War.* HarperCollins *Publishers.* ISBN 0 00 637666 5

Gilbert, Martin. (1974, 1996) *Atlas of the Arab-Israeli Conflict.* Routledge, London. ISBN 0-415-15130-9

Gilbert, Martin. (2010) *In Ishmael's House, A History of Jews in Muslim Lands.* Yale University Press. ISBN 978-0-300-16715-3

Ginzburg, L. (1920) *The Gaon, Rabbi Elijah.* London.

Glubb, Sir John. B. (1967) *The Middle East Crisis. A Personal Interpretation.* Hodder & Stoughton, London.

Glubb, Sir John. B. (1957) *A Soldier with the Arabs.* Hodder & Stoughton, London.

Goitein, Solomon D. (1973) *Letters of Medieval Jewish Traders.* Princeton University Press.

Goldhagen, Daniel Jonah. (1996) *Hitler's Willing Executioners.* Abacus. ISBN 379 17 866 6

Grant, Michael. (1984) *A History of Ancient Israel,* Gale Group, London.

Gribetz, Greenstein, Stein. (1994) *The Timetables of Jewish History.* Touchstone Simon & Schuster. 0 671-88577-4

Grossman, Vasily. (2006) *A Writer At War.* Pimlico edition. ISBN 9781845950156

Harkabi, Yehoshafat. (1972) *Arab Attitudes to Israel.* Keter Publishing House, Jerusalem.

Hart, B.H. Liddell. (1938). *T.E. Lawrence to His Biographer.* Greenwood Publishing Group, Inc. NY.

Harvey, Oliver. *The Diplomatic Diaries of Oliver Harvey 1941 - 1945.* WilliamCollins Sons & Co. Ltd. London. (ed) John Harvey.

Heikal, Mohammed. (1973) *The Cairo Documents.* Doubleday. NY.

Heikal, Mohammed. (1975) *The Road to Ramadan.* Collins. London.

Hertzberg, Arthur. (1960) *The Zionist Ideal,* A Historical Analysis. Jewish Publication Society, USA.

Hertzberg, Arthur. (1968). *The French Enlightenment and the Jews.* Columbia University Press, NY.

Herzog, Chaim. (1984) *The Arab-Israeli Wars.* Vintage Books. ISBN 0-394-71746-5

Herzog, Chaim (1975) *War of Atonement.* Weidenfeld and Nicholson. London.

Herzog, Chaim; Gichon, Mordechai. (1997). *Battles of the Bible.* Greenhill Books, London ISBN 1-85367-266-1

Hoebel, E.A. (1954) *The Law of Primitive Man.* Harvard University Press, NY.

Hoffman, Edward (2008) *The Wisdom of Maimonides.* Trumpeter Books ISBN 978-1-59030-517-1

Horowitz, David. (1953) *The State in the Making.* Alfred A Knopf, NY.

Hussein, King of Jordan (1969). *My 'War' with Israel.* Peter Owen, London.

Isaacson, Walter. (2008) *Einstein His Life and Universe.* Simon & Schuster ISBN-13: 978-0-7432-6474-7

Israel Pocket Library. (1973) *History until 1880.* Keter Books. ISBN 0 7065 1321 5

Israel Pocket Library. (1973) *Jerusalem*. Keter Books. ISBN 0 7065 1325 8

Jacoby, Ruth; Talgam, Rina *Ancient Jewish Synagogues*. Architectural Glossary. Hebrew University of Jerusalem.

Jarvis, Major C S. (1938) *Desert and Delta*. John Murray. Albemarle street, W London.

Johnson, Paul. (1987). *A History of the Jews*. Weidenfeld & Nicholson 0-06-091533-1

Johnson, Paul. (1993) *A History of the Modern World 1917 -1980's*. Weidenfeld & Nicholson, London. ISBN 0 297 78475 7

Johnson, Paul. (1991) *The Birth of the Modern 1815 -1830*. Weidenfeld & Nicholson. ISBN 0 297 81207 6

Join-Lambert, Michel. (1958) *Jerusalem*. Elek Books, London.

Josephus, Flavius *The Jewish War*. The New English Library. (1996).

Keller, Werner. (1956) *The Bible as History*. Hodder & Stroughton. London.

Kimche, John. (1950) *Seven Fallen Pillars: The Middle East, 1915-1950*. Secker & Warburg, London.

King-Clark, R. (1988) *Free for a Blast*. Grenville Publishing Co. Limited, London. ISBN 0-903243-07-5

King-Clark, R. (1997) *Jack Churchill 'Unlimited Boldness'*. Fleur-de-Lys Publishing, Cheshire. ISBN 1 873907 06 0

Kochan, Lionel. (1977) *The Jew and His History*. Schocken Books, London.

Lacquer, Walter. (1974) *Confrontation 1973: The Model East War and the Great Powers*. Wildwood House. London.

Lacquer, Walter. (1969) *The Israel-Arab Reader*. Weidenfeld and Nicholson. London.

Lehman, Johannes. (1977) *The Hittites*. Collins, London ISBN 0-00216314-4. German edition (1975)

Lewis, Bernard. (1984) *The Jews of Islam*. Routledge and Kegan Paul, London.

Lewis, Bernard. (1995, 2001). *The Middle East*. Phoenix Press Paperback. ISBN 1 84212 0174

Lewis, Bernard. (2001) *What Went Wrong?* Phoenix Press Paperback. ISBN 075381 675X

Lewis, Jon E. (2010) *Rome The Autobiography* Constable-Robinson Ltd., ISBN 978-1-84901-083-2

Lorch, Nathanel. (1961) *The Edge of the Sword: War of Independence, 1947 - 1949*. Putnam, London and NY.

MacArthur, John (1997) *The MacArthur Study Bible*. Word Publishing. USA ISBN 0-8499-1222-9

Mace, D.R. (1953) *Hebrew Marriage*. NY.

MacMillan, Margaret. (2002). *Paris 1919: Six Months that Changed the World*. Random House, NY.

Mardor, Meir (Munya) (1957) *Secret Missions, Chapters of Special Operations of the Hagana*. (Hebrew). IDF Printing Press.

Maimonides. *The Guide for the Perplexed*. Dover Publications NY (1956)

McDonald, James G. (1951) *My Mission in Israel. 1948–1951*. Victor Gollancz, London. pp. 22, 23.

Meeks, Wayne (1984) *The First Urban Christians, The Social World of the Apostle Paul*. Yale University Press.

Meinertzhagen, Colonel Richard. (1959) *Middle East Diary, 1917-1956*. The Cresset Press, London. Thomas Yoseloff, NY.

Meir, Golda. (1975) *My Life*. Weidenfeld and Nicholson, London.

Moore, G.F. (1927) *Judaism in the First Centuries of the Christian Era*. Hendrickson Publishers, Inc.

Morse, Arthur. (1967) *While Six Million Died, A Chronicle of American Apathy*. Random House, NY.

Mumford, Lewis. (1961, 1966) *The City in History.* Pelican Books, Cox & Wyman Ltd. London.

National Geographic Society, (1969) *The Age of Chivalry.* NGS.

National Geographic Society, (1967) *Everyday Life in Bible Times.* NGS ISBN 0-87044-131-0

National Geographic Society. (1997) *Atlas of World History.* NGS. ISBN 0-7922-7048-7

Neguib, Mohammed (1955). *Egypt's Destiny.* Gollancz, London.

Nordau. Max. (1884) *The Conventional Lies of Our Civilization.* L. Schick, Chicago.

Noth, Martin. (1960) *The History of Biblical Israel.* Harper Collins, London.

Oliphant, Lawrence. (1887) *Haifa or Life in Modern Palestine, 1882 - 1885.* London. Reprint Canaan Publishing House Jerusalem.

Parry, Rabbi Aaron. (2004) *The Complete IDIOT'S Guide to The Talmud.* Alpha (Penguin), ISBN 1-59257-202-2

Pa'il, Meir. (1987) *The Emergence of the Zionist Defense Forces in Eretz Israel.* (Hebrew) Ministry of Defense, Israel. 965-5-0298.

Palgi, Yoel. (2003) *Into the Inferno.* Rutgers University Press.

Perlman, Moshe and Yannai, Yaacov (1964) *Historical Sites in Israel.* London.

Peters, Joan. (1984, 2000) *From Time Immemorial.* Harper & Row, USA ISBN 0-9636242-0-2

Pickthall, Mohammed Marmaduke. (1953) Translation. *The Meaning of The Glorious Koran.* Mentor Books, NY.

Pinner, Walter. (1959) *How Many Arab Refugees?* London.

Pipes, Daniel. (1983) *In the Path of God: Islam and Political Power.* Basic Books, NY.

Pohoryles, Samuel. (1975) *Agricultural Adjustment in Semi-Arid Areas.* Tel Aviv University.

Prawer, Joshua. (1972) *The Latin Kingdom of Jerusalem.* Weidenfeld and Nicholson, London. ISBN 0 297 99397 6

Prawer, Joshua. (1972) *The World of the Crusaders.* Weidenfeld and Nicholson, London. ISBN 0 297 99537-5.

Prittie, Terence. (1968) *Israel: Miracle in the Desert.* Frederick A. Praeger, NY.

Rabin, Yitzhak. (1979) *The Rabin Memoirs.* Weidenfeld and Nicholson, London.

Rabinovich, Itamar. (2004) *Waging Peace.* Princeton University Press.

Richardson, Peter. (1996) *Herod King of the Jews, Friend of the Romans.* Univ. of South Carolina 1996 ISBN 157003-136-3

Rogan, Eugene. (2015) *The Fall of the Ottomans.* Allen Lane ISBN 978-1-846-14438-7

Ross, Dennis. (2004) *The Missing Peace: Inside Story of the Fight for Middle East Peace.* Farrar, Straus and Giroux.

Roth, Cecil. (1936, 1959). *A Short History of the Jewish People.* The East and West Library, London.

Runican, Steven. (1965) *A History of the Crusades.* Harmondsworth, Middlesex, UK.

Sandel, Samuel. (1977) *Judaism and Christian Beginnings.* Oxford University Press.

Sanders, E.P. (1977) *Paul and Palestinian Judaism, a Comparison of Patterns of Religion.* Fortress Press, Minneapolis.

Sanders, Ronald. (1984) *The High Walls of Jerusalem.* HRW, NY.

Schama, Simon. (1978) *Two Rothschilds and the Land of Israel.* Alfred A Knopf, NY.

Schechtman, Joseph. (1965) *The Mufti and the Fuhrer: The Rise and Fall of Haj Amin el-Husseini.* NY.

Shachar, Howard. (1976) *History of Israel, from the Rise of Zionism to Our Time.* Alfred A Knopf, NY.

Shahar, Howard. (1966) *Europe leaves the Middle East 1936 - 1954.* Alfred A Knopf, NY.

Shalev, Aryeh. (1993) *Israel and Syria: Peace and Security on the Golan* (Hebrew). Tel Aviv University.

Shelev, Aryeh. (2006) *The Israeli Intelligence Assessment on the Eve of the Yom Kippur War* (Hebrew). Ministry of Defense, Israel.

Shapiro, S. (1988) *Jews in Old China.* Hippocrene Books, NY.

Silver-Brody, Vivienne. (1998) *Documentors of the Dream.* The Jewish Publication Society, Philadelphia ISBN0-8276-0657-5.

Smith, George Adam. (1931) *The Historical Geography of the Holy Land.* Reprint Harper London (1996).

Tal, Eliezer. (1964) *Naval Operations in the Israel War of Independence.* (Hebrew) Ministry of Defense, Israel.

Taylor, A.J.P. (1996) *Origin of the Second World War.* Readers Union, NY.

Torah/Prophets/Writings. Tanach. (1996, 1998) The Stone Edition, Mesorah Publications, Ltd. NY. ISBN 0-89906-269-5.

Torrey, Charles. C. (1967) *The Jewish Foundation of Islam.* Jewish Institute of Religion Press, NY.

Treece, Henry. (1964) *The Crusades.* Souvenir Press. ISBN 0285 62347 8

Tsidon-Chatto, Yoash. (2001). *Israel-Arabia. Eye to Eye with the Future.* ACPR Publishers, Shaarei Tikva. Israel.

Tuchman, Barbara W. (1985) *Sand Against the Wind.* Futura Publications. ISBN 0 7088 1990 7

Tuchman, Barbara W. (1976) *The Proud Tower.* PAPERMAC. ISBN 0 333 30646 5. Alfred A Knopf, NY.

Tuchman, Barbara W. (1978) *A Distant Mirror, The Calamitous 14th Century* PAPERMAC ISBN 0 333 33414 0

Turki, Fawaz. (1972) *The Disinherited: Journal of a Palestinian Exile.* Monthly Review Press, NY.

Twain, Mark. (1881) *The Innocence Abroad* (New American Library, 1997).

Vilnay, Zev. (1955, 1985). *The Guide to Israel.* Ahiever, Jerusalem.

Wasserstein, Bernard. (1979) *Britain and the Jews of Europe 1939 - 1945.* Oxford University Press.

Wavel, Field Marshal Alfred P. *The Palestine Campaigns.*

Waxman, Meyer. (1958) *Judaism: Religion and Ethics.* T. Yoseloff, NY.

Weinberg, Gerhard. L. (1995) *A World at Arms, A Global History of World War II.* Cambridge University Press. ISBN 0 521 44317 2.

Weizman, Ezer. (1981) *The Battle for Peace.* Bantam Books, NY.

Weizmann, Chaim. (1949) *Trial and Error, The Autobiography of Chaim Weizmann.* Harpers & Brothers, NY.

Wigoder, Geoffrey (1991) *Dictionary of Jewish Biography.* Simon & Schuster, NY.

Woolley, Leonard. (1954) *Ur Excavations.* The British Museum. London.

Woolley, Leonard. (1954) *The Sumarians.* Barnes and Noble (reprint 1955).

Wright, Quincey. (1930) *Mandates Under the League of Nations.* Chicago.

Yadin, Yigal. (1966, 1967). *Masada.* Weidenfeld and Nicholson. London.

Yadin, Yigal. (1975). Hazor: *The Rediscovery of a Great Citadel of the Bible.* Random House, NY.

Yerushalmi, Y. H. (1989) *Zakhor: Jewish History and Jewish Memory.* Schocken, NY.

Author's Profile
Adrian Wolff

Born in London, and after graduating BA Honours in Economics from the University of Cape Town, immigrated to Israel and worked in the field of economics and marketing. Having had an exhaustive interest in history since childhood, he returned to academic life, graduated from the official Israeli Tourist Guide course which became the impetus to further study and research on the history of Israel, including a study of the Bible.

He served in the Israel Defense Forces, rising to the rank of major.

When not traveling, lecturing or reading he can be found playing the clarinet, participating in various national cycling activities, being a grandfather or the general handyman at home.

He was the Israel co-coordinator of an annual One-to-One charity bicycle ride around the Kinneret (Sea of Galilee) which raises money for Israel's Victims of Terror and Disadvantaged Youth. Furthermore, am a member of The Israel Military History Society, and Cyclenix, off-road cycling club.

He is married with two daughters and grandchildren.